THE HUTCHINSON
BOOK OF
Essays

Also by Frank Delaney

The Hutchinson Book of
ESSAYS

CHOSEN AND INTRODUCED
BY
Frank Delaney

WITH ENGRAVINGS
BY
Reynolds Stone

HUTCHINSON
London Sydney Auckland Johannesburg
1990

For my son, Bryan

Introduction, selection and editorial matter
© *The Folio Society Ltd 1990*
All rights reserved

This edition first published in 1990 by Hutchinson

Century Hutchinson Ltd, 20 Vauxhall Bridge Road,
London SW1V 2SA

Century Hutchinson Australia (Pty) Ltd
20 Alfred Street, Milsons Point,
Sydney NSW 2061, Australia

Century Hutchinson New Zealand Limited
PO Box 40–086, Glenfield, Auckland 10, New
Zealand

Century Hutchinson South Africa (Pty) Ltd
PO Box 337, Bergvlei, 2012 South Africa

Set in Bembo by Fakenham Photosetting Ltd
Printed and bound in Great Britain
at The Bath Press, Avon.
Typography by Malcolm Harvey Young

British Library Cataloguing in Publication Data
Hutchinson book of essays.
I. Delaney, Frank, *1942–*
824'.008

ISBN 0–09–173911–X (hardcased)
ISBN 0–09–1745500 (paperback)

Contents

PART THREE
ON THE PLEASURES OF THE FLESH

PART FOUR
ON THE PLEASURES OF THE MIND

Editorial Note

American spelling has been retained in those essays where it was felt
that to change it would alter the flavour of the piece.

Introduction

According to Virginia Woolf: 'There is no room for the impurities of literature in an Essay. Somehow or other, by dint of labour or bounty of nature, or both combined, the Essay must be pure—pure like water or pure like wine, but pure from dullness, deadness and deposits of extraneous matter.'

To Mrs Woolf's insistence on purity add another quality—flexibility. Ever since it became established four centuries ago, the Essay has proven itself as one of the most flexible and versatile shapes in literature, variable to a philanthropic degree in length, context, mood or subject matter—light and popular, through pretentious and contentious, to truly inspirational and seminal.

The combination of excellent writing and the capacity to address any imaginable topic makes the Essay as continually formidable a weapon as the writer's armoury contains. It can go anywhere, do anything, fit innumerable wearers. As Alexander Pope demonstrated with his *Moral Essays*, it can even be expressed in verse. In the more habitual prose form it can make a few hundred terse Baconian words, or expand to entire volume length, as with Doctor Locke's *Essay concerning Human Understanding*, published in 1690.

In its long and changeful history virtually all significant writers (and a myriad others) have written Essays, even if certain historical connotations of the word have suggested from time to time that the formal Essay no longer takes exercise. Not so: the mannered intellectual statement and political and social moralising of the eighteenth century in London may have been conducted in pieces of writing deliberately called 'Essays'. We immediately recall Addison and Steele and the famous periodicals to which they contributed so memorably, *The Spectator* and *Tatler*, and before them Bacon and Cornwallis, and after them Defoe, and Johnson in *The Rambler*, and then Lamb and Hazlitt. Obviously their language now feels antique, as dated as the wearing of evening gloves by gentlemen. Duly they may have become, through their own brilliance, embalmed in educators' curricula. However, they have served to inspire rather than inhibit the legions of authors, scholars, critics and journalists who, whatever generic name they call the form of their contributions today, write with all the purity demanded by Virginia Woolf and all the flexibility which the Essay, as a literary form, bestows.

The word itself came generally into currency under the pen of Michel de Montaigne in 1580 with the publication of his *Essais*. He saw them as a means of autobiography, in which he carried out 'trials' (that is to say, *essais*) of his responses to a variety of circumstances and topics. In these he attempted to discover what he thought, what he felt, what he believed, what he was. He scrutinised his own judgements and opinions, considered their permanence or instability, and used this system of judiciousness (in his very own term, *judicieux*) to reach for a greater knowledge of himself.

Montaigne, though, did not invent the form; his innovation consisted in using this method for the purposes of self-enquiry and in then attaching to it the word which became 'Essay'. Discursive prose of such a nature, though without any collective titular description, had long existed and, indeed, had inspired him. He clearly acknowledged the influence of, for instance, Marcus Aurelius Antoninus's *Meditations*, and, four and a half centuries before him, Theophrastus's *Characters*, published in 319 BC. Sir Francis Bacon, having in 1590 published a collection of 'Essaies', acknowledged that perspective when he observed, 'the word is late but the thing is ancient', and both his and Montaigne's immediate successors, inferring a long tradition, referred copiously to Cicero, Plato, Seneca, Plutarch.

In the standard sense, Montaigne and Bacon, a decade apart, were the progenitors of the essay form. That is to say, both men carried on their discussions with clarity and power and rigorousness, in recognisable sequences of enquiry, discovery, expansion, challenge and conclusion, all conducted with reason and addressed to any subject that took their fancy. Bacon wrote about Gardens, Love, Death, Revenge, Adversity, Praise, Boldness, Goodness, Seditions, Cunning, Fortune; Montaigne addressed himself to Sorrow, Liars, Custom, Imagination, Cannibals, Drunkenness, the Affection of Fathers, the Resemblance of Children to their Fathers, Repentance, Conversation, Cripples, Imagination.

Furthermore, the French grandee and the English statesman marked out deliciously wide boundaries in style and demonstrated that the Essay permitted personal expression as freely as a poem. Montaigne conversed, informal and friendly; Bacon lectured, didactically and often brusquely. Montaigne happily used up several thousand words; Bacon often no more than a page and a half. Montaigne said that he intended his *Essais* to display him comprehensively—'All the world knows me in my book and my book in me'; Bacon describes his own *Essaies* as 'grains of salt which will rather give an appetite than offend with satiety'.

Two more diverse poles to which the early form may be moored could scarcely be found—Bacon aloof, particular, scientific, strict and political; Montaigne intimate, vagarious, practical, incontinent and innocent. By example a definition of the form emerged from their pages: they brought the purity of their intellects, displayed in their language as well as in their arguments, to bear on a wide choice of subject matter. In that fusion of rigorousness and flexibility all material seemed improved, concerns of weight appeared more profound and even light business sparkled.

Imitators materialised. Within two decades of Montaigne's *Essais*, within a decade of Bacon's, and opening (as it were) for the seventeenth century, Sir William Cornwallis's *Essayes* appeared—light, unremarkable observations, notable principally for their acknowledgement of this new form rather than for their individualism or depth. Several others followed, on different plateaux of quality. In 1604, Nicholas Breton, a prolific writer of romantic and satirical verse, published *Fantasticks: Serving for a Perpetuall Prognostication*, a collection of observations on mankind and the natural world which he arranged in the sequence of the calendar. In 1614, Sir Thomas Overbury, who died in the Tower of London (Bacon prosecuted his trial), wrote *Characters*, with acknowledgements to Theophrastus.

As the seventeenth century progressed, works appeared by John Earle, the Restorationist, whose observations pursued Overbury's and conflicted with them; by Abraham Cowley who, like Montaigne, asked discursive questions of himself, scrutinising his own attitudes to gold, poverty, greed. Swift's friend, Sir William Temple, the diplomat-politician, discussed 'Of Health and Long Life', and 'Of Heroic Virtue', and 'Of Ancient and Modern Learning': he wrote, 'Books, like proverbs, receive their chief value from the stamp and esteem of ages through which they have passed'. Most excellent of all these was John Dryden—'the father of English criticism', as Johnson called him, who utilised the Essay brilliantly to practise his trials of Satire, Ben Jonson and Shakespeare. In his *Essay of Dramatic Poesy*, published in 1668, Dryden characteristically pushed the boundaries a little further, by writing it, his first major work of criticism, as a colloquy. (He later wrote, in the same year, 'A Defence of an Essay'.)

Between 1704 and 1713 Daniel Defoe's *Review* carried many essays which he first tested on the populace—by reading them aloud at street-corners for political as well as commercial reasons—before publishing them. Concurrently, the *Tatler* and *The Spectator* allowed

Joseph Addison and Richard Steele full rein, with such prominence that their reputations as leading progenitors of the Essay have long overpraised their actual literary talents—as Dr Johnson accurately perceived when he described Addison's prose as 'the model of the middle style; on grave subjects not formal, on light occasions not grovelling'.

What actually took place was an expansion of the Essay popularly rather than intellectually: Addison decided that fine writing sprang from sentiments which are 'natural without being obvious'. He and Steele became famous not for the power of their work but because the topics they chose made the hitherto rather lofty Essay more access-ible. Addison, indeed, saw his own contribution in populist rather than solely intellectual or literary terms: 'I shall be ambitious to have it said of me, that I have brought philosophy out of closets and libraries, schools and colleges, to dwell in clubs and assemblies, at tea-tables and coffee-houses.'

Admiration for his contribution to the stature of the Essay has lasted. Virginia Woolf, who called his essays 'perfect', summarised his place in the history of the form. 'Whether it was a high thing or a low thing, whether an epic is more profound or a lyric more passion-ate, undoubtedly it is due to Addison that prose is now prosaic—the medium which makes it possible for people of ordinary intelligence to communicate their ideas to the world.' Cyril Connolly, though disagreeing (to put it mildly), none the less understood that Addison had established a presence. In *Enemies of Promise*, where he called him 'the first Man of Letters', Connolly went on to dissect: 'Addison was responsible for many of the evils from which English has since suffered. He made prose artful and whimsical, he made it sonorous when sonority was not needed, affected when it did not require affectation . . . He had the misuse of an extensive vocabulary and so was able to invalidate a great number of words and expressions; the quality of his mind was inferior to the language in which he expressed it.' Likewise Sir Richard Steele, soldier and courtier, whimsically considered domestic life and sentimental concerns and gained a split verdict: 'a scholar among rakes and a rake among scholars,' wrote Macaulay (in an Essay).

Without question Addison and Steele, while observing the Theophrastus/Montaigne/Bacon tradition by way of form, had addressed content beyond the purlieu of their predecessors. They wrote about ladies' hats, childhood memories, popular foibles and mimicries, sentimental and public curios, such as the tombs in West-minster Abbey and the Cries of London. Essentially they made the Essay available in the popular marketplace by widening it to embrace domestic and social concerns where previously it had addressed literature, philosophy or politics. They wrote at a time when literacy had begun to spread and, taking credit for a body of work which reached deeper than their capacity but with which they were none the less perceived to be associated, they may be likened to the projectionists during the early days of Cinema. These gentlemen entered the auditorium in front of the screen, took a bow to thunderous applause and then walked up through the aisles to begin showing the film.

The field had now opened wide, from thoughtfulness to levity. The Montaigne and Bacon parallels continued in the Essay throughout the eighteenth century practised, for instance, by Swift, ferocious; Johnson, admonitory and moral, and his friend Goldsmith, pleasant and mischievous. Publications which accommodated the Essay—were created to serve it—proliferated: *The Englishman, The Reader, The Plebeian, The Gentleman's Magazine, The Universal Chronicle: or Weekly Gazette*, to which Johnson contributed the 'Idler' papers. *The Rambler*, Johnson's own periodical, which appeared twice a week from March 1750 to March 1752, 208 editions in all, existed solely to exhibit the versatility of subject matter in the hands of Johnson. Goldsmith also published his own essays in *The Bee*, which he initiated in 1759.

The Essay, now confidently and authoritatively established, flourished through the rest of the eighteenth century and into the nineteenth and twentieth. Almost *de rigueur* leading writers of whatever literary discipline, by contributing prolifically, ensured their immortality in the form, and at the same time claimed their obvious right to be viewed in philosophical and intellectual lights while displaying their versatility of thought and style. Some balanced both, seeing the perceived ability to 'turn out' the Essay as proof of a Renaissance roundness—essential in a literary man. Their efforts appeared in a wide variety of publications, newspapers, learned journals, popular weekly magazines and in the combined traditions of Montaigne and Bacon, Addison and Steele, Johnson and Goldsmith, addressed every conceivable topic on every imaginable level. More than a few such writers then published their Collected Essays, a flourishing exclamation mark of comprehensiveness in any wide bibliography. Some made it the major form in their canon: Lamb and Leigh Hunt and Hazlitt. Some added to their other reputations: Coleridge and Matthew Arnold and Robert Louis Stevenson. Others, such as Walter Pater (much of his later output collected in the 1893 volume *Plato and Platonism*), Oscar Wilde (influenced by Pater's *Essay on Style*), John Ruskin and George Bernard Shaw, performed *tours de force* as critics and commentators, so that the Essay turned the corner of the twentieth century in excellent health and gaining in weight.

Not all of this four-century, lively pathway ran smooth; the use of the Essay in education caused disenchantment from time to time. It proved perfect teaching material—after all, it possessed the quality of thought in the standard of language from the calibre of writer to which any student must surely, ideally, aspire. Pedagogues thrilled to it, and in the nineteenth century began to load it into their curricula— a certain loftiness, a feeling of aspiration, encouraging young minds upwards, etc. The Essay had become official.

Writers reacted. It was not that they never wrote Essays again, but they twitched and became shy. The approval of any establishment habitually breeds suspicion in artistic minds: to this day many writers, dreading the conformity inferred by such official acceptance—as well as fearing embalmment—dislike having their works selected for school texts. Anything over-praised tends to lose favour: even the Essay's declared literary qualities of precise grammar, faultless syntax, economy of expression proved too approved. By the middle of the nineteenth century the form had become a fixture in every textbook in every place of learning and, further, a required part of instruction in writing, hated by students who had no aptitude for it. Anyone who went to school in western Europe within the last century must have encountered such terms as, 'The perfect Essay describes a circle'; 'The perfect Essay contains no cluttered thoughts'; 'The perfect Essay enables the reader to understand without asking any further questions what the writer means, and yet encourages debate onwards beyond the writer's arguments.' When such sentiments take to the air, the word 'worthy' begins to lurk not far off.

In *Our Mutual Friend*, Charles Dickens teasingly interpreted this petty elevation of the Essay when he described the schoolmistress: 'Small, shining, neat, methodical and buxom was Miss Peecher; cheery-cheeked and tuneful of voice. A little pincushion, a little housewife, a little book, a little workbox, a little set of tables and weights and measures and a little woman all in one. She could write a little Essay on any subject, exactly a slate long, beginning at the left-hand top of one side and ending at the right-hand bottom of the other, and the Essay should be strictly according to rule. If Mr Bradley Headstone had addressed a written proposal of marriage to her, she would probably have replied in a complete little Essay on the theme, exactly a slate long, but would certainly have replied yes. For she loved him.'

'Small, shining, neat, methodical . . . a little pincushion, a little workbox, a little set of tables and weights and measures . . . exactly a slate long' etc.—the Essay answered all of these descriptions. But it survived them too; when not being imposed on the weary benches it continued to function with its twin disciplines of clarity and elasticity and, individual and collected, it romped on into the twentieth century, unabated.

Its political application, flexed by Defoe and Swift, flourished, as Fabians and anarchists and socialists and political theorists and fabulists of all hues filled national newspapers, weekly politicals and their own dedicated publications with discussions and expositions. Every new twist and turn in the political life of the world brought forward the researched, thoughtful paper. Often these latter-day Essays went on at some length and Dr Johnson's definition of the Essay as 'an irregular undigested piece, but now said of a composition more or less elaborate in style, though limited in range' frequently proved deadly accurate.

Vigorous literary application burnished it further. In 1918 Lytton Strachey, already an Essayist who published widely in the periodicals, made an important advance both in biography and the Essay itself with *Eminent Victorians*. This collection of four pieces examined the diverse lives of Cardinal Henry Manning, Thomas Arnold of Rugby School, Florence Nightingale and General Gordon of Khartoum. In 1925 Virginia Woolf published *The Common Reader* addressing herself to *The Modern Essay* and *On Not Knowing Greek*, while Belloc and Chesterton pursued the Essay more directly in what amounted, both in form and content, to an observance of the eighteenth-century tradition; Max Beerbohm likewise, though in a lighter, more Addisonian tone. In 1932 T. S. Eliot published his *Selected Essays*; in 1946 George Orwell's *Selected Essays* appeared; in 1951, Graham Greene's *Lost Childhood, and Other Essays*; in 1956, Aldous Huxley's *Adonis and the Lost Alphabet*; in 1963, W. H. Auden's *The Dyer's Hand*. Other contributors included Harold Nicolson who, along with J. B. Priestley and James Stephens, the Irish writer, took the Essay into a new field, in the form of the broadcast talk. In the 1970s and 1980s John Updike and Gore Vidal stood foremost among the later Americans who, under the guise of literary criticism or political commentary, wrote Essays in their truest form, sometimes at considerable length.

During this period too, emanating from the turmoil of the 1960s, a hot hybrid emerged, collectively called *The New Journalism*, which, in the hands of American writers such as Hunter S. Thompson and Tom Wolfe, observed, beneath the skin, all the traditions of Bacon and Montaigne. The writers not only examined subjects but put themselves inside them; Thompson travelled with the Hell's Angels;

Wolfe's four essays for the magazine *Esquire* called *The Right Stuff* appeared, as Strachey's biographical essays had done, in book form, and then took the Essay into the cinema with the eponymous film. A neat circle may thus (if a little fancifully) be perceived—where Montaigne entered the inner space of his own self, Wolfe followed the first astronauts into outer space.

Today Essayists still abound, though perhaps with different job descriptions—journalists, commentators, critics. Many 'pieces', in daily newspapers, in weekly news magazines, reveal splendid writers observing all the principles of the Essayist—'content to begin in doubts, ending in certainties' like Bacon, even putting up 'trials' like Montaigne. The intent is what decides, not the placing of the piece or the logistical requirements of publication. 'Posterity will be astonished when it is told,' wrote Boswell of *The Rambler* and its author/publisher, 'upon the authority of Johnson himself, that many of these discourses, which we should suppose had been laboured with all the slow attention of literary leisure, were written in haste as the moment pressed, without even being read over by him before they were printed.'

Given that wide application throughout its history, the Essay's great versatility makes difficult the exercise of nailing the form to a simple definition. The attractiveness of Montaigne's term, *essai*, heightens if used as related to 'assay', in the sense of the trial of metals. For the amusing purposes of any general definition we may begin accurately by saying something like this: 'An Essay is an exercise in prose which uses an elegant and concise non-fiction form to convey and establish opinions, whether criticism, review, appreciation, interpretation, elaboration, point of view, argument, observation, idea, instruction or challenge, without obstructing the nature of the writer's mind or character.' Reach for a shorter definition—'the Essay is a piece of elegant prose expressing the thought-out opinions of the writer upon a fact, subject or concept'. Tighten further, to a shorthand view coined by the biographer Michael Holroyd: 'a non-fiction short story.' The scope implicit in all of these definitions supports further the Essay's claim to belong at the heart of literature as a composing art: if the novel reflects the human condition, then perhaps the Essay records it.

Example, however, provides the best definition of all: to meet it is to know it. An Essay may be recognised in the same way as a concerto or a collage or an arabesque or a sonnet. Part of the appeal lies in that recognition—Thoreau said of poetry: 'We do not enjoy poetry unless we know it to be poetry.' Even if it has changed down the course of the years the Essay may still be recognised by the first hallmarks—purity of writing addressing variety of subject. Any anthologising will *de facto* result in a large and clear collected definition, both of Mrs Woolf's ideas on the purity of form and the historically untrammelled content. The selection should prove generally that lucidly written discussions On Getting Respected in Inns and Hotels may sit with the same ease and vitality beside The Reach of the Imagination: National Prejudice may be contemplated with the same calm as hot-water bottles in girls' boarding-schools.

The essence of anthology consists in personal taste. Balance is a major component of taste. Discipline achieves balance. To begin with I approached this book in the simplest way—to donate to myself a volume which agreed with Virginia Woolf's terms; 'The principle which controls [the Essay] is simply that it should give pleasure; the desire which impels us when we take it from the shelf is simply to receive pleasure.' All of the writers selected should also have the capacity to say, in an agreeably elegant, and sometimes brilliant, way, things which I found I wanted to read and return to. They should perform on a scale which ran from at least interesting right up to indispensable. Therefore I came to the task with that dangerous possession—a feeling of great freedom. It seemed simple enough: select from a diet I have relished since childhood, and serve up all the dishes which have nourished me.

The trap shut with a clang. Entire forests would have had to be cut down to print everything I wanted to include. I moved, therefore, from the variety half of the equation that forms the Essay, to the rigorousness half (and in the process discarded a million and a half words). Interesting preferences emerged both in the discarding and the retaining. Just as the Oxford English Dictionary now has within its huge computerised range the capacity to compile entire other strands of lexicography, such as legal terminology, or the language of Jane Austen, or handbooks of, say, North American language, so the range, the database, from which these essays have been collected has many other divisions and sub-divisions. For example, I had to correct all throughout a lingering imbalance in favour of those Essays discussing Writers and Writing. Other bulges also needed ironing—the Arts generally, then History, Travel. Anthologies must certainly appear most interesting when reflecting the personal choice of the anthologist, but not so as to over-egg the pudding.

Anyway, nothing gets lost. When the *farceur* Ben Travers objected gently that the line which a director was about to remove from his play in rehearsal was 'rather good', the director said genially, 'A "rather good" line? My dear fellow, it is an absolutely splendid line. Keep it. Use it in another play.'

Anthologies have a most attractive place, portable permanent exhibitions, private bedside museums. Ideally they should occupy a place on the bookshelf to which, like the Bible or Shakespeare, the reader returns without thinking, knowing what awaits. And essays perform a not dissimilar function: release and escape, provocation into contemplation, the impression at least (and who cares if it is an illusion) of beneficial result. 'Everything in an essay'—see Mrs Woolf in *The Modern Essay*—'must be subdued to that end. It should lay us under a spell with its first word, and we should only wake, refreshed, with its last. In the interval we may pass through the most various experiences of amusement, surprise, interest, indignation; we may soar to the heights of fantasy with Lamb or plunge to the depths of wisdom with Bacon.' Upon which, read, for instance, Bertrand Russell's opening sentence, inherited from Samuel Butler: 'Will machines destroy emotions or will emotions destroy machines?' Or Graham Greene, always likely to make a literary point, who observes, having given copious examples from *Two Bad Mice*, 'It is curious that Beatrix Potter's method of paragraphing has never been imitated.' Collecting all of these strange bedfellows between one set of covers has a delicious appeal—they form not a chorus but an auditorium full of soloists.

Which is as it should be: if the form has any use, it is best of all at charting the thoughts, emotions, beliefs and enquiries of cultivated man, a projector of the mind since the moment at which civilisation turned to literature as a means of self-expression. It is as if man, looking around for something, some convenient vessel to carry his thoughts in, discovered a wonderful product of civilisation, the Essay, by whatever name. After all, the Essayist takes his reader into the most civilised of all legislations, an ideal state where, within absolute freedom of choice, only one law exists—that law of purity, 'pure like water or pure like wine, but pure from dullness, deadness and deposits of extraneous matter.'

FRANK DELANEY

PART ONE
On Age, Young and Old

THE DIVISIONS in this anthology, though as personal as the choice of Essays, are intended to correspond generally with major themes that Essayists have addressed—beginning with Time and the ageing process, a preoccupation of all art. Nine writers from four centuries comprise this section, one seventeenth-century, Owen Felltham, one eighteenth-century, Richard Steele, one nineteenth-, the agreeable Stevenson, and the rest from across the twentieth century.

Youth and old age obviously form the boundaries of their discussions. Shuttling back and forth, from the dictatorship of adults to which the child is subject, through the growing pains of independence, to the dependency and recollected musings of old age, charming patterns unfold, both physical and spiritual. For instance, the corporal manifestations of ageing produce a touching defiance. These travellers, sincerely interested in the journey, prefer to see thinning blood, greying hair, creaking bones as signs of how far they have come, rather than how far remains to go. 'Not a day's illness, we boast,' writes V. S. Pritchett, 'except a winter cough or a twinge of arthritis or gout; we speak of these twitches as medals we have won.'

Spiritually the resistance becomes even more poignant, an escape into personal memorials of joy long ago or the treachery of those habitually sunny days or the (now enjoyable) difficulty of growing up, school and the like. In such matters the capacity for recollection counts for more than its accuracy. 'We, that are very old,' says Richard Steele in *Recollections of Childhood*, 'are better able to remember things which befell us in our distant youth, than the passages of later days.' All retrospectives look at where their author came from in order to guess where he might be going, and how, and why: how to give ourselves the story of our own lives thus far in order that we may attempt some influence upon the story of our future.

Recollections of Childhood

RICHARD STEELE

Dies, ni fallor, adest, quem semper acerbum,
Semper honoratum, sic dii voluistis, habebo.
VIRGIL, *Aeneid*, v. 49

There are those among mankind, who can enjoy no relish of their being, except the world is made acquainted with all that relates to them, and think everything lost that passes unobserved; but others find a solid delight in stealing by the crowd, and modelling their life after such a manner, as is as much above the approbation as the practice of the vulgar. Life being too short to give instances great enough of true friendship or good will, some sages have thought it pious to preserve a certain reverence for the names of their deceased friends; and have withdrawn themselves from the rest of the world at certain seasons, to commemorate in their own thoughts such of their acquaintance who have gone before them out of this life. And indeed, when we are advanced in years, there is not a more pleasing entertainment, than to recollect in a gloomy moment the many we have parted with, that have been dear and agreeable to us, and to cast a melancholy thought or two after those, with whom, perhaps, we have indulged ourselves in whole nights of mirth and jollity. With such inclinations in my heart I went to my closet yesterday in the evening, and resolved to be sorrowful; upon which occasion I could not but look with disdain upon myself, that though all the reasons which I had to lament the loss of many of my friends are now as forcible as at the moment of their departure, yet did not my heart swell with the same sorrow which I felt at the time; but I could, without tears, reflect upon many pleasing adventures I have had with some, who have long been blended with common earth. Though it is by the benefit of nature, that length of time thus blots out the violence of afflictions; yet, with tempers too much given to pleasure, it is almost necessary to revive the old places of grief in our memory; and ponder step by step on past life, to lead the mind into that sobriety of thought which poises the heart, and makes it beat with due time, without being quickened with desire, or retarded with despair, from its proper and equal motion. When we wind up a clock that is out of order, to make it go well for the future, we do not immediately set the hand to the present instant, but we make it strike the round of all its hours, before it can recover the regularity of its time. Such, thought I, shall be my method this evening; and since it is that day of the year which I dedicate to the memory of such in another life as I much delighted in when living, an hour or two shall be sacred to sorrow and their memory, while I run over all the melancholy circumstances of this kind which have occurred to me in my whole life.

The first sense of sorrow I ever knew was upon the death of my father, at which time I was not quite five years of age; but was rather amazed at what all the house meant, than possessed with a real understanding why nobody was willing to play with me. I remember I went into the room where his body lay, and my mother sat weeping alone by it. I had my battledore in my hand, and fell a-beating the coffin, and calling Papa; for, I know not how, I had some slight idea that he was locked up there. My mother caught me in her arms, and, transported beyond all patience of the silent grief she was before in, she almost smothered me in her embraces; and told me in a flood of tears, Papa could not hear me, and would play with me no more, for they were going to put him under ground, whence he could never come to us again. She was a very beautiful woman, of a noble spirit, and there was a dignity in her grief amidst all the wildness of her transport, which, methought, struck me with an instinct of sorrow, that, before I was sensible of what it was to grieve, seized my very soul, and has made pity the weakness of my heart ever since. The mind in infancy is, methinks, like the body in embryo; and receives impressions so forcible, that they are as hard to be removed by reason, as any mark with which a child is born is to be taken away by any future application. Hence it is, that good nature in me is no merit; but having been so frequently overwhelmed with her tears before I knew the cause of any affliction, or could draw defences from my own judgement, I imbibed commiseration, remorse, and an unmanly gentleness of mind, which has since ensnared me into ten thousand calamities; and from whence I can reap no advantage, except it be, that, in such a humour as I am now in, I can the better indulge myself in the softnesses of humanity, and enjoy that sweet anxiety which arises from the memory of past afflictions.

We, that are very old, are better able to remember things which befell us in our distant youth, than the passages of later days. For this reason it is, that the companions of my strong and vigorous years present themselves more immediately to me in this office of sorrow. Untimely and unhappy deaths are what we are most apt to lament; so little are we able to make it indifferent when a thing happens, though we know it must happen. Thus we groan under life, and bewail those who are relieved from it. Every object that returns to our imagination raises different passions, according to the circumstance of their departure. Who can have lived in an army, and in a serious hour reflect upon the many gay and agreeable men that might long have flourished in the arts of peace, and not join with the imprecations of the fatherless and widows on the tyrant to whose ambition they fell sacrifices? But gallant men, who are cut off by the sword, move rather our veneration than our pity; and we gather relief enough from their own contempt of death, to make that no evil, which was approached with so much cheerfulness, and attended with so much honour. But when we turn our thoughts from the great parts of life on such occasions, and instead of lamenting those who stood ready to give death to those from whom they had the fortune to receive it; I say, when we let our thoughts wander from such noble objects, and consider the havoc which is made among the tender and the innocent, pity enters with an unmixed softness, and possesses all our souls at once.

Here (were there words to express such sentiments with proper tenderness) I should record the beauty, innocence, and untimely death, of the first object my eyes ever beheld with love. The beauteous virgin! how ignorantly did she charm, how carelessly excel? Oh death! thou hast right to the bold, to the ambitious, to the high, and to the haughty; but why this cruelty to the humble, to the meek, to the undiscerning, to the thoughtless? Nor age, nor business, nor distress, can erase the dear image from my imagination. In the same week I saw her dressed for a ball, and in a shroud. How ill did the habit of death become the pretty trifler? I still behold the smiling earth—A large train of disasters were coming on to my memory, when my servant knocked at my closet-door, and interrupted me with a letter, attended with a hamper of wine, of the same sort with that which is to be put to sale on Thursday next, at Garraway's coffee-house. Upon the receipt of it, I sent for three of my friends. We are so intimate, that we can be company in whatever state of mind we meet, and can entertain each other without expecting always to rejoice. The wine we found to be generous and warming, but with such a heat as moved us rather to be cheerful than frolicsome. It revived the spirits, without firing the blood. We commended it until two of the clock this morning; and having today met a little before dinner, we found, that though we drank two bottles a man, we had much more reason to recollect than forget what had passed the night before.

Living on Capital

JONATHAN RABAN

I suppose that everyone is really the father of their own family. We make them up, these private sanctuaries, prisons and sunny utopias. Visiting other people's families, I've always found it hard to square what I've seen with the legend as it was told to me in the car on the way. The characters are always much bigger or smaller, nicer or nastier, than they ought to be. It's like seeing a play performed by a weekly rep working from the wrong text. One's own legend is doubly distrustable. One has all the ruthless impartiality of a critic writing up a show in which he has been both casting director and one of the stars. Legend it must be, not accountancy or gritty realism; and like all genesis myths, its garden, its rib and its fruit of the tree are symbols. When it comes to his own family, no one can afford to be a fundamentalist.

Once upon a time, before the idea of 'family' ever took hold, there was just my mother and I. We lived in a sweet cocoon, and it was much like having an idyllic extra-marital affair. My father was away 'in the war': he was a photograph on the mantelpiece; he was the morning post; he was part of the one o'clock news on the wireless. He was not so much my father as the complaisant husband of the woman I lived with—and I dreaded his return. Meanwhile, we made hay while the sun shone. I had contracted a wasting disease called coeliac, and I was fed, like a privileged lover, on specially imported bananas and boiled brains. We learned to read together, so that I could spell out paragraphs from *The Times* before my third birthday. We stoved in the bottoms of eggshells, so that witches wouldn't be able to use them as boats. We saved up our petrol rations, and drove to my grandmother's house in Sheringham. My mother's Ford Eight, AUP 595, had been bought in 1939 with money she'd earned writing love stories for women's magazines, and it was the perfect vehicle for conducting a romance. Bowling along Norfolk lanes at a hair-raising thirty, with the windows down and the smell of pollen, leather and motor oil in my nose, I felt that this was the life. I meant to keep on as I had started; riding in the front seat with kisses and confessions, and the Ribena bottle conveniently near the top of the hamper.

I was a bag of bones. But I had already acquired the manner of a practised gigolo. My illness gave me the right to constant attention. With my forehead in my mother's hands, I was sick until my throat bled. When I wasn't being sick, I was being loquacious. Since my mother had only me to talk to, I'd picked up an impressive vocabulary which I was perpetually airing and adding to. Too weak to play with other children—whom I regarded from a distance as rough, untutored creatures—I looked to grown-ups for the concern and admiration that were clearly my due. I feared the mockery of the few children who were allowed ('No rough games, mind!') to enter my bone-china world. My one friend was the doctor's son, who'd been crippled with polio and went about in a steel frame that was almost as big as himself. When I was three, my mother told me that children like him and me would go on scholarships to nice schools, but that the village children would all go to knocky-down schools like the one up the road. I saw myself and my mother sailing out in my scholar ship, its sail filling with the offshore wind on the beach at Sheringham, its prow headed into a romantic sunset, away from the line of jeering, unkempt children on the shore.

I hadn't reckoned with my father. I had once made my mother cry, when I had enquired whether he was likely to be killed by Germans; and I was often puzzled by the depth of her engrossment when a new batch of letters arrived from North Africa, then Italy, then Palestine. Curiously, I have no memory at all of my father coming back on leave. He must have blended into the other occasional visitors— many of them in uniform—to our house. Was he the man who took us both out to lunch one Sunday at a Fakenham hotel, where I remember the stringy rhubarb and a fit of sickness in the lavatory? I'm not sure.

At any rate, he was a complete stranger when he turned up late one morning, carrying a khaki kitbag across Hempton Green—the moment at which family life began for me. My first impression of him was of an unprepossessing roughness. The photo on the mantelpiece showed a junior officer so boyish he looked too young to shave. My father's jowl was the colour and texture of emery paper. His demob suit, too, seemed to have been woven out of corn-stubble. When my mother and he embraced, right there in the open on the green, I was mortified. I studied the faded white lettering on his bag: Major J. P. C. P. Raban R.A. By what right did this tall soldier in his ill-fitting civilian suit horn in on our household? The question took me several years to even begin to answer.

My father must have been a bit shaken too. His spindly, solemn son can hardly have been the beamish three-year-old he might have looked forward to. He was obviously unused to children anyway, and had had no practice at dealing with precocious little invalids who cried when he spoke to them. He brought with him the affectedly hearty manners of the mess, and tried to make friends with me rather as he might have jollied along a particularly green subaltern. On the afternoon of his arrival, he carried me by my feet and suspended me over the water-butt in the back garden. As I hung, screaming, over this black soup of mosquito larvae, my mother rushed out of the house to my defence.

'Only a game,' said my father. 'We were just having a game.' But I knew otherwise. This terrifying Visigoth, fresh from the slaughter, had tried to murder me before we'd even reached teatime. I ran bleating to my mother, begging her to send this awful man back to the war where he so clearly belonged. My father's fears were also confirmed: unless something pretty firm in the way of paternal influence was applied here and now, I was going to turn out a first-rate milksop, an insufferable little wet.

My father's feelings about 'wets' may have been streaked with anxieties of his own. Before the war, he had been a shy young man who had scraped through School Certificate at a minor public school. From there he had gone to a teachers' training college, and had done a probationary year of teaching (at which he had not been a success) before enlisting in the Territorial Army. In the army, he blossomed. He was rapidly promoted. He got married. He found himself suddenly a figure of some considerable poise and authority. When the war ended, he had hoped to transfer to the Regular Army but had been discouraged from doing so. By the time we met, he was twenty-seven, already at the end of a career he had been able to shine at. He had, along with his forced officer-style jocularity, a kind of preternatural gravity; he had learned to carry his own manliness with the air of an acolyte bearing an incense-boat. My father in his twenties was a profoundly responsible young man who had grown up late and then too quickly. He was stiff, avuncular and harsh by turns. I think that he felt my namby-pamby nature obscurely threatened his own manhood, and he set about toughening me up.

I was frightened of him. I was afraid of his irritable, headachey silences; afraid of his sudden gusts of good humour; afraid of his inscrutable, untouchable air; and afraid, most of all, of his summary beatings, which were administered court-martial fashion in his study. A toy left overnight in the path of the car got me a spanking; so did being unable to remember whether I had said 'thank you' to my hostess after a four-year-old's birthday party. He introduced me to a new cold world of duties and punishments—a vastly complicated, unforgiving place in which the best one could hope for was to pass without comment. Perhaps my father had cause to believe that the world really was like this, and was simply doing his best to rescue me from the fool's paradise unwittingly created for me by my mother. I felt then that he was just jealous of my intimacy with her, and was taking his revenge.

For weeks after the war he hung about the house and garden. He clacked out letters to potential employers on my mother's old portable Olivetti. He practised golf swings. He rambled round and round the birdbath in his demob suit. He made gunnery calculations on his slide rule. I played gooseberry—a sullen child lurking in passageways, resentfully spying on my parents. I felt cuckolded, and showed it. When my father eventually found a job, as the local area secretary of TocH, his work took him out of the house most evenings: when he drove off to Wisbech and Peterborough and King's Lynn, I would try to seduce my mother back to the old days of our affair. We listened to *Dick Barton* on the wireless over cocoa, and then I would launch into an avalanche of bright talk, hoping to buy back her attention and distract her from the clock. I felt her joy at having my father home, and I think I did sense her distress at my conspicuous failure to share it. I also felt a twinge or two of shame at our snugness. From my father, I was beginning to learn that my behaviour was distinctly unmanly, and these cocoon-evenings were clouded with guilt. When my father said, as he did several times a week, 'You are going to have to learn to stand up for yourself, old boy,' I shrank from the idea but knew it to be unarguably right.

But my father and I grew grim with the responsibilities that had been placed on our shoulders. I think we both felt helpless. He had inherited a role in life which he could only conceive in the most old-fashioned terms: he had to become a Victorian husband and father, a pillar of the family, the heir to the fading Raban fortunes. I had inherited *him*. And we both chafed under the weight of these legacies, both of us too weak to carry them off with any style. He bullied me, and he in turn was bullied by the family dead. If I feared him, he had Furies of his own—the ancestors and elderly relations who had set him standards by which he could do nothing except fail.

My father was not an eldest son, nor was his father. It must have been just his seriousness, his air of being the sort of young man who could take responsibility, his obvious dutifulness towards his own father, that marked him out. Whatever it was, it seemed that every dotty uncle and crusty great-aunt had named him as an executor of their wills. Whenever anyone in the family died, my father got busy with auctioneers and lawyers; and our house began to fill with heirlooms. Vans arrived with furniture and pictures and papers in tin boxes. Things went 'into store', then had to be brought out because it cost too much to keep them in the repository. We were swamped by my father's ancestors.

They looked down on us disapprovingly from every wall. In vast, bad, oxidised oil portraits, in pencil-and-wash sketches, in delicate miniatures, in silhouettes, they glared dyspeptically from their frames. There was the Recorder of Bombay. There was General Sir Edward. There was Cousin Emma at her writing desk. There were countless Indian Army colonels and mean-mouthed clerics. There were General Sir Edward's military honours mounted on velvet in a glass case. On top of the wireless stood the family coat of arms (a raven, a boar's head, some battlements and a motto that I don't remember). They were joyless, oppressive trophies. They represented a hundred-and-something years of dim middle-class slogging through the ranks of the army and the church. The faces of these ancestors were like their furniture—stolid, graceless but well-made in that provincial English fashion which equates worth with bulk. There was no fun in them, and only the barest modicum of intelligence. They looked like people who had found the going hard, but had come through by sticking to the principles that had been drummed into them at boarding school.

We revered them, these implacable household gods. We tiptoed around their hideous furniture ('*Don't* play on the games table; it's an *antique*—'); we ate our fish fingers with their crested forks; we obediently tidied our own lives into the few humble corners that were left behind by the importunate family dead. My father bought books on genealogy (*How to Trace Your Family Tree* by L. G. Pine), and buried himself in index cards and the 1928 edition of *Burke's Landed Gentry*. Summer holidays turned into sustained bouts of ancestor-worship of a kind that might have been more appropriate to a pious Chinese than to an English middle-class family on its uppers. In a Bradford Jowett van (my mother's Ford had been sold, and I now rode second class, in the back) we trailed through Somerset, hunting for churchyards where remote cousins were supposed to have been buried. My father scraped the lichens off tombstones with a kitchen knife, while I looked for slow worms under fallen slates. On wet days, he took himself off to the record offices in Taunton and Exeter, where he ploughed through parish registers, checking births, marriages and deaths in eighteenth-century villages. 'We come', he said, 'from yeoman stock. Good yeoman stock.'

Then there were the living to visit. Most seemed to be elderly women living with a 'companion', and they stretched, like a row of hill forts, across southern England from Sussex to Devon. Each holiday, my father appeared to discover a new great-aunt. Their houses were thatched, and smelled of must and dog. The ladies themselves were mannish, always up to something in the garden with a hoe and trug. The few men were immobilised, wrapped up in rugs, and talked in fluting falsetto voices. My grandfather, Harry Priaulx Raban (grown-ups called him 'H.P.'), had retired from his parish in Worcestershire to a Hampshire cottage where, on his good days, he used to celebrate an Anglo-Catholic mass of his own devising in a little room that he'd turned into an alfresco shrine. I sometimes acted as his server on these occasions, piping the responses to his piped versicles. A plain crucifix hung above the improvised altar, sur-rounded by framed photographs of Edwardian boys at Clifton College. At Prime and Compline and Communion, my grandfather paid homage to his own past in a way that had come to seem to me perfectly natural—for anyone in our family.

My father was barely thirty, yet we lived almost exclusively in the company of the old and the dead. Sometimes his old regimental friends would call, and there was a steady stream of youngish clergy-men and colleagues from TocH; these contemporaries brought a boisterous, irresponsible air into the house, a hint of fun which seemed alien to it. Its proper visitors were aunts and elderly cousins—people who nodded at the portraits on the walls and left their sticks in the rack by the front door. In private with my mother, my father had a lightness I have not done justice to. He liked *Punch*, and told stories, and spent a lot of time in the garage tinkering with the car: there was a boyishness about him which was always being forcibly squashed. The lugubrious solemnity was practised as a duty. He behaved as if it was incumbent on him to appear older, stuffier, more deferential than he really was. The silly world of gaiety and feeling was my mother's province, and I think my father felt a stab of guilt every time he entered it. It was *not manly*, not quite worthy of a serious Raban. So he overcompensated, with a surfeit of aunts and ancestors, and made his amends by constructing a vast family tree which he kept rolled up in a cardboard tube. Each year, new lines appeared; forgotten cousins many times removed were resurrected; our yeoman stock inched steadily back through the Georges and into the reigns of Queen Anne and Charles II.

I was five, then six, when my younger brothers were born. These additions to the tree struck me as needless. With ancestors like ours, who needed children? But I had been cuckolded before, and had learned to live with infidelity. Our household was already bulging with family, and my brothers simply added to the clutter. Though my own status was eroded. My mother constantly mixed up our names, and the two leaking babies and I got rechristened, for convenience's sake, as 'the boys', a title that made me cringe with humiliation. I hated their swaddled plumpness, their milky smell, and felt that their babyhood somehow defeated what little progress I had made in the direction of manliness. Lined up with them on the back seat of the Bradford van, surrounded by their cardigans, their leggings, their bootees, their plastic chamber pots and teated bottles, I used to daydream myself into a state of haughty solitude. I acquired a habitual manner of grossly injured dignity.

If I have a single image of family life, it is of a meal table. There is a high chair in the picture, dirty bibs, spilt apple puree, food chaotically laid out in saucepans, a squeal, a smack, my father's suffering brow creased with migraine, my mother's harassed face ('Oh, *blow*!'), and the line 'William's made a smell' spoken by my younger brother through his adenoids. And over all this, the ancestors glower from their frames and the crested silver mocks from the tabletop. It isn't just the noise, the mess, the intrusive intimacies; it is that hopeless collision between the idea of Family as expounded by my father and the facts of family as we lived them out. We had ideas that were far beyond our means.

At this time my father must have been earning about £600 a year. Like most other lower-middle-class households, we were overcrowded, we had to make do on a shoestring budget and we had neither the money, the time nor the space for the dignities and civilities that my father craved. 'We are', he reminded us, 'a family of *gentlemen*.' Was my teacher at school, I asked, a gentleman? No. A nice man, certainly, but not quite a gentleman. Was Mr Banham up the road a gentleman? No: Mr Banham was in trade. People in trade were not gentlemen: gentlemanliness, it was explained, had nothing to do with money; it was a matter of caste, taste and breeding—and we were gentlemen. This distinction caused me a great deal of anxiety. The few friends I made never turned out to be gentlemen. Some were 'almost'; most were 'not quite'. Their fathers were often much better paid than mine, their accents (to my ears) just as clear. My mother was always keen to stretch the point and allow all sorts and conditions of men into our privileged class; but my father was a stickler for accuracy and knew a parvenu when he saw one. Consequently I was ashamed of my friends, though my mother always welcomed them, at least into the garden if not into the house. They didn't have ancestors and family trees like ours, and I half-despised and half-envied them their undistinguished ordinariness. Once or twice I was unwise enough to let on that I was marked by a secret distinction invisible to the eye—and the consequences tended to support my parents' conviction that the state system of education was barbarous and fit only for young hooligans. I was, predictably (especially since I started to get asthma the moment I stopped having coeliac), a thoroughly unpopular child. At primary school, I started to keep a score of the number of days I had lasted without crying in the playground. It stayed at zero, and I gave it up. But I always believed that I was bullied because I was 'special'. That too happened to you because you were a gentleman.

There was another family on our horizon. Uncle Peter—my mother's brother—lived on the suburban outskirts of Birmingham, and we saw him twice or three times a year. I was his godson, and after I was seven or eight I was occasionally allowed to stay at his house. For me, he was pure legend. Balding, affable, blasé, he would drop in and out of the blue in a Jaguar car, smelling of soap and aftershave. Like my mother, Uncle Peter had been brought up by my grandmother in Switzerland, in the last days of servants; but somehow he had managed to escape being a gentleman. He'd taken a degree in engineering at Birmingham University, and during the war had served in the RNVR. If Macmillan had wanted a symbol of postwar meritocratic affluence in the age of You've-Never-Had-It-So-Good, he might well have chosen Uncle Peter, with his car, his sailing boat, his first-in-the-road TV set and his centrally heated suburban villa. Uncle Peter had real class—with a flat *a*—but he was entirely innocent of the suffocating class snobbery which ruled our roost.

Staying at Uncle Peter's was like being admitted to Eden. There was no smell of guilt in the air, no piety to a lost past. Where we had ancestors, he had Peter Scott bird-paintings and framed photos of ocean racing yachts on his walls. Where we had shelves of family books (sermons, Baker's *Sport in Bengal*, *The Royal Kalendar*, first editions of Jane Austen, a Victorian *Encyclopedia Britannica*), Uncle Peter had copies of the *National Geographic* magazine, *Reader's Digest* condensed books and greenback Penguins. I had often been enchanted by the bright theatre of an illuminated department store window at dusk—the impossibly soft rugs, the virgin upholstery of the three-piece suite, the bottles and glasses set ready on gleaming coffee tables, the glow of steel standing lamps . . . a room designed for immaculate people without memories or consciences. The inside of Uncle Peter's house was like one of those windows come to life. It was my Brideshead. I was dazzled by its easy, expensive philistinism; dazzled, too, by my girl cousins with their bicycles and tennis rackets and the casual, bantering way in which they talked to their parents.

On Sunday morning, no one went to church. I half expected a thunderbolt to strike us down for our audacity, but in Uncle Peter's family church was for weddings, funerals, baptisms and Christmas. Instead, we sat out on the breakfast patio, sunbathing. Uncle Peter stretched himself out on a scarlet barcalounger, put on dark glasses, and settled into his *Sunday Express*. I was nearly delirious. I hadn't realised that it was possible to break so many taboos at once, and Uncle Peter was breaking them all without so much as a flicker of acknowledgement that he was doing anything out of the ordinary. I also felt ashamed. I was so much grubbier, more awkward, more screwed-up than these strange people with their Californian ease and negligent freedom; like any trespasser in Eden, I was always expecting to be given the boot.

Given his belief in stock and blood-lines, it would have been hard for my father to be too openly critical of Uncle Peter. My mother's family (doctors and Shetland crofters) was, of course, not quite up to Raban standards, but Uncle Peter was still definitely a gentleman. So my father limited himself to a few warning shots delivered from a safe distance. 'Don't suppose he gets more than fifteen to the gallon out of *that car*.' 'Can't think what he must be paying for moorings for *that boat*.'

'He's always going abroad to conferences,' said my mother.

'One conference, dear. One conference that we actually *know* of.'

To me, he was spoken of as '*your* Uncle Peter', which gave me a certain pride of possession, as I happily took responsibility for the 3.8 Jag, the decanter of Scotch and *that boat*. At Christmas and on my birthday he sent postal orders, and I was briefly *nouveau riche*, happily about to squander the money on status symbols on my own account, like fixed-spool fishing reels and lacquered cork floats. 'You'd better put *that* in your post-office savings. Hadn't you, old boy?' So Uncle Peter was laid up where neither moth nor rust corrupted. I loathed my savings-book. When, years later, I first heard the phrase 'The Protestant Ethic', I knew exactly what it meant: it was my father's lectures on the subject of my post-office savings account.

'It's all very well, old boy, your wanting to throw your money down the drain in inessentials now. But when it comes to the time, what are you going to do about the Big Things, eh? Now, that money you've got in the post office; that *grows*. Sixpence in the pound mounts up, you know. Suppose . . . suppose, in, say, three or four years you want a bicycle. Where do you imagine that bicycle is going to come from? I'm afraid, old boy, that bicycles do not grow on trees.'

But in Selly Oak I had ridden in the Jag, and skipped church on Sunday, and a splinter of doubt had lodged in my mind. There were, I now knew, places in the world where bicycles did grow on trees.

When it was announced ('Daddy has had a calling') that my father was going to seek ordination, I lay on the floor and howled with laughter. I can't remember why—it certainly wasn't in any spirit of satire. I think it may have been straightforward nervous hysteria in the face of the fact that my father was on such intimate terms with God. The question had been put to Him, and He had made His position clear. It all sounded a bit like having an interview with one's bank manager. But I was awed and proud. We were high Anglicans—so high that we could almost rub noses with the Romans. The priest, in his purple and gold vestments, was a figure of glorious authority. He was attended by boys swinging incense. He chanted services in plainsong. High in the pulpit, his surplice billowing round him, he exercised a mystique of a kind that, say, a politician could not hope to match. Had my father said that he was going to stand for parliament, I would have been impressed; when he said he was going to be a priest, I was awestruck. I grew intensely vain on the strength of his vocation. I was not only a gentleman; I was about to be the son of a priest. When bullied in the playground, I now thought of myself as a holy martyr, and my brows touched heaven. 'Daddy's vocation' had singled him out from the ruck of common men, just as I expected soon to be singled out myself. I waited for my calling, and pitied my persecutors. At night, I had vivid fantasies in which God and I were entwined in a passionate embrace. By day, I spent my time staring out of the classroom window in a fog of distraction. I was not a clever child. My distinction was a secret between myself, my ancestors and God.

My father was thirty-three—a year younger than I am now—when he became a theological student. For the first time in my life, I realised that he was not actually as old as he had always seemed. We took a rented house on the outskirts of Bognor, and my father bicycled the six miles between there and his college in Chichester, staying in the house only at weekends. He wore a college scarf and went about in cycle clips; he played for the college cricket team and swotted up his notes. Now that he was more often away from the family than inside it, he lost his irritable hauteur, and I began to lose my fear of him. On Saturday afternoons, my mother brought my brothers and me to support his team from the boundary, where we were the centre of a group of pious, hearty young men with the arms of their white sweaters tied round their necks. At college, I think my father must have recaptured some of the ease that he'd felt in his wartime regiment. Most of the other students were younger than him, and he was like an easygoing adjutant among subalterns. I sensed—again for the first time—that he was proud of his family, and we were proud of him.

For those two years we were 'living on capital'—an ominous phrase which meant, in effect, that my parents were blueing their post-office savings; and this hectic, once-in-a-lifetime gesture seemed to liberate and frighten them in equal parts. They went on a spree of economies, putting one gallon of petrol at a time in the car and buying everything in quantities so small that my mother appeared to be going shopping round the clock. They also hatched what was as far as I was concerned their greatest folly. They decided to scrape their last pennies together and send me to public school.

For once, I was happy at school. At Rose Green Primary I had made some friends (no gentlemen, but with my father now a student we were turning into daring bohemians). With private coaching, I muddled, a little improbably, through the eleven-plus, and had a place waiting for me at the grammar school in Chichester. But my parents were expecting to move house at least twice within the next three years, and at ten I had already attended four different schools (a dame, a prep and two primaries). That was the rational side. The irrational side was all to do with ancestors, gentility and manliness.

'Take this business of your asthma, old boy. It's all psychosomatic, you know. Psychosomatic. Know what psychosomatic means? In the head. It's all in the head. It means you bring it on yourself. Public school will clear that one up in no time.'

The brochure arrived. My father had been at King's in the 1930s, and we pored over the blotchy photos of rugger pitches and the cathedral green. My father showed a new, alarming levity; we were boys together as he pitched into a slightly mad peroration about the joys of doing 'The Classics' and taught me the basic rules of rugger on the drawing-room carpet.

'Pass the ball behind you—like this. Always pass the ball behind, never in front.'

His own fondest memory of King's had to do with being put into a laundry basket and having his arm broken. Somehow as my father told it it came out as pure pleasure. Every Sunday we checked over the public-school rugby results where they were listed in small print at the back of the *Sunday Times*. When King's won, there was a celebratory air around the breakfast table; when they lost we were downcast too. My mother had some Cash's name-tapes made up: J. M. H. P. RABAN SCHOOL HOUSE. In the evenings, she sewed them into piles of socks, pants, shirts and towels, checking each item against the matron's printed list.

When we made our annual trek from aunt to aunt, I basked in the phrase, repeated like a litany, 'Ah—Jonathan's off to public school, you know.' God, I was special. Suddenly elevated out of 'the boys', I towered with distinction. I could barely speak to my old friends at Rose Green—common little boys who played soccer and went on Sundays, if they went at all, to nonconformist churches.

At my confirmation service, the Bishop of Chichester preached on a text from Paul's Epistle to the Ephesians:

> *I therefore, the prisoner of the Lord, beseech you*
> *that ye walk worthy of the vocation wherewith ye are called.*

No one that year was walking more worthily than me. Already I was nursing my own calling and talking regularly to God. I walked in imaginary vestments, a halo of distinction faintly glowing round my person.

As my father pointed out, sending me to public school was going to mean sacrifices—enormous sacrifices. My mother was not going to be able to buy clothes; my brothers would have to live in hand-me-downs; with the price of tobacco as it was, my father was going to have to think seriously about giving up his pipe. This did frighten me. Despite the fact that I was living in an ever-inflating bubble of persecuted egotism, it did break in on me that the probable result of all this sacrifice was going to be that I was going to let everybody down. At nights, I strained to see myself sprinting away from the scrum towards the touch-line to score the winning try for School House; but the picture would never quite come right. When my father talked about the famous 'house spirit', I was troubled by a stubborn image of myself skulking grubbily, shame-faced, on the fringe of things. I had always been the last to be picked for any side. Would public school really change that? I tried fervently to believe so but some germ of realism made me doubt it. Certainly I felt singled out for peculiar honours, but my vocation was for something priestly and solitary; it wasn't for team games. I was scared by the other children whom I now affected to despise—and the prospect of living in a whole houseful of my contemporaries was frightening. I was beginning to suspect that I had my limits, and my faith in miracles was shaky. But with General Sir Edward and his cronies on one side, and the hand-me-downs and shiny skirts on the other, I went off to King's, teased by the notion that it was I who was the sacrifice.

One memory of being miserable at boarding school is much like another—and none are quite believable. I went when I was eleven; I left when I was sixteen; and I spent an unhealthy proportion of that five years wishing that I was dead. The usual story. For the holidays, I came home to beat my puzzled younger brothers black and blue. I was their monitor; they were my fags. So I was able to share with my family some of the benefits of going to public school.

Our family life seemed full of anomalies and bad fits. There was the problem of my father's age—one moment he was boyish, the next testily patriarchal. There was the mismatch between our actual circumstances and our secret splendour. There was the constant conflict between the superior Victorian family to which we were supposed to belong and the squally muddle of our everyday life. We were short on education, short on money, short on manners; and the shorter we got, the taller grew our inward esteem. In the Anglican Church, and in the succession of clergy-houses that we moved to, we found a kind of objective correlative for our private family paradoxes.

In the 1950s, the Church of England had not changed all that much since George Herbert was a parish priest. It hadn't yet been hit by 'existential theology' or the decadent tomfoolery of the Charismatic Movement. It still stood firm on Parson's Freehold and the idea that the priest was third in line to the squire and the doctor. Even on urban housing estates, where churches were plonked down in the middle to be vandalised before they'd had a chance to be consecrated, the vicar was expected to behave as he would in an agricultural village. The Church was smiled on by the housing authorities presumably because it was felt that it might introduce a cheery, villagey note of 'community' into these godforsaken places. Put a beaming cleric in dog-collar and cassock in Churchill Crescent or Keynes Road, and you are halfway to creating another Tiddlepuddle Magna. In one sense, the clergyman was expressly hired to be an anomaly. Like our family, the Church had a grand past but was down on its luck. Like our family, it was succoured by a sense of its own inner virtue and stature in the face of utter indifference from ninety per cent of the rest of the world. Like my own, its public face was one of superior injured dignity.

My father was given the curacy of a council estate just outside Winchester, and we turned into a parsonage family. To begin with, the ancestors were moved into a council house, disdainfully slumming it in the cramped lounge-diner. They had probably known worse. Long-suffering, ox-like men, their schools, like mine, had prepared them for temporary quarters and outposts of Empire. The Weeke Estate was much like an Indian hill station, with hard rations, lousy architecture and nothing to speak of in the way of society. It was no accident that the one author whose works we possessed in their entirety, in the uniform Swastika edition, was Kipling.

The parsonage was an island. People came to it when they wanted *rites de passage*—to be baptised, married and buried. Or they were in distress: tramps with tall stories on the look-out for a soft touch; pregnant girls, dragged there by grave, ashamed parents; middle-aged women who cried easily; and lots of shadowy people, talking in low confessional voices beyond the closed door of my father's study. When they came to the house, their manners were formal; often they had put on best suits for the occasion. What is it that people want from a priest? Understanding, surely, but not ease or intimacy. Most of all, I suspect, they feel that only a priest can clothe a bitter private hurt or mess with the gravity and dignity that they would like it to deserve.

My father seemed cold and inhibited towards me as if he found our biological connection an embarrassment. But to his parishioners he was able to show a sympathy, even a warmth, that perhaps depended on the formal distance which lay between him and them. In mufti, he was often stiff and blundering. In the uniform of his cassock and his office, he was gentle and considerate. The very things that might have marked him as a misfit outside the priesthood enabled him to be a good priest. I've known a number of people who have told me how much they have admired him, been grateful to him, and thought of him as a consummately good man.

At that time, though, for me he was pure Jekyll and Hyde. I thought of him as a hypocritical actor. Offstage, he seemed to be perpetually irritable, perpetually swallowing aspirins, never to be disturbed. His study—a chaos of papers under a blue pall of St Bruno Rough Cut tobacco smoke—was a place I was summoned to, for a long series of awkward, sometimes tearful, occasionally violent interviews. Once I tried to knock him down, and in my memory he collapses in an amazed heap among the parish magazines, narrowly avoiding cracking his skull on the duplicating machine. But that is probably an Oedipal fantasy. What really happened, I'm afraid, is that the amazement was on my face, and that the collapse too was mine—into weeping apologies. Usually, though, these confrontations followed a pattern as cold and stereotyped as a chess gambit. I stood; my father sat, shuffling papers, filling his pipe. While he stared beyond me out of the window, he would talk with tired logic about my misdemeanours (terrible school reports, insolence, laziness in the house, rumours of girls). The final line was always the same.

'I'm afraid that the trouble with you . . . old boy . . . is that you appear to have no thought for anyone except yourself.'

Long, long pause. Sound of pipe dottle bubbling in a stem. A faint groan from my father. A muttered monosyllable from me.

'What did you say?'

'Sorry.'

'Sorry—*what?*'

'Sorry . . . *Daddy.*'

Another pause, while my father gazes sadly out over a landscape of sandpiles, stray dogs and upturned tricycles.

'I do wish you'd make *some* sort of an effort.'

I did see his point. The sacrifices that were being made on my behalf were all too visible. My father's clothes had been worn to a bluebottle sheen. His shoes gaped. And I was at public school. Worse, I knew that I was wrong, perhaps even evil, when I accused him of hypocrisy. Here he was, wearing himself through on my behalf, and driving himself to nervous exhaustion in the parish; what right had I to ask even more of a man who was clearly two-thirds of the way to being a living saint? It was further evidence—as if I needed any more—of my own selfishness. With the help of a Penguin book on psychology I diagnosed myself as a psychopath.

The parsonage became a refuge for a number of people who, as social casualties go, were the walking wounded. Most had been left stranded—as we had—in the wrong age or the wrong class. Schoolmistresses, social workers, district nurses, they attached themselves to the fringe of the family, dropping in unannounced with small presents and staying on into the night talking with my father. The closest, most persistent ones were made honorary aunts, and they liked to busy themselves in the house, clucking over my brothers, 'helping' my mother, and making strained conversation with me, until my father, his cassock flapping round his heels, came home from his rounds.

'Hello, dear!' Having spotted the parked Morris Minors round the corner, he had the cheeriness of someone walking through the French windows in a drawing-room comedy. He always discovered the lurking aunts with delighted surprise. 'Ah, Elspeth!' And Miss Stockbridge, or Miss Winnall, or Miss Crawley, glandularly mountainous in tweeds, would produce a tiny, astonished little Bo-Beep voice—'Oh, hel*lo*, Peter!'—as if their meeting was a stroke of wild coincidence. From my room upstairs, I would hear my father's

'Hmmn ... hmmn ... yes ... yes ... yes ... *Oh*, dear. Ah, ha-ha,' while the high, put-upon frequency of the adoptive aunt was lost to all except my father and the neighbourhood dogs.

Much later, when they'd gone, I'd hear my mother's voice. 'Oh, poor old Elspeth—the *poor* soul!' And my father would answer, 'I'm afraid the trouble with *that* one ...'

The social worker's dealings with his client do have some formal limits. But with a clergyman, nothing is out of bounds. People came to my father for reassurances of a kind no doctor or psychiatrist could offer. This meant that everyone who arrived at the parsonage—even those who came in the guise of my parents' friends—presented themselves as crocks and casualties. The ones who came and came again had things wrong with them that were far too vague to ever cure. They were spiritual things—weaknesses and discontents for which the doctrine of the Resurrection was the only answer. My father had put himself in the position of Miss Lonelyhearts, but he had more pride and less saving cynicism than the columnist in Nathanael West's novel; and his view of this world to which he'd opened our door was one of compassionate condescension.

'We in the parsonage ...' 'In the parsonage family ...' 'As a son of the parsonage ...' My father's lectures nearly always started out with one or other of these riders. We were expected to be exemplary. Our standards of moral and social decorum—unlike those of the natives among whom we'd been posted—were supposed to be beyond either criticism or pity. Another favourite was 'More people know Tom Fool than Tom Fool knows'; and I went about the council estate aware that it was full of spies behind curtains. One slip from me, and my father's standing in his parish could come a cropper. On the estate as on the rugger field, I was always letting our side down. At twelve and thirteen, up to no particular good with boys of my own age from the youth club, I sometimes came face to face with my father on his rounds, and pretended not to see him. He misinterpreted these gestures, and thought I was trying to 'cut' him. I wasn't. I was simply ashamed to be caught fraternising with the children of his problem families—boys who, as he pointed out, had not had my advantages, and whose obvious shortcomings deserved compassion, not uncritical collusion.

On the far fringes of the parish, where the houses stood back from the road behind trees and rhododendrons, the gentry lived. Like the ancestors, they were retired colonels and commanders, admirals and generals. Their children went to boarding schools. Their houses smelled of flowers, dry sherry and wax polish. They weren't problem families; and we visited them shyly when bidden, like poor cousins, trying as best we could to tiptoe through their loud gravel. It usually took fifteen minutes for me to find myself out on the back lawn with their daughter, where we would both stand awkwardly scuffing our heels and smiling fiendishly.

'Do you play tennis?'

'No.'

'Oh, what a pity. When Henry's here, we play a lot of tennis. But Henry's at Dartmouth, you know.'

'Oh, dear.'

'Mummy said she thought you might play tennis.'

'I'm sorry.'

'Oh—not to worry!'

Desperation. With an hour to kill, we would inspect abandoned tree-houses like a pair of undertakers visiting a cemetery on their day off.

'I say, you didn't hear a bell, did you?'

'I don't think so.'

'I could have sworn . . . I suppose Mrs Hawkins must be late with tea. Awfully boring for you, I'm afraid.'

'Oh, no! No, no, no!'

'Are you in YF?'

'Er . . . I don't think so.'

'Ah, there's the bell. Good-oh.'

Then, quite suddenly in the middle of the 1950s, a lot of bells began to ring. The first one I remember hearing was Frankie Lymon singing 'I'm not a juvenile delinquent', which went to the top of the hit parade sometime in 1955, I think. Bill Haley and his Comets made their first British tour, and in Worcester, where I was at school, there was hardly a seat left intact after *Rock Around the Clock* was shown at the Gaumont. I read *Look Back in Anger*, Joyce's *Portrait of the Artist*, and Anouilh's *Antigone*, and somehow managed to muddle them together into a single work of which I was the hero. There was the Chris Barber band and the Beaulieu Jazz Festival. There was C.N.D., which for me meant the triumphant end of the C.C.F. All at once it was possible to think of oneself as a member of a generation and not as a member of a family; and the generation provided me with new standards that were even more liberated than Uncle Peter's. It seemed that overnight my minuses had all changed to pluses. The generation loathed my ancestors even more than I did; it despised team games; its heroes were sulky, sickly solitaries like Juliette Greco in her death-mask phase. At sixteen, I discovered that the inchoate mess of my relations with my father had been all the time, unknown to me, a key battle in the coming revolution. And I was on the winning side. It was like having my dream of scoring the winning try in the house match come true. We continued to have rows—about my wearing a C.N.D. badge at family meals, about bringing *that* rag into *this* house (the *New Statesman* into the vicarage), about girls ('Not really the kind of girl you'd wish to introduce to Mummy, is she?'), about the width of my trouser-bottoms (eighteen was permissible, but sixteen was 'teddy boy'). But I too now wore an expression of distant superiority through these wrangles. An outsider looking in might have seen us as a pair of quarrelling mirror-images—two glazed faces speaking in the accents of the same old school.

I was much too absorbed in the enthralling process of my own adolescence to notice that bells had begun to ring for my father too. Something happened. Perhaps it came about on his parish rounds, as he found himself drawn in to the tangle of other people's lives, unable, finally, to maintain his distance. Perhaps it had to do with the difficulties he found himself in when he skirmished with the local worthies who regarded the church as an extension of their own drawing-rooms. Perhaps he just strayed one day from under the oppressive shadow of the family past and found the air clearer and the going easier. At any rate, he changed. The first thing to go was his Anglo-Catholicism, which he dropped in favour of a kind of basic, ecumenical Christianity. Sometime in the 1960s, he slipped out of his ancestral family toryism and became a Labour voter. He exchanged his living in a Hampshire village for a vast parish of tower blocks in Southampton. His passion for ancestor-hunting turned into a scholarly interest in social history. On holiday one year, he grew a beard. It was as if a row of buttons on a tight waistcoat had suddenly given way.

I have written about him as if he was dead—the Oedipal fantasy again. But when we see each other now, I find it hard to detect more than shadows of the man I remember as my father. The ancestors are still hanging on the walls of his vicarage, but they have the air of inherited lumber now, and have lost their power to hex. We talk easily. We both think of ourselves as victims of our upbringing—and beneficiaries of it too. The solitariness of his priesthood and my writing is a shared legacy: we have each had to learn how to be alone in society in the practice of our odd, anomalous crafts. A little more than ten years ago, we both suddenly realised that we were chips off the same family block—and I think that the discovery surprised him as much as it did me. When I showed my father this piece in galley proof, he said: 'What you've written here is really a confession on my behalf.'

It is certainly a confession on mine. Looking at the other man, it occurs to me that he may have been a wilful invention of my own. Did I conceive him on the green when I was three as a jealous, defensive fiction? And did I let this fiction die only when I was old enough to leave the family and do without a father to be afraid of?

Perhaps. I don't know. 'There's some *slight* exaggeration—I hope,' my father said, handing me back my galley sheets. I'm afraid so.

An Irish Schooling

SEÁN O'FAOLÁIN

The school I speak of was the Lancasterian School in the town of Cork, one of the first, and maybe the first, Bell and Lancaster schools founded in Ireland. This I did not discover, until long afterwards, for we all associated it with the enemies of the Tudors, and the good monks who taught us, being mentally and emotionally rather like children themselves, did not, I imagine, discover it at any time. It was originally a barrack or a poorhouse, or maybe a madhouse, but at any rate it was born weary like a Buddhist in his fourth transmigration, and should never have been used in our time for any purpose whatever. I do not know when it was founded, but I am certain that it defied all the change and alteration that overtook schooling since the days of Wordsworth, and I know that the hoary, dusty, cobwebbed atmosphere of the place remained to the end the atmosphere of Carleton rather than of Joyce—the atmosphere, that is, of an enormous hedge-school in what, so bizarre was the life there, must surely have been a discarded asylum.

At the centre of the school was the Big Room, what wealthier folk would have called the *Aula Maxima*. The roof was broken on either side of the roof-tree by a clerestory composed of hundreds upon hundreds of patches of glass; beneath this clerestory, 'dreadful and dizzy to cast one's eyes so low', four or five classes would 'toe the line' in different parts of the hall, curved about a horseshoe, chalked on the floor, at whose centre stood the black-robed monk in charge. Every second boy was barelegged, with the mud drying between his toes and zoomorphic tracery on his shins from sitting in the ashes of his laneway home. At playtime, when other classes were howling in the yard, we would stand thus, each boy with a little penthouse balanced on his head, an open book, to protect him from the penalty of falling glass. For the great game in the yard outside was what I have since heard called the Roof Game. It began with the throwing of a ball, a thing of paper and twine, sideways on the slates, and it ended with a mad tangle fighting under the gutters to catch the ball, when, where, and if it fell.

East and west were the aisles to this nave, sheltering one or two more classes each, as well as the science-room, which was also office, drawing-room, monks' lunch-room, and place of more painful and less modest corporal punishment. The Infants were tucked away behind the apse; there was a black-hole where chronic offenders were sometimes flung to whimper among the coals and the rats; a gravelled yard ran on each side of the building; the foul jakes lined it behind; and there was, finally, the caretaker's cottage where he stored thrown-out copy-books for fuel and broke up old desks for firewood.

I shall always associate this school with Lowood School in *Jane Eyre*, not because we ever had any Reverend Mr Brocklehurst, but because in spite of much vermin, some disease, and no external beauty, in spite of the cold and the smells, we managed to create inside that crumbling hole a faery world of our own—and by *we*, I mean the monks and the children together, for these Brothers were truly brothers to us and I think we really loved them. They were country lads with buttermilk complexions, hats prevented from extinguishing their faces only by the divine prescience of ears, hands still rough from the spade and feet still heavy with the clay. I recall their complete lack of self-consciousness with us—which did not prevent them from being shy and blushing in the presence of other monks—the complete absence of the keep-the-boy-in-his-place rule which (perhaps largely in self-defence) is so common in High Schools. Some, to be sure, were disliked—it is not in the nature of small boys to hate—and because they were mincing or had no sense of fun we called them names like Cinderella or Sloppy Dan.

But in general it is their simplicity that I recall now, their jokes that were not made simple for our benefit but were born simple of simple parents, the games they played with us so lustily with bits of stick or cloth-balls in the rough yard, their inquisitiveness about our home lives, their natural piety that threw a benignity over all our days. I recall their general and particular ignorance with a general and particular delight. I once wrote a childish essay on Fishing for my Brother Josephus in which I cheekily described how I went fishing up the Lee and fished up a girl; and I still remember the utter joy with which they all crowded about that essay, gloating in their own knowledge of worldly wickedness. And, to reverse the roles, how innocent Brother Patrick seemed to us when he began to warn us about the great temptations of the summer time and how he actually knew little boys who went swimming without any bathing-drawers at all! As they grew older and were instructed better they gradually moved on to High School or Secondary School where with the increase in their 'little learning' they often became priggish and unlikeable; and they often became unhappy, and between comic and tragic like the two poor men, who for all their thirty years or more we used to watch throwing their eyes mawkishly after girls. One was always hearing of this or that monk who left the Order or was about to leave it, though I find it hard to imagine how they could ever earn a living after being so long cloistered away from the competing world.

As to their particular ignorance, I remember it, I hope, not with the slightest feeling of superiority but because, even then, we knew that their weight of knowledge did not prevent them from being very near our ignorance. They—the pronoun is colloquial and exclusive—commonly mispronounced words and place-names in frequent use, saying NewFOUNDland, HanOVER, *coincídence*; were free with superfluous syllables as in *cathedaral*; failed to recess the accent as in *contráry*—it is the natural conservatism of the provincial which still says *tay* for *tea*, that says *demónstrate* for *démonstrate*; they were hopelessly muddled by *shall* and *will*; the use of the Gaelic present-habitual for the English present, *They do be* for *They are*, was widespread, and so on—lapses which are all easily remembered because forgotten with difficulty among the 'little gents' of the higher school. I can scarcely believe my memory when I seem to recall being told by Brother Josephus that combustion is due to phlogiston; that Brother Philip told us that circumcision was a small circle cut out on the forehead of Jewish children; clearly his reading misled him; but I do know, having verified it by the memory of others, that we were told there were twelve minerals and we were given their names, and that was that. On the other hand I always think admiringly of old Brother Magnus, who offered sixpence to anybody who would extract salt from the seawater in the harbour, and when one or two did it, offered a silver watch to any boy who would extract sugar from a turnip.

The point is, we all worked together as in a family, conspiring for example against inspectors from the Board of Education, or even against the headmaster. I remember one Inspector of Hygiene who came to lecture us on cleanliness—a badly needed lecture in that school—about nails, and hair and teeth and so forth, while our Brother Josephus stood in the background with a slow smile about his lips. When the man of cleanliness was finished Josephus showed him out coldly and then, turning back to us, swept us together into his bosom for ever and ever in one wave of indignation by saying in contempt of all inspectors: 'Boys! He thinks ye're filth!' When more important inspectors were coming how we worked in preparation, often copying in reams from old boys' essays, in the full knowledge that it was all a 'racket'; and after the inspection, during which the poor little monks stood about pale and trembling, we would crowd about our particular Josephus to know if we had done well—well by

him, that is—rejoicing if he told us mildly that we had done quite
well, then pulling us up short in the sudden effort to recapture his
sadly damaged authority.

I know I am doing them all an injustice, and doing those years an
injustice too. It is another world, not only gone for ever now, but not
to be recaptured even in memory. All I did and learned there was
done and learned for the love of the thing. In the High School, life and
learning became (and have ever since remained) complicated by the
importunity of those two heritages of Adam, the conscience and the
will. From that complicated world to look back on a world where
these genii did not exist is to look into a blinding light. Life there was
a succession of dream-days which now as a writer—self-conscious
like all my tribe—I envy almost to tears, because they were the only
days of my life that were really lived. Then there were, in our minds,
no strivings towards an end, as in school later (or towards perfection,
as in the conscience of the grown man, writer or artisan), to annotate
the joys of living by reminders of the seriousness of life. Far otherwise, all the seriousness of life was annotated by the sheer, unconscious joy of being simply alive. I had not eaten of the apple of
ambition and was unaware of nakedness.

Do not imagine that a child does not enjoy 'being simply alive', or
that when a man says he recalls pleasant times at school that he means
anything but times that seemed pleasant then. Indeed, the *recherche du
temps perdu* is always melancholy with a sense of loss where the *temps*
itself glowed with immediacy.

What of those wet southern days when few children dared come to
school and the feeling of comradeship among those that came was so
great that we hated to return home? Where the rain lashed the patched
windows in the clerestory and we crowded over the fire to talk of the
tawny rivers of the city rising in flood! When we rounded our cheeks
and rolled our eyes and said Oooh! to the wind under the door! Yes!
One could weep now because never again can one say Oooh! to the
wind under the door, but then it was all sheer delight in the delights of
Delight itself. And then there were days before breaking-up at sum-
mer-time, when all fear of inspectors was vanished, and we did
nothing for days but clean the white ink-wells, and roll up the maps,
and disclose on the walls behind them sudden stored blasts of light,
and shoved dusters down one another's backs, and crushed closer
than ever about the skirts of the Brothers to talk of our home, and our
holidays, and their homes and their holidays, and our future—which
meant next year—and theirs that meant, alas, poor adults, so much
more. You looked back at the last moment at the crumb-laden floors,
and the dust under the desks, all empty, and you felt the crumbs at the

47

bottom of your school-sack that suddenly having lost all its import smelt only of vanished days; and you turned away as to a long exile.

It's the sense of wonder which is gone now, I suppose, the capacity of enjoyment killed by constant ratiocination, by too much thinking of things instead of doing them. Even those casualties from falling glass, or stones flung in yard-fights, were welcome because you were led out by an elder boy to be stitched or bandaged at the hospital, a pleasantly terrifying experience, during which you wondered if you were really going to die. These breaks were typical of that school; it was a delight to be sent making up the rolls, doing all the adding and subtracting and compiling that the Head was too lazy to do himself; to be sent out to the street just before roll-call to see if any laggards were coming, in which case you certainly told the shivering wretch that Sloppy Dan would KILL him when he got inside; magical to be sent in search of a missing pupil down among the penthouse lanes of the city, in and out of Featherbed or Cut-throat where the shifts and shawls drying from window to window made the colours of a canopy in a papal procession, where every dark doorway under the thatch, shot by its blob of firelight, delayed further your already slow-lingering steps.

One may think that it was not a good school, but I think it was—fairly good. Its great drawback was that a clever boy fell at once into habits of idleness there for lack of competition; the pace was set, perforce, for slowcoaches. But the great point about the place was that it was not even faintly 'respectable' and though the teaching was serious it was never solemn. We learned there that learning can be an interesting occupation, and we learned to enjoy without question, as equals, one another's company. When I think of the other kind of school, your High, Secondary, or Public School, where the little gentlemen are critical of one another without rest, and think of learning only as a means to an end, I sigh with relief at being free of it as one sighs on waking from a painful dream.

Not that my school was not cold and cheerless and had not some bad hours. I can never forget that one or two of these monks were rude, brutal men who terrified the very heart out of us at times. I am thinking particularly of one huge fellow in the Third, or Fourth class, I forget which, who had a throat and a voice like a bull, and a strong right arm coming down with the leather-strap, half an inch thick, on our palms. He used, at one period, to collect bread from the monks' lunch-room, and after school set two of his bigger boys, newsboys by night, schoolchildren by day, fighting with bare fists and bare to the waist, for these scraps of food; and withheld the bread one afternoon because they were either not hungry enough, or were too hungry, to take part in his circus. I saw him in the street, years later, when I was in the university, and I looked at his dark jowl with sideward glance, almost in fear.

The place is gone now; not a stone remains upon a stone, and a boot factory in red brick stands where it stood. A new, modern school replaces it, all white tiles and parquet, very anodyne and aseptic. That is all to the good, but it is not that which gives it an advantage over the old place. It is beside fields, and below it there are trees through which one sees the flowing river with cows in other fields beyond. In our old place there were a few ragged trees growing out of asphalt but not a blade of grass to be seen anywhere; and a school without a field is a prison.

If I were a child again and both schools stood, to which would I go? If not to some sterner, more ambitious school than either of them? It is a question à hausser les épaules. Certainly, if it is a matter of getting on in the world, to neither. But if one places more value on other things, then this type of school is ideal, and according as you value these 'other things' the more, then the more reason to go to some old shack like mine where, although one learned little about the world, one imbibed a great deal about life—and perhaps a little about the next life, too.

Hot-Water-Bottle Love

Cheltenham Ladies' College

THEODORA BENSON

I would have liked it better if I had been better liked. And looking back on the year I spent there I cannot help thinking that it was nice of people to like me even as much as they did.

I had been educated at day schools so when I arrived there at the age of seventeen I was completely ignorant of boarding schools and their ways. I thought the others very queer; they thought me very queer; both sides were about right. But the staff were not queer. How they preserved their sanity coping with those battalions of girls I don't know, but they did. I suppose they must have got a lot of quiet fun out of it sometimes, but they must often have felt exasperated. Certainly it never occurred to us that they thought us funny, that we could be the objects of the mistresses' senses of humour. We supposed it to be the other way round, though I cannot recollect that we really made much fun of them. We spoke very cavalierly of most of the staff behind their backs. In their presence we would become subdued and anxious to please. Relieved of their presence, reaction would set in and we would break down into shrieks of giggling.

> When the sands are all dry he's as gay as a lark
> And will talk in contemptuous tones of the shark,
> But when the sea's in and sharks are around
> His voice has a timid and tremulous sound.

Of the ways in which I gave offence by not conforming, some come back to me as quite intolerable and some as mere accidents for which I could not have foreseen blame. To the latter class belongs the matter of the bag in which I carried my books from the residential house to the College. Every other girl in my house used a stereotyped leather bag, carrier, satchel, or whatever it was called, costing I forget how many shillings. I had a bag of just the same convenient size made of matting and ornamented pictorially with three blue geese. It was a nice bag, given to me by a bishop. Not only would it have been a very dull waste of money to have bought another, but I would then have

shared everyone else's difficulty in picking out my own bag from the
mass where they were dumped before lunch after morning school. I
did not know till several years after that my use of that bag was taken
personally and with bitterness by all.

On the other hand I had not even success to justify my attempts to
give myself *soigné* and sophisticated airs. I have not mastered either of
those attributes since; how much less then, with ten years of con-
scientious labour ahead instead of behind me! Perhaps I would have
found the atmosphere of a rather silly and gawkish finishing school in
Paris more congenial. My sister 'came out' while I was still being
educated, and my mind was on parties, clothes, cosmetics, young
men, none of which I knew anything about. My sister had been very
kind to me, consequently so had some of her young men. Two of
these heroes had given me a cocktail at their club, fully chaperoned.
The cocktail was a bronx, the club was the Wellington: dear Wellington, it is still sacred to me. And was I proud of this, or was I proud?
Shortly after my arrival at Cheltenham I said to a group of girls:

'Oh, does anyone happen to remember the address of the Wellington Club? I must get this letter off to Ronnie. Grosvenor something. Really I shall be forgetting my own name next. When I think of
the times that I've drunk cocktails there!'

On another occasion someone remarked that she was going to buy
some vanishing cream and I called out superbly: 'Now there's a thing
I could give you some useful advice about.'

The advice, very rightly, was not asked for. And this was just as
well, for I had none to give.

I got my sister to give me photographs of all her young men with
which to decorate my mantelpiece. My classmates behaved admirably; they never encouraged me by making any comment at all. Since
those days I have so often been accused of affectation, though it
comes quite naturally to me, that I shudder to think how affected I
must have been at a time when I deliberately tried to lounge about
with feline and film-star grace—all elbows and Anglo-Saxon attitudes. Then on one occasion I did myself a bit of no good by telling a
cowardly, flustered and futile lie. I had a few friends to tea in my
room and was doing, as girls will, a crossing the channel act when the
housemistress came in at the noisiest and most displeasing bit. I
muttered into the midst of an awkward silence that I had had a fit of
coughing.

That I think covers their side of the matter. The rest of the things
they had against me seem to me to be moot points. One sees a
photograph of me and thinks that I was wrong to try and do my hair
attractively. One sees a photograph of them and thinks that I was

right. Then as to the question of games, I was intolerant about their heartiness and they were equally intolerant because I took all my exercise on long walks. It cancels out.

Before I go on to my side of the matter there is something that I must stress. The student of modern school literature who expects the stuff to be served up really hot is going to be disappointed. We were almost incredibly innocent. Most of us were eighteen or nineteen, a few of us seventeen or even twenty. I believe that hardly anyone knew what are so exclusively called THE facts of life. Even I was among the more knowing. One of the girls once asked me how babies came. I had a sort of hazy idea but was not very sure of my ground, so I benevolently answered that I thought I should only embarrass both of us by telling her. The usual rules and regulations which belong to the residential section of girls' schools were to us quite silly and meaningless. I think our childish ignorance was almost excessive, and that we might have been a little less foolish if we had known a little more. But I cannot find that this innocence did any of us any harm. All of us that I have come across since have turned out as normal as can be.

It being understood that they were all very nice, very harmless young ladies, I must admit that I had every excuse for being amazed and disgusted at their capacity for heroine worship. I had heard of little girls having tiresome devotions to older ones, of older girls adoring some particular mistress. At my kindergarten I had myself so admired the scripture mistress as to paint her Christmas cards all the year round of holly and plum puddings or of the birth of Christ, and to send her shoe boxes full of flowers. I had sometimes loved the little boys, generally getting engaged to them and on one occasion knocking out a rival for the sake of my simpering small hero. But I simply did not know until I went to Cheltenham Ladies' College that one grown girl could dote to idolatry upon another girl of her own age. These affections, known in the College as 'raves', had all the emotional aspects of calf love or the flutters between a young man and a maid. It seemed kind of odd to me.

They were painful, these raves, and tearful, and, since the College was the world to us who lived therein, they were for the time being important. The ravers would give the ravees anonymous presents of cakes and sweets, and then look conscious. They would be in heaven if accorded a smile as their inamoratas passed them in a passage. They would entreat me to snoop round the bedrooms and spy out who held converse with who. Generally the beloveds loathed it, but sometimes they were touched or flattered at the beginning, encouraged their admirers, then found the thing palled woefully, and got landed in a pretty how-do-you-do of scenes and recriminations. Since I had never been to a boarding school before, these ecstasies were beyond my reach, though I did once unexpectedly find myself a snake in the grass, playing in fact that well-known role the false female friend.

What endless discussions of tactics and strategy we used to hold after supper! I still think I gave very good advice to those love-lorn maidens on how to deal with each other. But whenever the advice happened to be 'hold off for a bit', like many wiser and older they couldn't take it. One of my afflicted friends I think bound all raves into a nutshell when she said to me:

'It's so heartless to like Patsy better than me, when you think how I filled her hot-water-bottle for her every night of the winter term. I don't think Patsy would have filled her hot-water-bottle for her every night—at least I'm sure she wouldn't have done it in quite the same way.'

The other thing I still hold against my fellow students is that they used at breakfast not only to smell their perfectly good boiled eggs, but to pass them round the tables for their friends to smell and pass opinions on too.

Girls *en masse* are quite apt to produce that morbid atmosphere of raves and there is nothing the authorities can do about it. I have a deep distrust of hero or heroine worship in any walk of life. I dislike anything that tends to make people substitute emotion for reason as a regular thing, or to lose themselves in the luxury of hanging on to something else, or to make another human being their brain or their conscience. I would rather see them standing on their own feet and choosing wrong than being towed along in the right direction. Anything of the rave nature always strikes me as unhealthy. But the raves of my school-fellows were no more than a phase of growing up. They were of no significance in the post-College life of the girls. 'They came and went and are not, and come no more anew.' There was nothing sinister about them. We must all be silly sometimes and that was the revolting way a little passing silliness took my contemporaries at College.

The egg business, of course, is inexcusable.

In trying to recapture the atmosphere of my school days and give an account of Cheltenham Ladies' College, I have only been able to talk of myself and my school-fellows. For when it comes to the organisation of the College and the residential houses, and to the teaching, I have nothing that is not pleasant and efficient to report and who wants to read about that? I will get it over very quickly. The food, with the exception of one pudding which we got about twice in three weeks made of liquid blancmange and something tasting like dog biscuits, was excellent. It was good, plentiful, nice and varied. The accommodation was all we could wish. We were allowed a fair degree of liberty. There were parts of the town where we could go alone, and we could visit most of it if we went two or three together. Two or three together could go long walks or bicycle expeditions into the country. There were places that were out of bounds, among them not unreasonably the race course, the polo ground and the boys' college football ground, but this I fortunately did not discover till two-thirds of the way through my time there so I was not greatly inconvenienced. Prayers were short, and involved a nice bit of hymn singing. Only one church service was compulsory on Sundays. We had a grand library at the College and a fair amount of time for browsing in it. The teaching was so stimulating and good that most of us felt inspired to read quite a lot of good stuff we needn't have read at all. My housemistress was kindness itself to me. I remember with great respect and affection both the head of my class room and the Principal of the College, while one of my teachers was among the most interesting, intelligent and delightful women that I have ever met. For the first time in my life I worked hard and enjoyed work. And though I forgot everything I'd learnt within a month of leaving for good, I have always thought that it is better to have known and forgotten than never to have known at all.

I began by saying that had I been more popular I should have been happier at Cheltenham. I think this is true. During my last term I had a few established friendships and I think I was happier. Though I passed through another tiresome stage then, natural this time rather than affected, a sort of Madcap-Molly-the-Pride-of-the-Fourth business which would, had I been in a book, have made me very popular but which in actual fact made no difference either way. I got up sweepstakes on horse races, and brought out a ribald newspaper which was instantly suppressed.

It is such fun reminiscing. When I visited Cheltenham again, years after, with a friend who knew it not, I had so lovely a time recounting anecdotes, showing her round, telling her the nicknames for this place and that place, pointing out where we bought cream buns and sugar biscuits at eleven o'clock in the black and white marble corridor, that were I given to kidding myself in that sort of way I could easily have made the preposterous announcement that my school days had been the happiest time of my life. Really that weekend of revisiting the old haunts and meeting again the old friends, acquaintances and enemies was wholly delightful. There were my fellow students looking pretty and nicely dressed, talking amusingly and sanely. It seemed incredible. What was so particularly strange was to be at Cheltenham with all the same people and not to find them completely and utterly humourless.

As regards humour they compelled my respect and my gratitude. I had put a school in my first novel, a hash-up of every school that I had ever heard anything about, much of the material borrowed from my own school and all of it guyed. I felt some embarrassment at facing all the Cheltonians, but they scored off me. I think the school in that novel very funny. I was not surprised that the staff of Cheltenham thought it funny and congratulated me cordially; they must often have wanted to say the same things. But I was surprised that my fellow students, many of whom were most obviously ragged in this novel, thought it a very funny and entirely justifiable joke. I even felt a little humbled!

I have related, perhaps too incoherently, all that I remember of my year at Cheltenham. All the bad, which seems slight and ludicrous; all the good, which seems sufficient and solid. The fact remains that I disliked my time there on the whole, and that not only did I, the fish out of water, dislike my school days, but that many of the others, in spite of conforming to type, of being used to schools, of playing games, of having *esprit de corps*, disliked it or were more or less unhappy.

But many modern writers make out that schools, and unhappiness at schools, have dire effects on the characters and futures of the pupils. It just isn't so. People don't grow up warped or embittered or the victims of complexes because they had a few good cries in the cloakroom or somebody once snubbed them. I know quite well that my own character is my own fault, and I'd rather have it that way than push the responsibility on to my upbringing. At sixteen I was happy, from seventeen to twenty I was fairly unhappy, from twenty on I grew steadily happier, and now—let me put it on record while it lasts—I am very happy. I should be the same me whether I had been to Cheltenham or not, and if I ever try to blame anything concerning me off on to the old school I shall be a liar.

Not Cricket

MICHAEL HOLROYD

Some people use sheep: I bowl. Along the years, lying in my bed, I must have sent down hundreds of overs—leg-breaks, mostly, mixed with my own version of the googly. If I am rarely successful, either at taking wickets or at inducing sleep, this does not make me feel wretched. I enjoy the rhythm, persistent, floating . . . and since everything can be contained in the reading of a wicket, my thoughts are seldom pierced by dark knives in the night. Many an old man's dream, I suspect, is lit up by white-flannelled figures on a field of glorious green: and then rained off by his crying failure, at the age of eighteen, to make the team. So deep are these regrets for some they overshadow everything.

But not for me. When very young I seemed hedged with such momentous promise as to incapacitate me from doing anything at all. I seldom spoke or was seen to take any initiative, but there was an air (or so I later assumed) of miracles to come: and it was on the cricket pitch that I brought this promise to its tightest knot of suspense. At my private school I was the secret weapon of our First XI—a weapon so secret that few of our opponents could decipher me. It was not (good heavens!) that I scored boundaries or flourished the bat in any stylish way; my bowling, oscillating haphazardly between fast and slow, was seldom called upon; my fielding already showed the resentment I felt for the hardness of the ball. My contribution was independent of all this activity. I stood. As opening batsman, my favourite score at the culmination of the match was nought-not-out. I was still standing. Fast bowlers, it was said, broke their hearts against me.

My conservatism as a batsman had a complicated history. I had been sent to the same school as my father, and his brother before him. But there was a difference. In the interval the family had run out of money. As a result, though appearances were to be kept up, they could not afford all the equipment I needed. I never had, for example, proper pads or a bat. Instead I made do with my uncle's—the bat and pads he had employed with moderate success at university in the 1920s. The pads were deeply yellow and reached almost to my shoulders. I peeped out from them unafraid. The bat was a mature instrument, well-bound and fully-seasoned, giving out a deep note when struck, like a groan. I admired that bat—but I could not lift it. I was ten or twelve: the bat was more than a quarter-of-a-century old. Dressed like some odd laboratory assistant, I would drag it to the crease and then, as it were, leave it there. As I took guard, there occurred a total eclipse of the stumps. The bowler had not even a bail to aim at—no wonder I was so disheartening. After that, there was in effect no more to be done and I was the very person to do it. I had, so to speak, made my statement and there was little refuting it. We stood there, my uncle's bat and I, keeping our end up, while runs flowed and wickets fell at the other end. I had a good eye and would watch the balls swinging my way with great keenness, making lightning decisions as to what shots I could play. But I never played them except in my imagination. If I tried anything, it invariably led to my being given out either hit-wicket or leg-before-wicket—depending on which, the umpire decided, had happened first.

Occasionally, over the seasons, the ball would glance the edge of my uncle's bat and flutter into the slips bringing me a run. But it had to go far to enable me to reach the other end in those pads. In the slips I began to notice a curious figure among one of the teams we played regularly from schools nearby. He merited my attention since it was through his feet that most of my meagre totals would come. He was a large crouching boy, with a round face, hawk-like nose, hanging arms and curiously intent brown eyes. Though he appeared to miss nothing that was going on, he nevertheless also appeared to take no part in any of it. His expression was alert, yet blank, and he looked like a perpetual twelfth man. He was the only other player, I observed, who regularly scored nought-not-out. This was because he went in last and, whatever the circumstances, never received a ball, though he would prod the pitch expertly and swish his bat about a bit from the non-striking end, indicating his keenness. Everything considered, this keenness seemed remarkable and had earned him, I felt, his place in the team. He would blunder on to the field first, ahead of his captain, whirl his arms around and reach the slips long before everyone else arrived at their positions. Then he would wait. He did as much waiting as I did standing. Of course we never really spoke to each other, just nodded; but I warmed to him when, during one of the tea intervals, he put aside his cake for a moment and addressed a few words to my uncle's bat, as one might encourage a dog or cat. You could see it had set him thinking. The blankness of his expression intensified, and he wandered off.

I don't think there was any question of my deliberately steering the ball towards this figure in the slips: I was incapable of such refinements. But I observed, during my last summer at this school, how the bowlers, desperate to get past my uncle's bat, were tending to aim the ball at its very edge—from which it would slump off, with a thunderous groan, towards the slips. There were two consequences to this. It brought that strange hanging figure into the game as he had never been before. Often at the end of an over he would be left with the ball. It was from him therefore that the next bowler had to receive it; or via him that the captain was obliged to indicate a change of bowler. From all this hubbub I learnt his name, which I shall call Philipps. To spectators who did not know the game but might be watching it from the boundary, Philipps must have seemed the most important person on the field. If they knew no one else, they knew him. Sometimes, too, I noticed that he actually despatched the ball to the next bowler by bowling it along himself, as if to suggest something. I think he appreciated his new prominence in the team and I felt gratified that my uncle's bat had been instrumental in bringing him into it. I noticed, too, a peculiar smile sometimes stretch across his oval face. It gave him an odd look: almost ironic.

The second consequence of this constant edging of the ball seemed much more grave. My uncle's bat, like an old ship after a tempest, was beginning to break up. Splinters would fly off like sparks, scattering the fielders and adding to my already legendary reputation. The wound, it appeared, was a deep one and no amount of the bandaging, glueing and patching I applied could long delay the end. I felt the pathos. If only, I thought, it could have held out another five or ten years. I would have grown into it and then all those miracles-to-come might actually have burst forth. But it was a great-hearted bat and somehow it survived to the end of the season, its off-side edge like a cliff face.

Next year I went to Eton. My father had been there, and his brother before him. Unlike them I went there on a double mortgage—but without the bat. To prepare me for school my father had invited a local grocer to give me a few evening nets. There were just the two of us, the grocer and I, in a large field at evening when the bat finally cracked up. The pads, too, by that time were sprouting various materials: it seemed sensible to lay them to rest at the same time. So we hoisted the lot on to a rubbish dump, gave up and went home.

My father was anxious that I do well at Eton. A robust chap now of forty, he had been delicate in his 'teens, and lay for part of this time in Switzerland, recovering. All that he had missed then took hold of his imagination: it seemed that things like success had been somewhere else while he lay breathing in Switzerland. When had he ever heard applause, been thumped on the back, won anything? He had breasted no tapes; catapulted over no crossbars; above all he had scored no centuries. I was his second chance. He had had me padded up when I was three or four, and out on the lawn practising regardless of my aunt's flowerbeds. We were interrupted somewhat by the Second World War, I remember, but my grandmother was under instructions to push the ball at me through those years, though her terrier seemed to gain more from this exercise than I.

I went to Eton not long after the war had ended and my father returned. He had done his bit and now settled down to see me do mine, using some of his demobilisation pay to buy me a bright new bat, gleaming pads, dazzling gloves: everything a chap could want. It was now up to me.

On the first afternoon at Eton the new boys in our house were given tea. Our parents came, joked with one another, then slunk guiltily and gratefully off, leaving us alone with our housemaster, 'Purple' Parr. It was then that someone suddenly said something to me. I jumped, not being used to such attention (indeed, having gone a long way in a dozen years to avoid it), then saw that it was Philipps, the round-faced crouching boy in the slips. He had some cake still in his hand and was asking me about my uncle's bat. I told him; he understood at once; and we got to talking. I knew rather a lot about cricket, but Philipps knew more. He knew everything. His command of bowling analyses, going back years, was extraordinarily impressive. Batting, in this respect, was also no problem to him. He threw off wicket-keeping statistics too as if he had been the wicket-keeper in Calcutta or Melbourne himself. I don't think I ever caught him out with a question—I would have backed him against anyone in a quiz. But his information was never dull. When he spoke, these figures danced, sang, lived for him. He spoke with a passion that touched even tennis players and oarsmen. It was as if all the striving, hope, enjoyment, pain of life had been ritualised and fitted into the rhythms and processions of a cricket match. Life might shrink a little, but the game expanded.

Philipps knew about cricket, but cricketers did not know about Philipps. They knew about me. In Surrey, Berkshire, even parts of Middlesex, Stonewall Holroyd and his uncle's bat had been spoken of. I was a useful man to have on the losing side—I might even force a draw. So, while Philipps was despatched to some obscure pitch on the periphery of the school, I went straight to the top game. But I went without my uncle's bat—and without that I was lost. Approaching the crease in my blinding new gear I seemed to be walking on air. Where was my ballast, my anchor? Taking guard, I felt absurdly exposed to the fast bowlers. I had never realised what a dangerous sport cricket could be. My new bat wouldn't keep still. It sent the first ball I received for an astonishing four through the covers. I felt like apologising. After all, I had done no more than contemplate a cover-drive: the bat had done the rest. To the second ball it offered a leg-glance, and I walked back with it off the field while the wicket-keeper righted my leg-stump.

People, I realised, were angry with me. I had acted completely out of character and they felt cheated. I was dropped from the top game and, after a couple of attempted sixes over the bowler's head, fell from the second to the third. In that top game cricket had been played with frightful earnestness. To excel here was the principal ambition of many boys, and the *raison d'être* of their school careers—they had not come to learn algebra. They dreamed of being capped and their emotional energy revolved round the glamour, the aesthetic brilliance of the white flannels and pristine blazer trimmed with blue. Really, nothing mattered after that.

I put away my new bat and took to leg-breaks and my own version of the googly. This, I can now reveal, consisted of 'presenting' the batsman with another monstrously obvious leg-break—then reversing my wrist at the last moment and hoping he wouldn't spot it. It seemed easier than bringing the ball out of the back of the hand—a risky business at best and a danger to the umpire. I was trained at the nets by the head of our house and captain of games, a tall thin boy who later compensated for having narrowly missed the First XI by becoming a top dog at Sotheby's. My bowling was unusual, but no legend adhered to it as it had to my uncle's bat. Nobody used leg-breaks and there was no place for such bowlers in most teams. They were expensive; they were unfashionable; they were perpetually almost getting wickets while in the intervals being regularly hit for four or six. For more than a decade it used to be said of England's leg-break 'merchant' D. V. P. Wright that he was the unluckiest bowler alive. I could well believe it. The head of our house, I reckon, was the second most unlucky; then there was me. Technically, we were fascinating: but people wanted to win their matches. As no one could demonstrate better than Philipps, D. V. P. Wright had got amazingly far; the head of our house even made Eton's Second XI (or 'twenty-two' as it was called); I gave up.

But Philipps did not give up. His keenness was never blunted by the continual drudgery of his experiences. While I sweated at those special nets, it now shames me to remember, he volunteered to come up and field the balls clouted over my head. We used to talk on our way up (not so much going back) and he told me that his parents were divorced. One of the results of this, it appeared, was that he did not own a pair of cricket boots. It did not matter in the sort of games he played. Nothing mattered. They were less cricket matches than exhibitions of anarchy. Gym shoes would do as well as any other. No one bothered if you turned up or didn't. Philipps always turned up early. Sometimes he had to wait almost an hour before enough people ambled along to make up a couple of scratch teams. In the evenings he tuned his bat against the day when he would be invited to use it.

I do not think I can be claiming too much when I say that 'Purple' Parr's was by far the worst house in the school when Philipps and I were its stars. For two years I was its captain of games despite the fact that I had given up cricket and did no rowing. I had taken savagely to non-team games such as squash. I would have played racquets too if my family could have afforded it; I would have played tennis if I could have found the courts. As it was, I settled for squash and as Keeper of Squash walked the streets wearing a dark blue cap with minute crossed rackets in gold that mystified everyone. Mystery had become my form of glamour, and elusiveness my publicity. For the players (it seems probable) cricket is a game; for literary gentlemen it becomes a metaphor. Like chess, it later absorbed much of my interest. But I play neither. That way I do not get too agitated. I am remorselessly involved but, at the same time, detached. I participate as a spectator.

Philipps took his role as spectator on to the centre of the field. He knew more than anyone there and he remained there, year after year, waiting to use his knowledge. I would see him in the summer afternoons setting off to the fields like clockwork, and I would think of Sisyphus and his stone. Possibly because of his divorced parents, he never got a new bat or pads or anything else during his five years at Eton. In a sense they weren't needed. Everything looked new: but smaller. By his last year all this miniature paraphernalia with which he stood waiting to try his luck looked Lilliputian.

My father had done all he could to conceal his disappointment in me, despite my having no Swiss alibi. Squash was all right of course; but it was not (he pointed out) cricket. This worried him. It even worried 'Purple' Parr, who came to my room one evening to explain the ridicule that attached to him personally for having a captain of games in his house who played no games. I felt sorry (it was the least I could feel) but I could do little about it. 'Purple' Parr himself did nothing, which was often his way; but my father found a devious means of keeping his vicarious hopes alive—he transferred them to Philipps. He had met him once or twice at tea and, like many before him, been moved by his statistics. Soon he began to press me with questions, often unanswerable. I remember how irritated I would be by his habit of getting my friend's name wrong. 'How's your friend Frobisher?' he would suddenly demand. 'Playing much, is he?' Or: 'Potter scored any runs yet?' If there was any pathos here I was not susceptible to it. But although I felt irritated, I also felt guilty and used to go up now and then to watch Philipps in the hope of providing my father with something nourishing to chew over. It wasn't easy. I may even have invented a little. But I did note a small change in Philipps's field manners. Whenever he had the ball, he liked to send it back to the bowler with a short fizzing action that spun it fiercely off the ground and out of the bowler's pleading fingers. That was all. He said nothing; his gestures revealed nothing; and I had nothing to report. But my father's curiosity persisted and, grateful to see it diverted from me in this way, I did my best to squeeze some drops of interest from that succession of dryly uneventful afternoons. I felt as if Philipps had in some way become my alter ego.

By our last year 'Purple' Parr had given us all up and retired to drink and geometry in his study. We were a hopeless generation of which Philipps, it seemed, was our finest representative. But my father's instinct probed deeper and was spectacularly rewarded. At the end of that last summer at Eton a special match had been arranged—rather a grand matter it was, peopled largely by First and Second XI players. Philipps had somehow secured the job of scorer. This was something he did well, and it came as a surprise to me that he had been asked to do it. That reflected my opinion, I dare say, of school cricket. The match took place on our last full day and shortly before it was due to start, Philipps blundered up to me with a curious request. Would I take his place as scorer? Someone had fallen out of the game, and he had been accepted as the replacement providing he could find someone to score. So, if I took his place, he would be playing that afternoon, he added matter-of-factly.

I scored. Philipps's side fielded first. It was not supposed to be a wholly serious game—more an exhibition of some of the school's most talented players. I was scoring quietly, sharpening the pencils, lining up the rubbers, humming a little, when all at once the captain threw the ball to Philipps. It must have been pure end-of-season intoxication: or a mistake. In any event there was no chance of changing his mind. Philipps thundered like a steam engine to the wicket, rubbing the ball as he'd seen everyone else do. I could not imagine what he felt. I found it difficult to decipher my own feelings and did not trust myself to write down his name until after he had sent down his first ball. He bowled off-cutters and almost bagged a wicket with this first ball. After that he was played with puzzled caution. His action looked innocent enough: not a long run (he did not have time for that) but with something of the swaying indecision of a rocking-horse—then the delivery, rather sudden at almost medium pace and given little air. His first over was a maiden so there was no option but to keep him on. By the end of the innings he had bowled some twenty tight overs, taken three wickets and conceded only about fifteen runs. There was, I appreciated, a hoard of hidden learning behind that bowling. Years of close observation, years of studying *Wisden* went into each delivery. It was concentrated scholarship we were witnessing and a triumph of theory over experience. Batsmen got out through the impertinence of trying to score off him. They did not realise what a studious attack was being aimed at them: and it was an *attack*.

Philipps's expression was buoyantly blank when he came off the field. No one who did not know him well could have told anything from it. Certainly there was no aspect of surprise there. I was astonished. But there was an even greater shock to come. Philipps had replaced an opening batsman. Instead of shifting up the whole order and establishing him in his normal place at the end, the captain simply asked Philipps to go in first. The world had gone topsy-turvy.

Had I not been scorer, I would have left then. I had seen his success: there were enough marvels here to repeat to my father for years. I wished 'Purple' Parr had been able to see them: but as usual he had not arrived. Like the Ancient Mariner's wedding guest, I was held there to act as witness for all: I could not choose but look.

I saw, with sinking heart, Philipps walk out with that midget bat and ridiculous pads. He actually tripped over on his way to the crease. I wrote his name down: and then it began. The first ball missed his bat, missed the wicket, the wicket-keeper's gloves and went for four byes. It appeared to have gone through everything, and so fast I could not tell whether Philipps realised what had happened. The next ball also shot to the boundary, this time from the top of Philipps's bat and over the heads of the slips. Four runs—to the best of my knowledge his best score that decade. That he had luck I think there was no doubt. But then he was owed luck. For the next hour-and-a-half, he *hammered* the bowling; he crashed the ball between them, above them, beyond them all. He seemed to be teasing the fielders. At first these champion bowlers with their gleaming flannels and hyphenated names may not have taken this onslaught so seriously; but before long they were trying all they knew to remove him. He kept them continually on the run. God knows how he did it. I had never seen anything like it before and never have again. But then I knew the years of frustration and inactivity behind it. A number of people stopped to watch, conscious that something unusual was happening. Philipps did not score a century, about seventy-five was his total and it easily won the game. We stood up, the few of us there, gave a dry cheer and clapped raggedly as he came out. He looked severe and sphinx-like sitting down to unstrap his pads; then for a moment that peculiar smile stretched silently across his face and seemed to engulf him.

Next day we left school. His parents being divorced, Philipps did not go up to university and nor did I. I never saw him play another game, though I would meet him from time to time and he would pass items of cricketing news my way—some record from New Zealand perhaps or curiosity from Canada. Once I reminded him of his schoolboy romance in that last match. He listened with what appeared deep pleasure to the story before rebuking me for having exaggerated everything. So perhaps, after all, I am re-writing rather than re-living the past. Anyway, it's the story my father likes to hear.

Shortly after he married, Philipps remarked to me that he was thinking of raising a complete eleven. Most of his children, it turned out, were girls. I don't think this mattered. In a few years, I predict, his name will be terrible to the women cricketers of Australia. And I shall have something new to tell my father.

Single-handed and Untrained

PHILIP LARKIN

In autumn 1943 the Ministry of Labour wrote to ask what I was doing. I could have answered that, having finished with the university and English literature, I was living at home writing a novel, but I rightly judged the enquiry to be a warning that I had better start doing something. Picking up the day's *Birmingham Post* (the paper we took in those days), I soon discovered an advertisement by a small urban district council for a Librarian. The salary was £175 per annum (plus cost-of-living bonus, Whitley Scale, of £45 10s for men, £36 8s for women), and the duties included 'those usual to the operation of a Lending Library (open access), and Reading Room supervision'.

Recourse to a gazetteer revealed that the town was about twelve miles from a school where a college friend of mine had recently taken a job as a temporary assistant master and was also writing a novel. This seemed a good omen, and I applied. In due course I was asked to attend for interview, and it occurred to me I had better find out something about the operation of a lending library (open access). A friendly senior assistant at the local one was kind enough to spend a morning showing me how books were ordered, accessioned and catalogued, and then given little pockets with individual tickets in them that were slipped into borrowers' cards when the book was lent. 'Come back tomorrow', she said, 'and I'll tell you about inter-library loans.'

My father, with remote amusement, handed me a green-covered report that had come out in the previous year entitled *The Public Library System of Great Britain*, and I took it with me in the train on 13 November, the day of the interview. Rain smashed against the carriage windows as I read the author's summary dismissals of sample libraries serving populations between 20,000 and 30,000: 'Old buildings, drab stocks and bad traditions of support ... antiquated methods include a really filthy indicator [what was that?] ... the reference library consists of two small cases of quite useless items. ...' The account of library 'I' seemed particularly intimidating: 'the children's books are much dirtier even than those provided for the adults. There is no proper counter; the single-handed librarian is untrained.' I fancied that the authority to which I had applied was in a smaller population category than this: would its library be worse? Certainly its potential Librarian looked like being single-handed, and could hardly have been more untrained.

Mr McColvin, the author of the trenchant sentences just quoted, would not in all probability have been much kinder about it. The council had adopted the Library Acts, and built a Library to celebrate the coronation of Edward VII. It was a simple two-storey building, with a reading room and a boiler room on the ground floor and a lending library, with a rudimentary office-cum-reference room, upstairs; its handsome stone façade was inscribed PUBLIC LIBRARY and recorded why it was erected and when (I think the date was 1903). A librarian-caretaker, son of a failed Wolverhampton bookseller, was appointed. When I turned up forty years later (for my application was successful), the astonishing thing was that almost nothing had changed. The librarian-caretaker was still there, by now a courtly old gentleman of at least seventy, who wore a hat indoors and uttered from time to time an absent-minded blowing noise, like a distant trombone. For many years he had washed the floors and lighted the boiler every morning in addition to his professional duties, and may have done so to the end. After leaving he never used the Library, and I saw him only once again; he called when it was shut ('Anyone in? It's only the old blackguard'), and we chatted, mostly about his inadequate pension and his funeral arrangements ('I've told the wife to stay at home and drink whisky'). I wondered uneasily if my life would be anything like his.

In 1903 the Library had, of course, been closed access; in the Thirties an effort had been made to modernise its methods, opening the doors to readers and constructing an issue desk. There had even been purchased a copy of the current edition of Dewey. Otherwise it remained antiquated. The boiler (which I had to stoke, if not light) did little to heat the radiators, which were in any case poorly placed; the real warmth of the building came from the gas lights, that had to be illumined with long tapers that dropped wax over the floors, and even on myself until I learned how to handle them. There was no telephone. The stock amounted to about 4,000 books, 3,000 of which were fiction and the rest non-fiction and juvenile (the admission of children had been a severe blow to my predecessor). The shelves were high, but even so layers of long-withdrawn books, thick with dust, were piled on top of them. I wish I had taken more detailed notes both of them and of the current stock: in all, it was like the advertisement pages of late nineteenth- and early twentieth-century novels come to life. A substantial body of the readers were elderly people who found the stairs difficult, but were still prepared to face them for Mrs Henry Wood, Florence L. Barclay, Silas K. Hocking, Rosa M. Carey and many others. The rest were either children or hopeful adults, some of them strangers to the town and used to better things.

My day began with collecting the day's papers and journals and setting them out in the reading room in time to open its doors at 9 AM. Then I retreated to the closed lending department and dealt with the post, such as it was, making out applications for inter-library loans and parcelling up volumes to be returned (the post office was, fortunately, directly opposite). From then until 3 PM when the first of the two-hour lending-library 'operations' began, my time was my own; landladies did not really want to provide fires in the morning, and I wrote my novel in the Library before taking it back with me to work at after lunch. After another session from 6 to 8 PM I finished reshelving and sorted the issue in time to close the reading room at 8.30 PM. It was a long day, and in some respects a tiring one. Quite early on I recorded a week when I issued 928 books in twenty hours, or one about every seventy-seven seconds—not much, perhaps, but an equal number had to be reshelved, and some of the shelves could be reached only by ladder. At first my hand was blistered from stamping books.

It was clear that the premises, stock and staff of the Library were totally inadequate for the potential, or even actual, demands of its readers. At the same time it was difficult to know what to do about it—difficult, because I really had no idea of how to come to grips with the council in order to, for instance, appoint a couple of assistants, double or treble the book grant (I don't think, in fact, that there was one), create a catalogue, modernise the building and so on, and even if I had there would have been, in the middle of the war, no money to do so. My committee, however, was sympathetic, chaired by a friendly and forward-looking headmaster, and they did what they could. New books began to appear on the shelves (I heard that I was 'filling the Library with dirty books'—not in the McColvin sense, but with Lawrence, Forster, Joyce, Isherwood, *et al.*), and after a year and three-quarters I got an assistant, enabling the Lending Library to 'operate' in the mornings. Readership increased to about twice the original number. Issues did likewise, from 3,000 to 6,000 a month. My most dramatic increase was in inter-library loans, from sixty-eight in the year I came to 499 in the year I left: these were chiefly to sixth formers, and those readers with precise interests and courses of study. Most of the books came from the huge and generous Birmingham City Libraries, at that time presided over by H. M.

Cashmore, surely one of the most indefatigable correspondents among chief Librarians. Hardly a day passed when I did not receive a letter signed by him correcting me about the details of an application, or pointing out that a parcel had been badly tied. Other librarians I met later confirmed this experience.

The Library should, of course, have been absorbed into the county system, and the county was anxious to do this: it already sent us a consignment of perhaps 300 books that was changed every few months, and these alone kept readers from complete apathy. Since the council had adopted the Library Acts in 1901 or so, however, it could not be compulsorily taken over, and there was enough local patriotism to believe that with 'the new young man' a proper library service could be offered. Of course improvements took place: almost anything one did was an improvement (one of my early reports states 'the Library has joined the official waiting list for *The Times Literary* and *Educational Supplements*'), and readers responded so eagerly in those book-hungry days that I could never stop trying, but in fact little could be done compared with what was needed. I consoled myself with my novel (having finished the first, I had begun a second), and started a correspondence course for Library Association qualifications.

My appointment there lasted two and three-quarter years. About three years after I left, the council did, in fact, surrender its powers, and 'my' Library became a county branch. Subsequently it was remodelled and enlarged, and in 1962 became a headquarters; to my surprise, I was asked to open it. Usually I avoid such undertakings, but the implication that I was not regarded by those concerned as an unfortunate episode best forgotten was so gratifying that I gladly accepted. The architect had done his work well, so that it was impossible to see where the boiler room had been, or the poky stairs, or the cobwebbed and dingy lavatory, on the walls of which my aged predecessor had pencilled a series of dates, a reference to a brand of pills, and a name that looked like 'Marley Mount'. Split-level and splendid, the Library now had proper staff quarters, a record listening room, a separate children's library and an electric book lift.

As I listened to the other speakers (my old chairman among them, still in office), I wondered what I had done to justify my presence at the ceremony. I had achieved nothing lasting: union with the county system had been delayed only a few years, and it might be said that I had made it inevitable. I found myself thinking of individual readers: the boy I had introduced to the Sherlock Holmes stories, the old lady who sent a messenger for her books and whose final note I still have: 'Owing to failing sight, I have decided no longer to be a Member of the "Free Library". Please accept of my grateful thanks for kindness choosing books for me during the past years . . .' and others, such as the lady who gave me ten 'Cogent' cigarettes at Christmas (product of the Scottish Co-operative Wholesale Society). I thought, too, of the knowledgeable 'graduate trainees' of today, with their year in a university library followed by a year at library school, and wondered further if there were any libraries left as backward as this one had been, or any librarians as unqualified as myself when appointed to it. If not, as seemed probable, this was no doubt the most comforting reflection available.

'Virginibus Puerisque'
On Marriage

ROBERT LOUIS STEVENSON

With the single exception of Falstaff, all Shakespeare's characters are what we call marrying men. Mercutio, as he was own cousin to Benedick and Biron, would have come to the same end in the long run. Even Iago had a wife, and, what is far stranger, he was jealous. People like Jacques and the Fool in *Lear*, although we can hardly imagine they would ever marry, kept single out of a cynical humour or for a broken heart, and not, as we do nowadays, from a spirit of incredulity and preference for the single state. For that matter, if you turn to George Sand's French version of *As You Like It* (and I think I can promise you will like it but little), you will find Jacques marries Celia just as Orlando marries Rosalind.

At least there seems to have been much less hesitation over marriage in Shakespeare's days; and what hesitation there was was of a laughing sort, and not much more serious, one way or the other, than that of Panurge. In modern comedies the heroes are mostly of Benedick's way of thinking, but twice as much in earnest, and not one quarter so confident. And I take this diffidence as a proof of how sincere their terror is. They know they are only human after all; they know what gins and pitfalls lie about their feet; and how the shadow of matrimony waits, resolute and awful, at the crossroads. They would wish to keep their liberty; but if that may not be, why, God's will be done! 'What, are you afraid of marriage?' asks Cécile, in *Maître Guerin*. 'Oh, mon Dieu, non!' replies Arthur; 'I should take chloroform.' They look forward to marriage much in the same way as they prepare themselves for death: each seems inevitable; each is a great Perhaps, and a leap into the dark, for which, when a man is in the blue devils, he has specially to harden his heart. That splendid scoundrel, Maxime de Trailles, took the news of marriages much as an old man hears the deaths of his contemporaries. '*C'est désespérant*,' he cried, throwing himself down in the armchair at Madame Schontz's; '*c'est désespérant, nous nous marions tous!*' Every marriage was like another grey hair on his head; and the jolly church bells seemed to taunt him with his fifty years and fair round belly.

The fact is, we are much more afraid of life than our ancestors, and cannot find it in our hearts either to marry or not to marry. Marriage is terrifying, but so is a cold and forlorn old age. The friendships of men are vastly agreeable, but they are insecure. You know all the time that one friend will marry and put you to the door; a second accept a situation in China, and become no more to you than a name, a reminiscence, and an occasional crossed letter, very laborious to read; a third will take up with some religious crotchet and treat you to sour looks thenceforward. So, in one way or another, life forces men apart and breaks up the goodly fellowships for ever. The very flexibility and ease which make men's friendships so agreeable while they endure, make them the easier to destroy and forget. And a man who has a few friends, or one who has a dozen (if there be anyone so wealthy on this earth), cannot forget on how precarious a base his happiness reposes; and how by a stroke or two of fate—a death, a few light words, a piece of stamped paper, a woman's bright eyes—he may be left, in a month, destitute of all. Marriage is certainly a perilous remedy. Instead of on two or three, you stake your happiness on one life only. But still, as the bargain is more explicit and complete on your part, it is more so on the other; and you have not to fear so many contingencies; it is not every wind that can blow you from your anchorage; and so long as Death withholds his sickle, you will always have a friend at home. People who share a cell in the Bastille, or are thrown together on an uninhabited isle, if they do not immediately fall to fisticuffs, will find some possible ground of compromise. They will learn each other's ways and humours, so as to know where they must go warily, and where they may lean their whole weight. The discretion of the first years becomes the settled habit of the last; and so, with wisdom and patience, two lives may grow indissolubly into one.

But marriage, if comfortable, is not at all heroic. It certainly narrows and damps the spirits of generous men. In marriage, a man becomes slack and selfish, and undergoes a fatty degeneration of his moral being. It is not only when Lydgate misallies himself with Rosamond Vincy, but when Ladislaw marries above him with Dorothea, that this may be exemplified. The air of the fireside withers out all the fine wildings of the husband's heart. He is so comfortable and happy that he begins to prefer comfort and happiness to everything else on earth, his wife included. Yesterday he would have shared his last shilling; today 'his first duty is to his family', and is fulfilled in large measure by laying down vintages and husbanding the health of an invaluable parent. Twenty years ago this man was equally capable of crime or heroism; now he is fit for neither. His soul is asleep, and you may speak without constraint; you will not wake him. It is not for nothing that Don Quixote was a bachelor and Marcus Aurelius married ill. For women, there is less of this danger. Marriage is of so much use to a woman, opens out to her so much more of life, and puts her in the way of so much more freedom and usefulness, that, whether she marry ill or well, she can hardly miss some benefit. It is true, however, that some of the merriest and most genuine of women are old maids; and that those old maids, and wives who are unhappily married, have often most of the true motherly touch. And this would seem to show, even for women, some narrowing influence in comfortable married life. But the rule is none the less certain: if you wish the pick of men and women, take a good bachelor and a good wife.

I am often filled with wonder that so many marriages are passably successful, and so few come to open failure, the more so as I fail to understand the principle on which people regulate their choice. I see women marrying indiscriminately with staring burgesses and ferret-faced, white-eyed boys, and men dwell in contentment with noisy scullions, or taking into their lives acidulous vestals. It is a common answer to say the good people marry because they fall in love; and of course you may use and misuse a word as much as you please, if you have the world along with you. But love is at least a somewhat hyperbolical expression for such lukewarm preference. It is not here, anyway, that Love employs his golden shafts; he cannot be said, with any fitness of language, to reign here and revel. Indeed, if this be love at all, it is plain the poets have been fooling with mankind since the foundation of the world. And you have only to look these happy couples in the face, to see they have never been in love, or in hate, or in any other high passion all their days. When you see a dish of fruit at dessert, you sometimes set your affections upon one particular peach or nectarine, watch it with some anxiety as it comes round the table, and feel quite a sensible disappointment when it is taken by someone else. I have used the phrase 'high passion'. Well, I should say this was about as high a passion as generally leads to marriage. One husband hears after marriage that some poor fellow is dying of his wife's love. 'What a pity!' he exclaims; 'you know I could so easily have got another!' And yet that is a very happy union. Or again: A young man was telling me the sweet story of his loves. 'I like it well enough as long as her sisters are there,' said this amorous swain; 'but I don't know what to do when we're alone.' Once more: A married lady was debating the subject with another lady. 'You know, dear,' said the first, 'after ten years of marriage, if he is nothing else, your husband is always an old friend.' 'I have many old friends,' returned the other, 'but I prefer them to be nothing more.' 'Oh, perhaps I might *prefer* that also!' There is a common note in these three illustrations of the modern idyll; and it must be owned the god goes among us with a limping gait and blear eyes. You wonder whether it was so always; whether desire was always equally dull and spiritless, and possession equally cold. I cannot help fancying most people make, ere they marry, some such table of recommendations as Hannah Godwin wrote to her brother William anent her friend, Miss Gay. It is so charmingly comical, and so pat to the occasion, that I must quote a few phrases. 'The young lady is in every sense formed to make one of your disposition really happy. She has a pleasing voice, with which she accompanies her musical instrument with judgement. She has an easy politeness in her manners, neither free nor reserved. She is a good housekeeper and a good economist, and yet of a generous disposition. As to her internal accomplishments, I have reason to speak still more highly of them: good sense without vanity, a pene-trating judgement without a disposition to satire, with about as much religion as my William likes, struck me with a wish that she was my William's wife.' That is about the tune: pleasing voice, moderate good looks, unimpeachable internal accomplishments after the style of the copybook, with about as much religion as my William likes; and then, with all speed, to church.

To deal plainly, if they only married when they fell in love, most people would die unwed; and among the others, there would be not a few tumultuous households. The Lion is the King of Beasts, but he is scarcely suitable for a domestic pet. In the same way, I suspect love is rather too violent a passion to make, in all cases, a good domestic sentiment. Like other violent excitements, it throws up not only what is best, but what is worst and smallest, in men's characters. Just as some people are malicious in drink, or brawling and virulent under the influence of religious feeling, some are moody, jealous, and exacting when they are in love, who are honest, downright, good-hearted fellows enough in the everyday affairs and humours of the world.

How then, seeing we are driven to the hypothesis that people choose in comparatively cold blood, how is it they choose so well? One is almost tempted to hint that it does not much matter whom you marry; that, in fact, marriage is a subjective affection, and if you have made up your mind to it, and once talked yourself fairly over, you could 'pull it through' with anybody. But even if we take matrimony at its lowest, even if we regard it as no more than a sort of friendship recognised by the police, there must be degrees in the freedom and sympathy realised, and some principle to guide simple folk in their selection. Now what should this principle be? Are there no more definite rules than are to be found in the Prayer Book? Law and religion forbid the banns on the ground of propinquity or consanguinity; society steps in to separate classes; and in all this most critical matter, has common sense, has wisdom, never a word to say? In the absence of more magisterial teaching, let us talk it over between friends: even a few guesses may be of interest to youths and maidens.

In all that concerns eating and drinking, company, climate, and ways of life, community of taste is to be sought for. It would be trying, for instance, to keep bed and board with an early riser or a vegetarian. In matters of art and intellect, I believe it is of no consequence. Certainly it is of none in the companionships of men, who will dine more readily with one who has a good heart, a good cellar, and a humorous tongue, than with another who shares all their favourite hobbies and is melancholy withal. If your wife likes Tupper, that is no reason why you should hang your head. She thinks with the majority, and has the courage of her opinions. I have always suspected public taste to be a mongrel product, out of affectation by dogmatism; and felt sure, if you could only find an honest man of no special literary bent, he would tell you he thought much of Shakespeare bombastic and most absurd, and all of him written in very obscure English and wearisome to read. And not long ago I was able to lay by my lantern in content, for I found the honest man. He was a fellow of parts, quick, humorous, a clever painter, and with an eye for certain poetical effects of sea and ships. I am not much of a judge of that kind of thing, but a sketch of his comes before me sometimes at night. How strong, supple, and living the ship seems upon the billows! With what a dip and rake she shears the flying sea! I cannot fancy the man who saw this effect, and took it on the wing with so much force and spirit, was what you call commonplace in the last recesses of the heart. And yet he thought, and was not ashamed to have it known of him, that Ouida was better in every way than William Shakespeare. If there were more people of his honesty, this would be about the staple of lay criticism. It is not taste that is plentiful, but courage that is rare. And what have we in place? How many, who think no otherwise than the young painter, have we not heard disbursing second-hand hyperboles? Have you never turned sick at heart, O best of critics! when some of your own sweet adjectives were returned on you before a gaping audience? Enthusiasm about art is become a function of the average female being, which she performs with precision and a sort of haunting sprightliness, like an ingenious and well-regulated machine. Sometimes, alas! the calmest man is carried away in the torrent, bandies adjectives with the best, and out-Herods Herod for some shameful moments. When you remember that, you will be tempted to put things strongly, and say you will marry no one who is not like George II, and cannot state openly a distaste for poetry and painting.

The word 'facts' is, in some ways, crucial. I have spoken with Jesuits and Plymouth Brethren, mathematicians and poets, dogmatic republicans and dear old gentlemen in bird's-eye neckcloths; and each understood the word 'facts' in an occult sense of his own. Try as I might, I could get no nearer the principle of their division. What was essential to them, seemed to me trivial or untrue. We could come to no compromise as to what was, or what was not, important in the life of man. Turn as we pleased, we all stood back to back in a big ring, and saw another quarter of the heavens, with different mountain-tops along the skyline and different constellations overhead. We had each of us some whimsy in the brain, which we believed more than anything else, and which discoloured all experience to its own shade. How would you have people agree, when one is deaf and the other blind? Now this is where there should be community between man and wife. They should be agreed on their catchword in 'facts of religion', or 'facts of science', or 'society, my dear'; for without such an agreement all intercourse is a painful strain upon the mind. 'About as much religion as my William likes', in short, that is what is necessary to make a happy couple of any William and his spouse. For there are differences which no habit nor affection can reconcile, and the Bohemian must not intermarry with the Pharisee. Imagine Consuelo as Mrs Samuel Budget, the wife of the successful merchant! The best of men and the best of women may sometimes live together all their lives, and, for want of some consent on fundamental questions, hold each other lost spirits to the end.

A certain sort of talent is almost indispensable for people who would spend years together and not bore themselves to death. But the talent, like the agreement, must be for and about life. To dwell happily together, they should be versed in the niceties of the heart, and born with a faculty for willing compromise. The woman must be talented as a woman, and it will not much matter although she is talented in nothing else. She must know her *métier de femme*, and have a fine touch for the affections. And it is more important that a person should be a good gossip, and talk pleasantly and smartly of common friends and the thousand and one nothings of the day and hour, than that she should speak with the tongues of men and angels; for a while together by the fire, happens more frequently in marriage than the presence of a distinguished foreigner to dinner. That people should laugh over the same sort of jests, and have many a story of 'grouse in the gun-room', many an old joke between them which time cannot wither nor custom stale, is a better preparation for life, by your leave, than many other things higher and better sounding in the world's ears. You could read Kant by yourself, if you wanted; but you must share a joke with someone else. You can forgive people who do not follow you through a philosophical disquisition; but to find your wife laughing when you had tears in your eyes, or staring when you were in a fit of laughter, would go some way towards a dissolution of the marriage.

I know a woman who, from some distaste or disability, could never so much as understand the meaning of the word *politics*, and has given up trying to distinguish Whigs from Tories; but take her on her own politics, ask her about other men or women and the chicanery of everyday existence—the rubs, the tricks, the vanities on which life turns—and you will not find many more shrewd, trenchant, and humorous. Nay, to make plainer what I have in mind, this same woman has a share of the higher and more poetical understanding, frank interest in things for their own sake, and enduring astonishment at the most common. She is not to be deceived by custom, or made to think a mystery solved when it is repeated. I have heard her say she could wonder herself crazy over the human eyebrow. Now in a world where most of us walk very contentedly in the little lit circle of their own reason, and have to be reminded of what lies without by specious and clamant exceptions—earthquakes, eruptions of Vesuvius, banjos floating in mid-air at a séance, and the like—a mind so fresh and unsophisticated is no despicable gift. I will own I think it a better sort of mind than goes necessarily with the clearest views on public business. It will wash. It will find something to say at an odd moment. It has in it the spring of pleasant and quaint fancies. Whereas I can imagine myself yawning all night long until my jaws ached and the tears came into my eyes, although my companion on the other side of the hearth held the most enlightened opinions on the franchise or the ballot.

The question of professions, in as far as they regard marriage, was only interesting to women until of late days, but it touches all of us now. Certainly, if I could help it, I would never marry a wife who wrote. The practice of letters is miserably harassing to the mind; and after an hour or two's work, all the more human portion of the author is extinct; he will bully, backbite, and speak daggers. Music, I hear, is not much better. But painting, on the contrary, is often highly sedative; because so much of the labour, after your picture is once begun, is almost entirely manual, and of that skilled sort of manual labour which offers a continual series of successes, and so tickles a man, through his vanity, into good humour. Alas! in letters there is nothing of this sort. You may write as beautiful a hand as you will, you have always something else to think of, and cannot pause to notice your loops and flourishes; they are beside the mark, and the first law stationer could put you to the blush. Rousseau, indeed, made some account of penmanship, even made it a source of livelihood, when he copied out the *Héloïse* for dilettante ladies; and therein showed that strange eccentric prudence which guided him among so many thousand follies and insanities. It would be well for all of the *genus irritabile* thus to add something of skilled labour to intangible brain-work. To find the right word is so doubtful a success and lies so near to failure, that there is no satisfaction in a year of it; but we all know when we have formed a letter perfectly; and a stupid artist, right or wrong, is almost equally certain he has found a right tone or a right colour, or made a dexterous stroke with his brush. And, again, painters may work out of doors; and the fresh air, the deliberate seasons, and the 'tranquillising influence' of the green earth, counterbalance the fever of thought, and keep them cool, placable, and prosaic.

A ship captain is a good man to marry if it is a marriage of love, for absences are a good influence in love and keep it bright and delicate; but he is just the worst man if the feeling is more pedestrian, as habit is too frequently torn open and the solder has never time to set. Men who fish, botanise, work with the turning-lathe, or gather sea-weeds, will make admirable husbands; and a little amateur painting in water-colour shows the innocent and quiet mind. Those who have a few intimates are to be avoided; while those who swim loose, who have their hat in their hand all along the street, who can number an infinity of acquaintances and are not chargeable with any one friend, promise an easy disposition and no rival to the wife's influence. I will not say they are the best of men, but they are the stuff out of which adroit and capable women manufacture the best of husbands. It is to be noticed that those who have loved once or twice already are so much the better educated to a woman's hand; the bright boy of fiction is an odd and most uncomfortable mixture of shyness and coarseness, and needs a deal of civilising. Lastly (and this is, perhaps, the golden rule), no woman should marry a teetotaller, or a man who does not smoke. It is not for nothing that this 'ignoble tabagie', as Michelet calls it, spreads over all the world. Michelet rails against it because it renders you happy apart from thought or work; to provident women this will seem no evil influence in married life. Whatever keeps a man in the front garden, whatever checks wandering fancy and all inordinate ambition, whatever makes for lounging and contentment, makes just so surely for domestic happiness.

These notes, if they amuse the reader at all, will probably amuse him more when he differs than when he agrees with them; at least they will do no harm, for nobody will follow my advice. But the last word is of more concern. Marriage is a step so grave and decisive that it attracts light-headed, variable men by its very awfulness. They have been so tried among the inconstant squalls and currents, so often sailed for islands in the air or lain becalmed with burning heart, that they will risk all for solid ground below their feet. Desperate pilots, they run their sea-sick, weary bark upon the dashing rocks. It seems as if marriage were the royal road through life, and realised, on the instant, what we have all dreamed on summer Sundays when the bells ring, or at night when we cannot sleep for the desire of living. They think it will sober and change them. Like those who join a brotherhood, they fancy it needs but an act to be out of the coil and clamour for ever. But this is a wile of the devil's. To the end, spring winds will sow disquietude, passing faces leave a regret behind them, and the whole world keep calling and calling in their ears. For marriage is like life in this—that it is a field of battle, and not a bed of roses.

The Misery of Being Old and Ignorant

OWEN FELLTHAM

It is a capital misery for a man to be at once both old and ignorant. If he were only old, and had some knowledge, he might abate the tediousness of decrepit age, by the divine raptures of contemplation. If he were young, though he knew nothing, yet his years would serve him to labour and learn; whereby, in the winter of his time, he might beguile the weariness of his pillow and chair. But now his body being withered by the stealing length of his days, and his limbs wholly disabled, for either motion or exercise; these, together with a mind unfurnished of those contenting speculations of admired science, cannot but delineate the portraiture of a man wretched. A gray head with a wise mind, is a treasure of great precepts, experience, and judgement; but foolish old age is a barren vine in Autumn; or an university to study folly in: every action is a pattern of infirmity: while his body sits still, he knows not how to find his mind action: and tell me, if there be any life more irksome than idleness? I have numbered yet but a few days; and those, I know, I have neglected: I am not sure they shall be more, nor can I promise my head, it shall have a snowy hair. What then? Knowledge is not hurtful, but helps a good mind: anything that is laudable, I desire to learn. If I die tomorrow, my life, today, shall be somewhat the sweeter for knowledge: and if my day prove a Summer one, it shall not be amiss to have provided something, that, in the evening of my age, may make my mind my companion. Notable was the answer that *Antisthenes* gave, when he was asked what fruit he had reaped of all his studies? 'By them', saith he, 'I have learned both to live and to talk with myself.'

As Old as the Century

V. S. PRITCHETT

Since my boyhood I have been vain of being born just before the end of 1900 and at every birthday thinking of myself as pretty well as old as the century. I was at ease with its assumptions for fourteen years: after that, two dreadful wars, huge social changes, technological revolution, the disappearance of British power, the rise of the Welfare State, a decade or two of 'peace' in the world abroad, dramatic threats once more.

Now I am eighty I see I have been shaken up like a dice in a box, if not as brutally as people born ten years earlier than myself. Many are still alive and in voice. I am abashed by my survival rather than proud of it; there is no merit in it. The credit goes to those secretive gamblers we call the genes.

I come of long-lived forebears among whom there were few defaulters on the Yorkshire side. Also, because of the great advances of medical science and hygiene, the average expectation of life in Great Britain has enormously increased in the past fifty years or more. The old are no longer revered curiosities; on the contrary, often a social problem. We swarm in cities and resorts, ancient mariners who square our shoulders as we pick one another out at a glance in the pubs, the shops, the park seats, the planes and the tourist buses. Our skins do not yet give off the eerie smell of senility. That glance of ours is often frisky, conspiratorial and threatening, warning you that we could a tale unfold if we should happen to get a grip on your wrist.

Not a day's illness—we boast—except a winter cough or a twinge of arthritis or gout; we speak of these twitches as medals we have won. Smoke like fish (we go on), drink like a chimney, pity people who do not work a twelve-hour day, who have not ducked their heads through two world wars or known the good old hard times. And as for this new thing called sex . . .!

As our tongues wag and our metaphors mix we turn into actors on our conspicuous stage. We are good at pretending to be modest; we refuse to acknowledge we are ever in the wrong or incompetent. A brisk eighty-year-old electrician came to do a job at my house six

80

years ago and serenely drove his drill clean through a hidden water pipe I had warned him of. He turned accusingly on me as the water spouted over us. Like all us oldies he congratulated himself and boasted he had never done such a thing to a water pipe. He and I still greet each other as we rush by in the street, equals in conceit and folly, and say how young we feel.

Our acting is, of course, a defence against our fear of senility and death. What shall we be like in our nineties? Are we for the old folks' home? We have seen so many of our friends paralysed, collapsing in mind and physically humiliated. Shall we escape? Yet, behind our acting there is also the knowledge that age does not march mathematically year by year with the calendar. One's real age stands still for large blocks of time.

My hair is now white and veins stand out on my temples, I have dark brown spots on my hands, my arms shrink, but to my mind I seem to be much what I was at fifty: at fifty-seven I looked despairingly bleak, ill and flaccid, to judge from a photograph, less brisk than I became in my sixties, seventies or today. Middle age was more agonising and trying than the later years have been, but perhaps my age has always gone up and down because I am one of those who 'live on their nerves'. I know one thing for certain: I was far, far younger in my thirties than I had been in my twenties, because my heart was fuller at thirty, my energies knew their direction, chiefly due to a happy marriage. It has lasted forty-four years. There is nothing like a *coup de foudre* and absorption in family responsibility for maturing the male and pulling his scattered wits together. I became physically stronger after years of bad health. Yet I had not lost what I valued in my twenties: living for the liberation of the moment.

Today I still go fast up the four flights of steep stairs to my study in our tall late-Nash house, every day of the week, at nine o'clock in the morning, Saturdays and Sundays included, cursing the Inland Revenue and inflation, groaning at the work I have to do, crying out dishonestly for leisure, thinking of this year's holiday and the ten-mile walks on the cliffs of North Cornwall, complaining that surely at my age I should be able to get some time off.

Why, even when I travel, do I still have to work? But the moment I've cleaned my pipe and put pen to paper the groans stop. I am under the spell of language which has ruled me since I was ten. A few minutes later—four hours' writing have washed out all sense of time—my wife calls me down to a delicious lunch. She has spent the morning typing what I wrote the day before, laughing at my bad spelling, inserting sportive words when she can't read my insectile hand—that has got smaller—and knowing she'll have to do the whole damn thing over again two or three times because I cover each page with an ants' colony of corrections; she is a perfectionist too. We enjoy working together; she has a better memory than I have and I depend on her criticism. It is she who charms away the swarms of people who telephone, the speculators who think I exist for reading their theses and books, for more and more reviews, for giving interviews or lectures or signing their applications for grants. She has also driven off the droppers-in, the Mormons and Jehovah's Witnesses and other enemies of a writer's life. She is much younger and more decisive than I am.

After lunch I have a nap for an hour, do some household shopping in Camden Town where I pass as an old pensioner called Pritchard— very suited to a writer's double life—and return to take up tea and then back to work about four until seven and then a couple of Martinis, eat, try to catch up with letters and bills or in good weather go out and work in the garden. Unless we are going out we are in bed by ten. I sleep pretty well, dream wildly; the bad nights are those when I go on writing in my sleep, in English mostly but often, out of vanity, in Spanish, French or in dog-German which I stopped learning when I left school at fifteen. For Latin I have to rely on my wife.

I am a very lucky man, of course. If our pleasant house among the old trees of the quiet terrace is too large for us now our family have grown up, after twenty-five years here where else could we go with thousands of books? Would that frozen Buddha—the freezer that has changed our lives—fit in a new kitchen? Moving would betray our furniture and new draughts often kill old men.

I am lucky to be able to work at home, to commute upstairs instead of by train or bus. It is lucky I am still able to earn my living as a writer which I dreamed of when I was a boy. Thomas Hardy, in his old age, told Virginia Woolf that to write poetry was simply a matter of physical strength. So is writing prose. And that energy I was given by my parents: my Kentish Town mother's energy was nervous, my father's had the obdurate Yorkshire self-will. I cannot claim credit as an heir to this enlivening mixture of fortune which has generated in me a mixture of fantasy and wry common sense.

I am fortunate in these times which are hard for many workers— especially the pensioned-off or redundant—to be 'in work'. Many a pensioner, forced to be idle against his will, has greater reserves of character than I have. I do have my occasional days of leisure, but for the most part I have to carry what Keats called the indispensable sense of 'negative capability' about with me and then, as he also said, work makes 'the disagreeables evaporate'.

I look back now at my 'evaporations' with astonishment. If I spent my boyhood in the low Kippsian regions of Edwardian Britain, the British assurance and locality had given an elegance to British comedy. The 'man of letters' I aspired to be was pre-eminent, if poor, in English periodical writing. Also modest families like mine were beneficiaries of the Education Act of the 1870s. Disagreeable to have education cut short at fifteen, but there had been a brief evaporation into foreign languages at a grammar school, language of any kind being my obsession.

It was disagreeable at first to be put into the malodorous leather trade, but the animality of skins fascinated me and so did the Bermondsey leather dressers and fellmongers. The smell of that London of my boyhood and bowler-hatted youth is still with me. I coughed my way through a city stinking, rather excitingly, of coal smoke, gas escapes, tanyards, breweries, horse manure and urine. Flies swarmed, people scratched their fleas. The streets smelled of beer; men and boys reeked of hair oil, vaseline, strong tobacco, powerful boot polish, mackintoshes and things like my father's voluptuous cachous.

The smell of women was racy and scented. Clothes were heavy; utterances—in all classes—were sententious whether witty or not. Music hall songs were epigrammatic stories. 'Lurve' had not yet killed them. Artful euphemism hid a secret archive of bad language. If a 'bloody' broke through, people would say 'Language, I hear,' disapproving as they admired. Hypocrisy was a native fruit, if then overripe.

By 1918 the skirts of the liberated girls who had worked in ammunition factories and offices were shortened a few inches. One now saw their erotic ankles and sex broke out; not as yet in plain Anglo-Saxon, but soon Latinised as copulation in the classier Twenties, for youths like myself who had moved on to Aldous Huxley. I had read enormously, most of Scott, Dickens, most of the Victorian novelists, caught up with Chesterton and Bennett and was heading for *Anna Karenina* and *Madame Bovary*.

I might have stuck in leather all my life but 1918 liberated me. Travel was cheap; I 'evaporated' to Paris, earned my living in the shellac and glue trade and discovered I could write sketches. I became the autodidact abroad and education was open to me at last.

It was even good luck to grow up among non-intellectual people, all in trades; better luck, to have a vocation fixed in my mind—so few boys have—to grow up in a period when the printed language was the dominant teacher and pleasure-giver. Good luck to escape, by going abroad, the perpetual British 'no' to the new boy; good luck to meet the American 'yes' to my first bits of writing. France, Ireland,

Spain were for six years my universities. They taught me European history and the conflicts of cultures and quickly got me clear of the hurdles of the then sticky English class system. Once they have made their bid, all kinds of artists—writers, painters, sculptors, musicians, educated or not—are free of that. It is also half-native in our tribe that we can talk and listen to anyone in his language. Among writers Kipling is an exemplar of what travel does for this faculty.

Since the wilful Twenties, the committals of the Thirties, it seems to me that my life as a man and as a writer has been spent on crossing and recrossing frontiers and that is at the heart of any talent I have. It cheers me that I live on the frontier of Camden Town and Regent's Park. Frontier life has been nourishing to me. Throwing something of oneself away is a way of becoming, for the moment, other people, and I have always thought that unselfing oneself, speaking for others, justifying those who cannot speak, giving importance to the fact that they live, is especially the privilege of the storyteller, and even the critic—who is also an artist.

And here, at the age of forty when the Second World War seemed that it would ruin my life as a short story writer, novelist and critic, I found that my early life in trade was an advantage: it prepared me for another evaporation. I had to divide my time between serious criticism in the *New Statesman* every week and studies of factories, mines, shipyards, railway sidings and industrial towns. I did my literary work in trains. I have always been wary of what used to be called 'committal' to the social and political ideologies which numbers of my contemporaries preached and now in war my foreignness abated: I began to know once more how my own people lived: that abstraction called The People dissolved as I saw real people living lives in conditions unlike my own but with passions like mine and as proud of something unique in them.

The decisive books of the period about English life for me were Jack Common's *The Freedom of the Streets* and—on the Spanish war— Borkenau's *The Spanish Cockpit*. I found my own *raison d'être* in some words of Dostoevsky's that 'without art a man might find his life on earth unliveable'.

If as a storyteller I have had an ear for how people speak and my travelling, bookish nature turned me into that now fading type, a man of letters, how do I see the changes that have slowly come about in the past forty years? In a searching way these changes were predicted in the late Thirties by Lewis Mumford in his absorbing book *The Culture of Cities*. My London has become a megalopolis. It has turned into a fantastic foreign bazaar. The Third World is replacing the traditional European immigrants.

Mumford argued that social betterment has been outstripped every decade by technology. We have become, or feel we have become, anonymous items in a mass society at once neutral and bizarre. As for technology the printed word no longer predominates in popular taste and, as Auden said, literature is now turning into 'a cottage industry'. The descendants of ordinary people who read their Dickens and the Victorian and Edwardian periodicals have given up the printed word for the instant sensation of sight and sound, for pictures on the screen.

One can tell this, if by nothing else, from popular speech in which half the vowels and consonants are missing, and in which a sentence becomes like one slurred word, a telegraphic message. The schools have turned out a large number of grown men and women who cannot read or write, for machines have made this unnecessary for them. I suppose the small core of addicted readers will remain, just as Latin remained for the medieval clerks, but the outlook for prose is not good. The new generation faces the attack of spoken and visual drama which cuts out our prose.

No professional writer becomes famous until his work has been televised or filmed: the rest of us may have to live in the conceit of being like the lamenting figures in the chorus of the Greek drama. That chorus was, in its tedious, humble way, the indispensable gang of prosing human moralists chanting the general dismay as they watched the impersonal and violent passions murderously at work on a stage without backcloth. We may of course become Aristophanic fabulists mocking the ruling cliques of a State Machine. Anthony Burgess and Angus Wilson are revelling in this at the moment.

There is another danger to literary culture: it comes from the technological habits of academic criticism. Scholars have been for ages the traditional conservers of literary tradition, but under the powerful influences of technology and the sciences, linguistics, psychology, sociology, philosophy, they are now using a new and portentous verbiage. They detach themselves from life and reduce it to an esoteric game or treat it as a kind of engineering. Their commentaries are full of self-important and comic irrelevancies. Their specialised ironmongery may be good training for engineers, scientists and spacemen, but it has little relation to imaginative literature.

I speak from experience for—to my astonishment as one who had never been inside any university until I was turned fifty—I have found myself teaching at Princeton, Berkeley, Columbia and the delightful Smith College, in the United States. I suppose to give their tormented Faculties a rest while I unloaded a chattering mind that has always read for delight. I like teaching because it wakes me up and teaches *me* and I am grateful to those institutions for giving me the free time an imaginative writer needs and which I get little of in England.

From my earliest days I have liked the natural readiness and openness of the American temperament and I had been brought up in childhood a good deal on the classic American writers and their direct response to the world they lived in. If American seriousness is often exhausting, the spontaneous image-making vernacular and wit are excellent. American short stories have often an archaic directness more striking than our own. I must also say that some of the most illuminating and helpful remarks about my own writing have come from American critics who, unlike so many of our own, are not out to display themselves rather than the authors they are dealing with. As for the American student—naive and earnest he may sometimes be, as I was when young; but he is continuously expectant and is without the European sneer.

At eighty I look at the horrible state of our civilisation. It seems to be breaking up and returning to the bloody world of Shakespeare's Histories which we thought we had outgrown. But public, like private life, proceeds in circles. The Third World is reliving history we have forgotten and indeed brings its violence to our cities. I am a humanist but I do not think human beings are rational: their greeds and passions are not quickly outgrown. We have now to school ourselves to deal with danger and tragedy.

I have some stoicism but I have often thought lately of a courageous friend of mine, now dead, an adventurous explorer, mountaineer and rather reckless yachtsman. He was one of those born to test his fears. I once sailed in a wild gale with him—much against my will—and was terrified, for I am afraid of the sea and have never learned to swim more than ten yards. He was not afraid. Or, if he feared, his fears exhilarated him and, in fact, vanished in danger because (he said) he was always 'thinking of the next thing to do'. (I suppose this is what I do, when I leave land for the perils of writing prose in which there have been so many shipwrecks.) In physical danger I am capable only of identifying myself with my evil: not as good a recourse as his, but it helps.

I have another friend, eighty-six years old, who has lately been hit by a tragedy in his family. He said he wanted to die at once—but not, he added, until he had seen what happened next in Poland and after that in Iran. At eighty I find myself on the lookout expectantly for the unexpected and am more than half allured by it.

Am I wiser in my old age? I don't know. I am not yet old enough to know loneliness and that puts one to the tests of folly and rage. But I am more tolerant than when I was young. I was not an affectionate young man and indeed I was thought of as fierce—a bolting pony, someone once said. But passionate love made me affectionate. I am deeply touched by the affection I now receive. It is one of the rewards of old age. I suppose I am slowly growing up. I am not a man's man for I owe much to women since my boyhood when my mother fascinated me by the whirligig of her humour and her emotions. And what about serenity? I see that many old women have it. In men it is more often torpor and I am drawn to activity and using myself. And to laughter, which wakes up the mind.

Strangely, laughter seems to me like the sexual act which is perhaps the laughter of two bodies. Whatever there is to be said for serenity there is not much opportunity for it in the modern world; and indeed I know by watching myself that old people are liable to fantasies of sadistic vengeance. The old should not look at the news on television at night.

The pleasures of old age are of the lingering kind, love itself becomes more mysterious, tender and lasting. The great distress of old age is the death of friends, the thinning ranks of one's generation. The air grows cold in the gaps. Something of oneself is drained away when friends go, though in mourning for them we learn to revalue a past we had more than half forgotten, and to bring them walking back to keener life in our memory. We have been members of one another. In old age we increasingly feel we are strangers and we warm to those who treat us as if we are not.

The new sensation is that living people are a wonder. Have you noticed how old people stare at groups of talkers, as if secretly or discreetly joining them silently at a distance? This does not happen to me much for I am always on the move, but I am aware of it. I used to sit long over my beer in pubs and clubs; now I swallow a double gin and run. I don't know why. Trying to pack more into the day? No: I just want to get home.

A sign of old age in myself is that, knowing my time is limited, I find myself looking at streets and their architecture much longer and more intensely and at Nature and landscape. I gaze at the plane tree at the end of the garden, studying its branches and its leaves. I look a long time at flowers. And I am always on the watch for the dramatic changes in the London sky. I have always liked to sketch formations of clouds. I store up the procession of headlands and terrifying ravines of North Cornwall and of all the landscapes that have formed me: the shapes of the Yorkshire Fells and the Downs in Sussex and Wiltshire, the tableland of Castile.

I have no religious faith. I am no pantheist or sentimentalist in my love of Nature but simply an idolater of leaf, hill, stream and stone. I came across a line of Camus which drily describes people like myself: 'One of our contemporaries is cured of his torment simply by contemplating a landscape.' That, and lately falling into the habit of reading Gibbon's *Decline and Fall* on Sunday evenings, 'evaporates the disagreeables' of history that now advance on us: the irony of the learned Gibbon excites the sense of tragi-comedy and is, except for its lack of poetic sense, close to the feeling I have about the present and the past.

PART TWO
On Men, Women and Human Nature

THIS SECTION contains ten Essayists, whose chronology runs from Plutarch, to Montaigne himself, with noted later contributors to the form, including Dr Johnson, David Hume and Charles Lamb. It comes as far up to date as that wacky Irishman, the late Patrick Campbell, whose antic public face concealed a surreal edge. Rather than make a collective point they all contribute to a composite observation.

If the novelist portrays life in oils, then the Essayist photographs it and keeps it in a kind of filing-cabinet of whims, characterisations, abstract impressions, humours. This does not mean that the Essay lacks excitement or novelty—quite the contrary. Could Jane Austen have bettered Lytton Strachey on Lady Hester Stanhope? 'The Pitt nose', he begins, 'has a curious history.'

When Essayists turn to self-examination they too have the benefit of allowing the reader to share in the inner life of the writer. Stendhal's daydream of 10 April 1840 specifies, among many other desirable things, that, according to the condition of Article 20, 'The privileged one [i.e., Stendhal himself] will never be more unhappy than he has been from 1 August 1839 to 1 April 1840'. A novelist would probably have an obligation to tell us how, or why, this unhappiness arose; the Essayist leaves us to our curiosity, and sympathy, and perhaps identification with him.

Another advantage lies in being able to perceive the writer in relation to his own time. A novel may, as one of its ingredients, include a deliberate re-distribution of time—we must travel with, say, a Russian soldier in his freezing column, or an English country gentleman to the sunny house of a prospective wife. The prosaic-ness of the Essay enables us to view the writer at the very moment he is writing—we can intercept him and consider his condition on that day, and therefore have room to wonder at the rest of him. Furthermore the concentration does not get as easily diffused: David Hume or Dr Johnson may dwell specifically on their meannesses and sorrows without being dragged off to attend to plot or narrative or characterisation. As a result the same demands are not made upon the reader's imagination either. Not that the demands are less, just different.

The Privileges of 10 April 1840

STENDHAL

translated by Cyril Connolly

May God grant me the following diploma:

ARTICLE 1

Never any serious pain right up to advanced old age; then, no pain but sudden death in bed from apoplexy, during sleep, without any moral or physical distress.

Every year, not more than three days of ill-health. The body and all its by-products to be quite odourless.

ARTICLE 2

The following miracles will neither be observed nor suspected by anyone.

ARTICLE 3

Whenever desired, the member to be as the index finger in regard to firmness and agility. Its shape two inches more than the big toe and of the same thickness, but pleasure by means of the said member to take place only twice a week. Twenty times a year the privileged one to be able to change himself into the being he wishes, provided that that being exists. A hundred times a year he will speak for twenty-four hours any language he wishes.

ARTICLE 4

The privileged one having a ring on his finger and pinching this ring while looking at a woman, she will fall passionately in love with him as we know Eloise did with Abelard. If the ring is slightly moistened with saliva, the woman becomes only a tender and devoted friend. By looking at a woman and taking the ring from the finger, all sentiments inspired by virtue of the foregoing privileges shall cease. By looking at a hostile being and stroking the ring on the finger hate changes into goodwill.

These miracles can only take place four times a year for *l'amour passion*; eight times for friendship; twenty times for the disappearance of hate, and fifty times to inspire simple goodwill.

ARTICLE 5

Fine hair, a good skin, excellent fingers which never peel, a delicate and gentle body odour. The 1st of February and the 1st of June every year the clothes of the privileged one revert to the condition they were at the third time he wore them.

ARTICLE 6

Miracles in the eyes of all who don't know him: the privileged one shall have the face of General Debelle, who died in St Domingo, but without any imperfection. He shall play faultlessly whisk [*sic*], écarté, billiards, chess, but never make more than a hundred francs at them. As a pistol shot, a horseman and a fencer he shall be perfect.

ARTICLE 7

Four times a year he can change himself into any animal he wishes, and afterwards change back into a man. Four times a year he can change himself into any man he wishes and furthermore concentrate that man's life into that of an animal. In case of death or impediment to the being into which he has changed, he shall revert immediately to the shape of the privileged one. Thus the privileged one can, four times a year, and for an unlimited time, in each case, occupy two bodies at the same time.

ARTICLE 8

When the privileged one is wearing on his person or his finger for two minutes a ring which he has kept for a moment in his mouth, he shall become invulnerable for the time he has decided upon. Ten times a year he shall possess the sight of an eagle and be able in running to make five leagues in an hour.

ARTICLE 9

Every day at two o'clock in the morning the privileged one shall find in his pocket a gold napoleon plus the value of forty francs in ready money in the currency of the country in which he finds himself. Any money of which he has been robbed will be found the following night at two o'clock in the morning on a table in front of him. Murderers at the moment of striking or giving him poison will have a violent access of cholera for eight days. The privileged one can shorten these pains by saying, 'I entreat that so-and-so's sufferings stop altogether or are diminished in severity'.

Thieves will be seized with an access of extreme cholera for two days at the moment when they shall be ready to perform the theft.

ARTICLE 10

Eight times a year while out hunting a little flag shall reveal to the privileged one an hour in advance what game there is and its exact location. One second before the game takes to flight the little flag will be luminous. It is understood that the flag shall be invisible to anyone except the privileged one.

ARTICLE 11

A small flag shall point out to the privileged one statues hidden underground, under water or by walls. Also what these statues are, when and by whom made and the price one could receive for them after discovery. The privileged one can change these statues into a ball of lead of the weight of a quarter of an ounce. The miracle of the flag and the successive changing of the statue into a small ball and back again into a statue to take place not more than eight times a year.

ARTICLE 12

The beast which the privileged one mounts or which draws the carriage in which he travels will never fall ill or fall down. The privileged one can unite himself with this animal in such a way as to inspire him with his wishes while participating in his sensations. Thus the privileged one when riding a horse will make but one animal with him and dictate his own will. The animal thus united with the privileged one will have three times the strength and courage which it possesses in its normal state.

The privileged one transformed into a fly, for example, and united with an eagle will form one being with that eagle.

ARTICLE 13

The privileged one is unable to pilfer; if he tries to do so, his organs would not permit the action. He can kill ten human beings a year, but no one to whom he shall have spoken. For the first year he can kill a human being provided he has not spoken to him more than twice.

ARTICLE 14

Should the privileged one wish to relate or reveal one of the articles of this diploma, his mouth would be unable to form any sound and he will have toothache for twenty-four hours.

ARTICLE 15

The privileged one taking a ring in his finger and saying, 'I entreat that noxious insects be annihilated', all insects within six metres of the ring in every direction to be smitten with death. These insects are fleas, bed-bugs, lice of every description, crabs, gnats, flies, rats, etc.

Snakes, vipers, lions, tigers, wolves and all poisonous animals, seized with fear, will take flight and shall withdraw to a league's distance.

ARTICLE 16

Wherever he is, the privileged one, after having said, 'I pray for my food', shall find: two pounds of bread, a steak done to a turn, a leg of mutton *idem*, a dish of spinach *idem*, a bottle of St Julien, a carafe of water, dessert and ice-cream and a *demi-tasse* of coffee. This prayer to be granted twice every twenty-four hours.

ARTICLE 17

Ten times a year by request the privileged one will never miss either with rifle or pistol or with a blow from any kind of weapon. Ten times a year he can perform feats of arms with twice the strength of his opponent, but he shall be incapable of administering any deadly wound or one which causes pain or disablement for more than a hundred hours.

ARTICLE 18

Ten times a year the privileged one by request will be able to diminish by three-quarters the suffering of anyone he sees; or this person being at the point of death, he can prolong his life by ten days while diminishing his actual suffering by three-quarters. He can also by request obtain for the person in pain a sudden and painless death.

ARTICLE 19

The privileged one can change a dog into a beautiful or an ugly woman: this woman will offer him her arm and will have the intelligence of Madame Ancilla★ and the heart of Melanie.† This miracle can renew itself twenty times a year.

The privileged one can change a dog into a man who will have the

★Madame Ancellot.

†Melanie Louason with whom he was in love in 1808. At fifty-nine years of age after thirty-two years of separation it is worth noting this reference in his wishful thinking.

figure of Pepin de Bellisle and the intelligence of Monsieur Koreff, the Jewish doctor.

ARTICLE 20

The privileged one will never be more unhappy than he has been from the 1st of August 1839 to the 1st of April 1840. Two hundred times a year the privileged one can reduce his sleep to two hours which will produce the physical effects of eight hours. He will have the eyes of a lynx and the agility of Debureau.

ARTICLE 21

Twenty times a year the privileged one can read the thoughts of everyone who is around him up to twenty metres distance. A hundred times a year he can see exactly what the person he wishes is doing, with the complete exception of the woman whom he loves the most.

There is also an exception for dirty or disgusting actions.

ARTICLE 22

The privileged one can earn no more money than his sixty francs a day by means of the privileges here announced. One hundred and fifty times a year he can obtain by request that such and such a person entirely forgets his existence.

ARTICLE 23

Ten times a year the privileged one can be transported to any place he wishes at the rate of one hundred leagues an hour. During the journey he will sleep.

On the Power of the Imagination

MONTAIGNE

translated by J. M. Cohen

'A strong imagination brings on the event,' say the scholars. I am one of those who are very much affected by the imagination. Everyone feels its impact, but some are knocked over by it. On me it makes an intense impression, and my practice is rather to avoid it than to resist it. I wish I could consort only with the healthy and the cheerful, for the sight of another's anguish gives me real pain, and my body has often taken over the sensations of some person I am with. A perpetual cougher irritates my lungs and my throat; and I am more reluctant to visit a sick man to whom I am bound by duty and interest than one who has a smaller claim on my attention and consideration. As I observe a disease, so I catch it and give it lodging in myself. It is no surprise to me that the imagination should bring fevers and death to those who allow it free play and encourage it. Simon Thomas was a great physician in his day, and I remember meeting him once at the house of a rich old man who suffered with his lungs. When the patient asked him how he could be cured, Master Thomas answered that one way would be for him to infect me with a liking for his company. Then if he were to fix his gaze on the freshness of my complexion, and his thoughts on the youthful gaiety and vigour with which I overflowed, and if he were to feast his senses on my flourishing state of health, his own condition might well improve. What he forgot to say was that mine might at the same time deteriorate.

Gallus Vibius so taxed his mind to understand the nature and periodicity of insanity that he completely lost his senses and was never able to recover them; he might have boasted that he had gone mad by learning. There are some who from fear anticipate the executioner's hand; and there was one who, when they unbound his eyes so that his pardon might be read to him, was found to be stark dead on the scaffold, slain by no other stroke than that of his imagination. We sweat, we tremble, we turn pale, we flush, beneath our imagination's impact; deep in our feather-beds, we feel our bodies shaken by its onslaughts, sometimes almost to the point of death; and fervent youth grows so heated in its sleep that it satisfies its amorous desires even in dreams,

Ut quasi transactis saepe omnibus rebus profundant
*fluminis ingentes fluctus, vestemque cruentent.**

Although there is nothing strange in seeing horns grow in the night on foreheads that had none at bedtime, there is something memorable about the case of Cippus, King of Italy. During the day he had been a passionate spectator at the bull-fight, and all night long he had worn horns in his dreams. His forehead had actually sprouted them by the power of the imagination. Anger gave Croesus' son† the voice that Nature had denied him, and Antiochus fell into a fever because Stratonice's beauty had become too deeply imprinted on his mind. Pliny says that he saw Lucius Cossitius change from a woman into a man on his wedding-day; and Pontanus and others record similar metamorphoses that have occurred in Italy in more recent times. By his own vehement desire and his mother's,

Vota puer solvit, qui femina voverat Iphis.‡

Passing through Vitry-le-François, I was shown a man whom the Bishop of Soissons had confirmed under the name of Germain, but whom all the village's inhabitants had both known and seen to be a girl, and who had been called Marie up to the age of twenty-two. He was then old, had a heavy growth of beard, and was unmarried. He said that as he was straining to take a jump his male organs appeared; and the girls of that neighbourhood still sing a song in which they warn one another not to take long strides or they may turn into boys, like Marie Germain. It is not very surprising that this sort of accident happens frequently, for the imagination is so continually drawn to this subject that, supposing it has any power over such things, it would be better for it to incorporate the virile member in a girl once and for all, rather than subject her so often to the same thoughts and the same violence of desire.

Some people attribute the scars of King Dagobert and St Francis§ to the power of the imagination. It is said sometimes to lift bodies from their places. Celsus tells of a priest whose soul was ravished by such an ecstasy that his body would remain for a long time without breath

---

* 'As if they were performing the entire act, the mighty wave gushes forth and stains their garments.' Lucretius, IV, 1305.

† According to Herodotus, he had been dumb from birth, but had found his voice when he saw his father in peril of death.

‡ 'Iphis as a man fulfilled the vows he had made as a woman.' Ovid, *Metamorphoses*, IX, 793.

§ Dagobert's scars were caused by fear of the gangrene; St Francis's were the stigmata.

or feeling. St Augustine makes mention of another who no sooner heard some melancholy or doleful cry than he would fall into a sudden swoon, and be so violently transported out of himself that it was no use shaking him or shouting at him, pinching him or scorching him, until he came to of his own accord. Then he would say that he had heard voices, but as if from far away, and would become aware of his bruises and burns. That this was no obstinate pretence, no concealment of his real sensations, was shown by the fact that all the time he had neither pulse nor breath.

It is probable that the belief in miracles, visions, enchantments, and such extraordinary occurrences springs in the main from the power of the imagination acting principally on the minds of the common people, who are the more easily impressed. Their beliefs have been so strongly captured that they think they see what they do not. I am also of the opinion that those comical impediments which so embarrass our society that they talk of nothing else are most likely caused by apprehensions and fears. I have personal knowledge of the case of a man for whom I can answer as for myself, and who could not fall under the least suspicion of impotence or of being under a spell. He had heard a comrade of his tell of an extraordinary loss of manhood that had fallen on him at a most inconvenient moment; and, when he was himself in a like situation, the full horror of this story had suddenly struck his imagination so vividly that he suffered a similar loss himself. Afterwards the wretched memory of his misadventure so devoured and tyrannised over him that he became subject to relapses. He found some remedy for this mental trick in another trick; by himself confessing this weakness of his and declaring it in advance, he relieved the strain on his mind and the mishap being expected, his responsibility for it diminished and weighed upon him less. When he had an opportunity of his own choosing—his thought being disengaged and free and his body in its normal state—he would have his virility tested, seized, and taken unawares, by previous arrangement with the other party. He was then completely and immediately cured of his infirmity. For once a man has been capable with a certain woman, he will never be incapable with her again unless out of real impotence.

This mishap is only to be feared in an enterprise where the mind is immoderately torn between desire and respect, and particularly when the opportunity is unforeseen and urgent. There is no way of overcoming the trouble. I know someone who found it a help to come to it with his body already partially sated elsewhere. Thus the heat of his passion was allayed. Now, in old age, he finds himself less impotent because less potent. And I know another man who was greatly helped by a friend's assurance that he was furnished with a counter-battery of enchantments, certain to protect him. But it would be better if I were to explain how this came about.

A count of very good family and an intimate friend of mine married a beautiful lady who had been courted by someone who was present at the marriage feast. This greatly perturbed his friends, and especially one old lady, a relation of his, who was presiding over the festivities and in whose house they were given. She was very much afraid of these sorceries and told me of her fears. I asked her to rely on me. Luckily, I had in my luggage a small flat piece of gold, with celestial figures engraved on it, as a charm against sunstroke and a remedy for headaches. It had to be worn just on the suture of the skull and, to keep it in place, a ribbon was sewn on to it, to be tied under the chin: a fantastic notion, but relevant to the subject we are discussing. Jacques Pelletier★ had given me this odd present, and I decided to put it to good use. I warned the count that he might encounter the same bad luck as other men had, certain persons being present who would like to play him a trick, but that he could boldly go to bed since I would act as his friend. I promised him that at need I would not withhold a miracle, which it was in my power to perform, provided that he would swear on his honour to keep it absolutely secret. He was merely to let me know by a certain sign when they brought in the midnight refreshment, if things had gone badly with him. This idea had been so dinned into his ears and into his brain that he found himself impeded by his disturbed imagination, and made me the sign. I told him then to get up under pretence of chasing us from the room and, as if in sport, to pull off the bed-robe I was wearing—we were much of a height. This he was to put on himself, and wear it until he carried out my instructions. These were that, when we had gone, he should retire to make water, repeat certain prayers three times and go through certain motions. On each of these three occasions he must tie round his waist the ribbon that I put in his hands and very carefully place the medal which was attached to it over his kidneys with the figure in a certain position. After that, having made the ribbon quite tight so that it could not get untied or fall out of place, he should return to the business in hand, and not forget to throw my robe on to the bed, so that it covered them both.

These monkey-tricks play the main part in the matter, for we cannot get it out of our minds that such strange practices must be based on some occult knowledge. Their absurdity lends them weight and gains them respect. In short, my talisman certainly proved itself

★Jacques Pelletier (1517-82), physician, mathematician, and humanist.

more Venerian than Solar, more active than preventive. It was a sudden and odd impulse that led me to do a thing so alien to my nature. I am an enemy to all subtle deeds of deception, and I hate to take part in trickery, not only in sport but even to obtain an advantage; if the action is not wicked, the way to it is.

Amasis, King of Egypt, married a very beautiful Greek girl called Laodice, but though he had shown himself a regular gallant everywhere else, he found himself unable to enjoy her. Believing that there was some sorcery in this, he threatened to kill her. But she, considering his trouble to be of the imagination, sent him to his devotions. He made his vows and promises to Venus, and on the first night after the performance of his oblations and sacrifices found his potency divinely restored.

It is wrong of women to receive us with pouting, querulous, and shrinking looks that quell us even as they kindle us. The daughter-in-law of Pythagoras said that a woman who goes to bed with a man ought to lay aside her modesty with her skirt, and put it on again with her petticoat. The mind of the assailant, disturbed by so many different alarms, is easily dismayed; and once the imagination has subjected a man to this disgrace—and it never does so except at the first encounter, because the desires are then more turbulent and strong, and because at the outset one has a much greater fear of failing—the fact that he has begun badly throws him into a fever, and vexation at his mischance carries over to succeeding occasions.

Married men, with time at their command, need not hurry, nor need they attempt the enterprise if they are not ready. It is better to accept the disgrace and refrain from inaugurating the marriage-bed when feverish and full of agitations, and to await another more private and less disturbed opportunity, than to be thrown into a perpetual misery by the surprise and disappointment of an initial failure. Before possession is taken, one who suffers from the imagination should by sallies at different times make gentle essays and overtures without any strain or persistence, in order definitely to convince himself of his powers. Those who know their members to be obedient by nature need only take care to out-manoeuvre the imagination.

We have reason to remark the untractable liberties taken by this member, which intrudes so tiresomely when we do not require it and fails us so annoyingly when we need it most, imperiously pitting its authority against that of the will, and most proudly and obstinately refusing our solicitations both mental and manual. Yet if on being rebuked for rebellion and condemned on that score he were to engage me to plead his cause, I might perhaps cast some suspicion on our other members, his fellows, of having framed this fictitious case against him out of pure envy of the importance and pleasure attached to his functions. I might arraign them for plotting to make the world his enemy by maliciously blaming him alone for their common fault. For I ask you to consider whether there is a single part of our bodies that does not often refuse to work at our will, and does not often operate in defiance of it. Each one of them has its own passions that rouse it and put it to sleep without our leave.

How often do the involuntary movements of our features reveal what we are secretly thinking and betray us to those about us! The same cause that governs this member, without our knowing it governs the heart, the lungs, and the pulse, the sight of a charming object imperceptibly spreading within us the flame of a feverish emotion. Are these the only muscles and veins that swell and subside without the consent, not only of our will, but even of our thoughts? We do not command our hair to stand on end, or our skin to quiver with desire or fear. The hand often goes where we do not send it. The tongue is paralysed and the voice choked, each at its own time. Even when, having nothing to cook, we could gladly prevent it, the appetite for food and drink does not fail to stir those parts that are subject to it, in just the same way as this other appetite; and it forsakes us just as unseasonably when it chooses to. The organs that serve to discharge the bowels have their own dilations and contractions outside the control of the wishes and contrary to them, as have those that serve to relieve our kidneys. And though, to vindicate the supreme power of our will, St Augustine claims to have seen a man who could command his bottom to break wind as often as he wished, and Vives, his commentator, caps him with another case from his own day of a man who could synchronise his blasts to the metre of verses that were read to him, this does not imply the complete obedience of this organ. For usually it is most unruly and mutinous. Indeed, I know one such that is so turbulent and so intractable that for the last forty years it has compelled its master to break wind with every breath. So unremittingly constant is it in its tyranny that it is even now bringing him to his death.

But let us take our will, on whose behalf we are preferring this charge. How much more justifiably can we brand it with rebellion and sedition, on account of its constant irregularities and disobedience! Does it always desire what we wish it to desire? Does it not often desire, to our obvious disadvantage, what we forbid it to? Does it let itself be guided, either, by the conclusions of our reason?

In short, I ask you on behalf of my noble client kindly to reflect that, although his case in this matter is inseparably and indistinguishably joined with that of an accomplice, nevertheless he alone is attacked, and with such arguments and accusations as, seeing the condition of the parties, cannot possibly appertain to or concern the said accomplice. Wherefore the malice and manifest injustice of his accusers is apparent.

Be that as it may, protesting that the wranglings and sentences of lawyers and judges are in vain, nature will go her own way. Yet she would have been quite justified in endowing that member with some special privileges, since it is the author of the sole immortal work of mortal man. For this reason Socrates held that procreation is a divine act, and love a desire for immortality as well as an immortal spirit.

One man, perhaps, by this working of the imagination, may leave the king's evil behind him, while his companion carries it back to Spain. That is why in such cases the mind must generally be prepared in advance. Why do doctors begin by practising on the credulity of their patients with so many false promises of a cure, if not to call the powers of the imagination to the aid of their fraudulent concoctions? They know, as one of the masters of their craft has given it to them in writing, that there are men on whom the mere sight of medicine is operative.

All this nonsense has come into my head through my recalling a tale told me by an apothecary who served in the household of my late father. He was a simple man and a Swiss—a people not much given to vanity and lying. He had known, some years before, a merchant of Toulouse who was sickly and subject to stone, and who often resorted to enemas, which he had made up for him by the physicians in different ways according to the phases of his disease. When they were brought to him none of the usual formalities was omitted; and he often tried them to see if they were too hot. Imagine him then, lying on his stomach, with all the motions gone through except that no application had been made! This ceremonial over, the apothecary would retire, and the patient would be treated just as if he had taken the enema; the effect was the same as if he actually had. And if the doctor found the action insufficient, he would administer two or three more in precisely the same way. My witness swears that when, to save the expense—for he paid for the enemas as if he had really taken them—the patient's wife tried to make do with warm water, the result betrayed fraud; this method was found useless and they had to return to the first.

A certain woman, imagining that she had swallowed a pin with her bread, shrieked and writhed as if she had an unbearable pain in her gullet, where she thought she could feel it sticking. But, there being no swelling and no outward sign, a clever fellow concluded that this was just fancy, and that the idea had been suggested by a piece of crust that had scraped her throat as it went down. So he made her vomit, and stealthily threw a bent pin into what she threw up. Believing that she had thrown up the pin, the woman was immediately relieved of her pain. I know of a gentleman too who, three or four days after having entertained a large party in his house, bragged, by way of a joke—for there was nothing in it—that he had made them eat cat in a pasty. One young lady in the company was thereupon so horrified that she was seized with a severe dysentery and fever, and nothing could be done to save her. Even animals can be seen, like us, to be subject to the power of the imagination, as witness those dogs who pine away with grief for the loss of their masters. We also see them barking and trembling, and horses whinnying and struggling, in their dreams.

But all this may be attributed to the close connection between the mind and the body, whose fortunes affect one another. It is another matter when the imagination works, as it sometimes does, not on one's own body but on someone else's. Just as one body passes a disease to its neighbour, as we see in the case of plague, smallpox, and pink-eye, which one person catches from another—

> Dum spectant oculi laesos, laeduntur et ipsi,
> multaque corporibus transitione nocent,*

so, when the imagination is violently disturbed, it launches shafts that may hit a distant object. The ancients believed that certain women in Scythia, if aroused and angry with a man, could kill him with a single glance. Tortoises and ostriches hatch their eggs merely by looking at them—a proof that their eyes have some ejaculative power. And as for sorcerers, they are said to have an evil eye, which is capable of working mischief:

> Nescio quis teneros oculus mihi fascinat agnos.†

I do not put much trust in magic. But we know by experience that women imprint the marks of their fancies on the children they are carrying in their womb, as witness the mother who gave birth to a blackamoor.‡ And there was that girl from a village near Pisa, who was all rough and hairy. When she was presented to the Emperor Charles, King of Bohemia, her mother said the child had been

* When their eyes behold others in pain, they feel pain themselves, and so many ills pass from body to body.' Ovid, De Remedio Amoris, 615.

† 'Some evil eye has bewitched my young lambs.' Virgil, Eclogues, III, 103.

‡ An anecdote related by St Jerome.

conceived like that because of a picture of St John the Baptist that hung above her bed.

It is the same with animals, as witness Jacob's sheep, and those partridges and hares that are turned white by the snow on the mountains. Someone in my house recently saw a cat watching a bird at the top of a tree. After they had gazed fixedly at one another for some time, the bird dropped, apparently dead, between the cat's paws, either stupefied by its own imagination or drawn by some power of attraction in the cat. Lovers of hawking have heard the story of the falconer who fixed his glance firmly on a kite in the air, and wagered that he would bring it down simply by the power of his eyes. They say that he did so.

For the anecdotes that I borrow I rely on the consciences of those from whom I have them. The inferences are my own, and depend on the evidence of common reasoning, not of experience. Anyone may add his own examples, and if he has none, the number and variety of occurrences being so great, he may still be sure that plenty exist. If my own comments are not sound, let someone else comment for me. In this study of our manners and behaviour that I am undertaking, fabulous incidents are as good as true ones, so long as they are feasible. Whether they happened or not, in Paris or in Rome, to John or to Peter, there is always some turn of the human mind about which they give me useful information. I note and draw profit from these anecdotes, whether they are shadowy or substantial. Of the various readings that the histories often provide, I make use of the most unusual and memorable. There are some authors whose purpose is to relate actual events. Mine, if I could fulfil it, would be to tell what might happen. The schools are rightly permitted to invent examples when they have none. I do not do this, however, and in that respect I surpass the most faithful historians in scrupulous reverence for truth. In the examples which I am drawing here from what I have heard, done, or said, I have refused to be so bold as to change even the most trivial and unimportant details. Consciously I do not falsify one iota; I cannot answer for my knowledge.

In this connection I sometimes wonder whether it can be right for a prudent theologian, philosopher, or other such person of precise and delicate conscience to write history. How can they pledge their word on a popular belief? How can they answer for the thoughts of unknown persons, and advance their own conjectures as valid coin? They would refuse to give sworn testimony before a magistrate concerning actions involving several parties that had actually taken place before their eyes; and there is nobody whom they know so intimately that they would undertake to answer fully for his intentions. I consider it less dangerous, however, to write of the past than of present affairs, in as much as the writer has then only to produce some borrowed facts. Some people urge me to write a chronicle of my own times. They consider that I view things with eyes less disturbed by passion than other men, and at closer range, because fortune has given me access to the heads of various factions. But they do not realise that I would not undertake the task for all the fame of Sallust; that I am a sworn foe to constraint, assiduity, and perseverance; and that nothing is so foreign to my style as an extended narrative. So often I break off for lack of breath. I have no proper skill in composition or development, and am more ignorant than a child of the words and phrases used for the most ordinary things. Therefore I have undertaken to say only what I can say, suiting my matter to my powers. Were I to select some subject that I had to pursue, I might not be able to keep up with it. Besides, the liberties I take being so complete, I might publish opinions that reason, and even my own judgement, would find unwarrantable and blameworthy. Plutarch would readily tell us that if the examples he cites in his works are wholly and in every way true the credit is due to other writers; if they are of use to posterity, on the other hand, and are presented with a brilliance that lights us on the way to virtue, the credit for that is his own. An ancient tale is not like a medicinal drug; whether it is so or so, there is no danger in it.

On Sorrow

DR SAMUEL JOHNSON

Quanquam his solatiis acquiescam, debilitor et frangor eadem illa humanitate quae me, ut hoc ipsum permitterem, induxit. Non ideo tamen velim durior fieri: nec ignoro alios huiusmodi casus nihil amplius vocare quam damnum; eoque sibi magnos homines et sapientes videri. Qui an magni sapientesque sint, nescio: homines non sunt. Hominis est enim affici dolore, sentire: resistere tamen, et solatia admittere; non solatiis non egere.

PLINY

These proceedings have afforded me some comfort in my distress; not-withstanding which, I am still dispirited and unhinged by the same motives of humanity that induced me to grant such indulgences. However, I by no means wish to become less susceptible of tenderness. I know these kind of misfortunes would be estimated by other persons only as common losses, and from such sensations they would conceive themselves great and wise men. I shall not determine either their greatness or their wisdom; but I am certain they have no humanity. It is the part of a man to be affected with grief; to feel sorrow, at the same time that he is to resist it, and to admit of comfort.

EARL OF ORRERY

Of the passions with which the mind of man is agitated, it may be observed, that they naturally hasten towards their own extinction, by inciting and quickening the attainment of their objects. Thus fear urges our flight, and desire animates our progress; and if there are some which perhaps may be indulged till they outgrow the good appropriated to their satisfaction, as it is frequently observed of avarice and ambition, yet their immediate tendency is to some means of happiness really existing, and generally within the prospect. The miser always imagines that there is a certain sum that will fill his heart to the brim; and every ambitious man, like King Pyrrhus, has an acquisition in his thoughts that is to terminate his labours, after which he shall pass the rest of his life in ease or gaiety, in repose or devotion.

Sorrow is perhaps the only affection of the breast that can be excepted from this general remark, and it therefore deserves the particular attention of those who have assumed the arduous province of preserving the balance of the mental constitution. The other passions are diseases indeed, but they necessarily direct us to their proper cure. A man at once feels the pain, and knows the medicine, to which he is carried with greater haste as the evil which requires it is more excruciating, and cures himself by unerring instinct, as the wounded stags of Crete are related by Aelian to have recourse to vulnerary herbs. But for sorrow there is no remedy provided by nature; it is often occasioned by accidents irreparable, and dwells upon objects that have lost or changed their existence; it requires what it cannot hope, that the laws of the universe should be repealed; that the dead should return, or the past should be recalled.

Sorrow is not that regret for negligence or error which may animate us to future care or activity, or that repentance of crimes for which, however irrevocable, our Creator has promised to accept it as an atonement; the pain which arises from these causes has very salutary effects, and is every hour extenuating itself by the reparation of those miscarriages that produce it. Sorrow is properly that state of the mind in which our desires are fixed upon the past, without looking forward to the future, an incessant wish that something were otherwise than it has been, a tormenting and harassing want of some enjoyment or possession which we have lost, and which no endeavours can possibly regain. Into such anguish many have sunk upon some sudden diminution of their fortune, an unexpected blast of their reputation, or the loss of children or of friends. They have suffered all sensibility of pleasure to be destroyed by a single blow, have given up for ever the hopes of substituting any other object in the room of that which they lament, resigned their lives to gloom and despondency, and worn themselves out in unavailing misery.

Yet so much is this passion the natural consequence of tenderness and endearment, that, however painful and however useless, it is justly reproachful not to feel it on some occasions; and so widely and constantly has it always prevailed, that the laws of some nations, and the customs of others, have limited a time for the external appearances of grief caused by the dissolution of close alliances, and the breach of domestic union.

It seems determined, by the general suffrage of mankind, that sorrow is to a certain point laudable, as the offspring of love, or at least pardonable, as the effect of weakness; but that it ought not to be suffered to increase by indulgence, but must give way, after a stated time, to social duties, and the common avocations of life. It is at first unavoidable, and therefore must be allowed, whether with or without our choice; it may afterwards be admitted as a decent and affectionate testimony of kindness and esteem; something will be extorted by nature, and something may be given to the world. But all beyond the bursts of passion, or the forms of solemnity, is not only useless, but culpable; for we have no right to sacrifice, to the vain longings of affection, that time which providence allows us for the task of our station.

Yet it too often happens that sorrow, thus lawfully entering, gains such a firm possession of the mind, that it is not afterwards to be ejected; the mournful ideas, first violently impressed, and afterwards willingly received, so much engross the attention, as to predominate in every thought, to darken gaiety, and perplex ratiocination. An habitual sadness seizes upon the soul, and the faculties are chained to a single object, which can never be contemplated but with hopeless uneasiness.

From this state of dejection it is very difficult to rise to cheerfulness and alacrity, and therefore many who have laid down rules of intellectual health, think preservatives easier than remedies, and teach us not to trust ourselves with favourite enjoyments, not to indulge the luxury of fondness, but to keep our minds always suspended in such indifference, that we may change the objects about us without inconvenience or emotion.

An exact compliance with this rule might, perhaps, contribute to tranquillity, but surely it would never produce happiness. He that regards none so much as to be afraid of losing them, must live for ever without the gentle pleasures of sympathy and confidence; he must feel no melting fondness, no warmth of benevolence, nor any of those honest joys which nature annexes to the power of pleasing. And as no man can justly claim more tenderness than he pays, he must forfeit his share in that officious and watchful kindness which love only can dictate, and those lenient endearments by which love only can soften life. He may justly be overlooked and neglected by such as have more warmth in their heart; for who would be the friend of him, whom, with whatever assiduity he may be courted, and with whatever services obliged, his principles will not suffer to make equal returns, and who, when you have exhausted all the instances of goodwill, can only be prevailed on not to be an enemy?

An attempt to preserve life in a state of neutrality and indifference, is unreasonable and vain. If by excluding joy we could shut out grief, the scheme would deserve very serious attention; but since, however we may debar ourselves from happiness, misery will find its way at many inlets, and the assaults of pain will force our regard, though we may withhold it from the invitations of pleasure, we may surely endeavour to raise life above the middle point of apathy at one time, since it will necessarily sink below it at another.

But though it cannot be reasonable not to gain happiness for fear of losing it, yet it must be confessed, that in proportion to the pleasure of possession, will be for some time our sorrow for the loss; it is therefore the province of the moralist to inquire whether such pains may not quickly give way to mitigation. Some have thought that the most certain way to clear the heart from its embarrassment is to drag it by force into scenes of merriment. Others imagine, that such a transition is too violent, and recommend rather to soothe it into tranquillity, by making it acquainted with miseries more dreadful and afflictive, and diverting to the calamities of others the regards which we are inclined to fix too closely upon our own misfortunes.

It may be doubted whether either of those remedies will be sufficiently powerful. The efficacy of mirth is not always easy to try, and the indulgence of melancholy may be suspected to be one of those medicines, which will destroy, if it happens not to cure.

The safe and general antidote against sorrow, is employment. It is commonly observed, that among soldiers and seamen, though there is much kindness, there is little grief; they see their friend fall without any of that lamentation which is indulged in security and idleness, because they have no leisure to spare from the care of themselves; and whoever shall keep his thoughts equally busy, will find himself equally unaffected with irretrievable losses.

Time is observed generally to wear out sorrow, and its effects might doubtless be accelerated by quickening the succession and enlarging the variety of objects.

> *Si tempore longo*
> *Leniri poterit luctus, tu sperne morari,*
> *Qui sapiet sibi tempus erit.*   GROTIUS

> *'Tis long ere time can mitigate your grief;*
> *To wisdom fly, she quickly brings relief.*
> F. LEWIS

Sorrow is a kind of rust of the soul, which every new idea contributes in its passage to scour away. It is the putrefaction of stagnant life, and is remedied by exercise and motion.

Pierce Penniless: Of Greediness

THOMAS NASHE

Famine, Lent and Desolation sit in onion-skinned jackets before the door of his indurance, as a Chorus in *The Tragedy of Hospitality*, to tell Hunger and Poverty there's no relief for them there. And in the inner part of this ugly habitation stands Greediness, prepared to devour all that enter, attired in a capouch of written parchment, buttoned down before with labels of wax, and lined with sheep's fells for warmness; his cap furred with cats' skins, after the Muscovy fashion, and all to-be-tasselled with angle-hooks, instead of aglets, ready to catch hold of all those to whom he shows any humbleness. For his breeches, they were made of the lists of broadcloths, which he had by letters patents assured him and his heirs, to the utter overthrow of bowcases and cushion makers; and bombasted they were, like beer barrels, with statute merchants and forfeitures. But of all, his shoes were the strangest, which, being nothing else but a couple of crab shells, were toothed at the toes with two sharp sixpenny nails that digged up every dunghill they came by for gold, and snarled at the stones as he went in the street, because they were so common for men, women, and children to tread upon, and he could not devise how to wrest an odd fine out of any of them.

Thus walks he up and down all his lifetime, with an iron crow in his hand instead of a staff, and a sergeant's mace in his mouth, which night and day he still gnaws upon, and either busies himself in setting silver lime twigs to entangle young gentlemen, and casting forth silken shraps to catch woodcocks, or in sieving of muckhills and shop dust, whereof he will bolt a whole cartload to gain a bowed pin.

Of the Dignity or
Meanness of Human Nature

DAVID HUME

There are certain sects which secretly form themselves in the learned world, as well as factions in the political; and though sometimes they come not to an open rupture, they give a different turn to the ways of thinking of those who have taken part on either side. The most remarkable of this kind are the sects founded on the different sentiments with regard to the *dignity of human nature;* which is a point that seems to have divided philosophers and poets, as well as divines, from the beginning of the world to this day. Some exalt our species to the skies, and represent man as a kind of human demigod, who derives his origin from heaven, and retains evident marks of his lineage and descent. Others insist upon the blind sides of human nature, and can discover nothing, except vanity, in which man surpasses the other animals, whom he affects so much to despise. If an author possess the talent of rhetoric and declamation, he commonly takes part with the former: if his turn lie towards irony and ridicule, he naturally throws himself into the other extreme.

I am far from thinking that all those who have depreciated our species have been enemies to virtue, and have exposed the frailties of their fellow creatures with any bad intention. On the contrary, I am sensible that a delicate sense of morals, especially when attended with a splenetic temper, is apt to give a man a disgust of the world, and to make him consider the common course of human affairs with too much indignation. I must, however, be of opinion, that the sentiments of those who are inclined to think favourably of mankind, are more advantageous to virtue than the contrary principles, which give us a mean opinion of our nature. When a man is prepossessed with a high notion of his rank and character in the creation, he will naturally endeavour to act up to it, and will scorn to do a base or vicious action which might sink him below that figure which he makes in his own imagination. Accordingly we find, that all our polite and fashionable moralists insist upon this topic, and endeavour to represent vice unworthy of man, as well as odious in itself.★

We find few disputes that are not founded on some ambiguity in the expression; and I am persuaded that the present dispute, concerning the dignity or meanness of human nature, is not more exempt from it than any other. It may therefore be worth while to consider what is real, and what is only verbal, in this controversy.

That there is a natural difference between merit and demerit, virtue and vice, wisdom and folly, no reasonable man will deny: yet it is evident that, in affixing the term, which denotes either our approbation or blame, we are commonly more influenced by comparison than by any fixed unalterable standard in the nature of things. In like manner, quantity, and extension, and bulk, are by everyone acknowledged to be real things: but when we call any animal *great* or *little*, we always form a secret comparison between that animal and others of the same species; and it is that comparison which regulates our judgement concerning its greatness. A dog and a horse may be of the very same size, while the one is admired for the greatness of its bulk, and the other for the smallness. When I am present, therefore, at any dispute, I always consider with myself whether it be a question of comparison or not that is the subject of controversy; and if it be, whether the disputants compare the same objects together, or talk of things that are widely different.

In forming our notions of human nature, we are apt to make a comparison between men and animals, the only creatures endowed with thought that fall under our senses. Certainly this comparison is favourable to mankind. On the one hand, we see a creature whose thoughts are not limited by any narrow bounds, either of place or time; who carries his researches into the most distant regions of this globe, and beyond this globe to the planets and heavenly bodies; looks backward to consider the first origin, at least the history of the human race; casts his eye forward to see the influence of his actions upon posterity, and the judgements which will be formed of his character a thousand years hence; a creature, who traces causes and effects to a great length and intricacy; extracts general principles from particular appearances; improves upon his discoveries; corrects his mistakes; and makes his very errors profitable. On the other hand, we are presented with a creature the very reverse of this; limited in its observations and reasonings to a few sensible objects which surround

---

★Women are generally much more flattered in their youth than men, which may proceed from this reason among others, that their chief point of honour is considered as much more difficult than ours, and requires to be supported by all that decent pride which can be instilled into them.

it; without curiosity, without foresight; blindly conducted by instinct, and attaining, in a short time, its utmost perfection, beyond which it is never able to advance a single step. What a wide difference is there between these creatures! And how exalted a notion must we entertain of the former, in comparison of the latter.

There are two means commonly employed to destroy this conclusion: First, by making an unfair representation of the case, and insisting only upon the weakness of human nature. And, secondly, by forming a new and secret comparison between man and beings of the most perfect wisdom. Among the other excellences of man, this is one, that he can form an idea of perfections much beyond what he has experience of in himself; and is not limited in his conception of wisdom and virtue. He can easily exalt his notions, and conceive a degree of knowledge, which, when compared to his own, will make the latter appear very contemptible, and will cause the difference between that and the sagacity of animals, in a manner, to disappear and vanish. Now this being a point in which all the world is agreed, that human understanding falls infinitely short of perfect wisdom, it is proper we should know when this comparison takes place, that we may not dispute where there is no real difference in our sentiments. Man falls much more short of perfect wisdom, and even of his own ideas of perfect wisdom, than animals do of man; yet the latter difference is so considerable, that nothing but a comparison with the former can make it appear of little moment.

It is also usual to compare one man with another; and finding very few whom we can call wise or virtuous, we are apt to entertain a contemptible notion of our species in general. That we may be sensible of the fallacy of this way of reasoning, we may observe, that the honourable appellations of wise and virtuous are not annexed to any particular degree of those qualities of wisdom and virtue, but arise altogether from the comparison we make between one man and another. When we find a man who arrives at such a pitch of wisdom as is very uncommon, we pronounce him a wise man: so that to say there are few wise men in the world, is really to say nothing; since it is only by their scarcity that they merit that appellation. Were the lowest of our species as wise as Tully or Lord Bacon, we should still have reason to say that there are few wise men. For in that case we should exalt our notions of wisdom, and should not pay a singular homage to anyone who was not singularly distinguished by his talents. In like manner, I have heard it observed by thoughtless people, that there are few women possessed of beauty in comparison of those who want it; not considering that we bestow the epithet of beautiful only on such as possess a degree of beauty that is common to them with a few. The same degree of beauty in a woman is called deformity, which is treated as real beauty in one of our sex.

As it is usual, in forming a notion of our species, to *compare* it with the other species above or below it, or to compare the individuals of the species among themselves; so we often compare together the different motives or actuating principles of human nature, in order to regulate our judgement concerning it. And, indeed, this is the only kind of comparison which is worth our attention, or decides anything in the present question. Were our selfish and vicious principles so much predominant above our social and virtuous, as is asserted by some philosophers, we ought undoubtedly to entertain a contemptible notion of human nature. ★

There is much of a dispute of words in all this controversy. When a man denies the sincerity of all public spirit or affection to a country and community, I am at a loss what to think of him. Perhaps he never felt this passion in so clear and distinct a manner as to remove all his doubts concerning its force and reality. But when he proceeds afterwards to reject all private friendship, if no interest or self-love intermix itself; I am then confident that he abuses terms, and confounds the ideas of things; since it is impossible for anyone to be so selfish, or rather so stupid, as to make no difference between one man and another, and give no preference to qualities which engage his approbation and esteem. Is he also, say I, as insensible to anger as he pretends to be to friendship? And does injury and wrong no more affect him than kindness or benefits? Impossible: he does not know himself: he has forgotten the movements of his heart; or rather, he makes use of a different language from the rest of his countrymen, and calls not things by their proper names. What say you of natural affection? (I subjoin), Is that also a species of self-love? Yes; all is self-love. *Your* children are loved only because they are yours: *your* friend for a like reason: and *your* country engages you only so far as it has a connection with *yourself*. Were the idea of self removed, nothing would affect you: you would be altogether inactive and insensible: or, if you ever give yourself any movement, it would only be from vanity, and a desire of fame and reputation to this same self. I am willing, reply I, to receive your interpretation of human actions,

★I may perhaps treat more fully of this subject in some future Essay. In the meantime I shall observe, what has been proved beyond question by several great moralists of the present age, that the social passions are by far the most powerful of any, and that even all the other passions receive from them their chief force and influence. Whoever desires to see this question treated at large, with the greatest force of argument and eloquence, may consult my Lord Shaftesbury's *Inquiry concerning Virtue.*

provided you admit the facts. That species of self-love which displays itself in kindness to others, you must allow to have great influence over human actions, and even greater, on many occasions, than that which remains in its original shape and form. For how few are there, having a family, children, and relations, who do not spend more on the maintenance and education of these than on their own pleasures? This, indeed, you justly observe, may proceed from their self-love, since the prosperity of their family and friends is one, or the chief, of their pleasures, as well as their chief honour. Be you also one of these selfish men, and you are sure of everyone's good opinion and good-will; or, not to shock your ears with these expressions, the self-love of everyone, and mine among the rest, will then incline us to serve you, and speak well of you.

In my opinion, there are two things which have led astray those philosophers that have insisted so much on the selfishness of man. In the *first* place, they found that every act of virtue or friendship was attended with a secret pleasure; whence they concluded, that friendship and virtue could not be disinterested. But the fallacy of this is obvious. The virtuous sentiment or passion produces the pleasure, and does not arise from it. I feel a pleasure in doing good to my friend, because I love him; but do not love him for the sake of that pleasure.

In the *second* place, it has always been found, that the virtuous are far from being indifferent to praise; and therefore they have been represented as a set of vainglorious men, who had nothing in view but the applauses of others. But this also is a fallacy. It is very unjust in the world, when they find any tincture of vanity in a laudable action, to depreciate it upon that account, or ascribe it entirely to that motive. The case is not the same with vanity, as with other passions. Where avarice or revenge enters into any seemingly virtuous action, it is difficult for us to determine how far it enters, and it is natural to suppose it the sole actuating principle. But vanity is so closely allied to virtue, and to love the fame of laudable actions approaches so near the love of laudable actions for their own sake, that these passions are more capable of mixture, than any other kinds of affection; and it is almost impossible to have the latter without some degree of the former. Accordingly we find, that this passion for glory is always warped and varied according to the particular taste or disposition of the mind on which it falls. Nero had the same vanity in driving a chariot, that Trajan had in governing the empire with justice and ability. To love the glory of virtuous deeds is a sure proof of the love of virtue.

Concerning Busybodies

PLUTARCH

translated by T. G. Tucker

If a house is stuffy, dark, chilly, or unhealthy, it is perhaps best to get out of it. But if long association makes you fond of the place, you may alter the lights, shift the stairs, open a door here and close one there, and so make it brighter, fresher, and more wholesome. Even cities have sometimes been improved by such rearrangement. For instance, it is said that my own native town, which used to face the west and receive the full force of the afternoon sun from Parnassus, was turned by Chairon so as to front the east. Empedocles, the natural philosopher, once blocked up a mountain gorge, which sent a destructive and pestilential south wind blowing down upon the plains. By this means, it was thought, he shut the plague out of the district.

Well, since there are certain injurious and unhealthy states of mind which chill and darken the soul, it would be best to get rid of them—to make a clean sweep of the foundations, and give ourselves the benefit of a clear sky, light, and pure air to breathe. If not, we should reform and readjust them by turning them some other way about.

We may take the vice of the busybody as an instance in point. It is a love of prying into other people's troubles, a disease tainted—we may believe—with both envy and malice.

> Why so sharp-eyed, my most malignant sir,
> For others' faults, yet overlook your own?

Pray turn your pryingness the other way about, and make it face inwards. If you are so fond of the business of inquiring into defects, you will find plenty to occupy you at home.

'Abundant as leaves on the oak or the water that rolls from Alizon' will you find the errors in your conduct, the disorders in your heart and mind, and the lapses in your duty.

According to Xenophon, a good householder has a special place for the utensils of sacrifice, and a special place for those of the table; agricultural implements are stored in one room, weapons of war in another. In your own case you have one stock of faults arising from envy, another from jealousy, another from cowardice, another from meanness. These are the faults for you to inspect and examine. Block up the windows and alleys of your inquisitiveness on the side towards your neighbours, and open others which look into your own house— the male quarters, the female quarters, the living-rooms of the servants. Our busy curiosity will find occupation of a profitable and salutary, instead of a useless and malicious, kind, if each one will say to himself:

How have I err'd? What deed have I done? What duty neglected?

As it is, we are all of us like the Lamia in the fable, of whom we are told that at home she is asleep and blind, with her eyes stowed away in a jar, but that when she comes abroad she puts them in and can see. Outside, and in dealing with others, we furnish our malice with an eye in the shape of our meddlesomeness, but we are continually being tripped up by our own misdeeds and vices, of which we are unaware, because we provide ourselves with no light or vision to perceive them. It follows that the busybody is a better friend to his enemies than to himself. While censoriously reproving their shortcomings and showing them what they ought to avoid or amend, he is so taken up with faults outside that he overlooks most of those at home.

Odysseus refused even to talk to his mother, until he had got his answer from the seer concerning the business which had brought him to Hades. When he had received the information, he turned to her, and also began to put questions to the other women, asking who Tyro was, and the beautiful Chloris, and why Epicaste met her death by

Tying a sheer-hung noose from the height of the lofty roof-tree.

Not so we. While treating our own concerns with the greatest indifference, ignorance, and neglect, we begin discussing other people's pedigrees—how our neighbour's grandfather was a Syrian and his grandmother a Thracian. 'So-and-So owes more than seven hundred pounds, and cannot pay the interest.' We also make it our business to inquire about such matters as where So-and-So got his wife from, and what private talk was that between A and B in the corner. Socrates, on the other hand, went about inquiring, 'By what arguments did Pythagoras carry conviction?' So Aristippus, when he met Ischomachus at Olympia, proceeded to ask by what kind of conversation Socrates affected the Athenians as he did. When he had gleaned a few seeds or samples of his talk, he was so moved that he suffered a physical collapse, and became quite pale and thin. In the end he set sail for Athens, and slaked his thirst with draughts from the fountain-head, studying the man, his discourses and his philosophy, of which the aim was to recognise one's own vices and get rid of them.

But there are some to whom their own life is a most distressing spectacle, and who therefore cannot bear to look at it nor to reflect the light of reason upon themselves. Their soul is so fraught with all manner of vices, that, shuddering with horror at what lies within, it darts away from home, and goes prowling round other men's concerns, where it lets its malice batten and grow fat.

It often happens that a domestic fowl, though there is plenty of food lying at its disposal, will slink into a corner and scratch

Whereso appeareth, mayhap, one barley-grain in a dunghill.

It is much the same with the busybody. Ignoring the topics and questions which are open to all, and which no one prevents him from asking about or is annoyed with him if he does ask, he goes picking out of every house the troubles which it is endeavouring to bury out of sight . But surely it was a neat answer which the Egyptian made to the man who asked him what he was carrying in that wrapper. 'That', said he, 'is why it *is* in a wrapper.' And why, pray, are you so inquisitive about a thing which is being concealed? If it had not been something undesirable, there would have been no concealment. It is not usual to walk into another man's house without knocking at the door. Nowadays there are doorkeepers—formerly knockers were beaten upon the doors in order to give warning—the intention being that the stranger shall not surprise the lady of the house or her daughter in the open, or come upon a slave receiving punishment, or the handmaids screaming. But these are exactly the things which the busybody steals in to see. At a staid and quiet household he would have no pleasure in looking, even if he were invited. His object is to uncover and make public those things to which keys, bolts, and the street-door owe their existence. 'The winds which vex us most', says Ariston, 'are those which pull up our cloaks.' But the busybody strips off not only our mantles and tunics, but our walls; he spreads our doors wide open, and makes his way like a piercing wind through the 'maiden of tender skin', prying and sneaking into her bacchic revels, her dances, and her all-night festivals.

As Cleon in the comedy had

His hands in Askthorpe and his thoughts in Thefton,

so the busybody's thoughts are at one and the same time in the houses of the rich and the hovels of the poor, in the courts of kings and the chambers of the newly-wed. He searches into everybody's business—business of strangers, and business of potentates. Nor is his search without danger. If one were to take a taste of aconite because he was inquisitive as to its properties, he would find that he had killed the learner before he got his lesson. So those who pry into the troubles of the great destroy themselves before discovering what they seek. If anyone is not satisfied with the beams which the sun lavishes so abundantly upon all, but audaciously insists upon gazing unabashed at the orb itself and probing the light to its heart, the result is blindness. It was therefore wise of Philippides, the comic poet, when King Lysimachus once asked him, 'What can I give you of mine?' to reply, 'Anything, sire, but your secrets.' The finest and most pleasant aspects of royalty are those displayed outwardly—its banquets, wealth, pomps and shows, graces and favours. But if a king has any secret, keep away from it and leave it alone. A king does not conceal his joy when prosperous, nor his laughter when jocose, nor his intention to do a kindness or confer a boon. When he hides a thing, when he is glum, unsmiling, unapproachable, it is time for alarm. It means that he has been storing up anger, and that it is festering; or that he is sullenly meditating a severe punishment; or that he is jealous of his wife, or suspicious of his son, or distrustful of a friend. Run, run from that cloud which is gathering so black! You cannot possibly miss the thunder and lightning, when the matter which is now a secret bursts out in storm.

How, then, are we to escape this vice? By turning our inquisitiveness—as we have said—the other way round, and, as far as possible, directing our minds to better and more interesting objects. If you are to pry, pry into questions connected with sky, earth, air, or sea. You are by nature fond of looking either at little things or at big things. If at big things, apply your curiosity to the sun; ask where he sets and whence he rises. Inquire into the changes of the moon, as if she were a human being. Ask where she loses so much of her light, and whence she gets it back; how

> Once dim she first comes forth and makes
> Her young face beauteous, gathering to the full,
> And, when her greatest splendours she hath shown,
> Fades out, and passes into naught again.

These, too, are secrets—the secrets of Nature; but Nature has no grievance against those who find them out. Are the big things beyond you? Then pry into the smaller ones. Ask how it is that some plants are always flourishing and green, proudly displaying their wealth at every season, while others are at one moment as good as these, but at another have squandered their abundance all at once, like some human spendthrift, and are left bare and beggared. Why, again, do some plants produce elongated fruits, some angular, some round and globe-like?

But perhaps you will have no curiosity for such concerns, because there is nothing wrong about them. Well, if inquisitiveness absolutely must be always browsing and passing its time among things sordid, like a maggot among dead matter, let us introduce it to history and story, and supply it with bad things in abundance and without stint. For there it will find

Fallings of men and spurnings-off of life,

seductions of women, assaults by slaves, slanderings of friends, concoctions of poisons, envies, jealousies, shipwrecks of homes, overthrows of rulers. Take your fill, enjoy yourself, and cause no annoyance or pain to any of those with whom you come in contact.

Apparently, however, inquisitiveness finds no pleasure in scandals which are stale; it wants them hot and fresh. And while it enjoys the spectacle of a novel tragedy, it takes no sort of interest in the comedy or more cheerful side of life. Consequently the busybody lends but a careless and indifferent ear to the account of a wedding, a sacrifice, or a complimentary 'farewell'. He says he has already heard most of the details, and urges the narrator to cut them short or omit them. But if anyone will sit by him and tell him the news about the corruption of a girl or the unfaithfulness of a wife or an impending action at law or a quarrel between brothers, there is no sleepiness or hurry about him, but

More words still doth he ask, and proffers his ears to receive them.

As applied to the busybody, the words

How much more apt to reach the ear of man
An ill thing than a happy!

are a true saying. As a cupping-glass sucks from the flesh what is worst in it, so the inquisitive ear draws to itself the most undesirable topics. To vary the figure: cities have certain 'Accursed' or 'Dismal' gates, through which they take out criminals on their way to death and throw the refuse and offscourings of purification, while nothing sacred or undefiled goes in or out through them. So with the ears of the busybody. They give passage to nothing fine or useful, but serve only as the pathway of gruesome communications, with their load of foul and polluted gossip.

No chance brings other minstrel to my roof,
But always Lamentation.

That is the one Muse and Siren of the busybody, the most pleasant of all music to his ear. For his vice is a love of finding out whatever is secret and concealed, and no one conceals a good thing when he has one; on the contrary, he will pretend to one which has no existence. Since therefore it is troubles that the busybody is eager to discover, the disease from which he suffers is malignant gloating—own brother to envy and spite. For envy is pain at another's good; malignity is pleasure at another's harm; and the parent of both is ill-nature—the feeling of a savage or a brute beast.

So painful do we all find it to have our troubles revealed, that there are many who would rather die than tell a physician of a secret disease. Imagine Herophilus or Erasistratus, or Asclepius himself—when he was a mortal man—calling from house to house with his drugs and his instruments, and asking whether a man had a fistula or a woman a cancer in the womb! Inquisitiveness in their profession may, it is true, save a life. None the less, I presume, everyone would have scouted such a person, for coming to investigate other people's ailments without waiting till he was required and sent for. Yet our busybody searches out precisely these, or even worse, ailments; and, since he does so not by way of curing them, but merely of disclosing them, he deserves the hatred he gets.

We are annoyed and indignant with the collector of customs, not when he picks out and levies on those articles which we import openly, but when, in the search for hidden goods, he ransacks among baggage and merchandise which are not in question. Yet the law permits him to do so, and he is the loser if he does not. On the other hand, the busybody lets his own concerns go to ruin, while he is occupying himself with those of other people. He rarely takes a walk to the farm; it is too lonely, and he cannot bear the quiet and silence. And if, after a time, he does chance along, he has a keener eye for his neighbour's vines than for his own. He proceeds to ask how many of his neighbour's cattle have died, or how much of his wine turned sour. After a good meal of such news he is quickly off and away.

Your true and genuine type of farmer has no desire to hear even the news which finds its own way from the city. Says he:

> Then, while he digs, he'll tell
> The terms o' the treaty. He must now, confound him,
> Go round and poke his nose in things like that!

But to your busybody country life is a stale and uninteresting thing with nothing to fuss about. He therefore flees from it, and pushes into the Exchange, the Market, or the Harbour. 'Is there any news?' 'Why, weren't you at market early this morning?' 'Do you imagine there has been a revolution in three hours?' If, however, anyone has a piece of news to tell, down he gets from his horse, grasps the man's hand, kisses him, and stands there listening. But if someone meets him and says there is nothing fresh, he exclaims, as if he were annoyed: 'What? Haven't you been at market? Haven't you been near the Boardroom? And haven't you met the new arrivals from Italy?'

The Locrian magistrates therefore did the right thing in fining anyone who, after being out of town, came up and asked, 'Is there any news?' As the butchers pray for a good supply of animals, and fishermen for a good supply of fish, so busybodies pray for a good supply of calamities, for plenty of troubles, for novelties and changes. They must always have their fish to catch or carcass to cut up.

Another good rule was that of the legislator of Thurii, who forbade the lampooning of citizens on the stage, with the exception of adulterers and busybodies. The one class bears a resemblance to the other, adultery being a sort of inquisitiveness into another's pleasure, and a prying search into matters protected from the general eye, while inquisitiveness is the illicit denuding and corrupting of a secret. While a natural consequence of much learning is having much to say, and therefore Pythagoras enjoined upon the young a five years' silence, which he called 'Truce to Speech', the necessary concomitant of curiosity is speaking evil. What the curious delight to hear, they delight to talk about; what they take pains to gather from others, they joy in giving out to new hearers. It follows that, besides its other drawbacks, their disease actually stands in the way of its own desires. For everyone is on his guard to hide things from them, and is reluctant to do anything when the busybody is looking, or to say anything when he is listening. People put off a consultation and postpone the consideration of business until such persons are out of the way. If, when a secret matter is towards, or an important action is in the doing, a busybody appears upon the scene, they take it away and hide it, as they would a piece of victuals when the cat comes past. Often, therefore, he is the only person not permitted to hear or see what others may see and hear.

For the same reason the busybody can find no one to trust him. We would rather trust our letters, papers, or seals to a slave or a stranger than to an inquisitive relation or friend. Bellerophon, though the writing which he carried was about himself, would not broach it, but showed the same continence in keeping his hands off the king's letter as in keeping them off his wife.

Yes, inquisitiveness is as incontinent as adultery, and not only incontinent, but terribly silly and foolish. To pass by so many women who are public property, and to struggle to get at one who is kept under lock and key, who is expensive, and perhaps ugly to boot, is the very height of insanity. The busybody is just as bad. He passes by much that is admirable to see and hear, many an excellent discourse or discussion, to dig into another man's poor little letter or clap his ear to his neighbour's wall, listening to slaves and womenfolk whispering together, and incurring danger often, and discredit always.

Well, if he wishes to get rid of his vice, the busybody will find nothing so helpful as to think over the discoveries he has hitherto made. Simonides used to say that, in opening his boxes after a lapse of time, he found the fee-box always full and the thanks-box always empty. So, if one were to open the store-room of inquisitiveness after an interval, and to contemplate all the useless, futile, and uninviting things with which it is filled, he would probably become sick of the business, so nauseating and senseless would it appear.

Suppose a person to run over the works of our old writers and pick out their faultiest passages, compiling and keeping a book full of such things as 'headless' lines of Homer, solecisms in the tragedians, the indecent and licentious language to women by which Archilochus made a sorry show of himself. Does he not deserve the execration in the tragedy:

Perish, thou picker-up of miseries!

Execration apart, his treasury, filled with other men's faults, possesses neither beauty nor use. It is like the town which Philip founded with the rudest riff-raff, and which he called Knaveborough.

With the busybody, however, it is not from lines of poetry, but from lives, that he goes gleaning and gathering blunders and slips and solecisms, till the memory which he carries about is the dullest and dreariest record-box, crammed with ugly things.

At Rome, there are those who set no store by the paintings, the statues, or—failing these—the handsome children or women on sale, but who haunt the monster-market, examining specimens with no calves to their legs, or with weasel-elbows, three eyes, or ostrich-heads, and looking out for the appearance of any

Commingled shape and misformed prodigy.

Yet if you keep on showing them such sights, they will soon become surfeited and sick of it all. In the same way those who make it their business to pry into other people's failures in their affairs, blots on their pedigree, disturbances and delinquencies in their homes, will do well to remind themselves how thankless and unprofitable their previous discoveries have proved.

The most effective way, however, of preventing this weakness is to form a habit—to begin at an early stage and train ourselves systematically to acquire the necessary self-control. It is by habit that the vice increases, the advance of the disease being gradual. How this is, we shall see, in discussing the proper method of practice.

Let us make a beginning with comparatively trifling and insignificant matters.

On the roads it can be no difficult matter to abstain from reading the inscriptions on the tombs. Nor in the promenades can there be any hardship in refusing to let the eye linger upon the writings on the walls. You have only to tell yourself that they contain nothing useful or entertaining. There is A expressing his 'kind sentiments' towards B; So-and-So described as 'the best of friends'; and much mere twaddle of the same kind. No doubt it seems as if the reading of them does you no harm; but harm you it does, without your knowing it, by inducing a habit of inquiring into things which do not concern you. Hunters do not permit young hounds to turn aside and follow up every scent, but pull them sharply back with the leash, so as to keep their power of smell in perfectly clean condition for their proper work, and make it stick more keenly to the tracks:

With nostril a-search for the trail that the beast gives forth from its body.

The same watchfulness must be shown in suppressing, or in diverting to useful ends, the tendency of an inquisitive person to run off the track and wander after everything that he can see or hear. An eagle or a lion gathers its talons in when it walks, so as not to wear the sharp edge from their tips. Similarly let us treat the inquiring spirit as the keen edge to our love of learning, and refrain from wasting or blunting it upon objects of no value.

In the next place let us train ourselves, when passing another's door, to refrain from looking in, or from letting our inquisitive gaze clutch at what is passing inside. Xenocrates said—and we shall do well to keep the remark in mind—that whether we set foot or set eyes in another man's house makes no difference. Not only is such prying unfair and improper; we get no pleasure from the spectacle.

Unsightly, stranger, are the sights within,

is a saying which is generally true of what we see inside—a litter of pots and pans, or servant-girls sitting about, but nothing of any importance or interest. This furtive throwing of sidelong glances, which at the same time gives a kind of squint to the mind, is ugly, and the habit of it demoralising. When the Olympian victor Dioxippus was making a triumphal entry in a chariot, and could not drag his eyes from a beautiful woman among the spectators, but kept turning half round and throwing side glances in her direction, Diogenes—who saw it all—remarked, 'See how a bit of a girl gets the neck-grip of our great athlete!' Inquisitive people, however, are to be seen gripped by the neck and twisted about by any kind of sight, when they once develop a habit of squandering their glances in all directions.

This is assuredly no right use of the faculty of vision. It should not go gadding about like some ill-trained maid-servant; but when the mind sends it upon an errand, it should make haste to reach its destination, deliver its message, and then come quietly home again to wait upon the commands of the reason. Instead of this, the case is as in Sophocles:

> *Thereon the Aenean driver's hard-mouthed colts*
> *Break from control.*

When the faculty of vision has not been tutored and trained in the proper manner as above described, it runs away, drags the mind with it, and often brings it into disastrous collisions.

There is a story that Democritus deliberately destroyed his sight by fixing his eyes upon a red-hot mirror and allowing its heat to be focussed upon them. His object, it is said, was to block up the windows towards the street, and thus prevent the disturbance of his intellect by repeated calls from outside, enabling it to stay at home and devote itself to pure thinking. Though the story is a fiction, nothing is more true than that those who make most use of their mind make few calls upon the senses. Note how our halls of learning are built far out from the towns, and how night has been styled the 'well-minded', from a belief that quiet and the absence of distraction are a powerful aid to intellectual discovery and research.

Suppose, again, that people are quarrelling and abusing each other in the market-place. It requires no great effort of self-denial to keep at a distance. When a crowd is running towards a certain spot, it is easy for you to remain seated, or else, if you lack the necessary strength of mind, to get up and go away. There is no advantage to be got from mixing yourself with busybodies, whereas you will derive great benefit from putting a forcible check upon your curiosity and training it to obey the commands of the reason.

We may now go a step further, and tax ourselves more severely. It is good practice, when a successful entertainment is going on in a public hall, to pass it by; when our friends invite us to a performance by a dancer or comedian, to decline; when there is a roar in the raceground or the circus, to take no notice. Socrates used to urge the avoidance of all foods and drinks which tempt one to eat when he is not hungry or to drink when he is not thirsty. In the same way we shall do well to shun carefully all appeals to eye or ear, when, though they are no business of ours, their attractions prove too much for us.

Cyrus refused to see Panthea, and when Araspes talked of her remarkable beauty, his answer was: 'All the more reason for keeping away from her. If I took your advice and went to see her, she might perhaps tempt me to be visiting her again when I could not spare the time, and to be sitting and looking at her to the neglect of much important business.' In the same way Alexander refused to set eyes on Darius' wife, who was said to be strikingly handsome. Though he visited the mother—an elderly woman—he would not bring himself to see her young and beautiful daughter. But what we do is to peep into women's litters and hang about their windows, finding nothing improper in encouraging our curiosity and allowing it such dangerous and unchecked play.

Note how you may train yourself for other virtues. To learn justice you should sometimes forgo an honest gain, and so accustom yourself to keep aloof from dishonest ones. Similarly, to learn continence, you should sometimes hold aloof from your own wife, and so secure yourself against temptation from another's. Apply this habit to inquisitiveness. Endeavour occasionally to miss hearing or seeing things which concern yourself. When something happens at home, and a person wishes to tell you of it, put the matter off; and when things have been said which appear to affect yourself, refuse to hear them. Remember how Oedipus was brought into the direst disasters by over-curiosity. Finding he was no Corinthian, but an alien, he set to work to discover who he was, and so he met with Laius. He killed him, married his own mother, with the throne for dowry, and then, while apparently blessed by fortune, began his search once more. The endeavours of his wife to prevent him only made him question still more closely, and in the most peremptory way, the old man who was in the secret. And at last, when circumstances are already bringing him to suspect, and the old man cries:

Alas! I stand on the dread brink of speech!

he is nevertheless in such a blaze or spasm of passion that he replies:

And I of hearing; and yet hear I must.

So bitter-sweet, so uncontrollable, is the excitement of curiosity—like the tickling of a wound, at which one tears till he makes it bleed. Meanwhile if we are free from that malady, and mild by nature, we shall ignore a disagreeable thing and say:

Sovran Oblivion, how wise art thou!

We must therefore train ourselves to this end. If a letter is brought to us, we must not show all that hurry and eagerness to open it which most people display, when they bite the fastenings through with their teeth, if their hands are too slow. When a messenger arrives from somewhere or other, we must not run to meet him, nor get up from our seats. If a friend says, 'I have something new to tell you,' let us reply: 'Better, if you have something useful or profitable.' When I was once lecturing at Rome, the famous Rusticus—who was afterwards put to death by Domitian out of jealousy at his reputation—was among my hearers. A soldier came through the audience and handed him a note from the emperor. There was a hush, and I made a pause, to allow of his reading the letter. This, however, he refused to do, nor would he open it, until I had finished my discourse and the audience broke up. The incidence caused universal admiration at his dignified behaviour.

But when one feeds his inquisitiveness upon permissible material until he makes it robust and headstrong, he no longer finds it easy to master, when force of habit urges it towards forbidden ground. Such persons will stealthily open their friends' missives, will push their way into a confidential meeting, will get a view of rites which it is an impiety to see, will tread in hallowed places, and will pry into the doings and sayings of a king.

Now with a despot—who is compelled to know everything—there is nothing that makes him so detested as the crew known as his 'ears' and 'jackals'. 'Listeners' were first instituted by Darius the Younger, who had no confidence in himself and looked upon everyone with fear and suspicion. 'Jackals' were the creation of the Dionysii, who distributed them among the people of Syracuse. Naturally, when the revolution came, these were the first to be seized and cudgelled to death by the Syracusans.

Blackmailers and informers are a breed belonging to the Busybody clan; they are members of the family. But, whereas the informer looks to see if his neighbours have done or plotted any mischief, the busybody brings to book and drags into public even the misfortunes for which they are not responsible. It is said that the outcast derived his name of *aliterios* in the first instance from being a busybody. It appears that when a severe famine once occurred at Athens, and when those who were in possession of wheat, instead of bringing it in to the public stock, used to grind it *(alein)* secretly by night in their houses, certain persons, who went round watching for the noise of the mills, were in consequence called *aliterioi*. It was in the same way, we are told, that the informer won his name of *sykophantes*. The export of figs *(syka)* being prohibited, those who gave information *(phainein)* and impeached the offenders were called *sykophantai*. Busybodies would do well to reflect upon this fact. It may make them ashamed of the family likeness between their own practices and those of a class which is a special object of loathing and anger.

The Superannuated Man

CHARLES LAMB

Sera tamen respexit
Libertas.   VIRGIL

A Clerk I was in London gay.
            O'KEEFE

If peradventure, Reader, it has been thy lot to waste the golden years of thy life—thy shining youth—in the irksome confinement of an office; to have thy prison days prolonged through middle age down to decrepitude and silver hairs, without hope of release or respite; to have lived to forget that there are such things as holidays, or to remember them but as the prerogatives of childhood; then, and then only, will you be able to appreciate my deliverance.

It is now six-and-thirty years since I took my seat at the desk in Mincing Lane. Melancholy was the transition at fourteen from the abundant playtime, and the frequently-intervening vacations of school days, to the eight, nine, and sometimes ten hours' a day attendance at the Counting House. But time partially reconciles us to anything. I gradually became content—doggedly contented, as wild animals in cages.

It is true I had my Sundays to myself; but Sundays, admirable as the institution of them is for purposes of worship, are for that very reason the very worst adapted for days of unbending and recreation. In particular, there is a gloom for me attendant upon a city Sunday, a weight in the air. I miss the cheerful cries of London, the music, and the ballad-singers—the buzz and stirring murmur of the streets. Those eternal bells depress me. The closed shops repel me. Prints, pictures, all the glittering and endless succession of knacks and gewgaws, and ostentatiously displayed wares of tradesmen, which make a weekday saunter through the less busy parts of the metropolis so delightful—are shut out. No bookstalls deliciously to idle over— no busy faces to recreate the idle man who contemplates them ever passing by—the very face of business a charm by contrast to his temporary relaxation from it. Nothing to be seen but unhappy countenances—or half-happy at best—of emancipated 'prentices and little tradesfolks, with here and there a servant-maid that has got leave to go out, who, slaving all the week, with the habit has lost almost the capacity of enjoying a free hour; and livelily expressing the hollowness of a day's pleasuring. The very strollers in the fields on that day look anything but comfortable.

But besides Sundays, I had a day at Easter, and a day at Christmas, with a full week in the summer to go and air myself in my native fields of Hertfordshire. This last was a great indulgence; and the prospect of its recurrence, I believe, alone kept me up through the year, and made my durance tolerable. But when the week came round, did the glittering phantom of the distance keep touch with me, or rather was it not a series of seven uneasy days, spent in restless pursuit of pleasure, and a wearisome anxiety to find out how to make the most of them? Where was the quiet, where the promised rest? Before I had a taste of it, it was vanished. I was at the desk again, counting upon the fifty-one tedious weeks that must intervene before such another snatch would come. Still the prospect of its coming threw something of an illumination upon the darker side of my captivity. Without it, as I have said, I could scarcely have sustained my thraldom.

Independently of the rigours of attendance, I have ever been haunted with a sense (perhaps a mere caprice) of incapacity for business. This, during my latter years, had increased to such a degree, that it was visible in all the lines of my countenance. My health and my good spirits flagged. I had perpetually a dread of some crisis, to which I should be found unequal. Besides my daylight servitude, I served over again all night in my sleep, and would awake with terrors of imaginary false entries, errors in my accounts, and the like. I was fifty years of age, and no prospect of emancipation presented itself. I had grown to my desk, as it were; and the wood had entered into my soul.

My fellows in the office would sometimes rally me upon the trouble legible in my countenance; but I did not know that it had raised the suspicions of any of my employers, when, on the 5th of last month, a day ever to be remembered by me, L——, the junior partner in the firm, calling me on one side, directly taxed me with my bad looks, and frankly inquired the cause of them. So taxed, I honestly made confession of my infirmity, and added that I was afraid I should eventually be obliged to resign his service. He spoke some words of course to hearten me, and there the matter rested. A whole week I remained labouring under the impression that I had acted imprudently in my disclosure; that I had foolishly given a handle against myself, and had been anticipating my own dismissal. A week passed in this manner—the most anxious one, I verily believe, in my whole life—when on the evening of the 12th of April, just as I was about quitting my desk to go home (it might be about eight o'clock), I received an awful summons to attend the presence of the whole assembled firm in the formidable back parlour. I thought now my time is surely come, I have done for myself, I am going to be told that they have no longer occasion for me. L——, I could see, smiled at the terror I was in, which was a little relief to me—when to my utter astonishment B——, the eldest partner, began a formal harangue to me on the length of my services, my very meritorious conduct during the whole of the time (the deuce, thought I, how did he find out that? I protest I never had the confidence to think as much). He went on to descant on the expediency of retiring at a certain time of life (how my heart panted!) and asking me a few questions as to the amount of my own property, of which I have little, ended with a proposal, to which his three partners nodded a grave assent, that I should accept from the house, which I had served so well, a pension for life to the amount of two-thirds of my accustomed salary—a magnificent offer! I do not know what I answered between surprise and gratitude, but it was understood that I accepted their proposal, and I was told that I was free from that hour to leave their service. I stammered out a bow, and at just ten minutes after eight I went home—for ever. This noble benefit—gratitude forbids me to conceal their names—I owe to the kindness of the most munificent firm in the world—the house of Boldero, Merryweather, Bosanquet, and Lacy.

Esto perpetua!

For the first day or two I felt stunned—overwhelmed. I could only apprehend my felicity; I was too confused to taste it sincerely. I wandered about, thinking I was happy, and knowing that I was not. I was in the condition of a prisoner in the old Bastille, suddenly let loose after a forty years' confinement. I could scarce trust myself with myself. It was like passing out of Time into Eternity—for it is a sort of Eternity for a man to have all his Time to himself. It seemed to me that I had more Time on my hands than I could ever manage. From a poor man, poor in Time, I was suddenly lifted up into a vast revenue; I could see no end of my possessions; I wanted some steward, or judicious bailiff, to manage my estates in Time for me. And here let me caution persons grown old in active business, not lightly, nor without weighing their own resources, to forgo their customary employment all at once, for there may be danger in it. I feel it by myself, but I know that my resources are sufficient; and now that those first giddy raptures have subsided, I have a quiet home-feeling of the blessedness of my condition. I am in no hurry. Having all holidays, I am as though I had none. If Time hung heavy upon me, I could walk it away; but I do *not* walk all day long, as I used to do in those old transient holidays, thirty miles a day, to make the most of them. If Time were troublesome, I could read it away; but I do *not* read in that violent measure, with which, having no Time my own but candlelight Time, I used to weary out my head and eyesight in bygone winters. I walk, read, or scribble (as now) just when the fit seizes me. I no longer hunt after pleasure; I let it come to me. I am like the man

> *. . . that's born, and has his years come to him,*
> *In some green desert.*

'Years!' you will say; 'what is this superannuated simpleton calculating upon? He has already told us he is past fifty.'

I have indeed lived nominally fifty years, but deduct out of them the hours which I have lived to other people, and not to myself, and you will find me still a young fellow. For *that* is the only true Time, which a man can properly call his own—that which he has all to himself; the rest, though in some sense he may be said to live it, is other people's Time, not his. The remnant of my poor days, long or short, is at least multiplied for me threefold. My ten next years, if I stretch so far, will be as long as any preceding thirty. 'Tis a fair rule-of-three sum.

Among the strange fantasies which beset me at the commencement of my freedom, and of which all traces are not yet gone, one was, that a vast tract of time had intervened since I quitted the Counting House. I could not conceive of it as an affair of yesterday. The partners, and the clerks with whom I had for so many years, and for so many hours in each day of the year, been closely associated—being suddenly removed from them—they seemed as dead to me. There is a fine passage, which may serve to illustrate this fancy, in a Tragedy by Sir Robert Howard, speaking of a friend's death:

> *'Twas but just now he went away;*
> *I have not since had time to shed a tear;*
> *And yet the distance does the same appear*
> *As if he had been a thousand years from me.*
> *Time takes no measure in Eternity.*

To dissipate this awkward feeling, I have been fain to go among them once or twice since; to visit my old desk-fellows—my co-brethren of the quill—that I had left below in the state militant. Not all the kindness with which they received me could quite restore to me that pleasant familiarity, which I had heretofore enjoyed among them. We cracked some of our old jokes, but methought they went off but faintly. My old desk; the peg where I hung my hat, were appropriated to another. I knew it must be, but I could not take it kindly. D——l take me, if I did not feel some remorse—beast, if I had not—at quitting my old compeers, the faithful partners of my toils for six-and-thirty years, that soothed for me with their jokes and conundrums the ruggedness of my professional road. Had it been so rugged then, after all? or was I a coward simply? Well, it is too late to repent; and I also know that these suggestions are a common fallacy of the mind on such occasions. But my heart smote me. I had violently broken the bands betwixt us. It was at least not courteous. I shall be some time before I get quite reconciled to the separation. Farewell, old cronies, yet not for long, for again and again I will come among ye, if I shall have your leave. Farewell, Ch——, dry, sarcastic, and friendly! Do——, mild, slow to move, and gentlemanly! Pl——, officious to do, and to volunteer, good services!—and thou, thou dreary pile, fit mansion for a Gresham or a Whittington of old, stately house of Merchants; with thy labyrinthine passages, and light-excluding, pent-up offices, where candles for one-half the year supplied the place of the sun's light; unhealthy contributor to my weal, stern fosterer of my living, farewell! In thee remain, and not in the obscure collection of some wandering bookseller, my 'works!' There let them rest, as I do from my labours, piled on thy massy shelves, more MSS in folio than ever Aquinas left, and full as useful! My mantel I bequeath among ye.

A fortnight has passed since the date of my first communication. At that period I was approaching to tranquillity, but had not reached it. I boasted of a calm indeed, but it was comparative only. Something of the first flutter was left; an unsettling sense of novelty; the dazzle to weak eyes of unaccustomed light. I missed my old chains, forsooth, as if they had been some necessary part of my apparel. I was a poor Carthusian, from strict cellular discipline suddenly by some revolution returned upon the world. I am now as if I had never been other than my own master. It is natural for me to go where I please, to do what I please. I find myself at eleven o'clock in the day in Bond Street, and it seems to me that I have been sauntering there at that very hour for years past. I digress into Soho, to explore a bookstall. Methinks I have been thirty years a collector. There is nothing strange nor new in it. I find myself before a fine picture in the morning. Was it ever otherwise? What is become of Fish Street Hill? Where is Fenchurch Street? Stones of old Mincing Lane, which I have worn with my daily pilgrimage for six-and-thirty years, to the footsteps of what toil-worn clerk are your everlasting flints now vocal? I indent the gayer flags of Pall Mall. It is 'Change time, and I am strangely among the Elgin marbles. It was no hyperbole when I ventured to compare the change in my condition to passing into another world. Time stands still in a manner to me. I have lost all distinction of season. I do not know the day of the week or of the month. Each day used to be individually felt by me in its reference to the foreign post days; in its distance from, or propinquity to, the next Sunday. I had my Wednesday feelings, my Saturday nights' sensations. The genius of each day was upon me distinctly during the whole of it, affecting my appetite, spirits, etc. The phantom of the next day, with the dreary five to follow, sat as a load upon my poor Sabbath recreations. What charm has washed that Ethiop white? What is gone of Black Monday? All days are the same. Sunday itself—that unfortunate failure of a holiday, as it too often proved, what with my sense of its fugitiveness, and over-care to get the greatest quantity of pleasure out of it—is melted down into a week-day. I can spare to go to church now, without grudging the huge cantle which it used to seem to cut out of the holiday. I have time for everything. I can visit a sick friend. I can interrupt the man of much occupation when he is busiest. I can insult over him with an invitation to take a day's pleasure with me to Windsor this fine May morning. It is Lucretian pleasure to behold the poor drudges, whom I have left behind in the world, carking and caring; like horses in a mill, drudging on in the same eternal round—and what is it all for? A man can never have too much Time to himself, nor too little to do. Had I a little son, I would christen him NOTHING-TO-DO; he should do nothing. Man, I verily believe, is out of his element as long as he is operative. I am altogether for the life contemplative. Will no kindly earthquake come and swallow up those accursed cotton-mills? Take me that lumber of a desk there, and bowl it down

As low as to the fiends.

I am no longer ******, clerk to the Firm of, etc. I am Retired Leisure. I am to be met with in trim gardens. I am already come to be known by my vacant face and careless gesture, perambulating at no fixed pace, nor with any settled purpose. I walk about; not to and from. They tell me, a certain *cum dignitate* air, that has been buried so long with my other good parts, has begun to shoot forth in my person. I grow into gentility perceptibly. When I take up a newspaper, it is to read the state of the opera. *Opus operatum est.* I have done all that I came into this world to do. I have worked task-work, and have the rest of the day to myself.

Country Congregations

WILLIAM COWPER

Delicta majorum immeritus lues,
Romane, donec templa refeceris
Aedesque labentes deorum, et
Foeda nigro simulacra fumo.

HORACE

Dear cousin,

The country at present, no less than the metropolis, abounding with politicians of every kind, I began to despair of picking up any intelligence that might possibly be entertaining to your readers. However, I have lately visited some of the most distant parts of the kingdom with a clergyman of my acquaintance: I shall not trouble you with an account of the improvements that have been made in the seats we saw according to the modern taste, but proceed to give you some reflections, which occurred to us on observing several country churches, and the behaviour of the congregations.

The ruinous condition of some of these edifices gave me great offence; and I could not help wishing that the honest vicar, instead of indulging his genius for improvements, by enclosing his gooseberry bushes within a Chinese rail, and converting half an acre of his glebe-land into a bowling-green, would have applied part of his income to the more laudable purpose of sheltering his parishioners from the weather, during their attendance on divine service. It is no uncommon thing to see the parsonage well thatched, and in exceeding good repair, while the church perhaps has scarce any other roof than the ivy that grows over it. The noise of owls, bats, and magpies makes the principal part of the church music in many of these ancient edifices; and the walls, like a large map, seem to be portioned out into capes, seas, and promontories, by the various colours by which the damps have stained them. Sometimes, the foundation being too weak to support the steeple any longer, it has been expedient to pull down that part of the building, and to hang the bells under a wooden shed on the ground beside it. This is the case in a parish in Norfolk, through which I lately passed, and where the clerk and the sexton, like the two figures at St Dunstan's, serve the bells in capacity of clappers, by striking them alternately with a hammer.

In other churches I have observed, that nothing unseemly or ruinous is to be found, except in the clergyman, and the appendages of his person. The squire of the parish, or his ancestors, perhaps to testify their devotion, and leave a lasting monument of their magnificence, have adorned the altar-piece with the richest crimson velvet, embroidered with vine leaves and ears of wheat; and have dressed up the pulpit with the same splendour and expense; while the gentleman who fills it, is exalted in the midst of all this finery, with a surplice as dirty as a farmer's frock, and a periwig that seems to have transferred its faculty of curling to the band which appears in full buckle beneath it.

But if I was concerned to see several distressed pastors, as well as many of our country churches, in a tottering condition, I was more offended with the indecency of worship in others. I could wish that the clergy would inform their congregations, that there is no occasion to scream themselves hoarse in making the responses; that the town-crier is not the only person qualified to pray with due devotion; and that he who bawls the loudest may nevertheless be the wickedest fellow in the parish. The old women too in the aisle might be told, that their time would be better employed in attending to the sermon, than in fumbling over their tattered testaments till they have found the text; by which time the discourse is near drawing to a conclusion: while a word or two of instruction might not be thrown away upon the younger part of the congregation, to teach them that making posies in summer time, and cracking nuts in autumn, is no part of the religious ceremony.

The good old practice of psalm-singing is, indeed, wonderfully improved in many country churches since the days of Sternhold and Hopkins; and there is scarce a parish clerk who has so little taste as not to pick his staves out of the New Version. This has occasioned great complaint in some places, where the clerk has been forced to bawl by himself, because the rest of the congregation cannot find the psalm at the end of their prayer-books; while others are highly disgusted at the innovation, and stick as obstinately to the Old Version as to the Old Style. The tunes themselves have also been new set to jiggish measures; and the sober drawl, which used to accompany the two first staves of the hundredth psalm, with the *gloria patri,* is now split into as many quarters as an Italian air. For this purpose there is in every county an itinerant band of vocal musicians, who make it their business to go round to all the churches in their turns, and, after a prelude with the pitch-pipe, astonish the audience with hymns set to the new Winchester measure, and anthems of their own composing. As these new-fashioned psalmodists are necessarily made up of young men and maids, we may naturally suppose, that there is a perfect concord and symphony between them: and, indeed, I have known it happen that these sweet singers have more than once been brought into disgrace, by too close an unison between the thorough-bass and the treble.

It is a difficult matter to decide, which is looked upon as the greatest man in a country church, the parson or his clerk. The latter is most certainly held in higher veneration, where the former happens to be only a poor curate, who rides post every Sabbath from village to village, and mounts and dismounts at the church door. The clerk's office is not only to tag the prayers with an Amen, or usher in the sermon with a stave; but he is also the universal father to give away the brides, and the standing godfather to all the new-born bantlings. But in many places there is a still greater man belonging to the church, than either the parson or the clerk himself. The person I mean is the squire; who, like the king, may be styled Head of the Church in his own parish. If the benefice be in his own gift, the vicar is his creature, and of consequence entirely at his devotion; or, if the care of the church be left to a curate, the Sunday fees of roast beef and plum pudding, and a liberty to shoot in the manor, will bring him as much under the squire's command as his dogs and horses. For this reason the bell is often kept tolling and the people waiting in the churchyard an hour longer than the usual time; nor must the service begin until the squire has strutted up the aisle, and seated himself in the great pew in the chancel. The length of the sermon is also measured by the will of the squire, as formerly by the hour-glass: and I know one parish where the preacher has always the complaisance to conclude his discourse, however abruptly, the minute that the squire gives the signal, by rising up after his nap.

In a village church, the squire's lady or the vicar's wife are perhaps the only females that are stared at for their finery: but in the larger cities and towns, where the newest fashions are brought down weekly by the stage-coach or wagon, all the wives and daughters of the most topping tradesmen vie with each other every Sunday in the elegance of their apparel. I could even trace their gradations in their dress, according to the opulence, the extent, and the distance of the place from London. I was at a church in a populous city in the North, where the mace-bearer cleared the way for Mrs Mayoress, who came sidling after him in an enormous fan-hoop, of a pattern which had never been seen before in those parts. At another church, in a corporation town, I saw several negligées with furbelowed aprons, which had long disputed the prize of superiority; but these were most woefully eclipsed by a burgess's daughter, just come from London, who appeared in a Trollope or Slammerkin, with treble ruffles to the cuffs, pinked and gimped, and the sides of the petticoat drawn up in festoons. In some lesser borough towns, the contest, I found, lay between three or four black and green bibs and aprons; at one, a grocer's wife attracted our eyes, by a new-fashioned cap, called a Joan; and at another, they were wholly taken up by a mercer's daughter in a nun's hood.

I need not say anything of the behaviour of the congregations in these more polite places of religious resort; as the same genteel ceremonies are practised there, as at the most fashionable churches in town. The ladies, immediately on their entrance, breathe a pious ejaculation through their fan-sticks, and the beaux very gravely address themselves to the haberdashers' bills, glued upon the linings of their hats. This pious duty is no sooner performed, than the exercise of bowing and curtsying succeeds; the locking and unlocking of the pews drowns the reader's voice at the beginning of the service; and the rustling of silks, added to the whispering and tittering of so much good company, renders him totally unintelligible to the very end of it.

I am, dear cousin, yours, etc.

Lady Hester Stanhope

LYTTON STRACHEY

The Pitt nose has a curious history. One can watch its trans-
migrations through three lives. The tremendous hook of old Lord
Chatham, under whose curve empires came to birth, was succeeded
by the bleak upward-pointing nose of William Pitt the younger—the
rigid symbol of an indomitable *hauteur*. With Lady Hester Stanhope
came the final stage. The nose, still with an upward tilt in it, had lost
its masculinity; the hard bones of the uncle and the grandfather had
disappeared. Lady Hester's was a nose of wild ambitions, of pride
grown fantastical, a nose that scorned the earth, shooting off, one
fancies, towards some eternally eccentric heaven. It was a nose, in
fact, altogether in the air.

Noses, of course, are aristocratic things; and Lady Hester was the
child of a great aristocracy. But, in her case, the aristocratic impulse,
which had carried her predecessors to glory, had less fortunate
results. There has always been a strong strain of extravagance in the
governing families of England; from time to time they throw off
some peculiarly ill-balanced member, who performs a strange
meteoric course. A century earlier, Lady Mary Wortley Montagu
was an illustrious example of this tendency: that splendid comet, after
filling half the heavens, vanished suddenly into desolation and darkness. Lady Hester Stanhope's spirit was still more uncommon; and
she met with a most uncommon fate.

She was born in 1776, the eldest daughter of the extraordinary Earl
Stanhope, Jacobin and inventor, who made the first steamboat and
the first calculating machine, who defended the French Revolution in
the House of Lords and erased the armorial bearings—'damned
aristocratical nonsense'—from his carriages and his plate. Her
mother, Chatham's daughter and the favourite sister of Pitt, died
when she was four years old. The second Lady Stanhope, a frigid
woman of fashion, left her stepdaughters to the care of futile gover-
nesses, while 'Citizen Stanhope' ruled the household from his laboratory with the violence of a tyrant. It was not until Lady Hester was
twenty-four that she escaped from the slavery of her father's house,
by going to live with her grandmother, Lady Chatham. On Lady

Chatham's death, three years later, Pitt offered her his protection, and she remained with him until his death in 1806.

Her three years with Pitt, passed in the very centre of splendid power, were brilliant and exciting. She flung herself impetuously into the movement and the passion of that vigorous society; she ruled her uncle's household with high vivacity; she was liked and courted; if not beautiful, she was fascinating—very tall, with a very fair and clear complexion, and dark-blue eyes, and a countenance of wonderful expressiveness. Her talk, full of the trenchant nonchalance of those days, was both amusing and alarming: 'My dear Hester, what are you saying?' Pitt would call out to her from across the room. She was devoted to her uncle, who warmly returned her affection. She was devoted, too—but in a more dangerous fashion—to the intoxicating Antinous, Lord Granville Leveson Gower. The reckless manner in which she carried on this love-affair was the first indication of something overstrained, something wild and unaccountable, in her temperament. Lord Granville, after flirting with her outrageously, declared that he could never marry her, and went off on an embassy to St Petersburg. Her distraction was extreme; she hinted that she would follow him to Russia; she threatened, and perhaps attempted, suicide; she went about telling everybody that he had jilted her. She was taken ill, and then there were rumours of an accouchement, which, it was said, she took care to *afficher,* by appearing without rouge and fainting on the slightest provocation. In the midst of these excursions and alarums there was a terrible and unexpected catastrophe. Pitt died. And Lady Hester suddenly found herself a dethroned princess, living in a small house in Montague Square on a pension of £1200 a year.

She did not abandon society, however, and the tongue of gossip continued to wag. Her immediate marriage with a former lover, Mr Hill, was announced: 'il est bien bon,' said Lady Bessborough. Then it was whispered that Canning was 'le régnant'—that he was with her 'not only all day, but almost all night.' She quarrelled with Canning and became attached to Sir John Moore. Whether she was actually engaged to marry him—as she seems to have asserted many years later—is doubtful; his letters to her, full as they are of respectful tenderness, hardly warrant the conclusion; but it is certain that he died with her name on his lips. Her favourite brother, Charles, was killed beside him; and it was natural that under this double blow she should have retired from London. She buried herself in Wales; but not for long. In 1810 she set sail for Gibraltar with her brother James, who was rejoining his regiment in the Peninsula. She never returned to England.

There can be no doubt that at the time of her departure the thought of a lifelong exile was far from her mind. It was only gradually, as she moved further and further eastward, that the prospect of life in England—at last even in Europe—grew distasteful to her; as late as 1816 she was talking of a visit to Provence. Accompanied by two or three English fellow travellers, her English maid, Mrs Fry, her private physician, Dr Meryon, and a host of servants, she progressed, slowly and in great state, through Malta and Athens, to Constantinople. She was conveyed in battleships, and lodged with governors and ambassadors. After spending many months in Constantinople, Lady Hester discovered that she was 'dying to see Napoleon with her own eyes', and attempted accordingly to obtain passports to France. The project was stopped by Stratford Canning, the English minister, upon which she decided to visit Egypt, and, chartering a Greek vessel, sailed for Alexandria in the winter of 1811. Off the island of Rhodes a violent storm sprang up; the whole party were forced to abandon the ship, and to take refuge upon a bare rock, where they remained without food or shelter for thirty hours. Eventually, after many severe privations, Alexandria was reached in safety; but this disastrous voyage was a turning-point in Lady Hester's career. At Rhodes she was forced to exchange her torn and dripping raiment for the attire of a Turkish gentleman—a dress which she never afterwards abandoned. It was the first step in her orientalisation.

She passed the next two years in a triumphal progress. Her appearance in Cairo caused the greatest sensation, and she was received in state by the Pasha, Mehemet Ali. Her costume on this occasion was gorgeous: she wore a turban of cashmere, a brocaded waistcoat, a priceless pelisse, and a vast pair of purple velvet pantaloons embroidered all over in gold. She was ushered by chamberlains with silver wands through the inner courts of the palace to a pavilion in the harem, where the Pasha, rising to receive her, conversed with her for an hour. From Cairo she turned northwards, visiting Jaffa, Jerusalem, Acre, and Damascus. Her travelling dress was of scarlet cloth trimmed with gold, and, when on horseback, she wore over the whole a white-hooded and tasselled burnous. Her maid, too, was forced, protesting, into trousers, though she absolutely refused to ride astride. Poor Mrs Fry had gone through various and dreadful sufferings—shipwreck and starvation, rats and black-beetles unspeakable—but she retained her equanimity. Whatever her ladyship might think fit to be, *she* was an Englishwoman to the last, and Philippaki was Philip Parker and Mustapha Mr Farr.

Outside Damascus, Lady Hester was warned that the town was the most fanatical in Turkey, and that the scandal of a woman entering it in man's clothes, unveiled, would be so great as to be dangerous. She was begged to veil herself, and to make her entry under cover of darkness. 'I must take the bull by the horns,' she replied, and rode into the city unveiled at midday. The population were thunderstruck; but at last their amazement gave way to enthusiasm, and the incredible lady was hailed everywhere as queen, crowds followed her, coffee was poured out before her, and the whole bazaar rose as she passed. Yet she was not satisfied with her triumphs; she would do something still more glorious and astonishing; she would plunge into the desert and visit the ruins of Palmyra, which only half-a-dozen of the boldest travellers had ever seen. The Pasha of Damascus offered her a military escort, but she preferred to throw herself upon the hospitality of the Bedouin Arabs, who, overcome by her horsemanship, her powers of sight, and her courage, enrolled her a member of their tribe. After a week's journey in their company, she reached Palmyra, where the inhabitants met her with wild enthusiasm, and under the Corinthian columns of Zenobia's temple crowned her head with flowers. This happened in March 1813; it was the apogee of Lady Hester's life. Henceforward her fortunes gradually but steadily declined.

The rumour of her exploits had spread through Syria, and from the year 1813 onwards, her reputation was enormous. She was received everywhere as a royal, almost as a supernatural, personage: she progressed from town to town amid official prostrations and popular rejoicings. But she herself was in a state of hesitation and discontent. Her future was uncertain; she had grown scornful of the West—must she return to it? The East alone was sympathetic, the East alone was tolerable—but could she cut herself off for ever from the past? At Laodicea she was suddenly struck down by the plague, and, after months of illness, it was borne in upon her that all was vanity. She rented an empty monastery on the slopes of Mount Lebanon, not far from Sayda (the ancient Sidon), and took up her abode there. Then her mind took a new surprising turn; she dashed to Ascalon, and, with the permission of the Sultan, began excavations in a ruined temple with the object of discovering a hidden treasure of three million pieces of gold. Having unearthed nothing but an antique statue, which, in order to prove her disinterestedness, she ordered her appalled doctor to break into little bits, she returned to her monastery. Finally, in 1816, she moved to another house, further up Mount Lebanon, and near the village of Djoun; and at Djoun she remained until her death, more than twenty years later.

Thus, almost accidentally as it seems, she came to the end of her wanderings, and the last, long, strange, mythical period of her existence began. Certainly the situation that she had chosen was sublime. Her house, on the top of a high bare hill among great mountains, was a one-storied group of buildings, with many ramifying courts and outhouses, and a garden of several acres surrounded by a rampart wall. The garden, which she herself had planted and tended with the utmost care, commanded a glorious prospect. On every side but one the vast mountains towered, but to the west there was an opening, through which, in the far distance, the deep blue Mediterranean was revealed. From this romantic hermitage, her singular renown spread over the world. European travellers who had been admitted to her presence brought back stories full of Eastern mystery; they told of a peculiar grandeur, a marvellous prestige, an imperial power. The precise nature of Lady Hester's empire was, indeed, dubious; she was in fact merely the tenant of her Djoun establishment, for which she paid a rent of £20 a year. But her dominion was not subject to such limitations. She ruled imaginatively, transcendentally; the solid glory of Chatham had been transmuted into the phantasy of an Arabian Night. No doubt she herself believed that she was something more than a chimerical empress. When a French traveller was murdered in the desert, she issued orders for the punishment of the offenders; punished they were, and Lady Hester actually received the solemn thanks of the French Chamber. It seems probable, however, that it was the sultan's orders rather than Lady Hester's which produced the desired effect. In her feud with her terrible neighbour, the Emir Beshyr, she maintained an undaunted front. She kept the tyrant at bay; but perhaps the emir, who, so far as physical force was concerned, held her in the hollow of his hand, might have proceeded to extremities if he had not received a severe admonishment from Stratford Canning at Constantinople. What is certain is that the ignorant and superstitious populations around her feared and loved her, and that she, reacting to her own mysterious prestige, became at last even as they. She plunged into astrology and divination; she awaited the moment when, in accordance with prophecy, she should enter Jerusalem side by side with the Mahdi, the Messiah; she kept two sacred horses, destined, by sure signs, to carry her and him to their last triumph. The Orient had mastered her utterly. She was no longer an Englishwoman, she declared; she loathed England; she would never go there again; and if she went anywhere, it would be to Arabia, to 'her own people'.

Her expenses were immense—not only for herself but for others, for she poured out her hospitality with a noble hand. She ran into debt, and was swindled by the moneylenders; her steward cheated her, her servants pilfered her; her distress was at last acute. She fell into fits of terrible depression, bursting into dreadful tears and savage cries. Her habits grew more and more eccentric. She lay in bed all day, and sat up all night, talking unceasingly for hour upon hour to Dr Meryon, who alone of her English attendants remained with her, Mrs Fry having withdrawn to more congenial scenes long since. The doctor was a poor-spirited and muddle-headed man, but he was a good listener; and there he sat while that extraordinary talk flowed on—talk that scaled the heavens and ransacked the earth, talk in which memories of an abolished past—stories of Mr Pitt and of George III, vituperations against Mr Canning, mimicries of the Duchess of Devonshire—mingled phantasmagorically with doctrines of Fate and planetary influence, and speculations on the Arabian origin of the Scottish clans, and lamentations over the wickedness of servants; till the unaccountable figure, with its robes and its long pipe, loomed through the tobacco-smoke like some vision of a Sibyl in a dream. She might be robbed and ruined, her house might crumble over her head; but she talked on. She grew ill and desperate; yet still she talked. Did she feel that the time was coming when she should talk no more?

Her melancholy deepened into a settled gloom when the news came of her brother James's death. She had quarrelled with all her English friends, except Lord Hardwicke—with her eldest brother, with her sister, whose kind letters she left unanswered; she was at daggers drawn with the English consul at Alexandria, who worried her about her debts. Ill and harassed, she hardly moved from her bedroom, while her servants rifled her belongings and reduced the house to a condition of indescribable disorder and filth. Three dozen hungry cats ranged through the rooms, filling the courts with frightful noises. Dr Meryon, in the midst of it all, knew not whether to cry or laugh. At moments the great lady regained her ancient fire; her bells pealed tumultuously for hours together; or she leapt up, and arraigned the whole trembling household before her, with her Arab war-mace in her hand. Her finances grew more and more involved—grew at length irremediable. It was in vain that the faithful Lord Hardwicke pressed her to return to England to settle her affairs. Return to England, indeed! To England, that ungrateful, miserable country, where, so far as she could see, they had forgotten the very name of Mr Pitt! The final blow fell when a letter came from the English authorities threatening to cut off her pension for the payment of her debts. Upon that, after despatching a series of furious missives to Lord Palmerston, to Queen Victoria, to the Duke of Wellington, she renounced the world. She commanded Dr Meryon to return to Europe, and he—how could he have done it? —obeyed her. Her health was broken, she was over sixty, and, save for her vile servants, absolutely alone. She lived for nearly a year after he left her—we know no more. She had vowed never again to pass through the gate of her house; but did she sometimes totter to her garden—that beautiful garden which she had created, with its roses and its fountains, its alleys and its bowers—and look westward at the sea? The end came in June 1839. Her servants immediately possessed themselves of every moveable object in the house. But Lady Hester cared no longer: she was lying back in her bed—inexplicable, grand, preposterous, with her nose in the air.

Mr Smyllie, Sir

PATRICK CAMPBELL

When, in these trying times, it's possible to work on the lower slopes of a national newspaper for several weeks without discovering which of the scurrying executives is the editor, I count myself fortunate to have served under one who wore a green sombrero, weighed twenty-two stone, sang parts of his leading articles in operatic recitative, and grew the nail on his little finger into the shape of a pen nib, like Keats.

Even the disordered band of unemployed cooks, squabbling like crows over the Situations Vacant columns in the front office files, knew that he was Robert Maire Smyllie, Editor of the *Irish Times,* and fell silent as he made his swift rush up the stairs.

He was a classical scholar, at home among the Greek philosophers. He was the incorruptible champion of the fading Protestant cause in holy Ireland. His political and humanitarian views won international respect, and he spent most of his time on the run from the importunities of such characters as Chloral O'Kelly and Twitchy Doyle.

They lay in wait for him every evening in their chosen lairs in the front office and threw themselves in his path, as though to halt a rushing locomotive, as soon as he appeared at the door.

Chloral O'Kelly was a deeply melancholic youth who drank disinfectant, and was in constant need of 3*s* 9*d* for another bottle. Twitchy Doyle was a little old man with a straggly, jumping moustache who lived by reviewing reprints of Zane Grey. The moment the Editor burst through the front door they closed on him with urgent appeals, battling for position with Deirdre of the Sorrows, an elderly woman who believed for twelve years that she was being underpaid for her contributions to the Woman's Page. The Editor shot through them, weaving and jinking, crying: 'No—not tonight—tomorrow—goodbye'—and put on an extra burst of speed which carried him up the stairs to the safety of his own room, there to deliver his unforgettable cry: 'Pismires! Warlocks! Stand aside!'

I looked up 'pismire' once in the dictionary and found it meant an ant. It pictured, vividly, the unrelenting tenacity of his hangers-on.

For four years, six nights a week, I worked beside this enormous, shy, aggressive, musical, childlike, cultured and entirely unpredictable human being, separated from him by only a wooden partition, in a monastic life cut off almost completely from the world.

We worked in a high, dusty room topped by an opaque glass dome. There were no outside windows, so that the lights burned day and night. Alec Newman, the assistant editor, and Bill Fleming, the theatre critic, shared the outside part. Then came the Editor's office, partitioned off by battered wooden panelling. I had a tiny box jammed between him and the wall, with a sliding hatch between us for the purposes of communication. When it was open I got a portrait view of the great head, hair brushed smoothly back, brick-red face, snub nose supporting glasses and a ginger moustache enclosing the stem of a curved pipe the size of a flower-pot. 'Mr Campbell, we do not wish to be observed,' was the signal for the hatch to be closed.

Alec, Bill and I got in about nine-thirty every night and started to scratch around for leader subjects in the English papers. At ten o'clock the Editor burst in like a charging rhino, denounced pismires and warlocks, and went to ground in his own room.

At ten-thirty came the inevitable inquiry:'Well, gentlemen—?'

Alec assumed the responsibility of answering for all of us. 'Nothing, Mr Smyllie, sir. All is sterility and inertia.'

The reply was automatic. 'Ten-thirty, and not a strumpet in the house painted! Art is long, gentlemen, but life is shuddering shorter than you think.' 'Shuddering' and 'shudder' were favourite words of complaint.

Alec made his set protest. 'You're hard, Mr Smyllie, sir. Hard!'

'Mr Newman?'

'Sir?'

'Take your King Charles's head outside and suck it.'

I never discovered the origin of this extraordinary injunction, but it meant that some disagreement had taken place between them during the afternoon and that Alec had better be careful from now on. My own orders came floating over the partition.

'Mr Campbell?'

'Sir?'

'Prehensilise some Bosnian peasants.'

'Immediately, sir.'

The cryptic order had a simple origin. The Editor, seeking once to commend a piece of writing that clung closely, without irrelevant deviation, to its theme, had hit upon the word prehensile, which passed immediately into the language of our private nocturnal life. Somerset Maugham, for instance, was a prehensile writer, Henry James unprehensile in the extreme. From here it was a short step to prehensilising an untidily written contribution. Reprehensilisation covered a second re-write. We didn't even notice we were saying it after a week or two.

The Bosnian peasant came from a discovery of mine on the back page of the *Manchester Guardian*—an exceedingly improbable story about a Balkan shepherd who'd tripped over a railway line and derailed a train with his wooden leg. The shepherd, in addition, had only one eye, and was carrying a live salmon in his arms. I cannot imagine, now, how even a short fourth leader could have been written on such a theme, but for months I was dependent on the *Guardian's* Balkan correspondent for my ideas. Acceptance of this *argot* led me once to frighten the life out of the Bishop—I think—of Meath.

I'd come in very late and burst straight into the Editor's room. 'I'm sorry I got held up, Mr Smyllie, sir!' I cried. 'I can always reprehensilise some one-eyed Bosnian bastards!' It was only then that I saw the bishop sitting in the visitors' chair with his top hat on his knee. I've never seen a man so profoundly affected by a sentence containing only eight words.

If pursuing his personal, King Charles's head war with Alec, the Editor would suddenly give him the first, interminable leader to write on some political theme, while doing the second and shorter one himself.

Silence settled in for about an hour, with the four typewriters rattling away. Sometimes, then, we got: 'Cold—cold—cold—'

Almost anything could start it off, from the mere weather conditions to some philosophic reflection that had entered the Editor's mind. His typewriter stopped. The rest of us paused, too, expectant in our boxes. The voice rose, high and ghostly, from the Editor's compartment:

'Cold—cold—cold—'

We echoed it, still higher and thinner:

'Cold—cold—cold—'

The Editor's voice took on a deeper, tragically declamatory note:

> *'Cold as a frog in an ice-bound pool,*
> *Cold as a slew of gooseberry fool,*
> *Colder than charity—'*

There was a long pause, while we stuffed our handkerchiefs into our mouths, struggling to remain silent. The next line came out with rasping cynicism:

'And that's pretty chilly—'

He allowed this to sink in, then returned to the dramatic narrative form:

'*But it isn't as cold as poor Brother Billy—*'

We all joined in, vying with one another to achieve the maximum in greasy self-satisfaction, on the last line:

'*Cause he's DAID!*'

There was another pause, while we savoured the dying echoes. 'Get on with it, gentlemen,' said the Editor, and the four typewriters started again. But now that his appetite for music had been aroused—and he was a profoundly musical man, with a fine baritone voice—he would give us an encore, singing the words of his leader in a long recitative, like a chant:

> '*O, the Dublin Corporation had decided*
> *In its wis-***dum—**'

We joined in, like a Greek chorus, in the background:

> '*In its wis-***dum**. . .*its wis-***dum**. . .'
> '*To sign the death warrant*
> *Of the traam-***ways—**'
> '*Traam-***ways**. . .*traam-ways*. . .'
> '*A measure with which we find ourselves*
> *In agree-ment—*'
> '*In agree-ment*. . .*agree-ment*. . .'

There'd be a sudden break in the mood. The voice came out with a snap. 'Thank you, gentlemen, and give my regards to your poor father, too.'

When he was writing the words poured out of him in a flood, without correction, and at times, indeed, without much thought. He'd been doing it too long. But there were occasions when he bent the whole of his courageous and intelligent mind to denouncing the rising tide of parochial Irish republicanism—notably on the death of George V.

This long-drawn-out decline was being charted much more thoroughly by the *Irish Times,* without its Unionist sympathies, than by the other newspapers. Night after night Smyllie put a new touch to his obituary leader, after the routine inquiry, 'Has the poor old shudderer passed on?' Finally, the king died and the leader was sent out for setting. We were all in the Editor's room when the first edition came off the machines. He tore open the leader page to see how it looked, and gave a scream like a wounded bull when he saw the second half of it, possibly inadvertently, had been printed upside down. Pismires and warlocks that morning were relegated to the ends of hell.

This concern for the English king got us into scattered forays with the IRA, leading once to the windows of the office in Cork being broken by a shower of stones. When the news reached the Editor he made, taking as his framework, 'They cannot intimidate me by shooting my lieutenants,' one of the most carefully formulated battle-cries I've ever heard in my life.

We were in the office at the time. He instructed me to give him the noggin of brandy, filed under B in his correspondence cabinet, and took a steady pull. 'These shudderers', said Robert Maire Smyllie, 'cannot intimidate me by throwing half-bricks through the windows of the branch office while my lieutenants are taking a posset of stout in the shebeen next door.'

When we left, round about two o'clock the following morning, however, he was in a noticeable hurry to mount his bicycle. As he swung his massive weight into the saddle one of the pedals snapped off clean. He fell off, sprang up again, shouted, 'Mr Campbell, as your superior officer I order you to give me your velocipede!'— snatched it out of my hand, leaped aboard and sped off into the darkness. I limped after him on the broken one. When we got back to his house we drank Slivovitz until breakfast, in further defiance of 'the porter-slopping shudderers from Ballydehob'.

In the office there was indeed at this time the feeling of a beleaguered garrison, one which prompted all of us to remain in the place until daylight, rather than face the dark streets on our bicycles. Those were the great nights of the domino games that kept us locked in combat over the Editor's desk until the charwomen came in in the morning.

'A little pimping, Mr Smyllie, sir?' Alec would suggest, after the paper had gone to bed.

'A little pimping, Mr Newman, would be acceptable.'

No one could ever remember how it came to be called pimping, with the additional refinement of 'hooring', to describe the act of blocking the game with a blank at both ends, but because of Smyllie's complete purity of mind these technicalities added a notable spice to the game.

I can see him now, his green, wide-brimmed hat set square on his head, the great pipe fuming and a glass of brandy by his side, delicately picking up his tiles with the pen-nib finger-nail raised in the air.

The unspoken purpose of the three of us was to do him down by a concerted onslaught, all playing into one another's hands to present him with a blank, when his turn came to play, on both ends.

'Pimp, Mr Newman, pimp,' I would urge Alec, sitting on my right. We always used these formal titles when in play.

Alec would close one end. 'Hoor, Mr Campbell, hoor!'

If, happily, I had a suitable blank I would lose no time in playing it, then we all burst into a triumphant cry:

'Hoored, Mr Smyllie, sir—hoored! Take a little snatch from the bucket!'

With an expressionless face, and the dainty finger-nail raised in the air, the great man would draw some more tiles from the middle, on occasion being lucky enough to find a natural seven, and then lay it with an elegant flick of the wrist, like an eighteenth-century gallant. 'That, gentlemen,' he would say, 'should wipe the shuddering grins off your kissers. *Nemo me impune lacessit*—and best wishes to all at home.'

I left the *Irish Times* under rather dubious circumstances, intending, in fact, only to take a week's holiday in London, but I was also writing a column for the Irish edition of the *Sunday Dispatch* at this time, and thought it might be interesting to call in at headquarters. As a result of this I wrote a piece about the English scene which they used in all editions, and paid me a little more than five times what I was getting for a whole week's work at home. I sent Smyllie a telegram, saying I'd been held up, and hoped to be back soon. He countered with a letter saying he would be delighted to see the last of me if I'd send him a year's salary, in lieu of notice. I replied that I'd see my bank manager about it. I remained on in London, and the correspondence came to an end.

In the next three years I returned fairly frequently to Dublin, without daring to go and call on him, until one day, coming back in an aeroplane, I opened the *Irish Times* and saw a paragraph in his Saturday diary column, which he wrote under the name of Nichevo.

It was very short. 'My spies tell me', it read, 'that Paddy Campbell is back again in Dublin, after a long safari looking for tsetse fly in the bush. He is now preparing a definitive biography of Schopenhauer, and is doing a lot of field research on the subject in the back bar of Jammet's, and the Dolphin Hotel.'

It was an intimation that peace had been declared. But he was dead before I could say, 'Good evening, Mr Smyllie, sir,' again.

PART THREE
On the Pleasures of the Flesh

THE BALANCE in this section leans towards the first half of the twentieth century, with earlier contributions from Bacon and Cobbett. The nine Essays are about concrete experience rather than abstract discussion; when it comes to the pleasures of the flesh Essayists prefer to discuss experience rather than theory. And a suspicion arises that they treat their other subjects more profoundly—suggesting that the flesh and its pleasures have, as their principal value, diversion from serious and cerebral matters. The pieces here largely consider eating, drinking and sleeping, three of the four primary pleasures of the flesh. (The fourth has been ignored, not through any false delicacy, but through a shortage of Essayists on the subject, or at least a lack of writers who have shown any—forgive me—penetration.) The outdoors gets a mention too, though its inclusion as a pleasure of the flesh may hoist an eyebrow or two, past and present.

Corporal pleasure was one of our earliest responses; the flesh had in any case long been alerted to such fun, the shrewd gods encouraging procreation. How we civilise ourselves now, how we show our success, is still measured by how we cosset or otherwise enjoy ourselves physically. It even has psychological connotations: the Americans have a phrase to describe those who find sensual enjoyment in serious shopping—'retail therapy'. Sophistication may therefore be defined, on one level anyway, as the degree to which we bring the mind to bear upon giving pleasure to the body. Some moralists may call it decadence: writers consequently love it as a topic or ingredient.

In the Essays on the subject, no doubt exists that body and soul must be counted in the workings of the same engine. When Bacon discusses the garden, a physical experience, in terms of 'the greatest refreshment to the spirit of man', he acknowledges that the pleasures of the body revive the soul and the intellect. Does this mean that the more rigorous the soul the more splendid must be its refreshment? Or the exact opposite—eating asparagus with Milne, drinking tea in the East, brewing your own beer according to Cobbett or, like Chesterton—'Lying in bed would be an altogether perfect and supreme experience if only one had a coloured pencil long enough to draw on the ceiling'? Any selection from the myriad essays written to applaud fleshly enjoyment must mirror the thing itself—transient (even if taken seriously), occasionally gleeful and never threateningly memorable.

Of Gardens

FRANCIS BACON

God Almighty first planted a garden. And indeed it is the purest of human pleasures. It is the greatest refreshment to the spirits of man; without which, buildings and palaces are but gross handyworks: and a man shall ever see that when ages grow to civility and elegancy, men come to build stately sooner than to garden finely; as if garden-ing were the greater perfection. I do hold it, in the royal ordering of gardens, there ought to be gardens for all the months in the year; in which, severally, things of beauty may be then in season. For December and January and the latter part of November, you must take such things as are green all winter: holly; ivy; bays; juniper; cypress trees; yew; pineapple trees; fir trees; rosemary; lavender; periwinkle, the white, the purple, and the blue; germander; flags; orange trees, lemon trees, and myrtles, if they be stoved; and sweet marjoram, warm set. There followeth, for the latter part of January and February, the mezereon tree, which then blossoms; crocus ver-nus, both the yellow and the gray; primroses; anemones; the early tulippa; hyacinthus orientalis; chamaïris; fritillaria. For March, there come violets, specially the single blue, which are the earliest; the yellow daffadil; the daisy; the almond tree in blossom; the peach tree in blossom; the cornelian tree in blossom; sweet-briar. In April follow, the double white violet; the wallflower; the stock-gilly-flower; the cowslip; flower-delices, and lilies of all natures; rosemary flowers; the tulippa; the double piony; the pale daffadil; the French honeysuckle; the cherry tree in blossom; the dammasin and plum trees in blossom; the white-thorn in leaf; the lilac tree. In May and June come pinks of all sorts, specially the blush pink; roses of all kinds, except the musk, which comes later; honeysuckles; strawber-ries; bugloss; columbine; the French marygold; flos Africanus; cherry tree in fruit; ribes; figs in fruit; rasps; vine flowers; lavender in flowers; the sweet satyrian, with the white flower; herba muscaria; lilium convallium; the apple tree in blossom. In July come gilly-flowers of all varieties; musk-roses; the lime tree in blossom; early pears and plums in fruit; ginnitings; quadlins. In August come plums of all sorts in fruit; pears; apricocks; berberries; filberds; muskmelons; monks-hoods, of all colours. In September come grapes; apples; poppies of all colours; peaches; melocotones; nectarines; cornelians; wardens; quinces. In October and the beginning of November come services; medlars, bullises; roses cut or removed to come late; hollyokes; and such like. These particulars are for the climate of London; but my meaning is perceived, that you may have *ver perpetuum*, as the place affords.

And because the breath of flowers is far sweeter in the air (where it comes and goes, like the warbling of music) than in the hand, therefore nothing is more fit for that delight, than to know what be the flowers and plants that do best perfume the air. Roses, damask and red, are fast flowers of their smells; so that you may walk by a whole row of them, and find nothing of their sweetness; yea, though it be in a morning's dew. Bays likewise yield no smell as they grow. Rosemary little; nor sweet marjoram. That which above all others yields the sweetest smell in the air, is the violet; specially the white double violet, which comes twice a year; about the middle of April, and about Bartholomewtide. Next to that is the musk-rose. Then the strawberry-leaves dying, which yield a most excellent cordial smell. Then the flower of the vines; it is a little dust, like the dust of a bent, which grows upon the cluster in the first coming forth. Then sweet-briar. Then wallflowers, which are very delightful to be set under a parlour or lower chamber window. Then pinks and gillyflowers, specially the matted pink and clove gillyflower. Then the flowers of the lime tree. Then the honeysuckles, so they be somewhat afar off. Of bean flowers I speak not, because they are field flowers. But those which perfume the air most delightfully, not passed by as the rest, but being trodden upon and crushed, are three: that is, burnet, wild thyme, and water-mints. Therefore you are to set whole alleys of them, to have the pleasure when you walk or tread.

For gardens (speaking of those which are indeed prince-like, as we have done of buildings), the contents ought not well to be under thirty acres of ground, and to be divided into three parts: a green in the entrance; a heath or desert in the going forth; and the main garden in the midst; besides alleys on both sides. And I like well that four acres of ground be assigned to the green; six to the heath; four and four to either side; and twelve to the main garden. The green hath two pleasures: the one, because nothing is more pleasant to the eye than green grass kept finely shorn; the other, because it will give you a fair alley in the midst, by which you may go in front upon a stately hedge, which is to enclose the garden. But because the alley will be long, and, in great heat of the year or day, you ought not to buy the shade in the garden by going in the sun thorough the green, therefore you are, of either side the green, to plant a covert alley, upon carpenter's work, about twelve foot in height, by which you may go in shade into the garden. As for the making of knots or figures with divers-coloured earths, that they may lie under the windows of the house on that side which the garden stands, they be but toys: you may see as good sights many times in tarts. The garden is best to be square; encompassed, on all the four sides, with a stately arched hedge. The arches to be upon pillars of carpenter's work, of some ten foot high and six foot broad; and the spaces between of the same dimension with the breadth of the arch. Over the arches let there be an entire hedge, of some four foot high, framed also upon carpenter's work; and upon the upper hedge, over every arch, a little turret, with a belly, enough to receive a cage of birds; and over every space between the arches some other little figure, with broad plates of round coloured glass, gilt, for the sun to play upon. But this hedge I intend to be raised upon a bank, not steep, but gently slope, of some six foot, set all with flowers. Also I understand that this square of the garden should not be the whole breadth of the ground, but to leave, on either side, ground enough for diversity of side alleys; unto which the two covert alleys of the green may deliver you. But there must be no alleys with hedges at either end of this great enclosure: not at the hither end, for letting your prospect upon this fair hedge from the green; nor at the further end, for letting your prospect from the hedge, through the arches, upon the heath.

For the ordering of the ground within the great hedge, I leave it to variety of device; advising, nevertheless, that whatsoever form you cast it into, first, it be not too busy or full of work. Wherein I, for my part, do not like images cut out in juniper or other garden stuff: they be for children. Little low hedges, round, like welts, with some pretty pyramids, I like well; and in some places, fair columns upon frames of carpenter's work. I would also have the alleys spacious and fair. You may have closer alleys upon the side grounds, but none in the main garden. I wish also, in the very middle, a fair mount, with three ascents, and alleys, enough for four to walk abreast: which I would have to be perfect circles, without any bulwarks or embossments; and the whole mount to be thirty foot high; and some fine banqueting house, with some chimneys neatly cast, and without too much glass.

For fountains, they are a great beauty and refreshment; but pools mar all, and make the garden unwholesome and full of flies and frogs. Fountains I intend to be of two natures: the one, that sprinkleth or spouteth water; the other, a fair receipt of water, of some thirty or forty foot square, but without fish, or slime, or mud. For the first, the ornaments of images gilt, or of marble, which are in use, do well: but the main matter is, so to convey the water, as it never stay, either in the bowls or in the cistern; that the water be never by rest discoloured, green or red or the like, or gather any mossiness or putrefaction. Besides that, it is to be cleansed every day by the hand. Also some steps up to it, and some fine pavement about it, doth well. As for the other kind of fountain, which we may call a bathing pool, it may admit much curiosity and beauty, wherewith we will not trouble ourselves: as, that the bottom be finely paved, and with images; the sides likewise; and withal embellished with coloured glass, and such things of lustre; encompassed also with fine rails of low statuas. But the main point is the same which we mentioned in the former kind of fountain; which is, that the water be in perpetual motion, fed by a water higher than the pool, and delivered into it by fair spouts, and then discharged away under ground, by some equality of bores, that it stay little. And for fine devices, of arching water without spilling, and making it rise in several forms (of feathers, drinking glasses, canopies, and the like), they be pretty things to look on, but nothing to health and sweetness.

For the heath, which was the third part of our plot, I wish it to be framed, as much as may be, to a natural wildness. Trees I would have none in it; but some thickets, made only of sweet-briar and honeysuckle, and some wild vine amongst; and the ground set with violets, strawberries, and primroses. For these are sweet, and prosper in the shade. And these to be in the heath, here and there, not in any order. I like also little heaps, in the nature of molehills (such as are in wild heaths), to be set, some with wild thyme; some with pinks; some with germander, that gives a good flower to the eye; some with periwinkle; some with violets; some with strawberries; some with cowslips; some with daisies; some with red roses; some with lilium convallium; some with sweet williams red; some with bear's foot; and the like low flowers, being withal sweet and sightly. Part of which heaps to be with standards of little bushes pricked upon their top, and part without. The standards to be roses; juniper; holly; berberries (but here and there, because of the smell of their blossom); red currans; gooseberries; rosemary; bays; sweet-briar; and such like. But these standards to be kept with cutting, that they grow not out of course.

For the side grounds, you are to fill them with variety of alleys, private, to give a full shade, some of them, wheresoever the sun be. You are to frame some of them likewise for shelter, that when the wind blows sharp, you may walk as in a gallery. And those alleys must be likewise hedged at both ends, to keep out the wind; and these closer alleys must be ever finely gravelled, and no grass, because of going wet. In many of these alleys likewise, you are to set fruit trees of all sorts; as well upon the walls as in ranges. And this would be generally observed, that the borders, wherein you plant your fruit trees, be fair and large, and low, and not steep; and set with fine flowers, but thin and sparingly, lest they deceive the trees. At the end of both the side grounds, I would have a mount of some pretty height, leaving the wall of the enclosure breast high, to look abroad into the fields.

For the main garden, I do not deny but there should be some fair alleys, ranged on both sides with fruit trees; and some pretty tufts of fruit trees, and arbours with seats, set in some decent order; but these to be by no means set too thick; but to leave the main garden so as it be not close, but the air open and free. For as for shade, I would have you rest upon the alleys of the side grounds, there to walk, if you be disposed, in the heat of the year or day; but to make account that the main garden is for the more temperate parts of the year; and in the heat of summer, for the morning and the evening, or overcast days.

For aviaries, I like them not, except they be of that largeness as they may be turfed, and have living plants and bushes set in them; that the birds may have more scope and natural nestling, and that no foulness appear in the floor of the aviary. So I have made a platform of a princely garden, partly by precept, partly by drawing, not a model, but some general lines of it; and in this I have spared for no cost. But it is nothing for great princes, that, for the most part, taking advice with workmen, with no less cost set their things together; and sometimes add statuas, and such things, for state and magnificence, but nothing to the true pleasure of a garden.

The Gardener's August

KAREL ČAPEK

August usually is the time when the amateur gardener forsakes his garden of wonder and goes on leave. The whole year long he vehemently swore that this year he would not go anywhere, that a garden is worth more than all summer resorts, and that he, the gardener, was not such a fool and ass as to be harassed by trains and all the devils; nevertheless, when summer sets in even he deserts the town, either because the nomadic instinct has awakened in him or to keep his neighbours from talking. He departs, however, with a heavy heart, full of fears and cares for his garden; and he will not go until he has found a friend or relation to whom he entrusts his garden for that time.

'Look here,' he says, 'there is nothing to be done now in the garden in any case; if you come and look once in three days, that will be quite enough, and if something here and there is not in order, you must write me a card, and I will come. So, I am relying on you then? As I said, five minutes will be enough, just a glance round.'

Then he leaves, having laid his garden upon the heart of an obliging fellow-creature. Next day the fellow-creature receives a letter: 'I forgot to tell you that the garden must be watered every day, the best times for doing it are five in the morning and towards seven in the evening. It is practically nothing, you only fasten the hose to the hydrant and water for a few moments. Will you please water the conifers all over as they stand, and thoroughly, and the lawn as well? If you see any weeds, pull them out. That's all.'

A day after: 'It is frightfully dry, will you give every rhododendron about two buckets of tepid water, and each conifer five buckets, and other trees about four buckets? The perennials, which are now in flower, ought to have a good deal of water—write by return post what is in flower. Withered stalks must be cut off! It would be a good thing if you loosened all the beds with a hoe; the soil breathes much better then. If there are plant-lice on the roses, buy tobacco extract, and syringe them with it while the dew is on, or after a rain. Nothing else need be done at present.'

The third day: 'I forgot to tell you that the lawn must be cut; you

163

can do it easily with the mower, and what the mower does not take, you cut with clippers. But beware! after mowing the grass it must be well raked, and afterwards *swept with a sweeper*! Otherwise the lawn gets bald patches! And water, plenty of water!'

The fourth day: 'If a storm comes, will you please run and look at my garden? A heavy rain sometimes causes damage, and it is good to be on the spot. If mildew appears on the roses, sprinkle them early in the morning while the dew is still on them with flowers of sulphur. Tie high perennials to sticks so that the wind does not break them. It is glorious here, mushrooms are growing and the swimming is beautiful. Don't forget to water every day the ampelopsis near the house, it is too dry for it there. Keep for me in a packet the seeds of Papaver nudicaule. I hope that you have already mown the lawns. You needn't do anything else, but destroy earwigs.'

The fifth day: 'I am sending you a box of plants, which I dug up here in a wood. They are various orchids, wild lilies, Pasque flowers, pirolas, bugworts, anemones, and others. Immediately you have got the box, open it, and damp the seedlings, and plant them somewhere in a shady place! Add peat and leafmould! Plant immediately and water three times a day! Please cut the side branches of the roses.'

The sixth day: 'I am sending you by express post a box of plants from the country ... They must go into the ground at once ... At night you ought to go into the garden with a lamp and destroy snails. It would be good to weed the paths. I hope that looking after my garden doesn't take up much of your time, and that you are enjoying it.'

In the meantime the obliging fellow-creature, conscious of his responsibilities, waters, mows, tills, weeds, and wanders round with a box of seedlings looking where the devil he can plant them; he sweats, and is muddied all over; he notices with horror that here some damned plant is fading, and there some stalks are broken, and that the lawn has become rusty, and that the whole garden is somehow looking blasted, and he curses the moment when he took upon himself this burden, and he prays to heaven for autumn to come.

And in the meantime the owner of the garden thinks with uneasiness of his flowers and lawns, sleeps badly, curses because the obliging fellow-creature is not sending him reports every day on the state of the garden, and he counts the days to his return, posting every other day a box of plants from the country and a letter with a dozen urgent commands. Finally he returns; still with the baggage in his hands he rushes into his garden and looks round with damp eyes—

'That laggard, that dolt, that pig,' he thinks bitterly, 'he has made a mess of my garden!'

'Thank you,' he says dryly to his fellow-creature, and like a living reproach he snatches the hose to water the neglected garden. (That idiot, he thinks in the bottom of his heart, to trust him with anything! Never in my life will I be such a fool and ass to go away for holidays!)

As for the wild plants, the garden maniac digs them somehow out of the soil, to incorporate them in his garden; it is more difficult with other natural objects. 'Damn!' thinks the gardener, looking at the Matterhorn or on the Gerlachovka; 'if only I had this mountain in my garden; and this bit of forest with its enormous trees, and this clearing, and the stream here, or perhaps this lake; that luxuriant meadow would also look nice in my garden, or a strip of seashore and a ruin of a Gothic cloister would be splendid. And I should like to have that ancient lime tree there, and that antique fountain would also do quite well; and how about a herd of stags, or some chamois, or at least this avenue of old poplars; that rock there, this river, that oak grove, or that foaming waterfall, or at least this quiet and green dell—'

If it were possible to make a compact with the devil, who would then gratify every wish, the gardener would sell him his own soul; but for this soul the poor devil would pay damnably dear. 'You miserable fellow,' he would say at the end, 'rather than slave like this, get yourself gone to paradise—in any case it's the only place for you.' And lashing his tail in irritation, till he knocked off the flowers of the feverfew and helenium with it, he would go on his business, and leave the gardener to his immodest and inexhaustible desires.

Understand that I am talking of the real gardener and not of apple-growers and market gardeners. Let the apple-grower beam over his apples and pears, let the market gardener rejoice at the superhuman height of his kohlrabi, marrows, and celery; a real gardener feels in his bones that August is already a turning-point. What is in flower hastens to be over; autumn asters and chrysanthemums are still to come, and then good night! But you, shining phlox, the flower of rectory gardens, you, golden groundsel and golden rod, golden rudbeckia and golden harpalium, golden sunflower, you and I, we shall not go under yet, not we! All the year round is spring, and all through life is youth; there is always something which may flower. One only says that it is autumn; we are merely flowering in other ways, we grow beneath the earth, we put forth new shoots; and always there is something to do. Only those who keep their hands in their pockets say that it is getting worse; but who flowers and bears fruit, even in November, knows nothing of the autumn, but of the golden summer; knows nothing of decay, but of germination. Autumnal aster, dear man, the year is so long that you can't see its end.

Going Out for a Walk

MAX BEERBOHM

It is a fact that not once in all my life have I gone out for a walk. I have
been taken out for walks; but that is another matter. Even while I
trotted prattling by my nurse's side I regretted the good old days
when I had, and wasn't, a perambulator. When I grew up it seemed to
me that the one advantage of living in London was that nobody ever
wanted me to come out for a walk. London's very drawbacks—its
endless noise and hustle, its smoky air, the squalor ambushed everywhere in it—assured this one immunity. Whenever I was with
friends in the country, I knew that at any moment, unless rain were
actually falling, some man might suddenly say 'Come out for a walk!'
in that sharp imperative tone which he would not dream of using in
any other connection. People seem to think there is something
inherently noble and virtuous in the desire to go for a walk. Anyone
thus desirous feels that he has a right to impose his will on whomever
he sees comfortably settled in an armchair, reading. It is easy to say
simply 'No' to an old friend. In the case of a mere acquaintance one
wants some excuse. 'I wish I could, but '—nothing ever occurs to me
except 'I have some letters to write'. This formula is unsatisfactory in
three ways. 1. It isn't believed. 2. It compels you to rise from your
chair, go to the writing-table, and sit improvising a letter to somebody until the walkmonger (just not daring to call you liar and
hypocrite) shall have lumbered out of the room. 3. It won't operate
on Sunday mornings. 'There's no post out till this evening' clinches
the matter; and you may as well go quietly.

Walking for walking's sake may be as highly laudable and exemplary a thing as it is held to be by those who practise it. My objection
to it is that it stops the brain. Many a man has professed to me that his
brain never works so well as when he is swinging along the high road
or over hill and dale. This boast is not confirmed by my memory of
anybody who on a Sunday morning has forced me to partake of his
adventure. Experience teaches me that whatever a fellow-guest may
have of power to instruct or to amuse when he is sitting on a chair, or
standing on a hearthrug, quickly leaves him when he takes one out for
a walk. The ideas that come so thick and fast to him in any room,

where are they now? where that encyclopedic knowledge which he bore so lightly? where the kindling fancy that played like summer lightning over *any* topic that was started? The man's face that was so mobile is set now; gone is the light from his fine eyes. He says that A. (our host) is a thoroughly good fellow. Fifty yards further on, he adds that A. is one of the best fellows he has ever met. We tramp another furlong or so, and he says that Mrs A. is a charming woman. Presently he adds that she is one of the most charming women he has ever known. We pass an inn. He reads vapidly aloud to me: 'The Kings Arms. Licensed to sell Ales and Spirits.' I foresee that during the rest of the walk he will read aloud any inscription that occurs. We pass a milestone. He points at it with his stick, and says 'Uxminster. 11 Miles.' We turn a sharp corner at the foot of a hill. He points at the wall, and says 'Drive Slowly.' I see far ahead, on the other side of the hedge bordering the high road, a small notice-board. He sees it too. He keeps his eye on it. And in due course 'Trespassers', he says, 'Will Be Prosecuted.' Poor man!—mentally a wreck.

Luncheon at the As, however, salves him and floats him in full sail. Behold him once more the life and soul of the party. Surely he will never, after the bitter lesson of this morning, go out for another walk. An hour later, I see him striding forth, with a new companion. I watch him out of sight. I know what he is saying. He is saying that I am rather a dull man to go a walk with. He will presently add that I am one of the dullest men he ever went a walk with. Then he will devote himself to reading out the inscriptions.

How comes it, this immediate deterioration in those who go walking for walking's sake? Just what happens? I take it that not by his reasoning faculties is a man urged to this enterprise. He is urged, evidently, by something in him that transcends reason; by his soul, I presume. Yes, it must be the soul that raps out the 'Quick march!' to the body.—'Halt! Stand at ease!' interposes the brain, and 'To what destination,' it suavely asks the soul, 'and on what errand, are you sending the body?'—'On no errand whatsoever,' the soul makes answer, 'and to no destination at all. It is just like you to be always on the lookout for some subtle ulterior motive. The body is going out because the mere fact of its doing so is a sure indication of nobility, probity, and rugged grandeur of character.'—'Very well, Vagula, have your own wayula! But I', says the brain, 'flatly refuse to be mixed up in this tomfoolery. I shall go to sleep till it is over.' The brain then wraps itself up in its own convolutions, and falls into a dreamless slumber from which nothing can rouse it till the body has been safely deposited indoors again.

Even if you go to some definite place, for some definite purpose, the brain would rather you took a vehicle; but it does not make a point of this; it will serve you well enough unless you are going *for a walk*. It won't, while your legs are vying with each other, do any deep thinking for you, nor even any close thinking; but it will do any number of small odd jobs for you willingly—provided that your legs, also, are making themselves useful, not merely bandying you about to gratify the pride of the soul. Such as it is, this essay was composed in the course of a walk, this morning. I am not one of those extremists who must have a vehicle to every destination. I never go out of my way, as it were, to avoid exercise. I take it as it comes, and take it in good part. That valetudinarians are always chattering about it, and indulging in it to excess, is no reason for despising it. I am inclined to think that in moderation it is rather good for one, physically. But, pending a time when no people wish me to go and see them, and I have no wish to go and see anyone, and there is nothing whatever for me to do off my own premises, I never will go out for a walk.

Food of the Gods

A. A. MILNE

To write properly of asparagus one needs a fine feathery pen. Mine has had a hair in it for a week. Somebody ought to look into this question of superfluous hair in pens. Whence does it come, whither does it go? or, more profitably, why does it never go? Start the morning with a hair in your pen, and there are two of you writing for the rest of the session. I apologise for my collaborator.

Asparagus. A beautiful word to which the poets have never done justice. When Longfellow wrote 'The Wreck of the Hesperus' he must have—wait a moment. *Did* Longfellow write 'The Wreck of the Hesperus'? I am shaky on wrecks; there are too many of them in literature.

> *It was the schooner Hesperus*
> *That sailed the wintry sea;*
> *The boy stood on its burning deck*
> *Whence all had fled but he—*
> *'By thy long beard and glittering eye,*
> *Now wherefore stoppest thou me?'*
> *Toll for the brave.*

You see how easily one gets confused. Well, when Southey wrote 'The Wreck of the Hesperus', did he ever stop and think to himself, 'How much better this would be if I could make it something about asparagus'? I suppose not. When the Rev. J. M. Neale wrote 'Jerusalem the Golden', did *he*— No, obviously not. I oughtn't to have asked the question. But breathes there a bard with soul so dead, who *never* to himself has said, 'If I can write of asphodel, why not asparagus as well'? I cannot believe it. *Asparagus, or the Works, Human and Divine*, of Robert Herrick.

Even our novelists have been reticent, though there may be a reason for that. Asparagus is just a little—is it not?—obvious. We should suspect a novelist who took his heroine to the Savoy and gave her asparagus. We should say, 'This man dines once a week at the Regent Palace Hotel. He knows nothing of high life, and is playing for safety.' For what we like to read about is that little dinner *à deux,* *chez* Casani (or Casini or Casooni), at which, as he unfolds his napkin, the hero can remark casually to the admiring heroine, 'I always say that Casani's is the only place in London where they know how to do a *sole à la bonne femme.*' Then, since he is 'one of the few men in London to whom M. Casani attended personally', he dismisses François or Josef or Mario with a nod, and settles down to it with the great man himself. Probably they decide to follow the sole with a *poulet en casserole* and an *omelette aux fines herbes;* to the disappointment of the heroine, who lives on a poultry farm in the country, and is going to tell her younger sister all about it when she gets back.

No asparagus at dinner then. What about lunch? We flip our way through a thousand novels, alert for the magic word, and what do we get? 'Cold grouse and a salad, washed down by a pint of Chablis.' Just that; always that. You and I, if I may suppose you to have attended the same school of manners, were taught not to drink with our mouth full, but, it appears now, mistakenly taught. Perhaps, though, our teacher never envisaged Chablis for us. It is only with Chablis that an obstinate mouthful may be washed down; and only when he has so washed it down that the hero may 'carefully select a cigarette'. You and I (to bring you in again) have little scope for selection in our cigarette-case, provided that we left the bent one at home before coming out. Nobody sells us 'ten assorted' for sixpence; they are all brothers in the packet. But it may be—indeed, I often think it must be—that the proofs of these novels get passed too hastily, and that what the author has intended was no more than this: 'Rochester drew out his dainty enamelled case and carefully selected a cigarette-end,' having had, we may suppose, a particularly good morning in the Park.

On this question, then, of asparagus (to come back to it with my collaborator's permission) we shall get no help from other so-called writers. We must do our own thinking. Now, if you live in the country, you can grow your own asparagus; or your gardener can grow his—however you put it to each other. At least you would think so. But now I must tell you something; and as it is the only piece of real information in this article, you should turn off the loud-speaker for a moment. Theoretically an asparagus bed takes three years to mature. Practically what happens is that after the second lean year you decide, very naturally, to grow carrots instead (which also wave at the top), and after two years of carrots you decide, again very naturally, to give asparagus one more chance, and after giving it one more chance for another two barren years you decide (and who shall blame you?) on spinach, which doesn't wave, but gets down to it quickly. So in a little while you will have been trying to grow asparagus for eight years, and you will have come to the conclusion (as I have) that the thing cannot be done. You can buy asparagus, you can eat asparagus (heavens, yes), but you can't grow it, and you can't read about it.

When I say that you can't read about it, I mean that you can't read about it unless I am writing. I shall continue, therefore, to write. There was a character in one of Anthony Hope's books who was of opinion that, though port tasted better without the conflicting aroma of tobacco, and though a cigar tasted better without the conflicting savour of port, yet port and cigar together gave a better combined taste than either of them separately. A little subtle, perhaps, but if you have not yet resumed the 'headphones', you may get it. Well, I feel the same way about asparagus and *Hollandaise* sauce. I am aware that such an announcement may get me into trouble with the *gourmet* and the *gourmand*. Resisting an attempt by my collaborator to digress into a contemplation of the exact difference between a *gourmet* and a *gourmand*, as to whether, for instance, it is or is not more marked than the difference between an egoist and an egotist, I will tell these gentlemen that all which they are aching to say about melted butter is known to me. I remain unmoved. A man who loves *Hollandaise* sauce as I do must get at it somehow, and asparagus is the perfect vehicle.

As between French and English asparagus there is no argument. The French sort, which gives you a genteel suck at one end and burns your fingers at the other, is not under discussion. Real asparagus must be eaten to the hilt, so that the last bite imperils the thumb. Now, however unemotional you remain during the encounter, however steeled your nerve, however steady your hand, yet tender fragments, precious seedlings, will crumble off from each shoot as you lave it in the sauce, and be left, green islets in a golden sea, marooned upon the plate. These must be secured at any cost—with the fingers, a spoon, a piece of bread, an old envelope, it matters not. When you are eating asparagus, you are eating asparagus. Reserve your breeding for the brussels sprouts.

As to the last inch of the stalk, whether you eat it or not, circumstances must guide you. It happens sometimes that, when husband and wife have helped themselves from a common dish and there is an odd number of shoots left, so that none can say whether the wife or the husband is to benefit, then they will fall to counting the thumb stalks upon their plates, whereby they hope to remedy any original unfairness in the first helping. It will occur to you that, if you have disposed completely of this or that number of stalks, then by so much you will advantage yourself in any later readjustment. For, in the presence of asparagus, a man must think for himself, and think quickly.

And now I would give you my 'Ode to Asparagus', but it is not yet written, and time presses. Yet, since the earlier poets have been (I suppose) too busy eating it to sing of it, I must do what I can, if it be no more than four lines of tribute:

> *Asparagus, in hours of ease,*
> *A pleasing substitute for peas,*
> *When pain and anguish wring the brow*
> *The* only *vegetable, thou.*

The Church Supper

ROBERT BENCHLEY

The social season in our city ends up with a bang for the summer when the Strawberry Festival at the Second Congregational Church is over. After that you might as well die. Several people have, in fact.

The Big Event is announced several weeks in advance in that racy sheet known as the 'church calendar', which is slipped into the pews by the sexton before anyone has a chance to stop him. There, among such items as a quotation from a recent letter from Mr and Mrs Wheelock (the church's missionaries in China who are doing a really splendid work in the face of a shortage of flannel goods), and the promise that Elmer Divvit will lead the Intermediate Christian Endeavor that afternoon, rain or shine, on the subject of 'What Can I Do to Increase the Number of Stars in My Crown?' we find the announcement that on Friday night, June the 8th, the Ladies of the Church will unbelt with a Strawberry Festival to be held in the vestry and that, furthermore, Mrs William Horton MacInting will be at the head of the Committee in Charge. Surely enough good news for one day!

The Committee is then divided into commissary groups, one to provide the shortcake, another to furnish the juice, another the salad, and so on, until everyone has something to do except Mrs MacInting, the chairman. She agrees to furnish the paper napkins and to send her car around after the contributions which the others are making. Then, too, there is the use of her name.

The day of the festival arrives, bright and rainy. All preparations are made for a cosy evening in defiance of the elements; so when, along about four in the afternoon, it clears and turns into a nice hot day, everyone is caught with rubbers and steamy mackintoshes, to add to the fun. For, by four o'clock in the afternoon, practically everyone in the parish is at the vestry 'helping out', as they call it.

'Helping out' consists of putting on an apron over your good clothes, tucking up the real lace cuffs, and dropping plates. The scene in the kitchen of the church at about five-thirty in the afternoon is one to make a prospective convert to Christianity stop and think. Between four and nine thousand women, all wearing aprons over black silk dresses, rush back and forth carrying platters of food, bumping into each other, hysterical with laughter, filling pitchers with hot coffee from a shiny urn, and poking good-natured fun at Mr Numaly and Mr Dow, husbands who have been drafted into service and who, amid screams of delight from the ladies, have also donned aprons and are doing the dropping of the heavier plates and ice-cream freezers.

'Look at Mr Dow!' they cry. 'Some good-looking girl you make, Mr Dow!'

'Come up to my house, Mr Numaly, and I'll hire you to do our cooking.'

'Alice says for Mr Numaly to come up to her house and she'll hire him as a cook! Alice, you're a caution!'

And so it goes, back and forth, good church-members all, which means that their banter contains nothing off-color and, by the same token, nothing that was coined later than the first batch of buffalo nickels.

In the meantime, the paying guests are arriving out in the vestry and are sniffing avidly at the coffee aroma, which by now has won its fight with the smell of musty hymn books which usually dominates the place. They leave their hats and coats in the kindergarten room on the dwarfed chairs and wander about looking with weekday detachment at the wall-charts showing the startling progress of the Children of Israel across the Red Sea and the list of gold-star pupils for the month of May. Occasionally they take a peek in at the kitchen and remark on the odd appearance of Messrs Numaly and Dow, who by this time are just a little fed up on being the center of the taunting and have stopped answering back.

The kiddies, who have been brought in to gorge themselves on indigestible strawberry concoctions, are having a gay time tearing up and down the vestry for the purpose of tagging each other. They manage to reach the door just as Mrs Camack is entering with a platter full of cabbage salad, and later she explains to Mrs Reddy while the latter is sponging off her dress that this is the last time she is going to have anything to do with a church supper at which those Basnett children are allowed. The Basnett children, in the meantime, oblivious of this threat, are giving all their attention to slipping pieces of colored chalk from the blackboard into the hot rolls which have just been placed on the tables. And, considering what small children they are, they are doing remarkably well at it.

At last everyone is ready to sit down. In fact, several invited guests do sit down, and have to be reminded that Dr Murney has yet to arrange the final details of the supper with heaven before the chairs can be pulled out. This ceremony, with the gentle fragrance of strawberries and salad rising from the table, is one of the longest in the whole list of church rites; and when it is finally over there is a frantic scraping of chairs and clatter of cutlery and babble of voices which means that the hosts of the Lord have completed another day's work in the vineyard and are ready, nay, willing, to toy with several tons of foodstuffs.

The adolescent element in the church has been recruited to do the serving, but only a few of them show up at the beginning of the meal. The others may be found by any member of the committee frantic enough to search them out, sitting in little groups of two on the stairs leading up to the organ loft or indulging in such forms of young love as tie-snatching and braid-pulling up in the study.

The unattached youths and maids who are induced to take up the work of pouring coffee do it with a vim but very little skill. Pouring coffee over the shoulder of a person sitting at a long table with dozens of other people is a thing that you ought to practise weeks in advance for, and these young people step right in on the job without so much as a dress rehearsal. The procedure is, or should be, as follows:

Standing directly behind the person about to be served, say in a loud but pleasant voice: 'Coffee?' If the victim wishes it, he or she will lift the cup from the table and hold it to be filled, with the left forefinger through the handle and bracing the cup against the right upper-arm. The pourer will then have nothing to do but see to it that the coffee goes from the pitcher to the cup.

Where the inexperienced often make a mistake is in reaching for the cup themselves and starting to pour before finding out if the victim wants coffee. This results in nine cases out of six in the victim's turning suddenly and saying: 'No coffee, thank you, please!', jarring the arm of the pourer and getting the coffee on the cuff.

For a long time nothing is heard but the din of religious eating and then gradually, one by one, forks slip from nerveless fingers, chairs are scraped back, and the zealots stir heavily to their feet. All that remains is for the committee to gather up the remains and congratulate themselves on their success.

The next event in the calendar will not be until October, when the Men's Club of the church will prepare and serve a supper of escalloped oysters and hot rolls. Join now and be enrolled for labor in the vineyard in the coming year.

The Cup of Humanity

OKAKURA-KAKUZO

Tea began as a medicine and grew into a beverage. In China, in the eighth century, it entered the realms of poetry as one of the polite amusements. The fifteenth century saw Japan ennoble it into a religion of aestheticism—Teaism. Teaism is a cult founded on the adoration of the beautiful among the sordid facts of everyday existence. It inculcates purity and harmony, the mystery of mutual charity, the romanticism of the social order. It is essentially a worship of the Imperfect, as it is a tender attempt to accomplish something possible in this impossible thing we know as life.

The Philosophy of Tea is not mere aestheticism in the ordinary acceptance of the term, for it expresses conjointly with ethics and religion our whole point of view about man and nature. It is hygiene, for it enforces cleanliness; it is economics, for it shows comfort in simplicity rather than in the complex and costly; it is moral geometry, inasmuch as it defines our sense of proportion to the universe. It represents the true spirit of Eastern democracy by making all its votaries aristocrats in taste.

The long isolation of Japan from the rest of the world, so conducive to introspection, has been highly favourable to the development of Teaism. Our home and habits, costume and cuisine, porcelain, lacquer, painting—our very literature—all have been subject to its influence. No student of Japanese culture could ever ignore its presence. It has permeated the elegance of noble boudoirs and entered the abode of the humble. Our peasants have learned to arrange flowers, our meanest labourer to offer his salutation to the rocks and waters. In our common parlance we speak of the man 'with no tea' in him, when he is insusceptible to the serio-comic interests of the personal drama. Again we stigmatise the untamed aesthete who, regardless of the mundane tragedy, runs riot in the springtide of emancipated emotions, as one 'with too much tea' in him.

The outsider may indeed wonder at this seeming much ado about nothing. What a tempest in a tea-cup! he will say. But when we consider how small after all the cup of human enjoyment is, how soon overflowed with tears, how easily drained to the dregs in our quenchless thirst for infinity, we shall not blame ourselves for making so much of the tea-cup. Mankind has done worse. In the worship of Bacchus, we have sacrificed too freely; and we have even transfigured the gory image of Mars. Why not consecrate ourselves to the queen of the Camellias, and revel in the warm stream of sympathy that flows from her altar? In the liquid amber within the ivory-porcelain, the initiated may touch the sweet reticence of Confucius, the piquancy of Laotse, and the ethereal aroma of Sakyamuni himself.

Those who cannot feel the littleness of great things in themselves are apt to overlook the greatness of little things in others. The average Westerner, in his sleek complacency, will see in the tea ceremony but another instance of the thousand and one oddities which constitute the quaintness and childishness of the East to him. He was wont to regard Japan as barbarous while she indulged in the gentle arts of peace: he calls her civilised since she began to commit wholesale slaughter on Manchurian battlefields. Much comment has been given lately to the Code of the Samurai—the Art of Death which makes our soldiers exult in self-sacrifice; but scarcely any attention has been drawn to Teaism, which represents so much of our Art of Life. Fain would we remain barbarians, if our claim to civilisation were to be based on the gruesome glory of war. Fain would we await the time when due respect shall be paid to our art and ideals.

When will the West understand, or try to understand, the East? We Asiatics are often appalled by the curious web of facts and fancies which has been woven concerning us. We are pictured as living on the perfume of the lotus, if not on mice and cockroaches. It is either impotent fanaticism or else abject voluptuousness. Indian spirituality has been derided as ignorance, Chinese sobriety as stupidity, Japanese patriotism as the result of fatalism. It has been said that we are less sensible to pain and wounds on account of the callousness of our nervous organisation!

Why not amuse yourselves at our expense? Asia returns the compliment. There would be further food for merriment if you were to know all that we have imagined and written about you. All the glamour of the perspective is there, all the unconscious homage of wonder, all the silent resentment of the new and undefined. You have been loaded with virtues too refined to be envied, and accused of crimes too picturesque to be condemned. Our writers in the past— the wise men who knew—informed us that you had bushy tails somewhere hidden in your garments, and often dined off a fricassee of new-born babes! Nay, we had something worse against you: we used to think you the most impracticable people on the earth, for you were said to preach what you never practised.

Such misconceptions are fast vanishing amongst us. Commerce has forced the European tongues on many an Eastern port. Asiatic youths are flocking to Western colleges for the equipment of modern education. Our insight does not penetrate your culture deeply, but at least we are willing to learn. Some of my compatriots have adopted too much of your customs and too much of your etiquette, in the delusion that the acquisition of stiff collars and tall silk hats comprised the attainment of your civilisation. Pathetic and deplorable as such affectations are, they evince our willingness to approach the West on our knees. Unfortunately the Western attitude is unfavourable to the understanding of the East. The Christian missionary goes to impart, but not to receive. Your information is based on the meagre translations of our immense literature, if not on the unreliable anecdotes of passing travellers. It is rarely that the chivalrous pen of a Lafcadio Hearn or that of the author of *The Web of Indian Life* enlivens the Oriental darkness with the torch of our own sentiments.

Perhaps I betray my own ignorance of the Tea Cult by being so outspoken. Its very spirit of politeness exacts that you say what you are expected to say, and no more. But I am not to be a polite Teaist. So much harm has been done already by the mutual misunderstanding of the New World and the Old, that one need not apologise for contributing his tithe to the furtherance of a better understanding. The beginning of the twentieth century would have been spared the spectacle of sanguinary warfare if Russia had condescended to know Japan better. What dire consequences to humanity lie in the contemptuous ignoring of Eastern problems! European imperialism, which does not disdain to raise the absurd cry of the Yellow Peril, fails to realise that Asia may also awaken to the cruel sense of the White Disaster. You may laugh at us for having 'too much tea', but may we not suspect that you of the West have 'no tea' in your constitution?

Let us stop the continents from hurling epigrams at each other, and be sadder if not wiser by the mutual gain of half a hemisphere. We have developed along different lines, but there is no reason why one should not supplement the other. You have gained expansion at the cost of restlessness; we have created a harmony which is weak against aggression. Will you believe it?—the East is better off in some respects than the West!

Strangely enough humanity has so far met in the tea-cup. It is the only Asiatic ceremonial which commands universal esteem. The white man has scoffed at our religion and our morals, but he has accepted the brown beverage without hesitation. The afternoon tea is now an important function in Western society. In the delicate clatter of trays and saucers, in the soft rustle of feminine hospitality, in the common catechism about cream and sugar, we know that the Worship of Tea is established beyond question. The philosophic resignation of the guest to the fate awaiting him in the dubious decoction proclaims that in this single instance the Oriental spirit reigns supreme.

The earliest record of tea in European writing is said to be found in the statements of an Arabian traveller, that after the year 879 the main sources of revenue in Canton were the duties on salt and tea. Marco Polo records the deposition of a Chinese minister of finance in 1285 for his arbitrary augmentation of the tea-taxes. It was at the period of the great discoveries that the European people began to know more about the extreme Orient. At the end of the sixteenth century the Hollanders brought the news that a pleasant drink was made in the East from the leaves of a bush. The travellers Giovanni Batista Ramusio (1559), L. Almeida (1576), Maffeno (1588), Tareira (1610), also mentioned tea.* In the last-named year ships of the Dutch East India Company brought the first tea into Europe. It was known in France in 1636, and reached Russia in 1638.† England welcomed it in 1650 and spoke of it as 'That excellent and by all physicians approved China drink, called by the Chineans Tcha, and by other nations Tay, alias Tee.'

Like all the good things of the world, the propaganda of Tea met with opposition. Heretics like Henry Savile (1678) denounced drinking it as a filthy custom. Jonas Hanway (*Essays on Tea*, 1756) said that men seemed to lose their stature and comeliness, women their beauty through the use of tea. Its cost at the start (about fifteen or sixteen shillings a pound) forbade popular consumption, and made it 'regalia for high treatments and entertainments, presents being made thereof to princes and grandees.' Yet in spite of such drawbacks tea drinking spread with marvellous rapidity. The coffee-houses of London in the early half of the eighteenth century became, in fact, tea-houses, the resort of wits like Addison and Steele, who beguiled themselves over their 'dish of tea'. The beverage soon became a necessary of life—a taxable matter. We are reminded in this connection what an important part it plays in modern history. Colonial America resigned herself to oppression until human endurance gave way before the heavy duties laid on tea. American independence dates from the throwing of tea-chests into Boston harbour.

There is subtle charm in the taste of tea which makes it irresistible and capable of idealisation. Western humorists were not slow to

*Paul Kransel, *Dissertations*, Berlin, 1902.

†*Mercurius Politicus*, 1656.

mingle the fragrance of their thoughts with its aroma. It has not the arrogance of wine, the self-consciousness of coffee, nor the simpering innocence of cocoa. Already in 1711, says the *Spectator*: 'I would therefore in a particular manner recommend these my speculations to all well-regulated families that set apart an hour every morning for tea, bread and butter; and would earnestly advise them for their good to order this paper to be punctually served up and to be looked upon as a part of the tea-equipage.' Samuel Johnson draws his own portrait as 'a hardened and shameless tea-drinker, who for twenty years diluted his meals with only the infusion of the fascinating plant; who with tea amused the evening, with tea solaced the midnight, and with tea welcometh the morning'.

Charles Lamb, a professed devotee, sounded the true note of Teaism when he wrote that the greatest pleasure he knew was to do a good action by stealth, and to have it found out by accident. For Teaism is the art of concealing beauty that you may discover it, of suggesting what you dare not reveal. It is the noble secret of laughing at yourself, calmly yet thoroughly, and is thus humour itself—the smile of philosophy. All genuine humorists may in this sense be called tea-philosophers—Thackeray, for instance, and, of course, Shakespeare. The poets of Decadence (when was not the world in decadence?), in their protests against materialism, have, to a certain extent, also opened the way to Teaism. Perhaps nowadays it is in our demure contemplation of the Imperfect that the West and the East can meet in mutual consolation.

The Taoists relate that at the great beginning of the No-Beginning, Spirit and Matter met in mortal combat. At last the Yellow Emperor, the Sun of Heaven, triumphed over Shuhyung, the demon of darkness and earth. The Titan, in his death agony, struck his head against the solar vault and shivered the blue dome of Jade into fragments. The stars lost their nests, the moon wandered aimlessly among the wild charms of the night. In despair the Yellow Emperor sought far and wide for the repairer of the heavens. He had not to search in vain. Out of the Eastern sea rose a queen, the divine Niuka, horn-crowned and dragon-tailed, resplendent in her armour of fire. She welded the fire-coloured rainbow in her magic cauldron and rebuilt the Chinese sky. But it is also told that Niuka forgot to fill two tiny crevices in the blue firmament. Thus began the dualism of love—two souls rolling through space and never at rest until they join together to complete the universe. Everyone has to build anew his sky of hope and peace.

The heaven of modern humanity is indeed shattered in the Cyclopean struggle for wealth and power. The world is groping in the shadow of egotism and vulgarity. Knowledge is bought through a bad conscience, benevolence practised for the sake of utility. The East and West, like two dragons tossed in a sea of ferment, in vain strive to regain the jewel of life. We need a Niuka again to repair the grand devastation; we await the great Avatar. Meanwhile, let us have a sip of tea. The afternoon glow is brightening the bamboos, the fountains are bubbling with delight, the soughing of the pines is heard in our kettle. Let us dream of evanescence, and linger in the beautiful foolishness of things.

Brewing Beer

WILLIAM COBBETT

Before I proceed to give any directions about brewing, let me mention some of the inducements to do the thing. In former times, to set about to show to Englishmen that it was good for them to brew beer in their houses, would have been as impertinent as gravely to insist that they ought to endeavour not to lose their breath; for, in those times (only forty years ago), to have a house and not to brew was a rare thing indeed. Mr Ellman, an old man and a large farmer, in Sussex, has recently given in evidence, before a Committee of the House of Commons, this fact; that, forty years ago, there was not a labourer in his parish that did not brew his own beer; and that now there is not one that does it, except by chance the malt be given him. The causes of this change have been the lowering of the wages of labour, compared with the price of provisions, by the means of paper-money; the enormous tax upon the barley when made into malt; and the increased tax upon hops. These have quite changed the customs of the English people as to their drink. They still drink beer, but in general it is of the brewing of common brewers, and in public-houses, of which the common brewers have become the owners, and have thus, by the aid of paper-money, obtained a monopoly in the supplying of the great body of the people with one of those things which, to the hard-working man, is almost a necessary of life.

These things will be altered. They must be altered. The nation must be sunk into nothingness, or a new system must be adopted: and the nation will not sink into nothingness. The malt now pays a tax of 4s 6d a bushel, and the barley costs only 3s. This brings the bushel of malt to 8s including the maltster's charge for malting. If the tax were taken off the malt, malt would be sold, at the present price of barley, for about 3s 3d a bushel; because a bushel of barley makes more than a bushel of malt, and the tax, besides its amount, causes great expenses of various sorts to the maltster. The hops pay a tax of 2d a pound; and a bushel of malt requires, in general, a pound of hops; if these two taxes were taken off, therefore, the consumption of barley and of hops would be exceedingly increased; for double the present quantity would be demanded, and the land is always ready to send it forth.

It appears impossible that the landlords should much longer submit to these intolerable burdens on their estates. In short, they must get off the malt tax or lose those estates. They must do a great deal more, indeed; but that they must do at any rate. The paper-money is fast losing its destructive power; and things are, with regard to the labourers, coming back to what they were forty years ago, and therefore we may prepare for the making of beer in our own houses, and take leave of the poisonous stuff served out to us by common brewers. We may begin immediately; for, even at present prices, home-brewed beer is the cheapest drink that a family can use, except milk, and milk can be applicable only in certain cases.

The drink which has come to supply the place of beer has, in general, been tea. It is notorious that tea has no useful strength in it; that it contains nothing nutritious; that it, besides being good for nothing, has badness in it, because it is well known to produce want of sleep in many cases, and in all cases, to shake and weaken the nerves. It is, in fact, a weaker kind of laudanum, which enlivens for the moment and deadens afterwards. At any rate it communicates no strength to the body; it does not in any degree assist in affording what labour demands. It is, then, of no use. And now, as to its cost, compared with that of beer. I shall make my comparison applicable to a year, or three hundred and sixty-five days. I shall suppose the tea to be only five shillings the pound, the sugar only sevenpence, the milk only twopence a quart. The prices are at the very lowest. I shall suppose a tea-pot to cost a shilling, six cups and saucers two shillings and sixpence, and six pewter spoons eighteen-pence. How to esti-mate the firing I hardly know, but certainly there must be in the course of the year two hundred fires made that would not be made, were it not for tea drinking. Then comes the great article of all, the time employed in this tea-making affair. It is impossible to make a fire, boil water, make the tea, drink it, wash up the things, sweep up the fire-place, and put all to rights again in a less space of time, upon an average, than two hours. However, let us allow one hour; and here we have a woman occupied no less than three hundred and sixty-five hours in the year; or thirty whole days at twelve hours in the day; that is to say, one month out of the twelve in the year, besides the waste of the man's time in hanging about waiting for the tea! Needs there any-thing more to make us cease to wonder at seeing labourers' children with dirty linen and holes in the heels of their stockings? Observe, too, that the time thus spent is, one half of it, the best time of the day. It is the top of the morning, which, in every calling of life, contains an hour worth two or three hours of the afternoon. By the time that the clattering tea-tackle is out of the way, the morning is spoiled, its prime is gone, and any work that is to be done afterwards lags heavily along. If the mother have to go out to work, the tea affair must all first be over. She comes into the field, in summer time, when the sun has gone a third part of his course. She has the heat of the day to encounter, instead of having her work done and being ready to return home at an early hour. Yet early she must go too; for there is the fire again to be made, the clattering tea-tackle again to come forward; and even in the longest day she must have candle light, which never ought to be seen in a cottage (except in case of illness) from March to September.

Now, then, let us take the bare cost of the use of tea. I suppose a pound of tea to last twenty days, which is not nearly half an ounce every morning and evening. I allow for each mess half a pint of milk. And I allow three pounds of the red dirty sugar to each pound of tea. The account of expenditure would then stand very high; but to these must be added the amount of the tea-tackle, one set of which will, upon an average, be demolished every year. To these outgoings must be added the cost of beer at the public-house; for some the man will have, after all, and the woman too, unless they be upon the point of actual starvation. Two pots a week is as little as will serve in this way; and here is a dead loss of ninepence a week, seeing that two pots of beer, full as strong, and a great deal better, can be brewed at home for threepence. The account of the year's tea drinking will then stand thus:

	£	s	d
18lb of tea	4	10	0
54lb of sugar	1	11	6
365 pints of milk	1	10	0
Tea-tackle	0	5	0
200 fires	0	16	8
30 days' work	0	15	0
Loss by going to public-house . .	1	19	0
	£11	7	2

I have here estimated everything at its very lowest. The entertain-ment which I have here provided is as poor, as mean, as miserable, as anything short of starvation can set forth; and yet the wretched thing amounts to a good third part of a good and able labourers' wages! For this money he and his family may drink good and wholesome beer; in a short time, out of the mere savings from this waste, may drink it out of silver cups and tankards. In a labourer's family, wholesome beer, that has a little life in it, is all that is wanted in general. Little children, that do not work, should not have beer. Broth, porridge, or something in that way, is the thing for them. However, I shall suppose, in order to make my comparison as little complicated as possible, that he brews nothing but beer as strong as the generality of beer to be had at the public-house, and divested of the poisonous drugs which that beer but too often contains; and I shall further suppose that he uses in his family two quarts of this beer every day from the first of October to the last day of March inclusive; three quarts a day during the months of June and September; and five quarts a day during the months of July and August; and if this be not enough, it must be a family of drunkards. Here are 1,097 quarts, or 274 gallons. Now, a bushel of malt will make eighteen gallons of better beer than that which is sold at the public-houses. And this is precisely a gallon for the price of a quart. People should bear in mind, that the beer bought at the public-house is loaded with a beer tax, with the tax on the public-house keeper, in the shape of licence, with all the taxes and expenses of the brewer, and with all taxes, rent, and other expenses of the publican, and with all the profits of both brewer and publican; so that when a man swallows a pot of beer at a public-house, he has all these expenses to help to defray, besides the mere tax on the malt and on the hops.

Well, then, to brew this ample supply of good beer for a labourer's family, these 274 gallons, requires fifteen bushels of malt and (for let us do the thing well) fifteen pounds of hops. The malt is now eight shillings a bushel, and very good hops may be bought for less than a shilling a pound. The grains and yeast will amply pay for the labour and fuel employed in the brewing; seeing that there will be pigs to eat the grains, and bread to be baked with the yeast. The account will then stand thus:

	£	s	d
15 bushels of malt	6	0	0
15 pounds of hops	0	15	0
Wear of utensils	0	10	0
	£7	5	0

Here, then, is the sum of four pounds two shillings and twopence saved every year. The utensils for brewing are, a brass kettle, a mashing tub, coolers (for which washing tubs may serve), a half hogs-head, with one end taken out, for a tun tub, about four nine-gallon casks, and a couple of eighteen-gallon casks. This is an ample supply of utensils, each of which will last, with proper care, a good long lifetime or two, and the whole of which, even if purchased new from the shop, will only exceed by a few shillings, if they exceed at all, the amount of the saving, arising *the very first year*, from quitting the troublesome and pernicious practice of drinking tea. The saving of each succeeding year would, if you chose it, purchase a silver mug to hold half a pint at least. However, the saving would naturally be applied to purposes more conducive to the well-being and happiness of a family.

It is not, however, the mere saving to which I look. This is, indeed, a matter of great importance, whether we look at the amount itself, or at the ultimate consequences of a judicious application of it; for four pounds make a great hole in a man's wages for the year; and when we consider all the advantages that would arise to a family of children from having these four pounds, now so miserably wasted, laid out upon their backs, in the shape of a decent dress, it is impossible to look at this waste without feelings of sorrow, not wholly unmixed with those of a harsher description.

But I look upon the thing in a still more serious light. I view the tea drinking as a destroyer of health, an enfeebler of the frame, an engenderer of effeminacy and laziness, a debaucher of youth and a maker of misery for old age. In the fifteen bushels of malt there are 570 pounds weight of sweet; that is to say, of nutritious matter, unmixed with anything injurious to health. In the 730 tea messes of the year there are 54 pounds of sweet in the sugar, and about 30 pounds of matter equal to sugar in the milk. Here are eighty-four pounds instead of five hundred and seventy, and even the good effect of these eighty-four pounds is more than over-balanced by the corrosive, gnawing, and poisonous powers of the tea.

It is impossible for anyone to deny the truth of this statement. Put it to the test with a lean hog: give him the fifteen bushels of malt, and he will repay you in ten score of bacon or thereabouts. But give him the 730 tea messes, or rather begin to give them to him, and give him nothing else, and he is dead with hunger, and bequeaths you his skeleton, at the end of about seven days. It is impossible to doubt in such a case. The tea drinking has done a great deal in bringing this nation into the state of misery in which it now is; and the tea drinking, which is carried on by 'dribs' and 'drabs', by pence and farthings going out at a time; this miserable practice has been gradually introduced by the growing weight of the taxes on malt and on hops, and by the everlasting penury amongst the labourers, occasioned by the paper-money.

We see better prospects, however, and therefore let us now rouse ourselves, and shake from us the degrading curse, the effects of which have been much more extensive and infinitely more mischievous than men in general seem to imagine.

It must be evident to everyone, that the practice of tea drinking must render the frame feeble and unfit to encounter hard labour or severe weather, while, as I have shown, it deducts from the means of replenishing the belly and covering the back. Hence succeeds a softness, an effeminacy, a seeking for the fire-side, a lurking in the bed, and, in short, all the characteristics of idleness, for which, in this case, real want of strength furnishes an apology. The tea drinking fills the public-house, makes the frequenting of it habitual, corrupts boys as soon as they are able to move from home, and does little less for the girls, to whom the gossip of the tea-table is no bad preparatory school for the brothel. At the very least, it teaches them idleness. The everlasting dawdling about with the slops of the tea-tackle gives them a relish for nothing that requires strength and activity. When they go from home, they know how to do nothing that is useful. To brew, to bake, to make butter, to milk, to rear poultry; to do any earthly thing of use they are wholly unqualified. To shut poor young creatures up in manufactories is bad enough: but there, at any rate, they do something that is useful; whereas the girl that has been brought up merely to boil the tea-kettle, and to assist in the gossip inseparable from the practice, is a mere consumer of food, a pest to her employer, and a curse to her husband, if any man be so unfortunate as to fix his affections upon her.

But is it in the power of any man, any good labourer who has attained the age of fifty, to look back upon the last thirty years of his life, without cursing the day in which tea was introduced into England? Where is there such a man, who cannot trace to this cause a very considerable part of all the mortifications and sufferings of his life? When was he ever too late at his labour; when did he ever meet with a frown, with a turning off, and pauperism on that account, without being able to trace it to the tea-kettle? When reproached with lagging in the morning, the poor wretch tells you that he will make up for it by working during his breakfast time! I have heard this a hundred and a hundred times over. He was up time enough; but the tea-kettle kept him lolling and lounging at home; and now instead of sitting down to a breakfast upon bread, bacon, and beer, which is to carry him on to the hour of dinner, he has to force his limbs along under the sweat of feebleness, and at dinner-time to swallow his dry bread, or slake his half-feverish thirst at the pump or the brook. To the wretched tea-kettle he has to return at night, with legs hardly sufficient to maintain him: and thus he makes his miserable progress towards that death which he finds ten or fifteen years sooner than he would have found it had he made his wife brew beer instead of making tea. If he now and then gladdens his heart with the drugs of the public-house, some quarrel, some accident, some illness, is the probable consequence; to the affray abroad succeeds an affray at home; the mischievous example reaches the children, corrupts them or scatters them, and misery for life is the consequence.

On Lying in Bed

G. K. CHESTERTON

Lying in bed would be an altogether perfect and supreme experience
if only one had a coloured pencil long enough to draw on the ceiling.
This, however, is not generally a part of the domestic apparatus on
the premises. I think myself that the thing might be managed with
several pails of Aspinall and a broom. Only if one worked in a really
sweeping and masterly way, and laid on the colour in great washes, it
might drip down again on one's face in floods of rich and mingled
colour like some strange fairy rain; and that would have its disadvan-
tages. I am afraid it would be necessary to stick to black and white in
this form of artistic composition. To that purpose, indeed, the white
ceiling would be of the greatest possible use; in fact, it is the only use I
think of a white ceiling being put to.

But for the beautiful experiment of lying in bed I might never have
discovered it. For years I have been looking for some blank spaces in a
modern house to draw on. Paper is much too small for any really
allegorical design; as Cyrano de Bergerac says, '*Il me faut des géants.*'
But when I tried to find these fine clear spaces in the modern rooms
such as we all live in I was continually disappointed. I found an
endless pattern and complication of small objects hung like a curtain
of fine links between me and my desire. I examined the walls; I found
them to my surprise to be already covered with wallpaper, and I
found the wallpaper to be already covered with very uninteresting
images, all bearing a ridiculous resemblance to each other. I could not
understand why one arbitrary symbol (a symbol apparently entirely
devoid of any religious or philosophical significance) should thus be
sprinkled all over my nice walls like a sort of smallpox. The Bible
must be referring to wallpapers, I think, when it says, 'Use not vain
repetitions, as the Gentiles do.' I found the Turkey carpet a mass of
unmeaning colours, rather like the Turkish empire, or like the sweet-
meat called Turkish Delight. I do not know exactly what Turkish
Delight really is; but I suppose it is Macedonian massacres. Everywhere that I went forlornly, with my pencil or my paint brush, I
found that others had unaccountably been before me, spoiling the

walls, the curtains and the furniture with their childish and barbaric designs.

Nowhere did I find a really clear space for sketching until this occasion when I prolonged beyond the proper limit the process of lying on my back in bed. Then the light of that white heaven broke upon my vision, that breadth of mere white which is indeed almost the definition of Paradise, since it means purity and also means freedom. But alas! like all heavens, now that it is seen it is found to be unattainable; it looks more austere and more distant than the blue sky outside the window. For my proposal to paint on it with the bristly end of a broom has been discouraged—never mind by whom; by a person debarred from all political rights—and even my minor proposal to put the other end of the broom into the kitchen fire and turn it into charcoal has not been conceded. Yet I am certain that it was from persons in my position that all the original inspiration came for covering the ceilings of palaces and cathedrals with a riot of fallen angels or victorious gods. I am sure that it was only because Michelangelo was engaged in the ancient and honourable occupation of lying in bed that he ever realised how the roof of the Sistine Chapel might be made into an awful imitation of a divine drama that could only be acted in the heavens.

The tone now commonly taken towards the practice of lying in bed is hypocritical and unhealthy. Of all the marks of modernity that seem to mean a kind of decadence, there is none more menacing and dangerous than the exaltation of very small and secondary matters of conduct at the expense of very great and primary ones, at the expense of eternal ties and tragic human morality. If there is one thing worse than the modern weakening of major morals it is the modern strengthening of minor morals. Thus it is considered more withering to accuse a man of bad taste than of bad ethics. Cleanliness is not next to godliness nowadays, for cleanliness is made an essential and godliness is regarded as an offence. A playwright can attack the institution of marriage so long as he does not misrepresent the manners of society, and I have met Ibsenite pessimists who thought it wrong to take beer but right to take prussic acid. Especially this is so in matters of hygiene; notably such matters as lying in bed. Instead of being regarded, as it ought to be, as a matter of personal convenience and adjustment, it has come to be regarded by many as if it were a part of essential morals to get up early in the morning. It is upon the whole part of practical wisdom; but there is nothing good about it or bad about its opposite.

Misers get up early in the morning; and burglars, I am informed, get up the night before. It is the great peril of our society that all its mechanism may grow more fixed while its spirit grows more fickle. A man's minor actions and arrangements ought to be free, flexible, creative; the things that should be unchangeable are his principles, his ideals. But with us the reverse is true; our views change constantly; but our lunch does not change. Now, I should like men to have strong and rooted conceptions, but as for their lunch, let them have it sometimes in the garden, sometimes in bed, sometimes on the roof, sometimes in the top of a tree. Let them argue from the same first principles, but let them do it in a bed, or a boat, or a balloon. This alarming growth of good habits really means a too great emphasis on those virtues which mere custom can ensure, it means too little emphasis on those virtues which custom can never quite ensure, sudden and splendid virtues of inspired pity or of inspired candour. If ever that abrupt appeal is made to us we may fail. A man can get used to getting up at five o'clock in the morning. A man cannot very well get used to being burnt for his opinions; the first experiment is commonly fatal. Let us pay a little more attention to these possibilities of the heroic and the unexpected. I dare say that when I get out of this bed I shall do some deed of an almost terrible virtue.

For those who study the great art of lying in bed there is one emphatic caution to be added. Even for those who can do their work in bed (like journalists), still more for those whose work cannot be done in bed (as, for example, the professional harpooners of whales), it is obvious that the indulgence must be very occasional. But that is not the caution I mean. The caution is this: if you do lie in bed, be sure you do it without any reason or justification at all. I do not speak, of course, of the seriously sick. But if a healthy man lies in bed, let him do it without a rag of excuse; then he will get up a healthy man. If he does it for some secondary hygienic reason, if he has some scientific explanation, he may get up a hypochondriac.

A Few Thoughts on Sleep

LEIGH HUNT

This is an article for the reader to think of when he or she is warm in a bed, a little before he goes to sleep, the clothes at his ear, and the wind moaning in some distant crevice.

'Blessings', exclaimed Sancho, 'on him that first invented sleep! It wraps a man all round like a cloak.' It is a delicious moment certainly—that of being well nestled in bed, and feeling that you shall drop gently to sleep. The good is to come, not past: the limbs have been just tired enough to render the remaining in one posture delightful: the labour of the day is done. A gentle failure of the perceptions comes creeping over one: the spirit of consciousness disengages itself more and more, with slow and hushing degrees, like a mother detaching her hand from that of her sleeping child—the mind seems to have a balmy lid closing over it, like the eye—'tis closing—'tis more closing—'tis closed. The mysterious spirit has gone to take its airy rounds.

It is said that sleep is best before midnight: and Nature herself, with her darkness and chilling dews, informs us so. There is another reason for going to bed betimes; for it is universally acknowledged that lying late in the morning is a great shortener of life. At least, it is never found in company with longevity. It also tends to make people corpulent. But these matters belong rather to the subject of early rising than of sleep.

Sleep at a late hour in the morning is not half so pleasant as the more timely one. It is sometimes, however, excusable, especially to a watchful or overworked head; neither can we deny the seducing merits of 't'other doze'—the pleasing wilfulness of nestling in a new posture, when you know you ought to be up, like the rest of the house. But then you cut up the day, and your sleep the next night.

In the course of the day few people think of sleeping, except after dinner; and then it is often rather a hovering and nodding on the borders of sleep than sleep itself. This is a privilege allowable, we think, to none but the old, or the sickly, or the very tired and careworn; and it should be well understood before it is exercised in company. To escape into slumber from an argument; or to take it as an affair of course, only between you and your biliary duct; or to assent with involuntary nods to all that you have just been disputing, is not so well; much less, to sit nodding and tottering beside a lady; or to be in danger of dropping your head into the fruit-plate or your host's face; or of waking up, and saying 'Just so' to the bark of a dog; or 'Yes, madam,' to the black at your elbow.

Careworn people, however, might refresh themselves oftener with day-sleep than they do; if their bodily state is such as to dispose them to it. It is a mistake to suppose that all care is wakeful. People sometimes sleep, as well as wake, by reason of their sorrow. The difference seems to depend upon the nature of their temperament; though in the *most* excessive cases, sleep is perhaps Nature's never-failing relief, as swooning is upon the rack. A person with jaundice in his blood shall lie down and go to sleep at noonday, when another of a different complexion shall find his eyes as uncloseable as a statue's, though he has had no sleep for nights together. Without meaning to lessen the dignity of suffering, which has quite enough to do with its waking hours, it is this that may often account for the profound sleeps enjoyed the night before hazardous battles, executions, and other demands upon an over-excited spirit.

The most complete and healthy sleep that can be taken in the day is in the summertime, out in a field. There is, perhaps, no solitary sensation so exquisite as that of slumbering on the grass or hay, shaded from the hot sun by a tree, with the consciousness of a fresh but light air running through the wide atmosphere and the sky stretching far overhead upon all sides. Earth, and heaven, and a placid humanity seem to have the creation to themselves. There is nothing between the slumberer and the naked and glad innocence of nature.

Next to this, but at a long interval, the most relishing snatch of slumber out of bed is the one which a tired person takes before he retires for the night, while lingering in his sitting-room. The conciousness of being very sleepy, and of having the power to go to bed immediately, gives great zest to the unwillingness to move. Sometimes he sits nodding in his chair; but the sudden and leaden jerks of the head to which a state of great sleepiness renders him liable, are generally too painful for so luxurious a moment; and he gets into a more legitimate posture, sitting sideways with his head on the chair-back, or throwing his legs up at once on another chair, and half reclining. It is curious, however, to find how long an inconvenient posture will be borne for the sake of this foretaste of repose. The worst of it is, that on going to bed the charm sometimes vanishes; perhaps from the colder temperature of the chamber; for a fireside is a great opiate.

Speaking of the painful positions into which a sleepy lounger will get himself, it is amusing to think of the more fantastic attitudes that so often take place in bed. If we could add anything to the numberless things that have been said about sleep by the poets, it would be upon this point. Sleep ever shows himself a greater leveller. A man in his waking moments may look as proud and self-possessed as he pleases. He may walk proudly, he may sit proudly, he may eat his dinner proudly; he may shave himself with an air of infinite superiority; in a word, he may show himself grand and absurd upon the most trifling occasions. But Sleep plays the petrifying magician. He arrests the proudest lord as well as the humblest clown in the most ridiculous postures: so that if you draw a grandee from his bed without waking him, no limb-twisting fool in a pantomime should create wilder laughter. The toy with the string between its legs is hardly a posture-master more extravagant. Imagine a despot lifted up to the gaze of his valets, with his eyes shut, his mouth open, his left hand under his right ear, his other twisted and hanging helplessly before him like an idiot's, one knee lifted up, the other leg stretched out, or both knees huddled up together—what a scarecrow to lodge majestic power in!

But Sleep is kindly even in his tricks; and the poets have treated him with proper reverence. According to the ancient mythologists he had even one of the Graces to wife. He had a thousand sons, of whom the chief were Morpheus, or the Shaper; Icelos, or the Likely; Phantasus, the Fancy; and Phobetor, the Terror. His dwelling some writers place in a dull and darkling part of the earth; others, with greater compliment, in heaven; and others, with another kind of propriety, by the sea-shore. There is a good description of it in Ovid; but in these abstracted tasks of poetry the moderns outvie the ancients; and there is nobody who has built his bower for him so finely as Spenser. Archimago, in the first book of the *Faerie Queene* (Canto I, st. 39), sends a little spirit down to Morpheus to fetch him a Dream:

> *He, making speedy way through spersed ayre,*
> *And through the world of waters, wide and deepe,*
> *To Morpheus' house doth hastily repaire.*
> *Amid the bowels of the earth full steepe*
> *And low, where dawning day doth never peepe,*
> *His dwelling is. There, Tethys his wet bed*
> *Doth ever wash; and Cynthia still doth steepe*
> *In silver dew his ever-drouping head,*
> *Whiles sad Night over him her mantle black doth spred.*

> *And more to lull him in his slumber soft*
> *A trickling streame from high rocke tumbling downe,*

Mixed with a murmuring winde, much like the soune
Of swarming bees, did cast him in a swoune.
No other noise, nor people's troublous cryes,
As still are wont to annoy the wallèd towne,
Might there be heard; but careless Quiet lyes,
Wrapt in eternall silence, far from enimyes.

Chaucer has drawn the cave of the same god with greater simplicity; but nothing can have a more deep and sullen effect than his cliffs and cold running waters. It seems as real as an actual solitude, or some quaint old picture in a book of travels in Tartary. He is telling the story of Ceyx and Alcyone in the poem called his Dream. Juno tells a messenger to go to Morpheus and 'bid him creep into the body' of the drowned king, to let his wife know the fatal event by his apparition.

This messenger tooke leave, and went
Upon his way; and never he stent
Till he came to the dark valley,
That stant betweene rockes twey.
There never yet grew corne, ne gras.
Ne tree, ne naught that aught was.
Beast, ne man, ne naught else;
Save that there were a few wells
Came running fro the cliffs adowne,
That made a deadly sleeping soune,
And runnen downe right by a cave,
That was under a rocky grave,
Amid the valley, wonder-deepe.
There these goddis lay asleepe,
Morpheus and Eclympasteire,
That was the god of Sleepis heire,
That slept and did none other worke.

Where the credentials of this new son and heir, Eclympasteire, are to be found, we know not; but he acts very much, it must be allowed, like an heir-presumptive, in sleeping and doing 'none other work'.

We dare not trust ourselves with many quotations upon sleep from the poets; they are so numerous as well as beautiful. We must content ourselves with mentioning that our two most favourite passages are one in the *Philoctetes* of Sophocles, admirable for its contrast to a scene of terrible agony, which it closes; and the other the following address in Beaumont and Fletcher's tragedy of *Valentinian*, the hero of which is also a sufferer under bodily torment. He is in a chair, slumbering; and these most exquisite lines are gently sung with music:

Care-charming Sleep, thou easer of all woes,
Brother to Death, sweetly thyself dispose
On this afflicted prince. Fall like a cloud
In gentle showers: give nothing that is loud
Or painful to his slumbers: easy, sweet,
And as a purling stream, thou son of Night,
Pass by his troubled sense; sing his pain
Like hollow murmuring wind, or silver rain:
Into this prince, gently, oh gently slide,
And kiss him into slumbers, like a bride.

How earnest and prayer-like are these pauses! How lightly sprinkled, and yet how deeply settling, like rain, the fancy! How quiet, affectionate, and perfect the conclusion!

Sleep is most graceful in an infant; soundest, in one who has been tired in the open air; completest, to the seaman after a hard voyage; most welcome, to the mind haunted with one idea; most touching to look at, in the parent that has wept; lightest, in the playful child; proudest, in the bride adored.

PART FOUR

On the Pleasures of the Mind

SEVERAL of the ten writers in this section, Swift, Fielding, Huxley, Russell, have had a lasting intellectual and philosophical influence on the civilisation of the West. Some, Thackeray, Thurber, Jefferies, have at least carved unique niches in the literary consciousness of their own countries. Their activity—bringing the mind to bear on the mind—represents the very cornerstone of civilisation, the quintessence of intelligence.

Ever since Bacon, who by his own admission followed the Platonic and Socratic themes, Essayists have considered the mind, in terms of subject matter, in two ways—as a serious cerebral terrain to be mapped, and secondarily as a means of providing intellectual refreshment. When the mind and its produce is being considered seriously, the lighter vein, the diversion, balances it and makes sweet the use of the Essay. And when the two strands are taken and interwoven they provide a pleasing alternation, like current, in the mind's working.

Thus, Swift may despair of ever getting beyond the ideas stage with things so perfect as 'a true friend, a good marriage, a perfect form of government', but he understands the pleasure in contemplating them. For Richard Jefferies one pleasure of the mind derives from another—he can never read out of doors in summer; 'The eye wanders away, and rests lovingly on greensward and green lime leaves. The mind wanders yet deeper and farther in the dreamy mystery of the azure sky.'

Then, when the Essay uses the mind to map the future, powerful suggestions may arise which both employ and divert, above and below the surface of the text. Bertrand Russell clearly anticipated the eventual sophistication of a machine in whose construction man had so outreached himself that not quite knowing what he had done he could not undo it. Therefore a pleasure of the mind may be defined for the purposes of this anthology as something which entertains as it stimulates, that absorbs as it enquires—and all simultaneously.

The Reach of Imagination

JACOB BRONOWSKI

For three thousand years, poets have been enchanted and moved and perplexed by the power of their own imagination. In a short and summary essay I can hope at most to lift one small corner of that mystery; and yet it is a critical corner. I shall ask, What goes on in the mind when we imagine? You will hear from me that one answer to this question is fairly specific: which is to say, that we can describe the working of the imagination. And when we describe it as I shall do, it becomes plain that imagination is a specifically *human* gift. To imagine is the characteristic act, not of the poet's mind, or the painter's, or the scientist's, but of the mind of man.

My stress here on the word *human* implies that there is a clear difference in this between the actions of men and those of other animals. Let me then start with a classical experiment with animals and children which Walter Hunter thought out in Chicago about 1910. That was the time when scientists were agog with the success of Ivan Pavlov in forming and changing the reflex actions of dogs, which Pavlov had first announced in 1903. Pavlov had been given a Nobel prize the next year, in 1904; although in fairness I should say that the award did not cite his work on the conditioned reflex, but on the digestive glands.

Hunter duly trained some dogs and other animals on Pavlov's lines. They were taught that when a light came on over one of three tunnels out of their cage, that tunnel would be open; they could escape down it, and were rewarded with food if they did. But once he had fixed that conditioned reflex, Hunter added to it a deeper idea: he gave the mechanical experiment a new dimension, literally—the dimension of time. Now he no longer let the dog go to the lighted tunnel at once; instead, he put out the light, and then kept the dog waiting a little while before he let him go. In this way Hunter timed how long an animal can remember where he has last seen the signal light to his escape route.

The results were and are staggering. A dog or a rat forgets which one of the three tunnels has been lit up within a matter of seconds—in Hunter's experiment, ten seconds at most. If you want such an animal to do much better than this, you must make the task much simpler: you must face him with only two tunnels to choose from. Even so, the best that Hunter could do was to have a dog remember for five minutes which one of two tunnels had been lit up.

I am not quoting these times as if they were exact and universal: they surely are not. Hunter's experiment, more than fifty years old now, had many faults of detail. For example, there were too few animals, they were oddly picked, and they did not all behave consistently. It may be unfair to test a dog for what he *saw*, when he commonly follows his nose rather than his eyes. It may be unfair to test any animal in the unnatural setting of a laboratory cage. And there are higher animals, such as chimpanzees and other primates, which certainly have longer memories than the animals that Hunter tried.

Yet when all these provisos have been made (and met, by more modern experiments) the facts are still startling and characteristic. An animal cannot recall a signal from the past for even a short fraction of the time that a man can—for even a short fraction of the time that a child can. Hunter made comparable tests with six-year-old children, and found, of course, that they were incomparably better than the best of his animals. There is a striking and basic difference between a man's ability to imagine something that he saw or experienced, and an animal's failure.

Animals make up for this by other and extraordinary gifts. The salmon and the carrier pigeon can find their way home as we cannot: they have, as it were, a practical memory that man cannot match. But their actions always depend on some form of habit: on instinct or on learning, which reproduce by rote a train of known responses. They do not depend, as human memory does, on calling to mind the recollection of absent things.

Where is it that the animal falls short? We get a clue to the answer, I think, when Hunter tells us how the animals in his experiment tried to fix their recollection. They most often pointed themselves at the light before it went out, as some gun dogs point rigidly at the game they scent—and get the name *pointer* from the posture. The animal makes ready to act by building the signal into its action. There is a primitive imagery in its stance, it seems to me; it is as if the animal were trying to fix the light in its mind by fixing it in its body. And indeed, how else can a dog mark and (as it were) name one of three tunnels, when he has no such words as *left* and *right*, and no such numbers as *one, two, three*? The directed gesture of attention and readiness is perhaps the only symbolic device that the dog commands to hold on to the past, and thereby to guide himself into the future.

I used the verb *to imagine* a moment ago, and now I have some ground for giving it a meaning. *To imagine* means to make images and to move them about inside one's head in new arrangements. When you and I recall the past, we imagine it in this direct and homely sense. The tool that puts the human mind ahead of the animal is imagery. For us, memory does not demand the preoccupation that it demands in animals, and it lasts immensely longer, because we fix it in images or other substitute symbols. With the same symbolic vocabulary we spell out the future—not one but many futures, which we weigh one against another.

I am using the word *image* in a wide meaning, which does not restrict it to the mind's eye as a visual organ. An image in my usage is what Charles Pierce called a *sign*, without regard for its sensory quality. Pierce distinguished between different forms of signs, but there is no reason to make his distinction here, for the imagination works equally with them all, and that is why I call them all images.

Indeed, the most important images for human beings are simply words, which are abstract symbols. Animals do not have words, in our sense: there is no specific centre for language in the brain of any animal, as there is in the human brain. In this respect at least we know that the human imagination depends on a configuration in the brain that has only evolved in the last one or two million years. In the same period, evolution has greatly enlarged the front lobes in the human brain, which govern the sense of the past and the future; and it is a fair guess that they are probably the seat of our other images. (Part of the evidence for this guess is that damage to the front lobes in primates reduces them to the state of Hunter's animals.) If the guess turns out to be right, we shall know why man has come to look like a highbrow or an egg-head: because otherwise there would not be room in his head for his imagination.

The images play out for us events which are not present to our senses, and thereby guard the past and create the future—a future that does not yet exist, and may never come to exist in that form. By contrast, the lack of symbolic ideas, or their rudimentary poverty, cuts off an animal from the past and the future alike, and imprisons him in the present. Of all the distinctions between man and animal, the characteristic gift which makes us human is the power to work with symbolic images: the gift of imagination.

This is really a remarkable finding. When Philip Sidney in 1580 defended poets (and all unconventional thinkers) from the Puritan charge that they were liars, he said that a maker must imagine things that are not. Halfway between Sidney and us, William Blake said, 'What is now proved was once only imagin'd.' About the same time, in 1796, Samuel Taylor Coleridge for the first time distinguished between the passive fancy and the active imagination, 'the living Power and prime Agent of all human Perception'. Now we see that they were right, and precisely right: the human gift is the gift of imagination—and that is not just a literary phrase.

Nor is it just a literary gift; it is, I repeat, characteristically human. Almost everything that we do that is worth doing is done in the first place in the mind's eye. The richness of human life is that we have many lives; we live the events that do not happen (and some that cannot) as vividly as those that do; and if thereby we die a thousand deaths, that is the price we pay for living a thousand lives. (A cat, of course, has only nine.) Literature is alive to us because we live its images, but so is any play of the mind—so is chess: the lines of play that we foresee and try in our heads and dismiss are as much a part of the game as the moves that we make. John Keats said that the unheard melodies are sweeter, and all chess players sadly recall that the combinations that they planned and which never came to be played were the best.

I make this point to remind you, insistently, that imagination is the manipulation of images in one's head; and that the rational manipulation belongs to that, as well as the literary and artistic manipulation. When a child begins to play games with things that stand for other things, with chairs or chessmen, he enters the gateway to reason and imagination together. For the human reason discovers new relations between things not by deduction, but by that unpredictable blend of speculation and insight that scientists call induction, which—like other forms of imagination—cannot be formalised. We see it at work when Walter Hunter inquires into a child's memory, as much as when Blake and Coleridge do. Only a restless and original mind would have asked Hunter's questions and could have conceived his experiments, in a science that was dominated by Pavlov's reflex arcs and was heading towards the behaviorism of John Watson.

Let me find a spectacular example for you from history. What is the most famous experiment that you had described to you as a child? I will hazard that it is the experiment that Galileo is said to have made in Sidney's age, in Pisa about 1590, by dropping two unequal balls from the Leaning Tower. There, we say, is a man in the modern mold, a man after our own hearts; he insisted on questioning the authority of Aristotle and St Thomas Aquinas, and seeing with his own eyes whether (as they said) the heavy ball would reach the ground before the light one. Seeing is believing.

Yet seeing is also imagining. Galileo did challenge the authority of Aristotle, and he did look hard at his mechanics. But the eye that

Galileo used was the mind's eye. He did not drop balls from the Leaning Tower of Pisa—and if he had, he would have got a very doubtful answer. Instead, Galileo made an imaginary experiment in his head, which I will describe as he did years later in the book he wrote after the Holy Office silenced him: the *Discorsi . . . intorno à due nuove scienze*, which was smuggled out to be printed in the Netherlands in 1638.

Suppose, said Galileo, that you drop two unequal balls from the tower at the same time. And suppose that Aristotle is right—suppose that the heavy ball falls faster, so that it steadily gains on the light ball, and hits the ground first. Very well. Now imagine the same experiment done again, with only one difference: this time the two unequal balls are joined by a string between them. The heavy ball will again move ahead, but now the light ball holds it back and acts as a drag or brake. So the light ball will be speeded up and the heavy ball will be slowed down; they must reach the ground together because they are tied together, but they cannot reach the ground as quickly as the heavy ball alone. Yet the string between them has turned the two balls into a single mass which is heavier than either ball—and surely (according to Aristotle) this mass should therefore move faster than either ball? Galileo's imaginary experiment has uncovered a contradiction; he says trenchantly:

You see how, from your assumption that a heavier body falls more rapidly than a lighter one, I infer that a (still) heavier body falls more slowly.

There is only one way out of the contradiction: the heavy ball and the light ball must fall at the same rate, so that they go on falling at the same rate when they are tied together.

This argument is not conclusive, for nature might be more subtle (when the two balls are joined) than Galileo has allowed. And yet it is something more important: it is suggestive, it is stimulating, it opens a new view—in a word, it is imaginative. It cannot be settled without an actual experiment, because nothing that we imagine can become knowledge until we have translated it into, and backed it by, real experience. The test of imagination is experience. But then, that is as true of literature and the arts as it is of science. In science, the imaginary experiment is tested by confronting it with physical experience; and in literature, the imaginative conception is tested by confronting it with human experience. The superficial speculation in science is dismissed because it is found to falsify nature: and the shallow work of art is discarded because it is found to be untrue to our own nature. So when Ella Wheeler Wilcox died in 1919, more people were reading her verses than Shakespeare's; yet in a few years her work was dead. It had been buried by its poverty of emotion and its trivialness of thought: which is to say that it had been proved to be as false to the nature of man as, say, Jean Baptiste Lamarck and Trofim Lysenko were false to the nature of inheritance. The strength of the imagination, its enriching power and excitement, lies in its interplay with reality—physical and emotional.

I doubt if there is much to choose here between science and the arts: the imagination is not much more free, and not much less free, in one than in the other. All great scientists have used their imagination freely, and let it ride them to outrageous conclusions without crying 'Halt!' Albert Einstein fiddled with imaginary experiments from boyhood, and was wonderfully ignorant of the facts that they were supposed to bear on. When he wrote the first of his beautiful papers on the random movement of atoms, he did not know that the Brownian motion which it predicted could be seen in any laboratory. He was sixteen when he invented the paradox that he resolved ten years later, in 1905, in the theory of relativity, and it bulked much larger in his mind than the experiment of Albert Michelson and Edward Morley which had upset every other physicist since 1881. All his life Einstein loved to make up teasing puzzles like Galileo's, about falling lifts and the detection of gravity; and they carry the nub of the problems of general relativity on which he was working.

Indeed, it could not be otherwise. The power that man has over nature and himself, and that a dog lacks, lies in his command of imaginary experience. He alone has the symbols which fix the past and play with the future, possible and impossible. In the Renaissance, the symbolism of memory was thought to be mystical, and devices that were invented as mnemonics (by Giordano Bruno, for example, and by Robert Fludd) were interpreted as magic signs. The symbol is the tool which gives man his power, and it is the same tool whether the symbols are images or words, mathematical signs or mesons. And the symbols have a reach and a roundness that goes beyond their literal and practical meaning. They are the rich concepts under which the mind gathers many particulars into one name, and many instances into one general induction. When a man says *left* and *right*, he is out-distancing the dog not only in looking for a light; he is setting in train all the shifts of meaning, the overtones and the ambiguities, between *gauche* and *adroit* and *dexterous*, between *sinister* and the sense of right. When a man counts *one*, *two*, *three*, he is not only doing mathematics; he is on the path to the mysticism of numbers in Pythagoras and Vitruvius and Kepler, to the Trinity and the signs of the Zodiac.

I have described imagination as the ability to make images and to move them about inside one's head in new arrangements. This is the faculty that is specifically human, and it is the common root from which science and literature both spring and grow and flourish together. For they do flourish (and languish) together: the great ages of science are the great ages of all the arts, because in them powerful minds have taken fire from one another, breathless and higgledy-piggledy, without asking too nicely whether they ought to tie their imagination to falling balls or a haunted island. Galileo and Shakespeare, who were born in the same year, grew into greatness in the same age; when Galileo was looking through his telescope at the moon, Shakespeare was writing *The Tempest*; and all Europe was in ferment, from Johannes Kepler to Peter Paul Rubens, and from the first table of logarithms by John Napier to the Authorised Version of the Bible.

Let me end with a last and spirited example of the common inspiration of literature and science, because it is as much alive today as it was three hundred years ago. What I have in mind is man's ageless fantasy, to fly to the moon. I do not display this to you as a high scientific enterprise; on the contrary, I think we have more important discoveries to make here on earth than wait for us, beckoning, at the horned surface of the moon. Yet I cannot belittle the fascination which that little ice-blue journey has had for the imagination of men, long before it drew us to our television screens to watch the tumbling of astronauts. Plutarch and Lucian, Ariosto and Ben Jonson wrote about it, before the days of Jules Verne and H. G. Wells and science fiction. The seventeenth century was heady with new dreams and fables about voyages to the moon. Kepler wrote one full of deep scientific ideas, which (alas) simply got his mother accused of witchcraft. In England, Francis Godwin wrote a wild and splendid work, *The Man in the Moone*, and the astronomer John Wilkins wrote a wild and learned one, *The Discovery of a New World*. They did not draw a line between science and fancy; for example, they all tried to guess just where in the journey the earth's gravity would stop. Only Kepler understood that gravity has no boundary, and put a law to it— which happened to be the wrong law.

All this was a few years before Isaac Newton was born, and it was all in his head that day in 1666 when he sat in his mother's garden, a young man of twenty-three, and thought about the reach of gravity. This was how he came to conceive his brilliant image, that the moon is like a ball which has been thrown so hard that it falls exactly as fast as the horizon, all the way round the earth. The image will do for any satellite, and Newton modestly calculated how long therefore an astronaut would take to fall round the earth once. He made it ninety minutes, and we have all seen now that he was right; but Newton had no way to check that. Instead he went on to calculate how long in that case the distant moon would take to round the earth, if indeed it behaves like a thrown ball that falls in the earth's gravity, and if gravity obeyed a law of inverse squares. He found that the answer would be twenty-eight days.

In that telling figure, the imagination that day chimed with nature, and made a harmony. We shall hear an echo of that harmony on the day when we land on the moon, because it will be not a technical but an imaginative triumph, that reaches back to the beginning of modern science and literature both. All great acts of imagination are like this, in the arts and in science, and convince us because they fill out reality with a deeper sense of rightness. We start with the simplest vocabulary of images, with *left* and *right* and *one*, *two*, *three*, and before we know how it happened the words and the numbers have conspired to make a match with nature: we catch in them the pattern of mind and matter as one.

Hints Toward an Essay on Conversation

JONATHAN SWIFT

I have observed few obvious subjects to have been so seldom, or at least so slightly, handled as this; and indeed I know few so difficult to be treated as it ought, nor yet, upon which there seems so much to be said.

Most things pursued by men for the happiness of public or private life, our wit or folly have so refined, that they seldom subsist but in idea; a true friend, a good marriage, a perfect form of government, with some others, require so many ingredients, so good in their several kinds, and so much niceness in mixing them, that for some thousands of years men have despaired of reducing their schemes to perfection: but, in conversation, it is, or might be otherwise; for here we are only to avoid a multitude of errors, which, although a matter of some difficulty, may be in every man's power, for want of which it remains as mere an idea as the other. Therefore it seems to me, that the truest way to understand conversation, is to know the faults and errors to which it is subject, and from thence every man to form maxims to himself whereby it may be regulated, because it requires few talents to which most men are not born, or at least may not acquire, without any great genius or study. For nature has left every man a capacity of being agreeable, though not of shining in company; and there are a hundred men sufficiently qualified for both, who, by a very few faults, that they might correct in half an hour, are not so much as tolerable.

I was prompted to write my thoughts upon this subject by mere indignation, to reflect that so useful and innocent a pleasure, so fitted for every period and condition of life, and so much in all men's power, should be so much neglected and abused.

And in this discourse it will be necessary to note those errors that are obvious, as well as others which are seldomer observed, since there are few so obvious, or acknowledged, into which most men, some time or other, are not apt to run.

For instance: nothing is more generally exploded than the folly of talking too much; yet I rarely remember to have seen five people together, where someone among them has not been predominant in that kind, to the great constraint and disgust of all the rest. But among such as deal in multitudes of words, none are comparable to the sober deliberate talker, who proceeds with much thought and caution, makes his preface, branches out into several digressions, finds a hint that puts him in mind of another story, which he promises to tell you when this is done; comes back regularly to his subject, cannot readily call to mind some person's name, holding his head, complains of his memory; the whole company all this while in suspense; at length says, it is no matter, and so goes on. And, to crown the business, it perhaps proves at last a story the company has heard fifty times before; or, at best, some insipid adventure of the relater.

Another general fault in conversation, is that of those who affect to talk of themselves; some, without any ceremony, will run over the history of their lives; will relate the annals of their diseases, with the several symptoms and circumstances of them; will enumerate the hardships and injustice they have suffered in court, in parliament, in love, or in law. Others are more dexterous, and with great art will lie on the watch to hook in their own praise; they will call a witness to remember they always foretold what would happen in such a case, but none would believe them; they advised such a man from the beginning, and told him the consequences, just as they happened; but he would have his own way. Others make a vanity of telling their faults; they are the strangest men in the world; they cannot dissemble; they own it is a folly; they have lost abundance of advantages by it; but if you would give them the world, they cannot help it; there is something in their nature that abhors insincerity and constraint; with many other insufferable topics of the same altitude.

Of such mighty importance every man is to himself, and ready to think he is so to others; without once making this easy and obvious reflection, that his affairs can have no more weight with other men, than theirs have with him; and how little that is, he is sensible enough.

Where a company has met, I often have observed two persons discover, by some accident, that they were bred together at the same school or university; after which the rest are condemned to silence, and to listen while these two are refreshing each other's memory, with the arch tricks and passages of themselves and their comrades.

I know a great officer of the army, who will sit for some time with a supercilious and impatient silence, full of anger and contempt for those who are talking; at length, of a sudden, demanding audience, decide the matter in a short dogmatical way; then withdraw within himself again, and vouchsafe to talk no more, until his spirits circulate again to the same point.

There are some faults in conversation, which none are so subject to as the men of wit, nor ever so much as when they are with each other. If they have opened their mouths, without endeavouring to say a witty thing, they think it is so many words lost: it is a torment to the hearers, as much as to themselves, to see them upon the rack for invention, and in perpetual constraint, with so little success. They must do something extraordinary, in order to acquit themselves, and answer their character, else the standers-by may be disappointed, and be apt to think them only like the rest of mortals. I have known two men of wit industriously brought together, in order to entertain the company, where they have made a very ridiculous figure, and provided all the mirth at their own expense.

I know a man of wit, who is never easy but where he can be allowed to dictate and preside: he neither expects to be informed or entertained, but to display his own talents. His business is to be good company, and not good conversation; and therefore he chooses to frequent those who are content to listen, and profess themselves his admirers. And, indeed, the worst conversation I ever remember to have heard in my life, was that at Will's coffee-house, where the wits (as they were called) used formerly to assemble; that is to say, five or six men who had writ plays, or at least prologues, or had share in a miscellany, came thither, and entertained one another with their trifling composures, in so important an air, as if they had been the noblest efforts of human nature, or that the fate of kingdoms depended on them; and they were usually attended with an humble audience of young students from the inns of court, or the universities; who, at due distance, listened to these oracles, and returned home with great contempt for their law and philosophy, their heads filled with trash, under the name of politeness, criticism, and *belles lettres*.

By these means, the poets, for many years past, were all overrun with pedantry. For, as I take it, the word is not properly used; because pedantry is the too frequent or unseasonable obtruding our own knowledge in common discourse, and placing too great a value upon it; by which definition, men of the court, or the army, may be as guilty of pedantry, as a philosopher or a divine; and it is the same vice in women, when they are over copious upon the subject of their petticoats, or their fans, or their china. For which reason, although it be a piece of prudence, as well as good manners, to put men upon talking on subjects they are best versed in, yet that is a liberty a wise man could hardly take; because, beside the imputation of pedantry, it is what he would never improve by.

The great town is usually provided with some player, mimic, or buffoon, who has a general reception at the good tables; familiar and domestic with persons of the first quality, and usually sent for at every meeting to divert the company; against which I have no objection. You go there as to a farce or a puppet-show; your business is only to laugh in season, either out of inclination or civility, while this merry companion is acting his part. It is a business he has undertaken, and we are to suppose he is paid for his day's work. I only quarrel, when, in select and private meetings, where men of wit and learning are invited to pass an evening, this jester should be admitted to run over his circle of tricks, and make the whole company unfit for any other conversation, beside the indignity of confounding men's talents at so shameful a rate.

Raillery is the finest part of conversation; but, as it is our usual custom to counterfeit and adulterate whatever is too dear for us, so we have done with this, and turned it all into what is generally called repartee, or being smart; just as when an expensive fashion comes up, those who are not able to reach it, content themselves with some paltry imitation. It now passes for raillery to run a man down in discourse, to put him out of countenance, and make him ridiculous; sometimes to expose the defects of his person or understanding; on all which occasions, he is obliged not to be angry, to avoid the imputation of not being able to take a jest. It is admirable to observe one who is dexterous at this art, singling out a weak adversary, getting the laugh on his side, and then carrying all before him. The French, from whence we borrow the word, have a quite different idea of the thing, and so had we in the politer age of our fathers. Raillery, was to say something that at first appeared a reproach or reflection, but, by some turn of wit, unexpected and surprising, ended always in a compliment, and to the advantage of the person it was addressed to. And surely one of the best rules in conversation is, never to say a thing which any of the company can reasonably wish we had rather left unsaid; nor can there anything be well more contrary to the ends for which people meet together, than to part unsatisfied with each other or themselves.

There are two faults in conversation, which appear very different, yet arise from the same root, and are equally blameable; I mean an impatience to interrupt others; and the uneasiness of being interrupted ourselves. The two chief ends of conversation are to entertain and improve those we are among, or to receive those benefits ourselves; which whoever will consider, cannot easily run into either of these two errors; because, when any man speaks in company, it is to be supposed he does it for his hearers' sake, and not his own; so that common discretion will teach us not to force their attention, if they are not willing to lend it; nor, on the other side, to interrupt him who is in possession, because that is in the grossest manner to give the preference to our own good sense.

There are some people, whose good manners will not suffer them to interrupt you, but, what is almost as bad, will discover abundance of impatience, and lie upon the watch until you have done, because they have started something in their own thoughts, which they long to be delivered of. Meantime, they are so far from regarding what passes, that their imaginations are wholly turned upon what they have in reserve, for fear it should slip out of their memory; and thus they confine their invention, which might otherwise range over a hundred things full as good, and that might be much more naturally introduced.

There is a sort of rude familiarity, which some people, by practising among their intimates, have introduced into their general conversation, and would have it pass for innocent freedom or humour; which is a dangerous experiment in our northern climate, where all the little decorum and politeness we have, are purely forced by art, and are so ready to lapse into barbarity. This, among the Romans, was the raillery of slaves, of which we have many instances in Plautus. It seems to have been introduced among us by Cromwell, who, by preferring the scum of the people, made it a court entertainment, of which I have heard many particulars; and, considering all things were turned upside down, it was reasonable and judicious: although it was a piece of policy found out to ridicule a point of honour in the other extreme, when the smallest word misplaced among gentlemen ended in a duel.

There are some men excellent at telling a story, and provided with a plentiful stock of them, which they can draw out upon occasion in all companies; and, considering how low conversation runs now among us, it is not altogether a contemptible talent; however, it is subject to two unavoidable defects, frequent repetition, and being soon exhausted; so that, whoever values this gift in himself, has need of a good memory, and ought frequently to shift his company, that he may not discover the weakness of his fund; for those who are thus endued have seldom any other revenue, but live upon the main stock.

Great speakers in public are seldom agreeable in private conversation, whether their faculty be natural, or acquired by practice, and often venturing. Natural elocution, although it may seem a paradox, usually springs from a barrenness of invention, and of words; by which men who have only one stock of notions upon every subject, and one set of phrases to express them in, they swim upon the superficies, and offer themselves on every occasion; therefore, men of much learning, and who know the compass of a language, are generally the worst talkers on a sudden, until much practice has inured and emboldened them; because they are confounded with plenty of matter, variety of notions and of words, which they cannot readily choose, but are perplexed and entangled by too great a choice; which is no disadvantage in private conversation; where, on the other side, the talent of haranguing is, of all others, most unsupportable.

Nothing has spoiled men more for conversation, than the character of being wits; to support which, they never fail of encouraging a number of followers and admirers, who list themselves in their service, wherein they find their accounts on both sides by pleasing their mutual vanity. This has given the former such an air of superiority, and made the latter so pragmatical, that neither of them are well to be endured. I say nothing here of the itch of dispute and contradiction, telling of lies, or of those who are troubled with the disease called the wandering of the thoughts, so that they are never present in mind at what passes in discourse; for whoever labours under any of these possessions, is as unfit for conversation as a madman in Bedlam.

I think I have gone over most of the errors in conversation that have fallen under my notice or memory, except some that are merely personal, and others too gross to need exploding; such as lewd or profane talk; but I pretend only to treat the errors of conversation in general, and not the several subjects of discourse, which would be infinite. Thus we see how human nature is most debased, by the abuse of that faculty which is held the great distinction between men and brutes: and how little advantage we make of that, which might be the greatest, the most lasting, and the most innocent, as well as useful pleasure of life: in default of which, we are forced to take up with those poor amusements of dress and visiting, or the more pernicious ones of play, drink, and vicious amours; whereby the nobility and gentry of both sexes are entirely corrupted both in body and mind, and have lost all notions of love, honour, friendship, generosity; which, under the name of fopperies, have been for some time laughed out of doors.

This degeneracy of conversation, with the pernicious consequences thereof upon our humours and dispositions, has been owing, among other causes, to the custom arisen, for some time past, of excluding women from any share in our society, farther than in parties at play, or dancing, or in the pursuit of an amour. I take the highest period of politeness in England (and it is of the same date in France) to have been the peaceable part of King Charles I's reign; and from what we read of those times, as well as from the accounts I have formerly met with from some who lived in that court, the methods then used for raising and cultivating conversation were altogether different from ours: several ladies, whom we find celebrated by the poets of that age, had assemblies at their houses, where persons of the best understanding, and of both sexes, met to pass the evenings in discoursing upon whatever agreeable subjects were occasionally started; and although we are apt to ridicule the sublime platonic notions they had, or personated, in love and friendship, I conceive their refinements were grounded upon reason, and that a little grain of the romance is no ill ingredient to preserve and exalt the dignity of human nature, without which it is apt to degenerate into everything that is sordid, vicious, and low. If there were no other use in the conversation of ladies, it is sufficient that it would lay a restraint upon those odious topics of immodesty and indecencies, into which the rudeness of our northern genius is so apt to fall. And, therefore, it is observable in those sprightly gentlemen about the town, who are so very dexterous at entertaining a vizard mask in the park or the playhouse, that in the company of ladies of virtue and honour they are silent and disconcerted, and out of their element.

There are some people who think they sufficiently acquit themselves, and entertain their company, with relating facts of no consequence, nor at all out of the road of such common incidents as happen every day; and this I have observed more frequently among the Scots than any other nation, who are very careful not to omit the minutest circumstances of time or place; which kind of discourse, if it were not a little relieved by the uncouth terms and phrases, as well as accent and gesture, peculiar to that country, would be hardly tolerable. It is not a fault in company to talk much; but to continue it long is certainly one; for, if the majority of those who are got together be naturally silent or cautious, the conversation will flag, unless it be often renewed by one among them, who can start new subjects (provided he does not dwell upon them) that leave room for answers and replies.

Of the Love of Books

RICHARD DE BURY

It transcends the power of human intellect, however deeply it may have drunk of the Pegasean fount, to develop fully the title of the present chapter. Though one should speak with the tongue of men and angels, though he should become a Mercury or Tully, though he should grow sweet with the milky eloquence of Livy, yet he will plead the stammering of Moses, or with Jeremiah will confess that he is but a boy and cannot speak, or will imitate Echo rebounding from the mountains. For we know that the love of books is the same thing as the love of wisdom. Now this love is called by the Greek word *philosophy*, the whole virtue of which no created intelligence can comprehend; for she is believed to be the mother of all good things: Wisdom vii. She as a heavenly dew extinguishes the heats of fleshly vices, the intense activity of the mental forces relaxing the vigour of the animal forces, and slothfulness being wholly put to flight, which being gone all the bows of Cupid are unstrung.

Hence Plato says in the *Phaedo*: The philosopher is manifest in this, that he dissevers the soul from communion with the body. Love, says Jerome, the knowledge of the scriptures, and thou wilt not love the vices of the flesh. The godlike Xenocrates showed this by the firmness of his reason, who was declared by the famous hetaera Phryne to be a statue and not a man, when all her blandishments could not shake his resolve, as Valerius Maximus relates at length. Our own Origen showed this also, who chose rather to be unsexed by the mutilation of himself, than to be made effeminate by the omnipotence of women— though it was a hasty remedy, repugnant alike to nature and to virtue, whose place it is not to make men insensible to passion, but to slay with the dagger of reason the passions that spring from instinct.

Again, all who are smitten with the love of books think cheaply of the world and wealth; as Jerome says to Vigilantius: The same man cannot love both gold and books. And thus it has been said in verse:

> No iron-stained hand is fit to handle books,
> Nor he whose heart on gold so gladly looks:
> The same men love not books and money both,

And books thy herd, O Epicurus, loathe;
Misers and bookmen make poor company,
Nor dwell in peace beneath the same roof-tree.

No man, therefore, can serve both books and Mammon.

The hideousness of vice is greatly reprobated in books, so that he who loves to commune with books is led to detest all manner of vice. The demon, who derives his name from knowledge, is most effectually defeated by the knowledge of books, and through books his multitudinous deceits and the endless labyrinths of his guile are laid bare to those who read, lest he be transformed into an angel of light and circumvent the innocent by his wiles. The reverence of God is revealed to us by books, the virtues by which He is worshipped are more expressly manifested, and the rewards are described that are promised by the truth, which deceives not, neither is deceived. The truest likeness of the beatitude to come is the contemplation of the sacred writings, in which we behold in turn the Creator and the creature, and draw from streams of perpetual gladness. Faith is established by the power of books; hope is strengthened by their solace, insomuch that by patience and the consolation of scripture we are in good hope. Charity is not puffed up, but is edified by the knowledge of true learning, and, indeed, it is clearer than light that the Church is established upon the sacred writings.

Books delight us when prosperity smiles upon us; they comfort us inseparably when stormy fortune frowns on us. They lend validity to human compacts, and no serious judgements are propounded without their help. Arts and sciences, all the advantages of which no mind can enumerate, consist in books. How highly must we estimate the wondrous power of books, since through them we survey the utmost bounds of the world and time, and contemplate the things that are as well as those that are not, as it were in the mirror of eternity. In books we climb mountains and scan the deepest gulfs of the abyss; in books we behold the finny tribes that may not exist outside their native waters, distinguish the properties of streams and springs and of various lands; from books we dig out gems and metals and the materials of every kind of mineral, and learn the virtues of herbs and trees and plants, and survey at will the whole progeny of Neptune, Ceres, and Pluto.

But if we please to visit the heavenly inhabitants, Taurus, Caucasus, and Olympus are at hand, from which we pass beyond the realms of Juno and mark out the territories of the seven planets by lines and circles. And finally we traverse the loftiest firmament of all, adorned with signs, degrees, and figures in the utmost variety. There we inspect the antarctic pole, which eye hath not seen, nor ear heard; we admire the luminous Milky Way and the Zodiac, marvellously and delightfully pictured with celestial animals. Thence by books we pass on to separate substances, that the intellect may greet kindred intelligences, and with the mind's eye may discern the First Cause of all things and the Unmoved Mover of infinite virtue, and may immerse itself in love without end. See how with the aid of books we attain the reward of our beatitude, while we are yet sojourners below.

Why need we say more? Certes, just as we have learnt on the authority of Seneca, leisure without letters is death and the sepulture of the living, so contrariwise we conclude that occupation with letters or books is the life of man.

Again, by means of books we communicate to friends as well as foes what we cannot safely entrust to messengers; since the book is generally allowed access to the chambers of princes, from which the voice of its author would be rigidly excluded, as Tertullian observes at the beginning of his *Apologeticus*. When shut up in prison and in bonds, and utterly deprived of bodily liberty, we use books as ambassadors to our friends, and entrust them with the conduct of our cause, and send them where to go ourselves would incur the penalty of death. By the aid of books we remember things that are past, and even prophesy as to the future; and things present, which shift and flow, we perpetuate by committing them to writing.

The felicitous studiousness and the studious felicity of the all-powerful eunuch, of whom we are told in the Acts, who had been so mightily kindled by the love of the prophetic writings that he ceased not from his reading by reason of his journey, had banished all thought of the populous palace of Queen Candace, and had forgotten even the treasures of which he was the keeper, and had neglected alike his journey and the chariot in which he rode. Love of his book alone had wholly engrossed this domicile of chastity, under whose guidance he soon deserved to enter the gate of faith. O gracious love of books, which by the grace of baptism transformed the child of Gehenna and nursling of Tartarus into a Son of the Kingdom!

Let the feeble pen now cease from the tenor of an infinite task, lest it seem foolishly to undertake what in the beginning it confessed to be impossible to any.

On a Lazy Idle Boy

WILLIAM MAKEPEACE THACKERAY

I had occasion to pass a week in the autumn in the little old town of Coire or Chur, in the Grisons, where lies buried that very ancient British king, saint, and martyr, Lucius,* who founded the Church of St Peter, on Cornhill. Few people note the church nowadays, and fewer ever heard of the saint. In the cathedral at Chur, his statue appears surrounded by other sainted persons of his family. With tight red breeches, a Roman habit, a curly brown beard, and a neat little gilt crown and sceptre, he stands, a very comely and cheerful image: and from what I may call his peculiar position with regard to Cornhill, I beheld this figure of St Lucius with more interest than I should have bestowed upon personages who, hierarchically, are, I daresay, his superiors.

The pretty little city stands, so to speak, at the end of the world—of the world of today, the world of rapid motion, and rushing railways, and the commerce and intercourse of men. From the northern gate, the iron road stretches away to Zürich, to Basle, to Paris, to home. From the old southern barriers, before which a little river rushes, and around which stretch the crumbling battlements of the ancient town, the road bears the slow diligence or lagging vetturino by the shallow Rhine, through the awful gorges of the Via Mala, and presently over the Splügen to the shores of Como.

I have seldom seen a place more quaint, pretty, calm, and pastoral, than this remote little Chur. What need have the inhabitants for walls and ramparts, except to build summer-houses, to trail vines, and hang clothes to dry on them? No enemies approach the great mouldering gates: only at morn and even the cows come lowing past them, the village maidens chatter merrily round the fountains, and babble like the ever-voluble stream that flows under the old walls. The

---

* Stow quotes the inscription still extant 'from the table fast chained in St Peter's Church, Cornhill'; and says, 'he was after some chronicle buried at London, and after some chronicle buried at Glowcester'—but, oh! these incorrect chroniclers! when Alban Butler, in the *Lives of the Saints*, v. 12, and Murray's *Handbook*, and the Sacristan at Chur, all say Lucius was killed there, and I saw his tomb with my own eyes.

schoolboys, with book and satchel, in smart uniforms, march up to
the gymnasium, and return thence at their stated time. There is one
coffee-house in the town, and I see one old gentleman goes to it.
There are shops with no customers seemingly, and the lazy tradesmen look out of their little windows at the single stranger sauntering
by. There is a stall with baskets of queer little black grapes and apples,
and a pretty brisk trade with half-a-dozen urchins standing round.
But, beyond this, there is scarce any talk or movement in the street.
There's nobody at the bookshop. 'If you will have the goodness to
come again in an hour,' says the banker, with his mouth full of dinner
at one o'clock, 'you can have the money.' There is nobody at the
hotel, save the good landlady, the kind waiters, the brisk young cook
who ministers to you. Nobody is in the Protestant church—(oh!
strange sight, the two confessions are here at peace!)—nobody in the
Catholic church: until the sacristan, from his snug abode in the
cathedral close, espies the traveller eyeing the monsters and pillars
before the old shark-toothed arch of his cathedral, and comes out
(with a view to remuneration possibly) and opens the gate, and shows
you the venerable church, and the queer old relics in the sacristy, and
the ancient vestments (a black velvet cope, amongst other robes, as
fresh as yesterday, and presented by that notorious 'pervert', Henry
of Navarre and France), and the statue of St Lucius who built St
Peter's Church, on Cornhill.

What a quiet, kind, quaint, pleasant, pretty old town! Has it been
asleep these hundreds and hundreds of years, and is the brisk young
Prince of the Sidereal Realms in his screaming car drawn by his
snorting steel elephant coming to waken it? Time was when there
must have been life and bustle and commerce here. Those vast,
venerable walls were not made to keep out cows, but men-at-arms,
led by fierce captains, who prowled about the gates, and robbed the
traders as they passed in and out with their bales, their goods, their
pack-horses, and their wains. Is the place so dead that even the clergy
of the different denominations can't quarrel? Why, seven or eight, or
a dozen, or fifteen hundred years ago (they haven't the register at St
Peter's up to that remote period. I daresay it was burnt in the fire of
London)—a dozen hundred years ago, when there was some life in
the town, St Lucius was stoned here on account of theological
differences, after founding our church in Cornhill.

There was a sweet pretty river walk we used to take in the evening
and mark the mountains round glooming with a deeper purple; the
shades creeping up the golden walls; the river brawling, the cattle
calling, the maids and chatterboxes round the fountains babbling and
bawling; and several times in the course of our sober walks we

overtook a lazy slouching boy, or hobbledehoy, with a rusty coat, and trousers not too long, and big feet trailing lazily one after the other, and large lazy hands dawdling from out the tight sleeves, and in the lazy hands a little book, which my lad held up to his face, and which I daresay so charmed and ravished him, that he was blind to the beautiful sights around him; unmindful, I would venture to lay any wager, of the lessons he had to learn for tomorrow; forgetful of mother waiting supper, and father preparing a scolding—absorbed utterly and entirely in his book.

What was it that so fascinated the young student, as he stood by the river shore? Not the *Pons Asinorum*. What book so delighted him, and blinded him to all the rest of the world, so that he did not care to see the apple-woman with her fruit, or (more tempting still to sons of Eve) the pretty girls with their apple-cheeks, who laughed and prattled round the fountain! What was the book? Do you suppose it was Livy, or the Greek grammar? No; it was a NOVEL that you were reading, you lazy, not very clean, good-for-nothing, sensible boy! It was D'Artagnan locking up General Monk in a box, or almost succeeding in keeping Charles I's head on. It was the prisoner of the Château d'If cutting himself out of the sack fifty feet under water (I mention the novels I like best myself—novels without love or talking, or any of that sort of nonsense, but containing plenty of fighting, escaping, robbery, and rescuing)—cutting himself out of the sack, and swimming to the island of Monte Cristo. O Dumas! O thou brave, kind, gallant old Alexandre! I hereby offer thee homage, and give thee thanks for many pleasant hours. I have read thee (being sick in bed) for thirteen hours of a happy day, and had the ladies of the house fighting for the volumes. Be assured that lazy boy was reading Dumas (or I will go so far as to let the reader here pronounce the eulogium, or insert the name of his favourite author); and as for the anger, or it may be, the reverberations of his schoolmaster, or the remonstrances of his father, or the tender pleadings of his mother that he should not let the supper grow cold—I don't believe the scapegrace cared one fig. No! figs are sweet, but fictions are sweeter.

Have you ever seen a score of white-bearded, white-robed warriors, or grave seniors of the city, seated at the gate of Jaffa or Beyrout, and listening to the storyteller reciting his marvels out of *Antar* or the *Arabian Nights*? I was once present when a young gentleman at table put a tart away from him, and said to his neighbour, the Younger Son (with rather a fatuous air), 'I never eat sweets.'

'Not eat sweets! and do you know why?' says T.

'Because I am past that kind of thing,' says the young gentleman.

'Because you are a glutton and a sot!' cries the Elder (and Juvenis winces a little). 'All people who have natural , healthy appetites, love sweets; all children, all women, all Eastern people, whose tastes are not corrupted by gluttony and strong drink.' And a plateful of raspberries and cream disappeared before the philosopher.

You take the allegory? Novels are sweets. All people with healthy literary appetites love them—almost all women—a vast number of clever, hard-headed men. Why, one of the most learned physicians in England said to me only yesterday, 'I have just read *So-and-So* for the second time' (naming one of Jones's exquisite fictions). Judges, bishops, chancellors, mathematicians, are notorious novel-readers; as well as young boys and sweet girls, and their kind tender mothers. Who has not read about Eldon, and how he cried over novels every night when he was not at whist?

As for that lazy naughty boy at Chur, I doubt whether *he* will like novels when he is thirty years of age. He is taking too great a glut of them now. He is eating jelly until he will be sick. He will know most plots by the time he is twenty, so that *he* will never be surprised when the Stranger turns out to be the rightful earl—when the old Water-man, throwing off his beggarly gabardine, shows his stars and the collars of his various orders, and clasping Antonia to his bosom, proves himself to be the prince, her long-lost father. He will recog-nise the novelist's same characters, though they appear in red-heeled pumps and *ailes-de-pigeon*, or the garb of the nineteenth century. He will get weary of sweets, as boys of private schools grow (or used to grow, for I have done growing some little time myself, and the practice may have ended too)—as private schoolboys used to grow tired of the pudding before their mutton at dinner.

And pray what is the moral of this apologue? The moral I take to be this: the appetite for novels extending to the end of the world; far away in the frozen deep, the sailors reading them to one another during the endless night—far away under the Syrian stars, the solemn sheiks and elders hearkening to the poet as he recites his tales; far away in the Indian camps, where the soldiers listen to —'s tales, or —'s, after the hot day's march; far away in little Chur yonder where the lazy boy pores over the fond volume, and drinks it in with all his eyes: the demand being what we know it is, the merchant must supply it, as he will supply saddles and pale ale for Bombay or Calcutta.

But as surely as the cadet drinks too much pale ale, it will disagree with him; and so surely, dear youth, will too much novels cloy on thee. I wonder, do novel-writers themselves read many novels? If you go into Gunter's you don't see those charming young ladies (to whom I present my most respectful compliments) eating tarts and ices, but at the proper eventide they have good plain wholesome tea and bread and butter. Can anybody tell me does the author of the *Tale of Two Cities* read novels? does the author of the *Tower of London* devour romances? does the dashing *Harry Lorrequer* delight in *Plain or Ringlets* or *Sponge's Sporting Tour*? Does the veteran, from whose flowing pen we had the books which delighted our young days, *Darnley*, and *Richelieu*, and *Delorme*,★ relish the works of Alexandre the Great, and thrill over the *Three Musqueteers*? Does the accomplished author of *The Caxtons* read the other tales in *Blackwood*? (For example that ghost story printed last August, and which for my part, though I read it in the public reading-room at the 'Pavilion Hotel' at Folkestone, I protest frightened me so that I scarce dared look over my shoulder.) Does *Uncle Tom* admire *Adam Bede*; and does the author of the *Vicar of Wrexhill* laugh over *The Warden* and the *Three Clerks*? Dear youth of ingenuous countenance and ingenuous pudor! I make no doubt that the eminent parties above named all partake of novels in moderation—eat jellies—but mainly nourish themselves upon wholesome roast and boiled.

Here, dear youth aforesaid! our *Cornhill Magazine* owners strive to provide thee with facts as well as fiction; and though it does not become them to brag of their Ordinary, at least they invite thee to a table where thou shalt sit in good company. That story of the *Fox*† was written by one of the gallant seamen who sought for poor Franklin under the awful Arctic Night: that account of China‡ is told by the man of all the empire most likely to know of what he speaks: those pages regarding Volunteers§ come from an honoured hand that has borne the sword in a hundred famous fields, and pointed the British guns in the greatest siege in the world.

Shall we point out others? We are fellow-travellers, and shall make acquaintance as the voyage proceeds. In the Atlantic steamers, on the first day out (and on high and holy days subsequently), the jellies set down on table are richly ornamented; *medioque in fonte leporum* rise the American and British flags nobly emblazoned in tin. As the passengers remark this pleasing phenomenon, the captain no doubt

---

★ By the way, what a strange fate is that which befell the veteran novelist! He was appointed her Majesty's Consul-General in Venice, the only city in Europe where the famous 'Two Cavaliers' cannot by any possibility be seen riding together.

† *The Search for Sir John Franklin.* (From the Private Journal of an Officer of the *Fox*.)

‡ *The Chinese and the Outer Barbarians.* By Sir John Bowring.

§ *Our Volunteers.* By Sir John Burgoyne.

improves the occasion by expressing a hope, to his right and left, that the flag of Mr Bull and his younger Brother may always float side by side in friendly emulation. Novels having been previously compared to jellies—here are two (one perhaps not entirely saccharine, and flavoured with an *amari aliquid* very distasteful to some palates)—two novels★ under two flags, the one that ancient ensign which has hung before the well-known booth of *Vanity Fair*; the other that fresh and handsome standard which has lately been hoisted on *Barchester Towers*. Pray, sir, or madam, to which dish will you be helped?

So have I seen my friends Captain Lang and Captain Comstock press their guests to partake of the fare on that memorable 'First day out', when there is no man, I think, who sits down but asks a blessing on his voyage, and the good ship dips over the bar, and bounds away into the blue water.

★ *Lovel the Widower* and *Framley Parsonage.*

225

The Town Week

E. V. LUCAS

It is odd that 'Mondayish' is the only word which the days of the
week have given us; since Monday is not alone in possessing a
positive and peculiar character. Why not 'Tuesdayish' or 'Wednes-
dayish'? Each word would convey as much meaning to me, 'Tuesdayish' in particular, for Monday's cardinal and reprehensible error
of beginning the business week seems to me almost a virtue compared with Tuesday's utter flatness. To begin a new week is no fault at
all, though tradition has branded it as one. To begin is a noble
accomplishment; but to continue dully, to be the tame follower of a
courageous beginner, to be the second day in a week of action, as in
Tuesday's case—that is deplorable, if you like.

Monday can be flat enough, but in a different way from Tuesday.
Monday is flat because one has been idling, perhaps unconsciously
absorbing notions of living like the lilies; because so many days must
pass before the week ends; because yesterday is no more. But Tuesday has the sheer essential flatness of nonentity; Tuesday is nothing. If
you would know how absolutely nothing it is, go to a weekend hotel
at, say Brighton, and stay on after the Saturday-to-Monday population has flitted. On Tuesday you touch the depths. So does the
menu—no *chef* ever exerted himself for a Tuesday guest. Tuesday is
also very difficult to spell, many otherwise cultured ladies putting
the *e* before the *u*: and why not? What right has Tuesday to any
preference?

With all its faults, Monday has a positive character. Monday brings
a feeling of revolt; Tuesday, the base craven, reconciles us to the
machine. I am not surprised that the recent American revivalists held
no meetings on Mondays. It was a mark of their astuteness; they
knew that the wear and tear of overcoming the Monday feeling of the
greater part of their audience would exhaust them before their magnetism began to have play; while a similarly stubborn difficulty
would confront them in the remaining portion sunk in apathy by the
thought that tomorrow would be Tuesday. It is this presage of certain
tedium which has robbed Monday evening of its 'glittering star'. Yet
since nothing so becomes a flat day as the death of it, Tuesday

evening's glittering star (it is Wordsworth's phrase) is of the brightest—for is not the dreary day nearly done, and is not tomorrow Wednesday the bland?

With Wednesday, the week stirs itself, turns over, begins to wake. There are matinées on Wednesday; on Wednesdays some of the more genial weekly papers come out. The very word has a good honest round air—Wednesday. Things, adventures, might happen very naturally on Wednesday; but that nothing ever happened on a Tuesday I am convinced. In summer Wednesday has often close finishes at Lord's, and it is a day on which one's friends are pretty sure to be accessible. On Monday they may not have returned from the country; on Friday they have begun to go out of town again; but on Wednesday they are here, at home—are solid. I am sure it is my favourite day.

(Even politicians, so slow as a rule to recognise the kindlier, more generous, side of life, realised for many years that Wednesday was a day on which they had no right to conduct their acrimonious business for more than an hour or so. Much of the failure of the last Government may be traced to their atheistical decision no longer to remember Wednesday to keep it holy.)

On Thursday the week falls back a little; the stirring of Wednesday is forgotten; there is a return to the folding of the hands. I am not sure that Thursday has not become the real day of rest. That it is a good honest day is the most that can be said for it. It is certainly not Thor's day any longer—if my reading of the character of the blacksmith-god is true. There is nothing strong and downright and fine about it. Compared with Tuesday's small beer, Thursday is almost champagne; but none the less they are related. One can group them together. If I were a business man, I should, I am certain, sell my shares at a loss on Monday and at a profit on Wednesday and Friday, but on Tuesday and Thursday I should get for them exactly what I gave.

I group Friday with Wednesday as a day that can be friendly to me, but it has not Wednesday's quality. Wednesday is calm, assured, urbane; Friday allows itself to be a little flurried and excited. Wednesday stands alone; Friday to some extent throws in its lot with Saturday. Friday is too busy. Too many papers come out, too many bags are packed, on Friday. But herein, of course, is some of its virtue; it is the beginning of the end, the forerunner of Saturday and Sunday. If anticipation, as the moralists say, is better than the realisation, Friday is perhaps the best day of the week, for one spends much of it in thinking of the morrow and what of good it should bring forth. Friday's greatest merit is perhaps that it paves the way to

Saturday and the cessation of work. That it ever was really unlucky I greatly doubt.

And so we come to Saturday and Sunday. But here the analyst falters, for Saturday and Sunday pass from the region of definable days. Monday and Tuesday, Wednesday and Thursday and Friday, these are days with a character fixed more or less for all. But Saturday and Sunday are what we individually make of them. In one family they are friends, associates; in another as ill-assorted as Socrates and Xantippe. For most of us Saturday is not exactly a day at all, it is a collection of hours, part work, part pleasure, and all restlessness. It is a day that we plan for, and therefore it is often a failure. I have no distinct and unvarying impression of Saturday, except that trains are full and late and shops shut too early.

Sunday even more than Saturday is different as people are different. To the godly it is a day of low tones, its minutes go by muffled; to the children of the godly it is eternity. To the ungodly it is a day jeopardised by an interest in barometers that is almost too poignant. To one man it is an interruption of the week; to another it is the week itself, and all the rest of the days are but preparations for it. One cannot analyse Saturday and Sunday.

But Monday? There we are on solid ground again. Monday—but I have discussed Monday already: that is one of its principal characteristics, that it is always coming round again, pretending to be new. It is always the same in reality.

Meadow Thoughts

RICHARD JEFFERIES

The old house stood by the silent country road, secluded by many a long, long mile, and yet again secluded within the great walls of the garden. Often and often I rambled up to the milestone which stood under an oak, to look at the chipped inscription low down—'To London, 79 miles.' So far away, you see, that the very inscription was cut at the foot of the stone, since no one would be likely to want that information. It was half hidden by docks and nettles, despised and unnoticed. A broad land this seventy-nine miles—how many meadows and cornfields, hedges and woods, in that distance?—wide enough to seclude any house, to hide it like an acorn in the grass. Those who have lived all their lives in remote places do not feel the remoteness. No one else seemed to be conscious of the breadth that separated the place from the great centre, but it was, perhaps, that consciousness which deepened the solitude to me. It made the silence more still; the shadows of the oaks yet slower in their movement; everything more earnest. To convey a full impression of the intense concentration of Nature in the meadows is very difficult—everything is so utterly oblivious of man's thought and man's heart. The oaks stand—quiet, still—so still that the lichen loves them. At their feet the grass grows, and heeds nothing. Among it the squirrels leap, and their little hearts are as far away from you or me as the very wood of the oaks. The sunshine settles itself in the valley by the brook, and abides there whether we come or not. Glance through the gap in the hedge by the oak, and see how concentrated it is—all of it, every blade of grass, and leaf, and flower, and living creature, finch or squirrel. It is mesmerised upon itself. Then I used to feel that it really was seventy-nine miles to London, and not an hour or two only by rail, really all those miles. A great, broad province of green furrow and ploughed furrow between the old house and the city of the world. Such solace and solitude seventy-nine miles thick cannot be painted; the trees cannot be placed far enough away in perspective. It is necessary to stay in it like the oaks to know it.

Lime tree branches overhung the corner of the garden wall, whence a view was easy of the silent and dusty road, till over-arching

229

oaks concealed it. The white dust heated by the sunshine, the green hedges, and the heavily massed trees, white clouds rolled together in the sky, a footpath opposite lost in the fields, as you might thrust a stick into the grass, tender lime leaves caressing the cheek, and silence. That is, the silence of the fields. If a breeze rustled the boughs, if a greenfinch called, if the cart-mare in the meadow shook herself, making the earth and air tremble by her with the convulsion of her mighty muscles, these were not sounds, they were the silence itself. So sensitive to it as I was, in its turn it held me firmly, like the fabled spells of old time. The mere touch of a leaf was a talisman to bring me under the enchantment, so that I seemed to feel and know all that was proceeding among the grass-blades and in the bushes. Among the lime trees along the wall the birds never built, though so close and sheltered. They built everywhere but there. To the broad coping-stones of the wall under the lime boughs speckled thrushes came almost hourly, sometimes to peer out and reconnoitre if it was safe to visit the garden, sometimes to see if a snail had climbed up the ivy. Then they dropped quietly down into the long strawberry patch immediately under. The cover of strawberries is the constant resource of all creeping things; the thrushes looked round every plant and under every leaf and runner. One toad always resided there, often two, and as you gathered a ripe strawberry you might catch sight of his black eye watching you take the fruit he had saved for you.

Down the road skims an eave-swallow, swift as an arrow, his white back making the sun-dried dust dull and dingy; he is seeking a pool for mortar, and will waver to and fro by the brook below till he finds a convenient place to alight. Thence back to the eave here, where for forty years he and his ancestors built in safety. Two white butterflies fluttering round each other rise over the limes, once more up over the house, and soar on till their white shows no longer against the illumined air. A grasshopper calls on the sward by the strawber-ries, and immediately fillips himself over seven leagues of grass blades. Yonder a line of men and women file across the field, seen for a moment as they pass a gateway, and the hay changes from hay-colour to green behind them as they turn the under but still sappy side upwards. They are working hard, but it looks easy, slow, and sunny. Finches fly out from the hedgerow to the overturned hay. Another butterfly, a brown one, floats along the dusty road—the only travel-ler yet. The white clouds are slowly passing behind the oaks, large puffed clouds, like deliberate loads of hay, leaving little wisps and flecks behind them caught in the sky. How pleasant it would be to read in the shadow! There is a broad shadow on the sward by the strawberries cast by a tall and fine-grown American crab tree. The very place for a book; and although I know it is useless, yet I go and fetch one and dispose myself on the grass.

I can never read in summer out of doors. Though in shadow the bright light fills it, summer shadows are broadest daylight. The page is so white and hard, the letters so very black, the meaning and drift not quite intelligible, because neither eye nor mind will dwell upon it. Human thoughts and imaginings written down are pale and feeble in bright summer light. The eye wanders away, and rests more lovingly on greensward and green lime leaves. The mind wanders yet deeper and farther into the dreamy mystery of the azure sky. Once now and then, determined to write down that mystery and delicious sense while actually in it, I have brought out table and ink and paper, and sat there in the midst of the summer day. Three words, and where is the thought? Gone. The paper is so obviously paper, the ink so evidently ink, the pen so stiff; all so inadequate. You want colour, flexibility, light, sweet low sound—all these to paint it and play it in music, at the same time you want something that will answer to and record in one touch the strong throb of life and the thought or feeling, or whatever it is that goes out into the earth and sky and space, endless as a beam of light. The very shade of the pen on the paper tells you how utterly hopeless it is to express these things. There is the shade and the brilliant gleaming whiteness; now tell me in plain written words the simple contrast of the two. Not in twenty pages, for the bright light shows the paper in its common fibre-ground, coarse aspect, in its reality, not as a mind-tablet.

The delicacy and beauty of thought or feeling is so extreme that it cannot be inked in; it is like the green and blue of field and sky, of veronica flower and grass blade, which in their own existence throw light and beauty on each other, but in artificial colours repel. Take the table indoors again, and the book: the thoughts and imaginings of others are vain, and of your own too deep to be written. For the mind is filled with the exceeding beauty of these things, and their great wondrousness and marvel. Never yet have I been able to write what I felt about the sunlight only. Colour and form and light are as magic to me. It is a trance. It requires a language of ideas to convey it. It is ten years since I last reclined on that grass plot, and yet I have been writing of it as if it was yesterday, and every blade of grass is as visible and as real to me now as then. They were greener towards the house, and more brown tinted on the margin of the strawberry bed, because towards the house the shadow rested longest. By the strawberries the fierce sunlight burned them.

The sunlight put out the books I brought into it just as it put out the fire on the hearth indoors. The tawny flames floating upwards could not bite the crackling sticks when the full beams came pouring on them. Such extravagance of light overcame the little fire till it was screened from the power of the heavens. So here in the shadow of the American crab tree the light of the sky put out the written pages. For this beautiful and wonderful light excited a sense of some likewise beautiful and wonderful truth, some unknown but grand thought hovering as a swallow above. The swallows hovered and did not alight, but they were there. An inexpressible thought quivered in the azure overhead; it could not be fully grasped, but there was a sense and feeling of its presence. Before that mere sense of its presence the weak and feeble pages, the small fires of human knowledge, dwindled and lost meaning. There was something here that was not in the books. In all the philosophies and searches of mind there was nothing that could be brought to face it, to say, This is what it intends, this is the explanation of the dream. The very grass-blades confounded the wisest, the tender lime leaf put them to shame, the grasshopper derided them, the sparrow on the wall chirped his scorn. The books were put out, unless a screen were placed between them and the light of the sky—that is, an assumption, so as to make an artificial mental darkness. Grant some assumptions—that is, screen off the light— and in that darkness everything was easily arranged, this thing here and that yonder. But Nature grants no assumptions, and the books were put out. There is something beyond the philosophies in the light, in the grass-blades, the leaf, the grasshopper, the sparrow on the wall. Some day the great and beautiful thought which hovers on the confines of the mind will at last alight. In that is hope, the whole sky is full of abounding hope. Something beyond the books, that is consolation.

The little lawn beside the strawberry bed, burned brown there, and green towards the house shadow, holds how many myriad grass-blades? Here they are all matted together, long and dragging each other down. Part them, and beneath them are still more, overhung and hidden. The fibres are intertangled, woven in an endless basket work and chaos of green and dried threads. A blamable profusion this; a fifth as many would be enough; altogether a wilful waste here. As for these insects that spring out of it as I press the grass, a hundredth part of them would suffice. The American crab tree is a snowy mount in spring; the flakes of bloom, when they fall, cover the grass with a film—a bushel of bloom, which the wind takes and scatters afar. The extravagance is sublime. The two little cherry trees are as wasteful; they throw away handfuls of flower: but in the meadows the careless, spendthrift ways of grass and flower and all things are not to be expressed. Seeds by the hundred million float with absolute indifference on the air. The oak has a hundred thousand more leaves than necessary, and never hides a single acorn. Nothing utilitarian—everything on a scale of splendid waste. Such noble, broadcast, open-armed waste is delicious to behold. Never was there such a lying proverb as 'Enough is as good as a feast'. Give me the feast; give me squandered millions of seeds, luxurious carpets of petals, green mountains of oak leaves. The greater the waste, the greater the enjoyment—the nearer the approach to real life. Casuistry is of no avail; the fact is obvious; Nature flings treasures abroad, puffs them with open lips along on every breeze, piles up lavish layers of them in the free open air, packs countless numbers together in the needles of a fir tree. Prodigality and superfluity are stamped on everything she does. The ear of wheat returns a hundredfold the grain from which it grew. The surface of the earth offers to us far more than we can consume—the grains, the seeds, the fruits, the animals, the abounding products are beyond the power of all the human race to devour. They can, too, be multiplied a thousandfold. There is no natural lack. Whenever there is lack among us it is from artificial causes, which intelligence should remove.

From the littleness, and meanness, and niggardliness forced upon us by circumstances, what a relief to turn aside to the exceeding plenty of Nature! There are no bounds to it, there is no comparison to parallel it, so great is this generosity. No physical reason exists why every human being should not have sufficient, at least, of necessities. For any human being to starve, or even to be in trouble about the procuring of simple food, appears, indeed, a strange and unaccountable thing, quite upside down, and contrary to sense, if you do but consider a moment the enormous profusion the earth throws at our feet. In the slow process of time, as the human heart grows larger, such provision, I sincerely trust, will be made that no one need ever feel anxiety about mere subsistence. Then, too, let there be some imitation of this open-handed generosity and divine waste. Let the generations to come feast free of care, like my finches on the seeds of the mowing-grass, from which no voice drives them. If I could but give away as freely as the earth does!

The white-backed eave-swallow has returned many, many times from the shallow drinking-place by the brook to his half built nest. Sometimes the pair of them cling to the mortar they have fixed under the eave, and twitter to each other about the progress of the work. They dive downwards with such velocity when they quit hold that it seems as if they must strike the ground, but they shoot up again, over the wall and the lime trees. A thrush has been to the arbour yonder twenty times; it is made of crossed laths, and overgrown with 'tea-plant', and the nest is inside the lath-work. A sparrow has visited the rose tree by the wall—the buds are covered with aphides. A brown tree-creeper has been to the limes, then to the cherries, and even to a stout lilac stem. No matter how small the tree, he tries all that are in his way. The bright colours of a bullfinch were visible a moment just now, as he passed across the shadows farther down the garden under the damson trees and into the bushes. The grasshopper has gone past and along the garden path, his voice is not heard now; but there is another coming. While I have been dreaming, all these and hundreds out in the meadow have been intensely happy. So concentrated on their little work in the sunshine, so intent on the tiny egg, on the insect captured, on the grass-tip to be carried to the eager fledglings, so joyful in listening to the song poured out for them or in pouring it forth, quite oblivious of all else. It is in this intense concentration that they are so happy. If they could only live longer!—but a few such seasons for them—I wish they could live a hundred years just to feast on the seeds and sing and be utterly happy and oblivious to every-thing but the moment they are passing. A black line has rushed up from the espalier apple yonder to the housetop thirty times at least. The starlings fly so swiftly and so straight that they seem to leave a black line along the air. They have a nest in the roof, they are to and fro it and the meadow the entire day, from dawn till eve. The espalier apple, like a screen, hides the meadow from me, so that the descend-ing starlings appear to dive into a space behind it. Sloping down-wards the meadow makes a valley; I cannot see it, but know that it is golden with buttercups, and that a brook runs in the groove of it.

Afar yonder I can see a summit beyond where the grass swells upwards to a higher level than this spot. There are bushes and elms whose height is decreased by distance on the summit, horses in the shadow of the trees, and a small flock of sheep crowded, as is their wont, in the hot and sunny gateway. By the side of the summit is a deep green trench, so it looks from here, in the hillside: it is really the course of a streamlet worn deep in the earth. I can see nothing between the top of the espalier screen and the horses under the elms on the hill. But the starlings go up and down into the hollow space, which is aglow with golden buttercups, and, indeed, I am looking over a hundred finches eagerly searching, sweetly calling, happy as the summer day. A thousand thousand grasshoppers are leaping, thrushes are labouring, filled with love and tenderness, doves coo-ing—there is as much joy as there are leaves on the hedges. Faster than the starling's flight my mind runs up to the streamlet in the deep green trench beside the hill.

Pleasant it was to trace it upwards, narrowing at every ascending step, till the thin stream, thinner than fragile glass, did but merely slip over the stones. A little less and it could not have run at all, water could not stretch out to greater tenuity. It smoothed the brown growth on the stones, stroking it softly. It filled up tiny basins of sand and ran out at the edges between minute rocks of flint. Beneath it went under thickest brooklime, blue flowered, and serrated water-parsnips, lost like many a mighty river for a while among a forest of leaves. Higher up masses of bramble and projecting thorn stopped the explorer, who must wind round the grassy mound. Pausing to look back a moment there were meads under the hill with the shortest and greenest herbage, perpetually watered, and without one single buttercup, a strip of pure green among yellow flowers and yellowing corn. A few hollow oaks on whose boughs the cuckoos stayed to call, two or three peewits coursing up and down, larks singing, and for all else silence. Between the wheat and the grassy mound the path was almost closed, burdocks and brambles thrust the adventurer outward to brush against the wheatears. Upwards till suddenly it turned, and led by steep notches in the bank, as it seemed, down to the roots of the elm trees. The clump of elms grew right over a deep and rugged hollow; their branches reached out across it, roofing in the cave.

Here was the spring, at the foot of a perpendicular rock, moss-grown low down, and overrun with creeping ivy higher. Green thorn bushes filled the chinks and made a wall to the well, and the long narrow hart's-tongue streaked the face of the cliff. Behind the thick thorns hid the course of the streamlet, in front rose the solid rock, upon the right hand the sward came to the edge—it shook every now and then as the horses in the shade of the elms stamped their feet—on the left hand the ears of wheat peered over the verge. A rocky cell in concentrated silence of green things. Now and again a finch, a starling, or a sparrow would come meaning to drink—athirst from the meadow or the cornfield—and start and almost entangle their wings in the bushes, so completely astonished that anyone should be there. The spring rises in a hollow under the rock imperceptibly, and without bubble or sound. The fine sand of the shallow basin is undisturbed—no tiny water-volcano pushes up a dome of particles. Nor is there any crevice in the stone, but the basin is always full and always running over. As it slips from the brim a gleam of sunshine falls through the boughs and meets it. To this cell I used to come once now and then on a summer's day, tempted, perhaps, like the finches, by the sweet cool water, but drawn also by a feeling that could not be analysed. Stooping, I lifted the water in the hollow of my hand—carefully, lest the sand might be disturbed—and the sunlight gleamed on it as it slipped through my fingers. Alone in the green-roofed cave, alone with the sunlight and the pure water, there was a sense of something more than these. The water was more to me than water, and the sun than sun. The gleaming rays on the water in my palm held me for a moment, the touch of the water gave me something from itself. A moment, and the gleam was gone, the water flowing away, but I had had them. Beside the physical water and physical light I had received from them their beauty; they had communicated to me this silent mystery. The pure and beautiful water, the pure, clear, and beautiful light, each had given me something of their truth.

So many times I came to it, toiling up the long and shadowless hill in the burning sunshine, often carrying a vessel to take some of it home with me. There was a brook, indeed; but this was different, it was the spring; it was taken home as a beautiful flower might be brought. It is not the physical water, it is the sense of feeling that it conveys. Nor is it the physical sunshine; it is the sense of inexpressible beauty which it brings with it. Of such I still drink, and hope to do so still deeper.

Machines and the Emotions

BERTRAND RUSSELL

Will machines destroy emotions, or will emotions destroy machines? This question was suggested long ago by Samuel Butler in *Erewhon*, but it is growing more and more actual as the empire of machinery is enlarged.

At first sight, it is not obvious why there should be any opposition between machines and emotions. Every normal boy loves machines; the bigger and more powerful they are, the more he loves them. Nations which have a long tradition of artistic excellence, like the Japanese, are captivated by Western mechanical methods as soon as they come across them, and long only to imitate us as quickly as possible. Nothing annoys an educated and travelled Asiatic so much as to hear praise of 'the wisdom of the East' or the traditional virtues of Asiatic civilisation. He feels as a boy would feel who was told to play with dolls instead of toy automobiles. And like a boy, he would prefer a real automobile to a toy one, not realising that it may run over him.

In the West, when machinery was new, there was the same delight in it, except on the part of a few poets and aesthetes. The nineteenth century considered itself superior to its predecessors chiefly because of its mechanical progress. Peacock, in its early years, makes fun of the 'steam intellect society', because he is a literary man, to whom the Greek and Latin authors represent civilisation; but he is conscious of being out of touch with the prevailing tendencies of his time. Rousseau's disciples with the return to Nature, the Lake Poets with the medievalism, William Morris with his *News from Nowhere* (a country where it is always June and everybody is engaged in haymaking), all represent a purely sentimental and essentially reactionary opposition to machinery. Samuel Butler was the first man to apprehend intellectually the non-sentimental case against machines, but in him it may have been no more than a *jeu d'esprit*—certainly it was not a deeply held conviction. Since his day numbers of people in the most mechanised nations have been tending to adopt in earnest a view similar to that of the Erewhonians; this view, that is to say, has been latent or explicit in the attitude of many rebels against existing industrial methods.

237

Machines are worshipped because they are beautiful, and valued because they confer power; they are hated because they are hideous, and loathed because they impose slavery. Do not let us suppose that one of these attitudes is 'right' and the other 'wrong', any more than it would be right to maintain that men have heads but wrong to maintain that they have feet, though we can easily imagine Lilliputians disputing this question concerning Gulliver. A machine is like a Djinn in the Arabian Nights: beautiful and beneficent to its master, but hideous and terrible to his enemies. But in our day nothing is allowed to show itself with such naked simplicity. The master of the machine, it is true, lives at a distance from it, where he cannot hear its noise or see its unsightly heaps of slag or smell its noxious fumes; if he ever sees it, the occasion is before it is installed in use, when he can admire its force or its delicate precision without being troubled by dust and heat. But when he is challenged to consider the machine from the point of view of those who have to live with it and work it, he has a ready answer. He can point out that, owing to its operations, these men can purchase more goods—often vastly more—than their great-grandfathers could. It follows that they must be happier than their great-grandfathers—if we are to accept an assumption which is made by almost everyone.

The assumption is, that the possession of material commodities is what makes men happy. It is thought that a man who has two rooms and two beds and two loaves must be twice as happy as a man who has one room and one bed and one loaf. In a word, it is thought that happiness is proportional to income. A few people, not always quite sincerely, challenge this idea in the name of religion or morality; but they are glad if they increase their income by the eloquence of their preaching. It is not from a moral or religious point of view that I wish to challenge it; it is from the point of view of psychology and observation of life. If happiness is proportional to income, the case for machinery is unanswerable; if not, the whole question remains to be examined.

Men have physical needs, and they have emotions. While physical needs are unsatisfied, they take first place; but when they are satisfied, emotions unconnected with them become important in deciding whether a man is to be happy or unhappy. In modern industrial communities there are many men, women, and children whose bare physical needs are not adequately supplied; as regards them, I do not deny that the first requisite for happiness is an increase of income. But they are a minority, and it would not be difficult to give the bare necessaries of life to all of them. It is not of them that I wish to speak, but of those who have more than is necessary to support existence—

not only those who have much more, but also those who have only a little more.

Why do we, in fact, almost all of us, desire to increase our incomes? It may seem, at first sight, as though material goods were what we desire. But, in fact, we desire these mainly in order to impress our neighbours. When a man moves into a large house in a more genteel quarter, he reflects that 'better' people will call on his wife, and some unprosperous cronies of former days can be dropped. When he sends his son to a good school or an expensive university, he consoles himself for the heavy fees by thoughts of the social kudos to be gained. In every big city, whether of Europe or of America, houses in some districts are more expensive than equally good houses in other districts, merely because they are more fashionable. One of the most powerful of all our passions is the desire to be admired and respected. As things stand, admiration and respect are given to the man who seems to be rich. This is the chief reason why people wish to be rich. The actual goods purchased by their money play quite a secondary part. Take, for example, a millionaire who cannot tell one picture from another, but has acquired a gallery of old masters by the help of experts. The only pleasure he derives from his pictures is the thought that others know how much they have cost; he would derive more direct enjoyment from sentimental chromos out of Christmas numbers, but he would not obtain the same satisfaction for his vanity.

All this might be different, and has been different in many societies. In aristocratic epochs, men have been admired for their birth. In some circles in Paris, men are admired for their artistic or literary excellence, strange as it may seem. In a German university, a man may actually be admired for his learning. In India saints are admired; in China, sages. The study of these differing societies shows the correctness of our analysis, for in all of them we find a large percentage of men who are indifferent to money so long as they have enough to keep alive on, but are keenly desirous of the merits by which, in their environment, respect is to be won.

The importance of these facts lies in this, that the modern desire for wealth is not inherent in human nature, and could be destroyed by different social institutions. If, by law, we all had exactly the same income, we should have to seek some other way of being superior to our neighbours, and most of our present craving for material possessions would cease. Moreover, since this craving is in the nature of a competition, it only brings happiness when we out-distance a rival, to whom it brings correlative pain. A general increase of wealth gives no competitive advantage, and therefore brings no competitive happiness. There is, of course, *some* pleasure derived from the actual enjoyment of goods purchased, but, as we have seen, this is a very small part of what makes us desire wealth. And in so far as our desire is competitive, no increase of human happiness as a whole comes from increase of wealth, whether general or particular.

If we are to argue that machinery increases happiness, therefore, the increase of material prosperity which it brings cannot weigh heavily in its favour, except in so far as it may be used to prevent absolute destitution. But there is no inherent reason why it should be so used. Destitution can be prevented without machinery where the population is stationary; of this France may serve as an example, since there is very little destitution and much less machinery than in America, England, and pre-war Germany. Conversely, there may be much destitution where there is much machinery; of this we have examples in the industrial areas of England a hundred years ago and of Japan at the present day. The prevention of destitution does not depend upon machines, but upon quite other factors—partly density of population, and partly political conditions. And apart from prevention of destitution, the value of increasing wealth is not very great.

Meanwhile, machines deprive us of two things which are certainly important ingredients of human happiness, namely spontaneity and variety. Machines have their own pace, and their own insistent demands; a man who has expensive plant must keep it working. The great trouble with the machine, from the point of view of the emotions, is its *regularity*. And, of course, conversely, the great objection to the emotions, from the point of view of the machine, is their *irregularity*. As the machine dominates the thoughts of people who consider themselves 'serious', the highest praise they can give to a man is to suggest that he has the quality of a machine—that he is reliable, punctual, exact, etc. And an 'irregular' life has come to be synonymous with a bad life. Against this point of view Bergson's philosophy was a protest—not, to my mind, wholly sound from an intellectual point of view, but inspired by a wholesome dread of seeing men turned more and more into machines.

In life, as opposed to thought, the rebellion of our instincts against enslavement to mechanism has hitherto taken a most unfortunate direction. The impulse to war has always existed since men took to living in societies, but it did not, in the past, have the same intensity or virulence as it has in our day. In the eighteenth century, England and France had innumerable wars, and contended for the hegemony of the world; but they liked and respected each other the whole time. Officer prisoners joined in the social life of their captors, and were honoured guests at their dinner-parties. At the beginning of our war with Holland in 1665, a man came home from Africa with atrocity stories about the Dutch there; we (the British) persuaded ourselves that his story was false, punished him, and published the Dutch denial. In the late war we should have knighted him, and imprisoned anyone who threw doubt on his veracity. The greater ferocity of modern war is attributable to machines, which operate in three different ways. First, they make it possible to have larger armies. Secondly, they facilitate a cheap Press, which flourishes by appealing to men's baser passions. Thirdly—and this is the point that concerns us—they starve the anarchic, spontaneous side of human nature, which works underground, producing an obscure discontent, to which the thought of war appeals as affording possible relief. It is a mistake to attribute a vast upheaval like the late war merely to the machinations of politicians. In Russia, perhaps, such an explanation would have been adequate; that is one reason why Russia fought half-heartedly, and made a revolution to secure peace. But in England, Germany, and the United States (in 1917), no Government could have withstood the popular demand for war. A popular demand of this sort must have an instinctive basis, and for my part I believe that the modern increase in warlike instinct is attributable to the dissatis-faction (mostly unconscious) caused by the regularity, monotony, and tameness of modern life.

It is obvious that we cannot deal with this situation by abolishing machinery. Such a measure would be reactionary, and is in any case impracticable. The only way of avoiding the evils at present asso-ciated with machinery is to provide breaks in the monotony, and every encouragement to high adventure during the intervals. Many men would cease to desire war if they had opportunities to risk their lives in Alpine climbing; one of the ablest and most vigorous workers for peace that it has been my good fortune to know habitually spent his summer climbing the most dangerous peaks in the Alps. If every working man had a month in the year during which, if he chose, he could be taught to work an aeroplane, or encouraged to hunt for sapphires in the Sahara, or otherwise enabled to engage in some dangerous and exciting pursuit involving quick personal initiative, the popular love of war would become confined to women and invalids. I confess I know no method of making these classes pacific, but I am convinced that a scientific psychology would find a method if it undertook the task in earnest.

Machines have altered our way of life, but not our instincts. Consequently there is maladjustment. The whole psychology of the emotions and instincts is as yet in its infancy; a beginning has been made by psycho-analysis, but only a beginning. What we may accept from psycho-analysis is the fact that people will, in action, pursue various ends which they do not *consciously* desire, and will have an attendant set of quite irrational beliefs which enable them to pursue these ends without knowing that they are doing so. But orthodox psycho-analysis has unduly simplified our unconscious purposes, which are numerous, and differ from one person to another. It is to be hoped that social and political phenomena will soon come to be understood from this point of view, and will thus throw light on average human nature.

Moral self-control, and external prohibition of harmful acts, are not adequate methods of dealing with our anarchic instincts. The reason they are inadequate is that these instincts are capable of as many disguises as the devil in medieval legend, and some of these disguises deceive even the elect. The only adequate method is to discover what are the needs of our instinctive nature, and then to search for the least harmful way of satisfying them. Since spontaneity is what is most thwarted by machines, the only thing that can be *provided* is opportunity; the use made of opportunity must be left to the initiative of the individual. No doubt considerable expense would be involved; but it would not be comparable to the expense of war. Understanding of human nature must be the basis of any real improvements in human life. Science has done wonders in mastering the laws of the physical world, but our own nature is much less understood, as yet, than the nature of stars and electrons. When science learns to understand human nature, it will be able to bring a happiness into our lives which machines and the physical sciences have failed to create.

Selected Snobberies

ALDOUS HUXLEY

All men are snobs about something. One is almost tempted to add: There is nothing about which men cannot feel snobbish. But this would doubtless be an exaggeration. There are certain disfiguring and mortal diseases about which there has probably never been any snobbery. I cannot imagine, for example, that there are any leprosy snobs. More picturesque diseases, even when they are dangerous, and less dangerous diseases, particularly when they are the diseases of the rich, can be and very frequently are a source of snobbish self-importance. I have met several adolescent consumption-snobs, who thought that it would be romantic to fade away in the flower of youth, like Keats or Marie Bashkirtseff. Alas, the final stages of the consumptive fading are generally a good deal less romantic than these ingenuous young tubercle-snobs seem to imagine. To any who has actually witnessed these final stages, the complacent poeticising of these adolescents must seem as exasperating as they are profoundly pathetic. In the case of those commoner disease-snobs, whose claim to distinction is that they suffer from one of the maladies of the rich, exasperation is not tempered by very much sympathy. People who possess sufficient leisure, sufficient wealth, not to mention sufficient health, to go travelling from spa to spa, from doctor to fashionable doctor, in search of cures from problematical diseases (which, in so far as they exist at all, probably have their source in overeating) cannot expect us to be very lavish in our solicitude and pity.

Disease-snobbery is only one out of a great multitude of snobberies, of which now some, now others take pride of place in general esteem. For snobberies ebb and flow; their empire rises, declines, and falls in the most approved historical manner. What were good snobberies a hundred years ago are now out of fashion. Thus, the snobbery of family is everywhere on the decline. The snobbery of culture, still strong, has now to wrestle with an organised and active low-browism, with a snobbery of ignorance and stupidity unique, so far as I know, in the whole of history. Hardly less characteristic of our age is that repulsive booze-snobbery, born of American Prohibition. The malefic influences of this snobbery are rapidly spreading all over the world. Even in France, where the existence of so many varieties of delicious wine has hitherto imposed a judicious connoisseurship and has led to the branding of mere drinking as a brutish solecism, even in France the American booze-snobbery, with its odious accompaniments—a taste for hard drinks in general and for cocktails in particular—is making headway among the rich. Booze-snobbery has now made it socially permissible, and in some circles even rather creditable, for well-brought-up men and (this is the novelty) well-brought-up women of all ages, from fifteen to seventy, to be seen drunk, if not in public, at least in the very much tempered privacy of a party.

Modernity-snobbery, though not exclusive to our age, has come to assume an unprecedented importance. The reasons for this are simple and of a strictly economic character. Thanks to modern machinery, production is outrunning consumption. Organised waste among consumers is the first condition of our industrial prosperity. The sooner a consumer throws away the object he has bought and buys another, the better for the producer. At the same time, of course, the producer must do his bit by producing nothing but the most perishable articles. 'The man who builds a skyscraper to last for more than forty years is a traitor to the building trade.' The words are those of a great American contractor. Substitute motor car, boot, suit of clothes, etc., for skyscraper, and one year, three months, six months, and so on for forty years, and you have the gospel of any leader of any modern industry. The modernity-snob, it is obvious, is this industrialist's best friend. For modernity-snobs naturally tend to throw away their old possessions and buy new ones at a greater rate than those who are not modernity-snobs. Therefore it is in the producer's interest to encourage modernity-snobbery. Which in fact he does do—on an enormous scale and to the tune of millions and millions a year—by means of advertising. The newspapers do their best to help those who help them; and to the flood of advertisement is added a flood of less directly paid-for propaganda in favour of modernity-snobbery. The public is taught that up-to-dateness is one of the first duties of man. Docile, it accepts the reiterated suggestion. We are all modernity-snobs now.

Most of us are also art-snobs. There are two varieties of art-snobbery—the platonic and the unplatonic. Platonic art-snobs merely 'take an interest' in art. Unplatonic art-snobs go further and actually buy art. Platonic art-snobbery is a branch of culture-snobbery. Unplatonic art-snobbery is a hybrid or mule; for it is simultaneously a sub-species of culture-snobbery and of possession-snobbery. A collection of works of art is a collection of culture-symbols, and culture-symbols still carry social prestige. It is also a collection of wealth-symbols. For an art collection can represent money more effectively than a whole fleet of motor cars.

The value of art-snobbery to living artists is considerable. True, most art-snobs collect only the works of the dead; for an Old Master is both a safer investment and a holier culture-symbol than a living master. But some art-snobs are also modernity-snobs. There are enough of them, with the few eccentrics who like works of art for their own sake, to provide living artists with the means of subsistence.

The value of snobbery in general, its humanistic 'point', consists in its power to stimulate activity. A society with plenty of snobberies is like a dog with plenty of fleas: it is not likely to become comatose. Every snobbery demands of its devotees unceasing efforts, a succession of sacrifices. The society-snob must be perpetually lion-hunting; the modernity-snob can never rest from trying to be up-to-date. Swiss doctors and the Best that has been thought or said must be the daily and nightly preoccupation of all the snobs respectively of disease and culture.

If we regard activity as being in itself a good, then we must count all snobberies as good; for all provoke activity. If, with the Buddhists, we regard all activity in this world of illusion as bad, then we shall condemn all snobberies out of hand. Most of us, I suppose, take up our position somewhere between the two extremes. We regard some activities as good, others as indifferent or downright bad. Our approval will be given only to such snobberies as excite what we regard as the better activities; the others we shall either tolerate or detest. For example, most professional intellectuals will approve of culture-snobbery (even while intensely disliking most individual culture-snobs), because it compels the philistines to pay at least some slight tribute to the things of the mind and so helps to make the world less dangerously unsafe for ideas than it otherwise might have been. A manufacturer of motor cars, on the other hand, will rank the snobbery of possessions above culture-snobbery; he will do his best to persuade people that those who have fewer possessions, particularly possessions on four wheels, are inferior to those who have more possessions. And so on. Each hierarchy culminates in its own particular Pope.

How to Name a Dog

JAMES THURBER

Every few months somebody writes me and asks if I will give him a name for his dog. Several of these correspondents in the past year have wanted to know if I would mind the use of my own name for their spaniels. Spaniel owners seem to have the notion that a person could sue for invasion of privacy or defamation of character if his name is applied to a cocker without written permission, and one gentleman even insisted that we conduct our correspondence in the matter through a notary public. I have a way of letting communications of this sort fall behind my roll-top desk, but it has recently occurred to me that this is an act of evasion, if not, indeed, of plain cowardice. I have therefore decided to come straight out with the simple truth that it is as hard for me to think up a name for a dog as it is for anybody else. The idea that I was an expert in the business is probably the outcome of a piece I wrote several years ago, incautiously revealing the fact that I have owned forty or more dogs in my life. This is true, but it is also deceptive. All but five or six of my dogs were disposed of when they were puppies, and I had not gone to the trouble of giving to these impermanent residents of my house any names at all except Hey, You! and Cut That Out! and Let Go!

Names of dogs end up in 176th place in the list of things that amaze and fascinate me. Canine cognomens should be designed to impinge on the ears of the dogs and not to amuse neighbours, tradespeople, and casual visitors. I remember a few dogs from the past with a faint but lingering pleasure: a farm hound named Rain, a roving Airedale named Marco Polo, a female bull terrier known as Stephanie Brody because she liked to jump from moving motor-cars and second-storey windows, and a Peke called Darien; but that's about all. The only animals whose naming demands concentration, hard work, and ingenuity are the seeing-eye dogs. They have to be given unusual names because passers-by like to call to seeing-eyers—'Here, Sport', or 'Yuh, Rags', or 'Don't take any wooden nickels, Rin Tin Tin'. A blind man's dog with an ordinary name would continually be distracted from its work. A tyro at naming these dogs might make the mistake of picking Durocher or Teeftallow. The former is too much like Rover and the latter could easily sound like 'Here, fellow' to a dog.

Speaking of puppies, as I was a while back, I feel that I should warn inexperienced dog owners who have discovered to their surprise and dismay a dozen puppies in a hall closet or under the floors of the barn, not to give them away. Sell them or keep them, but don't give them away. Sixty per cent of persons who are given a dog for nothing bring him back sooner or later and plump him into the reluctant and unprepared lap of his former owner. The people say that they are going to Florida and can't take the dog, or that he doesn't want to go; or they point out that he eats first editions or lace curtains or spinets, or that he doesn't see eye to eye with them in the matter of house-breaking, or that he makes disparaging remarks under his breath about their friends. Anyway, they bring him back and you are stuck with him—and maybe six others. But if you charge ten or even five dollars for pups, the new owners don't dare return them. They are afraid to ask for their money back because they believe you might think they are hard up and need the five or ten dollars. Furthermore, when a mischievous puppy is returned to its former owner it invaria-bly behaves beautifully, and the person who brought it back is likely to be regarded as an imbecile or a dog hater or both.

Names of dogs, to get back to our subject, have a range almost as wide as that of the violin. They run from such plain and simple names as Spot, Sport, Rex, Brownie, and Rover—all originated by small boys—to such effete and fancy appellations as Prince Rudolph Her-tenberg Gratzheim of Darndorf-Putzelhorst, and Darling Mist o' Love III of Heather-Light-Holyrood—names originated by adults, all of whom in every other way, I am told, have made a normal adjustment to life. In addition to the plain and the fancy categories, there are the Cynical and the Coy. Cynical names are given by people who do not like dogs too much. The most popular cynical names during the war were Mussolini, Tojo, and Adolf. I never have been able to get very far in my exploration of the minds of people who call their dogs Mussolini, Tojo, and Adolf, and I suspect the reason is that I am unable to associate with them long enough to examine what goes on in their heads. I nod, and I tell them the time of day, if they ask, and that is all. I never vote for them or ask them to have a drink. The great Coy category is perhaps the largest. The Coy people call their pets Bubbles and Boggles and Sparkles and Twinkles and Doodles and Puffy and Lovums and Sweetums and Itsy-Bitsy and Betsy-Bye-Bye and Sugarkins. I pass these dog owners at a dog-trot, wearing a horrible fixed grin.

There is a special subdivision of the Coys that is not quite so awful, but awful enough. These people, whom we will call the Wits, own two dogs, which they name Pitter and Patter, Willy and Nilly, Helter and Skelter, Namby and Pamby, Hugger and Mugger, Hokery and Pokery, and even Wishy and Washy, Ups and Daisy, Fitz and Startz, Fetch and Carrie, and Pro and Connie. Then there is the Cryptic category. These people select names for some private reason or for no reason at all—except perhaps to arouse the visitor's curiosity, so that he will exclaim, 'Why in the world do you call your dog *that?*' The Cryptics name their dogs October, Bennett's Aunt, Three Fifteen, Doc Knows, Tuesday, Home Fried, Opus 38, Ask Leslie, and Thanks for the Home Run, Emil. I make it a point simply to pat these unfortunate dogs on the head, ask no questions of their owners, and go about my business.

This article has degenerated into a piece that properly should be entitled 'How Not To Name a Dog'. I was afraid it would. It seems only fair to make up for this by confessing a few of the names I have given my own dogs, with the considerable help, if not, indeed, the insistence, of their mistress. Most of my dogs have been females, and they have answered, with apparent gladness, to such names as Jeannie, Tessa, Julie, and Sophie. Sophie is a black French poodle whose kennel name was Christabel, but she never answered to Christabel, which she considers as foolish a name for a dog as Pamela, Jennifer, Clarissa, Jacqueline, Guinevere, and Shelmerdine. Sophie is opposed, and I am also, to Ida, Cora, Blanche, and Myrtle.

About six years ago, when I was looking for a house to buy in Connecticut, I knocked on the front door of an attractive home whose owner, my real estate agent had told me, wanted to sell it and go back to Iowa to live. The lady agent who escorted me around had informed me that the owner of this place was a man named Strong, but a few minutes after arriving at the house, I was having a drink in the living-room with Phil Stong, for it was he. We went out into the yard after a while and I saw Mr Stong's spaniel. I called to the dog and snapped my fingers but he seemed curiously embarrassed, like his master. 'What's his name?' I asked the latter. He was cornered and there was no way out of it. 'Thurber,' he said, in a small frightened voice. Thurber and I shook hands, and he didn't seem to me any more depressed than any other spaniel I have met. He had, however, the expression of a bachelor on his way to a party he has tried in vain to get out of, and I think it must have been this cast of countenance that had reminded Mr Stong of the dog I draw. The dog I draw is, to be sure, much larger than a spaniel and not so shaggy, but I confess, though I am not a spaniel man, that there are certain basic resemblances between my dog and all other dogs with long ears and troubled eyes.

The late Hendrik Van Loon was privy to the secret that the dog of my drawings was originally intended to look more like a bloodhound than anything else, but that he turned up by accident with legs too short to be an authentic member of this breed. This flaw was brought about by the fact that the dog was first drawn on a telephone memo pad which was not large enough to accommodate him. Mr Van Loon laboured under the unfortunate delusion that an actual bloodhound would fit as unobtrusively into the Van Loon living room as the drawn dog does in the pictures. He learned his mistake in a few weeks. He discovered that an actual bloodhound regards a residence as a series of men's rooms and that it is interested only in tracing things. Once, when Mr Van Loon had been wandering around his yard for an hour or more, he called to his bloodhound and was dismayed when, instead of coming directly to him, the dog proceeded to follow every crisscross of the maze its master had made in wandering about. 'That dog didn't care a damn about where I was,' Mr Van Loon told me. 'All he was interested in was how I got there.'

Perhaps I should suggest at least one name for a dog, if only to justify the title of this piece. All right, then, what's the matter with Stong? It's a good name for a dog, short, firm, and effective. I recommend it to all those who have written to me for suggestions and to all those who may be at this very moment turning over in their minds the idea of asking my advice in this difficult and perplexing field of nomenclature.

On Nothing

HENRY FIELDING

THE INTRODUCTION

It is surprising that, while such trifling matters employ the masterly pens of the present age, the great and noble subject of this essay should have passed totally neglected; and the rather, as it is a subject to which the genius of many of those writers who have unsuccessfully applied themselves to politics, religion, etc., is most peculiarly adapted.

Perhaps their unwillingness to handle what is of such importance may not improperly be ascribed to their modesty; though they may not be remarkably addicted to this vice on every occasion. Indeed I have heard it predicated of some, whose assurance in treating other subjects hath been sufficiently notable, that they have blushed at this. For such is the awe with which this Nothing inspires mankind, that I believe it is generally apprehended of many persons of very high character among us, that were title, power, or riches to allure them, they would stick at it.

But, whatever be the reason, certain it is, that except a hardy wit in the reign of Charles II, none ever hath dared to write on this subject: I mean openly and avowedly; for it must be confessed that most of our modern authors, however foreign the matter which they endeavour to treat may seem at their first setting out, they generally bring the work to this in the end. I hope, however, this attempt will not be imputed to me as an act of immodesty; since I am convinced there are many persons in this kingdom who are persuaded of my fitness for what I have undertaken. But as talking of a man's self is generally suspected to arise from vanity, I shall, without any more excuse or preface, proceed to my essay.

SECTION I

ON THE ANTIQUITY OF NOTHING

There is nothing falser than that old proverb which (like many other falsehoods) is in everyone's mouth:

Ex nihilo nihil fit.

Thus translated by Shakespeare, in *Lear*:

Nothing can come of nothing.

Whereas, in fact, from Nothing proceeds everything. And this is a truth confessed by the philosophers of all sects: the only point in controversy between them being, whether Something made the world out of Nothing, or Nothing out of Something. A matter not much worth debating at present, since either will equally serve our turn. Indeed the wits of all ages seem to have ranged themselves on each side of this question, as their genius tended more or less to the spiritual or material substance. For those of the more spiritual species have inclined to the former, and those whose genius hath partaken more of the chief properties of matter, such as solidity, thickness, etc., have embraced the latter.

But whether Nothing was the *artifex* or *materies* only, it is plain in either case, it will have a right to claim to itself the origination of all things.

And farther, the great antiquity of Nothing is apparent from its being so visible in the account we have of the beginning of every nation. This is very plainly to be discovered in the first pages, and sometimes books, of all general historians; and, indeed, the study of this important subject fills up the whole life of an antiquary, it being always at the bottom of his inquiry, and is commonly at last discovered by him with infinite labour and pains.

SECTION II

OF THE NATURE OF NOTHING

Another falsehood which we must detect in the pursuit of this essay is an assertion, 'That no one can have an idea on Nothing': but men who thus confidently deny us this idea either grossly deceive themselves, or would impose a downright cheat on the world: for, so far from having none, I believe there are few who have not many ideas of it; though perhaps they may mistake them for the idea of Something.

For instance, is there anyone who hath not an idea of immaterial substance?* Now what is immaterial substance, more than Nothing?

*The Author would not be here understood to speak against the doctrine of immateriality, to which he is a hearty well-wisher; but to point at the stupidity of those who, instead of immaterial *essence*, which would convey a rational meaning, have substituted immaterial *substance*, which is a contradiction in terms.

But here we are artfully deceived by the use of words: for, were we to ask another what idea he had of immaterial matter, or unsubstantial substance, the absurdity of affirming it to be Something would shock him, and he would immediately reply, it was Nothing.

Some persons perhaps will say, 'Then we have no idea of it'; but, as I can support the contrary by such undoubted authority, I shall, instead of trying to confute such idle opinions, proceed to show: first, what Nothing is; secondly, I shall disclose the various kinds of Nothing; and, lastly shall prove its great dignity, and that it is the end of everything.

As it is extremely hard to define Nothing in positive terms, I shall therefore do it in negative. Nothing then is not Something. And here I must object to a third error concerning it, which is, that it is in no place; which is an indirect way of depriving it of its existence; whereas indeed it possesses the greatest and noblest place on this earth, viz., the human brain. But indeed this mistake has been sufficiently refuted by many very wise men; who, having spent their whole lives in contemplation and pursuit of Nothing, have at last gravely concluded—*that there is Nothing in this world.*

Farther, as Nothing is not Something, so everything which is not Something is Nothing; and wherever Something is not Nothing is: a very large allowance in its favour, as must appear to persons well skilled in human affairs.

For instance, when a bladder is full of wind, it is full of something; but when that is let out, we aptly say, there is nothing in it.

The same may be as justly asserted of a man as of a bladder. However well he may be bedaubed with lace, or with title, yet, if he have not something in him, we may predicate the same of him as of an empty bladder.

But if we cannot reach an adequate knowledge of the true essence of Nothing, no more than we can of matter, let us, in imitation of the experimental philosophers, examine some of its properties or accidents.

And here we shall see the infinite advantages which Nothing hath over Something; for, while the latter is confined to one sense, or two perhaps at the most, Nothing is the object of them all.

For, first, Nothing may be seen, as is plain from the relation of persons who have recovered from high fevers, and perhaps may be suspected from some (at least) of those who have seen apparitions, both on earth and in the clouds. Nay, I have often heard it confessed by men, when asked what they saw at such a place and time, that they saw Nothing. Admitting then there are two sights, viz., a first and second sight, according to the firm belief of some, Nothing must be allowed to have a very large share of the first, and as to the second, it hath it all entirely to itself.

Secondly, Nothing may be heard, of which the same proofs may be given as of the foregoing. The Argive mentioned by Horace is a strong instance of this:

> *Fuit haud ignobilis Argis,*
> *Qui se credebat miros audire tragoedos,*
> *In vacuo laetus sessor plausorque theatro.*

That Nothing may be tasted and smelt is not only known to persons of delicate palates and nostrils. How commonly do we hear that such a thing smells or tastes of nothing! The latter I have heard asserted of a dish compounded of five or six savoury ingredients. And as to the former, I remember an elderly gentlewoman who had a great antipathy to the smell of apples, who, upon discovering that an idle boy had fastened some mellow apple to her tail, contracted a habit of smelling them whenever that boy came within her sight, though there were then none within a mile of her.

Lastly, feeling: and sure if any sense seems more particularly the object of matter only, which must be allowed to be Something, this doth. Nay, I have heard it asserted, and with a colour of truth, of several persons, that they can feel nothing but a cudgel. Notwithstanding which, some have felt the motions of the spirit, and others have felt very bitterly the misfortunes of their friends, without endeavouring to relieve them. Now these seem two plain instances that Nothing is an object of this sense. Nay, I have heard a surgeon declare, while he was cutting off a patient's leg, that *he was sure he felt Nothing*.

Nothing is as well the object of our passions as our senses. Thus there are many who love Nothing, some who hate Nothing, and some who fear Nothing, etc.

We have already mentioned three of the properties of a noun to belong to Nothing; we shall find the fourth likewise to be as justly claimed by it, and that Nothing is as often the object of the understanding as of the senses.

Indeed some have imagined that knowledge, with the adjective *human* placed before it, is another word for Nothing. And one of the wisest men in the world declared he knew Nothing.

But, without carrying it so far, this I believe may be allowed, that it is at least possible for a man to know Nothing. And whoever hath read over many works of our ingenious moderns, with proper attention and emoluments, will, I believe, confess that, if he understand them right, he understands Nothing.

This is a secret not known to all readers, and want of this knowledge hath occasioned much puzzling; for where a book or chapter or paragraph hath seemed to the reader to contain Nothing, his modesty hath sometimes persuaded him that the true meaning of the author hath escaped him, instead of concluding, as in reality the fact was, that the author in the said book, etc., did truly and *bona fide* mean Nothing. I remember once, at the table of a person of great eminence, and one no less distinguished by superiority of wit than fortune, when a very dark passage was read out of a poet famous for being so sublime that he is often out of the sight of his reader, some persons present declared they did not understand the meaning. The gentleman himself, casting his eye over the performance, testified a surprise at the dullness of his company, seeing Nothing could, he said, possibly be plainer than the meaning of the passage which they stuck at. This set all of us to puzzling again, but with like success; we frankly owned we could not find it out, and desired he would explain it. 'Explain it!' said the gentleman, 'why, he means Nothing.'

In fact, this mistake arises from a too vulgar error among persons unacquainted with the mystery of writing, who imagine it impossible that a man should sit down to write without any meaning at all! whereas, in reality, nothing is more common: for, not to instance in myself, who have confessedly set down to write this essay with Nothing in my head, or, which is much the same thing, to write about Nothing, it may be incontestably proved, *ab effectu*, that Nothing is commoner among the moderns. The inimitable author of a preface to the Posthumous Eclogues of a late ingenious young gentleman, says, 'There are men who sit down to write what they think, and others to think what they shall write.' But indeed there is a third and much more numerous sort, who never think either before they sit down or afterwards, and who, when they produce on paper what was before in their heads, are sure to produce Nothing.

Thus we have endeavoured to demonstrate the nature of Nothing, by showing first, definitively, *what it is not*; and, secondly, by describing *what it is*. The next thing therefore proposed is to show its various kinds.

Now some imagine these several kinds differ in name only. But, without endeavouring to confute so absurd an opinion, especially as these different kinds of Nothing occur frequently in the best authors, I shall content myself with setting them down, and leave it to the determination of the distinguished reader, whether it is probable, or indeed possible, that they should all convey one and the same meaning.

These are, Nothing *per se* Nothing; Nothing at all; Nothing in the least; Nothing in nature; Nothing in the world; Nothing in the whole world; Nothing in the whole universal world. And perhaps many other of which we say—Nothing.

SECTION III

OF THE DIGNITY OF NOTHING: AND AN ENDEAVOUR TO PROVE THAT IT IS THE END AS WELL AS BEGINNING OF ALL THINGS

Nothing contains so much dignity as Nothing. Ask an infamous worthless nobleman (if any such be) in what his dignity consists. It may not be perhaps consistent with his dignity to give you an answer, but suppose he should be willing to condescend so far, what could he in effect say? Should he say he had it from his ancestors, I apprehend a lawyer would oblige him to prove that the virtues to which his dignity was annexed descended to him. If he claims it as inherent in the title, might he not be told, that a title originally implied dignity, as it implied the presence of those virtues to which dignity is inseparably annexed; but that no implication will fly in the face of downright positive proof to the contrary. In short, to examine no farther, since his endeavour to derive it from any other fountain would be equally impotent, his dignity arises from Nothing, and in reality is Nothing. Yet, that this dignity really exists, that it glares in the eyes of men, and produces much good to the person who wears it, is, I believe, incontestable.

Perhaps this may appear in the following syllogism.

The respect paid to men on account of their titles is paid at least to the supposal of their superior virtues and abilities, or it is paid to Nothing.

But when a man is a notorious knave or fool it is impossible there should be any such supposal.

The conclusion is apparent.

Now, that no man is ashamed of either paying or receiving this respect I wonder not, since the great importance of Nothing seems, I think, to be pretty apparent: but that they should deny the Deity worshipped, and endeavour to represent Nothing as Something, is more worthy reprehension. This is a fallacy extremely common. I have seen a fellow, whom all the world knew to have Nothing in him, not only pretend to Something himself, but supported in that pretension by others who have been less liable to be deceived. Now whence can this proceed but from their being ashamed of Nothing? A modesty very peculiar to this age.

But, notwithstanding all such disguises and deceit, a man must have very little discernment who can live very long in courts, or populous cities, without being convinced of the great dignity of Nothing; and though he should, through corruption or necessity, comply with the vulgar worship and adulation, he will know to what it is paid; namely to Nothing.

The most astonishing instance of this respect, so frequently paid to Nothing, is when it is paid (if I may so express myself) to something less than Nothing; when the person who receives it is not only void of the quality for which he is respected, but is in reality notoriously guilty of the vices directly opposite to the virtues whose applause he receives. This is, indeed, the highest degree of Nothing, or (if I may be allowed the word), the Nothingest of all Nothings.

Here it is to be known, that respect may be aimed at Something and really light on Nothing. For instance, when mistaking certain things called gravity, canting, blustering, ostentation, pomp, and such like, for wisdom, piety, magnanimity, charity, true greatness, etc., we give to the former the honour and reverence due to the latter. Not that I would be understood so far to discredit my subject as to insinuate that gravity, canting, etc., are really Nothing; on the contrary, there is much more reason to suspect (if we judge from the practice of the world) that wisdom, piety, and other virtues, have a good title to that name. But we do not, in fact, pay our respect to the former, but to the latter: in other words, we pay it to that which is not, and consequently pay it to Nothing.

So far then for the dignity of the subject on which I am treating. I am now to show, that Nothing is the end as well as beginning of all things.

That everything is resolvable, and will be resolved into its first principles, will be, I believe, readily acknowledged by all philosophers. As, therefore, we have sufficiently proved the world came from Nothing, it follows that it will likewise end in the same: but as I am writing to a nation of Christians, I have no need to be prolix on this head; since every one of my readers, by his faith, acknowledges that the world is to have an end, *i.e.*, is to come to Nothing.

And, as Nothing is the end of the world, so is it of everything in the world. Ambition, the greatest, highest, noblest, finest, most heroic and godlike of all passions, what doth it end in?—Nothing. What did Alexander, Caesar, and all the rest of that heroic band, who have plundered and massacred so many millions, obtain by all their care, labour, pain, fatigue, and danger?—Could they speak for themselves must they not own, that the end of all their pursuit was Nothing? Nor is this the end of private ambition only. What is become of that proud mistress of the world—the *Caput triumphati orbis*—that Rome of which her own flatterers so liberally prophesied the immortality? In what hath all her glory ended? Surely in Nothing.

Again, what is the end of avarice? Not power, or pleasure, as some think, for the miser will part with a shilling for neither: not ease or happiness; for the more he attains of what he desires, the more uneasy and miserable he is. If every good in this world was put to him, he could not say he pursued one. Shall we say then he pursues misery only? That surely would be contradictory to the first principles of human nature. May we not therefore, nay, must we not confess, that he aims at Nothing? especially if he be himself unable to tell us what is the end of all this bustle and hurry, this watching and toiling, this self-denial and self-constraint?

It will not, I apprehend, be sufficient for him to plead that his design is to amass a large fortune, which he never can nor will use himself, nor would willingly quit to any other person: unless he can show us some substantial good which this fortune is to produce, we shall certainly be justified in concluding that his end is the same with that of ambition.

The great Mr Hobbes so plainly saw this, that as he was an enemy to that notable immaterial substance which we have here handled, and therefore unwilling to allow it the large province we have contended for, he advanced a very strange doctrine and asserted truly—That in all these grand pursuits the means themselves were the end proposed, viz., to ambition—plotting, fighting, danger, difficulty, and such like: to avarice—cheating, starving, watching, and the numberless painful arts by which this passion proceeds.

However easy it may be to demonstrate the absurdity of this opinion it will be needless to my purpose, since, if we are driven to confess that the means are the only end attained, I think we must likewise confess that the end proposed is absolutely Nothing.

As I have shown the end of our two greatest and noblest pursuits, one or other of which engages almost every individual of the busy part of mankind, I shall not tire the reader with carrying him through all the rest, since I believe the same conclusion may be easily drawn from them all.

I shall therefore finish this Essay with an inference, which aptly enough suggests itself from what hath been said: seeing that such is its dignity and importance, and that it is really the end of all those things which are supported with so much pomp and solemnity, and looked on with such respect and esteem, surely it becomes a wise man to regard Nothing with the utmost awe and adoration; to pursue it with all his parts and pains, and to sacrifice to it his ease, his innocence, and his present happiness. To which noble pursuit we have this great incitement, that we may assure ourselves of never being cheated or deceived in the end proposed. The virtuous, wise, and learned may then be unconcerned at all the changes of ministries and of government; since they may be well satisfied, that while ministers of state are rogues themselves, and have inferior knavish tools to bribe and reward, true virtue, wisdom, learning, wit, and integrity, will most certainly bring their possessors—Nothing.

PART FIVE

On the Arts (Mostly Writing)

ANY SELECTION of essays on the Arts (especially if 'mostly writing') lines up like a chain of mirrors—Montaigne used the original word *essai*, remember, as self-discussion. The twelve writers here constitute a kind of self-fulfilment. In life the arts provide a machinery of spiritual evaluation, of self-examination—the Essay is supposed to do the same. And it does: E. M. Forster, discussing the help available in times of need from the great minds of the past, points out that 'if we have read them, or have listened to good music, it is going to be some use'.

Art best deals with life when it mirrors it by making us, to take one example, examine beneath the surface, to look for what is not on display. Elizabeth Bowen, who helped to develop the short story in English so that it became the cantata or the fugue of the literary composing arts, addressed this exclusion: 'Experience, innate sense of his craft and a critical estimate of the work of others combine to teach the author that what may be most eloquent, sometimes, is the excluded word—or phrase, or paragraph, or it may be chapter.'

Essays on the arts perform another useful function in that they nail down the arts, freeze them, lepidopterise them there for us to see and when we return to the original we may view it fresher and more clearly. Will we ever again consider Leonardo's work without seeing him in the light Walter Pater shines on him? 'His life is one of sudden revolts in which he works not at all, or apart from the main scope of his work.' In which phase did he paint the Mona Lisa?

The Essay's wonderful flexibility lies in the comprehensiveness of its concerns. Essays on the arts take the form full circle, setting a thief to catch a thief. In all its elasticity the Essay shows life in the same wide variety found in the arts, and when therefore the Essay catches up on the arts the circle closes pleasingly, as it did when Shaw sat for Rodin: 'I wanted a portrait of myself by an artist capable of seeing me.'

A Note on the Way

E. M. FORSTER

After letting myself go lately on the depressing subject of military tattoos and tainted investments, I thought, as I often do, of a line of Matthew Arnold's: 'Who prop, thou ask'st, in these bad days, my mind?' It is a line that rather makes me smile. For one thing the difficulty of pronouncing 'skst' is almost insuperable, for another Matthew Arnold's 'bad days' are Halcyon when compared with our own. He belonged to an age which was concerned with problems of faith, doubt, and personal survival; he was worried by these, but the collapse of all civilisation, so realistic for us, sounded in his ears like a distant and harmonious cataract, plunging from Alpine snows into the eternal bosom of the Lake of Geneva. We are passing through a much rougher time, perhaps the roughest time that has ever been. And if we look back into the past for comfort, we see upon the faces of its great men a curious mixture of comprehension and of blankness. They seem at the same time to understand us and not to understand. If public violences increase and Geneva itself disappears—who is going to prop our minds? They? The great minds of the past? They, who imagined, at the worst, a local or a philosophic catastrophe?

Yes. They are going to do something. If we have read them, or have listened to good music, it is going to be some use. The individual who has been rendered sensitive by education will not be deserted by it in his hour of need. But the help won't be given as directly, as crudely, as Matthew Arnold thought. An educationist as well as a poet, he believed one could 'turn' to writers—to Homer, Epictetus and Sophocles in his own case—and by quoting their beauties or remembering their thoughts could steel oneself against injustice or cruelty. I don't think they are going to bring their help that way. Their gifts are received less consciously and often provoke no thanks. But it is a great mistake to assume that nothing is going on, and a great blunder to close one's mind to the past because the present is so large and so frightening. The past, through its very detachment, can re-interpret.

It is easier to catch it failing than succeeding, and a little experience of my own not long ago, when Beethoven failed to do his job, will, anyhow, indicate the area where the job lies. I was going to a Busch Quartet and much looking forward to it, but just before starting I heard a decent and straightforward story of misfortune—quite unprintable, even in these advanced columns. Much of what one hears and says can never be printed; that is why newspapers are so unreal. This particular story involved procreation, marriage, birth. I got to the Wigmore Hall so occupied and worried over it, that I could not listen to the music at all, and yet I heard the whole of the music. I could not be caught up to meet my Lord in the air, yet there Beethoven was, working away all the time, and seeming to be actually a few feet above my head, where I could not reach him. It is, perhaps, creditable to my heart that I couldn't, but exactly the same thing happened in the Queen's Hall a few years ago when I had received a notice that my evidence would be wanted in the *Well of Loneliness* case. Here my thoughts were purely selfish. I was so fidgeting as to what figure I should cut in the witness-box that again nothing came through. The arts are not drugs. They are not guaranteed to act when taken. Something as mysterious and as capricious as the creative impulse has to be released before they can prop our minds. Siegfried Sassoon calls them 'lamps for our gloom, hands guiding where we stumble', which quiet personal image suits them very well.

The propping quality in books, music, etc., is only a by-product of another quality in them; their power to give pleasure. Consequently, it is impossible to advise one's friends what to read in 'these bad days', and even more impossible to advise people whom one doesn't know. All I can suggest is that where the fire was thence will the light come; where there was intense enjoyment, grave or gay, thence will proceed the help which every individual needs. And I don't want to exaggerate that help. Art is not enough, any more than love is enough, and thought isn't stronger than artillery parks now, whatever it may have been in the days of Carlyle. But art, love and thought can all do something, and art, the most nervous of the three, mustn't be brushed aside like a butterfly. It is not all gossamer, what we have delighted in, it has become part of our armour, and we can gird it on, although there is no armour against fate.

> Fair as unshaded light, or as the day
> In its first birth, when all the year was May;
> Sweet as the altar's smoke, or as the new
> Unfolded bud, swelled by the early dew;

Smooth as the face of waters first appeared,
Ere tides began to strive or winds were heard—

I quote these lines, not because they are great poetry (it is only Sir William Davenant addressing Queen Henrietta Maria), nor because they bear on the matter in hand (he is only welcoming her to an evening at the Countess of Anglesey's), but because they have happened to deposit a grain of strength in my mind. They are so lovely in their little way, and they have helped towards that general belief in loveliness which is part of our outfit against brutality. And I thought I would try to bring this out in my present note rather than deal with 'actualities'. These lines of Davenant—not 'ready when wanted', yet serviceable somehow—have gone down to a region in me which Matthew Arnold and Beethoven have also reached.

In the 'great' war, books helped me enormously, they even helped men in the trenches. My own position was easy. I was comfortable in Egypt, yet could I have come through without those 'lamps for my gloom'? I did not seek help consciously—except on one occasion: from Browning, a poet whom I don't much admire, and Browning, knowing this, gave the help in a hard hygienic way, for the occasion only, and at the price of my reading his *Flight of the Duchess*. The people I really clung to were those who had nothing tangible to offer: Blake, William Morris, the early T. S. Eliot, J. K. Huysman, Yeats. They took me into a country where the will is not everything, and the braying patriots of the moment made no sound. They were personal guides, and if I mention their names and add César Franck's, it is not to give a tip to 1934, only to suggest some parallel. We are all harder and more disillusioned now than we were then, the League of Nations lies behind us instead of before, and no political creed except communism offers an intelligent man any hope. And those who are, like myself, too old for communism or too conscious of the blood to be shed before its problematic victory, turn to literature, because it is disinterested. Action? Yes, no objection to action if it tinkers in the right direction, stops tattoos for instance. But not action the Fascist anodyne:

> *Not milder is the general lot*
> *Because our spirits have forgot,*
> *In action's dizzying eddy whirl'd*
> *The something that infects the world.*

Matthew Arnold, the poet, felt and knew much more than Matthew Arnold, the prose-writer, succeeded in saying. His poetry stands up in the middle of the nineteenth century as a beacon to the twentieth, it is both an armoury and an enchanted garden. Literature as a retreat is rightly discredited; it is both selfish and foolish to bury one's head in the flowers. But herbs grow in the garden, too, and share in its magics, and from them is distilled the stoicism which we badly need today. Uneducated people have a quantity of valuable resources which are denied to people like ourselves, on whom much money has been spent, but that is no reason why we should despise our proper stock in trade. If we are accustomed to enjoy poetry Matthew Arnold may come in useful, and if I am on the right track it is not the didactic poems, like the great *Empedocles*, which will help, but the allusive wisdom of his lyrics. Anyone who cares to make an experiment might re-read the *Switzerland* series, which professes only to describe the parting between two lovers. Like Davenant, and more obviously, Arnold will deposit grains of strength. I have not the least wish to see him, or to put before him our troubles about tariff walls and aeroplanes. I know that he would be unhelpful, departmental. And I would no more consult him about conduct than I would a great poet who is actually alive: Professor A. E. Housman. Yet he props my mind. He writes to us because he is not writing about us, he can give us calm.

Exclusion

ELIZABETH BOWEN

Though one may speak of a novel in terms of its length or shortness, one has in mind something more—its effective size. The book's physical bulk, its number of pages by no means denote, or act as a measure for, the extent or depth of its hold on imagination. The content of the novel is what affects us; and the content, because it expands in the reader's mind, may by far exceed what is stated in the actual writing—this, in fact, is one evidence of creative power. In some few cases the giving of this expansive force may be a fluke of the author's genius, but more often it is considered aim; and—genius admittedly being rare—it is with the aim that we are concerned. Experience, innate sense of his craft and a critical estimate of the work of others combine to teach the author that what may be most eloquent, sometimes, is the excluded word—or phrase, or paragraph, or it may be chapter. He learns that elimination may serve expression. He comes to see how far the unstated builds up the content.

For, the author's purpose is not merely to tell much, it is to make known the whole—the whole being his concept, which is his novel. The making known, and its manner, is what concerns him. What kind of telling, and how much, can and should best go to the making known? Continuously the author must be deciding not only how but exactly *what* to tell. He will be seeking, somewhere within himself, the reasons for the statements he is to make and, not less, the reasons for his withholdings. That the withheld (from actual writing) is not necessarily the rejected cannot be made too clear: indeed, what is withheld plays a creative part—the author, by keeping some things back, is adding silent potentials to his story. He makes felt, in fact, what he feels but has never said. He says (or rather, writes and allows to stand) only what does gain, from his point of view, by being told in so many words. The gain is definite ground in the reader's memory—a base, perhaps, to take off from later on. There must *be* factual groundwork: statement takes care of fact. There is much that the reader relies upon being told, therefore much of writing is bound to be informative—as to what is happening, to whom, and where, and when. So much is the bone-structure of story-telling. Novel-writing, however, is more than that: it is when we come to the narrative's 'why's' and 'how's', the complex causes of action, the ripples of its effect, the shadowy ambience of the personality, that we touch what makes the essential *novel*. We pass outside the ranges of concrete fact: more will be needed, from now on, than direct telling. Perception, evaluation are called to come into play. From now on, the writer must cause the reader to perceive and evaluate for him-self—or at least, to imagine that he does so.

In so far as the writer has known more than he says, the reader will in his turn draw from the pages more than is there in print. More will appear to him to exist, more will appear to him to be going on than has been described or recounted. One assumes, of course, that the reader brings to the novel a certain capacity of his own—that he has not only knowledge but sense of life, ready to be stimulated further. He will have faculties ready to respond, a power of judgement gleaned from his own experience, and a wish that experience, as he already knows it, may perhaps yet yield up some more meaning. The reader, if he be of such a kind, will be predisposed to react to the novel fully (that is, if the novel has lifelike fullness) and with perhaps more intensity than he would to life. He cannot, however, add to the novel what is not already there—there, that is, in being known by the author, though not necessarily in words set down. For this reason, the whole of the novel *as* a whole—every possible aspect of the characters (not merely aspects relevant to the plot) and every possi-bility, implication, angle or incident of the plot (apart from the parts played by the characters)—ought to be an imaginative reality for the author, conceived absolutely, existing completely, circumstantial down to the last detail. Where the author has failed to know, there will be a vacuum, which cannot but become by the reader. The writer's failure to realise, at any point, may flaw the reality of the whole.

Here are instances of the demand for knowledge. It may sound a commonplace to say that the author should know his characters: do we grasp, though, what such knowingness comprehends? First, outwardly, all must be known *about* them—race, class, heredity, place and date of birth, the environment of the youth and childhood, education, profession, amount of income or salary, family life (if any), place and nature of residence and career or adventures up to the point where the character enters our given story. In fact, as to each of his men and women the author does well to compile a dossier, written or otherwise—if not written, kept ready in the file of the mind. Why? Because outer circumstance, in itself important, does also work on the inner being. And when it does come to the inner beings, the author must, in each of his cases, know those with a sort of passionless depth. His penetrating closeness to his characters can have the virtue (rarer with intimacies in real life) of being almost unclouded by emotion. And, in one way, he has the possibility of knowing them better than he knows himself; for he is unlikely to have the time, the occasion or inclination to watch himself either as continuously or with the same fervour as he watches them. It may, of course, be said that he is creating his characters *by* knowing them: in the early stage of his relations with them that may be true; but later they gain objective reality, turn round and begin to teach him about themselves. Complete and detached as beings, they reveal, as beings do, complexities, inconsistencies, contradictions; and, through being three-dimensional, they take on shadow. From then on, the author (who has become their chronicler, and nothing more) can do no more than apprehend them, guess at them. At the same time their conduct, the way they both act and are, begins to show variations and alternatives . . . Feeling that, the author must convey his sense of that to his reader. If he fails to feel that, his characters remain for the reader unrealised, 'thin'. At the same time, the reader demands that, for the plot, the characters should be so simplified as to be comprehensible.

For the plot, as related (or told) by the author to reader, an apparent simplicity is essential. And yet, what is told to have happened must gain significance, background from what is not told. The story's action, for instance, may take place on a Friday; but the reader must sense, through the author's knowing, what sort of Wednesday, Thursday, led up to it, and what sort of Saturday, Sunday are to follow. Also the alternatives to the plot, owing to the latent alternatives in the behaviour of the characters, must be felt by the reader up to the last moment—it is indeed in this that suspense consists; and no novel, whether the action in it be psychological or physical, ought to omit the factor of suspense. The existence, inside the author's mind, of a possible, far vaster range of the plot than is ever told gives what *is* told, for the reader, certainty and validity . . . The same is true with regard to the scenes of happenings, which must be by the author envisaged down to the final detail, though descriptions of them must not be categoric.

In short, the 'musts' and 'must nots' of effectual novel-writing entail embarkation, by the author, upon something far wider, deeper and longer than what, in print, *in statement*, he will eventually present. He will accumulate, in the course of his work, a mass of what is to him reality, with all the time the knowledge that much of it must remain, ultimately, extraneous. Extraneous to what? His aesthetic purpose. His eventual book is, he intends, to be wieldy, shapely and unencumbered: if statements are to make their expected point, he dare not clog the imagination of the reader with too much of them, or distract the mind of the reader by too many. As to the solution, nothing offers a rule but trained instinct or the immediate finding. The test of what *is* to be said, told, written (or, to remain in writing), is, its connection with what has been said before, its relevance to the aesthetic purpose and, not least, its power to make known, by suggestion or evocation of something further, what needs to be known without being told. From the unsaid, or from what does not remain in writing, comes a great part of the potency of the novel.

One speaks of what does, or does not, remain in writing, because of many authors who put work into pages they later destroy, or who complete scenes only to throw them out. I myself do so. I see that the sense or trend of what has been written almost always survives: it is there by inference—and further, expressive action which has been 'cut' still somehow makes its effect, from offstage. Other authors frame scenes or conceive of actions in their own minds only, yet with a thoroughness which, till they *are* abandoned, gives them the status of written work—and here, too, nothing goes quite for nothing. Master-novelists, Tolstoi, Balzac, give the impression of having held nothing back; their books' length tallies with their effective size. And less splendidly, that is so with Trollope and Thackeray. We, today, query whether actual writing can any longer carry the full charge: we have the art, the policy of exclusion. In their aim for size, our novels are partly silence: we seek what tells. By our own means, we seek to keep for the novel the veracity, the authority of the work of art.

Decline of the English Murder

GEORGE ORWELL

It is Sunday afternoon, preferably before the war. The wife is already asleep in the armchair, and the children have been sent out for a nice long walk. You put your feet up on the sofa, settle your spectacles on your nose, and open the *News of the World*. Roast beef and Yorkshire, or roast pork and apple sauce, followed up by suet pudding and driven home, as it were, by a cup of mahogany-brown tea, have put you in just the right mood. Your pipe is drawing sweetly, the sofa cushions are soft underneath you, the fire is well alight, the air is warm and stagnant. In these blissful circumstances, what is it that you want to read about?

Naturally, about a murder. But what kind of murder? If one examines the murders which have given the greatest amount of pleasure to the British public, the murders whose story is known in its general outline to almost everyone and which have been made into novels and re-hashed over and over again by the Sunday papers, one finds a fairly strong family resemblance running through the greater number of them. Our great period in murder, our Elizabethan period, so to speak, seems to have been between roughly 1850 and 1925, and the murderers whose reputation has stood the test of time are the following: Dr Palmer of Rugely, Jack the Ripper, Neill Cream, Mrs Maybrick, Dr Crippen, Seddon, Joseph Smith, Armstrong, and Bywaters and Thompson. In addition, in 1919 or thereabouts, there was another very celebrated case which fits into the general pattern but which I had better not mention by name, because the accused man was acquitted.

Of the above-mentioned nine cases, at least four have had successful novels based on them, one has been made into a popular melodrama, and the amount of literature surrounding them, in the form of newspaper write-ups, criminological treatises and reminiscences by lawyers and police officers, would make a considerable library. It is difficult to believe that any recent English crime will be remembered so long and so intimately, and not only because the violence of external events has made murder seem unimportant, but because the prevalent type of crime seems to be changing. The principal *cause célèbre* of the war years was the so-called Cleft Chin Murder, which has now been written up in a popular booklet*; the verbatim account of the trial was published some time last year by Messrs Jarrolds with an introduction by Mr Bechhofer Roberts. Before returning to this pitiful and sordid case, which is only interesting from a sociological and perhaps a legal point of view, let me try to define what it is that the readers of Sunday papers mean when they say fretfully that 'you never seem to get a good murder nowadays'.

In considering the nine murders I named above, one can start by excluding the Jack the Ripper case, which is in a class by itself. Of the other eight, six were poisoning cases, and eight of the ten criminals belonged to the middle class. In one way or another, sex was a powerful motive in all but two cases, and in at least four cases respectability—the desire to gain a secure position in life, or not to forfeit one's social position by some scandal such as a divorce—was one of the main reasons for committing murder. In more than half the cases, the object was to get hold of a certain known sum of money such as a legacy or an insurance policy, but the amount involved was nearly always small. In most of the cases the crime only came to light slowly, as the result of careful investigations which started off with the suspicions of neighbours or relatives; and in nearly every case there was some dramatic coincidence, in which the finger of Providence could be clearly seen, or one of those episodes that no novelist would dare to make up, such as Crippen's flight across the Atlantic with his mistress dressed as a boy, or Joseph Smith playing 'Nearer, my God, to Thee' on the harmonium while one of his wives was drowning in the next room. The background of all these crimes, except Neill Cream's, was essentially domestic; of twelve victims, seven were either wife or husband of the murderer.

With all this in mind one can construct what would be, from a *News of the World* reader's point of view, the 'perfect' murder. The murderer should be a little man of the professional class—a dentist or a solicitor, say—living an intensely respectable life somewhere in the suburbs, and preferably in a semi-detached house, which will allow the neighbours to hear suspicious sounds through the wall. He should be either chairman of the local Conservative Party branch, or a leading Nonconformist and strong Temperance advocate. He should go astray through cherishing a guilty passion for his secretary or the wife of a rival professional man, and should only bring himself to the point of murder after long and terrible wrestles with his conscience. Having decided on murder, he should plan it all with the utmost

---

* *The Cleft Chin Murder*, by R. Alwyn Raymond (Claude Morris, 1s 6d).

cunning, and only slip up over some tiny unforeseeable detail. The means chosen should, of course, be poison. In the last analysis he should commit murder because this seems to him less disgraceful, and less damaging to his career, than being detected in adultery. With this kind of background, a crime can have dramatic and even tragic qualities which make it memorable and excite pity for both victim and murderer. Most of the crimes mentioned above have a touch of this atmosphere, and in three cases, including the one I referred to but did not name, the story approximates to the one I have outlined.

Now compare the Cleft Chin Murder. There is no depth of feeling in it. It was almost chance that the two people concerned committed that particular murder, and it was only by good luck that they did not commit several others. The background was not domesticity, but the anonymous life of the dance-halls and the false values of the American film. The two culprits were an eighteen-year-old ex-waitress named Elizabeth Jones, and an American army deserter, posing as an officer, named Karl Hulten. They were only together for six days, and it seems doubtful whether, until they were arrested, they even learned one another's true names. They met casually in a teashop, and that night went out for a ride in a stolen army truck. Jones described herself as a strip-tease artist, which was not strictly true (she had given one unsuccessful performance in this line), and declared that she wanted to do something dangerous, 'like being a gun-moll'. Hulten described himself as a big-time Chicago gangster, which was also untrue. They met a girl bicycling along the road, and to show how tough he was Hulten ran over her with his truck, after which the pair robbed her of the few shillings that were on her. On another occasion they knocked out a girl to whom they had offered a lift, took her coat and handbag and threw her into a river. Finally, in the most wanton way, they murdered a taxi-driver who happened to have £8 in his pocket. Soon afterwards they parted. Hulten was caught because he had foolishly kept the dead man's car, and Jones made spontaneous confessions to the police. In court each prisoner incriminated the other. In between crimes, both of them seem to have behaved with the utmost callousness: they spent the dead taxi-driver's £8 at the dog races.

Judging from her letters, the girl's case has a certain amount of psychological interest, but this murder probably captured the headlines because it provided distraction amid the doodle-bugs and the anxieties of the Battle of France. Jones and Hulten committed their murder to the tune of V_1, and were convicted to the tune of V_2. There was also considerable excitement because—as has become usual in England—the man was sentenced to death and the girl to imprisonment. According to Mr Raymond, the reprieving of Jones caused widespread indignation and streams of telegrams to the Home Secretary: in her native town, 'SHE SHOULD HANG' was chalked on the walls beside pictures of a figure dangling from a gallows. Considering that only ten women have been hanged in Britain this century, and that the practice has gone out largely because of popular feeling against it, it is difficult not to feel that this clamour to hang an eighteen-year-old girl was due partly to the brutalising effects of war. Indeed, the whole meaningless story, with its atmosphere of dance-halls, movie-palaces, cheap perfume, false names and stolen cars, belongs essentially to a war period.

Perhaps it is significant that the most talked-of English murder of recent years should have been committed by an American and an English girl who had become partly Americanised. But it is difficult to believe that this case will be so long remembered as the old domestic poisoning dramas, product of a stable society where the all-prevailing hypocrisy did at least ensure that crimes as serious as murder should have strong emotions behind them.

Bohemia

ALAN COREN

English Bohemianism is a curiously unluscious fruit. It does not belong in the great, mad, steamy glasshouse in which so much of the art of the rest of the world seems to have flourished—or, at least, so much of the pseudo-art. Inside this hothouse, huge lascivious orchids slide sensually up the sweating windows, passion-flowers cross-pollinate in wild heliotrope abandon, lotuses writhe with poppies in the rich warm beds, kumquats ripen, tremble, and plop fatly to the floor—and outside, in a neat, trimly-hoed kitchen garden, English Bohemians sit in cold orderly rows, like carrots.

In our Bohemia, there are no beautifully crazy one-eared artists, no *sans culottes*, no castrated epistolarians, no genuine revolutionaries, no hopheads, no lunatics, not even any alcoholics of note; our seed-beds have never teemed with Rimbauds and Gauguins and Kafkas and d'Annunzios and Dostoievskys; we don't even have a Mailer or a Ginsberg to call our own. Our Bohemia is populated by Civil Servants like Chaucer and Spenser and Milton; by tough-nut professional penmongers like Shakespeare and Dryden and Johnson, who worried as much about underwear and rent as about oxymorons; by corpulent suburban family men like Thackeray and Dickens and Trollope. And whenever an English oddball raises, tentatively, his head, he's a pitifully pale imitation of the real thing—Thom. Gray, sad, thin Cambridge queer, Cowper, mad among his rabbits, Swinburne, a tiny fetishistic gnome as far from Leopold von Sacher-Masoch as water is from blood. The private lives of our great powerhouses of passion, Pope and Swift, were dreary and colourless in the extreme, and Emily Brontë divided her time between *Wuthering Heights* and the Haworth laundry-list. And history, though it may offer our only revolutionary poet the passing tribute of a literary footnote, will probably think of William Morris mainly as the Father of Modern Wallpaper.

There was, however, one brief moment in this socially unostentatious culture of ours when we were touched, albeit gingerly, by the spirit of Bohemia. I am not (how could you *think* a thing like that?) referring, of course, to the Wildean shenannigans at the *fin* of the last *siècle*, which were the product not of an authentic Bohemianism but of the need to dig up a literature and a *modus vivendi* you could wear with spats and a green carnation: that Café Royal crowd was the first Switched-On, With-It Generation England ever had, and the whole megillah should be taken with a pinch of pastis. No, the gang I have in mind are the Lake Poets, who had, for once, all the genuine consti-tuents of real adjustment problems, social malaise, illegitimate off-spring, numerous tracts, a hang-out, a vast literature, and, most important of all, a date: 1798. And since at first sight, and for several thereafter, the Lake District, a sopping place of sedge and goat, seems as unlikely a Bohemian ambience as you could shake a quill at, much can be gained by examining the area itself; one can do no better than take the career of its most eminent son, a William Wordsworth, and relate it (as all the local tourist offices do) to every cranny, sheep and sod between Windermere and the Scottish border.

I realise, naturally, that the aforementioned bard left a meticulous record of all that made him what he was, but since all writers are extraordinary liars, poseurs, distorters, and self-deceivers, I have chosen to ignore most of his farragos and interpretations; and for the background to this chapter, I am not indebted to *The Poetical Works Of William Wordsworth* (5 vols, Oxford 1940–49), *Wordsworth: A Re-interpretation* by F. W. Bateson (London 1954), *The Egotistical Sublime* by J. Jones (London 1954), or *Wordsworth and Coleridge* by H. G. Margoliouth (London 1953). In particular, I am not indebted to *Strange Seas of Thought: Studies in Wordsworth's Philosophy of Man and Nature* by N. P. Stallknecht (North Carolina 1945). However, I gather from friends in the trade that no work of serious scholarship is complete without a list of references and sources three times the size of the thing itself, so for devotees of this sort of *narrischkeit*, a fuller bibliography will be found sewn inside the lining of my old green hacking-jacket.

Cockermouth, Cumberland, was the spot where, on 7 April 1770, William Wordsworth first drew breath, and the location goes a long way towards explaining his characteristic lugubriousness. In the Old Hall, now derelict and seeping, Mary Queen of Scots was received after her defeat at Langside in 1568; her gloom was plumbless, and her host, Henry Fletcher, gave her thirteen ells of crimson velvet for a new dress. This could hardly have compensated for having her army trodden into the mud, but it ranks as one of history's nicer gestures to Mary. Nearby stands Harry Hotspur's house, contracts for which had just been exchanged when the new proprietor was butchered at Shrewsbury, in 1403, and within spitting distance can be found a few lumps of twelfth-century castle: this was captured in 1313 by Robert the Bruce, and spent the rest of the century under constant attack and bombardment by any Scots infantrymen who happened to be in the neighbourhood. During the Wars of the Roses, it was first Yorkist, then Lancastrian, and the catalogue of woe was finally brought to an end during the Civil War, when it was demolished by the Round-heads. A mile or so away, at Moorland Close, is the 1764 birthplace of Fletcher Christian, leader of the *Bounty* mutineers, and the 1766 birthplace of John Dalton, the physicist whose nefarious theories led ultimately to the destruction of Hiroshima.

Given this agglomerated misery, it isn't difficult to see how young Wordsworth could become aware, very early, of the general rotten-ness of intelligent bipeds, by comparison with whom the local trees, thorns, and general flora assume a commendable innocence. One imagines John Wordsworth taking his little offshoot on trots through the topography, pointing out the various scenes of butchery and nastiness, totting up the huge casualty list, and pondering aloud on the question of how long it would take that diabolical infant prodigy John Dalton to come up with a hydrogen bomb. It's little wonder that William decided early on who his friends were, and began associating with daffodils. Not that the idea of Nature possessing a mean streak escaped him, either; the news that Fletcher Christian got his come-uppance for interfering with the rights of breadfruit was undeniably traumatic for young Wm.—thereafter, as the *Prelude* indicates, he couldn't break a twig or step on a toadstool without feeling that the crime would be expunged in blood.

He went on to Hawkshead Grammar School, where little seems to have happened to him, except that he befriended a lad called John Tyson, who immediately died, aged twelve, to be later commemor-ated in 'There was a boy, / Ye knew him well, ye cliffs and islands of Winander ...' This drove Wordsworth even further towards the mountains and shrubbery, who were obviously bound to enjoy a longer life-span and weren't going to peg out just when William was getting to know them. This was now his period of greatest involve-ment with Nature, a time spent sculling about the lakes with which the area is infested and grubbing about in the undergrowth, one ear cocked for the song of earwig and slug, the other for That Still Sprit Shed From Evening Air. It rained most of the time. And, as the years rolled by and William grew to pubescence, talking the whiles to roots and knolls, he became more and more aware of humanity in general as a collection of blots and errors. One could rely on the crocus; every year it re-emerged from the turf, developed into its tiny, private perfection, and then quietly pegged out. And other mates of the poet, like Skiddaw and Scafell and Easedale Tarn, changed very little from year to year. But as the maturing bard pottered around Cumbria, he bumped inevitably into some of the area's human population, later immortalised and now available in paperback, who served only to convince him that after the fifth day, the Almighty's unerring talent for creating perfection deserted him: the life of Wordsworth the Teenager teemed with mad old women, decayed sailormen, idiot children, dispossessed cottars, impoverished leech-gatherers, bereaved lovers, unscrupulous potters, orphans, mutes, destitutes, and chronic bronchitics. Why the Lake District should have seethed with such sad misfits and sufferers to the point where Wordsworth never met anyone else is a question I gladly leave to medical historians or any similar forager with the necessary time on his hands. But I would just like to point out to all those scholars who have wondered why Wordsworth should have been a believer in metempsychosis (that dubiously scientific process whereby souls pass on from one corporeal form to another as the subsequent mortal coils get shuffled off) that he quite clearly needed the hope it offered: souls inhabiting the forms of Lake District inhabitants were so unfortunately lumbered, that only the belief in their ultimate transmogrification into a hollyhock or woodlouse sustained Wordsworth's faith in God's pervading goodness. There is, indeed, much evidence to show that the poet would have given his eye-teeth to have been a clump of heather.

In 1787, he went up to Cambridge. Everyone drank port and spoke Latin, and the nearest Cumberland beggar was three hundred miles to the NW. Wordsworth was desolate, left the university, utterly unnoticed, and took ship for the Continent. It was here that he burgeoned and ripened under the cucumber-glass of Italian culture and Gallic revolution, suddenly exposed to all that the Lake District was not: Bohemianism took root in the Cumbrian corpuscles, and in the general uproar following the coup of 1789, Wordsworth sang in the streets, went about with his shirt unbuttoned, and seduced the daughter of a French surgeon. Again, scholars have been baffled by the whole Annette Vallon business: why the mystery, the concealment of Wordsworth's bastard child, the failure to return with its father to England? What the scholars have in textual fidelity, they lack in imagination; even without dwelling on the unwholesome possibility that Wordsworth's boudoir techniques, picked up secondhand from observations of Esthwaite sheep, must have left much to be desired, we can make a fair guess at Annette's response to the poet's suggestion that she accompany him back to the fells to meet Mad Margaret, Peter Bell, Old Matthew, and the rest of the gang. At all events, Wordsworth came home alone, and unable to face the quiet of the Lakes, took Dorothy down to Somerset, which by now had got a reputation for having Coleridge on the premises. The two met up. Coleridge had already collected a Lake Poet, Robert Southey, and together they had concocted a form of early communism which they called Pantisocracy, so that by the time Wordsworth fixed his wagon to their star, the nub of Bohemianism had been unmistakably shaped: of these two ur-Marxists, Southey had already distinguished himself for his opposition to flogging, Coleridge was smoking pot and seeing visions, and the pair of them had been writing like things possessed. With Wordsworth in tow, the poetic output stepped up enormously, and in 1798, he and Coleridge hit the market with their *Lyrical Ballads*, and everyone took off for the Lake District. The years that followed were ambrosial for Wordsworth: at last he could stop mooning about and involving himself with the problems of the educationally sub-normal citizens of Westmorland and Cumberland, and throw himself into the serious business of Bohemianism. Night after night the fells echoed to revelry and pentameters as the wild poets of Cumbria entertained thinkers and versifiers from all over the civilised world. Scott came, and Lamb, and Hazlitt, and de Quincey, until the nights of riot and boozing and composition surpassed anything the literary world had seen since William Shagsper, Kit Marlowe, Francis Bacon, the Earl of Oxford and Robert Greene had all stabbed one another in the Mermaid Tavern, leaving the responsibility for Elizabethan drama entirely in the hands of a Mr W. H. Grobeley, the inn's landlord, who subsequently wrote it to avoid suspicion falling on his hostelry. No visit to Dove Cottage, Grasmere, is complete without examining the outhouse where Hazlitt's father, a Unitarian minister of strong liberal views, attempted to put his hand up Dorothy Wordsworth's skirt, and at Greta Hall, Keswick, can be seen the faded, bloody marks following a fight over the rent-book by its two most illustrious tenants, Coleridge and Southey.

But ultimately, as it will, Bohemianism died. Coleridge left in 1809, went south, and died of opium poisoning. Southey became Poet Laureate in 1813, and took to wearing hats and drinking lukewarm herb tea. In the same year, Wordsworth became the Distributor of Stamps for the County of Westmorland at £400 per annum, and as befitted a civil servant, moved to Rydal Mount, turned his back on liberalism, and finally petered out in 1850, leaving his cottage to de Quincey, who hadn't touched a drop for the past thirty years.

Today, there are few reminders of those high and far-off times: the occasional grocer with the ineradicable Hazlitt family nose, or the Coleridge lip; fading graffiti on some derelict farmhouse wall, retailing bizarre local legends in the language and forms set down in the famous *Preface* of 1798; the empty gin-bottles that have bobbed on Ullswater and Bassenthwaite for the past century and a half; a crumbling gazebo on the outskirts of Keswick, built by Southey and from which he would pounce on passing milkmaids. Naturally, there are far more memorials to the more respectable aspects of the Bohemians' life and work, and during the summer, the roads of the two counties are filled with coachloads of people from Bromley and Philadelphia being driven to Gowbarrow Park to look at the descendants of the original daffodils.

The traditions, too, are dead. Not only is the local population conspicuously sane, sober, ungrieving, unstarving and totally unlike the *dramatis personae* of Wordsworth's records, the visitors are similarly unpoetic and unBohemian. They throng the Lake District between April and October in great tweed crowds; they wear sensible shoes, and corduroy knee-breeches, headscarves and duffle-coats, balaclavas and plastic macs; they carry stolid-looking walking-sticks, and rucksacks, and notebooks for pressing bog asphodel and saxifrage in, and Aer Lingus bags containing tomato sandwiches and flasks of Bovril; they have rosy cheeks, and hearty, uncomplicated laughs, and sturdy calf-muscles; they eat ham teas, and hold singsongs in Youth Hostels, and go to bed at nine o'clock to listen to the wind in the eaves. Or else they come in Ford Cortinas and Bedford Dormobiles, with primus stoves and Calor Gas and tents from Gamages, to take their children boating on Windermere. And every year, they pay homage at the verdant shrine of someone whom they vaguely remember as being a poet, or something, simply because the guide book has led them to his grave, and because all tombs demand equal reverence. So they stand, heads bowed briefly, in St Oswald's churchyard, Grasmere.

Never for one moment realising that Wordsworth himself would have thrown up at the sight of them.

Beatrix Potter

GRAHAM GREENE

'It is said that the effect of eating too much lettuce is soporific.' It is with some such precise informative sentence that one might have expected the great Potter saga to open, for the obvious characteristic of Beatrix Potter's style is a selective realism, which takes emotion for granted and puts aside love and death with a gentle detachment reminiscent of Mr E. M. Forster's. Her stories contain plenty of dramatic action, but it is described from the outside by an acute and unromantic observer, who never sacrifices truth for an effective gesture. As an example of Miss Potter's empiricism, her rigid adherence to what can be seen and heard, consider the climax of her masterpiece *The Roly-Poly Pudding*, Tom Kitten's capture by the rats in the attic:

'Anna Maria,' said the old man rat (whose name was Samuel Whiskers), 'Anna Maria, make me a kitten dumpling roly-poly pudding for my dinner.'

'It requires dough and a pat of butter, and a rolling pin,' said Anna Maria, considering Tom Kitten with her head on one side.

'No,' said Samuel Whiskers. 'Make it properly, Anna Maria, with breadcrumbs.'

But in 1908, when *The Roly-Poly Pudding* was published, Miss Potter was at the height of her power. She was not a born realist, and her first story was not only romantic, it was historical. *The Tailor of Gloucester* opens:

In the time of swords and periwigs, and full-skirted coats with flowered lappets—when gentlemen wore ruffles and gold-lace waistcoats of paduasoy and taffeta—there lived a tailor in Gloucester.

In the sharp details of this sentence, in the flowered lappets, there is a hint of the future Potter, but her first book is not only hampered by its period setting but by the presence of a human character. Miss Potter is seldom at her best with human beings (the only flaw in *The Roly-Poly Pudding* is the introduction in the final pages of the authoress in person), though with one human character she succeeded triumphantly. I refer, of course, to Mr MacGregor, who made an elusive appearance in 1904 in *The Tale of Benjamin Bunny*, ran his crabbed earthmould way through *Peter Rabbit*, and met his final ignominious defeat in *The Flopsy Bunnies* in 1909. But the tailor of Gloucester cannot be compared with Mr MacGregor. He is too ineffective and too virtuous, and the atmosphere of the story—snow and Christmas bells and poverty—is too Dickensian. Incidentally in Simpkin Miss Potter drew her only unsympathetic portrait of a cat. The ancestors of Tom Thumb and Hunca-Munca play a humanitarian part. Their kind hearts are a little oppressive.

In the same year Miss Potter published *Squirrel Nutkin*. It is an unsatisfactory book, less interesting than her first, which was a good example of a bad *genre*. But in 1904, with the publication of *Two Bad Mice*, Miss Potter opened the series of her great comedies. In this story of Tom Thumb and Hunca-Munca and their wanton havoc of a doll's house, the unmistakable Potter style first appears.

It is an elusive style, difficult to analyse. It owes something to alliteration:

Hunca-Munca stood up in her chair and chopped at the ham with another lead knife.

'It's as hard as the hams at the Cheesemonger's,' said Hunca-Munca.

Something too it owes to the short paragraphs, which are fashioned with a delicate irony, not to complete a movement, but mutely to criticise the action by arresting it. The imperceptive pause allows the mind to take in the picture: the mice are stilled in their enraged attitudes for a moment, before the action sweeps forward.

Then there was no end to the rage and disappointment of Tom Thumb and Hunca-Munca. They broke up the pudding, the lobsters, the pears, and the oranges.

As the fish would not come off the plate, they put it into the red-hot crinkly paper fire in the kitchen; but it would not burn either.

It is curious that Beatrix Potter's method of paragraphing has never been imitated.

The last quotation shows another element of her later style, her love of a precise catalogue, her creation of atmosphere with still-life. One remembers Mr MacGregor's rubbish heap:

There were jam pots and paper bags and mountains of chopped

grass from the mowing machine (which always tasted oily), and some rotten vegetable marrows and an old boot or two.

The only indication in *Two Bad Mice* of a prentice hand is the sparsity of dialogue; her characters had not yet begun to utter those brief pregnant sentences, which have slipped, like proverbs, into common speech. Nothing in the early book equals Mr Jackson's 'No teeth. No teeth. No teeth.'

In 1904 too *The Tale of Peter Rabbit*, the second of the great comedies, was published, closely followed by its sequel, *Benjamin Bunny*. In Peter and his cousin Benjamin Miss Potter created two epic personalities. The great characters of fiction are often paired: Quixote and Sancho, Pantagruel and Panurge, Pickwick and Weller, Benjamin and Peter. Peter was a neurotic, Benjamin worldly and imperturbable. Peter was warned by his mother, 'Don't go into Mr MacGregor's garden; your father had an accident there; he was put in a pie by Mrs MacGregor.' But Peter went from stupidity rather than for adventure. He escaped from Mr MacGregor by leaving his clothes behind, and the sequel, the story of how his clothes were recovered, introduces Benjamin, whose coolness and practicality are a foil to the nerves and clumsiness of his cousin. It was Benjamin who knew the way to enter a garden: 'It spoils people's clothes to squeeze under a gate; the proper way to get in is to climb down a pear tree.' It was Peter who fell down head first.

From 1904 to 1908 were the vintage years in comedy; to these years belong *The Pie and the Patty Pan*, *The Tale of Tom Kitten*, *The Tale of Mrs Tiggy Winkle*, and only one failure, *Mr Jeremy Fisher*. Miss Potter had found her right vein and her right scene. The novels were now set in Cumberland; the farms, the village shops, the stone walls, the green slope of Catbells became the background of her pictures and her prose. She was peopling a countryside. Her dialogue had become memorable because aphoristic:

'I disapprove of tin articles in puddings and pies. It is most undesirable—(especially when people swallow in lumps).'

She could draw a portrait in a sentence:

'My name is Mrs Tiggy Winkle; oh yes if you please'm, I'm an excellent clear-starcher.'

And with what beautiful economy she sketched the first smiling villain of her gallery. Tom Kitten had dropped his clothes off the garden wall as the Puddle-Duck family passed:

'Come! Mr Drake Puddle-Duck,' said Moppet, 'Come and help us to dress him! Come and button up Tom!'

Mr Drake Puddle-Duck advanced in a slow sideways manner, and picked up the various articles.

But he put them on himself. They fitted him even worse than Tom Kitten.

'It's a very fine morning,' said Mr Drake Puddle-Duck.

Looking backward over the thirty years of Miss Potter's literary career, we see that the creation of Mr Puddle-Duck marked the beginning of a new period. At some time between 1907 and 1909 Miss Potter must have passed through an emotional ordeal which changed the character of her genius. It would be impertinent to inquire into the nature of the ordeal. Her case is curiously similar to that of Henry James. Something happened which shook their faith in appearance. From *The Portrait of a Lady* onwards, innocence deceived, the treachery of friends, became the theme of James's greatest stories. Mme Merle, Kate Croy, Mme de Vionnet, Charlotte Stant, these tortuous treacherous women are paralleled through the dark period of Miss Potter's art. 'A man can smile and smile and be a villain,' that, a little altered, was her recurrent message, expressed by her gallery of scoundrels: Mr Drake Puddle-Duck, the first and slightest, Mr Jackson, the least harmful with his passion for honey and his reiterated, 'No teeth. No teeth. No teeth', Samuel Whiskers, gross and brutal, and the 'gentleman with sandy whiskers' who may be identified with Mr Tod. With the publication of *Mr Tod* in 1912, Miss Potter's pessimism reached its climax. But for the nature of her audience *Mr Tod* would certainly have ended tragically. In *Jemima Puddle-Duck* the gentleman with sandy whiskers had at least a debonair impudence when he addressed his victim:

'Before you commence your tedious sitting, I intend to give you a treat. Let us have a dinner party all to ourselves!

'May I ask you to bring up some herbs from the farm garden to make a savoury omelette? Sage and thyme, and mint and two onions, and some parsley. I will provide lard for the stuff—lard for the omelette,' said the hospitable gentleman with sandy whiskers.

But no charm softens the brutality of Mr Tod and his enemy, the repulsive Tommy Brock. In her comedies Miss Potter had gracefully eliminated the emotions of love and death; it is the measure of her genius that when, in *The Tale of Mr Tod*, they broke the barrier, the form of her book, her ironic style, remained unshattered. When she could not keep death out she stretched her technique to include it.

Benjamin and Peter had grown up and married, and Benjamin's babies were stolen by Brock; the immortal pair, one still neurotic, the other knowing and imperturbable, set off to the rescue, but the rescue, conducted in darkness, from a house, 'something between a cave, a prison, and a tumbledown pig-sty', compares grimly with an earlier rescue from Mr MacGregor's sunny vegetable garden:

> The sun had set; an owl began to hoot in the wood. There were many unpleasant things lying about, that had much better have been buried; rabbit bones and skulls and chicken's legs and other horrors. It was a shocking place and very dark.

But *Mr Tod*, for all the horrors of its atmosphere, is indispensable. There are few fights in literature which can compare in excitement with the duel between Mr Tod and Tommy Brock (it was echoed by H. G. Wells in *Mr Polly*):

> Everything was upset except the kitchen table.
> And everything was broken, except the mantelpiece and the kitchen fender. The crockery was smashed to atoms.
> The chairs were broken, and the window, and the clock fell with a crash, and there were handfuls of Mr Tod's sandy whiskers.
> The vases fell off the mantelpiece, the canisters fell off the shelf; the kettle fell off the hob. Tommy Brock put his foot in a jar of raspberry jam.

Mr Tod marked the distance which Miss Potter had travelled since the ingenuous romanticism of *The Tailor of Gloucester*. The next year with *The Tale of Pigling Bland*, the period of the great near-tragedies came to an end. There was something of the same squalor, and the villain, Mr Thomas Piperson, was not less terrible than Mr Tod, but the book ended on a lyric note, as Pigling Bland escaped with Pig-Wig:

> They ran, and they ran, and they ran down the hill, and across a short cut on level green turf at the bottom, between pebble-beds and rushes. They came to the river, they came to the bridge—they crossed it hand in hand –

It was the nearest Miss Potter had approached to a conventional love story. The last sentence seemed a promise that the cloud had lifted, that there was to be a return to the style of the earlier comedies. But *Pigling Bland* was published in 1913. Through the years of war the author was silent, and for many years after it was over, only a few books of rhyme appeared. These showed that Miss Potter had lost none of her skill as an artist, but left the great question of whither her genius was tending unanswered. Then, after seventeen years, at the end of 1930, *Little Pig Robinson* was published.

The scene was no longer Cumberland but Devonshire and the sea. The story, more than twice as long as *Mr Tod*, was diffuse and undramatic. The smooth smiling villain had disappeared and taken with him the pungent dialogue, the sharp detail, the light of common day. Miss Potter had not returned to the great comedies. She had gone on beyond the great near-tragedies to her *Tempest*. No tortured Lear nor strutting Antony could live on Prospero's island, among the sounds and sweet airs and cloudcapt towers. Miss Potter too had reached her island, the escape from tragedy, the final surrender of imagination to safe serene fancy:

A stream of boiling water flowed down the silvery strand. The shore was covered with oysters. Acid-drops and sweets grew upon the trees. Yams, which are a sort of sweet potato, abounded ready cooked. The breadfruit tree grew iced cakes and muffins ready baked.

It was all very satisfying for a pig Robinson, but in that rarefied air no bawdy Tommy Brock could creep to burrow, no Benjamin pursue his feud between the vegetable-frames, no Puddle-Duck could search in wide-eyed innocence for a 'convenient dry nesting-place'.

Note. On the publication of this essay I received a somewhat acid letter from Miss Potter correcting certain details. *Little Pig Robinson*, although the last published of her books, was in fact the first written. She denied that there had been any emotional disturbance at the time she was writing *Mr Tod*: she was suffering however from the after-effects of flu. In conclusion she deprecated sharply 'the Freudian school' of criticism.

Cyril Connolly at Fifty

KENNETH TYNAN

Cyril Connolly is either a *bon viveur* with a passion for literature, or a
littérateur with a passion for high living. He has never quite made up
his mind, and his biography will be the story of his indecision. It is a
conflict of extremes, because his standards of living and writing are
both immensely high, too high for comfortable coexistence within
the same very self-critical human being: Brillat-Savarin and a fasting
friar might sooner inhabit the same cell. Whenever he revisits the
grands restaurants a nagging voice keeps reminding him of his own
dictum: 'The true function of a writer is to produce a masterpiece; no
other task is of any consequence.' Fancifully, one can picture him
echoing Ben Jonson's cry: 'O! If a man could restrain the fury of his
gullet and groin!' Only the best in food or art is good enough for him;
only what he calls 'alpha people' interest him, and nothing depresses
him more than an encounter with a thriving, contented, beta-plus,
best-selling novelist. Mediocre writing strikes him as several degrees
worse than no writing: 'The books I haven't written', he once said,
'are better than the books other people have.' For over twenty years
he has been pressing on his contemporaries the information that art is
a ferocious taskmistress, that the Muses do not welcome novices, but
(as Cocteau said) simply open the door and silently point at the
tightrope.

Immoderate faith in Connolly's pronouncements might persuade
any young author that literature was almost an impossibility: his
glum, lapidary admonitions produce an effect like that of reading a
medical textbook on the use of dangerous drugs, and it has been said
that the idea of modern English literature without him is as inconceivable as the idea of *Hamlet* without the Ghost. For him the test of a
piece of writing is: 'Would it amuse Horace or Milton or Swift or
Leopardi? Could it be read to Flaubert?' Writing under the shadow of
these appalling questions is naturally an exacting occupation and it is
no wonder that Connolly has been a miser of words, publishing only
five books of his own work in a lifetime of fifty years.

Horizon, the literary monthly which he ran from 1939 until 1950,
established him as a great editor, carrying on a rearguard action in the

service of letters at a time when art and frivolity were all but equated in the public mind. His anthology *The Golden Horizon* contains only one item, a brief questionnaire, written by himself, but the book bears his trademark on every page. Its flavour is wry, pungent and personal; the choice is that of a man to whom pomp, lushness and slogans are uniformly hateful. In *Ideas and Places*, a collection of his *Horizon* editorials, and in *The Unquiet Grave*, a quotation-peppered stew in which the modern intellectual's predicament is sadly anatomised, Connolly has stated his case against twentieth-century culture. The onlooker sees most of the game, but to Connolly the game is a war, with literature an open city being saturation-bombed by economic stress and betrayed from within by *Angst*—a cult word which he did more than anyone else to popularise. Sometimes one suspects that Connolly the physician is merely diagnosing his own ailment, and that the X-rays have been rigged to show only the cancers of guilt and indolence. He has tried and failed to cultivate what Lamb called 'a brawny defiance to the needles of a thrusting-in conscience'.

'His virtue as a critic', said one observer, 'has always been the directness that comes from treating all writings as the personal expression of a particular human being in particular circumstances . . .' How late did Baudelaire lie abed? What was Voltaire's digestion like? How important was sex to La Rochefoucauld? These are the questions which fascinate Connolly: in answering them, he has become the greatest living authority on good reasons for not writing. His lifework is a series of attempts to define the material and spiritual circumstances most propitious to the creation of good art. What pressures and solaces, how much drink, how much money, how much of the hermit's barrel and how much of the marriage bed, conduce to the nourishment of the creative mood? He has spent most of his career in search of the right solution.

'I have always disliked myself at any given moment,' he has written; 'the sum total of such moments is my life.' It began in England on 10 September 1903. Much later, in a completely unautobiographical context, he said, 'Thus astrologers find this love of perfection in those born under the sign of Virgo . . . between the end of August and the end of September.' His father was a soldier, of naval and military ancestry, and a collector of shells, a trait which has reproduced itself in Connolly's abiding love of hoarding exotic objects. His mother sprang from a line of gay Irish squirearchs, and in extreme youth, he says, 'I became a snob. The discovery that I was an earl's great-nephew was important to me . . .' He had a conventional English writer's childhood, which is to say, one that was geographically and genealogically bizarre, involving exposure to good books, the minor aristocracy and outposts of Empire—he visited South Africa twice before he was seven.

From private school, where his best friends were Cecil Beaton ('prettiness') and George Orwell ('intellect'), he went to Eton with a scholarship. He read intensively, became known as a wit, and suffered abominably. The evasiveness, the shrillness, the tendency to blink and stammer, which are to be found in most English intellectuals, can be traced directly to their public schools; and Connolly's account of the cliques and cruelty of Eton is characteristically alarming, as much in what it condones as in what it condemns. 'To this day', he wrote, 'I cannot bear to be sent for or to hear of anyone's wanting to see me about something without acute nervous dread.' He rejoiced when he was admitted to Pop, the Eton Society, much as he rejoiced when, years later, he was elected to White's Club, the Pop of St James's Street.

He took a degree in history at Oxford, and from this period dates his vision of himself as 'the boy who let the side down, the coming man who never came'. In 1926 he found a patron: the London refugee from Philadelphia, Logan Pearsall Smith, author of *Trivia* and like minor works, apprised of his brightness, offered him a secretarial job which proved to be less than exacting. *Chez* Pearsall Smith, he would rise at ten, spending the morning in a constantly replenished hot bath; at luncheon he would grumble politely if the wine insulted his palate; the afternoon might be occupied with yachting on the Solent; and then dinner, after which he customarily fell into a deep sleep.

He likens his subsequent career to a tree that has its destined shape but takes time to decide which branch is the main artery. He flourished ephemerally as a conversationalist, and more lastingly in the pages of the *New Statesman*, where his mentors were Raymond Mortimer and Desmond MacCarthy, who managed to rouse him from fits of what he calls 'mutinous and iconoclastic sloth'. His thirties' journalism is vivid, erudite, sharply metaphoric and only slightly cliquey: the best of it includes half a dozen lacerating burlesques, one of which, the playful·demolition of Aldous Huxley entitled 'Told in Gath', has been described as the most brilliant parody of the twentieth century. He also published a novel, *The Rock Pool*, which encapsulated the seedy, sub-Bohemian side of the French Riviera in the twenties, drably shivering under the blast of the mistral.

In 1930 he had married a not ill-heeled American, and was spared the necessity of sinking to the cheaper varieties of journalism. Analysing the blights afflicting the twentieth-century artist, he said, '... broadcasting, advertising, journalism and lecturing all pluck feathers from the blue bird of inspiration and cast them on the wind'. He more or less resisted all four, achieving instead considerable standing as guest, host, mimic, and Guardian of Values. Even now, it is difficult to leave his company without feeling determined to repel all forms of literary prostitution, a determination which can easily lead to inertia. He travelled, found acolytes, made friends and entertained them in Chelsea on champagne and sucking-pig.

'Favourite daydream,' he wrote in 1933, 'to edit a monthly magazine entirely subsidised by self. No advertisements. Harmless title. Deleterious contents.' In 1939 war broke out, and with it, like the rash sometimes produced by vaccination, *Horizon*, backed by Connolly's friend Peter Watson. From a chrysalis of journalism, fiction-writing and marriage (he was separated from his wife in 1939), an editor emerged, with views that were perfectionist without being pontifical, and for ten years the magazine spread its name around the world. In 1950, faced with a diminishing circulation, *Horizon* sank: 'only contributions continued to be delivered, like a suicide's milk,' Connolly wrote recently, 'and keep on coming'. He had lived lavishly during the forties, overspending on furniture, china and food; now he was jobless and in debt. A new self was called for.

'Stoic in adversity, Epicurean in prosperity'; thus he epitomised himself; now, obviously, was the Stoic's chance. Nineteen-fifty was a cashless year. He had just remarried, his new wife being the long, catlike, amazingly slim Barbara Skelton, whose circle of friends had formerly ranged from Peter Quennell to King Farouk. With her companionship, Connolly withdrew from London literary life, took an isolated cottage in Kent, acridly illuminated by oil lamps, and became an ascetic. The Spartan, antiseptic life of Oak Cottage was intended to sharpen his creative wits for the twenty years of literary activity which he believed were left to him: two decades to turn out the masterpiece, to put immortal flesh on the Ghost. 'I am', he said, 'a refugee from the business lunch and the *couche-tard* principle.'

The fleshed Ghost was and is a baggy, besandalled Buddha, with a pink child's face, slack jowls, a receding fuzz of hair skirmishing across his scalp, and somewhat sour, blank eyes which express the resignation of one who envisaged himself in a sedan chair sucking on a hubble-bubble and was fobbed off with secondhand Sheraton and cigars. Physically, a part for Charles Laughton at his driest and least expostulatory; intellectually, a logbook of his generation's voyages and discoveries—Freud in the twenties, the Left in the thirties, the preservative artistic Right in the late forties. In 1951 Connolly took a post as literary critic on the *Sunday Times*, a retreat to journalism but a concession to security. His vocation was still 'to make books', but his new job enabled him to vary the hermitage routine by spending one night a week at the Ritz, if only to get his pants pressed.

Last winter he concluded that his programme was 'to shed ballast, to cast off some of my selves—the Editor, the International Journalist, the Romantic Adolescent and the Diner-Out'. This last self was hastened to oblivion partly by Virginia Woolf's reference to him in her notebooks as 'that cocktail critic, C. Connolly', but more by Nancy Mitford's gentle parody of him in *The Blessing*, where he figures as the Captain, with a circle of handmaidens, sudden infatuations, and helplessly expensive tastes. 'I want to write myself out of journalism,' he says, 'as I have journalised myself out of editing.' His publications since his rural retirement have been three anthologies, two from *Horizon* and one of *Great English Short Novels*. 'I have read or reread about sixty or seventy novels for this selection,' he told his publishers. 'It has been a revelation to me and freed me at last from the bondage to French nineteenth-century writers, which has been holding me up for years and prevented me from writing more myself . . . I should like those who read this anthology to find all long books rather absurd.' He is now, not unexpectedly, working on a short novel ('form and shape and rapidity') about the murder of a man of letters. 'I write as a rule in the afternoons, using the mornings to rev up the engine,' he explains. 'I can go for long spells without working.' Sir Max Beerbohm has attested, among many others, that no writer enjoys writing. Connolly is reluctant to face the typewriter because, he says, the sheer *jouissance* of creation always burdens him with a profound, hungover sense of guilt. He cites, as a parallel, a fellow-critic who was told by a psychiatrist that his literary blockage was due to a subconscious identification of the desire to write with the desire to sleep with his mother.

Connolly fills the pre-lunch revving-up period with his other interests. He must feed his pet coati (a replacement for the lemurs whose distinctive stench pervaded most of his earlier homes); he must attend to his two Chinese ducks and his lovingly fattened guinea fowl. He gardens assiduously and adventurously, and next year he plans a 'Poison Corner'. His own list of hobbies runs: 'READING, travelling, talking, eating, drinking, motoring, gardening, thinking, planting shrubs and watching fishes, architecture, china, silver, paintings, furniture, reading, READING, READING.' His acquisitiveness is violent and endless: 'I am', he once said, 'one of nature's Rothschilds.' His afternoon bouts of creativeness produce the same concise, elegant, informal results as ever, laced with nodules of venom: he recently dismissed a volume of expendable memoirs with the phrase: 'wanly recommended'. He dines out seldom, but when he does he is ruthlessly critical of the food ('But the mashed potatoes were the best I've ever tasted,' or 'When will X learn that the champagne should *keep on coming*?') and more anxious than of old to get back home and read. Horace, Catullus, Flaubert, Lucretius, Stendhal, Molière, Firbank, Rabelais and Lamb are all within arm's length of his bed, the beloved collaborators on his 'culture picture'. 'A writer has to construct his shell, like the caddis worm, from the debris of the past.' The French finality of Connolly's style, at once supple and bleak, is one of the most glittering of English literary possessions, among which it shines like a crown jewel in a pawn-broker's shop.

It is hard to explain his influence to anyone who has not felt the impact of his personality. One might say that Alexander Woollcott was a vulgar, eunuchoid, ragtime caricature of Connolly, except that Connolly's earlier waspishness has mellowed with time. Nowadays, he says, 'things do not annoy me unless they are very badly made'. It is the making that worries him, the solitary toil of turning out a perfect sentence: but the hedonist in him forever militates against the anchorite. He wants to move up 'from the cottage class to the country-house class'; and thus, when his American publishers sent him a questionnaire with a final request for 'any other information about yourself . . . please do not be modest', his response was imme-diate: 'I could use a million dollars.' He loathes hearty, county people, but relishes the food they can afford. He is a journalist, but takes no newspapers. He detests easy fame, but wants to get rich quick. A fair description of Horace, Connolly's idol, might almost be a description of the idolater himself, but there is something irremediably comic about an English Horace in the 1950s. It conjures up a picture I cannot expunge from my mind: a draughty old Sunbeam Talbot being driven across country at breakneck speed in a rainstorm, Mrs Con-nolly furiously at the wheel, moodily grinding her teeth, and Con-nolly himself squatting in the back seat on what appeared to be a spare tyre and murmuring to me, in his fussy, tentative voice, 'By habit, of course, I am an Epicurean', as the needle touched seventy, the car lurched on a bend and an ominous banging was heard, as I remember, from the neighbourhood of the back axle.

Frying the Flag

LAWRENCE DURRELL

'Of course, if there had been any justice in the world,' said Antrobus depressing his cheeks grimly. 'If we ourselves had shown any degree of responsibility, the two old ladies would have been minced, would have been incinerated. Their ashes would have been trampled into some Serbian field or scattered in the sea off some Dalmatian island, like Drool or Snot. Or they would have been sold into slavery to the Bogomils. Or just simply crept up on from behind and murdered at their typewriters. I used to dream about it, old man.'

'Instead of which they got a gong each.'

'Yes. Polk-Mowbray put them up for an MBE. He had a perverted sense of humour. It's the only explanation.'

'And yet time softens so many things. I confess I look back on the old *Central Balkan Herald* with something like nostalgia.'

'Good heavens,' said Antrobus, and blew out his cheeks. We were enjoying a stirrup-cup at his club before taking a turn in the park. Our conversation, turning as it always did upon our common experiences abroad in the Foreign Service, had led us with a sort of ghastly inevitability to the sisters Grope; Bessie and Enid Grope, joint editor-proprietors of the *Central Balkan Herald* (circulation 500). They had spent all their lives in Serbia, for their father had once been Embassy chaplain and on retirement had elected to settle in the dusty Serbian plains. Where, however, they had inherited the old flat-bed press and the stock of battered Victorian faces, I cannot tell, but the fact remains that they had produced between them an extraordinary daily news-paper which remains without parallel in my mind after a comparison with newspapers in more than a dozen countries—'THE BALKAN HERALD KEEPS THE BRITISH FLAG FRYING'—that was the headline that greeted me on the morning of my first appearance in the Press Department. It was typical.

The reason for a marked disposition towards misprints was not far to seek; the composition room, where the paper was hand-set daily, was staffed by half a dozen hirsute Serbian peasants with greasy elf-locks and hands like shovels. Bowed and drooling and uttering weird eldrich-cries from time to time they went up and down the type-boxes with the air of half-emancipated baboons hunting for fleas. The master printer was called Icic (pronounced Itchitch) and he sat for-lornly in one corner living up to his name by scratching himself from time to time. Owing to such laborious methods of composition the editors were hardly ever able to call for extra proofs; even as it was the struggle to get the paper out on the streets was grandiose to watch. Some time in the early thirties it had come out a day late and that day had never been made up. With admirable single-mindedness the sisters decided, so as not to leave gaps in their files, to keep the date twenty-four hours behind reality until such times as, by a super-human effort, they could produce two newspapers in one day and thus catch up.

Bessie and Enid Grope sat in the editorial room which was known as the 'den'. They were both tabby in colouring and wore rusty black. They sat facing one another pecking at two ancient typewriters which looked as if they had been obtained from the Science Museum or the Victoria and Albert.

Bessie was News, Leaders, and Gossip; Enid was Features, Make-up and general Sub. Whenever they were at a loss for copy they would mercilessly pillage ancient copies of *Punch* or *Home Chat*. An occasional hole in the copy was filled with a ghoulish smudge—local block-making clearly indicated that somewhere a poker-work fanatic had gone quietly out of his mind. In this way the *Central Balkan Herald* was made up every morning and then delivered to the compo-sition room where the chain-gang rapidly reduced it to gibberish.

MINISTER FINED FOR KISSING IN PUBIC
WEDDING BULLS RING OUT FOR PRINCESS
QUEEN OF HOLLAND GIVES PANTY FOR EX-SERVICE MEN
MORE DOGS HAVE BABIES THIS SUMMER IN BELGRADE
BRITAIN'S NEW FLYING-GOAT

In the thirties this did not matter so much but with the war and the growth of interest in propaganda both the Foreign Office and the British Council felt that an English newspaper was worth keeping alive in the Balkans if only to keep the flag flying. A modest subsidy and a free news service went a long way to help the sisters, though of course there was nothing to be done with the crew down in the composition room. 'Mrs Schwartkopf has cast off clothes of every description and invites inspection', 'In a last desperate spurt the Cambridge crew, urged on by their pox, overtook Oxford'.

Every morning I could hear the whistles and groans and sighs as each of the secretaries unfolded his copy and addressed himself to his morning torture. On the floor above, Polk-Mowbray kept drawing his breath sharply at every misprint like someone who has run a splinter into his finger. At this time the editorial staff was increased by the addition of Mr Tope, an elderly catarrhal man who made up the news page, thus leaving Bessie free to follow her bent in paragraphs on gardening ('How to Plant Wild Bubs') and other extravagances. It was understood that at some time in the remotest past Mr Tope had been in love with Bessie but he 'had never Spoken'; perhaps he had fallen in love with both sisters simultaneously and had been unable to decide which to marry. At all events he sat in the 'den' busy with the world news; every morning he called on me for advice. 'We want the *Herald* to play its full part in the war effort,' he never failed to assure me gravely. 'We are all in this together.' There was little I could do for him.

At times I could not help feeling that the *Herald* was more trouble than it was worth. References, for example, to 'Hitler's nauseating inversion—the rocket-bomb' brought an immediate visit of protest from Herr Schpünk the German *chargé*, dictionary in hand, while the early stages of the war were greeted with BRITAIN DROPS BIG-GEST EVER BOOB ON BERLIN. This caused mild speculation as to who this personage might be. Attempts, moreover, to provide serious and authoritative articles for the *Herald* written by members of the Embassy shared the same fate. Spalding, the commercial attaché who was trying to negotiate on behalf of the British Mining Industry, wrote a painstaking survey of the wood resources of Serbia which appeared under the startling banner BRITAIN TO BUY SERBIAN TIT-PROPS, while the military attaché who was rash enough to contribute a short strategic survey of Suez found that the phrase 'Canal Zone' was printed without 'C' throughout. There was nothing one could do. 'One feels so desperately ashamed,' said Polk-Mowbray, 'with all the resources of culture and so on that we have— that a British newspaper abroad should put out such disgusting gibberish. After all, it's semi-official, the Council has subsidised it specially to spread the British Way of Life . . . It's not good enough.'

But there was nothing much we could do. The *Herald* lurched from one extravagance to the next. Finally in the columns of Theatre Gossip there occurred a series of what Antrobus called Utter Disasters. The reader may be left to imagine what the Serbian compositors would be capable of doing to a witty, urbane and deeply considered review of the 100,000th performance of *Charley's Aunt*.

The *Herald* expired with the invasion of Yugoslavia and the sisters were evacuated to Egypt where they performed prodigies of valour in nursing refugees. With the return to Belgrade, however, they found a suspicious Communist régime in power which ignored all their requests for permission to refloat the *Herald*. They brought their sorrows to the Embassy, where Polk-Mowbray received them with a stagey but absent-minded sympathy. He agreed to plead with Tito, but of course he never did. 'If they start that paper up again', he told his Chancery darkly, 'I shall resign.' 'They'd make a laughing stork out of you, sir,' said Spalding. (The pre-war mission had been returned almost unchanged.)

Mr Tope also returned and to everyone's surprise had Spoken and had been accepted by Bessie; he was now comparatively affluent and was holding the post which in the old days used to be known as Neuter's Correspondent—aptly or not who can say?

'Well, I think the issue was very well compounded by getting the old girls an MBE each for distinguished services to the British Way of Life. I'll never forget the investiture with Bessie and Enid in tears and Mr Tope swallowing like a toad. And all the headlines Spalding wrote for some future issues of the *Herald*: "Sister Roasted in Punk Champagne after solemn investiture".'

'It's all very well to laugh,' said Antrobus severely, 'but a whole generation of Serbs have had their English gouged and mauled by the *Herald*. Believe me, old man, only yesterday I had a letter from young Babic, you remember him?'

'Of course.'

'For him England is peppered with fantastic place-names which he can only have got from the *Herald*. He says he enjoyed visiting Henleg Regatta and Wetminster Abbey; furthermore, he was present at the drooping of the colour; he further adds that the noise of Big Bun striking filled him with emotion; and that he saw a film about Florence Nightingale called "The Lade With the Lump". No, no, old man, say what you will the *Herald* has much to answer for. It is due to sinister influences like the Gropes and Topes of this world that the British Council's struggle is such an uphill one. Care for another?'

On Shakespeare

BERNARD LEVIN

It seems unlikely, but I believe that I knew nothing at all of Shakespeare before I went away to boarding school at the age of eleven. I must have heard of him, I suppose, but certainly I had seen none of his plays (an easy enough claim to make, as I had never been to a theatre at all), or read any, either. My mother, to my retrospective astonishment, knew one Shakespeare passage, and would occasionally, *à propos* nothing very much, recite it:

> *A fool, a fool! I met a fool i' the forest*
> *A motley fool; a miserable world!*
> *As I do live by food, I met a fool;*
> *Who laid him down and bask'd him in the sun,*
> *And rail'd on Lady Fortune in good terms,*
> *In good set terms, and yet a motley fool.*
> *'Good morrow, fool', quoth I. 'No, sir', quoth he,*
> *'Call me not fool till heaven hath sent me fortune.'*
> *And then he drew a dial from his poke . . .*

She never mentioned, however, that it was from Shakespeare, and may not have remembered, as she must have learned it at school, and would certainly never have seen it acted. I committed it to memory from her recitation alone, but I had no idea what it was about, and naturally took 'fool' to have its modern meaning; what motley was, or what 'sans intermission' meant, or who was the aristocratic Lady Fortune, I could not imagine, and as for

> *My lungs began to crow like chanticleer*

it might have been a foreign language. But I can still hear the way she stressed 'goooood set terms', as I can hear the way she said my name. British usage puts the stress in 'Bernard' on the first syllable, American on the second; my mother is the only person I have ever known to make it a true spondee, stressing both evenly.

One of my uncles used to recite, in a very funny parody of an old-fashioned melodrama, Hubert's speech from the scene with Arthur in Act IV of *King John*:

Heat me these irons hot; and look thou stand
Within the arras: when I strike my foot
Upon the bosom of the ground, rush forth,
And bind the boy which you shall find with me
Fast to the chair: be heedful. Hence, and watch.

'Heat me these irons hot' became a family catchphrase; but of its Shakespearean provenance I was likewise unaware until later. There was no copy of Shakespeare in my earliest home; instead, the only books I can recall, apart from children's books and my grandfather's Hebrew bible, were some from a very motley uniform edition of long-forgotten authors who meant nothing to me, though I remember the look of the volumes, which had a disconcerting trick of falling to pieces, and their musty smell. I got my books from the local public library.

So presumably I first encountered Shakespeare at my boarding school, and as it chanced the first play I studied in class was *King John*; my delight and astonishment when we got to 'Heat me these irons hot' was greater even than what I felt when I later met Jaques in *As You Like It* and not only recognised my mother's recitation but found out what chanticleer meant. (Later still—much later, for the *Canterbury Tales* were considered grossly improper for my generation of public schoolboys, and we studied only the Prologue and that cautiously—I came on Chanticleer himself in the Nun's Priest's Tale.)

Much indignant breath and print has been expended, over the years, about the practice of making children study Shakespeare line by line for examinations; it is said to kill any possibility of a spontaneous love for him, by removing the excitement that comes from reading him straight through, and better still from seeing him acted, or even acting him. Perhaps; though I find the argument rather like the claim that television has killed the art of conversation, as though the people who sit comatose before their sets every hour of every evening would, if it had never been invented ('No good will come of this device,' said C. P. Scott, 'the word is half Greek and half Latin'), spend their time scintillating at one another like so many Sainte-Beuves or Dr Johnsons. I doubt it, as I doubt whether any child capable of responding to Shakespeare has been prevented from doing so by being obliged to understand him word by word and then to 'Write short notes on the characters of, a) Laertes, b) Rosencrantz and Guildenstern, c) Fortinbras'.

Anyway, when Sir Toby Belch declares that he 'would as lief be a Brownist as a politician' I discovered from such study not only what a Brownist was, but also that a politician was not what is now meant by the term (though the two meanings, as it happens, are today growing closer together again, which is a comment on the development of politics, not of language). And somewhere in the course of such study, I began to discover Shakespeare.

What was I responding to? I think it must have been the abrupt assault of emotion; more precisely of emotion I could feel in safety. Much later, when I discovered Wagner, the same thing happened, far more intensely, and it was not long before I realised consciously what was happening to me when I listened to *Tristan* or *The Ring* in the knowledge, simultaneously held and rejected, that this was not the real world but an opera house; for a few hours, no restraint on feeling was required, because for one thing it could be reimposed as soon as the performance ended, and for another and much more important thing it was too dark in the auditorium for anyone to see.

I am sure, though I was too young to wonder about it, let alone understand it, that Shakespeare offered me the same release. Though *King John* was the first Shakespeare play I studied at school, the first of the canon that I read as a 'set book' for an examination was *Twelfth Night*, and its music opened windows on such vistas of poetry, beauty and emotion that to this day I can recapture in their full strength my feelings as I gazed out upon the new, moonlit landscape. *Twelfth Night* is not really for children; they can enjoy the comics, of course, and the gulling of Malvolio (though no doubt they are still, as I was, steered rapidly past the appalling obscenity concealed in the most innocent line of the Letter Scene, which I was not only steered past but never spotted for myself either, finally learning it a quarter of a century later from a friend in the Chichester Festival Theatre during the interval of *The Wild Duck*), but the delicacy of the emotional relationship is too fragile and subtle for a schoolboy, and too often appears to him to be only 'soppy'.

I remember that some primitive instinct for self-preservation warned me to join in the jeering at Olivia and Viola, lest I should be thought as soppy as the play. But I *was* as soppy as the play; I had nothing to measure the feelings against, but when I got to

> *Make me a willow cabin at your gate,*
> *And call upon my soul within the house;*
> *Write loyal cantons of contemned love,*
> *And sing them loud even in the dead of night . . .*

I felt as though I was being drowned in a strange sea, the very existence of which I had not previously suspected, or which, if I had suspected it, I had instinctively denied.

This could not, I feel sure, have been the stirrings of adolescence; it was too early, and I was far too backward emotionally. I was vibrating to the sounds of a different music altogether, that of Shakespeare's unique ability to understand the human soul and its needs and powers, and to clothe that understanding in thoughts and words that enable his readers and listeners at least to glimpse what *he* sees in its entirety, which is what I mean when I say he allowed me to respond to the assaults of emotion. But that brings me to his understanding itself, and my discovery of it.

It is possible to learn a great deal about Shakespeare by reading him, and taking steps to ensure that you understand what you are reading. But there is a dimension to him that can only be discovered through seeing him acted. That is true, of course, in a fairly mundane sense as well as in the innermost feeling of all; however many times I had seen *Richard III* I could still never remember the Who's Who of Act IV, scene iv:

> '*I had an Edward, till a Richard kill'd him;*
> *I had a Harry, till a Richard kill'd him;*
> *Thou hadst an Edward, till a Richard kill'd him;*
> *Thou hadst a Richard, till a Richard kill'd him.*'

> '*I had a Richard too, and thou didst kill him;*
> *I had a Rutland too, thou holp'st to kill him.*'

> '*. . . Thy Edward he is dead, that kill'd my Edward;*
> *Thy other Edward dead, to quit my Edward . . .*
> *Thy Clarence he is dead that stabb'd my Edward . . .*'

Then, in the 1960s, the Royal Shakespeare Company staged, under the title of *The Wars of the Roses*, an extraordinary conflation of the three parts of *Henry VI* together with *Richard III*, and at last the scene made perfect sense, since all the killings to which the tragic women were referring had taken place before my eyes only a few hours before, and the dynastic relationships, as well as the killers' motives, were fresh in my mind.

But that is not what I meant when I said that Shakespeare has to be seen to be comprehended. The first productions I ever saw were also among the best I have ever seen, those magical performances in the Old Vic's days of glory in St Martin's Lane, and John Gielgud's last *Hamlet*, at the Haymarket Theatre in 1944, at the end of which I walked all the way home, a distance of some four miles, without being in any way conscious of my surroundings until I found myself, to my extreme astonishment, putting my key in the door. But Shakespeare was only one of the authors in the Old Vic's repertoire, and *Hamlet* was the only Shakespeare play in the Gielgud season, and of course this was many years before the Royal Shakespeare Company set up home in London as well as Stratford. So I had had no opportunity to see Shakespeare with any frequency or regularity, or to see more than a handful of the plays, or any of them more than once.

Not long after the war, however, Donald Wolfit took the old Bedford Music Hall, in Camden High Street, and announced an all-Shakespeare season of a month, with eight plays: *Hamlet*, *Othello*, *Lear*, *Macbeth*, *As You Like It*, *The Merchant of Venice*, *Twelfth Night* and *The Merry Wives of Windsor*. I went to more than twenty of the twenty-eight performances, and realised immediately that there was a very great deal more to Shakespeare than I had until then supposed, though exactly what it was I was unable to say. In a sense, my life ever since has been a quest for the meaning of Shakespeare, in which quest I am not by any means alone:

> *Others abide our question. Thou art free.*
> *We ask and ask: Thou smilest, and art still*
> *Out-topping knowledge . . .*

That, I suppose, is another way of drawing attention to Shakespeare's uniqueness, to the nature of which Emerson provides a useful clue:

What point of morals, of manners, of economy, of philosophy, of religion, of taste, of the conduct of life, has he not settled? What mystery has he not signified his knowledge of? What office, or function, or district of man's work, has he not remembered? What maiden has not found him finer than her delicacy? What sage has he not outseen?

The mystery of Shakespeare, the greatest and last of the mysteries that lie behind that lofty brow, is not that of his identity, for he was not Francis Bacon, or Christopher Marlowe, or the Earl of Oxford, though much more ingenuity and ink will be vainly spent, between now and the end of time, demonstrating that he was; nor is the mystery to be penetrated, the darkness significantly illuminated, by those who have sought to trace the origins of his learning or the roots of his philosophy; nor does it even lie in the astounding and undoubtedly unique breadth of his range, from Hamlet to Falstaff, from Iago to Prospero, from Imogen and Rosalind to Cressida and Lady Macbeth, from the Rialto to the walls of Troy, from the Forum to the Court of Navarre, from the sea coast of Bohemia to another part of the forest, from the death of King Lear to the birth of Queen Elizabeth, from Clarence's Dream to Bottom's Dream, from tennis to chess, from tinkers to tailors, from

. . . this my hand will rather
The multitudinous seas incarnadine

to

Making the green one red.

What, then, is the secret, where is the key that will fit the lock—the lock that I discovered at the Bedford Music Hall, seeing Shakespeare horribly travestied (not that I realised that at the time) by Wolfit and his dreadful company? It was a strange period for me anyway, Shakespeare or no Shakespeare, for the brief weeks of the Wolfit season coincided with the only period in my life after my buried infancy in which I had the direct acquaintance of my father, who then vanished entirely from my life; I possess no photograph of him, indeed no memento at all other than the inscription on the back of my watch, a handsome black-faced Movado with Arabic numerals (a rarity today), which he sent me (according to the inscription, though I have no recollection of his doing so) for my seventeenth birthday, and which still keeps perfect time. He and I went to one or two of the Wolfit productions together, though he had no knowledge of Shakespeare at all, except as the provider of plots for opera, about which he knew a little.

By then, I was a first-year undergraduate, and for several years had been a reader of eclectic tastes and almost insane voracity. I had read widely in the literature of eight languages beside my own (though very little of it, alas, in the original), and what I discovered—'sensed' would be a better word—in the dusty interior of the Bedford Music Hall, watching the 'acting versions' used by Wolfit (he used to bring the curtain down on *Hamlet* at '. . . and flights of angels sing thee to thy rest', lest he should not hold the centre of the stage to the last) and his scratch crew, was that the genius unfolding before me, in all its glory despite the conditions, was of a beauty, vigour, humanity, wisdom, wit, imagination, maturity, grace, feeling, profundity, richness and understanding that embraced all the qualities of everything of all the authors I had ever read put together, and a very great deal more besides.

That extraordinary truth I worked out only slowly; but in what I actually experienced on those evenings just round the corner from my childhood home I had leaped the argument and the evidence, and had arrived, without really knowing it, at the right conclusion.

Such actor-managing could not survive today; Ronald Harwood's shrewd and entertaining play *The Dresser*, which is plainly based on the character and career of Wolfit (Harwood started theatrical life as

Wolfit's dresser), gives an idea, and a good one, of what his work was like, and T. C. Worsley's description of his curtain speech (reproduced almost verbatim, incidentally, in *The Dresser*), with the old megalomaniac, as he thanked the audience, indulging in 'the same exhausted clutch of the curtain whether he had been laying himself out with Lear or trotting through twenty minutes of Touchstone', will also serve to remind those who saw Wolfit's productions of their nature.

None of that mattered in the least to an eighteen-year-old experiencing total immersion, for the first time, in Shakespeare acted. I did not know that the productions were grotesque, designed as a frame for Wolfit's own performances; I could not compare his interpretations with those of other actors, because the only play he did that I had seen before was *Hamlet*; I did not realise that the costumes were such as might have come from the nursery dressing-up basket in the home of a family that had come down in the world; as a matter of fact I had never so much as heard of Donald Wolfit before I read of the season he was about to present, and I was certainly not going, night after night, to see him, let alone his company. I was going to see—to see, hear, feel, drink, gorge myself upon—Shakespeare. That I did; and although it is the fashion now to decry Wolfit in retrospect, a fashion which I have myself here adopted, and although everything said about the awfulness of his work is true, I remain none the less devoted to his memory for that score of performances which still live so vividly in mine.

One of the very few sensible things Swinburne ever said, possibly the *only* sensible thing he ever said, was that the name of Bowdler should, so far from being an object of execration and derision, be honoured among the generations, because he made it possible for untold thousands if not millions of children, for the best part of a century, to become acquainted with the works of Shakespeare, which in an unexpurgated edition would never have been allowed in their hands. That is very like what I feel about Wolfit, and I cannot be alone in my debt to him. (I must, incidentally, be one of the few people to own a complete set of Bowdler's Shakespeare, and it is difficult to see, looking through it, why the good doctor should still arouse such ire; does it really matter very much if Shylock speaks not of one 'who, when the bagpipe sings i' the nose, cannot contain his urine' but of a less gross figure who 'cannot contain his choler'? Mind you, when the reader gets to *Measure for Measure* it *is* a little difficult to tell from the bowdlerised version just what it is that Angelo wants from Isabella.)

Take that list of plays I saw in the Bedford Music Hall: the four principal tragedies, plus *The Merchant of Venice* (another thing I didn't then know about Wolfit was that he would never refer to Hamlet, Shylock, Macbeth or Othello—in his mouth they were always The Dane, The Jew, The Thane and The Moor); two of the greatest comedies; and the Falstaff farce. I can remember details from almost every one of the productions. In *The Merry Wives*, for instance, when the search is going on in Ford's house and before Falstaff gets into the laundry basket, he tries to hide behind a wall hanging, but it turns out to be a *pair* of wall hangings, and his stomach protrudes between them into the room; in *Twelfth Night*, after Malvolio's final exit ('I'll be revenged on the whole pack of you'), Wolfit used the Duke's line 'Pursue him, and entreat him to a peace' as the cue for a dumb-show in which Malvolio is led back and reconciled, with Olivia hanging his chain of office, which he had torn off and hurled at her feet, round his neck again; playing The Jew, Wolfit ended the trial scene lying on the floor, writhing and weeping, but dragged himself to his feet, stumbled to the door and, before he left the courtroom and the play, looked right round the entire cast of his enemies and comprehensively spat at them all.

Those scenes have remained in my memory for more than thirty-five years; not because of Wolfit, but because of Shakespeare. For, much more vividly than these scenes, I remember the excitement that swept me along as the plays unfolded, the stupendous prodigality of the verse that flooded over me, the passion and the drama that seized me, the richness and variety of the gallery of characters that passed before me, the instinctive realisation which told me that this man was a being unlike all other writers in history.

When that I was, and a little tiny boy . . . Later, at some point, I began to understand consciously what Shakespeare meant to me. There was no single moment, no flinging open of the doors of perception, though I have never felt so completely part of Shakespeare, and so confident in my belief that I understood what was the nature of the effect he had on me, as I did at the production of *A Midsummer Night's Dream* which Peter Brook directed for the Royal Shakespeare Company in 1970. Here is an absurd test: if I were asked to select one single production of one single work on the dramatic or lyric stage as the richest and most profound experience I have ever had in any kind of theatre, I would choose that one. From the clash of cymbals to which the characters of the opening scene entered through the swing doors in the bare, white back wall, to the almost unbearably affecting yet gloriously appropriate final gesture of the cast making their exit through the auditorium, shaking hands with us as they went, it constituted the most complete and fruitful interpretation of any work of art I had, and have, ever seen interpreted. I

303

mention it for a particular reason: when the production opened, Brook gave an interview in which, discussing Shakespeare's use of the comic play-within-the-play as the climax of the work rather than as an interlude in the serious business of love, he said, 'By now, Shakespeare did nothing by accident.'

It is a haunting phrase, and it is surely true. Shakespeare's self-consciousness was greater than any other artist who ever lived; not Beethoven himself saw more deeply into his own heart. And he takes this to lengths that would be very dangerous in the hands of lesser men:

> *Not marble, nor the gilded monuments*
> *Of princes, shall outlive this powerful rhyme.*
>
> *So long as men can breathe, or eyes can see,*
> *So long lives this, and this gives life to thee.*
>
> *. . . How many ages hence*
> *Shall this our lofty scene be acted o'er,*
> *In states unborn and accents yet unknown!*
>
> *. . . I have bedimm'd*
> *The noontide sun, call'd forth the mutinous winds,*
> *And 'twixt the green sea and the azur'd vault*
> *Set roaring war; to the dread-rattling thunder*
> *Have I given fire and rifted Jove's stout oak*
> *With his own bolt: the strong-bas'd promontory*
> *Have I made shake; and by the spurs pluck'd up*
> *The pine and cedar: graves at my command*
> *Have wak'd their sleepers, op'd, and let them forth*
> *By my so potent art . . .*

The last of those extraordinary claims to immortality provides a clear test of Shakespeare's pre-eminence, for the passage is a reworking of part of a translation of Ovid's *Metamorphoses* by Arthur Golding, published in 1567, and although Golding certainly had great gifts, the difference between his talent and Shakespeare's transcendent genius becomes at once apparent when we watch him striking fire from Golding's clay. It is worth quoting the original at some length for a true comparison:

> *. . . Ye Elves of Hilles, of Brookes, of Woods alone,*
> *Of standing Lakes, and of the Night approche ye everychone.*
> *Through helpe of whom (the crooked banks much wondering at the thing)*
> *I have compelled streames to run cleane backward to their spring.*

By charmes I make the calme seas rough, & make the rough Seas plaine
And cover all the Skie with Cloudes, and chase them thence againe.
By charmes I raise and lay the windes, and burst the Vipers jawe:
And from the bowels of the Earth both stones and trees do drawe.
Whole woods and Forests I remove: I make the mountains shake,
And even the Earth itselfe to grone and fearfully to quake.
I call up dead men from their graves: and Thee O lightsome Moone
I darken oft . . .

No wonder that Shakespeare, contemplating Golding's earthbound
lines and his own soaring imagination, dared to claim immortality.
But many a lesser artist, many a poet and playwright without even a
slight gift, might put forward such a claim; indeed, many have, and it
is not enough to say, though it is true, that he has made good his claim
for four centuries, and will continue to do so for many more centuries
to come. He based his certainty that he was immortal on something
far deeper and more important than his understanding of the magnitude of his genius, and not only had he no need of Jonson's epitaph to
understand that he 'was not for an age, but for all time'; he knew
precisely why.

If he knew why, it seems likely that, whether deliberately or not,
he communicated the reason to us, his readers and audiences. And to
do so he had no occasion to resort to ciphers concealed in the text, nor
to publish accounts of his aims and methods, nor to commit such
reflections to diaries now lost. The mystery is explained in the works
themselves, which is where we would expect it to be explained, and
the explanation is not at all difficult to find, nor to understand when
found.

My own most striking experience of the discovery was also the
most striking Shakespearean experience I have ever had; it was much
more powerful than anything I have ever felt in any other performance or study of his work, not excluding the magical *Midsummer
Night's Dream*, and could hardly fail to be so, given the circumstances.

It has always been my practice, whenever going to see any Shakespeare play, to read it before setting out for the theatre, however many
times I have seen it and however well I know it. Many years ago, I
was due to see *Love's Labour's Lost* for the first time; it was the only
one of the canon that I had never seen staged, for I had by then
collected even the rarely-performed *Titus Andronicus*, in an astonishing production, also by Peter Brook, with Olivier in the title role,
which raised it from its gory gutter to the status of a true Roman
tragedy, and thus provided me with a valuable early lesson in the
truth that if we think little of any play of Shakespeare's, even the

slightest, the misunderstanding is more likely to be in us than in him. (The production also included a most striking *coup de théâtre*, still fresh in my mind decades later. In one of the battle scenes the action was shaped to suggest that the enemy was in the audience, and to our amazement the suggestion was suddenly borne out by a shower of arrows embedding themselves in the proscenium arch and the scenery. Brook had had the arrows fixed to their targets and painted so as to be invisible; then, at the moment they were to be 'fired', the unseen wires were all twitched simultaneously and the arrows instantly stood out at right angles, hypnotising the audience into the belief that they had been shot off from behind us and passed over our heads to do their work.)

In the afternoon, following my custom, I took down *Love's Labour's Lost* from the shelf and began to read. Before I had finished Act I, scene i, I had shut the book and put it away. For I had realised that not only had I never seen the play; I had never read it either. Now of course that is true for everyone, and for every play of Shakespeare's at some point; every Shakespeare-lover, from the most occasional theatre-goer to the editors of the *Variorum*, has had to discover the plays, one by one, and to be ignorant of them before doing so. But in this case, I was already familiar, to a greater or lesser degree, with all the other thirty-six; many I had known for years, and some intimately, both in performance and on the page. I could by then, for instance, recite some thousands of lines from the canon, and could tell you not only who Voltimand and Cornelius are, and in what play they appear, but could do the same for such far more recondite figures as Rugby, Capucius, Boult, Philario and Sir Oliver Martext, and in addition say where to find, as stage directions, both the famous *Exit, pursued by a bear* and the much less famous *Enter, and pass across the stage, a sewer.*

How *Love's Labour's Lost*, and that one alone, had escaped me I could not guess, and still cannot, but there lay the fact before me, and I knew at once what I was to do. That night, I had the pleasure (though the word is far too familiar to describe what I experienced) of seeing a new play of Shakespeare's as his contemporaries saw it when they were already familiar with his work in general. For me, that night, it was entirely new, just written and never before performed; I could measure it against his other plays but not against previous recollections of itself, as it unfolded on my delighted ear and eye and mind, and found there no preconceptions, no knowledge, no previous acquaintance with the characters or even the plot, to get in the way of its force, beauty and effect.

It so chanced that the production itself was a thing of vibrant imagination and loveliness; it was directed by David William, in the Open-Air Theatre at Regent's Park, and even the weather was perfect. The entrance of Mercade in the final scene of the play—and remember that until he spoke I did not know what he had come to announce—was miraculously staged. Dressed entirely in black, he emerged from the bushes at the back of the acting area; the scene of the Worthies had ended in a full-sized Court Ball, and for some time the messenger was unobserved. One by one, the revellers noticed him as he stood, silent and unmoving, surveying the mirth that he was so soon to bring to an end; one by one, they stopped their dancing, and eventually the whole stage was still, staring at him as the music faltered and died away. Then he advanced a few steps into the silence, and bowed to the new Queen:

> '*God save you, madam!*'

> '*Welcome, Mercade;*
> *But that thou interrupt'st our merriment.*'

> '*I am sorry, madam; for the news I bring*
> *Is heavy in my tongue. The king your father —*'

> '*Dead, for my life!*'

> '*Even so: my tale is told.*'

Did even Shakespeare ever give a character so few words (twenty-eight, for Mercade says nothing else and appears in no other scene) yet establish him instantly as a recognisable individual and at the heart of the drama? (Yes, he did. Popilius Lena, who appears only in Act III, scene i of *Julius Caesar*, has only *ten* words—'I wish your enterprise today may thrive ... fare you well'—spoken to Cassius immediately before the assassination, yet epitomising all those who speak ambiguously in dangerous affairs of state in order to ensure that whatever happens they may plausibly claim to have supported the winning side.)

Even at this point, of course, I did not know what was to follow, the vows demanded and given, the song—which I had long known as a poem without knowing its provenance or even its authorship—and that final, conclusive, eternally echoing curtain line:

> *The words of Mercury are harsh after the songs of Apollo.*
> *You, that way; we, this way.*

As I left the park, and made my way home through the silent night, I was being borne along on the extraordinary intensity of what had just happened to me, the experience of new-minted Shakespeare; and that river of glory, as it swept me, unresisting, with it, taught me, and teaches me still, whenever I conjure up the feelings I had that night, what is the greatest of all the pleasures and wonders and beauties and insights that Shakespeare provides.

No other writer, and with the exception of Mozart no other artist, has brought us so close to the heart of the ultimate mystery of the universe and of man's place in it; no other has felt and presented the numinous with such certainty and power, no other penetrated so deeply into the source from which he derived his genius and from which we all, including him, derive our humanity. The ultimate wonder of Shakespeare is the deep, sustaining realisation that his work, in addition to all its other qualities—poetical, dramatic, philo-sophical, psychological—is above all *true*. It is hardly surprising that he, alone among mortals, has conquered mortality, and still speaks directly to us from lips that have been dust for hundreds of years, and a heart that stopped beating to mortal rhythms on St George's Day, 1616. He alone had defeated the last enemy, that pitiless foe which he called 'cormorant devouring time'; no wonder that he knew it, and thought it no shame—'Not marble, nor the gilded monuments Of princes shall outlive this powerful rhyme'—to proclaim it.

Think of the old definition of tragedy: a man brought down by the quality that made him great. Then think of what it means in symbolic terms; the imperfection that lies within us all, and that we are on earth to work at until—perhaps, as the Buddhists believe, through many thousands of lifetimes—we wear it away entirely and become one with the perfection of the universe. Surely there is hardly an import-ant character (and in Shakespeare *every* character is important, includ-ing Mercade and Popilius Lena) who does not in some way reflect back to us the principle that informs the universe.

Why is Macbeth a villain? Because he commits murder? But what is the murder he commits, apart from being specially heinous as the murder of one to whom he owes the loyalty both of a subject and a host? It is an insult, in the sense of the word as it was used on Dylan Thomas's death certificate—'an insult to the brain'—to the universe, a deliberate attempt to disturb its order, its flow and its purpose. Why, unless we are psychopathically deranged, do we *always* know when we are doing wrong, whether we thereupon stay our hands or not? Because we are all attuned, deny it though we may, to the harmony of the spheres ('There's not the smallest orb which thou behold'st, But in his motion like an angel sings, Still quiring to the young-eyed cherubins'), and we know instantly when we have introduced a discord into this harmony ('But while this muddy vesture of decay Doth grossly close us in, we cannot hear it'). The 'order' speech of Ulysses in *Troilus and Cressida* is a statement, perhaps the noblest in the entire canon, of Shakespeare's own horror of anarchy and disorder. Shakespeare, however, was rarely quite so literal, and never two-dimensional; the speech, which in any case is obviously—more obviously than anything except Prospero's farewell and lines like Falstaff's 'I am not only witty in myself but the cause that wit is in other men'—Shakespeare himself speaking, is a statement of *why* he felt that horror.

Troilus and Cressida was written little more than a century after the Battle of Bosworth; when he was a boy there must have been men and women in Stratford whose fathers had fought there and told them of it, and of what it meant for their country, racked so long with civil war. That war, for Shakespeare, reflected the other, greater war in man's soul, which will continue until man makes his own peace by learning how to heal the split between those inner factions of White Rose and Red, and Ulysses describes precisely what must happen until that peace is made:

> *... untune that string*
> *And, hark! what discord follows; each thing meets*
> *In mere oppugnancy: the bounded waters*
> *Should lift their bosoms higher than the shores,*
> *And make a sop of all this solid globe:*
> *Strength should be lord of imbecility,*
> *And the rude son should strike his father dead:*
> *Force should be right; or rather, right and wrong –*
> *Between whose endless jar justice resides –*
> *Should lose their names, and so should justice too.*
> *Then every thing includes itself in power,*
> *Power into will, will into appetite;*
> *And appetite, an universal wolf,*
> *So doubly seconded with will and power,*
> *Must make perforce an universal prey,*
> *And last eat up himself ...*

The Bosworth within us all is real: 'Two loves I have of comfort and despair ... I guess one angel in another's hell'. Again and again, Shakespeare strikes the agonised balance between contrary impulses; he wrestled throughout his life with the Divine Rights of Kings, and in *Richard II*, most perfectly balanced of all the Histories, he stated the human dilemma in terms of Richard and Bolingbroke, king and subject, allegiance to an oath and allegiance to a country. He did it constantly, this offering of the stark choice we all have: what else is *Hamlet* but another such battlefield, on which the regiments are mother, father, the canon 'gainst self-slaughter *and* against murder, and on which the same interior dynastic struggle is being waged?

Aeschylus could solve the insoluble problem and free Orestes from the Furies by a *deus ex machina*; Wagner could square the circle of Wotan's impossible bargain by the creation of a new order out of the resultant chaos; Shakespeare knew better than both of them, and Lear must drain the cup to the last drop once the bitter wine is poured.

We are here to learn, and there is nothing we cannot learn from Shakespeare if we will only trust him. The feminine principle, yin for yang, he saw as the indispensable healing agent in the masculine, three centuries before modern psychology saw it too, and it is never stronger in Shakespeare than when it is literally disguised: there are no more complete women in all art than Rosalind-Ganymede, Viola-Cesario, Imogen-Fidele, Portia-Bellario, emphasising as they don their jerkins the incompleteness of one sex without the other, which is in turn another clue to our duty to be whole:

> . . . *Men must endure*
> *Their going hence, even as their coming hither;*
> *Ripeness is all.*

There is no play of his that will not, in the hands of a sufficiently imaginative director, yield up the same secret. When Trevor Nunn directed *The Comedy of Errors* for the Royal Shakespeare Company in the late 1970s, he knew that the play is almost always thought of as a feeble and unworthy work, thrown off without labour, and consequently incapable of making a modern audience laugh, or indeed of conveying anything but boredom. But Nunn knew also that fifteen years earlier, at Stratford, Clifford Williams had succeeded in making it an airy, delicate comedy, which suddenly, in the scene of reconciliation at the end, presided over by the Abbess (a true *dea ex machina*, conjured up by the deep necessity of the play's witness, not the shallower need of its plot), struck an entirely different note. This note was born of the pain that lay behind the comic confusions of the drama, and of the terrible threat to the fundamental regime of harmony and order that the unresolvable mystery poses until, when all the missing parts of the whole are assembled for the first time, we can see that there is no mystery and never was one; there was no more than a fragmentation, which needed only to be made whole.

That is what Clifford Williams did with the play; he divined what Shakespeare had done with it, and managed to convey that to the audience in unmistakable conviction. How was Trevor Nunn to do the same, to work the miracle again? At first sight, he seemed to have solved the problem by fleeing from it, by making the play only a ripe and dazzling farce, larded with such imaginative and pleasing business that we could do nothing but laugh helplessly throughout. But in that case, why did we feel not merely the benign warmth of laughter, but a sensation of extraordinary harmony even amid the whirling absurdities? Because he also had divined Shakespeare's purpose, and interpreted it by making the spinning farce truly centripetal, so that the reconciliation scene became, incredibly but undoubtedly, the only logical—the only *true*—way out of the impasse. It so happened that at the time of the first of these productions of *The Comedy of Errors* I was just coming to the end of a period of some years as a newspaper theatre critic, and at the time of the second I was just embarking on another such period. Of the first I wrote that 'at the end, it was like taking leave of a group of friends': of the second that if he could have seen it 'Shakespeare would have gone his way rejoicing, and so did I'. Both comments were reactions to the quality that Williams and Nunn, in their very different styles, had found in the play. But obviously they had only been able to find it because it was there. And if it is to be found in a play as slight as *The Comedy of Errors*, how much more clearly can it be seen in the principal tragedies, comedies and histories!

If we seek something in Shakespeare and cannot find it, it is not because what we seek is not there; it is because we have not sought it diligently enough.

I started reading *Much Ado About Nothing* when I was a schoolboy, and seeing it not much later, and I always enjoyed Benedick's catalogue of the attributes of his ideal woman—rich, wise, mild, noble, musical—ending with a shrug and the casual line, indicating his indifference to such considerations, 'And her hair shall be of what colour it please God'. Then I saw Robert Donat play it; he struck the last word a delicate blow, his voice falling half an octave on it—'her hair shall be of what colour it please *God*'—and instantly a joke, at the expense of women who touch up the silver with gold, that had lain buried for three and a half centuries, sprang to life. No wonder Mercutio dies punning.

The laughter of Shakespeare must not be rated low; if we think of it as no more than decoration we are in danger of missing not only the point of the laughter but the point of Shakespeare himself. Laughter is one of the deepest essences of mankind, one of the most significant clues to our humanity, for no other animal has the gift. Nobody has yet discovered what it is, not even physiologically, and we can only guess at the purpose it serves. But Shakespeare understood, and portrays, every variety of it, from the earthiness of Falstaff and Sir

Toby Belch to the delicate raillery of Beatrice and Benedick and all
the way to the bitter truth in the jests of Lear's Fool:

'Dost thou call me a fool, boy?'

*'All thy other titles thou hast given
away; that thou wast born with.'*

The first Falstaff I saw was Ralph Richardson; the finest, Hugh
Griffith (said to be the most difficult and uncolleaguely actor on the
stage, though this characteristic never communicated itself to the
audience—another proof that Shakespeare was right when he said
'There's no art to find the mind's construction in the face'); both gave
performances that vibrate still in the memory, because they went
straight through theory ('How do I get this laugh, why is this line
funny?') into Shakespeare's own understanding of the nature of
laughter. It is a truth not yet universally acknowledged that an actor
who trusts Shakespeare to know his business will have taken the
greatest single step towards success; this also applies, even more
strongly, to directors, though they are even further away from
understanding the necessity for the rule ('Shakespeare does nothing
by accident') than the actors.

I can remember my laughter at Shakespeare before any other of my
responses; Stanley Holloway was First Gravedigger to the Gielgud
Hamlet, and made me realise, again without understanding what the
realisation meant, that laughter is valuable at a level far deeper than
the enjoyment of the moment; young and unknown actors with any
sense ought to leap at the chance of playing Osric, or the Porter, or
the Clown in *Antony and Cleopatra*. (Though directors with any sense
will not let them do so, knowing that such tiny but vital parts must be
put in surer hands.)

Close behind the laughter came the excitement. There were no
Histories in that month of Wolfit, and only the two *Henry IV*s in
those early seasons of the Old Vic, though it is true that they gave me
Olivier's Hotspur; I did not see *Henry· V* until the young Richard
Burton, afire with youthful promise that was doomed never to be
fulfilled, played it at the Old Vic when the company had moved back
across the river to its own home at Waterloo, nor *Richard II* until I saw
it at Stratford with the young Guinness as Richard facing the young
Harry Andrews as Bolingbroke, nor *Henry VIII* until Tyrone Guth-
rie directed it as a loyal salute to the monarch in Coronation year,
1953, nor any of the *Henry VI*s until the Birmingham Repertory
Company brought them to London for a brief season. But even
collecting performances of them one by one over so long a period I

could realise what an important part of Shakespeare's life and work the Histories constitute.

There has been too much silly, modish chatter about 'Tudor propaganda' from critics and dons who seem incapable of sensing the greatness of the events the cycle of history plays depicts. There is carnage as well as splendour, treachery as well as honour, cowardice (though astonishingly little of it) as well as courage; but what we see is the forging of England on the anvil of history, and anyone who is, or, worse, affects to be, not at all stirred by pride as the metal is shaped and toughened has no idea of what a nation is, or why it matters to the people of it. Some day, a leading theatre company should stage all the ten Histories in a single season. I can think of no better way of explaining the first four of the most crucial five centuries of this country's history (alas, there was no Shakespeare to finish off the cycle with the Civil War and the Glorious Revolution, only the Restoration dramatists with their febrile, mincing wit) than by watching Shakespeare's immense tapestry unroll. When the RSC gave us *The Wars of the Roses* I recall that even the scenery entered into the spirit of the plays and their didactic purpose, its great slabs and joists of English oak and English steel making Shakespeare's point as vividly as Shakespeare's words did, and suffusing the theatre with the pleasure the audience took in its fitness.

And that is only the Histories: what of the excitement of *Macbeth*, of which Keats said that he didn't know how anyone alone in the house at two o'clock in the morning could even dare to read it? That first *Macbeth*, with Wolfit, seared my feelings with the power and electricity of the tale and the language in which it is clothed; who, however often he has seen it (and I suppose I must have seen it more than a score of times now), does not experience in himself, and not just vicariously, the sickened realisation that the witches are false when Macduff declares that he was from his mother's womb un-timely ripped, or does not feel the hair rising on the back of his neck when the servant announces that Birnam Wood is on the march to Dunsinane, or at the appearance of Banquo's ghost?

There is not a play of the thirty-seven without this excitement, the excitement that comes from seeing human beings facing apparently insoluble clashes between irresistible force and immovable object, whether these take the form of kingship and usurpation, or jealousy and fidelity, or belief and duty, or fathers and children, or cruelty and forgiveness, or dignity and humiliation, or truth and falsehood, or love and misunderstanding, or life and death.

Line after line rolls echoing round the mind on wheels of passion and arousal:

How all occasions do inform against me
And spur my dull revenge!

'Tis one thing to be tempted, Escalus,
Another thing to fall.

There was a man . . . dwelt by a churchyard.

I was not angry since I came to France,
Until this instant.

There is a world elsewhere.

> *Perdition catch my soul*
But I do love thee! and when I love thee not,
Chaos is come again.

Kill Claudio!

And the imperial votaress passed on,
In maiden meditation, fancy-free.

If every ducat in six thousand ducats
Were in six parts and every part a ducat,
I would not draw them: I would have my bond.

Good shepherd, tell this youth what 'tis to love.

I dare do all that may become a man;
Who dares do more is none.

'Tis the times' plague, when madmen lead the blind.

The last of all the Romans, fare thee well!

We feel the terror of Macbeth's cry 'Which of you have done this?', even if we know the play intimately, and even if the director or actor is clumsy, so that we see Banquo slipping into his place at the table, we still feel it undiminished. But why do we feel it so? Because for a moment we *are* Macbeth. That is why the question that works with all other playwrights and novelists—with which character do we identify?—simply makes no sense with Shakespeare, whose genius ensures that we are Iago as well as Othello, Hamlet and Claudius, Lear and his daughters, Montagues and Capulets, Posthumus and Iachimo, Shylock and Antonio, the Dark Lady and the lovely boy. And for the best of all reasons: these are all aspects of ourselves, and no man can contain Prospero without also encompassing Caliban.

And yet whatever of Shakespeare resides in his laughter, his excitement, his characters, his sense of history, his balance, his understanding, his universality, it is his poetry that provides the sea on which all these proud vessels sail; his music provides the most immediate, complete and enduring of all the pleasures he offers. There is no mood it cannot reflect or evoke, no feeling it cannot recall or inspire, no thought it cannot brighten, no sound it cannot make sweeter. In the words of Henry the Fifth it is always bright as noon; in the speeches of Iago it is dark and smoky as hell; in the ghostly tones of Oberon we are well-met by moonlight. And just as Shakespeare never ceases to remind us that we are at once king and rebel, Caesar and assassin, Leontes and Hermione, Timon and Athens, so the limitless flood of his verse is poured out for the knaves as well as the upright, the poltroons as well as the heroes, the corrupt as well as the pure, the solemn and the light-hearted, servant and master, country-man and courtier, clown and sexton, rich and poor, old and young, beautiful and ill-favoured.

Why do we smile at the story of the old lady who saw *Hamlet* for the first time and came out complaining that it was full of quotations? Shakespeare's unique ability was to convey a thought, original or familiar, profound or casual, in words that have rooted themselves in the innermost consciousness of millions, because his thoughts corres-pond to what is already, unexpressed, to be found there. If it were not so his words, however magnificent, could not have struck roots so deep and so tenacious; he found the soil fertile, and through his genius it has borne fruit.

'Truism' is a word of abuse, but it should not be, for the whole point of a truism is that it is true, and those Shakespearean phrases that have been worn away almost to dust remain alive in his mouth even if they do not in ours. If you cannot understand my argument, and declare 'It's Greek to me', you are quoting Shakespeare; if you claim to be more sinned against than sinning, you are quoting Shakespeare; if you recall your salad days, you are quoting Shakes-peare; if you act more in sorrow than in anger, if your wish is father to the thought, if your lost property has vanished into thin air, you are quoting Shakespeare; if you have ever refused to budge an inch or suffered from green-eyed jealousy, if you have played fast and loose, if you have been tongue-tied, a tower of strength, hoodwinked or in a pickle, if you have knitted your brows, made a virtue of necessity, insisted on fair play, slept not one wink, stood on ceremony, danced attendance (on your lord and master), laughed yourself into stitches, had short shrift, cold comfort or too much of a good thing, if you have seen better days or lived in a fool's paradise—why, be that as it may, the more fool you, for it is a foregone conclusion that you are (as good luck would have it) quoting Shakespeare; if you think it is early days and clear out bag and baggage, if you think it is high time and that that is the long and short of it, if you believe that the game is up and that truth will out even if it involves your own flesh and blood, if you lie low till the crack of doom because you suspect foul play, if you have your teeth set on edge (at one fell swoop) without rhyme or reason, then—to give the devil his due—if the truth were known (for surely you have a tongue in your head) you are quoting Shakespeare; even if you bid me good riddance and send me packing, if you wish I was dead as a doornail, if you think I am an eyesore, a laughing stock, the devil incarnate, a stony-hearted villain, bloody-minded or a blinking idiot, then—by Jove! O Lord! Tut, tut! for goodness' sake! what the dickens! but me no buts—it is all one to me, for you are quoting Shakespeare.

And the pleasure of Shakespeare's language is inextricably interwoven with what he says in it. His mind is an instrument of such stupendous understanding, depth and creativity that it towers over the human race, and to hear the contents of that mind clothed in that poetry provides a pleasure which consumes like fire.

> *Take him and cut him out in little stars,*
> *And he will make the face of heaven so fine*
> *That all the world will be in love with night,*
> *And pay no worship to the garish sun.*

When I hear those words spoken by a Juliet who knows how to ring Shakespeare's chimes (it happens, alas, all too rarely), I shiver in the ecstasy they provoke. But so I do when Coriolanus begins 'You common cry of curs', or Hotspur 'My lord, I did deny no prisoners', or Dogberry 'Dost thou not suspect my place?', or Petruchio 'Have I not in my time heard lions roar?', or Wolsey 'Farewell, a long farewell, to all my greatness'. For the ecstasy wells up from a level far below the ecstasy that comes from beauty or passion; it comes from the same spring as that which gives us life and meaning, which defines our humanity and our divinity, which makes us what we are and Shakespeare what he is. And that is why his last words apply to everything in the universe except him and what he serves:

> *The cloud-capped towers, the gorgeous palaces,*
> *The solemn temples, the great globe itself,*
> *Yea, all which it inherit, shall dissolve,*
> *And like this unsubstantial pageant faded,*
> *Leave not a wrack behind. We are such stuff*
> *As dreams are made on; and our little life*
> *Is rounded with a sleep.*

The Swirling Cape and the Low Bow

S. J. PERELMAN

If I live to be a hundred years old (a possibility that must have actuarial circles sick with fear), I doubt that I shall ever forget the winter of 1932. It needs no cup of lime-flower tea, macaroon or other Proustian accouterments to help me recall that that was the year I worked on a revue called *Sherry Flip*. It was also the year Rudy Vallee crooned his way to fame in a voice as seductive as mineral oil, the year Douglas MacArthur brilliantly routed the bonus marchers at Anacostia Flats, and the year those sparkling philosophers, Father Coughlin and Howard Scott, bedazzled the lunatic fringe, but all these calamities were trifling compared to *Sherry Flip*. Speaking dispassionately, I would say that the people responsible for that show—and I was as culpable as anyone—set the American theater back a hundred years.

The producer of *Sherry Flip* was a *bon vivant* named Avery Mapes, a one-time yacht broker riding out the depression on a cask of Courvoisier, and its creators were three: Lazlo Firkusny, a Budapest composer, a lyric writer named Lytton Swazey, and myself. Swazey, after years of grinding out special material for those willowy pianists who chant in cocktail bars at nightfall, had teamed up with Firkusny, who wrote popular airs under the pseudonym of Leonard Frayne. Together they confected a valiseful of show tunes, and it was on these, and half a dozen sketches I wrung out of a dry sponge I carried in my head, that the revue was based.

From the first week of rehearsals, it was obvious that the Furies had marked us down. The leading lady fell out with the composer, branded him a Hungarian meat ball, and went into nervous collapse. The comedians, who had made their reputation in burlesque, took a very dim view of my sketches, referring to me disdainfully as Percy Bysshe Shelley. They abandoned the material agreed on and began improvising routines in which they flimflammed a Polack from Scranton with a wallet stuffed with tissue paper, gave impersonations of humorous tramps, and spawned *double-entendres* that made the brain reel. Once embarked, no protestations, no appeals, could curb them; they girded themselves with grotesque rubber feet and boutonnières that spurted water, pursued squealing showgirls into the boxes

317

and thwacked their bottoms with rolled-up newspapers. Their behavior totally unnerved Wigmore, our director, a brilliant man around an Ibsen revival but a newcomer to the revue theater. The poor man fluttered about in a continual wax, pathetically wringing his hands like Zazu Pitts and endeavoring to assert his authority. In the dance division, there was a similar lack of co-ordination. The production numbers, two portentous ballets of the type informally known in dance circles as 'Fire in a Whorehouse', had got away out of hand. Muscle-bound youths stamped about bearing dryads who whinnied in ecstasy, shoals of coryphees fled helter-skelter across the stage, and the choreographer, wild-eyed with exhaustion, sat slumped in the apron, dreaming up new flights of symbolism. It was a holocaust.

We opened in Boston on the eve of Thanksgiving, a season associated from time immemorial with turkeys, and our *première*, I am told, is still spoken of along the Charles. The house curtain did not rise on *Sherry Flip* in the conventional fashion; instead, it billowed out and sank down over the orchestra, perceptibly muffling the overture. The musicians fiddled with might and main underneath, but Firkusny's score was too fragile and lilting to overcome the handicap. The comedy, on the other hand, was exceedingly robust, so much so that the police stepped in the next day and excised four sketches.

The tone of the reviews, by and large, was vengeful. One of the critics felt that we ought to be hunted down with dogs. Another, singling me out as the chief malefactor, stated he would be appeased by nothing short of my heart's blood. For the first time in its twenty-seven years of publication, *Variety* was guilty of a glaring omission. It forgot to review the show at all.

Two nights later, I was emerging from the stage door after a post-mortem when I heard my name called. Turning, I beheld one of our showgirls, a gazelle whose lavish *poitrine* was the despair of the wardrobe mistress and the lodestar of every male in the cast. She was accompanied by a vital, leathery taxpayer with protuberant eyes, opulently clad in a black astrakhan coat sporting a mink collar. His face was screwed around an unlit Partagas which he was savagely chewing into submission.

'My friend would like to know you,' said the winsome balloon smuggler. 'Meet Georgie Jessel.'

'Hello, kid,' said her escort hoarsely, seizing me in a paralysing handclasp. 'I've just been out front watching the performance. Does the name of George Armstrong Custer suggest anything to you?'

'Well—er—yes,' I said innocently. 'Isn't it usually identified with some massacre or other?'

'Indeed it is,' he affirmed. 'And as I sat there tonight, the walls of the theater receded and it seemed to me that I was back on the Little Big Horn. My friend,' he said, his voice solemn, 'the handwriting on the wall reads "*Mene mene tekel upharsin*". Your goose is cooked, the scuppers are awash. Get out of town while there's still time.'

'D-don't you see any hope at all?' I asked, trembling.

'Only for the Shuberts,' he said inexorably. 'They can always flood the auditorium and rent it out to hockey teams. As for yourself, go back to that job at the slaughterhouse. It's not glamorous work, but I can tell from your sketches that you have a career there. *Zei gezünt.*' He wrapped a proprietary arm around his date and swept her off to a hot bird and a cold bottle at Locke-Ober's. Desolate, I watched them go; then, hailing a jitney, I sped to Back Bay and boarded the midnight to New York.

Considering that I spent most of the ensuing decade in Hollywood writing scenarios, an occupation akin to stuffing kapok in mattresses, it was strange that I should not have encountered Jessel. The fact was, however, that he went there infrequently, for his services were not avidly sought by the movie satraps. He held them in rather low regard and his tongue was much too unruly to disguise his contempt. On one occasion, for example, he waspishly interrupted a panegyric someone was delivering about several production geniuses. 'Over-rated,' he snapped. 'They could put butter on the film and sell it.' Jessel's intimates begged him to be more politic, pointing out that other actors were being given parts he might have had, but the poniard flashed automatically out of the sheath. Typical was the evening he was taken to dine at the home of an M-G-M big wheel who was considering him for a role. Throughout dinner, Jessel was a model of tact and affability. After the walnuts and wine, the party adjourned to the rumpus room for a game of poker. All went well until the host's nine-year-old son, a particularly objectionable lad, entered and began kibitzing. Jessel gnawed his cheroot to ribbons in an effort to contain himself. At length he turned on the producer. 'Listen,' he rasped. 'Why don't you sling that punk across the bridge of your nose and tote him off to bed?' The name of Jessel, needless to add, was conspicuously absent from the cast of characters when the picture was released.

In the amnesty and repatriation that followed the accession of Zanuck I of the Skouras dynasty to the throne of Twentieth Century-Fox, Jessel suddenly confounded the wiseacres and bobbed up as one of the very clan he had derided for years. Whether he became a movie producer through hunger or sheer contrariness is uncertain, but he vanished from Times Square and the lush pastrami beds of the West Forties knew him not. It was whispered along the grapevine that the man was now a Zoroastrian and a food faddist, subsisting entirely on dates, bran, and blintzes made of soybeans, and engaged between times on projects clearly beyond mortal skill, such as translating the prose of Louella Parsons into English. Some even asserted that the real Jessel had succumbed a year before to steam poisoning in a Finnish bath, and that his studio was employing a double to impersonate him.

None of this kit-kit, happily, was true. A few weeks ago, lunching with a friend in the Twentieth Century-Fox commissary, I heard a familiar raucous voice upraised several tables away. 'Sure I like Grossinger's,' it was saying, 'but let me warn you—if you go up there, be sure and wear sunglasses. You can get snow blindness from the sour cream.' It was Jessel, right enough, and nothing had changed but his attire. He was clad in white sharkskin and a chocolate-colored shirt with pale-blue collar and cuffs, wore a coconut-fiber straw encircled by a puggree band, and rotated the inevitable perfecto in his cheek. Our eyes met at the same instant.

'Percy B. Shelley!' he gasped, springing toward me. No Siberian exiles could have exchanged more emotional salutations. 'What happened to that revue of yours in Boston? Is it still open?' I revealed that it had closed just prior to its nineteenth anniversary, and he shook his head. 'Oh, well, we all have flops,' he commiserated. 'Say, who's this interesting-looking fellow you're with?'

'Excuse me,' I apologised. 'Mr Jessel—John Keats.'

'A pleasure, Keats,' said Jessel. 'I've read your *Ode on a Grecian Urn*. There's a great picture in it; tell your agent to call me. Well,' he said, taking me by the arm, 'come on, I have to get back to my office. We can talk there.'

'But I haven't had my dessert,' I protested.

'Quiet,' he said under his breath. 'You don't want to be seen eating with starvelings—it's bad for you socially in Hollywood.' To save Keats's feelings, I told him that since he was jobless, a nonentity, and furthermore strongly suspected of being un-American, he could be of no earthly use to me, and ran after Jessel. Our chance meeting had thrown him into a reminiscent mood; his rhetoric as he expatiated on the early thirties grew more florid by the moment.

'Halcyon days, by Jove,' he declaimed. 'Gad, I was a picaresque fellow then, another Benvenuto Cellini. It was the day of the swirling cape and the low bow. What madcap escapades, what deeds of high emprise! Albeit my purse was empty, I was ever ready for a duel or a bout with the flagons. One look from Milady's eyes—'

'À propos of that,' I put in, 'whatever became of the pouter pigeon who introduced us?'

'She married into the peerage,' said Jessel impressively. 'The Turkish peerage. I sent them a box of halvah for the wedding.' His face took on a faraway expression. 'What a dainty waist that creature had!' he marveled. 'You could span it with your two hands. I spent the winter of '32 spanning it. Here we are.' The anteroom of his suite was a smoke-filled chamber resembling a vaudeville booking office. A handful of callers—a lush blonde, a small ulcerous agent, an insurance canvasser, and a carefully unobtrusive citizen who looked like a dice hustler—greeted Jessel effusively. When they had been disposed of, I rejoined him in his inner sanctum. The memorabilia accumulated in an extensive career as monologist and toastmaster overflowed the walls and furniture; testimonial letters from presidents, banquet scenes, signed cigarette boxes, and posters lay jumbled on his desk amid movie scripts, clippings, and a mountainous correspondence. He was shouting into a phone as I entered.

'How can I open the Santa Anita track that Friday?' he bellowed in anguish. 'I have to dedicate a new playground in Tel Aviv the next day! Yes, and emcee the Lambs' Gambol in New York two days after! I tell you, you're killing me, you're ruining my stomach—say no more, Harry, I'll be there.' He waved me into a chair, picked up a script, and began intoning over it. 'M-m-m. "Lucy, your eyes are like sesame seeds tonight, sesame and lilies. Anybody who says different is a liar". "Oh, Ruskin, don't, don't. What if my husband should come in from his destroyer?" No, that's too bald. The writer's using a javelin instead of a needle.' He blue-penciled the speech, and tossing aside the script, swung toward me.

'Why do I do it?' he demanded. 'Why does a gifted Thespian, a mummer in the great tradition of Burbage, Macready, and Booth, hock out his brains here for a lousy twenty-five hundred a week when he could be holding audiences spellbound with his magic? I should be playing Strindberg and Shaw in the different world capitals, not vegetating in this cactus-covered suburb!' He smote his breast, taking care not to muss his pocket handkerchief. 'When I remember those early days in the theater—the freedom, the bonhomie, the comradeship of those roaches in the dressing rooms! A man could live on nothing at all; I used to pay off my Chinese laundryman in lichee nuts. Today I've got a mansion overlooking the Pacific, with a library of the world's most expensive classics, a retinue of servants, a cellar of the finest French wines, brandies, and cordials, every luxury money can buy—and yet I'm like a bird in a gilded cage. Sometimes I'm tempted to kick over the whole shebang. If it wasn't for the crushing weight of responsibility, the whole studio on my shoulders—'

'Let someone else carry the load,' I advised. 'Get away from the artificiality and hypocrisy of Hollywood. Go down to Palm Springs.'

'No, it's too primitive, too remote,' he said uneasily. 'Sometimes it takes the *Hollywood Reporter* a whole day to reach there. Wait a minute, though,' he exclaimed. 'You gave me an idea. Have you ever been in Catalina? A Garden of Eden—a little fragment of Paradise in an emerald sea! How soon can you be back here?'

'I *am* here,' I replied, 'and what's more, I've seen Catalina. I went over there in 1938—'

'Look, I haven't got time to listen to travelogues, I'm a busy man,' Jessel broke in. 'Get some pajamas and a toothbrush, and meet me in an hour at Woloshin's delicatessen. I'll phone down to San Pedro for a boat, we'll pick up a cargo of lox and bagels, and I'll guarantee you a cruise that'll make Magellan look like a farmer.'

Naturally, I had no intention of abetting any such harebrained scheme, and I said so. I was still saying so about mid-afternoon as Jessel propelled me down a wharf at San Pedro toward a luxurious motor cruiser, all mahogany and brass, moored alongside it. My companion's innate flair for pageantry had impelled him to outfit us both with yachting caps and binoculars, and he was as salty as one of Joseph C. Lincoln's down-East skippers. The captain of the vessel, a stout foxy-nose in brown gabardine whom I would have cast more accurately as a defaulting bank cashier, welcomed us aboard and begged our indulgence. The starboard Diesel had broken down, but we should be under way within a few minutes. 'Take your time, Captain Applejack,' said Jessel negligently, stretching out in a chair under the awning. 'The others haven't showed up anyway.'

'What others?' I asked apprehensively.

'Oh, just some people I invited along to keep us company,' he returned. 'I figured we might as well play pinochle to while away the trip. How long can you look at the ocean, for God's sake? When you've seen one wave, you've seen 'em all.' Before I could invent some plausible excuse to disembark, like a ruptured appendix, our fellow passengers appeared in a peach-colored convertible, clad, to a man, in nylon windbreakers, Bermuda shorts, and berets. They all proved to be either former studio heads who were now agents or former agents who had just become studio heads, and their conversation was so cryptic that it might as well have been in Pawnee. The occasional monosyllables I caught, however, indicated that they were highly suspicious of each other and were only undertaking the voyage as a mark of esteem for Jessel. How profound this was I shortly discovered. One of them deserted the card table at which the rest sat engrossed in the pasteboards and joined me at the rail.

'A great guy, Georgie,' he observed emotionally. 'Salt of the earth.

You and I'll be lucky to have him read over us when our time comes.'
I did not quite grasp his meaning and begged for elucidation. 'The
eulogy,' he said impatiently. 'Haven't you ever heard him give an
address at a burial? Jeez, he'll make you bawl like a baby. I've heard
him speak at all kinds of dinners and affairs, but take it from me,
nobody can top that boy at a funeral.' He was launching into a hushed
account of Jessel's eloquence at the interment of some picture notable
when the captain reappeared with a long countenance. The engine
was hopelessly out of commission, and to further confound our
plans, an unexpected tidal wave had submerged Catalina and swallowed it up in the depths of the Pacific. The news acted like digitalis
on Jessel, whose mood had been growing progressively more somber
at the thought of putting to sea.

'Good riddance,' he commented exultantly, as we drove back into
Los Angeles. 'As a matter of fact, I was opposed to the trip from the
start—I only agreed to humor you. Now we can have a good juicy
steak and go to the fights.' The prospect of watching a number of
third-rate pugs maul each other into insensibility in a drafty armory
full of cigar smoke was an exhilarating one. Unluckily, I had a prior
engagement to dine with two other old friends in the movie colony,
Doc Johnson and Jamie Boswell, who were collaborating on a Biblical film at Paramount, and I did not feel I could let them down. The
mention of their names drew immediate approbation from Jessel. 'A
topflight comedy team,' he declared. 'Strictly with the boffs. Keep
this under your hat, but I'm planning a musical about Disraeli, with
Yvonne de Carlo as Queen Victoria, and I'd love to have those boys
write it. Tell their agent to call me.'

'Right,' I said, as we drew up before the Hollywood hotel where I
was bivouacked. 'Well, it's been a treat seeing you again, old man. By
the way, please don't bother to drive me out to the airport when I
leave, will you?'

'Of course not,' he said warmly. 'Now remember, any time you're
having a banquet, a christening, a wedding anniversary, or a shower,
don't forget Jessel. I've got speeches for all occasions, grave or
licentious as the case may be. I can tug at the heartstrings, I can tickle
the risibilities, and, if the caterer needs an extra man, I can even carry
chairs. *Lox vobiscum*, and give my regards to Broadway.' His custom-
built wig slid away from the curb and was lost in the stream of traffic.
On the sidewalk two urchins were turning handsprings, and somehow they provided a note of poetic justice. After all, nobody could
follow Jessel but acrobats.

The Opera

THOMAS CARLYLE

Music is well said to be the speech of angels; in fact, nothing among the utterances allowed to man is felt to be so divine. It brings us near to the Infinite; we look for moments, across the cloudy elements, into the eternal Sea of Light, when song leads and inspires us. Serious nations, all nations that can still listen to the mandate of Nature, have prized song and music as the highest; as a vehicle for worship, for prophecy, and for whatsoever in them was divine. Their singer was a *vates*, admitted to the council of the universe, friend of the gods, and choicest benefactor to man.

Reader, it was actually so in Greek, in Roman, in Moslem, Christian, most of all in Old-Hebrew times; and if you look how it now is, you will find a change that should astonish you. Good heavens, from a Psalm of Asaph to a seat at the London Opera in the Haymarket, what a road have men travelled! The waste that is made in music is probably among the saddest of all our squanderings of God's gifts. Music has, for a long time past, been avowedly mad, divorced from sense and the reality of things; and runs about now as an open Bedlamite, for a good many generations back, bragging that she has nothing to do with sense and reality, but with fiction and delirium only; and stares with unaffected amazement, not able to suppress an elegant burst of witty laughter, at my suggesting the old fact to her.

Fact nevertheless it is, forgotten, and fallen ridiculous as it may be. Tyrtaeus, who had a little music, did not sing Barbers of Seville, but the need of beating back one's country's enemies; a most true song, to which the hearts of men did burst responsive into fiery melody, followed by fiery strokes before long. Sophocles also sang, and showed in grand dramatic rhythm and melody, not a fable but a fact, the best he could interpret it; the judgements of Eternal Destiny upon the erring sons of men. Aeschylus, Sophocles, all noble poets were priests as well; and sang the *truest* (which was also the divinest) they had been privileged to discover here below. To 'sing the praise of God', that, you will find, if you can interpret old words, and see what new things they mean, was always, and will always be, the business of the singer. He who forsakes that business, and, wasting our divinest gifts, sings the praise of Chaos, what shall we say of him!

David, King of Judah, a soul inspired by divine music and much other heroism, was wont to pour himself in song; he, with seer's eye and heart, discerned the Godlike amid the Human; struck tones that were an echo of the sphere-harmonies, and are still felt to be such. Reader, art thou one of a thousand, able still to *read* a Psalm of David, and catch some echo of it through the old dim centuries; feeling far off, in thy own heart, what it once was to other hearts made as thine? To sing it attempt not, for it is impossible in this late time; only know that it once was sung. Then go to the Opera, and hear, with unspeakable reflections, what things men now sing! . . .

Of the Haymarket Opera my account, in fine, is this: Lustres, candelabras, painting, gilding at discretion; a hall as of the Caliph Alraschid, or him that commanded the slaves of the Lamp; a hall as if fitted-up by the genii, regardless of expense. Upholstery, and the outlay of human capital, could do no more. Artists, too, as they are called, have been got together from the ends of the world, regardless likewise of expense, to do dancing and singing, some of them even geniuses in their craft. One singer in particular, called Coletti or some such name, seemed to me, by the cast of his face, by the tones of his voice, by his general bearing, so far as I could read it, to be a man of deep and ardent sensibilities, of delicate intuitions, just sympathies; originally an almost poetic soul, or man of *genius*, as we term it; stamped by Nature as capable of far other work than squalling here, like a blind Samson, to make the Philistines sport!

Nay, all of them had aptitudes, perhaps of a distinguished kind; and must, by their own and other people's labour, have got a training equal or superior in toilsomeness, earnest assiduity and patient travail to what breeds men to the most arduous trades. I speak not of kings, grandees, or the like show-figures; but few soldiers, judges, men of letters, can have had such pains taken with them. The very ballet-girls, with their muslin saucers round them, were perhaps little short of miraculous; whirling and spinning there in strange mad vortexes, and then suddenly fixing themselves motionless, each upon her left or right great toe, with the other leg stretched out an angle of ninety degrees—as if you had suddenly pricked into the floor, by one of their points, a pair, or rather a multitudinous cohort, of mad restlessly jumping and clipping scissors, and so bidden them rest, with opened blades, and stand still, in the devil's name! A truly notable motion; marvellous, almost miraculous, were not the people there so used to it. Motion peculiar to the Opera; perhaps the ugliest, and surely one of the most difficult, ever taught a female creature in this world.

Nature abhors it; but Art does at least admit it to border on the impossible. One little Cerito, or Taglioni the Second, that night when I was there, went bounding from the floor as if she had been made of Indian-rubber, or filled with hydrogen gas, and inclined by positive levity to bolt through the ceiling; perhaps neither Semiramis nor Catherine the Second had bred herself so carefully.

Such talent, and such martyrdom of training, gathered from the four winds, was now here, to do its feat and be paid for it. Regardless of expense, indeed! The purse of Fortunatus seemed to have opened itself, and the divine art of Musical Sound and Rhythmic Motion was welcomed with an explosion of all the magnificences which the other arts, fine and coarse, could achieve. For you to think of some Rossini or Bellini in the rear of it, too: to say nothing of the Stanfields, and hosts of scene-painters, machinists, engineers, enterprisers—fit to have taken Gibraltar, written the History of England, or reduced Ireland into Industrial Regiments, had they so set their minds to it!

Alas, and of all these notable or noticeable human talents, and excellent perseverances and energies, backed by mountains of wealth, and led by the divine art of Music and Rhythm vouchsafed by heaven to them and us, what was to be the issue here this evening? An hour's amusement, not amusing either, but wearisome and dreary, to a high-dizened select populace of male and female persons, who seemed to me not much worth amusing! Could anyone have pealed into their hearts once, one true thought, and glimpse of self-vision: 'High-dizened, most expensive persons, Aristocracy so-called, or *Best* of the World, beware, beware what proofs you are giving here of betterness and bestness!' And then the salutary pang of conscience in reply: 'A select populace, with money in its purse, and drilled a little by the posture-master: good heavens! if that were what, here and everywhere in God's Creation, I *am*? And a world all dying because I am, and show myself to be, and to have long been, even that? John, the carriage, the carriage; swift! Let me go home in silence, to reflection, perhaps to sackcloth and ashes!' This, and not amusement, would have profited those high-dizened persons.

Amusement, at any rate, they did not get from Euterpe and Melpomene. These two Muses, sent-for regardless of expense, I could see, were but the vehicle of a kind of service which I judged to be Paphian rather. Young beauties of both sexes used their opera-glasses, you could notice, not entirely for looking at the stage. And, it must be owned, the light, in this explosion of all the upholsteries, and the human fine arts and coarse, was magical; and made your fair one an Armida—if you liked her better so. Nay, certain old Improper Females (of quality), in their rouge and jewels, even these looked some *reminiscence* of enchantment; and I saw this and the other lean domestic Dandy, with icy smile on his old worn face; this and the other Marquis Chatabagues, Prince Mahogany, or the like foreign Dignitary, tripping into the boxes of said females, grinning there awhile, with dyed moustachios and macassar-oil graciosity, and then tripping-out again—and, in fact, I perceived that Coletti and Cerito and the Rhythmic Arts were a mere accompaniment here.

Wonderful to see; and sad, if you had eyes! Do but think of it. Cleopatra threw pearls into her drink, in mere waste; which was reckoned foolish of her. But here had the Modern Aristocracy of men brought the divinest of its Arts, heavenly Music itself; and, piling all the upholsteries and ingenuities that other human art could do, had lighted them into a bonfire to illuminate an hour's flirtation of Chatabagues, Mahogany, and these improper persons! Never in Nature had I seen such waste before. O Coletti, you whose inborn melody, once of kindred, as I judged, to 'the Melodies Eternal', might have valiantly weeded-out this and the other false thing from the ways of men, and made a bit of God's Creation more melodious—they have purchased you away from that; chained you to the wheel of Prince Mahogany's chariot, and here you make sport for a macassar Chatabagues and his improper-females past the prime of life! Wretched spiritual Nigger, O, if you *had* some genius, and were not born a Nigger with mere appetite for pumpkin, should you have endured such a lot? I lament for you beyond all other expenses. Other expenses are light; you are the Cleopatra's pearl that should not have been flung into Mahogany's claret-cup. And Rossini, too, and Mozart and Bellini—O heavens! when I think that Music too is condemned to be mad, and to burn herself, to this end, on such a funeral pile—your celestial opera house grows dark and infernal to me! Behind its glitter stalks the shadow of Eternal death; through it too, I look not 'up into the divine eye', as Richter has it, 'but down into the bottomless eyesocket'—not up towards God, Heaven, and the Throne of Truth, but too truly down towards Falsity, Vacuity, and the dwelling-place of Everlasting Despair . . .

Good sirs, surely I by no means expect the Opera will abolish itself this year or the next. But if you ask me, Why heroes are not born now, why heroisms are not done now? I will answer you: It is a world all calculated for strangling of heroisms. At every ingress into life, the genius of the world lies in wait for heroisms, and by seduction or compulsion unweariedly does its utmost to pervert them or extinguish them. Yes; to its hells of sweating tailors, distressed needle-women and the like, this Opera of yours is the appropriate heaven! Of a truth, if you will read a Psalm of Asaph till you understand it, and then come hither and hear the Rossini-and-Coletti Psalm, you will find the ages have altered a good deal . . .

Nor do I wish all men to become Psalmist Asaphs and fanatic Hebrews. Far other is my wish; far other, and wider, is now my notion of this Universe. Populations of stern faces, stern as any Hebrew, but capable withal of bursting into inextinguishable laughter on occasion:—do you understand that new and better form of character? Laughter also, if it come from the heart, is a heavenly thing. But, at least and lowest, I would have you a Population abhorring phantasms—abhorring *unveracity* in all things; and in your 'amusements', which are voluntary and not compulsory things, abhorring it most impatiently of all . . .

Notes on Leonardo da Vinci

WALTER PATER

In Vasari's life of Leonardo da Vinci, as we now read it, there are
some variations from the first edition. There, the painter who has
fixed the outward type of Christ for succeeding centuries was a bold
speculator, holding lightly by other men's beliefs, setting philosophy
above Christianity. Words of his, trenchant enough to justify this
impression, are not recorded, and would have been out of keeping
with a genius of which one characteristic is a tendency to lose itself in
a refined and graceful mystery. The suspicion was but the time-
honoured form in which the world stamps its appreciation of one
who has thoughts for himself alone, his high indifferentism, his
intolerance of the common forms of things; and in the second edition
the image was changed into something fainter and more conventional. But it is still by a certain mystery in his work, and something
enigmatical beyond the usual measure of great men, that he fascinates, or perhaps half repels. His life is one of sudden revolts, with
intervals in which he works not at all, or apart from the main scope of
his work. By a strange fortune the works on which his more popular
fame rested disappeared early from the world, as the Battle of the
Standard; or are mixed obscurely with the work of meaner hands, as
the Last Supper. His type of beauty is so exotic that it fascinates a
larger number than it delights, and seems more than that of any other
artist to reflect ideas and views and some scheme of the world within,
so that he seemed to his contemporaries to be the possessor of some
unsanctified and secret wisdom, as to Michelet and others to have
anticipated modern ideas. He trifles with his genius, and crowds all
his chief work into a few tormented years of later life; yet he is so
possessed by his genius that he passes unmoved through the most
tragic events, overwhelming his country and friends, like one who
comes across them by chance on some secret errand.

His *legend*, as the French say, with the anecdotes which everyone
knows, is one of the most brilliant in Vasari. Later writers merely
copied it, until in 1804, Carlo Amoretti applied to it a criticism which
left hardly a date fixed, and not one of those anecdotes intact. And
now a French writer, M. Arsène Houssaye, gathering all that is

known about Leonardo in an easily accessible form, has done for the third of the three great masters what Grimm has done for Michelangelo, and Passavant, long since, for Raphael. Antiquarianism has no more to do. For others remain the editing of the thirteen books of his manuscripts, and the separation by technical criticism of what in his reputed works is really his, from what is only half his or the work of his pupils. But a lover of strange souls may still analyse for himself the impression made on him by those works, and try to reach through it a definition of the chief elements of Leonardo's genius. The legend, corrected and enlarged by its critics, may now and then intervene to support the results of this analysis.

His life has three divisions—thirty years at Florence, nearly twenty years at Milan, then nineteen years of wandering, till he sinks to rest under the protection of Francis I at the Château de Clou. The dishonour of illegitimacy hangs over his birth. Piero Antonio, his father, was of a noble Florentine house, of Vinci in the Val d'Arno, and Leonardo, brought up delicately among the true children of that house, was the love-child of his youth, with the keen puissant nature such children often have. We see him in his youth fascinating all men by his beauty, improvising music and songs, buying the caged birds and setting them free as he walked the streets of Florence, fond of odd bright dresses and spirited horses.

From his earliest years he designed many objects, and constructed models in relief, of which Vasari mentions some of women smiling. Signor Piero, thinking over this promise in the child, took him to the workshop of Andrea del Verrocchio, then the most famous artist in Florence. Beautiful objects lay about there—reliquaries, pyxes, silver images for the Pope's chapel at Rome, strange fancy-work of the Middle Age keeping odd company with fragments of antiquity, then but lately discovered. Another student Leonardo may have seen there—a boy into whose soul the level light and aerial illusions of Italian sunsets had passed, in after days famous as Perugino. Verrocchio was an artist of the earlier Florentine type, carver, painter, and worker in metals in one; designer, not of pictures only, but of all things, for sacred or household use, drinking-vessels, ambries, instruments of music, making them all fair to look upon, filling the common ways of life with the reflection of some far-off brightness; and years of patience had refined his hand till his work was now sought after from distant places.

It happened that Verrocchio was employed by the brethren of Vallombrosa to paint the Baptism of Christ, and Leonardo was allowed to finish an angel in the left-hand corner. It was one of those moments in which the progress of a great thing—here that of the art of Italy—presses hard and sharp on the happiness of an individual, through whose discouragement and decrease humanity, in more fortunate persons, comes a step nearer to its final success.

For beneath the cheerful exterior of the mere well-paid craftsman, chasing brooches for the copes of Santa Maria Novella, or twisting metal screens for the tombs of the Medici, lay the ambitious desire of expanding the destiny of Italian art by a larger knowledge and insight into things—a purpose in art not unlike Leonardo's still unconscious purpose; and often, in the modelling of drapery, or of a lifted arm, or of hair cast back from the face, there came to him something of the freer manner and richer humanity of a later age. But in this Baptism the pupil had surpassed the master; and Verrocchio turned away as one stunned, and as if his sweet earlier work must thereafter be distasteful to him, from the bright animated angel of Leonardo's hand.

The angel may still be seen in Florence, a space of sunlight in the cold, laboured old picture; but the legend is true only in sentiment, for painting had always been the art by which Verrocchio set least store. And as in a sense he anticipates Leonardo, so to the last Leonardo recalls the studio of Verrocchio, in the love of beautiful toys, such as the vessel of water for a mirror and lovely needlework about the implicated hands in the Modesty and Vanity, and of reliefs, like those cameos which in The Virgin of the Balances hang all round the girdle of St Michael, and of bright variegated stones, such as the agates in the Saint Anne, and in a hieratic preciseness and grace, as of a sanctuary swept and garnished. Amid all the cunning and intricacy of his Lombard manner this never left him. Much of it there must have been in that lost picture of Paradise, which he prepared as a cartoon for tapestry to be woven in the looms of Flanders. It was the apex of the older Florentine style of miniature painting, with patient putting of each leaf upon the trees and each flower in the grass, where the first man and woman were standing.

And because it was the perfection of that style, it awoke in Leonardo some seed of discontent which lay in the secret places of his nature. For the way to perfection is through a series of disgusts; and this picture—all that he had done so far in his life at Florence—was after all in the old slight manner. His art, if it was to be something in the world, must be weighted with more of the meaning of nature and purpose of humanity. Nature was 'the true mistress of higher intelligences'. So he plunged into the study of nature. And in doing this he followed the manner of the older students; he brooded over the hidden virtues of plants and crystals, the lines traced by the stars as they moved in the sky, over the correspondences which exist between the different orders of living things, through which, to eyes opened, they interpret each other; and for years he seemed to those about him as one listening to a voice silent for other men.

He learned here the art of going deep, of tracking the sources of expression to their subtlest retreats, the power of an intimate presence in the things he handled. He did not at once or entirely break with art; only he was no longer the cheerful objective painter, through whose soul, as through clear glass, the bright figures of Florentine life, only made a little mellower and more pensive by the transit, passed on to the white wall. He wasted many days in curious tricks of design, seeming to lose himself in the spinning of intricate devices of lines and colours. He was smitten with a love of the impossible—the perforation of mountains, changing the course of rivers, raising great buildings, such as Giovanni Church, in the air; all those feats for the performance of which natural magic professes to have the key. Later writers, indeed, see in these efforts an anticipation of modern mechanics; in him they were rather dreams, thrown off by the overwrought and labouring brain. Two ideas were especially fixed in him, as reflexes of things that had touched his brain in childhood beyond the measure of other impressions—the smiling of women and the motion of great waters.

And in such studies some interfusion of the extremes of beauty and terror shaped itself, as an image that might be seen and touched, in the mind of this gracious youth, so fixed, that for the rest of his life it never left him; and as catching glimpses of it in the strange eyes or hair of chance people, he would follow such about the streets of Florence till the sun went down, of whom many sketches of his remain. Some of these are full of a curious beauty, that remote beauty apprehended only by those who have sought it carefully; who, starting with acknowledged types of beauty, have refined as far upon these as these refine upon the world of common forms. But mingled inextricably with this there is an element of mockery also; so that, whether in sorrow or scorn, he caricatures Dante even. Legions of grotesques sweep under his hand; for has not nature, too, her grotesques—the rent rock, the distorting light of evening on lonely roads, the unveiled structure of man in the embryo or the skeleton?

All these swarming fancies unite in the Medusa of the Uffizi. Vasari's story of an earlier Medusa, painted on a wooden shield, is perhaps an invention; and yet, properly told, has more of the air of truth about it than anything else in the whole legend. For its real subject is not the serious work of a man, but the experiment of a child. The lizards and glow-worms and other strange small creatures which haunt an Italian vineyard bring before one the whole picture of a child's life in a Tuscan dwelling, half castle, half farm; and are as true to nature as the pretended astonishment of the father for whom the boy has prepared a surprise. It was not in play that he painted that other Medusa, the one great picture which he left behind him in Florence. The subject has been treated in various ways; Leonardo alone cuts to its centre; he alone realises it as the head of a corpse, exercising its power through all the circumstances of death. What we may call the fascination of corruption penetrates in every touch its exquisitely-finished beauty. About the dainty lines of the cheek a rabbit creeps unheeded. The delicate snakes seem literally strangling each other in terrified struggle to escape from the Medusa brain. The hue which violent death always brings with it is in the features— features singularly massive and grand, as we catch them inverted, in a dexterous foreshortening, sloping upwards, almost sliding down upon us, crown foremost, like a great calm stone against which the wave of serpents breaks. But it is a subject that may well be left to the beautiful verses of Shelley.

The science of that age was all divination, clairvoyance, unsubjected to our exact modern formulas, seeking in an instant of vision to concentrate a thousand experiences. Later writers, thinking only of the well-ordered treatise on painting which a Frenchman, Raffaelle du Fresne, a hundred years after, compiled from Leonardo's bewildered manuscripts, written strangely, as his manner was, from right to left, have imagined a rigid order in his inquiries. But such rigid order was little in accordance with the restlessness of his character; and if we think of him as the mere reasoner who subjects design to anatomy, and composition to mathematical rules, we shall hardly have of him that impression which those about him received from him. Poring over his crucibles, making experiments with colour, trying by a strange variation of the alchemist's dream to discover the secret, not of an elixir to make man's natural life immortal, but rather of giving immortality to the subtlest and most delicate effects of painting, he seemed to them rather the sorcerer or the magician, possessed of curious secrets and a hidden knowledge, living in a world of which he alone possessed the key. What his philosophy seems to have been most like is that of Paracelsus or Cardan; and much of the spirit of the older alchemy still hangs about it, with its confidence in short cuts and odd byways to knowledge. To him philosophy was to be something giving strange swiftness and double sight, divining the sources of springs beneath the earth or of expression beneath the human countenance, clairvoyant or occult gifts in common or uncommon things, in the reed at the brook-side or the star which draws near to us but once in a century. How in this way the clear purpose was overclouded, the fine chaser's hand perplexed, we but dimly see; the mystery which at no point quite lifts from Leonardo's life is thickest here. But it is certain that at one period of his life he had almost ceased to be an artist.

The year 1483—year of the birth of Raphael and the thirty-first of Leonardo's life—is fixed as the date of his visit to Milan by the letter in which he recommends himself to Ludovico Sforza, and offers to tell him for a price strange secrets in the art of war. It was that Sforza who murdered his young nephew by slow poison, yet was so susceptible to religious impressions that he turned his worst passions into a kind of religious cultus, and who took for his device the mulberry tree—symbol, in its long delay and sudden yielding of flowers and fruit together, of a wisdom which economises all forces for an opportunity of sudden and sure effect. The fame of Leonardo had gone before him, and he was to model a colossal statue of Francesco, the first duke. As for Leonardo himself, he came not as an artist at all, or careful of the fame of one; but as a player on the harp—strange harp of silver of his own construction, shaped in some curious likeness to a horse's skull. The capricious spirit of Ludovico was susceptible to the charm of music, and Leonardo's nature had a kind of spell in it. Fascination is always the word descriptive of him. No portrait of his youth remains; but all tends to make us believe that up to this time some charm of voice and aspect, strong enough to balance the disadvantage of his birth, had played about him. His physical strength was great; it was said that he could bend a horseshoe like a coil of lead.

The Duomo, work of artists from beyond the Alps, so fantastic to a Florentine used to the mellow, unbroken surfaces of Giotto and Arnolfo, was then in all its freshness; and below, in the streets of Milan, moved a people as fantastic, changeful, and dreamlike. To Leonardo least of all men could there be anything poisonous in the exotic flowers of sentiment which grew there. It was a life of exquisite amusements—Leonardo became a celebrated designer of pageants—and brilliant sins; and it suited the quality of his genius, composed in almost equal parts of curiosity and the desire of beauty, to take things as they came.

Curiosity and the desire of beauty! They are the two elementary forces in Leonardo's genius; curiosity often in conflict with the desire of beauty, but generating, in union with it, a type of subtle and curious grace.

The movement of the thirteenth century was twofold: partly the Renaissance, partly also the coming of what is called the modern spirit, with its realism, its appeal to experience; it comprehended a return to antiquity, and a return to nature. Raphael represents the return to antiquity, and Leonardo the return to nature. In this return to nature he was seeking to satisfy a boundless curiosity by her perpetual surprises, a microscopic sense of finish by her finesse, or delicacy of operation, that *subtilitas naturae* which Bacon notices. So we find him often in intimate relations with men of science, with Fra Luca Paccioli the mathematician, and the anatomist Marc Antonio della Torre. His observations and experiments fill thirteen volumes of manuscript; and those who can judge describe him as anticipating long before, by rapid intuition, the later ideas of· science. He explained the obscure light of the unilluminated part of the moon, knew that the sea had once covered the mountains which contain shells, and the gathering of the equatorial waters above the polar.

He who thus penetrated into the most secret parts of nature preferred always the more to the less remote, what, seeming exceptional, was an instance of law more refined, the construction about things of a peculiar atmosphere and mixed lights. He paints flowers with such curious felicity that different writers have attributed to him a fondness for particular flowers, as Clement the cyclamen, and Rio the jasmine; while at Venice there is a stray leaf from his portfolio dotted all over with studies of violets and the wild rose. In him first appears the taste for what is bizarre or *recherché* in landscape—hollow places full of the green shadow of bituminous rocks, ridged reefs of trap-rock which cut the water into quaint sheets of light—their exact antitype is in our own western seas—all solemn effects of moving water; you may follow it springing from its distant source among the rocks on the heath of the Madonna of the Balances, passing as a little fall into the treacherous calm of the Madonna of the Lake, next, as a goodly river below the cliffs of the Madonna of the Rocks, washing the white walls of its distant villages, stealing out in a network of divided streams in La Gioconda to the seashore of the Saint Anne—that delicate place, where the wind passes like the hand of some fine etcher over the surface, and the untorn shells lie thick upon the sand, and the tops of the rocks, to which the waves never rise, are green with grass grown fine as hair. It is the landscape, not of dreams or fancy, but of places far withdrawn, and hours selected from a thousand with a miracle of finesse. Through his strange veil of sight things reach him so; in no ordinary night or day, but as in faint light of eclipse, or in some brief interval of falling rain at daybreak, or through deep water.

And not into nature only; but he plunged also into human personality, and became above all a painter of portraits; faces of a modelling more skilful than has been seen before or since, embodied with a reality which almost amounts to illusion on dark air. To take a character as it was, and delicately sound its stops, suited one so curious in observation, curious in invention. So he painted the portraits of Ludovico's mistresses, Lucretia Crivelli and Cecilia Galerani the poetess, of Ludovico himself, and the Duchess Beatrice. The portrait of Cecilia Galerani is lost, but that of Lucretia Crivelli has been identified with La Belle Feronière of the Louvre, and Ludovico's pale, anxious face still remains in the Ambrosian. Opposite is the portrait of Beatrice d'Este, in whom Leonardo seems to have caught some presentiment of early death, painting her precise and grave, full of the refinement of the dead, in sad earth-coloured raiment, set with pale stones.

Sometimes this curiosity came into conflict with the desire of beauty; it tended to make him go too far below that outside of things in which art begins and ends. This struggle between the reason and its ideas and the senses, the desire of beauty, is the key to Leonardo's life at Milan—his restlessness, his endless retouchings, his odd experiments with colour. How much must he leave unfinished, how much recommence! His problem was the transmutation of ideas into images. What he had attained so far had been the mastery of that earlier Florentine style, with its naïve and limited sensuousness. Now he was to entertain in this narrow medium those divinations of a humanity too wide for it—that larger vision of the opening world which is only not too much for the great irregular art of Shakespeare; and everywhere the effort is visible in the work of his hands. This agitation, this perpetual delay, give him an air of weariness and ennui. To others he seems to be aiming at an impossible effect, to do something that art, that painting, can never do. Often the expression of physical beauty at this or that point seems strained and marred in the effort, as in those heavy German foreheads—too heavy and German for perfect beauty.

There was a touch of Germany in that genius which, as Goethe said, had 'müde sich gedacht', thought itself weary. What an anticipation of modern Germany, for instance, in that debate on the question whether sculpture or painting is the nobler art!* But there is this difference between him and the German, that, with all that curious science, the German would have thought nothing more was needed; and the name of Goethe himself reminds one how great for the artist may be the danger of overmuch science; how Goethe, who, in the *Elective Affinities* and the first part of *Faust*, does transmute ideas into

---

*How princely, how characteristic of Leonardo, the answer, 'Quanto più un' arte porta seco fatica di corpo, tanto più è vile!'

images, who wrought many such transmutations, did not invariably find the spell-word, and in the second part of *Faust*, presents us with a mass of science which has no artistic character at all. But Leonardo will never work till the happy moment comes—that moment of *bien-être*, which to imaginative men is a moment of invention. On this moment he waits; other moments are but a preparation or after-taste of it. Few men distinguish between them as jealously as he did. Hence so many flaws even in the choicest work. But for Leonardo the distinction is absolute, and in the moment of *bien-être* the alchemy complete; the idea is stricken into colour and imagery; a cloudy mysticism is refined to a subdued and graceful mystery, and painting pleases the eye while it satisfies the soul.

This curious beauty is seen above all in his drawings, and in these chiefly in the abstract grace of the bounding lines. Let us take some of these drawings, and pause over them awhile; and, first, one of those at Florence—the heads of a woman and a little child, set side by side, but each in its own separate frame. First of all, there is something exquisitely tender in the reappearance in the fuller curves of the child, of the sharper, more chastened lines of the worn and older face, which leaves no doubt that the heads are those of a little child and its mother, indicative of a feeling for maternity always characteristic of Leonardo; a feeling further indicated here by the half-humorous pathos of the diminutive rounded shoulders of the child. You may note a like tenderness in drawings of a young man, seated in a stooping posture, his face in his hands, as in sorrow; of a slave sitting in an uneasy attitude in some brief interval of rest; of a small Madonna and Child, peeping sideways in half-reassured terror, as a mighty griffin with bat-like wings—one of Leonardo's finest *inventions*—descends suddenly from the air to snatch up a lion wandering near them. But note in these, as that which especially belongs to art, the contour of the young man's hair, the poise of the slave's arm above his head, and the curves of the head of the child, following the little skull within, thin and fine as some sea-shell worn by the wind.

Take again another head, still more full of sentiment, but of a different kind—a little red chalk drawing, which everyone remembers who has seen the drawings at the Louvre. It is a face of doubtful sex, set in the shadow of its own hair, the cheek-line in high light against it, with something voluptuous and full in the eyelids and the lips. Another drawing might pass for the same face in childhood, with parched and feverish lips, but with much sweetness in the loose, short-waisted, childish dress, with necklace and bulla, and the daintily bound hair. We might take the thread of suggestion which these two drawings offer, thus set side by side, and following it through the drawings at Florence, Venice, and Milan, construct a sort of series, illustrating better than anything else Leonardo's type of womanly beauty. Daughters of Herodias, their fantastic head-dresses knotted and folded so strangely, to leave the dainty oval of the face disengaged, they are not of the Christian family, or of Raphael's. They are the clairvoyants, through whom, as through delicate instruments, one becomes aware of the subtler forces of nature, and the modes of their action, all that is magnetic in it, all those finer conditions wherein material things rise to that subtlety of operation which constitutes them spiritual, where only the finer nerve and the keener touch can follow; it is as if in certain revealing instances we actually saw them at their work on human flesh. Nervous, electric, faint always with some inexplicable faintness, they seem to be subject to exceptional conditions, to feel powers at work in the common air unfelt by others, to become, as it were, receptacles of them, and pass them on to us in a chain of secret influences.

But among the more youthful heads there is one at Florence which Love chooses for its own—the head of a young man, which may well be the likeness of Salaino, beloved of Leonardo for his curled and waving hair—*belli capelli ricci e inanellati*—and afterwards his favourite pupil and servant. Of all the interests in living men and women which may have filled his life at Milan, this attachment alone is recorded; and in return, Salaino identified himself so entirely with Leonardo, that the picture of St Anne, in the Louvre, has been attributed to him. It illustrates Leonardo's usual choice of pupils—men of some natural charm of person or intercourse, like Salaino; or men of birth and princely habits of life, like Francesco Melzi—men with just enough genius to be capable of initiation into his secret, for which they were ready to efface their own individuality. Among them, retiring often to the villa of the Melzi at Canonica al Vaprio, he worked at his fugitive manuscripts and sketches, working for the present hour, and for a few only, perhaps chiefly for himself. Other artists have been as careless of present or future applause, in self-forgetfulness, or because they set moral or political ends above the ends of art; but in him this solitary culture of beauty seems to have hung upon a kind of self-love, and a carelessness in the work of art of all but art itself. Out of the secret places of a unique temperament he brought strange blossoms and fruits hitherto unknown; and for him the novel impression conveyed, the exquisite effect woven, counted as an end in itself—a perfect end.

And these pupils of his acquired his manner so thoroughly, that though the number of Leonardo's authentic works is very small indeed, there is a multitude of other men's pictures, through which

we undoubtedly see him, and come very near to his genius. Sometimes, as in the little picture of the Madonna of the Balances, in
which, from the bosom of his mother, Christ weighs the pebbles of
the brook against the sins of men, we have a hand, rough enough by
contrast, working on some fine hint or sketch of his. Sometimes, as in
the subjects of the daughter of Herodias and the head of John the
Baptist, the lost originals have been re-echoed and varied upon again
and again by Luini and others. At other times the original remains,
but has been a mere theme or motive, a type of which the accessories
might be modified or changed; and these variations have but brought
out the more the purpose or expression of the original. It is so with
the so-called St John the Baptist of the Louvre—one of the few naked
figures Leonardo painted—whose delicate brown flesh and woman's
hair no one would go out into the wilderness to seek, and whose
treacherous smile would have us understand something far beyond
the outward gesture or circumstance. But the long reed-like cross in
the hand, which suggests John the Baptist, becomes faint in a copy at
the Ambrosian, and disappears altogether in another in the Palazzo
Rosso at Genoa. Returning from the last to the original, we are no
longer surprised by St John's strange likeness to the Bacchus, which
hangs near it, which set Gautier thinking of Heine's notion of decayed
gods, who, to maintain themselves, took employment in the new
religion. We recognise one of those symbolical inventions in which
the ostensible subject is used, not as matter for definite pictorial
realisation, but as the starting-point of a train of sentiment, subtle and
vague as a piece of music. No one ever ruled over his subject more
entirely than Leonardo, or bent it more dexterously to purely artistic
ends. And so it comes to pass that though he handles sacred subjects
continually, he is the most profane of painters; the given person or
subject, Saint John in the Desert, or the Virgin on the Knees of Saint
Anne, is often merely the pretext for a kind of work which carries one
quite out of the range of its conventional associations.

About the Last Supper, its decay and restorations, a whole literature has risen up, Goethe's pensive sketch of its sad fortunes being far
the best. The death in child-birth of the Duchess Beatrice, was
followed in Ludovico by one of those paroxysms of religious feeling
which in him were constitutional. The low, gloomy, Dominican
church of Saint Mary of the Graces had been the favourite shrine of
Beatrice. She had spent her last days there, full of sinister presenti-
ments; at last it had been almost necessary to remove her from it by
force. And now it was here that mass was said a hundred times a day
for her repose; and a mania for restoring churches took possession of
the duke. So on the damp wall of the refectory, oozing with mineral

salts, Leonardo painted the Last Supper. A hundred anecdotes were told about it, his retouchings and delays. They show him refusing to work except at the moment of invention, scornful of whoever thought that art was a work of mere industry and rule, often coming the whole length of Milan to give a single touch. He painted it, not in fresco, where all must be impromptu, but in oils, the new method which he had been one of the first to welcome, because it allowed of so many after-thoughts, such a refined working out of perfection. It turned out that on a plastered wall no process could have been less durable. Within fifty years it had fallen into decay. Protestants, who always found themselves much edified by a certain biblical turn in it, have multiplied all sorts of bad copies and engravings of it. And now we have to turn back to Leonardo's own studies—above all, to one drawing of the central head at the Brera, which in a union of tenderness and severity in the face-lines, reminds one of the monumental work of Mino da Fiesole—to trace it as it was.

It was another effort to set a thing out of the range of its conventional associations. Strange, after all the misrepresentations of the Middle Age, was the effort to see it, not as the pale host of the altar, but as one taking leave of his friends. Five years after, the young Raphael, at Florence, painted it with sweet and solemn effect in the refectory of Saint Onofrio; but still with all the mystical unreality of the school of Perugino. Vasari pretends that the central head was never finished. Well; finished or unfinished, or owing part of its effect to a mellowing decay, this central head does but consummate the sentiment of the whole company—ghosts through which you see the wall, faint as the shadows of the leaves upon the wall on autumn afternoons; this figure is but the faintest, most spectral of them all. It is the image of what the history it symbolises has been more and more ever since, paler and paler as it recedes from us. Criticism came with its appeal from mystical unrealities to originals, and restored no lifelike reality but these transparent shadows—spirits which have not flesh and bones.

The Last Supper was finished in 1497; in 1498 the French entered Milan, and whether or not the Gascon bowmen used it as a mark for their arrows,* the model of the Sforza certainly did not survive. Ludovico became a prisoner, and the remaining years of Leonardo's life are more or less years of wandering. From his brilliant life at court he had saved nothing, and he returned to Florence a poor man. Perhaps necessity kept his spirit excited: the next four years are one prolonged rapture or ecstasy of invention. He painted the pictures of

---

*M. Arsène Houssaye comes to save the credit of his countrymen.

the Louvre, his most authentic works, which came there straight from the cabinet of Francis I at Fontainebleau. One picture of his, the Saint Anne—not the Saint Anne of the Louvre, but a mere cartoon now in London—revived for a moment a sort of appreciation more common in an earlier time, when good pictures had still seemed miraculous; and for two days a crowd of people of all qualities passed in naïve excitement through the chamber where it hung, and gave him a taste of Cimabue's triumph. But his work was less with the saints than with the living women of Florence; for he moved still in the polished society that he loved, and in the salons of Florence, left perhaps a little subject to light thoughts by the death of Savonarola (the latest gossip is of an undraped Mona Lisa, found in some out-of-the-way corner of the late Orleans collection), he met Ginevra di Benci, and Lisa, the young third wife of Francesco del Giocondo. As we have seen him using incidents of the sacred legend, not for their own sake, or as mere subjects for pictorial realisation, but as a symbolical language for fancies all his own, so now he found a vent for his thoughts in taking one of these languid women, and raising her as Leda or Pomona, Modesty or Vanity, to the seventh heaven of symbolical expression.

La Gioconda is, in the truest sense, Leonardo's masterpiece—the revealing instance of his mode of thought and work. In suggestiveness, only the Melancholia of Dürer is comparable to it; and no crude symbolism disturbs the effect of its subdued and graceful mystery. We all know the face and hands of the figure, set in its marble chair, in that cirque of fantastic rocks, as in some faint light under sea. Perhaps of all ancient pictures time has chilled it least.★ As often happens with works in which invention seems to reach its limit, there is an element in it given to, not invented by, the master. In that inestimable folio of drawings, once in the possession of Vasari, were certain designs by Verrocchio—faces of such impressive beauty that Leonardo in his boyhood copied them many times. It is hard not to connect with these designs of the elder by-past master, as with its germinal principle, the unfathomable smile, always with a touch of something sinister in it, which plays over all Leonardo's work. Besides the picture is a portrait. From childhood we see this image defining itself on the fabric of his dreams; and but for express historical testimony, we might fancy that this was but his ideal lady, embodied and beheld at last. What was the relationship of a living Florentine to this creature of his thought? By what strange affinities had she and the dream

★ Yet for Vasari there was some further magic of crimson in the lips and cheeks, lost for us.

grown thus apart, yet so closely together? Present from the first incorporeal in Leonardo's thought, dimly traced in the designs of Verrocchio, she is found present at last in Il Giocondo's house. That there is much of mere portraiture in the picture is attested by the legend that by artificial means, the presence of mimes and flute-players, that subtle expression was protracted on the face. Again, was it in four years and by renewed labour never really completed, or in four months, as by stroke of magic, that the image was projected?

The presence that thus so strangely rose beside the waters is expressive of what in the ways of a thousand years man had come to desire. Hers is the head upon which all 'the ends of the world are come', and the eyelids are a little weary. It is a beauty wrought out from within upon the flesh—the deposit, little cell by cell, of strange thoughts and fantastic reveries and exquisite passions. Set it for a moment beside one of those white Greek goddesses or beautiful women of antiquity, and how would they be troubled by this beauty, into which the soul with all its maladies has passed? All the thoughts and experiences of the world have etched and moulded there in that which they have of power to refine and make expressive the outward form—the animalism of Greece, the lust of Rome, the reverie of the Middle Age with its spiritual ambition and imaginative loves, the return of the Pagan world, the sins of the Borgias. She is older than the rocks among which she sits; like the vampire, she has been dead, many times, and learned the secrets of the grave, and has been a diver in deep seas, and keeps their fallen day about her; and trafficked for strange webs with Eastern merchants; and, as Leda, was the mother of Helen of Troy, and, as Saint Anne, the mother of Mary; and all this has been to her but as the sound of lyres and flutes, and lives only in the delicacy with which it has moulded the changing linea-ments and tinged the eyelids and the hands. The fancy of a perpetual life, sweeping together ten thousand experiences, is an old one; and modern thought has conceived the idea of humanity as wrought upon by, and summing up in itself, all modes of thought and life. Cer-tainly, Lady Lisa might stand as the embodiment of the old fancy, the symbol of the modern idea.

During these years at Florence Leonardo's history is the history of his art; he himself is lost in the bright cloud of it. The outward history begins again in 1502, with a wild journey through central Italy, which he makes as the chief engineer of Caesar Borgia. The biographer, putting together the stray jottings of his manuscripts, may follow him through every day of it, up the strange tower of Siena, which looks towards Rome, elastic like a bent bow, down to the seashore at Piombino, each place appearing as fitfully as in a fever dream.

One other great work was left for him to do—a work all trace of which soon vanished—the Battle of the Standard, in which he had for his rival Michelangelo. The citizens of Florence, desiring to decorate the walls of the great council chambers, had offered the work for competition, and any subject might be chosen from the Florentine wars of the fifteenth century. Michelangelo chose for his cartoon an incident of the war with Pisa, in which the Florentine soldiers, bathing in the Arno, are surprised by the sound of trumpets, and run to arms. His design has reached us only in an old engraving, which perhaps would help us less than what we remember of the background of his Holy Family in the Uffizi to imagine in what superhuman form, such as might have beguiled the heart of an earlier world, those figures may have risen from the water. Leonardo chose an incident from the battle of Anghiari, in which two parties of soldiers fight for a standard. Like Michelangelo's, his cartoon is lost, and has come to us only in sketches and a fragment of Rubens. Through the accounts given we may discern some lust of terrible things in it, so that even the horses tore each other with their teeth; and yet one fragment of it, in a drawing of his at Florence, is far different—a waving field of lovely armour, the chased edgings running like lines of sunlight from side to side. Michelangelo was twenty-seven years old; Leonardo more than fifty; and Raphael, then nineteen years old, visiting Florence for the first time, came and watched them as they worked.

We catch a glimpse of him again at Rome in 1514, surrounded by his mirrors and vials and furnaces, making strange toys that seemed alive of wax and quicksilver. The hesitation which had haunted him all through life, and made him like one under a spell, was on him now with double force. No one had even carried political indifferentism farther; it had always been his philosophy to 'fly before the storm'; he is out with the Sforzas and in with the Sforzas as the tide of fortune turns. Yet now he was suspected by the anti-Gallican, Medicean society at Rome, of French leanings. It paralysed him to find himself among enemies; and he turned wholly to France, which had long courted him.

France was going to be an Italy more Italian than Italy itself. Francis I, like Louis XII before him, was attracted by the finesse of Leonardo's work. La Gioconda was already in his cabinet, and he offered Leonardo the little Château de Clou, with its vineyards and meadows, in the soft valley of the Masse—not too far from the great outer sea. M. Arsène Houssaye has succeeded in giving a pensive local colour to this part of his subject, with which, as a Frenchman, he could best deal. 'A Monsieur Lyonard, peinteur du Roy pour

ON THE ARTS (MOSTLY WRITING)

Amboyse,' so the letter of Francis I is headed. It opens a prospect—one of the most attractive in the history of art –where, under a strange mixture of lights Italian art dies away as a French exotic. M. Houssaye does but touch it lightly, and it would carry us beyond the present essay if we allowed ourselves to be seduced by its interest.

Two questions remain, after all busy antiquarianism, concerning Leonardo's death—the question of his religion, and the question whether Francis I was present at the time. They are of about equally little importance in the estimate of Leonardo's genius. The directions in his will about the thirty masses and the great candles for the church of St Florentin are things of course—their real purpose being immediate and practical; and on no theory of religion could such hurried candle-burning be of much consequence. We forget them in speculating how one who had been always so desirous of beauty, but desired it always in such precise and definite forms, as hands or flowers or hair, looked forward now into the vague land, and experienced the last curiosity.

Rodin

GEORGE BERNARD SHAW

In the year 1906 it was proposed to furnish the world with an authentic portrait-bust of me before I had left the prime of life too far behind. The question then arose: Could Rodin be induced to undertake the work? On no other condition would I sit, because it was clear to me that Rodin was not only the greatest sculptor then living, but the greatest sculptor of his epoch: one of those extraordinary persons who, like Michelangelo, or Phidias, or Praxiteles, dominate whole ages as fashionable favourites dominate a single London season. I saw, therefore, that any man who, being a contemporary of Rodin, deliberately allowed his bust to be made by anybody else, must go down to posterity (if he went down at all) as a stupendous nincompoop.

Also, I wanted a portrait of myself by an artist capable of seeing me. Many clever portraits of my reputation were in existence; but I have never been taken in by my reputation, having manufactured it myself. A reputation is a mask which a man has to wear just as he has to wear a coat and trousers: it is a disguise we insist on as a point of decency. The result is that we have hardly any portraits of men and women. We have no portraits of their legs and shoulders; only of their skirts and trousers and blouses and coats. Nobody knows what Dickens was like, or what Queen Victoria was like, though their wardrobes are on record. Many people fancy they know their faces; but they are deceived: we know only the fashionable mask of the distinguished novelist and of the queen. And the mask defies the camera. When Mr Alvin Langdon Coburn wanted to exhibit a full-length photographic portrait of me, I secured a faithful representation up to the neck by the trite expedient of sitting to him one morning as I got out of my bath. The portrait was duly hung before a stupefied public as a first step towards the realisation of Carlyle's antidote to political idolatry: a naked parliament. But though the body was my body, the face was the face of my reputation. So much so, in fact, that the critics concluded that Mr Coburn had faked his photograph, and stuck my head on somebody else's shoulders. For, as I have said, the mask cannot be penetrated by the camera. It is transparent only to the eye of a veritably god-like artist.

Rodin tells us that his wonderful portrait-busts seldom please the sitters. I can go further, and say that they often puzzle and disappoint the sitters' friends. The busts are of real men, not of the reputations of celebrated persons. Look at my bust, and you will not find it a bit like that brilliant fiction known as G. B. S. or Bernard Shaw. But it is most frightfully like me. It is what is really there, not what you think is there. The same with Puvis de Chavannes and the rest of them. Puvis de Chavannes protested, as one gathers—pointed to his mirror and to his photographs to prove that he was not like his bust. But I am convinced that he was not only like his bust, but that the bust actually was himself as distinct from his collars and his public manners. Puvis, though an artist of great merit, could not see himself. Rodin could. He saw me. Nobody else has done that yet.

Troubetskoi once made a most fascinating Shavian bust of me. He did it in about five hours, in Sargent's studio. It was a delightful and wonderful performance. He worked convulsively, giving birth to the thing in agonies, hurling lumps of clay about with groans, and making strange, dumb movements with his tongue, like a wordless prophet. He covered himself with plaster. He covered Sargent's carpets and curtains and pictures with plaster. He covered me with plaster. And, finally, he covered the block he was working on with plaster to such purpose that, at the end of the second sitting, lo! there stood Sargent's studio in ruins, buried like Pompeii under the scoriae of a volcano, and in the midst a spirited bust of one of my reputations, a little idealised (quite the gentleman, in fact) but recognisable a mile off as the sardonic author of *Man and Superman*, with a dash of Offenbach, a touch of Mephistopheles, and a certain aristocratic delicacy and distinction that came from Troubetskoi himself, he being a prince. I should like to have that bust; but the truth is, my wife cannot stand Offenbach-Mephistopheles; and I was not allowed to have the bust any more than I was allowed to have that other witty jibe at my poses, Neville Lytton's portrait of me as Velasquez's Pope Innocent.

Rodin worked very differently. He plodded along exactly as if he were a river-god doing a job of wall-building in a garden for three or four francs a day. When he was in doubt he measured me with an old iron dividers, and then measured the bust. If the bust's nose was too long, he sliced a bit out of it, and jammed the tip of it up to close the gap, with no more emotion or affectation than a glazier putting in a window pane. If the ear was in the wrong place, he cut it off and slapped it into its right place, excusing these ruthless mutilations to my wife (who half expected to see the already terribly animated clay bleed) by remarking that it was shorter than to make a new ear. Yet a succession of miracles took place as he worked. In the first fifteen minutes, in merely giving a suggestion of human shape to the lump of clay, he produced so spirited a thumbnail bust of me that I wanted to take it away and relieve him from further labour. It reminded me of a highly finished bust by Sarah Bernhardt, who is very clever with her fingers. But that phase vanished like a summer cloud as the bust evolved. I say evolved advisedly; for it passed through every stage in the evolution of art before my eyes in the course of a month. After that first fifteen minutes it sobered down into a careful representation of my features in their exact living dimensions. Then this representation mysteriously went back to the cradle of Christian art, at which point I again wanted to say: 'For heaven's sake, stop and give me that: it is a Byzantine masterpiece.' Then it began to look as if Bernini had meddled with it. Then, to my horror, it smoothed out into a plausible, rather elegant piece of eighteenth-century work, almost as if Houdon had touched up a head by Canova or Thorwaldsen, or as if Leighton had tried his hand at eclecticism in bust-making. At this point Troubetskoi would have broken it with a hammer, or given it up with a wail of despair. Rodin contemplated it with an air of callous patience, and went on with his job, more like a river-god turned plasterer than ever. Then another century passed in a single night; and the bust became a Rodin bust, and was the living head of which I carried the model on my shoulders. It was a process for the embryologist to study, not the aesthete. Rodin's hand worked, not as a sculptor's hand works, but as the Life Force works. What is more, I found that he was aware of it, quite simply. I no more think of Rodin as a celebrated sculptor than I think of Elijah as a well-known *littérateur* and forcible after-dinner speaker. His 'Main de Dieu' is his own hand. That is why all the stuff written about him by professional art-critics is such ludicrous cackle and piffle. I have been a professional art-critic myself, and perhaps not much of one at that (though I fully admit that I touched nothing I did not adorn), but at least I knew how to take off my hat and hold my tongue when my cacklings and pifflings would have been impertinences.

Rodin took the conceit out of me most horribly. Once he showed me a torso of a female figure; an antique. It was a beauty; and I swallowed it whole. He waited rather wistfully for a moment, to see whether I really knew chalk from cheese, and then pointed out to me that the upper half of the figure was curiously inferior to the lower half, as if the sculptor had taught himself as he went along. The difference, which I had been blind to a moment before, was so obvious when he pointed it out, that I have despised myself ever since for not seeing it. There never was such an eye for carved stone as

Rodin's. To the average critic or connoisseur half the treasures he collects seem nothing but a heap of old paving-stones. But they all have somewhere a scrap of modelled surface, perhaps half the size of a postage stamp, that makes gems of them. In his own work he shows a strong feeling for the beauty of marble. He gave me three busts of myself: one in bronze, one in plaster, one in marble. The bronze is me (growing younger now). The plaster is me. But the marble has quite another sort of life: it glows; and light flows over it. It does not look solid: it looks luminous; and this curious glowing and flowing keeps people's fingers off it; for you feel as if you could not catch hold of it. People say that all modern sculpture is done by the Italian artisans who mechanically reproduce the sculptor's plaster model in the stone. Rodin himself says so. But the peculiar qualities that Rodin gets in his marbles are not in the clay models. What is more, other sculptors can hire artisans, including those who have worked for Rodin. Yet no other sculptor produces such marbles as Rodin. One day Rodin told me that all modern sculpture is imposture; that neither he nor any of the others can use a chisel. A few days later he let slip the remark: 'Handling the chisel is very interesting.' Yet when he models a portrait-bust, his method is neither that of Michelangelo with his chisel nor of a modeller in the round, but that of a draughtsman outlining in clay the thousand profiles which your head would present if it were sliced a thousand times through the centre at different angles.

Rodin, like all great workmen who can express themselves in words, was very straight and simple, and disposed to be useful to those who listened to him, and not to waste their time. He knew what is important and what is not, and what can be taught and what cannot. After all, apart from the acquired skill of his hands, which he shared with any stonemason, he had only two qualifications to make him the divinest workman of his day. One was a profounder and more accurate vision than anyone else's. The other was an incorruptible veracity. That was all, ladies and gentlemen. Now I have told you his secret, you can all become great sculptors. It is as easy as any other sort of manual labour, and much pleasanter—if you can pick up those two simple qualifications.

PART SIX

On History and Politics

WHEN DEALING with such a huge concern as man's capacity to govern his world, the Essay rises to its busiest heights. If the range of the Essay constitutes an accurate record of western man's primary concerns, then the story of how we have managed ourselves in the places in which we found ourselves takes precedence over everything else: the endless failures, the prolix personalities, the hopeful theories, the inevitable atrocities.

Therefore logistical restrictions bite deepest in this section—this sliver of History and Politics could have run to a hundred thousand essays. As it is the nine writers chosen here deal with history and politics in concrete and abstract terms. Both are needed: history is unavoidably bound up with philosophical notions of practical territorial relationships. A modern English playwright put it another way—'history is geography'. The more concrete Essays here range from the discussion of prejudice, Goldsmith and Vidal, to the personalities, Lord Macaulay's Burleigh and Michael Foot's Enoch Powell. Those who write in the abstract seek to prove that our doing has been intended to enhance our being, and therefore the Essayists must also reflect personal understanding and hope, as does Adlai Stevenson.

The vital need for political ideas to be clear at once defined and confirmed the power of the Essay as a form of literary communication. As a bonus, Essays in these two genres collectively provide the same kind of museum of our intellectual progress at governing ourselves as W. N. P. Barbellion's putative storehouses where 'Small collections were made, but merely as the mementos of a soldier's campaign, or a mariner's curiosities, like the "gorilla" skins brought home from Africa...' Museums can never be definitive either; the glass cases can only show glimpses. And in those glimpses, given the connective nature of politics, we see the reflections of light cast by others, so that when Macaulay writes about Lord Burleigh we learn more about the Virgin Queen than from a thousand texts: 'Elizabeth, it is true, often spoke to her parliaments in language as haughty and imperious as that which the Great Turk would use to his divan.'

My View of History

ARNOLD TOYNBEE

My view of history is in itself a tiny piece of history; and this mainly other people's history and not my own; for a scholar's life-work is to add his bucketful of water to the great and growing river of knowledge fed by countless bucketfuls of the kind. If my individual view of history is to be made at all illuminating, or indeed intelligible, it must be presented in its origin, growth, and social and personal settings.

There are many angles of vision from which human minds peer at the universe. Why am I a historian, not a philosopher or a physicist? For the same reason that I drink tea and coffee without sugar. Both habits were formed at a tender age by following a lead from my mother. I am a historian because my mother was one before me; yet at the same time I am conscious that I am of a different school from hers. Why did I not exactly take my mother's cue?

First, because I was born by my mother into the next generation to hers, and my mind was, therefore, not yet set hard when history took my generation by the throat in 1914; and, secondly, because my education was more old-fashioned than my mother's had been. My mother—belonging as she did to the first generation, in England, of university women—had obtained an up-to-date education in modern Western history, with the national history of England itself as the principal guide-line. Her son, being a boy, went to an old-fashioned English public school and was educated, both there and at Oxford, almost entirely on the Greek and Latin classics.

For any would-be historian—and especially for one born into these times—a classical education is, in my belief, a priceless boon. As a training-ground, the history of the Graeco-Roman world has its conspicuous merits. In the first place, Graeco-Roman history is visible to us in perspective and can be seen by us as a whole, because it is over—in contrast to the history of our own Western world, which is a still-unfinished play of which we do not know the eventual ending and cannot even see the present general aspect from our own position as momentary actors on its crowded and agitated stage.

In the second place, the field of Graeco-Roman history is not encumbered and obscured by a surfeit of information, and so we can see the wood—thanks to a drastic thinning of the trees during the interregnum between the dissolution of the Graeco-Roman society and the emergence of or own. Moreover, the conveniently manageable amount of evidence that has survived is not overweighted by the state papers of parochial principalities, like those which, in our Western world, have accumulated, ton upon ton, during the dozen centuries of its pre-atomic-bomb age. The surviving materials for a study of Graceo-Roman history are not only manageable in quantity and select in quality; they are also well-balanced in their character. Statues, poems, and works of philosophy count here for more than the texts of laws and treaties; and this breeds a sense of proportion in the mind of a historian nursed on Graeco-Roman history; for—as we can see in the perspective given by lapse of time more easily than we can see it in the life of our own generation—the works of artists and men of letters outlive the deeds of business men, soldiers and statesmen. The poets and the philosophers outrange the historians; while the prophets and the saints overtop and outlast them all. The ghosts of Agamemnon and Pericles haunt the living world of today by grace of the magic words of Homer and Thucydides; and, when Homer and Thucydides are no longer read, it is safe to prophesy that Christ and the Buddha and Socrates will still be fresh in the memory of (to us) almost inconceivably distant generations of men.

The third, and perhaps greatest, merit of Graeco-Roman history is that its outlook is ecumenical rather than parochial. Athens may have eclipsed Sparta and Rome Samnium, yet Athens in her youth made herself the education of all Hellas, while Rome in her old age made the whole Graeco-Roman world into a single commonwealth. In Graeco-Roman history, surveyed from beginning to end, unity is the dominant note; and, when once I had heard this great symphony, I was no longer in danger of being hypnotised by the lone and outlandish music of the parochial history of my own country, which had once enthralled me when I listened to my mother telling it to me in instalments, night by night, as she put me to bed. The historical pastors and masters of my mother's generation, not only in England but in all Western countries, had been eagerly promoting the study of national history in the mistaken belief that it had a closer bearing on their countrymen's lives and was, therefore, somehow more readily accessible to their understanding than the history of other places and times (although it is surely evident that, in reality, Jesus' Palestine and Plato's Greece were more potently operative than Alfred's or Elizabeth's England in the lives of English men and women of the Victorian age).

Yet, in spite of this misguided Victorian canonisation—so alien

from the spirit of the father of English history, the Venerable Bede—
of the history of the particular country in which one happened to have
been born, the unconscious attitude of the Victorian Englishman
towards history was that of someone living outside history altogether. He took it for granted—without warrant— that he himself
was standing on *terra firma*, secure against being engulfed in that ever-
rolling stream in which Time had borne all of his less privileged sons
away. In his own privileged state of being emancipated, as he supposed, from history, the Victorian Englishman gazed with curiosity,
condescension, and a touch of pity, but altogether without apprehension, at the spectacle of less fortunate denizens of other places and
periods struggling and foundering in history's flood—in much the
same way as, in a medieval Italian picture, the saved lean over the
balustrade of heaven to look down complacently at the torments of
the damned in hell. Charles I—worse luck for him—had been in
history, but Sir Robert Walpole, though threatened with impeach-
ment, had just managed to scramble out of the surf, while we
ourselves were well beyond high-water mark in a snug coign of
vantage where nothing could happen to us. Our more backward
contemporaries might, perhaps, still be waist-high in the now receding tide, but what was that to us?

I remember, at the beginning of a university term during the
Bosnian crisis of 1908–9, Professor L. B. Namier, then an undergraduate at Balliol and back from spending a vacation at his family home
just inside the Galician frontier of Austria, saying to us other Balliol
men, with (it seemed to us) a portentous air: 'Well, the Austrian army
is mobilised on my father's estate and the Russian army is just across
the frontier, half-an-hour away.' It sounded to us like a scene from
The Chocolate Soldier, but the lack of comprehension was mutual, for
a lynx-eyed Central European observer of international affairs found
it hardly credible that these English undergraduates should not realise
that a stone's-throw away, in Galicia, their own goose, too, was
being cooked.

Hiking round Greece three years later on the trail of Epaminondas
and Philopoemen and listening to the talk in the village cafés, I learnt
for the first time of the existence of something called the foreign
policy of Sir Edward Grey. Yet, even then, I did not realise that we
too were still in history after all. I remember feeling acutely homesick
for the historic Mediterranean as I walked, one day in 1913, along the
Suffolk coast of a grey and uneventful North Sea. The general war of
1914 overtook me expounding Thucydides to Balliol undergraduates
reading for *Literae Humaniores*, and then suddenly my understanding
was illuminated. The experience that we were having in our world

now had been experienced by Thucydides in his world already. I was re-reading him now with a new perception—perceiving meanings in his words, and feelings behind his phrases, to which I had been insensible until I, in my turn, had run into the historical crisis that had inspired him to write his work. Thucydides, it now appeared, had been over this ground before. He and his generation had been ahead of me and mine in the stage of historical experience that we had respectively reached; in fact, his present had been my future. But this made nonsense of the chronological notation which registered my world as 'modern' and Thucydides' world as 'ancient'. Whatever chronology might say, Thucydides' world and my world had now proved to be philosophically contemporary. And, if this were the true relation between the Graeco-Roman and the Western civilisations, might not the relation between all the civilisations known to us turn out to be the same?

This vision—new to me—of the philosophical contemporaneity of all civilisations was fortified by being seen against a background provided by some of the discoveries of our modern Western physical science. On the time-scale now unfolded by geology and cosmogony, the five or six thousand years that had elapsed since the first emergence of representatives of the species of human society that we label 'civilisations' were an infinitesimally brief span of time compared to the age, up to date, of the human race, of life on this planet, of the planet itself, of our own solar system, of the galaxy in which it is one grain of dust, or of the immensely vaster and older sum total of the stellar cosmos. By comparison with these orders of temporal magnitude, civilisations that had emerged in the second millennium BC (like the Graeco-Roman), in the fourth millennium BC (like the Ancient Egyptian), and in the first millennium of the Christian era (like our own) were one another's contemporaries indeed.

Thus history, in the sense of the histories of the human societies called civilisations, revealed itself as a sheaf of parallel, contemporary, and recent essays in a new enterprise: a score of attempts up to date, to transcend the level of primitive human life at which man, after having become himself, had apparently lain torpid for some hundreds of thousands of years—and was still, in our day, so lying in out-of-the-way places like New Guinea, Tierra del Fuego and the north-eastern extremity of Siberia, where such primitive human communities had not yet been pounced upon and either exterminated or assimilated by the aggressive pioneers of other human societies that, unlike these sluggards, had now, though this only recently, got on the move again. The amazing present difference in cultural level between various extant societies was brought to my attention by the works of Professor Teggart of the University of California. This far-going differentiation had all happened within these brief last five or six thousand years. Here was a promising point to probe in investigating, *sub specie temporis*, the mystery of the universe.

What was it that, after so long a pause, had so recently set in such vigorous motion once again, towards some new and still unknown social and spiritual destination, those few societies that had embarked upon the enterprise called civilisation? What had roused them from a torpor that the great majority of human societies had never shaken off? This question was simmering in my mind when, in the summer of 1920, Professor Namier—who had already put Eastern Europe on my map for me—placed in my hands Oswald Spengler's *Untergang des Abendlandes*. As I read these pages teeming with firefly flashes of historical insight, I wondered at first whether my whole inquiry had been disposed of by Spengler before even the questions, not to speak of the answers, had fully taken shape in my own mind. One of my own cardinal points was that the smallest intelligible fields of historical study were whole societies and not arbitrarily insulated fragments of them like the nation-states of the modern West or the city states of the Graeco-Roman world. Another of my points was that the histories of all societies of the species called civilisations were in some sense parallel and contemporary; and both these points were also cardinal in Spengler's system. But when I looked in Spengler's book for an answer to my question about the geneses of civilisations, I saw that there was still work for me to do, for on this point Spengler was, it seemed to me, most unilluminatingly dogmatic and deterministic. According to him, civilisations arose, developed, declined, and foundered in unvarying conformity with a fixed time-table, and no explanation was offered for any of this. It was just a law of nature which Spengler had detected, and you must take it on trust from the master: *ipse dixit*. This arbitrary fiat seemed disappointingly unworthy of Spengler's brilliant genius; and here I became aware of a difference in national traditions. Where the German *a priori* method drew blank, let us see what could be done by English empiricism. Let us test alternative possible explanations in the light of the facts and see how they stood the ordeal.

Race and environment were the two main rival keys that were offered by would-be scientific nineteenth-century Western historians for solving the problem of the cultural inequality of various extant human societies, and neither key proved, on trial, to unlock the fast-closed door. To take the race theory first, what evidence was there that the differences in physical race between different members of the *genus homo* were correlated with differences on the spiritual plane which was the field of history? And, if the existence of this correlation were to be assumed for the sake of argument, how was it that members of almost all the races were to be found among the fathers of one or more of the civilisations? The black race alone had made no appreciable contribution up to date; but, considering the shortness of the time during which the experiment of civilisation had been on foot so far, this was no cogent evidence of incapacity; it might merely be the consequence of a lack of opportunity or a lack of stimulus. As for environment, there was, of course, a manifest similarity between the physical conditions in the lower Nile valley and in the lower Tigris-Euphrates valley, which had been the respective cradles of the Egyptian and Sumerian civilisations; but, if these physical conditions were really the cause of their emergence, why had no parallel civilisations emerged in the physically comparable valleys of the Jordan and the Rio Grande? And why had the civilisation of the equatorial Andean plateau had no African counterpart in the highlands of Kenya? The breakdown of these would-be scientific impersonal explanations drove me to turn to mythology. I took this turning rather self-consciously and shamefacedly, as though it were a provocatively retrograde step. I might have been less diffident if I had not been ignorant, as I was at that date, of the new ground broken by psychology during the war of 1914–18. If I had been acquainted at the time with the works of C. G. Jung, they would have given me the clue. I actually found it in Goethe's *Faust*, in which I had fortunately been grounded at school as thoroughly as in Aeschylus' *Agamemnon*.

Goethe's 'Prologue in Heaven' opens with the archangels hymning the perfection of God's creation. But, just because His works are perfect, the Creator has left Himself no scope for any further exercise of His creative powers, and there might have been no way out of this *impasse* if Mephistopheles—created for this very purpose—had not presented himself before the throne and challenged God to give him a free hand to spoil, if he can, one of the Creator's choicest works. God accepts the challenge and thereby wins an opportunity to carry His work of creation forward. An encounter between two personalities in the form of challenge and response: have we not here the flint and steel by whose mutual impact the creative spark is kindled?

In Goethe's exposition of the plot of the *Divina Commedia*, Mephistopheles is created to be diddled—as the fiend, to his disgust, discovers too late. Yet if, in response to the devil's challenge, God genuinely puts His created works in jeopardy, as we must assume that He does, in order to win an opportunity of creating something new, we are also bound to assume that the devil does not always lose. And thus, if the working of challenge-and-response explains the otherwise inexplicable and unpredictable geneses and growths of civilisations, it also explains their breakdowns and disintegrations. A majority of the score of civilisations known to us appear to have broken down already, and a majority of this majority have trodden to the end the downward path that terminates in dissolution.

Our *post mortem* examination of dead civilisations does not enable us to cast the horoscope of our own civilisation or of any other that is still alive. *Pace* Spengler, there seems to be no reason why a succession of stimulating challenges should not be met by a succession of victorious responses *ad infinitum*. On the other hand, when we make an empirical comparative study of the paths which the dead civilisations have respectively travelled from breakdown to dissolution, we do here seem to find a certain measure of Spenglerian uniformity, and this, after all, is not surprising. Since breakdown means loss of control, this in turn means the lapse of freedom into automatism, and, whereas free acts are infinitely variable and utterly unpredictable, automatic processes are apt to be uniform and regular.

Briefly stated, the regular pattern of social disintegration is a schism of the disintegrating society into a recalcitrant proletariat and a less and less effectively dominant minority. The process of disintegration does not proceed evenly; it jolts along in alternating spasms of rout, rally, and rout. In the last rally but one, the dominant minority succeeds in temporarily arresting the society's lethal self-laceration by imposing on it the peace of a universal state. Within the framework of the dominant minority's universal state the proletariat creates a universal church, and after the next rout, in which the disintegrating civilisation finally dissolves, the universal church may live on to become the chrysalis from which a new civilisation eventually emerges. To modern Western students of history, these phenomena are most familiar in the Graeco-Roman examples of the *Pax Romana* and the Christian Church. The establishment of the *Pax Romana* by Augustus seemed, at the time, to have put the Graeco-Roman world back upon firm foundations after it had been battered for several centuries by perpetual war, misgovernment, and revolution. But the Augustan rally proved, after all, to be no more than a respite. After two hundred and fifty years of comparative tranquillity, the empire suffered in the third century of the Christian era a collapse from which it never fully recovered, and at the next crisis, in the fifth and sixth centuries, it went to pieces irretrievably. The true beneficiary of the temporary Roman Peace was the Christian Church. The church seized this opportunity to strike root and spread; it was stimulated by persecution until the empire, having failed to crush it, decided, instead, to take it into partnership. And, when even this reinforcement failed to save the empire from destruction, the church took over the empire's heritage. The same relation between a declining civilisation and a rising religion can be observed in a dozen other cases. In the Far East, for instance, the Ts'in and Han Empire plays the Roman Empire's part, while the role of the Christian Church is assumed by the Mahayana school of Buddhism.

If the death of one civilisation thus brings on the birth of another, does not the at first sight hopeful and exciting quest for the goal of human endeavours resolve itself, after all, into a dreary round of vain repetitions of the Gentiles? This cyclic view of the process of history was taken so entirely for granted by even the greatest Greek and Indian souls and intellects—by Aristotle, for instance, and by the Buddha—that they simply assumed that it was true without thinking it necessary to prove it. On the other hand, Captain Marryat, in ascribing the same view to the ship's carpenter of HMS *Rattlesnake*, assumes with equal assurance that this cyclic theory is an extravaganza, and he makes the amiable exponent of it a figure of fun. To our Western minds the cyclic view of history, if taken seriously, would reduce history to a tale told by an idiot, signifying nothing. But mere repugnance does not in itself account for effortless unbelief. The traditional Christian beliefs in hell fire and in the last trump were also repugnant, yet they continued to be believed for generations. For our fortunate Western imperviousness to the Greek and Indian belief in cycles we are indebted to the Jewish and Zoroastrian contributions to our *Weltanschauung*.

In the vision seen by the Prophets of Israel, Judah, and Iran, history is not a cyclic and not a mechanical process. It is the masterful and progressive execution, on the narrow stage of this world, of a divine plan which is revealed to us in this fragmentary glimpse, but which transcends our human powers of vision and understanding in every dimension. Moreover, the Prophets, through their own experience, anticipated Aeschylus' discovery that learning comes through suffering—a discovery which we, in our time and circumstances, have been making too.

Shall we opt, then, for the Jewish-Zoroastrian view of history as against the Graeco-Indian? So drastic a choice may not, after all, be forced upon us, for it may be that the two views are not fundamentally irreconcilable. After all, if a vehicle is to move forward on a course which its driver has set, it must be borne along on wheels that turn monotonously round and round. While civilisations rise and fall and, in falling, give rise to others, some purposeful enterprise, higher than theirs, may all the time be making headway, and, in a divine plan, the learning that comes through the suffering caused by the failures of civilisations may be the sovereign means of progress. Abraham was an émigré from a civilisation *in extremis*; the Prophets were children of another civilisation in disintegration; Christianity was born of the sufferings of a disintegrating Graeco-Roman world. Will some comparable spiritual enlightenment be kindled in the 'displaced persons' who are the counterparts, in our world, of those Jewish exiles to whom so much was revealed in their painful exile by the waters of Babylon? The answer to this question, whatever the answer may be, is of greater moment than the still inscrutable destiny of our world-encompassing Western civilisation.

The Passion for Perpetuation

W. N. P. BARBELLION

Just as the ancient hunter shot a fish with a spear, so we may imagine the ancient philosopher separated the Thing, caught it up out of the Heracleitean flux and transfixed it with a name. With this first great preservative came the first great museum of language and logical thought. Ever since, we have been feverishly busy collecting, recording, and preserving the universe, or as much of it as is accessible. Perpetuation has become an all-absorbing passion.

It is only recently that certain interesting, not to say remarkable, refinements in the technique of the art have been developed and come into common use, such being, for example, the museum, the printing-press, the camera, the cinema film, the gramophone record. By the ancient Greeks and ancient Romans, the desire to collect, and above all to conserve, the moveable furniture of the earth was only indistinctly felt. As storehouses, museums were almost unknown. Small collections were made, but merely as the mementos of a soldier's campaign, or a mariner's curiosities, like the 'gorilla' skins brought home from Africa by Hanno.

The assembling of curiosities, drawing-room curios, bric-à-brac, and *objets de vertu*, was still the immature purpose of the conservator, even so late as the days of Sir Hans Sloane, Elias Ashmole, and John Hunter. Ashmole's gift to the University of Oxford was laconically described as 'twelve cartloads of curios'. Hunter's Museum, as everyone knows, was a gorgeous miscellany of stuffed birds, mammals, reptiles, fossils, plants, corals, shells, insects, bones, anatomical preparations, injected vascular preparations, preparations of hollow viscera, mercurial injections, injections in vermilion, minerals, coins, pictures, weapons, coats of mail. It is obvious that in those days the collector had not passed beyond the miscellany stage. According to his pleasure, he selected say a Japanese midzuire, a scarab of Rameses II, a porpentine's quill, a hair from the Grand Cham's beard, and saw the world as an inexhaustible Bagdad bazaar. Now he sees it as *exhaustible*, and is grimly determined to exhaust it as soon as may be.

Today everything is changed. Mankind is astride the globe from pole to pole, like Arion on the dolphin's back. With all the departments of human knowledge clearly mapped out in the likeness of his own mind, man now occupies himself with collecting and filling in the details. He ransacks heaven and earth; armies of collectors, brigaded under the different sciences and arts, labour incessantly for the salvation of the globe. All objects are being named, labelled, and kept in museums; all the facts are being enshrined in the libraries of books. We are embarked on an amazing undertaking. A well-equipped modern expedition apparently leaves nothing behind in the territory traversed save its broad physical features; and as Mont Blanc or the Andes cannot be moved even by scientific Mahomets, the geologist's hammer deftly breaks off a chip, and the fragment is carried off in triumph to the cabinet as a sample.

It is estimated that there are about seven millions of distinct species of insects, and naturalists the world over have entered upon a solemn league and covenant to catch at least one specimen of every kind which shall be pinned and preserved in perpetuity for as long as one stone shall stand upon another in the kingdom of man. There are already an enormous number of such types, as they are professionally called, not only of insects, but of all classes of animals and plants, jealously guarded and conserved by the zealous officials of the British Museum.

When I was a small boy I greedily saved up the names of naval vessels and inscribed each with a fair round hand in a M S book specially kept for the purpose. Now the financial or aesthetic motives that may be said to govern the boy collector of postage stamps, birds' eggs, cigarette cards must here be ruled out of court. For if half-a-dozen of the rarest unused surcharged Mauritius, a complete set of Wills' 'Cathedrals' or Players' 'Inventions', or a single blood alley of acknowledged virtue minister to the tingling acquisitiveness of the average schoolboy, it is difficult to say the same of the hunting down in newspapers and books of battle-ships, cruisers, and T.B.D.'s. At least I am inclined to think that my subconscious motive was a fear lest any of His Majesty's ships should be overlooked or lost, that it was indeed a good example of the instinct for simple conservation uncomplicated by the usual motives of the collector.

The joy of possession, the greed, vanity and self-aggrandisement of the collector proper, are deftly subverted to the use of the explorer and conservator of knowledge who, having a weak proprietorial sense—bloodless, anaemic it must seem to the enthusiastic connoisseur—is satisfied so long as somewhere by someone Things are securely saved. The purpose of the archconservator—his whole design and the rationale of his art—is to redeem, embalm, dry, cure, salt, pickle, pot every animal, vegetable and mineral, every stage in the history of the universe from nebular gas or planetismals down to the latest and most insignificant event reported in the newspapers. He would like to treat the globe as the experimental embryologist treats an egg—to preserve it whole in every hour of its development and then section it with a microtome.

People who are not in the habit of visiting or considering museums fail to realise how prodigiously within recent times the zeal for conservation, or—as Sir Thomas Browne puts it—the diuturnity of relics has increased all over the world in every centre of civilisation. A constant stream of objects flows into the great treasuries of human inheritance—about 400,000 separate objects per annum being received into the British Museum in Bloomsbury, and there is scarcely a capital in Europe or a big town in America in which congestion is not already being felt.

In a museum you shall find not only the loin cloth or feathers of the savage, but an almost perfect series of costumes worn by man down through the ages in any country. Man's past in particular is preserved with the tenderest care. It is possible to go and, with the utmost pride and self-satisfaction, observe the milestones of man's progress from the arrowhead to the modern rifle, from the Sedan-chair and hobby-horse to the motor cycle and aeroplane, from the spinning-wheel to the modern loom, from the Caxton printing-press to the linotype, from Stephenson's Rocket to the railway express engine, from the coracle to the latest ocean greyhound in miniature. It is all there: china, tobacco pipes, door handles, iron railings, bedsteads, clavichords, buttons, lamps, vases, sherds, bones, Babylonian and Hittite tablets, the Moabite stone, the autographs and MSS of everyone who was anybody since writing came into common practice, scarabs and coins, scarabs of the Rameses and Amenheteps, coins of Greece and Rome, coins of Arabia, coins of Cyrenaica, coins from Colophon, Tyre, Sidon—Nineveh's winged bulls.

I knew a police inspector who saved and docketed the cigar ashes of royalties, and I once heard of a distinguished chiropodist who saved their nail parings. Mr Pierpont Morgan owns the largest collection of watches in the world, and another American is the proud possessor of the only complete collection of 'Crusoes' in existence—*i.e.*, the editions of *Robinson Crusoe* by Daniel Defoe.

But not only is the past retrieved in fragments; in some museums and exhibitions and to a certain extent in historical plays, it is actually reconstructed: in London is displayed the interior of an apothecary's shop in the seventeenth century with its crocodile and bunches of herbs, or the shop of a barber surgeon, or a reconstruction of the laboratory used by Liebig, or the Bromley Room, or Shakespeare's Globe Theatre in exact facsimile, or Solomon's temple, while for the purposes of illustration, Madam Tussaud's must for the moment be classed with the Pantheon. The cinema is going to keep alive the persons and events of the present generation within the most sluggish imaginations of the next—for the benefit of those who perhaps don't read history or visit museums. This need not mean the gradual atrophy of the imagination as some Solomon Eagles portend—to discuss which would mean a digression. In any case, I fancy the most lively imagination would scarcely ignore the opportunity of seeing Dr Johnson, let us say, walk down Fleet Street tapping each lamp-post with his stick, if an authentic film of him were in existence, or of listening to a gramophone record of Rachel or Edmund Burke.

Wherever one turns, it is easy to see this thriving instinct of the human heart. There are enthusiastic leagues for preserving woods, forests, footpaths, commons, trees, plants, animals, ancient buildings, historical sites. In times to come, nearly every private house in London will have historical connections and bear a commemorative tablet. In anticipation of its extinction the hansom cab has already been lodged behind the portals of its last depository. Everywhere enthusiasts are expending a vast amount of energy in inducing people to stick to the old—pedants will have you use the old idioms and spellings, the language must be preserved in its original beauty; no ancient rite or custom can be allowed to lapse into desuetude but some cry of reprobation goes up to heaven in righteous anger. There are anniversaries, centenaries, bicentenaries, tercentenaries—glutinous tercentenaries!

Perhaps the most valuable instrument for perpetuation is the printing-press. No sooner is an event over, than it is reported in the daily press, and the newspaper preserved in the British Museum for all time. In future there will be no historical lacunae. In virtue of our elaborate precautions it is improbable that London will ever become a second Nineveh. Immediately a discovery is made or a research brought to its conclusion the world is copiously informed. In the present era of publicity, we need never fear that a man's secrets will die with him. It were safe to prophesy that there will never be another Mrs Stopes, for the good reason that his contemporaries will never let a second Shakespeare slip through their fingers so to speak. A lament like the scholar's over the loss of the Diakosmos of Demokritus will probably never be heard again. Within the sacred rotunda of the

British Museum reading room may be perused the novels of Charles Garvice as well as the great Chinese encyclopedia prepared for the Emperor K'ang-hi in 5020 volumes.

In books our knowledge to date is rounded up and displayed: you can read a book on a lump of coal, a grass blade, a sea worm, on hair combs, carpets, ships, sticks, sealing wax, cabbages, kings, cosmetics, Kant. A very thick volume indeed was published last year upon the anatomy of the *thorax* of the field-cricket. It would require a learned man to catalogue the literature that deals with such comparatively trivial subjects as the History of the Punch and Judy Show, or the History of Playing Cards.

At the present rapid rate of accumulation, the time must come when the British Museum, thousands of years hence, will occupy an area as large as London and the *Encyclopedia Britannica* be housed in a building as big as the Crystal Palace: an accumulation of learning to make Aristotle and Scaliger turn pale.

For let us not forget that man is only at the beginning of things. The first Egyptian dynasty began 7000 BC and we are now only in AD 1916. Every day sees the birth of entirely new things that must be collected and preserved, new babies, new wars, new books, new discoveries, so that—to take a moderate figure—by 3000 AD we shall have saved up such a prodigious quantity of the relics and minutiae of the past that only a relatively small fraction of it will be contained in the united consciousness of the men of that time. Everything will be there and accessible, but for reference only. Knowledge will be an amazing organisation (let us hope it will be done better than the Poor Law system), and battalions of men of the intellectual lineage of Diderot and D'Alembert will be continuously occupied in sifting and arranging our stores of information, whereby the curious, by handing a query over the counter, will be given all the knowledge in existence in any particular subject. Yet for the most part human knowledge will be left stranded high and dry in books: entombed, embalmed, labelled, and clean forgotten—unless the human brain becomes hypertrophied.

Conservation is a natural tendency of the mind. One might lay down a certain law of the conservation of consciousness to indicate our extreme repugnance to the idea of anything passing clean away into the void. What insinuating comfort in those words that every hair of our heads is numbered!

True, the chain of causation is unbroken, and in a sense every effect is the collection and preservation of all its past causes; and if to live can be said to exist in results, then no man ever dies, and no thought can perish, and every act is infinite in its consequences. Yet I fancy this transcendental flourish will not satisfy the brotherhood of salvation-ists, who desire to possess something more than the means embodied abstractly in the result; no consideration will ever cause them to abate one jot their feverish labours to forestall their common enemies: cormorant devouring Time, man's own leaky memory, Death's abhorred shears, the Futurist, the Hun, the Vandal, the carrion worm or the devil.

The instinct for conservation in different men has different origins. To the scientific man, Nature is higgledy-piggledy, until she is collected, classified, stored, and explained according to his own scheme; every phenomenon, unobserved or imperfectly compre-hended, escapes and flows past him, defeating his will to understand. In politics conservatism means a distrust of the unknown future suited to a comfortable habituation to current customs and current statecraft, or—to quote Fluellen—the ceremonies of it and the cares of it and the forms of it and the sobriety of it and the modesty of it. In still another direction, the desire to conserve is simply a sentiment for the old, for the old unhappy, far-off things. The flight of time, its likeness to a running stream, the great world spinning down the grooves of change, endless change and decay, have been food for the melancholy ruminations of philosophers and poets from the earliest times. '*Tout ce qui fut un jour et n'est plus aujourd'hui incline à la tristesse surtout ce qui fut très beau et très heureux,*' says Maeterlinck.

But regard for the old is not always vague sentiment alone. In one of his essays, Emerson remarks that Nature often turns to ornament what she once employed for use, illustrating his suggestion with certain sea shells, in which the parts which have for a time formed the mouth are at the next whorl of growth left behind as decorative nodes and spines. Subsequently, Herbert Spencer applied the idea to human beings, remarking how the material exuviae of past social states become the ornaments of the present—for example, ruined castles, old rites and ceremonies, old earthenware water-jars. The explana-tion of this metamorphosis simply is that so long as a thing is useful, its beauty goes for the most part unobserved. Beauty is the pursuit of leisure, and it was probably in those rhythmic periods of relaxation when the primitive potter or stone carver paused from his labour that the aesthetic sense according to some was given birth.

Now it is certain that there be some to whom the perpetuation of Stonehenge or the Diplodocus is a matter of large indifference, in whom arises no joy in the fruits of the conservator's art upon handling say a Syracusan tetradrachm or a folio of Shakespeare with 'the excessively rare title-page "for Richard Meigher"'. Yet over the question of self-perpetuation these same men will be as desirous as others. Few men save Buddhists relish the idea of self-extinction. No one likes the thought of the carrion worm in the seat of intellect. The Egyptians bravely fought the course of Nature and gained some solace we may assume by embalming. Christians if they resign themselves to the decay of the body, labour in its stead to save the soul. On his death, every man at least claims a tombstone. The surface of the earth is stippled with crosses (especially in France), with monuments, obelisks, mausoleums, pyramids, cenotaphs, tombs, tumuli, barrows, cairns designed to keep evergreen the memory of the dead, to forestall oblivion lurking like a ghoul in the background. Look at Keats's naive preoccupation with his future fame, his passionate desire to be grouped among the heirs of all eternity. If we are to believe Shakespeare and the Elizabethan sonneteers their common obsession was to combat brass and stone with their own immortal lines.

No doubt there are a few apparently sincere, high-minded gentlemen ('Rocky Mountain toughs' William James calls them) who emphatically declare that when they die they will, after cremation, have their ashes scattered to the winds of heaven,★ who scoff at the salvation of their souls and quote Haeckel's jibe about God as 'a gaseous vertebrate', who are indifferent to fame and spurn monuments that live no longer than the bell rings and the widow weeps. In short, since conservation must always be o'erswayed by sad mortality in the long run, they will have nothing of it. 'Give me my scallop shell of quiet,' they would say—and let the world pass on its primrose way to the everlasting bonfire.

But conservation cannot be so summarily set aside. Every man, willy-nilly, collects and preserves, his consciousness is of itself an automatic collecting instrument. The alert mind collects observations and impressions without being conscious of them. Then, later, when the note is struck, to our surprise they rise up into vision as if from nowhere. The memory is a preservative. After a life of it a

---

★In accordance with his wishes, the body of Samuel Butler (of *Erewhon*) was cremated and the ashes buried near some shrubs in the garden of the crematorium with nothing to mark the spot. Sir Thomas Browne said that at his death he meant to take a total adieu of the world, 'not caring for a Monument, Historie, or Epitaph, not so much as the bare memory of my name to be found anywhere but in the universal Register of God'. But, as a matter of fact, he was given a brass coffin-plate (with a curious inscription that has afforded matter for antiquarian controversy) as well as a mural monument.

man's mind is a museum, a palimpsest, a hold-all. In the heyday of manhood we may perhaps go adventuring on in lavish expenditure of life, nomads, careless of the day as soon as it is over. Yet he must be a very rare bird indeed, the veteran who when all the wheels are run down does not choose to write his memoirs or even to relate reminiscences around the fireside, the broken soldier who never shoulders his crutch, the barrister who never recalls his first brief. Two old men will haggle with one another over the fixation of a date, they will pull up a conversation and everyone must wait on account of a forgotten name... This morning I was delighted to hear myself burst out whistling a nocturne of Chopin, which I have not heard for twelve months, and then for the first time. I confess it was pleasant to think I had been entertaining an angel unawares all these months, and I like to believe that in the all too swift trajectory of one's career through life, nothing is really left behind, that all the phantasmagoria of our life which seems to be passing us by on each side for ever falls into line behind with the rest and follows on like a comet's tail. Much may be forgotten, yet nothing perhaps is ever lost; no impression once photographed upon the mind ever becomes obliterated—comfortable words, I apprehend, for the benefit of any diarist whose eyes these lines may catch. According to William James's attractive 'world-memory' idea, the whole history of the earth actually exists and some occultists indeed claim to have tapped such inaccessible material as life on the extinct continent of Atlantis or in Knossos.

In 1768, Fanny Burney made this entry in her Journal: 'I cannot express the pleasure I have in writing down my thoughts at the very moment ... and I am much deceived in my foresight if I shall not have very great delight in reading this living proof of my manner of passing my time ... there is something to me very unsatisfactory in passing year after year without even a memorandum of what you did, etc.' This is the true spirit of the habitual diarist speaking. At heart, everyone is a diarist. There is no child who has not kept a diary at some time or another, and there is no one who having given it up has not regretted it later on. The confirmed journal writer, however, possesses a psychology not altogether common, being one of those few persons who truly appraise the beauty, interest, and value of the present without having to wait until memory has lent the past its chromatic fringe.

When his youth died, wrote George Moore about his *Confessions of a Young Man*, the soul of the ancient Egyptians awoke in him. He had the idea of conserving his dead past in a work of art, embalming it with pious care in a memorial, he hoped, as durable as the pyramids of Rameses II! Poor George Moore!

It is strange that so many gallant knights clad in the armour of steely determination should fight on, unthinking, against such overwhelming odds. For the conservators in trying to dam back time, in resisting change and decay wrestle with the stars in their courses and dispute the very constitution of the universe. But the imperative instinct must be obeyed. The ominous warnings of Sir Thomas Browne are unavailing. 'There is no antidote for the opium of time.' 'Gravestones tell truth but a year.' 'We might just as well be content with six feet as with the moles of Adrianus.' And 'to subsist but in bones and be but pyramidally extant is a fallacy in duration'. To erect a monument is like trying to fix a stick into the bed of the Niagara. No memorial as large and wonderful as the Taj Mahal can stay the passage of grief, no pen can preserve an emotion held for a while in the sweet shackles of a sonnet's rules. Neither pen nor brush nor chisel knows the art of perpetuation.

As the torrent races past, frantic hands stretch out to snatch some memento from the flood—a faded letter, an old concert programme, a bullet, the railway labels jealously preserved on travellers' portmanteaux, a lock of hair. 'Only a woman's hair,' said Swift in the bitterness of his heart as he handled Stella's tress.

There are some things we can never hope to recall, even so long as the world lasts, except by divination or black magic. The hopeless science of Palaeontology offers its students no tiniest ray of comfort—a pterodactyl, a dinosaur or an archaeopteryx will never be disclosed to us in the flesh. There are many things lost for ever: Who was the Man in the Iron Mask? or the author of the *Letters of Junius*? or Mr W. H.?—the precious library burnt at Louvain? And so on by the score.

'All is vanity, feeding the wind and folly. Mummy is become merchandise, Mizraim cures wounds, and Pharaoh is sold for balsams'—to borrow once more from Sir Thomas Browne's organ music.

> *Tarry awhile lean earth!*
> *Rabble of Pharaohs and Arsacidae*
> *Keep their cold court within thee; thou hast sucked down*
> *How many Ninevehs and Hecatompyloi*
> *And perished cities whose great phantasmata*
> *O'erbrow the silent citizens of Dis.*

Life is expenditure. We must always be paying away. It is sad to behold the conservators—ecstatic hearts—following like eager camp followers in the trail of the whirlwind, collecting and saving the fragments so as to work them up into some pitiful history, poem, biography, monograph, or memorial.

Why pursue this hopeless task? What is the use in being precious and saving? Nature wastes a thousand seeds, experiments lightly with whole civilisations, and has abandoned a thousand planets that cycle in space forgotten and cold. Both collection and recollection are insufficient. The only perfect preservation is re-creation. Surely our zeal for conservation betokens a miserly close-fisted nature in us. It cannot be very magnanimous on our part to be so precious, since God and Nature are on the side of waste. Let us squander our life and energy in desire, love, experience. And, since so it is to be, let us without vain regrets watch the universe itself be squandered on the passing years, on earthquakes, and on wars. The world is an adventurer, and we try to keep him at home—in a museum. Let us not be niggardly over our planet nor over ourselves.

Yet it is easy but fatuous to sit at a writing desk and make suggestions for the alteration of human nature. Conservation is as deeply rooted as original sin.

Party Patches

JOSEPH ADDISON

About the middle of last winter I went to see an opera at the theatre in the Haymarket, where I could not but take notice of two parties of very fine women, that had placed themselves in the opposite side boxes, and seemed drawn up in a kind of battle-array one against another. After a short survey of them, I found they were patched differently; the faces, on one hand, being spotted on the right side of the forehead, and those upon the other on the left: I quickly perceived that they cast hostile glances upon one another; and that their patches were placed in those different situations, as party-signals to distinguish friends from foes. In the middle boxes, between these two opposite bodies, were several ladies who patched indifferently on both sides of their faces, and seemed to sit there with no other intention but to see the opera. Upon inquiry I found, that the body of Amazons on my right hand were Whigs, and those on my left, Tories; and that those who had placed themselves in the middle boxes were a neutral party, whose faces had not yet declared themselves. These last, however, as I afterwards found, diminished daily, and took their party with one side or the other; insomuch that I observed in several of them, the patches, which were before dispersed equally, are now all gone over to the Whig or the Tory side of the face. The censorious say, that the men whose hearts were aimed at, are very often the occasions that one part of the face is thus dishonoured, and lies under a kind of disgrace, while the other is so much set off and adorned by the owner; and that the patches turn to the right or to the left, according to the principles of the man who is most in favour. But whatever may be the motives of a few fantastical coquettes, who do not patch for the public good so much as for their own private advantage, it is certain, that there are several women of honour who patch out of principle, and with an eye to the interest of their country. Nay, I am informed that some of them adhere so steadfastly to their party, and are so far from sacrificing their zeal for the public to their passions for any particular person, that in a late draught of marriage-articles a lady has stipulated with her husband, that whatever his opinions are, she shall be at liberty to patch on which side she pleases.

I must here take notice, that Rosalinda, a famous Whig partisan, has most unfortunately a very beautiful mole on the Tory part of her forehead; which being very conspicuous, has occasioned many mistakes, and given an handle to her enemies to misrepresent her face, as though it had revolted from the Whig interest. But, whatever this natural patch may seem to insinuate, it is well known that her notions of government are still the same. This unlucky mole, however, has misled several coxcombs; and like the hanging out of false colours, made some of them converse with Rosalinda in what they thought the spirit of her party, when on a sudden she has given them an unexpected fire, that has sunk them all at once. If Rosalinda is unfortunate in her mole, Nigranilla is as unhappy in a pimple, which forces her, against her inclinations, to patch on the Whig side.

I am told that many virtuous matrons, who formerly have been taught to believe that this artificial spotting of the face was unlawful, are now reconciled by a zeal for their cause, to what they could not be prompted by a concern for their beauty. This way of declaring war upon one another, puts me in mind of what is reported of the tigress, that several spots rise in her skin when she is angry; or, as Mr Cowley has imitated the verses that stand as the motto of this paper,

She swells with angry pride.
And calls forth all her spots on every side.

When I was in the theatre the time above-mentioned, I had the curiosity to count the patches on both sides, and found the Tory patches to be about twenty stronger than the Whig; but to make amends for this small inequality, I the next morning found the whole puppet-show filled with faces spotted after the Whiggish manner. Whether or no the ladies had retreated hither in order to rally their forces, I cannot tell; but the next night they came in so great a body to the opera, that they outnumbered the enemy.

This account of party-patches will, I am afraid, appear improbable to those who live at a distance from the fashionable world; but as it is a distinction of a very singular nature, and what perhaps may never meet with a parallel, I think I should not have discharged the office of a faithful Spectator, had I not recorded it.

I have endeavoured to expose this party-rage in women, as it only serves to aggravate the hatred and animosities that reign among men, and in a great measure deprives the fair sex of those peculiar charms with which nature has endowed them.

When the Romans and Sabines were at war, and just upon the point of giving battle, the women who were allied to both of them, interposed with so many tears and entreaties, that they prevented the mutual slaughter which threatened both parties, and united them together in a firm and lasting peace.

I would recommend this noble example to our British ladies, at a time when their country is torn with so many unnatural divisions, that if they continue, it will be a misfortune to be born in it. The Greeks thought it so improper for women to interest themselves in competitions and contentions, that for this reason, among others, they forbade them, under pain of death, to be present at the Olympic games, notwithstanding these were the public diversions of all Greece.

As our English women excel those of all nations in beauty, they should endeavour to outshine them in all other accomplishments proper to the sex, and to distinguish themselves as tender mothers and faithful wives, rather than as furious partisans. Female virtues are of a domestic turn. The family is the proper province for private women to shine in. If they must be showing their zeal for the public, let it not be against those who are perhaps of the same family, or at least of the same religion or nation, but against those who are the open, professed, undoubted enemies of their faith, liberty, and country. When the Romans were pressed with a foreign enemy, the ladies voluntarily contributed all their rings and jewels to assist the government under the public exigence, which appeared so laudable an action in the eyes of their countrymen, that from thenceforth it was permitted by a law to pronounce public orations at the funeral of a woman in praise of the deceased person, which till that time was peculiar to men.

Would our English ladies, instead of sticking on a patch against those of their own country, show themselves so truly public-spirited as to sacrifice every one her necklace against the common enemy, what decrees ought not to be made in favour of them!

Since I am recollecting upon this subject such passages as occur to my memory out of ancient authors, I cannot omit a sentence in the celebrated funeral oration of Pericles, which he made in honour of those brave Athenians that were slain in a fight with the Lacedaemonians. After having addressed himself to the several ranks and orders of his countrymen, and shown them how they should behave themselves in the public cause, he turns to the female part of his audience; 'And as for you, (says he,) I shall advise you in very few words: aspire only to those virtues that are peculiar to your sex; follow your natural modesty, and think it your greatest commendation not to be talked of one way or other.'

On National Prejudices

OLIVER GOLDSMITH

As I am one of that sauntering tribe of mortals who spend the greatest part of their time in taverns, coffee-houses, and other places of public resort, I have thereby an opportunity of observing an infinite variety of characters, which to a person of a contemplative turn is a much higher entertainment than a view of all the curiosities of art or nature. In one of these my late rambles I accidentally fell into a company of half a dozen gentlemen, who were engaged in a warm dispute about some political affair, the decision of which, as they were equally divided in their sentiments, they thought proper to refer to me, which naturally drew me in for a share of the conversation.

Amongst the multiplicity of other topics, we took occasion to talk of the different characters of the several nations of Europe; when one of the gentlemen, cocking his hat, and assuming such an air of importance as if he had possessed all the merit of the English nation in his own person, declared, that the Dutch were a parcel of avaricious wretches; the French a set of flattering sycophants; that the Germans were drunken sots, and beastly gluttons; and the Spaniards proud, haughty, and surly tyrants; but that in bravery, generosity, clemency, and in every other virtue, the English excelled all the world.

This very learned and judicious remark was received with a general smile of approbation by all the company—all, I mean, but your humble servant, who, endeavouring to keep my gravity as well as I could, and reclining my head upon my arm, continued for some time in a posture of affected thoughtfulness, as if I had been musing on something else, and did not seem to attend to the subject of conversation; hoping by this means to avoid the disagreeable necessity of explaining myself, and thereby depriving the gentleman of his imaginary happiness.

But my pseudo-patriot had no mind to let me escape so easily. Not satisfied that his opinion should pass without contradiction, he was determined to have it ratified by the suffrage of everyone in the company; for which purpose, addressing himself to me with an air of inexpressible confidence, he asked me if I was not of the same way of thinking. As I am never forward in giving my opinion, especially when I have reason to believe that it will not be agreeable; so, when I am obliged to give it, I always hold it for a maxim to speak my real sentiments. I therefore told him that, for my own part, I should not have ventured to talk in such peremptory strain unless I had made the tour of Europe, and examined the manners of these several nations with great care and accuracy: that perhaps a more impartial judge would not scruple to affirm, that the Dutch were more frugal and industrious, the French more temperate and polite, the Germans more hardy and patient of labour and fatigue, and the Spaniards more staid and sedate, than the English; who, though undoubtedly brave and generous, were at the same time rash, headstrong, and impetuous; too apt to be elated with prosperity, and to despond in adversity.

I could easily perceive, that all the company began to regard me with a jealous eye before I had finished my answer, which I had no sooner done, than the patriotic gentleman observed, with a contemptuous sneer, that he was greatly surprised how some people could have the conscience to live in a country which they did not love, and to enjoy the protection of a government to which in their hearts they were inveterate enemies. Finding that by this modest declaration of my sentiments I had forfeited the good opinion of my companions, and given them occasion to call my political principles in question, and well knowing that it was in vain to argue with men who were so very full of themselves, I threw down my reckoning and retired to my own lodgings, reflecting on the absurd and ridiculous nature of national prejudice and prepossession.

Among all the famous sayings of antiquity, there is none that does greater honour to the author, or affords greater pleasure to the reader (at least if he be a person of a generous and benevolent heart), than that of the philosopher who, being asked what countryman he was, replied, that he was 'a citizen of the world'. How few are there to be found in modern times who can say the same, or whose conduct is consistent with such a profession! We are now become so much Englishmen, Frenchmen, Dutchmen, Spaniards, or Germans, that we are no longer citizens of the world; so much the natives of one particular spot, or members of one petty society, that we no longer consider ourselves as the general inhabitants of the globe, or members of that grand society which comprehends the whole human kind.

Did these prejudices prevail only among the meanest and lowest of the people, perhaps they might be excused, as they have few, if any, opportunities of correcting them by reading, travelling, or conversing with foreigners: but the misfortune is, that they infect the minds, and influence the conduct, even of our gentlemen; of those, I mean, who have every title to this appellation but an exemption from prejudice, which, however, in my opinion, ought to be regarded as the characteristical mark of a gentleman; for let a man's birth be ever so high, his station ever so exalted, or his fortune ever so large, yet if he is not free from national and other prejudices, I should make bold to tell him, that he had a low and vulgar mind, and had no just claim to the character of a gentleman. And, in fact, you will always find that those are most apt to boast of national merit, who have little or no merit of their own to depend on; than which, to be sure, nothing is more natural: the slender vine twists around the sturdy oak, for no other reason in the world but because it has not strength sufficient to support itself.

Should it be alleged in defence of national prejudice, that it is the natural and necessary growth of love to our country, and that there-fore the former cannot be destroyed without hurting the latter, I answer that this is a gross fallacy and delusion. That it is the growth of love to our country, I will allow; but that it is the natural and necessary growth of it, I absolutely deny. Superstition and enthu-siasm, too, are the growth of religion; but who ever took it in his head to affirm, that they are the necessary growth of this noble principle? They are, if you will, the bastard sprouts of this heavenly plant, but not its natural and genuine branches, and may safely enough be lopped off, without doing any harm to the parent stock: nay, perhaps, till once they are lopped off, this goodly tree can never flourish in perfect health and vigour.

Is it not very possible that I may love my own country, without hating the natives of other countries? that I may exert the most heroic bravery, the most undaunted resolution, in defending its laws and liberty, without despising all the rest of the world as cowards and poltroons? Most certainly it is; and if it were not—But why need I suppose what is absolutely impossible?—But if it were not, I must own I should prefer the title of the ancient philosopher, viz., a citizen of the world, to that of an Englishman, a Frenchman, an European, or to any other appellation whatever.

The Genealogy of Hitler

HUGH KINGSMILL

I

Most of the avoidable suffering in life springs from our attempts to escape the unavoidable suffering inherent in the fragmentary nature of our present existence. We expect immortal satisfactions from mortal conditions, and lasting and perfect happiness in the midst of universal change. To encourage this expectation, to persuade mankind that the ideal is realisable in this world, after a few preliminary changes in external conditions, is the distinguishing mark of all charlatans, whether in thought or action. In the middle of the eighteenth century Johnson wrote: 'We will not endeavour to fix the destiny of kingdoms: it is our business to consider what beings like us may perform.' A little later Rousseau wrote: 'Man is born free, and is everywhere in chains.' Johnson's sober truth kindled no one, Rousseau's seductive lie founded the secular religion which in various forms has dominated Europe since Rousseau's death.

Although tinged with a vague deism, Rousseau's religion of the natural man treated this life as essentially a complete and self-contained experience, a view which tends to stimulate both self-glorification and Utopianism. The *Confessions* of Rousseau opened with the claim that he was a unique individual. Frustrated and embittered, he could mitigate the unsatisfactoriness of his appearance on the stage of life only by pitting his singularity against the featureless mediocrity of the indifferent world. At the same time, partly out of a desire to blame circumstances for his wretchedness, and partly out of that feeling of solidarity with the general life which even the most obdurate egotist feels until he is required to translate it into action, Rousseau looked forward to an earthly paradise in which a liberated humanity would attain the felicity denied to those born, like him, into the night of privilege, tyranny and greed; for Utopianism is the transference to society of the individual's disappointed expectation of personal happiness.

Rousseau's gospel found its first practical expression in the French Revolution, which followed the usual course of Utopianism in action—wild rejoicing among the masses at the destruction of old abuses and the ruin of their oppressors, the improvisation of a new order, the necessity in the general confusion for ruthless methods of imposing it, the increasingly rapid elimination of those Utopians in whom humanity was stronger than practical sense, the welcome threat of foreign intervention and ensuing diversion of revolutionary passion, now a menace to the Utopians at the top, into patriotic fervour, and finally a military dictatorship and a series of crusades against reactionary neighbours. Out of this welter emerged a figure well suited to be the god of the new religion and the new century. Napoleon's first appeal to men's imaginations was as a liberator, and even after he mounted a higher throne than any he had overturned, he was still to millions the man of the people who had avenged their agelong sufferings and humiliations. This view of him, blurred during his later years of power, blossomed again as soon as he was dead. In 1814 the poet laureate, Robert Southey, called him 'Remorseless, godless, full of frauds and lies, and black with murders and with treacheries'; and the *Times* lamented that no description could more than faintly portray the foul and ghastly features of the grim idol worshipped by the French. A few years later, when the news of his death reached England, the *Times*, after regretting that he had not used his extraordinary gifts to better purpose, noted mildly that he was steady and faithful in his friendships, and not vindictive even when he could have been so with impunity. Since this could be written in 1821, it is not surprising that as the century advanced his exile became a martyrdom, and that before the close of the century Prometheus on his rock and even Christ in Gethsemane were being invoked to measure the extremity of Napoleon's dereliction on St Helena. Mixed with this view of him as a supremely tragic figure, the baffled liberator of mankind, was adoration of him as the Man of Destiny, the incarnation of will-power, ruthless and irresistible. The two aspects complemented each other, and together formed a god.

Byron soon joined Napoleon in the new pantheon. The uprush of energy in the second half of the eighteenth century had poured itself into poetry as well as action, and for a short period, poised between the age of reason and the age of romance, the mist which veils reality thinned in a few imaginations. Mozart and Beethoven, Blake and Goethe and Wordsworth, wrote as representatives of mankind, not as unique specimens of it; their work was inspired not by their own singularity but by the whole of which they felt themselves to be parts. It meant little to most people, and the stirring of men's minds and imaginations by the Revolution and Napoleon had to be satisfied on a different level.

Like Napoleon, Byron possessed the twofold appeal of a liberator and an embodiment of the untrammelled will. His politics were of the usual revolutionary kind. He expected nothing from the world as it was, and everything from the world as it was shortly to be—'Give me a republic. The king times are fast finishing; there will be blood shed like water and tears like mist, but the peoples will conquer in the end.' In the opinion of the public his death at Missolonghi proved the sincerity of his love for freedom; and his disinterestedness being thus established, it was possible to surrender without qualms to the spell of his egotism. In his essay on Byron Macaulay wondered why egotism, so distasteful in personal intercourse, should be so attractive in poetry. The explanation (to borrow one of Macaulay's formulas) is a very simple one. The reader identifies himself with the poet; and the readers of Byron, even when not in mere fact of noble birth and young and beautiful, fatal to all they loved, lonely wanderers over high mountains and misunderstood roamers on far-off strands, quickly became all these things in fancy. In the vacuum created by Napoleon's downfall Byron's image of himself enchanted all Europe, and the star-crossed lover took his place beside the star-crossed conqueror as the second of the two divinities presiding over the new age.

II

In his preface to *Ruy Blas*, which appeared in 1838, Victor Hugo wrote that the hero of the play was not Ruy Blas, but the people 'without a present, but looking to the future; humble in station, yet aspiring high, and with the premonition of genius'. Hugo, in the direct line of descent from Rousseau through Napoleon and Byron, was both a unique personality and a Utopian, but as this quotation suggests, he was aware that romantic individualism, symbolised by Ruy Blas, was on the wane, and that Utopianism was becoming the more important element in a great man's make-up. The age of progress had set in, applied science was multiplying the comforts of life, and the masses, temporarily suppressed after Waterloo, were beginning to stir again.

The rich, too, were looking to the future, but with a premonition of trouble, not of genius. Increasingly aware of the poor ever since the Revolution, they were trying to reassure themselves by crediting the man in the street with exactly those virtues which he had patently failed to exhibit during the Terror. As employees infer a fine nature in the head of a firm on evidence which would not raise the office boy in their esteem, so from 1789 onwards the well-to-do began to detect high qualities in what they now called 'the sovereign people'. 'Poor but honest', a realistic phrase previously in common use, was seldom heard after the Revolution, and the possessing classes inclined instead to the fallacy that because saints are usually poor men, therefore poor men are usually saints.

A less sweeping and majestic witness to the emergence of the people than Hugo, but a more perceptive one, was Heine. A German Jew, whose later years were spent in France, he had a wider range of experience than Hugo, and reflected the changing spirit of the age more completely perhaps than any other writer in the second quarter of the century. The heroes of his youth were Byron and Napoleon, Byron with his broken heart and unbroken will, and Napoleon who had abolished the Ghettos of Germany and scourged the hated Prussians, but had perished at last, as all great spirits perish, in vain conflict with the insensate hostility of the world. For Heine himself at this time the hostility of the world was expressed in the indifference to his love of a beautiful cousin, and the indifference to his poverty of her father, a rich Hamburg banker. A luckless Atlas bearing on his shoulders the whole world's woe was how he saw himself when he was feeling like Napoleon, and a poet whose songs and sorrows were on every German tongue when he was feeling like Byron. The charm of the Romantic age, as well as its closely interwoven foolishness, suffused these early verses, with their nostalgia for far-off lands and ages, their nightingales echoing the poet's pain, their moonlit waters and fairy-haunted woods, and at the end of every vista death, the goal of all desire because its only cure. But the poet lived on, and, like Byron in *Don Juan*, began to correct false sentiment with cynicism, using a jarring last line to let daylight into the moonshine. As his humour and his emotions became more harmonised he dropped this trick, which, however, expressed his permanent feeling of the antithesis between truth and beauty. Beauty was the romantic illusion he and his age had outgrown, truth the repulsive reality they could no longer evade; and by truth he meant the nature of things as they are experienced in the ordinary course of life. He was willing to believe that life could be beautiful in other lands, or had been beautiful in other ages, or even in his own youth when Byron and Napoleon were still on earth. But now the mob was in the ascendant, the drab era of the sovereign people was beginning. As a poet, and therefore by romantic convention an aristocrat, the prospect disgusted him. As a Utopian, a 'soldier in the liberation war of humanity', as he called himself, he welcomed it. For a year or two in the eighteen-forties he was a close friend of Karl Marx, whose political philosophy he condensed into a few stanzas of a satirical poem called 'Deutschland'. The people, that great booby (he wrote), had been fooled long enough by the old hymn of renunciation, the lullaby of heaven, with its promise of a world up there to recompense them for all their suffering below. He had a new, a better, hymn to sing. Let them build the kingdom of heaven here on earth. There was bread, and cakes, enough for every man. Leave heaven to the angels and the sparrows.

With this prevision of the Bolshevist millennium went the craving for violence which is induced by a glut of material well being, whether in fancy or in fact. In a famous passage he warned France to beware of the hammer of Thor which Germany, breaking through its crust of Christianity, would bring crashing down on the cathedrals of Christendom; but though he loved France and civilised life there was a note of exultation in the warning. Give me bloody and colossal crimes (he cried in one of his poems), but not this smug virtue of solvent traders; and in another poem he hailed Germany as a child whom its nurse, the sun, was suckling not with milk but with wild flames, and on whose forehead a diamond-studded crown would presently be sparkling.

III

While Heine was looking backwards with regret and forwards with a mixture of repulsion and excitement, Balzac was carving an epic out of the new age of money and machines. He was not a Utopian. With his vast appetite for the concrete, the present was feast enough for him. But he was intensely romantic. His ambition, he said, was to achieve with his pen what Napoleon had achieved with his sword. He wanted to pass the whole of life through his imagination, and stamp his picture of it on every mind. It was the hallucination of a man whose enormous natural vitality had been stimulated throughout a childhood and youth passed in Napoleon's world, and galvanised into delirium by the conquest of matter which in the second quarter of the century seemed to all Europe to prelude a millennium of earthly felicity. In England this illusion was still strongly tinged by Christianity. 'Commerce, till lately comparatively inert,' an Oxford graduate wrote in 1854, 'is springing and running and flying with a more rapid motion of every limb, no longer dependent on the slowness of road-travel or the fitfulness of breezes, but self-propelled by the living and roaring leviathan within her bosom . . . We have celebrated the festival of material civilisation in the great Exhibition of the nations' industry, and called all the ends of the earth to unite with us in patient and laborious progress. It was a noticeable fact, that in a bay of that Exhibition was a stand of books open to all readers; they were spread outside to attract the gaze of those who should pass by. It was the Book, the Word of God, the revelation of Christianity, published in more than a hundred languages of the nations of the earth. That fact is not a solitary or an isolated one; for coeval with the advance of commerce and of practical science there has taken place a mighty advance of Christianity.' This was not how Balzac felt about the conquest of matter. Though a Catholic and Royalist, he was neither of those things out of a tenderness for religion or the past, but because in a country subject to revolutions a conservative theory of society seemed to him a necessary safeguard against the disruption and dispersal of the individual will which was symbolised for him in Napoleon. Though his books pulsate with energy and teem with life, there are really only two men in them: the man who is like Napoleon and the man who isn't. The first may be a country solicitor, a money-lender, or a gossip-writer on the Parisian press, but Balzac blows him out into a daemonic creature, grappling with society in a life-and-death struggle. The other man is a cross between a village idiot and Balzac's idea of Christ, which it is not easy to distinguish from the ordinary idea of a village idiot. There are also two women: the one a ruthless, triumphant courtesan, the other a victimised Madonna.

The belief that goodness is due to an absence of will, not to a presence of spirit, expanded with the growing materialism of the age. Balzac, who died in 1850, could drop a tear over the hapless plight of virtue, but a few years later the philosophy deduced from Darwin's *Origin of Species* dignified egotism as the universal law of life. Confined within the material universe, spirit dismissed as an illusion, and matter elevated into the ultimate reality, the European mind turned to science as the sole repository of truth. The vastness of the universe, which so tormented Tennyson and which he was the first poet to feel and to express, became a part of the general consciousness. Space and time, now absolute realities, stretched behind and before into sickening distances, and a feeling of his inexpressible insignificance descended upon man. This did not last long. His insignificance bred a sense of irresponsibility, his sense of irresponsibility a sense of power, and the net result of realising that he measured about six feet from end to end, as compared with the x billion miles of the universe, was greatly to increase his self-conceit. Rid of God, he felt himself superior to anything that remained, or at least to anything within view. This, however, was a collective feeling rather than an individual one, a huddling together of the herd in the presence of a mechanistic universe.

The descent of man from a spiritual being to a self-dependent personality, and from a self-dependent personality to a unit of the collective consciousness, was quickening fast—a change which sounds catastrophic, but which in practice was immensely modified by the fact that the mass of mankind is always swaying about between the highest and lowest conceptions of its nature, with flashes of divinity in an age of atheism and flashes of devilry in an age of religion. Nevertheless, the change portended great disasters, which in the twenty to thirty years following the *Origin of Species* were foreshadowed by Dostoevsky and Nietzsche.

IV

The fundamental impulse in Dostoevsky's work was to dramatise the conflict in his nature between will-worship and spiritual freedom. When he wrote *Crime and Punishment,* will-worship was embodied for him in Napoleon and spiritual freedom in Christ; the hero of the book murdering an old woman in order to demonstrate his Napoleonic self-sufficiency, and repenting later under the influence of a prostitute who reads the Gospel of St John to him. In his last novel, *The Brothers Karamazov*, the conflict is less simply presented. There is a young priest, Alyosha, who is supposed to embody the spirit of universal love, but in spite of much effort by Dostoevsky he plays a minor and vapid part in the book. The true field of Dostoevsky's genius was not the heights of the human spirit but the depths of the human consciousness. He was most at home in the underworld, the literal one of St Petersburg, the metaphorical one of his own nature, and the most directly self-revealing of his stories, because the freest from false sentiment, is *Letters from the Underworld*, the confession of a small government official, shabby, insignificant and savagely resentful, whose longing for happiness and love is twisted into a devilish satisfaction in undeceiving and humiliating a prostitute who thinks she has found in him a refuge from the cruelty of life.

It was out of this inferno of perverted impulses, shot at intervals with gleams of spiritual insight, that the gospel of Dostoevsky rose into the upper air of the late nineteenth century, a strange exhalation which in the thickening twilight was mistaken for an apparition from heaven. Although what the Oxford graduate of 1854 had described as the triumph of patient and laborious progress was still in full spate, it inspired now less exultation than fear. In the more advanced countries of Europe the desire of the rich to think highly of the poor, to which Victor Hugo and Dickens had so freely ministered, was being more and more thwarted by the increasing demand of the poor for greater power and better conditions. No wonder, then, that in the closing decades of the century and the years before the war of 1914, western Europeans of the cultured classes turned with relief from labour organising itself for battle to Dostoevsky's vision of brotherly love among the uncomplaining Russian poor. It was among university professors and first-class civil servants, popular novelists of the better sort and the lettered members of great banking and commercial families, that Dostoevsky's most ardent admirers were to be found. 'The love which is in Dostoevsky's work', one of these admirers wrote, 'is so great, so bountiful, so overflowing that it is impossible to find a parallel to it, either in ancient or in modern literature. Supposing the Gospel of St John were to be annihilated and lost to us for ever, although nothing could replace it, Dostoevsky's work would go nearer to replacing it than any other books written by any other man.' What these enthusiasts divined in Dostoevsky was, on an enormously larger scale, their own guilt and fear and desire to placate an unknown and growing power. They, no more than Dickens or Victor Hugo or Dostoevsky, were attracted by the idea of self-chosen poverty. It was poverty as the great mass of mankind knows it that they wanted to be glorified as a privileged experience and a purifying destiny—a view of poverty which makes affluence seem almost a deprivation.

With the desire to idealise the masses is usually associated a desire to manage and use them, and it was this desire, stimulated by the growing collectivism of the age, which in Dostoevsky's last years blurred his earlier antithesis between Napoleon and Christ, producing a mixture of the two in which will-worship masqueraded as universal love. By this time Dostoevsky had become a fanatical nationalist, who was urging that Constantinople should be incorporated in the Russian Empire, beyond which relatively modest aim he saw the gradual absorption of the whole world by Russia. In a speech in honour of Pushkin, which he delivered just before his death and which aroused great popular enthusiasm, he said: 'What is the strength of the Russian national spirit other than an aspiration towards a universal spirit which shall embrace the whole world and the whole of mankind? . . . To be a real Russian must signify simply this: to strive to bring about a solution and an end to European conflicts; to show to Europe a way to escape from its anguish in the Russian soul, which is universal and all-embracing; to instil into her a brotherly love for all men, and in the end perhaps to utter the great and final word of universal harmony, the fraternal and lasting concord of all people according to the gospel of Christ.'

This totalitarian fantasy was his refuge from the panorama of malice, lust and despair which he displayed with all the intensity of his genius in *The Brothers Karamazov*. The clue to what in this last phase of his development he really felt about the masses is to be found not in his Pushkin speech but in the Legend of the Grand Inquisitor which he inserted in *The Brothers Karamazov*. In this legend Christ returns to earth in the sixteenth century, and is brought before the Grand Inquisitor in Seville. The Grand Inquisitor in a lengthy apologia presents himself as an enlightened sage, full of pity for the multitude, whom he directs and rules in their own interest, knowing them to be too weak for the burden of spiritual freedom imposed upon them by Christ. One would not, of course, expect a Calvin, a Torquemada or a Robespierre to present himself as a warped and savage soul which hates and seeks to destroy the happiness of others. But his true motives and impulses would be revealed incidentally as he talked. Dostoevsky's Grand Inquisitor is throughout unintermittently high-minded and disinterested, and even when he tells Christ that he must be killed, so that men may be saved from a gospel too hard for them, his majestic serenity remains unflawed by any gleam of satisfaction. Christ's response is to lean forward and kiss the Inquisitor on the lips; the Inquisitor shudders, and Christ passes out into the night, leaving the Inquisitor to roast his fellow-creatures in peace.

Like Dostoevsky's Christ, the Christs who round about this time made occasional appearances in the fiction of western Europe no longer contend against evil. Now and then a look of pain reveals their distress at wrong-doing, but their real business is to suggest that if the worst came to the worst, and there really should be another life, there would be loving-kindness enough to spare for everyone at the Day of Judgement.

V

The advisability of identifying oneself with some communal faith or activity was by the closing decades of the century clear to everyone who wished to bring himself to the notice of the public. After 1870 even Wagner, the most flamboyant of romantic individualists, aligned his music with the aspirations of the new Germany. Ten years later, Dostoevsky became a Russian idol overnight with his speech on Pushkin, and in the next fifty years or so all the world-wide reputations, both in literature and in action, were made by men who drew attention to themselves by denouncing the individual and exalting the community—Shaw, Kipling and Wells, Lenin, Mussolini and Hitler.

Nietzsche reached maturity just as this landslide of self-effacing self-advancement was beginning to gather momentum, but he did not slide along with the rest. There was nothing of the opportunist in him, no point of contact with ordinary men. Of clerical stock on both sides, even in his childhood he was remote from life, earnest, scrupulous and thoughtful, with a budding didacticism which led the other children to call him 'the little pastor'. Living entirely in his mind, he could have jogged through the world comfortably enough as a professor, but for his genius. There was an enormous power in him which could find nothing to feed on. His passions came to him in the form of ideas, he passed from one idea to another instead of from one experience to another, and for want of the balance between experience and thought which keeps genius sane collapsed at last under the unrelieved pressure of his thoughts on his emotions.

Looking at the world as a starving child looks through a window at people eating in a restaurant, he refused to blunt the pangs of his unsatisfied appetite with any hope of another life, or belief in a supernatural order. Matter was for him the only reality, the struggle and suffering of life were justified by the courage they evoked to endure them, only great individuals had any value, and the greatness of the individual was measured by the exaltation inspired in him by his tragic destiny. The philosophy which he based on this attitude and which he preached in his third and final stage was an extreme individualism, equally opposed to Christianity and to all forms of collectivism, democratic or nationalistic. Christianity he held to be a trick by which the herd had disarmed the aristocrat. Its humanitarianism was based not on love but on cowardice, it turned noble savages into sick monks, and hated and feared all that was strong and happy. Democracy, the modern secularised form of Christianity, levelled all superiorities. Slavery was essential to culture, and the enormous majority ought to be ruthlessly subjected to life's struggle, so that a select minority might expand without restraint. War he of course approved—'Man shall be trained for war, and woman for the recreation of the warrior.' Yet he disliked Prussian nationalism only less than democratic pacifism, denouncing 'this bovine nationalism' and warning Germany to free itself from 'this fatal Prussia with its repugnance to culture'. That the effective conduct of a war presupposes a strong collective emotion, and that nationalism is the form which a strong collective emotion necessarily takes when one country is fighting or preparing to fight another, clashed with his picture of glorious individuals hurling themselves into self-engendered frays. Reaching far out into the future, he found there a Utopia of his own, a world which had passed beyond the collectivism without tears of other founders of Utopia: 'There, where the State ceaseth—pray look thither, my brethren! Do ye not see it, the rainbow and the bridges of the Superman?' In this paradise of happy warriors, transfigured Caesar Borgias, resounding with 'the final, cheerfullest, exuberantly maddest and merriest Yea to life', there would be a supreme wisdom of soul and body, a perfect harmonisation of joy and strength—'light feet, wit, fire, grave grand logic, stellar dancing, wanton intellectuality'.

This vision brought him no readers, one by one his friends were estranged by his growing conviction that he was destined to be the second and final saviour of mankind, and in his despair he turned back from his distant dream to the Europe of the later eighties, congested with prosperity and sick of progress. What could save it, he asked himself, and found the answer in the prospect of huge socialistic crises which would throw up the barbarians of the twentieth century to refresh and renovate an outworn world. 'Would not the democratic movement itself', he wrote, 'find a sort of goal, salvation, and justification, if someone appeared who availed himself of it, so that at last, besides its new and sublime product, slavery (for this would be the end of European democracy), that higher species of ruling and Caesarian spirits might also be produced, which would stand upon it, hold to it, and elevate themselves through it?'

Not long after this greeting to the collective frenzies he had tried to escape from in the dream of a Superman, at the beginning of 1889, a few months before the birth of Hitler, Nietzsche became insane.

VI

In the year of Hitler's birth and Nietzsche's mental collapse, James Payn wrote to Conan Doyle, who had just brought out a story of the Monmouth Rebellion: 'How can you, how can you, waste your time and wits writing historical novels?' The solid domestic themes which had made Anthony Trollope the most representative novelist of the sixties and seventies were still, in the opinion of a novelist well acquainted with popular taste, the most likely to please the public. Nevertheless, the first rumbling of the eruption against peace and prosperity and all the values summed up in the Victorian aphorism that the true knight of the modern world was the knight of commerce could already be heard. Kipling's Indian stories were coming out, Stevenson had written *Treasure Island* and *Kidnapped,* Stanley Weyman's *A Gentleman of France*, ostensibly the history of a soldier of fortune in sixteenth-century France and really the daydream of a gentleman in late Victorian England, was soon to appear and sell in thousands, and Conan Doyle was about to become the medium through which the ordinary Englishman of the 1890s expressed most fully and variously his nostalgia for excitement and adventure. In his Sherlock Holmes stories Doyle peopled London with bizarre criminals, dotting a few over the countryside to suggest the horrors beneath its peaceful surface; and in other stories he ranged from diabolical pirates of the Spanish Main to murderous reanimated mummies. In his medieval romances he unrolled a landscape full of chivalrous knights and valiant bowmen, with here and there a flagel-lating hermit or white-livered clerk in holy orders. In *Rodney Stone* he pictured the bucks and bare-fist fighters of the Regency, and in his Napoleonic tales he resurrected the gigantic figure of Napoleon for, as he put it, 'you who live so gently and peacefully now'.

There was nothing of the revolutionary in Conan Doyle, a solid English individualist, or in Kipling, who early in his career attached himself to the ruling classes. In H. G. Wells, on the other hand, the element of violence was closely connected with his revolutionary sympathies. He was both generous and resentful by nature, but his early years of poverty deepened his resentment at the expense of his generosity. Overlooking the treatment saints and poets have received from churches and universities, he identified religion with the Church of England and culture with Oxford and Cambridge, and fell into a habit of disparaging the great men of the past as though they were merely dummies set up by snobs and pedants to intimidate the unlettered. His enthusiasm for science, a study disdained by the upper classes in his youth, was therefore not entirely impersonal, and his materialistic creed not the spontaneous exuberant materialism of the first half of the century, but a mixed product of a desire for power and of a dogged resistance to the spiritual element in his nature.

The hero of all his books, which fall into three categories, novels, scientific romances and Utopias, is the Little Man. In his early novels, based on his own youth, the Little Man is drawn with great humour, tenderness and warmth in his aspiration towards the happiness which life seems to hold for leisured and prosperous people. But Hoop-driver, Mr Lewisham and Kipps are not allowed to develop the confused poetry in their natures. Forced by his creed and by his own development to look for the kingdom of heaven anywhere except within the individual, Wells had either to give them money and position or leave them unblessed and unspoiled by prosperity. In his tenderness for them and deep obscure regret for what they still possessed and he had lost, he left them where they were, reserving for novels based, somewhat loosely, on his later years the transmogrifi-cation of the Little Man into a powerful figure in politics and big business. In his scientific romances, Wells transformed the Little Man into a magician, a being, that is, who concentrates on the mastery of natural forces and rejects spiritual development. Thus endowed, the Little Man ranges to the furthest limits of past and future time, flies to the moon, discovers the secret of invisibility, and turns himself into a giant. Some reality still adheres to him in these transformations. His powers do not bring him much happiness, and from time to time he misuses them in outbursts of rage and destructiveness. In the Utopian fantasies, put forward by Wells as valuable contributions to political thought, the Little Man, leaving all reality behind him, takes whole-sale vengeance on the insolent past, abolishing all nations, wiping out all religions, and erecting on the ruins a social order founded on applied science and enlightened sexual relations.

The Little Man as pictured by Wells in his best days passed away in 1914. Surfeited with the material triumphs of the previous hundred years, Europe was ready for an explosion, and the first effect of the war was a sense of overwhelming relief, to which the *Daily Mail* gave eloquent expression early in August 1914: 'We of this generation are destined to see hours glorious beyond hope and imagination; we are already entering upon them. We have passed from the twilight of sloth and indulgence into the clear day of action and self-sacrifice.' There was the same exaltation in Germany, where Thomas Mann spoke of the hearts of poets standing in flame, 'for now it is war! . . . Nothing better, more beautiful, happier could befall them in the whole world.' For the time being each of the warring nations was unified within itself, the external enemy became a symbol of the evil in life, the Little Man laid aside his resentments, and the rich man his pleasures and security.

Under the strain of the war revolution broke out in Russia, a worm-eaten autocracy ripe to yield to a new order in which the nineteenth-century illusions of progress and prosperity and the magi-cal benefits of applied science could find fresh soil to blossom in. In the highly industrialised nations of western Europe, which Karl Marx had considered sufficiently well organised to be transferred at the right moment from bourgeois-capitalist control to the control of the proletariat, the chief effect of the infinite suffering of the war was a deep disillusionment with all the hopes engendered by the previous century. Materialism, once a solid daylight faith, now took strange shapes, lapsing into the dark night of the unconscious, the world of dreams and atavistic impulses, in which blind guides, pillars of cloud by night, led their stumbling followers in circles.

The Little Man of this new world was Charlie Chaplin, whose inconsequential moods and actions, and alternations of hope and dejection, mirrored the general disintegration. His fame in the 1920s was universal. No one in his own lifetime had ever been known to so many millions, who in every land saw themselves in the forlorn little man in his battered bowler and huge shapeless boots, his trim officer's moustache an emblem of his social aspirations, his final disappearance beyond the twilit skyline the confession of his defeat.

Wearying at last of the pathos of failure, Chaplin in 1925 produced 'The Gold Rush', in which the Little Man triumphed both in love and in the pursuit of wealth. The film was revived in 1942, and as one watched the Little Man struggling in a world of husky toughs, one remembered how in the intervening years another down-and-out, with the same kind of moustache and a not much more impressive appearance, had overturned the whole planet, toughs and all. This parallel in mind, one followed the Little Man's search for gold in Alaska with a different kind of interest. The fantastically unsuitable get-up in which he braved the snowy wastes now seemed part of his technique. When, as he tottered along the edge of a precipice, a bear sniffed at him and turned away, one was relieved rather for the bear than for the Little Man. The gale that blew him back into Black Larsen's cabin, after Black Larsen had ejected him, seemed to come from a million lungs, and one was not surprised when Black Larsen later on ran into an Alaskan equivalent of the Night of the Long Knives. The huge bulk of the Little Man's partner seemed appropriate, and the happy ending inevitable—both of them multi-millionaires, the Little Man in fashionable clothes strutting up and down his suite on an ocean liner, and the beauty he has adored mute and blissful beside him.

What the Little Man of 'The Gold Rush' desired was money and women, what Hitler desired was power, these desires forming together the sum of what most men want from the world. Hitler, who was born in the same week of April 1889 as Chaplin, was his complement not his antithesis, the Napoleon of the mass-consciousness as Chaplin was its Byron, and therefore cast for the more ungrateful part, since it has fallen to him to demonstrate, on the widest possible scale, that the obverse of self-pity is not pity for others, but hatred, and that no one has less sympathy with the poor than the down-and-out who has managed to become an up-and-in.

After a century and a half of emptying the divine out of life, the epoch which opened with the uniqueness and Utopianism of Rousseau has collapsed in the self-deification and New Order of Hitler. Many remedies for a shattered world are now being offered to mankind, but they are all collective remedies, and collective remedies do not heal the ills produced by collective action. The purpose of this book is not to suggest the true remedy, except indirectly, but to illustrate in four famous examples the barren results of action and the destructive effect of power. Naturally, it is not disputed that benefits of a secondary order may flow from the achievements of able rulers; it was clearly to the advantage of England in the second half of the sixteenth century to be governed by Queen Elizabeth and not by

Queen Anne. But, on a much deeper level of reality, it was not to the advantage either of Elizabeth or of those who served her that she should set herself up as a semi-divine figure, a Virgin Queen exalted high above common humanity. What is divine in man is elusive and impalpable, and he is easily tempted to embody it in a concrete form—a church, a country, a social system, a leader—so that he may realise it with less effort and serve it with more profit. Yet, as even Lincoln proved, the attempt to externalise the kingdom of heaven in a temporal shape must end in disaster. It cannot be created by charters and constitutions nor established by arms. Those who set out for it alone will reach it together, and those who seek it in company will perish by themselves.

Pink Triangle and Yellow Star

GORE VIDAL

A few years ago on a trip to Paris, I read an intriguing review in *Le Monde* of a book called *Comme un Frère, Comme un Amant*, a study of 'Male Homosexuality in the American Novel and Theater from Herman Melville to James Baldwin', the work of one Georges-Michel Sarotte, a Sorbonne graduate and a visiting professor at the University of Massachusetts. I read the book, found it interesting; met the author, found him interesting. He told me that he was looking forward to the publication of his book in the United States by Anchor Press/Doubleday. What sort of response did I think he would have? I was touched by so much innocent good faith. There will be no reaction, I said, because no one outside of the so-called gay press will review your book. He was shocked. Wasn't the book serious? scholarly? with an extensive bibliography? I agreed that it was all those things; unfortunately, scholarly studies having to do with fags do not get reviewed in the United States (this was before the breakthrough of Yale's John Boswell, whose ferociously learned *Christianity, Social Tolerance and Homosexuality* obliged even the 'homophobic' *New York Times* to review it intelligently). If Sarotte had written about the agony and wonder of being female and/or Jewish and/or divorced, he would have been extensively reviewed. Even a study of black literature might have got attention (Sarotte is beige), although blacks are currently something of a nonsubject in these last days of empire.

I don't think that Professor Sarotte believed me. I have not seen him since. I also have never seen a review of his book or of Roger Austen's *Playing the Game* (a remarkably detailed account of American writing on homosexuality) or of *The Homosexual as Hero in Contemporary Fiction* by Stephen Adams, reviewed at much length in England and ignored here, or of a dozen other books that have been sent to me by writers who seem not to understand why an activity of more than casual interest to more than one-third of the male population of the United States warrants no serious discussion. That is to say, no serious *benign* discussion. All-out attacks on faggots are perennially fashionable in our better periodicals.

I am certain that the novel *Tricks* by Renaud Camus (recently translated for St Martin's Press by Richard Howard, with a preface by Roland Barthes) will receive a perfunctory and hostile response out there in book-chat land. Yet in France, the book was treated as if it were actually literature, admittedly a somewhat moot activity nowadays. So I shall review *Tricks*. But first I think it worth bringing out in the open certain curious facts of our social and cultural life.

The American passion for categorising has now managed to create two nonexistent categories—gay and straight. Either you are one or you are the other. But since everyone is a mixture of inclinations, the categories keep breaking down; and when they break down, the irrational takes over. You *have* to be one or the other. Although our mental therapists and writers for the better journals usually agree that those who prefer same-sex sex are not exactly criminals (in most of our states and under most circumstances they still are) or sinful or, officially, sick in the head, they must be, somehow, evil or inadequate or dangerous. The Roman Empire fell, didn't it? because of the fags?

Our therapists, journalists, and clergy are seldom very learned. They seem not to realise that most military societies on the rise tend to encourage same-sex activities for reasons that should be obvious to anyone who has not grown up ass-backward, as most Americans have. In the centuries of Rome's great military and political success, there was no differentiation between same-sexers and other-sexers; there was also a lot of crossing back and forth of the sort that those Americans who *do* enjoy inhabiting category-gay or category-straight find hard to deal with. Of the first twelve Roman emperors, only one was exclusively heterosexual. Since these twelve men were pretty tough cookies, rigorously trained as warriors, perhaps our sexual categories and stereotypes are—can it really be?—false. It was not until the sixth century of the empire that same-sex sex was proscribed by church and state. By then, of course, the barbarians were within the gates and the glory had fled.

Today, American evangelical Christians are busy trying to impose on the population at large their superstitions about sex and the sexes and the creation of the world. Given enough turbulence in the land, these natural fascists can be counted on to assist some sort of authoritarian—but never, never totalitarian—political movement. Divines from Santa Clara to Falls Church are particularly fearful of what they describe as the gay liberation movement's attempt to gain 'special rights and privileges' when all that the same-sexers want is to be included, which they are not by law and custom, within the framework of the Fourteenth Amendment. The divine in Santa Clara believes that same-sexers should be killed. The divine in Falls Church believes that they should be denied equal rights under the law. Meanwhile, the redneck divines have been joined by a group of New York Jewish publicists who belong to what they proudly call 'the new class' (né arrivistes), and these lively hucksters have now managed to raise fag-baiting to a level undreamed of in Falls Church—or even in Moscow.

In a letter to a friend, George Orwell wrote, 'It is impossible to mention Jews in print, either favorably or unfavorably, without getting into trouble.' But there are times when trouble had better be got into before mere trouble turns into catastrophe. Jews, blacks and homosexualists are despised by the Christian and Communist majorities of East and West. Also, as a result of the invention of Israel, Jews can now count on the hatred of the Islamic world. Since our own Christian majority looks to be getting ready for great adventures at home and abroad, I would suggest that the three despised minorities join forces in order not to be destroyed. This seems an obvious thing to do. Unfortunately, most Jews refuse to see any similarity between their special situation and that of the same-sexers. At one level, the Jews are perfectly correct. A racial or religious or tribal identity is a kind of fact. Although sexual preference is an even more powerful fact, it is not one that creates any particular social or cultural or religious bond between those so-minded. Although Jews would doubtless be Jews if there was no anti-Semitism, same-sexers would think little or nothing at all about their preference if society ignored it. So, there *is* a difference between the two estates. But there is no difference in the degree of hatred felt by the Christian majority for Christ-killers and Sodomites. In the German concentration camps, Jews wore yellow stars while homosexualists wore pink triangles. I was present when Christopher Isherwood tried to make this point to a young Jewish movie producer. 'After all,' said Isherwood, 'Hitler killed six hundred thousand homosexuals.' The young man was not impressed. 'But Hitler killed six *million* Jews,' he said sternly. 'What are you?' asked Isherwood. 'In real estate?'

Like it or not, Jews and homosexualists are in the same fragile boat, and one would have to be pretty obtuse not to see the common danger. But obtuseness is the name of the game among New York's new class. Elsewhere, I have described the shrill fag-baiting of Joseph Epstein, Norman Podhoretz, Alfred Kazin, and the Hilton Kramer Hotel. *Harper's* magazine and *Commentary* usually publish these pieces, though other periodicals are not above printing the odd exposé of the latest homosexual conspiracy to turn the United States over to the Soviet Union or to structuralism or to Christian Dior. Although the new class's thoughts are never much in themselves, and they themselves are no more than spear carriers in the political and cultural life of the West, their prejudices and superstitions do register in a subliminal way, making mephitic the air of Manhattan if not of the Republic.

A case in point is that of Mrs Norman Podhoretz, also known as Midge Decter (like Martha Ivers, *whisper* her name). In September of last year, Decter published a piece called 'The Boys on the Beach' in her husband's magazine, *Commentary*. It is well worth examining in some detail because she has managed not only to come up with every known prejudice and superstition about same-sexers but also to make up some brand-new ones. For sheer vim and vigour, 'The Boys on the Beach' outdoes its implicit model, *The Protocols of the Elders of Zion*.

Decter notes that when the 'homosexual-rights movement first burst upon the scene', she was 'more than a little astonished'. Like so many new-class persons, she writes a stilted sort of genteel-gentile prose not unlike—but not very like, either—the *New Yorker* house style of the 1940s and '50s. She also writes with the authority and easy confidence of someone who knows that she is very well known indeed to those few who know her.

Decter tells us that twenty years ago, she got to know a lot of pansies at a resort called Fire Island Pines, where she and a number of other new-class persons used to make it during the summers. She estimates that forty per cent of the summer people were heterosexual; the rest were not. Yet the 'denizens, homosexual and heterosexual alike, were predominantly professionals and people in soft, marginal businesses—lawyers, advertising executives, psychotherapists, actors, editors, writers, publishers, etc.' Keep this in mind. Our authoress does not.

Decter goes on to tell us that she is now amazed at the recent changes in the boys on the beach. Why have they become so politically militant—and so ill groomed? 'What indeed has happened to the homosexual community I used to know—they who only a few short years ago [as opposed to those manly 370-day years] were characterised by nothing so much as a sweet, vain, pouting, girlish attention to the youth and beauty of their bodies?' Decter wrestles with this problem. She tells us how, in the old days, she did her very best to come to terms with her own normal dislike for these half-men—and half-women, too: 'There were also homosexual women at the Pines, but they were, or seemed to be, far fewer in number. Nor, except for a marked tendency to hang out in the company of large and ferocious dogs, were they instantly recognisable as the men were.' Well, if I were a dyke and a pair of Podhoretzes came waddling towards me on the beach, copies of Leviticus and Freud in hand, I'd get in touch with the nearest Alsatian dealer pronto.

Decter was disturbed by the 'slender, seamless, elegant and utterly chic' clothes of the fairies. She also found it 'a constant source of wonder' that when the fairies took off their clothes, 'the largest number of homosexuals had hairless bodies. Chests, backs, arms, even legs were smooth and silky . . . We were never able to determine just why there should be so definite a connection between what is nowadays called their sexual preference [previously known to right-thinking Jews as an abomination against Jehovah] and their smooth feminine skin. Was it a matter of hormones?' Here Decter betrays her essential modesty and lack of experience. In the no doubt privileged environment of her Midwestern youth, she could not have seen very many gentile males without their clothes on. If she had, she would have discovered that gentile men tend to be less hairy than Jews except, of course, when they are not. Because the Jews killed our Lord, they are forever marked with hair on their shoulders—something that no gentile man has on *his* shoulders except for John Travolta and a handful of other Italian-Americans from the Englewood, New Jersey, area.

It is startling that Decter has not yet learned that there is no hormonal difference between men who like sex with other men and those who like sex with women. She notes, 'There is also such a thing as characteristic homosexual speech . . . it is something of an accent redolent of small towns in the Midwest whence so many homosexuals seemed to have migrated to the big city.' Here one detects the disdain of the self-made New Yorker for the rural or small-town American. 'Midwest' is often a code word for the flyovers, for the millions who do not really matter. But she is right in the sense that when a group chooses to live and work together, they do tend to sound and look alike. No matter how crowded and noisy a room, one can always detect the new-class person's whine.

Every now and then, Decter does wonder if, perhaps, she is generalising and whether this will 'no doubt in itself seem to many of the uninitiated a bigoted formulation'. Well, Midge, it does. But the spirit is upon her, and she cannot stop because 'one cannot even begin to get at the truth about homosexuals without this kind of generalisation. They are a group so readily distinguishable'. Except of course, when they are not. It is one thing for a group of queens, in 'soft, marginal' jobs, to 'cavort', as she puts it, in a summer place and be 'easily distinguishable' to her cold eye just as Jewish members of the new class are equally noticeable to the cold gentile eye. But it is quite another thing for those men and women who prefer same-sex sex to other-sex sex yet do not choose to be identified—and so are not. To begin to get at the truth about homosexuals, one must realise that the majority of those millions of Americans who prefer same-sex sex to other-sex sex are obliged, sometimes willingly and happily but often not, to marry and have children and to conform to the guidelines set down by the heterosexual dictatorship.

Decter would know nothing of this because in her 'soft, marginal' world, she is not meant to know. She does remark upon those fairies at the Pines who did have wives and children: 'They were for the most part charming and amusing fathers, rather like favorite uncles. And their wives . . . drank.' This dramatic ellipsis is most Decterian.

She ticks off Susan Sontag for omitting to mention in the course of an essay on camp 'that camp is of the essence of homosexual style, invented by homosexuals, and serving the purpose of domination by ridicule'. The word 'domination' is a characteristic new-class touch. The powerless are always obsessed by power. Decter seems unaware that all despised minorities are quick to make rather good jokes about themselves before the hostile majority does. Certainly Jewish humour, from the Book of Job (a laff-riot) to pre-*auteur* Woody Allen, is based on this.

Decter next does the ritual attack on Edward Albee and Tennessee Williams for presenting 'what could only have been homosexual relationships as the deeper truth about love in our time'. This is about as true as the late Maria Callas's conviction that you could always tell a Jew because he had a hump at the back of his neck—something Callas herself had in dromedarian spades.

Decter makes much of what she assumes to be the fags' mockery of the heterosexual men at the Pines: 'Homosexuality paints them [heterosexuals] with the color of sheer entrapment', while the fags' 'smooth and elegant exteriors, unmussed by traffic with the detritus of modern family existence, constituted a kind of sniggering reproach to their striving and harried straight brothers'. Although I have never visited the Pines, I am pretty sure that I know the 'soft, marginal' types, both hetero and homo, that hung out there in the 1960s. One of the most noticeable characteristics of the self-ghettoised same-sexer is his perfect indifference to the world of the other-sexers. Although Decter's blood was always at the boil when contemplating these unnatural and immature half-men, they were, I would suspect, serenely unaware of her and her new-class cronies, solemnly worshipping at the shrine of The Family.

To hear Decter tell it, fags had nothing to complain of then, and they have nothing to complain of now: 'Just to name the professions and industries in which they had, and still have, a significant presence is to define the boundaries of a certain kind of privilege: theater, music, letters, dance, design, architecture, the visual arts, fashion at every level—from head, as it were, to foot, and from inception to retail—advertising, journalism, interior decoration, antique dealing, publishing . . . the list could go on.' Yes. But these are all pretty 'soft, marginal' occupations. And none is 'dominated' by fags. Most male same-sexers are laborers, farmers, mechanics, small businessmen, schoolteachers, firemen, policemen, soldiers, sailors. Most female same-sexers are wives and mothers. In other words, they are like the rest of the population. But then it is hard for the new-class person to realise that Manhattan is not the world. Or as a somewhat alarmed Philip Rahv said to me after he had taken a drive across the United States, 'My God! There are so many of them!' In theory, Rahv had always known that there were a couple of hundred million gentiles out there, but to see them, in the flesh, unnerved him. I told him that I was unnerved, too, particularly when they start showering in the Blood of the Lamb.

Decter does concede that homosexuals have probably not 'established much of a presence in basic industry or government service or in such classic [new-classy?] professions as doctoring and lawyering but then for anyone acquainted with them as a group the thought suggests itself that few of them have ever made much effort in these directions'. Plainly, the silly billies are too busy dressing up and dancing the hully-gully to argue a case in court. Decter will be relieved to know that the percentage of same-sexers in the 'classic' activities is almost as high, proportionately, as that of Jews. But a homosexualist in a key position at, let us say, the Department of Labor will be married and living under a good deal of strain because he could be fired if it is known that he likes to have sex with other men.

Decter knows that there have always been homosexual teachers, and she thinks that they should keep quiet about it. But if they keep quiet, they can be blackmailed or fired. Also, a point that would really distress her, a teacher known to be a same-sexer would be a splendid role model for those same-sexers that he—or she—is teaching. Decter would think this an unmitigated evil because men and women were created to breed: but, of course, it would be a perfect good because we have more babies than we know what to do with while we lack, notoriously, useful citizens at ease with themselves. That is what the row over the schools is all about.

Like most members of the new class, Decter accepts without question Freud's line (*Introductory Lectures on Psychoanalysis*) that 'we actually describe a sexual activity as perverse if it has given up the aim of reproduction and pursues the attainment of pleasure as an aim independent of it.' For Freud, perversion was any sexual activity involving 'the abandonment of the reproductive function'. Freud also deplored masturbation as dangerous 'primal affliction'. So did Moses. But then it was Freud's curious task to try to create a rational, quasi-scientific basis for Mosaic law. The result has been not unlike the accomplishments of Freud's great contemporary, the ineffable and inexorable Mary Baker Eddy, whose First Church of Christ Scientist he was able to match with *his* First Temple of Moses Scientist.

Decter says that once faggots have 'ensconced' themselves in certain professions or arts, 'they themselves have engaged in a good deal of disciminatory practices against others. There are businesses and professions [which ones? She is congenitally short of data] in which it is less than easy for a straight, unless he makes the requisite gesture of propitiation to the homosexual in power, to get ahead.' This, of course, was Hitler's original line about the Jews: they had taken over German medicine, teaching, law, journalism. Ruthlessly, they kept out gentiles; lecherously, they demanded sexual favors. 'I simply want to reduce their numbers in these fields,' Hitler told Prince Philip of Hesse. 'I want them proportionate to their overall number in the population.' This was the early solution; the final solution followed with equal logic.

In the 1950s, it was an article of faith in new-class circles that television had been taken over by the fags. Now I happen to have known most of the leading producers of that time and of a dozen, the two who were interested in same-sex activities were both married to women who ... did not drink. Neither man dared mix sex with business. Every now and then an actor would say that he had not got work because he had refused to put out for a faggot producer, but I doubt very much if there was ever any truth to what was to become a bright jack-o'-lantern in the McCarthy *Walpurgisnacht*.

When I was several thousand words into Decter's tirade, I suddenly realised that she does not know what homosexuality is. At some level she may have stumbled, by accident, on a truth that she would never have been able to comprehend in a rational way. Although to have sexual relations with a member of one's own sex is a common and natural activity (currently disapproved of by certain elements in this culture), there is no such thing as a homosexualist any more than there is such a thing as a heterosexualist. That is one of the reasons there has been so much difficulty with nomenclature. Despite John Boswell's attempts to give legitimacy to the word 'gay', it is still a ridiculous word to use as a common identification for Frederick the

Great, Franklin Pangborn and Eleanor Roosevelt. What makes some people prefer same-sex sex derives from whatever impulse or conditioning makes some people prefer other-sex sex. This is so plain that it seems impossible that our Mosaic-Pauline-Freudian society has not yet figured it out. But to ignore the absence of evidence is the basis of true faith.

Decter seems to think that yesteryear's chic and silly boys on the beach and today's socially militant fags are simply, to use her verb, 'adopting' what she calls, in her tastefully appointed English, a lifestyle. On the other hand, 'whatever disciplines it might entail, heterosexuality is not something adopted but something accepted. Its woes—and they have of course nowhere been more exaggerated than in those areas of the culture consciously or unconsciously influenced by the propaganda of homosexuals—are experienced as the woes of life.'

'Propaganda'—another key word. 'Power.' 'Propitiation.' 'Domination.' What *does* the new class dream of?

Decter now moves in the big artillery. Not only are fags silly and a nuisance but they are, in the unrelenting hatred of heterosexuals, given to depicting them in their plays and films and books as a bunch of klutzes, thereby causing truly good men and women to falter— even question—that warm, mature heterosexuality that is so necessary to keeping this country great while allowing new-class persons to make it materially.

Decter is in full cry. Fags are really imitation women. Decter persists in thinking that same-sexers are effeminate, swishy, girlish. It is true that a small percentage of homosexuals is indeed effeminate, just as there are effeminate heterosexuals. I don't know why this is so. No one knows why. Except Decter. She believes that this sort 'of female imitation pointed neither to sympathy with nor flattery of the female principle'. Yet queens of the sort she is writing about tend to get on very well with women. But Decter can only cope with two stereotypes: the boys on the beach, mincing about, and the drab political radicals of gay liberation. The millions of ordinary masculine types are unknown to her because they are not identifiable by voice or walk and, most important, because they have nothing in common with one another except the desire to have same-sex relations. Or, put the other way round, since Lyndon Johnson and Bertrand Russell were both heterosexuals, what character traits did *they* have in common? I should think none at all. So it is with the invisible millions—now becoming less invisible—of same-sexers.

But Decter knows her Freud, and reality may not intrude: 'The desire to escape from the sexual reminder of birth and death, with its threat of paternity—that is, the displacement of oneself by others—was the main underlying desire that sent those Fire Island homosexuals into the arms of other men. Had it been the opposite desire—that is, the positive attraction to the manly—at least half the boutiques, etc.,' would have closed. Decter should take a stroll down San Francisco's Castro Street, where members of the present generation of fags look like off-duty policemen or construction workers. They have embraced the manly. But Freud has spoken. Fags are fags because they adored their mothers and hated their poor, hard-working daddies. It is amazing the credence still given this unproven, unprovable thesis.

Curiously enough, as I was writing these lines, expressing yet again the unacceptable obvious, I ran across Ralph Blumenthal's article in the *New York Times* (25 August), which used 'unpublished letters and growing research into the hidden life of Sigmund Freud' to examine 'Freud's reversal of his theory attributing neurosis in adults to sexual seduction in childhood'. Despite the evidence given by his parents, Freud decided that their memories of molestation were 'phantasies'. He then appropriated from the high culture (a real act of hubris) Oedipus the King, and made him a complex. Freud was much criticised for this theory at the time—particularly by Sandor Ferenczi. Now, as we learn more about Freud (not to mention about the sexual habits of Victorian Vienna as reported in police records), his theory is again under attack. Drs Milton Klein and David Tribich have written a paper titled 'On Freud's Blindness'. They have studied his case histories and observed how he ignored evidence, how 'he looked to the child and only to the child, in uncovering the causes of psychopathology'. Dr Karl Menninger wrote Dr Klein about these findings: 'Why oh why couldn't Freud believe his own ears?' Dr Menninger then noted, 'Seventy-five per cent of the girls we accept at the Villages have been molested in childhood by an adult. And that's today in Kansas! I don't think Vienna in 1900 was any less sophisticated.'

In the same week as Blumenthal's report on the discrediting of the Oedipus complex, researchers at the Kinsey Institute reported (the *Observer,* 30 August) that after studying 979 homosexuals ('the largest sample of homosexuals—black and white, male and female—ever questioned in an academic study') and 477 heterosexuals, they came to the conclusion that family life has nothing to do with sexual preference. Apparently, 'homosexuality is deep-rooted in childhood, may be biological in origin, and simply shows in more and more important ways as a child grows older. It is not a condition which therapy can reverse'. Also, 'homosexual feelings begin as much as three years before any sort of homosexual act, undermining theories that homosexuality is learned through experience'. There goes the teacher-as-seducer-and-perverter myth. Finally, 'Psychoanalysts' theories about smothering mum and absent dad do not stand investigation. Patients may tend to believe that they are true because therapists subtly coach them in the appropriate memories of their family life.'

Some years ago, gay activists came to *Harper's*, where Decter was an editor, to demonstrate against an article by Joseph Epstein, who had announced, 'If I had the power to do so, I would wish homosexuality off the face of the earth.' Well, that's what Hitler had the power to do in Germany, and did—or tried to do. The confrontation at *Harper's* now provides Decter with her theme. She tells us that one of the demonstrators asked, 'Are you aware of how many suicides you may be responsible for in the homosexual community?' I suspect that she is leaving out the context of this somewhat left-field *cri de coeur*. After all, homosexualists have more to fear from murder than suicide. I am sure that the actual conversation had to do with the sort of mischievous effect that Epstein's Hitlerian piece might have had on those fag-baiters who read it.

But Decter slyly zeroes in on the word 'suicide'. She then develops a most unusual thesis. Homosexualists hate themselves to such an extent that they wish to become extinct either through inviting murder or committing suicide. She notes that in a survey of San Francisco's homosexual men, half of them 'claimed to have had sex with at least five hundred people'. This 'bespeaks the obliteration of all experience, if not, indeed, of oneself'. Plainly Decter has a Mosaic paradigm forever in mind and any variation on it is abominable. Most men—homo or hetero—given the opportunity to have sex with 500 different people would do so, gladly; but most men are not going to be given the opportunity by a society that wants them safely married so that they will be docile workers and loyal consumers. It does not suit our rulers to have the proles tomcatting around the way that our rulers do. I can assure Decter that the thirty-fifth president went to bed with more than 500 women and that the well-known . . . but I must not give away the secrets of the old class or the newly-middle-class new class will go into shock.

Meanwhile, according to Decter, 'many homosexuals are nowadays engaged in efforts at self-obliteration . . . there is the appalling rate of suicide among them'. But the rate is not appreciably higher than that for the rest of the population. In any case, most who do commit—or contemplate—suicide do so because they cannot cope in a world where they are, to say the least, second-class citizens. But Decter is now entering uncharted country. She also has a point to make: 'What is undeniable is the increasing longing among the homosexuals to do away with themselves—if not in the actual physical sense then at least spiritually—a longing whose chief emblem, among others, is the leather bars.'

So Epstein will not be obliged to press that button in order to get rid of the fags. They will do it themselves. Decter ought to be pleased by this, but it is not in her nature to be pleased by anything that the same-sexers do. If they get married and have children and swear fealty to the family gods of the new class, their wives will . . . drink. If they live openly with one another, they have fled from women and real life. If they pursue careers in the arts, heteros will have to be on guard against vicious covert assaults on heterosexual values. If they congregate in the fashion business the way that Jews do in psychiatry, they will employ only those heterosexuals who will put out for them.

Decter is appalled by the fag 'takeover' of San Francisco. She tells us about the 'ever deepening resentment of the San Francisco straight community at the homosexuals' defiant displays and power ['power'!] over this city', but five paragraphs later she contradicts herself: 'Having to a very great extent overcome revulsion of common opinion, are they left with some kind of unappeased hunger that only their own feelings of hatefulness can now satisfy?'

There it is. *They are hateful.* They know it. That is why they want to eliminate themselves. 'One thing is certain.' Decter finds a lot of certainty around. 'To become homosexual is a weighty act.' She still has not got the point that one does not choose to have same-sex impulses; one simply has them, as everyone has, to a greater or lesser degree, other-sex impulses. To deny giving physical expression to those desires may be pleasing to Moses and Saint Paul and Freud, but these three rabbis are aberrant figures whose nomadic values are not those of the thousands of other tribes that live or have lived on the planet. Women's and gay liberation are simply small efforts to free men and women from this trio.

Decter writes, 'Taking oneself out of the tides of ordinary mortal existence is not something one does from any longing to think oneself ordinary (but only following a different "life-style").' I don't quite grasp this sentence. Let us move on to the next: 'Gay Lib has been an effort to set the weight of that act at naught, to define homosexuality as nothing more than a casual option among options.' Gay Lib has done just the opposite. After all, people are what they are sexually not through 'adoption' but because that is the way they are structured. Some people do shift about in the course of a life. Also, most of those with same-sex drives do indeed 'adopt' the heterosexual life-style because they don't want to go to prison or to the madhouse or become unemployable. Obviously, there *is* an option but it is a hard one that ought not to be forced on any human being. After all, homosexuality is only important when made so by irrational opponents. In this, as in so much else, the Jewish situation is precisely the same.

Decter now gives us not a final solution so much as a final conclusion: 'In accepting the movement's terms [hardly anyone has, by the way], heterosexuals have only raised to a nearly intolerable height the costs of the homosexuals' flight from normality.' The flight, apparently, is deliberate, a matter of perverse choice, a misunderstanding of daddy, a passion for mummy, a fear of responsibility. Decter threads her clichés like Teclas on a string. 'Faced with the accelerating round of drugs, S-M and suicide, can either the movement or its heterosexual sympathisers imagine they have done anyone a kindness?'

Although the kindness of strangers is much sought after, gay liberation has not got much support from anyone. Natural allies like the Jews are often virulent in their attacks. Blacks in their ghettos, Chicanos in their barrios, and rednecks in their pulpits also have been influenced by the same tribal taboos. That Jews and blacks and Chicanos and rednecks all contribute to the ranks of the same-sexers only increases the madness. But the world of the Decters is a world of perfect illogic.

Herewith the burden of 'The Boys on the Beach': since homosexualists choose to be the way they are out of idle hatefulness, it has been a mistake to allow them to come out of the closet to the extent that they have, but now that they are out (which most are not), they will have no choice but to face up to their essential hatefulness and abnormality and so be driven to kill themselves with promiscuity, drugs, S-M and suicide. Not even the authors of *The Protocols of the Elders of Zion* ever suggested that the Jews, who were so hateful to them, were also hateful to themselves. So Decter has managed to go one step further than the *Protocols'* authors; she is indeed a virtuoso of hate, and thus do pogroms begin.

Tricks is the story of an author—Renaud Camus himself—who has twenty-five sexual encounters in the course of six months. Each of these encounters involves a pick-up. Extrapolating from Camus's sexual vigour at the age of thirty-five, I would suspect that he has already passed the 500 mark and so is completely obliterated as a human being. If he is, he still writes very well indeed. He seems to be having a good time, and he shows no sign of wanting to kill himself, but then that may be a front he's keeping up. I am sure that Decter will be able to tell just how close he is to OD'ing.

From his photograph, Camus appears to have a lot of hair on his chest. I don't know about the shoulders, as they are covered, modestly, with a shirt. Perhaps he is Jewish. Roland Barthes wrote an introduction to *Tricks*. For a time, Barthes was much admired in American academe. But then, a few years ago, Barthes began to write about his same-sexual activities; he is now mentioned a bit less than he was in the days before he came out, as they say.

Barthes notes that Camus's book is a 'text that belongs to literature'. It is not pornographic. It is also not a Homosexual Novel in that there are no deep, anguished chats about homosexuality. In fact, the subject is never mentioned; it just is. Barthes remarks, 'Homosexuality shocks less [well, he is—or was—French], but continues to be interesting; it is still at that stage of excitation where it provokes what might be called feats of discourse [see 'The Boys on the Beach', no mean feat!]. Speaking of homosexuality permits those who aren't to show how open, liberal, and modern they are, and those who are to bear witness, to assume responsibility, to militate. Everyone gets busy, in different ways, whipping it up.' You can say that again! And Barthes does. But with a nice variation. He makes the point that you are never allowed *not* to be categorised. But then, 'say "I am" and you will be socially saved'. Hence the passion for the either/or.

Camus does not set out to give a panoramic view of homosexuality. He comments, in *his* preface, on the variety of homosexual expressions. Although there is no stigma attached to homosexuality in the French intellectual world where, presumably, there is no equivalent of the new class, the feeling among the lower classes is still intense, a memento of the now exhausted (in France) Roman Catholic Church's old dirty work ('I don't understand the French Catholics,' said John Paul II). As a result, many 'refuse to grant their tastes because they live in such circumstances, in such circles, that their desires are not only for themselves inadmissible but inconceivable, unspeakable'.

It is hard to describe a book that is itself a description, and that is what *Tricks* is—a flat, matter-of-fact description of how the narrator meets the tricks, what each says to each other, where they go, how the rooms are furnished, and what the men do. One of the tricks is nuts; a number are very hairy—the narrator has a Decterian passion for the furry; there is a lot of anal and banal sex as well as oral and floral sex. *Frottage* flows. Most of the encounters take place in France, but there is one in Washington, DC, with a black man. There is a good deal of comedy, in the Raymond Roussel manner.

Tricks will give ammunition to those new-class persons and red-neck divines who find promiscuity every bit as abominable as same-sex relations. But that is the way men are when they are given freedom to go about their business unmolested. One current Arab ruler boasts of having ten sexual encounters a day, usually with different women. A diplomat who knows him says that he exaggerates, but not much. Of course, he is a Moslem.

The family, as we know it, is an economic, not a biological, unit. I realise that this is startling news in this culture and at a time when the economics of both East and West require that the nuclear family be, simply, God. But our ancestors did not live as we do. They lived in packs for hundreds of millennia before 'history' began, a mere 5,000 years ago. Whatever social arrangements human society may come up with in the future, it will have to be acknowledged that those children who are needed should be rather more thoughtfully brought up than they are today and that those adults who do not care to be fathers or mothers should be let off the hook. This is beginning, slowly, to dawn. Hence, the rising hysteria in the land. Hence, the concerted effort to deny the human ordinariness of same-sexualists. A recent attempt to portray such a person sympathetically on television was abandoned when the Christers rose up in arms.

Although I would never suggest that Truman Capote's bright wit and sweet charm as a television performer would not have easily achieved for him his present stardom had he been a *hetero*-sexualist, I do know that if he had not existed in his present form, another would have been run up on the old sewing machine because that sort of *persona* must be, for a whole nation, the stereotype of what a fag is. Should some macho film star like Clint Eastwood, say, decide to confess on television that he is really into same-sex sex, the cathode tube would blow a fuse. That could never be allowed. That is all wrong. That is how the Roman Empire fell.

There is not much *angst* in *Tricks*. No one commits suicide—but there is one sad story. A militant leftist friend of Camus's was a teacher in the south of France. He taught fourteen-year-old members of that oldest of all the classes, the exploited laborer. One of his pupils saw him in a fag bar and spread the word. The students began to torment what had been a favorite teacher. 'These are little proles,' he tells Camus, 'and Mediterranean besides—which means they're obsessed by every possible macho myth, and by homosexuality as well. It's all they can think about.' One of the boys, an Arab, followed him down the street, screaming 'Faggot!' 'It was as if he had finally found someone onto whom he could project his resentment, someone he could hold in contempt with complete peace of mind.'

This might explain the ferocity of the new class on the subject. They know that should the bad times return, the Jews will be singled out yet again. Meanwhile, like so many Max Naumanns (Naumann was a German Jew who embraced Nazism), the new class passionately supports our ruling class—from the Chase Manhattan Bank to the Pentagon to the Op-Ed page of the *Wall Street Journal*—while holding in fierce contempt faggots, blacks (see Norman Podhoretz's 'My Negro Problem and Ours', *Commentary*, February 1963), and the poor (see Midge Decter's 'Looting and Liberal Racism', *Commentary*, September 1977). Since these neo-Naumannites are going to be in the same gas chambers as the blacks and the faggots, I would suggest a cease-fire and a common front against the common enemy, whose kindly voice is that of Ronald Reagan and whose less than kindly mind is elsewhere in the boardrooms of the Republic.

Faith, Knowledge, and Peace

ADLAI E. STEVENSON

If I were asked what the greatest danger is today in the conduct of democracy's affairs I suppose I would think first of war—but second, and immediately, of a very different kind of thing—of what seems to me the possibility that we in America are becoming so big, so organised, so institutionalised, so governmentalised—yes, and so standardised—that there is increasing danger that the individual and his precious diversity will get squeezed out completely.

Of freedom as an abstraction, as a concept, as a general principle, I know nothing new or different to say. Pericles stated freedom's character in his Funeral Oration in Athens in 430 B C. And its contemporary hazards and applications have been made pointedly and persuasively plain in enduring volumes written within the year by Elmer Davis, Henry Steele Commager, Erwin Griswold, Walter Lippmann, that brilliant Englishwoman, Barbara Ward, and others.

Freedom—effective freedom—does not exist as a formula which can be written out by some and then used by others. The term itself is used as an argument for everything from absolutism to anarchy. Freedom is not what the government does. It is not something that is either won or lost in the world's capitals or on its battlefields, or that can be preserved by law—except for a moment or two in history's expanse.

The freedom that counts is simply what is in the minds and hearts of millions of free people. It is nothing more than the total of the feelings of people as they are expressed in the way we, the people, deal with our own families and our own neighbors and associates. This is freedom's hope today on the other side of the iron curtain. And, paradoxically, it is part of freedom's danger here at home.

Someone said: 'The world is so big and I am so small, I do not like it, at all, at all.' But if all of us could only realise that *we*, as individuals, are the guardians of this thing called freedom, this 'Holy Light', that we as individuals are its makers, its destroyers, we might get rid of this debilitating illusion that we no longer count in a system of things that has gotten discouragingly big. If we could only realise that all freedom really amounts to is the way *we* think about and treat a non-conforming neighbor, a dissenting teacher, the minority view among us, people of different races and religions, people from the other side of town—then citizenship might become more meaningful, and freedom infinitely more secure.

My first point then may be very simply stated: It is that freedom begins at home. In the current phrase, this precious treasure has to be, by its very nature, a do-it-yourself business.

Yet to recognise freedom as essentially a personal thing is not to disregard the conditions of its endurance in society—of keeping the Holy Light burning. I think of three such primary conditions. Freedom, to change the figure, is a plant which grows only from *knowledge*. It must be watered by *faith*. It will come to leaf and fruit and flower only in the benevolent sunlight of *peace*.

We have long recognised in this country the essentiality of knowledge to freedom. We accept without dissent Jefferson's pronouncement that 'if a people expects to be both ignorant and free, it expects what never was and never will be'. We have accordingly made ourselves perhaps the most literate people in history. Our children go to school; not merely ten per cent of them as in many places; not half of them as in others, but *all* of them. We do a job of opening up to them civilisation's accumulated learning that is a far, far distant goal to most of mankind.

But that knowledge which is the seedbed of freedom is much more than the absence of ignorance, than the memorisation of the accumulated truths, facts, and assumptions which we call learning. It is the capacity for *new* learning that counts, for learning the things which are still unknown, for learning what mistakes we are making, what better answers there are. If knowledge is essential to freedom it is equally true that freedom is essential to learning, to new knowledge—freedom to criticise, to disagree, to dissent, to inquire, even to be wrong, to err in the attempt to be right or to discover truth.

We applaud in the fields of physical science this freedom to look for *new* truth. The whole urge there is to do things differently from the way they have been done before, to assume that old assumptions are wrong, to assert that there are four dimensions where only three have previously been recognised, to unlock particles of matter, and unleash immeasurable forces—to everlastingly probe and penetrate the unknown.

But in social and economic and political relationships our attitude is very different. The work of the heretic, the questioner, in science is applauded; but in society it is different. We grasped eagerly, desperate for the great new thoughts which came from Einstein and Oppenheimer about the relativity of matter, but their views on the relativity of men were suspect and unsafe. We seem to realise too little that the same kind of thinking which split the atom and is now controlling (I hope) the virus which caused polio may be needed to teach us how to control the use of the atom and to stop the virus which causes war.

We must come to the realisation that *new* knowledge, some criticism and some dissent and some new ideas, will be required to level out cycles of our economy, to merge our markets with the world's, to get 'farm surpluses' into empty stomachs, to replace men with machines and swords with plowshares without causing unemployment, and to create a more meaningful place in society for those whose life's work is done.

Our recent inclination to turn upon our thinkers, to sneer at intellectuals and to hold them up to ridicule, to suspect, denounce, and require oaths of them, is not just an attack on their dignity and freedom as individuals. It impairs, too, our hopes for the enlarged freedoms for all of us which could be the product of their unchallenged right to dissent and to explore. It seems so wrong to take a gun this way and blow out our brains.

May I add here just a footnote of further and not unrelated concern about the latter-day emphasis in our schools upon 'the well-adjusted individual'. I'm not coming out in favor of the maladjustment of individuals, but at the same time overemphasis on the 'well-rounded', 'well-adjusted', 'well-balanced' personality seems deliberately designed to breed mental neuters. In actual practice mental neutrality means docile support of the *status quo*. And when students and teachers alike are discouraged from a critical evaluation of society, we are taking a longer step into the Age of Conformity than we may wish.

I have not meant to seem either despondent or critical about our current attitude toward the knowledge element in freedom. It is probably just a feeling that we come so close to our goals in this area that prompts a kind of agonising about our falling short.

But, to move on, if knowledge is freedom's mind, its heart is faith. There must be a moral basis for asserting the worth of the individual, the essentiality of his freedom. This basis is for me, simply the belief that man is the child of God, that he holds within himself some portion of divinity, that he is the instrument for developing the meaningfulness of a divine order.

When we speak of individual freedom we hark back ultimately to the psalmist's words: 'Thou hast made him a little lower than the angels; Thou hast crowned him with glory and honor and hast set him over the work of thy hands.' Isn't this the sense of freedom?

There is cause for concern among freedom's friends, I think, that faith—the heart and meaning of freedom—has become less a part of our everyday life. We profess less, and perhaps share less, the religious faith of an earlier time which bade us love and trust one another—and accordingly respect each other's freedom. I recall that declining faith evoked Matthew Arnold's disheartened lines:

> The Sea of Faith
> Was once, too, at the full, and round earth's shore
> Lay like the folds of a bright girdle furl'd;
> But now I only hear
> Its melancholy long, withdrawing roar . . .

Another poet speaks of 'Freedom's Holy Light'. And it must be a holy light or it will be no light at all. It will glow only in a cherished faith that all men are brothers, and that they are brothers because each contains within himself a spark of the divine. It falls on each of us but only as it is reflected from the countenance of others. It can prosper and wax bright only in a widening dawn of human conscience, an awakening into a time when we become each day a little better able to see ourselves in each other.

But, in the immediate view of it, the keystone, the indispensable ingredient, of liberty is peace.

The international scene is calmer; the music of the doves, albeit a little hoarse and hesitant, has suddenly replaced the harsh words and threatening gestures of a couple of months ago. The days are brighter in Europe, and a softer sun comes up each morning out of China, ''cross the bay', or at least it appears to. For these new tunes here and abroad we are grateful.

Yet to speak of peace in terms of the demands of lasting freedom, to speak of it as members of the human race, is to think today far beyond a stalemate of arms, a cease-fire, a treaty. Peace means today facing squarely into the deadly, hypnotic eye of the hydrogen bomb—facing it and finding the answer. And there is only one sure answer.

With the unlocking of the atom, mankind crossed one of the great watersheds of history. We have entered uncharted lands. The maps of strategy and diplomacy by which we guided ourselves until yesterday no longer reveal the way. Fusion and fission revolutionised the entire foundation of human affairs. It has placed mankind, in the words of Sir Winston Churchill, 'in a situation both measureless and laden with doom'.

The words we use when we talk of this terrible force are so absolute as to be almost meaningless. We say that civilisation cannot survive an atomic war, that there can be no victory and no victors, that

nuclear weapons can annihilate all life on this planet. All these statements are true. But it is nearly impossible for us to understand them.

This scientific revolution in man's capacity for self-destruction
calls for an equivalent revolution in man's capacity for self-preservation and the conduct of our foreign affairs. It will not do to rely
only on the orthodox, time-tried methods of foreign policy which
the great states have used in the past; for war was one of these
methods; and today either war must become obsolete, or mankind
will.

In the long run nothing will meet the needs of the people of our
nation or of the world short of abolishing the very institution of war
as an arbiter of disputes or a tool of annihilation. We must, of course,
continue to preserve and build our alliances, to help free nations gain
strength to preserve their freedom, to develop our own armed
strength—indeed, until the aggressors come to tolerable terms we
must even continue building our own nuclear power.

But this is not enough. To stop here is to dwell still in the house of
the past, with a bomb ticking in the basement. We can no longer rest
contentedly on the framework of the old diplomacy and the old
strategy of preponderant or balanced power. We must move beyond
to that brighter day envisioned just ten years ago when the Nazi
nightmare died and the United Nations came to birth in San Francisco amid great rejoicing. We must resume the attack on the institution of war itself.

Let no one deceive himself about the enormity of this task. The
roots of war lie deep, not only in rivalries among peoples and
conflicts among nations and ideas, but in the dark, tormented depths
of the human heart. To abolish human rivalry and conflict would be a
utopian dream. But to try and make sure that human rivalry and
conflict will not abolish us is just not a possibility: it is an imperative
necessity.

The differences between ourselves and the Communists are great
and terrifying. They will not be easily resolved. I doubt if they will be
resolved in our lifetime. Our effort must be to make sure that their
resolution will take place, not in the old arena, where war was one of
the weapons, but in a new arena, under new rules, in a new spirit.
And the effort must be remorseless.

So, while we cannot yet control the sources of conflict, we can
perhaps, in this new mood of humility and understanding, try to
control the means of our annihilation.

Our national record in this field, I should say, has been a creditable
one. President Truman first proposed a system of enforced disarmament to be administered by the United Nations in 1945. In 1946 and

1950 and 1951 his administration proposed plans for the world-wide control of atomic weapons. In 1953 President Eisenhower affirmed his support for this policy of enforced disarmament. And recently he has named a special assistant to prosecute the search for arms limitation.

All this has been in the right direction. But I wonder if we have yet spelled out clearly to the world that we know that mankind has crossed a great divide, that, compared with the stake of survival, every other interest is minor and every other preoccupation petty. On this great issue, I fear we have too often been perfunctory where we should be passionate, more cynical than zealous, tepid and torpid where we should have dedicated our best energies and our highest purposes. And saber-rattling and bellicose speeches have all too frequently distorted and obscured America's peaceful purposes.

Let this phase be done with forever. Let us instead place effective arms control at the very core of our diplomacy and at the very heart of our communications with other lands. Surely if we could afford a crash program to build the hydrogen bomb, we can afford a crashing effort to control it . . .

What are the chances that we may get somewhere at last in our efforts to prevent a hydrogen war? I don't know. While there are signs that patience and strength are paying off, I have no illusions that our search for peace will succeed easily. Yet, in all conscience, our great nation has no choice other than to use its day of leadership to work remorselessly for peace—to do its best to make sure that the epoch of American power produces, not the final earthly holocaust, but a world of justice, security, and freedom.

Faith, knowledge, and peace—these will be the cornerstones of such a world. And, of these, none will avail if peace is lacking, if an atom split in anger turns out to be mankind's last reality.

Burleigh and his Times

THOMAS BABINGTON, LORD MACAULAY

Memoirs of the Life and Administration of the Right Honourable William Cecil Lord Burghley, Secretary of State in the Reign of King Edward the Sixth, and Lord High Treasurer of England in the Reign of Queen Elizabeth. Containing an Historical View of the Times in which he lived, and of the many eminent and illustrious Persons with whom he was connected; with Extracts from his Private and Official Correspondence and other Papers, now first published from the Originals. By the Reverend Edward Nares, DD, Regius Professor of Modern History in the University of Oxford. London: 1828, 1832.

The work of Dr Nares has filled us with astonishment similar to that which Captain Lemuel Gulliver felt when first he landed in Brobdingnag, and saw corn as high as the oaks in the New Forest, thimbles as large as buckets, and wrens of the bulk of turkeys. The whole book, and every component part of it, is on a gigantic scale. The title is as long as an ordinary preface: the prefatory matter would furnish out an ordinary book; and the book contains as much reading as an ordinary library. We cannot sum up the merits of the stupendous mass of paper which lies before us better than by saying that it consists of about two thousand closely printed quarto pages, that it occupies fifteen hundred inches cubic measure, and that it weighs sixty pounds avoirdupois. Such a book might, before the deluge, have been considered as light reading by Hilpa and Shalum. But unhappily the life of man is now threescore years and ten; and we cannot but think it somewhat unfair in Dr Nares to demand from us so large a portion of so short an existence.

Compared with the labour of reading through these volumes, all other labour, the labour of thieves on the treadmill, of children in factories, of negroes in sugar plantations, is an agreeable recreation. There was, it is said, a criminal in Italy, who was suffered to make his choice between Guicciardini and the galleys. He chose the history. But the war of Pisa was too much for him. He changed his mind, and went to the oar. Guicciardini, though certainly not the most amusing of writers, is a Herodotus or a Froissart, when compared with Dr Nares. It is not merely in bulk, but in specific gravity also, that these memoirs exceed all other human compositions. On every subject which the professor discusses, he produces three times as many pages as another man; and one of his pages is as tedious as another man's three. His book is swelled to its vast dimensions by endless repetitions, by episodes which have nothing to do with the main action, by quotations from books which are in every circulating library, and by reflections which, when they happen to be just, are so obvious that they must necessarily occur to the mind of every reader. He employs more words in expounding and defending a truism than any other writer would employ in supporting a paradox. Of the rules of historical perspective, he has not the faintest notion. There is neither foreground nor background in his delineation. The wars of Charles V in Germany are detailed at almost as much length as in Robertson's life of that prince. The troubles of Scotland are related as fully as in M'Crie's Life of John Knox. It would be most unjust to deny that Dr Nares is a man of great industry and research; but he is so utterly incompetent to arrange the materials which he has collected that he might as well have left them in their original repositories.

Neither the facts which Dr Nares has discovered, nor the arguments which he urges, will, we apprehend, materially alter the opinion generally entertained by judicious readers of history concerning his hero. Lord Burleigh can hardly be called a great man. He was not one of those whose genius and energy change the fate of empires. He was by nature and habit one of those who follow, not one of those who lead. Nothing that is recorded, either of his words or of his actions, indicates intellectual or moral elevation. But his talents, though not brilliant, were of an eminently useful kind; and his principles, though not inflexible, were not more relaxed than those of his associates and competitors. He had a cool temper, a sound judgment, great powers of application, and a constant eye to the main chance. In his youth he was, it seems, fond of practical jokes. Yet even out of these he contrived to extract some pecuniary profit. When he was studying the law at Gray's Inn, he lost all his furniture and books at the gaming table to one of his friends. He accordingly bored a hole in the wall which separated his chambers from those of his associate, and at midnight bellowed through this passage threats of damnation and calls to repentance in the ears of the victorious gambler, who lay sweating with fear all night, and refunded his winnings on his knees next day. 'Many other like the merry jests', says his old biographer, 'I have heard him tell, too long to be here noted.' To the last, Burleigh was somewhat jocose; and some of his sportive sayings have been recorded by Bacon. They show much more shrewdness than generosity, and are, indeed, neatly expressed reasons for exacting money rigorously, and for keeping it carefully. It must, however, be acknowledged that he was rigorous and careful for the public advantage as well as for his own. To extol his moral character as Dr Nares has extolled it is absurd. It would be equally absurd to represent him as a corrupt, rapacious, and bad-hearted man. He paid great attention to the interests of the state, and great attention also to the interest of his own family. He never deserted his friends till it was very inconvenient to stand by them, was an excellent Protestant when it was not very advantageous to be a Papist, recommended a tolerant policy to his mistress as strongly as he could recommend it without hazarding her favour, never put to the rack any person from whom it did not seem probable that useful information might be derived, and was so moderate in his desires that he left only three hundred distinct landed estates, though he might, as his honest servant assures us, have left much more, 'if he would have taken money out of the Exchequer for his own use, as many Treasurers have done'.

Burleigh, like the old Marquess of Winchester, who preceded him in the custody of the White Staff, was of the willow, and not of the oak. He first rose into notice by defending the supremacy of Henry VIII. He was subsequently favoured and promoted by the Duke of Somerset. He not only contrived to escape unhurt when his patron fell, but became an important member of the administration of Northumberland. Dr Nares assures us over and over again that there could have been nothing base in Cecil's conduct on this occasion; for, says he, Cecil continued to stand well with Cranmer. This, we confess, hardly satisfies us. We are much of the mind of Falstaff's tailor. We must have better assurance for Sir John than Bardolph's. We like not the security.

Through the whole course of that miserable intrigue which was carried on round the dying bed of Edward VI, Cecil so bemeaned himself as to avoid, first, the displeasure of Northumberland, and afterwards the displeasure of Mary. He was prudently unwilling to put his hand to the instrument which changed the course of the succession. But the furious Dudley was master of the palace. Cecil, therefore, according to his own account, excused himself from signing as a party, but consented to sign as a witness. It is not easy to describe his dexterous conduct at this most perplexing crisis, in language more appropriate than that which is employed by old Fuller. 'His hand wrote it as secretary of state,' says that quaint writer; 'but his heart consented not thereto. Yea, he openly opposed it;

though at last yielding to the greatness of Northumberland, in an age when it was present drowning not to swim with the stream. But as the philosopher tells us, that, though the planets be whirled about daily from east to west, by the motion of the *primum mobile,* yet have they also a contrary proper motion of their own from west to east, which they slowly, though surely, move at their leisure; so Cecil had secret counter-endeavours against the strain of the court herein, and privately advanced his rightful intentions against the foresaid duke's ambition.'

This was undoubtedly the most perilous conjuncture of Cecil's life. Wherever there was a safe course, he was safe. But here every course was full of danger. His situation rendered it impossible for him to be neutral. If he acted on either side, if he refused to act at all, he ran a fearful risk. He saw all the difficulties of his position. He sent his money and plate out of London, made over his estates to his son, and carried arms about his person. His best arms, however, were his sagacity and his self-command. The plot in which he had been an unwilling accomplice ended, as it was natural that so odious and absurd a plot should end, in the ruin of its contrivers. In the mean time, Cecil quietly extricated himself, and, having been successively patronised by Henry, by Somerset, and by Northumberland, continued to flourish under the protection of Mary.

He had no aspirations after the crown of martyrdom. He confessed himself, therefore, with great decorum, heard mass in Wimbledon Church at Easter, and, for the better ordering of his spiritual concerns, took a priest into his house. Dr Nares, whose simplicity passes that of any casuist with whom we are acquainted, vindicates his hero by assuring us that this was not superstition, but pure unmixed hypocrisy. 'That he did in some manner conform, we shall not be able, in the face of existing documents, to deny; while we feel in our own minds abundantly satisfied, that, during this very trying reign, he never abandoned the prospect of another revolution in favour of Protestantism.' In another place, the doctor tells us, that Cecil went to mass 'with no idolatrous intention'. Nobody, we believe, ever accused him of idolatrous intentions. The very ground of the charge against him is that he had no idolatrous intentions. We never should have blamed him if he had really gone to Wimbledon Church, with the feelings of a good Catholic, to worship the host. Dr Nares speaks in several places with just severity of the sophistry of the Jesuits, and with just admiration of the incomparable letters of Pascal. It is somewhat strange, therefore, that he should adopt, to the full extent, the jesuitical doctrine of the direction of intentions.

We do not blame Cecil for not choosing to be burned. The deep stain upon his memory is that, for differences of opinion for which he would risk nothing himself, he, in the day of his power, took away without scruple the lives of others. One of the excuses suggested in these Memoirs for his conforming, during the reign of Mary, to the Church of Rome, is that he may have been of the same mind with those German Protestants who were called Adiaphorists, and who considered the popish rites as matters indifferent. Melancthon was one of these moderate persons, and 'appears', says Dr Nares, 'to have gone greater lengths than any imputed to Lord Burleigh.' We should have thought this not only an excuse, but a complete vindication, if Cecil had been an Adiaphorist for the benefit of others as well as for his own. If the popish rites were matters of so little moment that a good Protestant might lawfully practise them for his safety, how could it be just or humane that a Papist should be hanged, drawn, and quartered, for practising them from a sense of duty. Unhappily these non-essentials soon became matters of life and death. Just at the very time at which Cecil attained the highest point of power and favour, an Act of Parliament was passed by which the penalties of high treason were denounced against persons who should do in sincerity what he had done from cowardice.

Early in the reign of Mary, Cecil was employed in a mission scarcely consistent with the character of a zealous Protestant. He was sent to escort the Papal Legate, Cardinal Pole, from Brussels to London. That great body of moderate persons who cared more for the quiet of the realm than for the controverted points which were in issue between the churches seem to have placed their chief hope in the wisdom and humanity of the gentle cardinal. Cecil, it is clear, cultivated the friendship of Pole with great assiduity, and received great advantage from the Legate's protection.

But the best protection of Cecil, during the gloomy and disastrous reign of Mary, was that which he derived from his own prudence and from his own temper, a prudence which could never be lulled into carelessness, a temper which could never be irritated into rashness. The Papists could find no occasion against him. Yet he did not lose the esteem even of those sterner Protestants who had preferred exile to recantation. He attached himself to the persecuted heiress of the throne, and entitled himself to her gratitude and confidence. Yet he continued to receive marks of favour from the queen. In the House of Commons, he put himself at the head of the party opposed to the court. Yet, so guarded was his language that, even when some of those who acted with him were imprisoned by the Privy Council, he escaped with impunity.

At length Mary died: Elizabeth succeeded; and Cecil rose at once to greatness. He was sworn in Privy Councillor and Secretary of State to the new sovereign before he left her prison of Hatfield; and he continued to serve her during forty years, without intermission, in the highest employments. His abilities were precisely those which keep men long in power. He belonged to the class of the Walpoles, the Pelhams, and the Liverpools, not to that of the St Johns, the Carterets, the Chathams, and the Cannings. If he had been a man of original genius and of an enterprising spirit, it would have been scarcely possible for him to keep his power or even his head. There was not room in one government for an Elizabeth and a Richelieu. What the haughty daughter of Henry needed, was a moderate, cautious, flexible minister, skilled in the details of business, competent to advise, but not aspiring to command. And such a minister she found in Burleigh. No arts could shake the confidence which she reposed in her old and trusty servant. The courtly graces of Leicester, the brilliant talents and accomplishments of Essex, touched the fancy, perhaps the heart, of the woman; but no rival could deprive the Treasurer of the place which he possessed in the favour of the queen. She sometimes chid him sharply; but he was the man whom she delighted to honour. For Burleigh, she forgot her usual parsimony both of wealth and of dignities. For Burleigh, she relaxed that severe etiquette to which she was unreasonably attached. Every other person to whom she addressed her speech, or on whom the glance of her eagle eye fell, instantly sank on his knee. For Burleigh alone, a chair was set in her presence; and there the old minister, by birth only a plain Lincolnshire esquire, took his ease, while the haughty heirs of the Fitzalans and the De Veres humbled themselves to the dust around him. At length having survived all his early coadjutors, and rivals, he died full of years and honours. His royal mistress visited him on his death-bed, and cheered him with assurances of her affection and esteem; and his power passed, with little diminution, to a son who inherited his abilities, and whose mind had been formed by his counsels.

The life of Burleigh was commensurate with one of the most important periods in the history of the world. It exactly measures the time during which the House of Austria held decided superiority and aspired to universal dominion. In the year in which Burleigh was born, Charles V obtained the imperial crown. In the year in which Burleigh died, the vast designs which had, during near a century, kept Europe in constant agitation, were buried in the same grave with the proud and sullen Philip.

The life of Burleigh was commensurate also with the period during which a great moral revolution was effected, a revolution the consequences of which were felt, not only in the cabinets of princes, but at half the firesides in Christendom. He was born when the great religious schism was just commencing. He lived to see that schism complete, and to see a line of demarcation, which, since his death, has been very little altered, strongly drawn between Protestant and Catholic Europe.

The only event of modern times which can be properly compared with the Reformation is the French Revolution, or, to speak more accurately, that great revolution of political feeling which took place in almost every part of the civilised world during the eighteenth century, and which obtained in France its most terrible and signal triumph. Each of these memorable events may be described as a rising up of the human reason against a caste. The one was a struggle of the laity against the clergy for intellectual liberty; the other was a struggle of the people against princes and nobles for political liberty. In both cases, the spirit of innovation was at first encouraged by the class to which it was likely to be most prejudicial. It was under the patronage of Frederic, of Catherine, of Joseph, and of the grandees of France, that the philosophy which afterwards threatened all the thrones and aristocracies of Europe with destruction first became formidable. The ardour with which men betook themselves to liberal studies, at the close of the fifteenth and the beginning of the sixteenth century, was zealously encouraged by the heads of that very church to which liberal studies were destined to be fatal. In both cases, when the explosion came, it came with a violence which appalled and disgusted many of those who had previously been distinguished by the freedom of their opinions. The violence of the democratic party in France made Burke a Tory and Alfieri a courtier. The violence of the chiefs of the German schism made Erasmus a defender of abuses, and turned the author of *Utopia* into a persecutor. In both cases, the convulsion which had overthrown deeply seated errors, shook all the principles on which society rests to their very foundations. The minds of men were unsettled. It seemed for a time that all order and morality were about to perish with the prejudices with which they had been long and intimately associated. Frightful cruelties were committed. Immense masses of property were confiscated. Every part of Europe swarmed with exiles. In moody and turbulent spirits zeal soured into malignity, or foamed into madness. From the political agitation of the eighteenth century sprang the Jacobins. From the religious agitation of the sixteenth century sprang the Anabaptists. The partisans of Robespierre robbed and murdered in the name of fraternity and equality. The followers of Kniperdoling robbed and murdered in the name of Christian liberty. The feeling of patriotism was, in many parts of Europe, almost wholly extinguished. All the old maxims of foreign policy were changed. Physical boundaries were superseded by moral boundaries. Nations made war on each other with new arms, with arms which no fortifications, however strong by nature or by art, could resist, with arms before which rivers parted like the Jordan, and ramparts fell down like the walls of Jericho. The great masters of fleets and armies were often reduced to confess, like Milton's warlike angel, how hard they found it

To exclude
Spiritual substance with corporeal bar.

Europe was divided, as Greece had been divided during the period concerning which Thucydides wrote. The conflict was not, as it is in ordinary times, between state and state, but between two omnipresent factions, each of which was in some places dominant and in other places oppressed, but which, openly or covertly, carried on their strife in the bosom of every society. No man asked whether another belonged to the same country with himself, but whether he belonged to the same sect. Party-spirit seemed to justify and consecrate acts which, in any other times, would have been considered as the foulest of treasons. The French emigrant saw nothing disgraceful in bringing Austrian and Prussian hussars to Paris. The Irish or Italian democrat saw no impropriety in serying the French Directory against his own native government. So, in the sixteenth century, the fury of theological factions suspended all national animosities and jealousies. The Spaniards were invited into France by the League; the English were invited into France by the Huguenots.

We by no means intend to underrate or to palliate the crimes and excesses which, during the last generation, were produced by the spirit of democracy. But, when we hear men zealous for the Protestant religion constantly represent the French Revolution as radically and essentially evil on account of those crimes and excesses, we cannot but remember that the deliverance of our ancestors from the house of their spiritual bondage was effected 'by plagues and by signs, by wonders and by war'. We cannot but remember that, as in the case of the French Revolution, so also in the case of the Reformation, those who rose up against tyranny were themselves deeply tainted with the vices which tyranny engenders. We cannot but remember that libels scarcely less scandalous than those of Hebert, mummeries scarcely less absurd than those of Clootz, and crimes scarcely less atrocious than those of Marat, disgrace the early history of Protestantism. The Reformation is an event long past. That volcano has spent its rage. The wide waste produced by its outbreak is forgotten. The landmarks which were swept away have been replaced. The ruined edifices have been repaired. The lava has covered with a rich incrustation the fields which it once devastated, and, after having turned a beautiful and fruitful garden into a desert, has again turned the desert into a still more beautiful and fruitful garden. The second great eruption is not yet over. The marks of its ravages are still around us. The ashes are still hot beneath our feet. In some directions, the deluge of fire still continues to spread. Yet experience surely entitles us to believe that this explosion, like that which preceded it, will fertilise the soil which it has devastated. Already, in those parts which have suffered most severely, rich cultivation and secure dwellings have begun to appear amidst the waste. The more we read of the history of past ages, the more we observe the signs of our own times, the more do we feel our hearts filled and swelled up by a good hope for the future destinies of the human race.

The history of the Reformation in England is full of strange problems. The most prominent and extraordinary phenomenon which it presents to us is the gigantic strength of the government contrasted with the feebleness of the religious parties. During the twelve or thirteen years which followed the death of Henry VIII, the religion of the state was thrice changed. Protestantism was established by Edward; the Catholic Church was restored by Mary; Protestantism was again established by Elizabeth. The faith of the nation seemed to depend on the personal inclinations of the sovereign. Nor was this all. An established church was then, as a matter of course, a persecuting church. Edward persecuted Catholics. Mary persecuted Protestants. Elizabeth persecuted Catholics again. The father of those three sovereigns had enjoyed the pleasure of persecuting both sects at once, and had sent to death, on the same hurdle, the heretic who denied the real presence, and the traitor who denied the royal supremacy. There was nothing in England like that fierce and bloody opposition which, in France, each of the religious factions in its turn offered to the government. We had neither a Coligny nor a Mayenne, neither a Moncontour nor an Ivry. No English city braved sword and famine for the reformed doctrines with the spirit of Rochelle, or for the Catholic doctrines with the spirit of Paris. Neither sect in England formed a League. Neither sect extorted a recantation from the sovereign. Neither sect could obtain from an adverse sovereign even a toleration. The English Protestants, after several years of domination, sank down with scarcely a struggle under the tyranny of Mary. The Catholics, after having regained and abused their old ascendency, submitted patiently to the severe rule of Elizabeth. Neither Protestants nor Catholics engaged in any great and well organised scheme of resistance. A few wild and tumultuous risings, suppressed as soon as they appeared, a few dark conspiracies in which only a small number of desperate men engaged, such were the utmost efforts made by these two parties to assert the most sacred of human rights, attacked by the most odious tyranny.

The explanation of these circumstances which has generally been given is very simple, but by no means satisfactory. The power of the crown, it is said, was then at its height, and was in fact despotic. This solution, we own, seems to us to be no solution at all. It has long been the fashion, a fashion introduced by Mr Hume, to describe the English monarchy in the sixteenth century as an absolute monarchy. And such undoubtedly it appears to a superficial observer. Elizabeth, it is true, often spoke to her parliaments in language as haughty and imperious as that which the Great Turk would use to his divan. She punished with great severity members of the House of Commons who, in her opinion, carried the freedom of debate too far. She assumed the power of legislating by means of proclamations. She imprisoned her subjects without bringing them to a legal trial. Torture was often employed, in defiance of the laws of England, for the purpose of extorting confessions from those who were shut up in her dungeons. The authority of the Star Chamber and of the Ecclesiastical Commission was at its highest point. Severe restraints were imposed on political and religious discussion. The number of presses was at one time limited. No man could print without a licence; and every work had to undergo the scrutiny of the Primate, or the Bishop of London. Persons whose writings were displeasing to the court were cruelly mutilated, like Stubbs, or put to death, like Penry. Nonconformity was severely punished. The queen prescribed the exact rule of religious faith and discipline; and whoever departed from that rule, either to the right or to the left, was in danger of severe penalties.

Such was this government. Yet we know that it was loved by the great body of those who lived under it. We know that, during the fierce contests of the sixteenth century, both the hostile parties spoke of the time of Elizabeth as of a golden age. That great queen has now been lying two hundred and thirty years in Henry VII's chapel. Yet her memory is still dear to the hearts of a free people.

The truth seems to be that the government of the Tudors was, with a few occasional deviations, a popular government, under the forms of despotism. At first sight, it may seem that the prerogatives of Elizabeth were not less ample than those of Louis XIV, and her parliaments were as obsequious as his parliaments, that her warrant had as much authority as his *lettre-de-cachet*. The extravagance with which her courtiers eulogised her personal and mental charms went beyond the adulation of Boileau and Molière. Louis would have blushed to receive from those who composed the gorgeous circles of Marli and Versailles such outward marks of servitude as the haughty Britoness exacted of all who approached her. But the authority of Louis rested on the support of his army. The authority of Elizabeth rested solely on the support of her people. Those who say that her power was absolute do not sufficiently consider in what her power consisted. Her power consisted in the willing obedience of her sub-jects, in their attachment to her person and to her office, in their respect for the old line from which she sprang, in their sense of the general security which they enjoyed under her government. These were the means, and the only means, which she had at her command for carrying her decrees into execution, for resisting foreign enemies, and for crushing domestic treason. There was not a ward in the city, there was not a hundred in any shire in England, which could not have overpowered the handful of armed men who composed her household. If a hostile sovereign threatened invasion, if an ambitious noble raised the standard of revolt, she could have recourse only to the train-bands of her capital and the array of her counties, to the citizens and yeomen of England, commanded by the merchants and esquires of England.

Thus, when intelligence arrived of the vast preparations which Philip was making for the subjugation of the realm, the first person to whom the government thought of applying for assistance was the Lord Mayor of London. They sent to ask him what force the city would engage to furnish for the defence of the kingdom against the Spaniards. The mayor and Common Council, in return, desired to know what force the Queen's Highness wished them to furnish. The answer was, fifteen ships and five thousand men. The Londoners deliberated on the matter, and, two days after, 'humbly intreated the council, in sign of their perfect love and loyalty to prince and country, to accept ten thousand men, and thirty ships amply furnished.'

People who could give such signs as these of their loyalty were by no means to be misgoverned with impunity. The English in the sixteenth century were, beyond all doubt, a free people. They had not, indeed, the outward show of freedom; but they had the reality. They had not as good a constitution as we have; but they had that without which the best constitution is as useless as the king's procla-mation against vice and immorality, that which, without any consti-tution, keeps rulers in awe, force, and the spirit to use it. Parliaments, it is true, were rarely held, and were not very respectfully treated. The great charter was often violated. But the people had a security against gross and systematic misgovernment, far stronger than all the parchment that was ever marked with the sign manual, and than all the wax that was ever pressed by the great seal.

It is a common error in politics to confound means with ends. Constitutions, charters, petitions of right, declarations of right, representative assemblies, electoral colleges, are not good government; nor do they, even when most elaborately constructed, necessarily produce good government. Laws exist in vain for those who have not the courage and the means to defend them. Electors meet in vain where want makes them the slaves of the landlord, or where superstition makes them the slaves of the priest. Representative assemblies sit in vain unless they have at their command, in the last resort, the physical power which is necessary to make their deliberations free, and their votes effectual.

The Irish are better represented in parliament than the Scotch, who indeed are not represented at all.* But are the Irish better governed than the Scotch? Surely not. This circumstance has of late been used as an argument against reform. It proves nothing against reform. It proves only this, that laws have no magical, no supernatural virtue; that laws do not act like Aladdin's lamp or Prince Ahmed's apple; that priestcraft, that ignorance, that the rage of contending factions, may make good institutions useless; that intelligence, sobriety, industry, moral freedom, firm union, may supply in a great measure the defects of the worst representative system. A people whose education and habits are such, that, in every quarter of the world, they rise above the mass of those with whom they mix, as surely as oil rises to the top of water, a people of such temper and self-government that the wildest popular excesses recorded in their history partake of the gravity of judicial proceedings, and of the solemnity of religious rites, a people whose national pride and mutual attachment have passed into a proverb, a people whose high and fierce spirit, so forcibly described in the haughty motto which encircles their thistle, preserved their independence, during a struggle of centuries, from the encroachments of wealthier and more powerful neighbours, such a people cannot be long oppressed. Any government, however constituted, must respect their wishes and tremble at their discontents. It is indeed most desirable that such a people should exercise a direct influence on the conduct of affairs, and should make their wishes known through

* It must be remembered that this was written before the passing of the Reform Act.

constitutional organs. But some influence, direct or indirect, they will assuredly possess. Some organ, constitutional or unconstitutional, they will assuredly find. They will be better governed under a good constitution than under a bad constitution. But they will be better governed under the worst constitution than some other nations under the best. In any general classification of constitutions, the constitution of Scotland must be reckoned as one of the worst, perhaps as the worst, in Christian Europe. Yet the Scotch are not ill governed. And the reason is simply that they will not bear to be ill governed.

In some of the Oriental monarchies, in Afghanistan for example, though there exists nothing which an European publicist would call a Constitution, the sovereign generally governs in conformity with certain rules established for the public benefit; and the sanction of those rules is, that every Afghan approves them, and that every Afghan is a soldier.

The monarchy of England in the sixteenth century was a monarchy of this kind. It is called an absolute monarchy, because little respect was paid by the Tudors to those institutions which we have been accustomed to consider as the sole checks on the power of the sovereign. A modern Englishman can hardly understand how the people can have had any real security for good government under kings who levied benevolences, and chid the House of Commons as they would have chid a pack of dogs. People do not sufficiently consider that, though the legal checks were feeble, the natural checks were strong. There was one great and effectual limitation on the royal authority, the knowledge that, if the patience of the nation were severely tried, the nation would put forth its strength, and that its strength would be found irresistible. If a large body of Englishmen became thoroughly discontented, instead of presenting requisitions, holding large meetings, passing resolutions, signing petitions, forming associations and unions, they rose up; they took their halberds and their bows; and, if the sovereign was not sufficiently popular to find among his subjects other halberds and other bows to oppose to the rebels, nothing remained for him but a repetition of the horrible scenes of Berkeley and Pomfret. He had no regular army which could, by its superior arms and its superior skill, overawe or vanquish the sturdy Commons of his realm, abounding in the native hardihood of Englishmen, and trained in the simple discipline of the militia.

It has been said that the Tudors were as absolute as the Caesars. Never was parallel so unfortunate. The government of the Tudors was the direct opposite to the government of Augustus and his successors. The Caesars ruled despotically, by means of a great standing army, under the decent forms of a republican constitution. They called themselves citizens. They mixed unceremoniously with other citizens. In theory they were only the elective magistrates of a free commonwealth. Instead of arrogating to themselves despotic power, they acknowledged allegiance to the senate. They were merely the lieutenants of that venerable body. They mixed in debate. They even appeared as advocates before the courts of law. Yet they could safely indulge in the wildest freaks of cruelty and rapacity, while their legions remained faithful. Our Tudors, on the other hand, under the titles and forms of monarchical supremacy, were essentially popular magistrates. They had no means of protecting themselves against the public hatred; and they were therefore compelled to court the public favour. To enjoy all the state and all the personal indulgences of absolute power, to be adored with Oriental prostrations, to dispose at will of the liberty and even of the life of ministers and courtiers, this the nation granted to the Tudors. But the condition on which they were suffered to be the tyrants of Whitehall was that they should be the mild and paternal sovereigns of England. They were under the same restraints with regard to their people under which a military despot is placed with regard to his army. They would have found it as dangerous to grind their subjects with cruel taxation as Nero would have found it to leave his praetorians unpaid. Those who inmmediately surrounded the royal person, and engaged in the hazardous game of ambition, were exposed to the most fearful dangers. Buckingham, Cromwell, Surrey, Seymour of Sudeley, Somerset, Northumberland, Suffolk, Norfolk, Essex, perished on the scaffold. But in general the country gentleman hunted and the merchant traded in peace. Even Henry, as cruel as Domitian, but far more politic, contrived, while reeking with the blood of the Lamiae, to be a favourite with the cobblers.

The Tudors committed very tyrannical acts. But in their ordinary dealings with the people they were not, and could not safely be, tyrants. Some excesses were easily pardoned. For the nation was proud of the high and fiery blood of its magnificent princes, and saw, in many proceedings which a lawyer would even then have condemned, the outbreak of the same noble spirit which so manfully hurled foul scorn at Parma and at Spain. But to this endurance there was a limit. If the government ventured to adopt measures which the people really felt to be oppressive, it was soon compelled to change its course. When Henry VIII attempted to raise a forced loan of unusual amount by proceedings of unusual rigour, the opposition which he encountered was such as appalled even his stubborn and imperious spirit. The people, we are told, said that, if they were treated thus, 'then were it worse than the taxes of France; and England should be bond, and not free'. The county of Suffolk rose in arms. The King prudently yielded to an opposition which, if he had persisted, would, in all probability, have taken the form of a general rebellion. Towards the close of the reign of Elizabeth, the people felt themselves aggrieved by the monopolies. The queen, proud and courageous as she was, shrank from a contest with the nation, and, with admirable sagacity, conceded all that her subjects had demanded, while it was yet in her power to concede with dignity and grace.

It cannot be imagined that a people who had in their own hands the means of checking their princes would suffer any prince to impose upon them a religion generally detested. It is absurd to suppose that, if the nation had been decidedly attached to the Protestant faith, Mary could have re-established the Papal supremacy. It is equally absurd to suppose that, if the nation had been zealous for the ancient religion, Elizabeth could have restored the Protestant Church. The truth is, that the people were not disposed to engage in a struggle either for the new or for the old doctrines. Abundance of spirit was shown when it seemed likely that Mary would resume her father's grants of church property, or that she would sacrifice the interests of England to the husband whom she regarded with unmerited tenderness. That queen found that it would be madness to attempt the restoration of the abbey lands. She found that her subjects would never suffer her to make her hereditary kingdom a fief of Castile. On these points she encountered a steady resistance, and was compelled to give way. If she was able to establish the Catholic worship and to persecute those who would not conform to it, it was evidently because the people cared far less for the Protestant religion than for the rights of property and for the independence of the English crown. In plain words, they did not think the difference between the hostile sects worth a struggle. There was undoubtedly a zealous Protestant party and a zealous Catholic party. But both these parties were, we believe, very small. We doubt, whether both together made up, at the time of Mary's death, the twentieth part of the nation. The remaining nineteen-twentieths halted between the two opinions, and were not disposed to risk a revolution in the government, for the purpose of giving to either of the extreme factions an advantage over the other.

We possess no data which will enable us to compare with exactness the force of the two sects. Mr Butler asserts that, even at the accession of James I, a majority of the population of England were Catholics. This is pure assertion; and is not only unsupported by evidence, but, we think, completely disproved by the strongest evidence. Dr

Lingard is of opinion that the Catholics were one-half of the nation in the middle of the reign of Elizabeth. Rushton says that, when Elizabeth came to the throne, the Catholics were two-thirds of the nation, and the Protestants only one-third. The most judicious and impartial of English historians, Mr Hallam, is, on the contrary, of opinion, that two-thirds were Protestants, and only one-third Catholics. To us, we must confess, it seems incredible that, if the Protestants were really two to one, they should have borne the government of Mary, or that, if the Catholics were really two to one, they should have borne the government of Elizabeth. We are at a loss to conceive how a sovereign who has no standing army, and whose power rests solely on the loyalty of his subjects, can continue for years to persecute a religion to which the majority of his subjects are sincerely attached. In fact, the Protestants did rise up against one sister, and the Catholics against the other. Those risings clearly showed how small and feeble both the parties were. Both in the one case and in the other the nation ranged itself on the side of the government, and the insurgents were speedily put down and punished. The Kentish gentlemen who took up arms for the reformed doctrines against Mary, and the great northern earls who displayed the banner of the Five Wounds against Elizabeth, were alike considered by the great body of their countrymen as wicked disturbers of the public peace.

The account which Cardinal Bentivoglio gave of the state of religion in England well deserves consideration. The zealous Catholics he reckoned at one-thirtieth part of the nation. The people who would without the least scruple become Catholics, if the Catholic religion were established, he estimated at four-fifths of the nation. We believe this account to have been very near the truth. We believe that the people, whose minds were made up on either side, who were inclined to make any sacrifice or run any risk for either religion, were very few. Each side had a few enterprising champions, and a few stout-hearted martyrs; but the nation, undetermined in its opinions and feelings, resigned itself implicitly to the guidance of the government, and lent to the sovereign for the time being an equally ready aid against either of the extreme parties.

We are very far from saying that the English of that generation were irreligious. They held firmly those doctrines which are common to the Catholic and to the Protestant theology. But they had no fixed opinion as to the matters in dispute between the churches. They were in a situation resembling that of those Borderers whom Sir Walter Scott has described with so much spirit,

Who sought the beeves that made their broth

In England and in Scotland both.

And who

Nine times outlawed had been
By England's king and Scotland's queen.

They were sometimes Protestants, sometimes Catholics; sometimes half Protestants half Catholics.

The English had not, for ages, been bigoted Papists. In the fourteenth century, the first and perhaps the greatest of the reformers, John Wickliffe, had stirred the public mind to its inmost depths. During the same century, a scandalous schism in the Catholic Church had diminished, in many parts of Europe, the reverence in which the Roman pontiffs were held. It is clear that, a hundred years before the time of Luther, a great party in this kingdom was eager for a change at least as extensive as that which was subsequently effected by Henry VIII. The House of Commons, in the reign of Henry IV, proposed a confiscation of ecclesiastical property, more sweeping and violent even than that which took place under the administration of Thomas Cromwell; and, though defeated in this attempt, they succeeded in depriving the clerical order of some of its most oppressive privileges. The splendid conquests of Henry V turned the attention of the nation from domestic reform. The Council of Constance removed some of the grossest of those scandals which had deprived the Church of the public respect. The authority of that venerable synod propped up the sinking authority of the Popedom. A considerable reaction took place. It cannot, however, be doubted, that there was still some concealed Lollardism in England; or that many who did not absolutely dissent from any doctrine held by the Church of Rome were jealous of the wealth and power enjoyed by her ministers. At the very beginning of the reign of Henry VIII, a struggle took place between the clergy and the courts of law, in which the courts of law remained victorious. One of the bishops, on that occasion, declared that the common people entertained the strongest prejudices against his order, and that a clergyman had no chance of fair play before a lay tribunal. The London juries, he said, entertained such a spite to the Church that, if Abel were a priest, they would find him guilty of the murder of Cain. This was said a few months before the time when Martin Luther began to preach at Wittenburg against indulgences.

As the Reformation did not find the English bigoted Papists, so neither was it conducted in such a manner as to make them zealous Protestants. It was not under the direction of men like that fiery

Saxon who swore that he would go to Worms, though he had to face as many devils as there were tiles on the houses, or like that brave Switzer who was struck down while praying in front of the ranks of Zurich. No preacher of religion had the same power here which Calvin had at Geneva and Knox in Scotland. The government put itself early at the head of the movement, and thus acquired power to regulate, and occasionally to arrest, the movement.

To many persons it appears extraordinary that Henry VIII should have been able to maintain himself so long in an intermediate position between the Catholic and Protestant parties. Most extraordinary it would indeed be, if we were to suppose that the nation consisted of none but decided Catholics and decided Protestants. The fact is that the great mass of the people was neither Catholic nor Protestant, but was, like its sovereign, midway between the two sects. Henry, in that very part of his conduct which has been represented as most capricious and inconsistent, was probably following a policy far more pleasing to the majority of his subjects than a policy like that of Edward, or a policy like that of Mary, would have been. Down even to the very close of the reign of Elizabeth, the people were in a state somewhat resembling that in which, as Machiavelli says, the inhabitants of the Roman Empire were, during the transition from heathenism to Christianity; *'sendo la maggior parte di loro incerti a quale Dio dovessero ricorrere.'* They were generally, we think, favourable to the royal supremacy. They disliked the policy of the Court of Rome. Their spirit rose against the interference of a foreign priest with their national concerns. The bull which pronounced sentence of deposition against Elizabeth, the plots which were formed against her life, the usurpation of her titles by the Queen of Scotland, the hostility of Philip, excited their strongest indignation. The cruelties of Bonner were remembered with disgust. Some parts of the new system, the use of the English language, for example, in public worship, and the communion in both kinds, were undoubtedly popular. On the other hand, the early lessons of the nurse and the priest were not forgotten. The ancient ceremonies were long remembered with affectionate reverence. A large portion of the ancient theology lingered to the last in the minds which had been imbued with it in childhood.

The best proof that the religion of the people was of this mixed kind is furnished by the drama of that age. No man would bring unpopular opinions prominently forward in a play intended for representation. And we may safely conclude, that feelings and opinions which pervade the whole dramatic literature of a generation, are feelings and opinions of which the men of that generation generally partook.

The greatest and most popular dramatists of the Elizabethan age treat religious subjects in a very remarkable manner. They speak respectfully of the fundamental doctrines of Christianity. But they speak neither like Catholics nor like Protestants, but like persons who are wavering between the two systems, or who have made a system for themselves out of parts selected from both. They seem to hold some of the Romish rites and doctrines in high respect. They treat the vow of celibacy, for example, so tempting, and, in later times, so common a subject for ribaldry, with mysterious reverence. Almost every member of a religious order whom they introduce is a holy and venerable man. We remember in their plays nothing resembling the coarse ridicule with which the Catholic religion and its ministers were assailed, two generations later, by dramatists who wished to please the multitude. We remember no Friar Dominic, no Father Foigard, among the characters drawn by those great poets. The scene at the close of the *Knight of Malta* might have been written by a fervent Catholic. Massinger shows a great fondness for ecclesiastics of the Romish Church, and has even gone so far as to bring a virtuous and interesting Jesuit on the stage. Ford, in that fine play which it is painful to read and scarcely decent to name, assigns a highly creditable part to the Friar. The partiality of Shakspeare for friars is well known. In *Hamlet*, the Ghost complains that he died without extreme unction, and, in defiance of the article which condemns the doctrine of purgatory, declares that he is

> *Confined to fast in fires,*
> *Till the foul crimes, done in his days of nature,*
> *Are burnt and purged away.*

These lines, we suspect, would have raised a tremendous storm in the theatre at any time during the reign of Charles II. They were clearly not written by a zealous Protestant, or for zealous Protestants. Yet the author of *King John* and *Henry VIII* was surely no friend to papal supremacy.

There is, we think, only one solution of the phenomena which we find in the history and in the drama of that age. The religion of the English was a mixed religion, like that of the Samaritan settlers, described in the Second Book of Kings, who 'feared the Lord, and served their graven images'; like that of the Judaising Christians who blended the ceremonies and doctrines of the synagogue with those of the church; like that of the Mexican Indians, who, during many generations after the subjugation of their race, continued to unite with the rites learned from their conquerors the worship of the grotesque idols which had been adored by Montezuma and Guatemozin.

These feelings were not confined to the populace. Elizabeth herself was by no means exempt from them. A crucifix, with wax-lights burning round it, stood in her private chapel. She always spoke with disgust and anger of the marriage of priests. 'I was in horror', says Archbishop Parker, 'to hear such words to come from her mild nature and Christian learned conscience, as she spake concerning God's holy ordinance and institution of matrimony.' Burleigh prevailed on her to connive at the marriages of churchmen. But she would only connive; and the children sprung from such marriages were illegitimate till the accession of James I.

That which is, as we have said, the great stain on the character of Burleigh is also the great stain on the character of Elizabeth. Being herself an Adiaphorist, having no scruple about conforming to the Romish Church when conformity was necessary to her own safety, retaining to the last moment of her life a fondness for much of the doctrine and much of the ceremonial of that church, she yet subjected that church to a persecution even more odious than the persecution with which her sister had harassed the Protestants. We say more odious. For Mary had at least the plea of fanaticism. She did nothing for her religion which she was not prepared to suffer for it. She had held it firmly under persecution. She fully believed it to be essential to salvation. If she burned the bodies of her subjects, it was in order to rescue their souls. Elizabeth had no such pretext. In opinion, she was little more than half a Protestant. She had professed, when it suited her, to be wholly a Catholic. There is an excuse, a wretched excuse, for the massacres of Piedmont and the *autos da fe* of Spain. But what can be said in defence of a ruler who is at once indifferent and intolerant?

If the great queen, whose memory is still held in just veneration by Englishmen, had possessed sufficient virtue and sufficient enlargement of mind to adopt those principles which More, wiser in speculation than in action, had avowed in the preceding generation, and by which the excellent L'Hospital regulated his conduct in her own time, how different would be the colour of the whole history of the last two hundred and fifty years! She had the happiest opportunity ever vouchsafed to any sovereign of establishing perfect freedom of conscience throughout her dominions, without danger to her government, without scandal to any large party among her subjects. The nation, as it was clearly ready to profess either religion, would, beyond all doubt, have been ready to tolerate both. Unhappily for her own glory and for the public peace, she adopted a policy from the effects of which the empire is still suffering. The yoke of the Established Church was pressed down on the people till they would bear it no longer. Then a reaction came. Another reaction followed. To the tyranny of the establishment succeeded the tumultuous conflict of sects, infuriated by manifold wrongs, and drunk with unwonted freedom. To the conflict of sects succeeded again the cruel domination of one persecuting church. At length oppression put off its most horrible form, and took a milder aspect. The penal laws which had been framed for the protection of the Established Church were abolished. But exclusions and disabilities still remained. These exclusions and disabilities, after having generated the most fearful discontents, after having rendered all government in one part of the kingdom impossible, after having brought the state to the very brink of ruin, have, in our times, been removed, but, though removed, have left behind them a rankling which may last for many years. It is melancholy to think with what ease Elizabeth might have united all conflicting sects under the shelter of the same impartial laws and the same paternal throne, and thus have placed the nation in the same situation, as far as the rights of conscience are concerned, in which we at last stand, after all the heart-burnings, the persecutions, the conspiracies, the seditions, the revolutions, the judicial murders, the civil wars, of ten generations.

This is the dark side of her character. Yet she surely was a great woman. Of all the sovereigns who exercised a power which was seemingly absolute, but which in fact depended for support on the love and confidence of their subjects, she was by far the most illustrious. It has often been alleged as an excuse for the misgovernment of her successors that they only followed her example, that precedents might be found in the transactions of her reign for persecuting the Puritans, for levying money without the sanction of the House of Commons, for confining men without bringing them to trial, for interfering with the liberty of parliamentary debate. All this may be true. But it is no good plea for her successors; and for this plain reason, that they were her successors. She governed one generation, they governed another; and between the two generations there was almost as little in common as between the people of two different countries. It was not by looking at the particular measures which Elizabeth had adopted, but by looking at the great general principles of her government, that those who followed her were likely to learn the art of managing untractable subjects. If, instead of searching the records of her reign for precedents which might seem to vindicate the mutilation of Prynne and the imprisonment of Eliot, the Stuarts had attempted to discover the fundamental rules which guided her conduct in all her dealings with her people, they would have perceived that their policy was then most unlike to hers, when to a superficial observer it would have seemed most to resemble hers. Firm, haughty, sometimes unjust and cruel, in her proceedings towards individuals or towards small parties, she avoided with care, or retracted with speed, every measure which seemed likely to alienate the great mass of the people. She gained more honour and more love by the manner in which she repaired her errors than she would have gained by never committing errors. If such a man as Charles I had been in her place when the whole nation was crying out against the monopolies, he would have refused all redress. He would have dissolved the parliament, and imprisoned the most popular members. He would have called another parliament. He would have given some vague and delusive promises of relief in return for subsidies. When entreated to fulfil his promises, he would have again dissolved the parliament, and again imprisoned his leading opponents. The country would have become more agitated than before. The next House of Commons would have been more unmanageable than that which preceded it. The tyrant would have agreed to all that the nation demanded. He would have solemnly ratified an act abolishing monopolies for ever. He would have received a large supply in return for this concession; and within half a year new patents, more oppressive than those which had been cancelled, would have been issued by scores. Such was the policy which brought the heir of a long line of kings, in early youth the darling of his countrymen, to a prison and a scaffold.

Elizabeth, before the House of Commons could address her, took out of their mouths the words which they were about to utter in the name of the nation. Her promises went beyond their desires. Her performance followed close upon her promise. She did not treat the nation as an adverse party, as a party which had an interest opposed to hers, as a party to which she was to grant as few advantages as possible, and from which she was to extort as much money as possible. Her benefits were given, not sold; and, when once given, they were never withdrawn. She gave them too with a frankness, an effusion of heart, a princely dignity, a motherly tenderness, which enhanced their value. They were received by the sturdy country gentlemen who had come up to Westminster full of resentment, with tears of joy, and shouts of 'God save the Queen'. Charles I gave up half the prerogatives of his crown to the Commons; and the Commons sent him in return the Grand Remonstrance.

We had intended to say something concerning that illustrious group

435

of which Elizabeth is the central figure, that group which the last of the bards saw in vision from the top of Snowdon, encircling the Virgin Queen,

> Many a baron bold,
> And gorgeous dames, and statesmen old
> In bearded majesty.

We had intended to say something concerning the dexterous Walsingham, the impetuous Oxford, the graceful Sackville, the all-accomplished Sydney; concerning Essex, the ornament of the court and of the camp, the model of chivalry, the munificent patron of genius, whom great virtues, great courage, great talents, the favour of his sovereign, the love of his countrymen, all that seemed to ensure a happy and glorious life, led to an early and an ignominious death; concerning Raleigh, the soldier, the sailor, the scholar, the courtier, the orator, the poet, the historian, the philosopher, whom we picture to ourselves, sometimes reviewing the queen's guard, sometimes giving chase to a Spanish galleon, then answering the chiefs of the country party in the House of Commons, then again murmuring one of his sweet love-songs too near the ears of her highness's maids of honour, and soon after poring over the Talmud, or collating Polybius with Livy. We had intended also to say something concerning the literature of that splendid period, and especially concerning those two incomparable men, the Prince of Poets, and the Prince of Philosophers, who have made the Elizabethan age a more glorious and important era in the history of the human mind than the age of Pericles, of Augustus, or of Leo. But subjects so vast require a space far longer than we can at present afford. We therefore stop here, fearing that, if we proceed, our article may swell to a bulk exceeding that of all other reviews, as much as Dr Nares's book exceeds the bulk of all other histories.

Enoch Powell

MICHAEL FOOT

All political lives, unless they are cut off in midstream at a happy juncture,
end in failure, because that is the nature of politics and of human affairs. The
career of Joseph Chamberlain was not an exception.

> Enoch Powell, in his *Joseph Chamberlain*
> (Thames & Hudson 1977)

Some of these reflections were first prompted by Roy Lewis's book *Enoch
Powell—Principle in Politics*, published by Cassell in 1979, but avuncular
sentiment and candour also make me recommend *The Rise of Enoch Powell*
by Paul Foot, published by Penguin in 1969.

I was astonished to discover that the word 'loner' had not found its
way into the *Oxford English Dictionary*, that final determinant of
political fashion, until the very last edition published in 1982. I had
thought that there had always been 'loners' at work in our political
system, men and women who preferred to act alone in the last resort,
who would always follow their own star or search out their own
circuitous destiny, who, for whatever reason, would find the associations of party loyalty too insulting or irksome to bear. I never saw
the definition, by the way, as one primarily of virtue or vice, but
rather of temperament and character. Some men or women—say,
General de Gaulle or Queen Elizabeth I—always made up their own
minds on great questions in the end; others no less great or estimable
had the gift of acting together with their closest companions, and
since party is an indispensable element in the British democratic
system, this for sure is a quality not to be spurned. However, even if
the word is novel, the political species is not.

Enoch Powell, it seems to me, has always been a loner—no doubt
his old leader and eternal enemy, Edward Heath, would concur—but
at once the assertion prompts some complicated questionings. He is
also the strong upholder of party ties and traditions, the sworn enemy
of coalitions in any shape and contrivance. He is, further, as anyone
who has ever had any personal dealings with him will testify, the soul
of honour and loyalty. No one so far as I know has ever accused him
of a personal breach of trust; not quite the claim which could be made

on behalf of some other leading 'loners', such as Joseph Chamberlain, for example, a man with whom Enoch Powell has sometimes been compared. We shall have special occasion in a moment to return to the comparison, but let us for a moment mark the contrast. When Chamberlain was called Judas, not even fellow disciples could repudiate the charge. No one ever dreamt of levelling any such accusation against Enoch Powell.

The examination of his political conduct has been persistent, especially in the form of political biographies. Few worthwhile books are written about living politicians, yet already there are several in which Powell appears as hero or villain, and each has helped to expose a corner of his mind and nature. No complete portrait emerges from any of them, and yet his magnetism loses none of its potency; so there will be more to come. He himself is (leaving aside for the moment any controversial attributes) the greatest master of clear exposition in British post-1945 politics; yet he has not explained himself. He seems to scorn excuses, apologia, memoirs, essays in autobiography. In the country at large he is a household word, a figure of fame or infamy; in the House of Commons, he can compel attention, even from those who detest what he appears to say or stand for, as no one else has done since Aneurin Bevan, almost alone, faced the all-powerful Winston Churchill with the wartime Parliament at his back. To elevate Enoch Powell into such company may at first seem a sacrilege, but most of those who have sat in the Parliaments of the past two decades would not dissent. And yet again, has there not been in his career, is there not in his character or perhaps his political philosophy, some indelible, inexorable flaw? The search for the truth about him remains absorbing and elusive.

Roy Lewis, a kindly, sympathetic and, one might guess, fully-converted Powellite disciple (even in the sense, as someone put it, that there's 'a Powell policy for everything'), chooses to start his book auspiciously with the tremendous moment when Powell refused to fight in the 'fraudulent' election of February 1974, called by Edward Heath. ('One might say his whole life had been a preparation for February 1974.') For the country at large, and for Powell's own constituency of Wolverhampton, the declaration was startling enough; for Powell himself, it must have been an indescribable agony. Maybe the action could be said to follow logically from some of his earlier quarrels with Heath, as Roy Lewis gropingly indicates; but how could this weigh in the balance against so much else? Powell cherished his individual association with his constituency as an essential part of his life and his parliamentary creed. He understood too, so much better than all the exponents of consensus and coalition politics, that allegiance to party is an essential ingredient of the British political system. He must have known that he would expose himself to charges of near-betrayal from his closest friends, apart even from the avalanche of Conservative fury which he invited upon his head.

Moreover, what hope could he have that he would ever survive the gamble? One of the oldest maxims of British politics is that politicians, and especially those who wish to take proper risks elsewhere, should guard their base: here was Powell, surrendering his without a fight, inexcusably, quixotically, wantonly. Many others before him have challenged their own party leaderships, left their own parties, crossed the floor of the House of Commons; but they have customarily done it with a reasonable and legitimate circumspection. Enoch Powell in February 1974 broke every such precedent and precaution. He did the deed in a manner likely (as most of us thought at the time) to inflict the minimum immediate injury on his opponents and the maximum lasting injury on himself.

Would he indeed ever return to the House of Commons; would he not be left to roam the political wilderness, a Hamlet without an Elsinore? He did not leave the path open for a return to his old party nor did he prepare to remodel his own party to suit his own design nor did he seek out the way to join a new one; the matchless trapeze artist of the age had fallen between three stools. He acted alone and indeed he selected a course where none of his followers could conceivably follow. Ambition should be made of a more willowy stuff; indeed, of a different fabric altogether.

Truly, one deduction to be drawn from this occasion, rightly raised to the place of honour in any record of his life, is that Enoch Powell cannot be intelligently defined as the high Tory turned populist, the opportunist without scruple, the arch-demagogue. Events have too often destroyed the accusation. Surely he likes applause and the proof of public support: is not this the meat on which all democratic politicians must feed? But often Powell seems ready to toss aside a popularity too easily gained, and to pursue some circuitous diversion in order to find his own solitary path. He has an unshakable, almost pedantic, sense of rectitude in personal dealings, and this strain does not accord readily with the notion of a ruthless, scheming careerist.

Turn aside for a moment from this aspect of his personality to one of his own esoteric writings, a learned essay contributed a few years ago to the *Historical Journal* on the subject of the so-called Kilmainham Treaty of 1882, agreed between Parnell and Gladstone, the essay being a by-product of Powell's own book on Joseph Chamberlain. Ever since reading that volume, I have nursed the suspicion that

Powell grew disenchanted with Chamberlain, maybe even after he had signed the contract and started the work. At first thought, the attraction for him of Chamberlain, as hero or exemplar, must have looked obvious and overpowering: the shared interest in Birmingham, Ireland, the unity of the United Kingdom, not to forget, of course, the common hazards courted by a politician challenging the leadership of his own party. But Powell's book falls very far short of hero-worship, and sometimes comes nearer to distaste or condemnation. His concluding sentences are surely not intended as an encomium. 'The pathos of Chamberlain's political life was not the less for his having never clearly perceived that he had turned his own weapons against himself. It was the pathos of Ajax, not an Achilles.'

And the later gratuitous contribution to the *Historical Journal* strikes a harsher note. It offers fresh evidence on how the wretched Captain O'Shea used and misused the relationship between his wife and Parnell for purposes of blackmail and deceit, and how Chamberlain himself was at least partly privy to these subterfuges. That Enoch Powell, the Unionist MP for South Down, should insist so fastidiously on setting the record straight, to the honour of the arch-Home Ruler Parnell and the dishonour of the arch-Unionist Chamberlain, shows a quality rare in a politician, or an historian for that matter. Nothing but a passion for truth could have persuaded him to write that learned treatise. Chamberlain was of a coarser breed altogether, and certainly no similar passion and no sense of scruple governed his conduct. Rather he left a stain of dissemblement wherever he went. No wonder the sympathy between subject and author proved so imperfect, despite their common cause.

But to return to Roy Lewis's biography and *his* hero; he paints no warts or weaknesses on that bold countenance; usually and wisely he lets Powell's natural eloquence speak for itself. It is an impressive spectacle on a series of stages: the Powell of the 1960s anticipating by more than a decade the intellectual triumph of the monetarists among the Conservatives; another Powell of the same epoch forecasting the collapse of the Americans in Vietnam and indeed the evaporation of another empire nearer home; the Powell of the 1970s defining more dazzlingly than any rival or associate the threat of the Common Market to the British Constitution and then the same Powell living to see his prophecies fulfilled in the spirit, if not the letter; the Powell of the late 1970s, with one hand seeking to purge the Ulster cause of its Paisleyite fanaticism, and then, with the other, hurling the hardest stones against Scottish and Welsh devolution—and this too from the Ulster glasshouse; or the Powell of the 1980s stating the case against the nuclear deterrent with a crystal logic no one else could equal: these and more. Considering the range of leading topics on which he has not shirked the test of offering settled and far-reaching judgements, it is an accomplishment of the first order. No one of his generation has done so much to check the subordination of the art of politics to the dictates of the technocrats, the managers, the crushing bureaucracies—the modern equivalent of what Edmund Burke berated as the rule of sophisters, economists and calculators.

Yet some qualifications of major consequence are required; we must dig deeper into the mystery than any of his biographers have yet attempted. Other aspects of the man and his politics must be explored by future biographers—or present-day politicians. 'We are all monetarists now,' is the slogan sometimes paraded as the new conventional wisdom, and if the claim were ever proved valid and the doctrine were applied *and found successful,* Enoch Powell would be entitled to the credit in a degree so far not even hinted at even in his own perorations. It is true that he had seen the blinding light before Keith Joseph or Nigel Lawson had ever heard there was any such place as Damascus. It is true that he has put the case in better English than Mrs Thatcher's best speech-writers will ever contrive. It is true that it is pleasanter to let Powell expound the pure milk of the word than to be condemned to endure Hayek, Friedman, Schumpeter and the rest all conglomerated into one or even that assortment of American or Middle European prophets of the 1920s who preached the same monetarist gospel with much the same assurance—and calamitous results. And as the old doctrine is applied, and the results are hardly less calamitous, Enoch Powell must bear the guilt no less than his late-developing pupils, the Jacks and Jills now in office.

It is not by these dead doctrines that the economic life of our nation, and indeed of the Western world, can be revived, and if they continue to be applied, with the full rigour of Powellite logic, great stretches of our beloved country will be wiped off the industrial map altogether—most of Ebbw Vale and much of Ulster, for a start. I long for the moment when he might stop and look at what is happening. It would be part of my thesis, if I ever contributed to a volume on the lives of Enoch Powell, that he became a wiser man when he crossed the Irish sea. And what would he do if he saw with his own eyes how the needs of the living nation, and more particularly that precious part of it which he represents so skilfully and loyally at Westminster, clashed with his suffocating economic theory? It would be a Powellite speech to outdo all that had gone before: that one assuredly will be worth reading many, many times as he invites us to do with the others.

The last burning topic is left till the end; it is almost too hot and too tender to touch: the item omitted from the list of great prophecies cited earlier and yet the most devastating of them all. Would Enoch Powell ever have made his reputation on the spacious scale now acknowledged if it had not been for the 'race' speech delivered in Birmingham in 1968, if he alone of all British politicians had not dared to treat the question in the terms and style he did? Roy Lewis, his biographer, has little difficulty in proving that the speech was not, on Powell's part, the calculated sensation designed to challenge Heath and the Tory leadership which some, like Lord Hailsham for example, have alleged. He can prove that in playing 'the numbers game', Powell has sometimes been right about the figures. He can show that Powell is no racist, a man obsessed with hatred for others with different coloured skins. Nor was that speech the act of an opportunist reaching for the popular cry—that would be the most shameful explanation of all, and is surely one belied by the whole of the rest of Powell's political life. So why did he do it? Why did the man who made another of his reputations with the Hola speech allow his imagination to desert him? Why did he fail to comprehend what fears and hatreds and antagonisms his words would help to spread, what furies and divisions and ferocities in the nation he wished to serve? Why did he harden his heart, like some Ancient Pharaoh?

I do not know the answers; one day a great biography or autobiography may give us the true ones. Meantime, I believe it is the tragic irony of Enoch Powell's political life—or the pathos, to use his own word about Chamberlain—that the issue which made him famous is also the one which has barred his path to the highest office in the state. Without the Birmingham speech, the Tory kingdom would sooner or later have been his to command, for he had all the shining qualities which the others lacked. Heath would never have outmanoeuvred him; Thatcher would never have stepped into the vacant shoes. It was a tragedy for Enoch, and a tragedy for the rest of us too.

Once—but only once, so far as I can see—he did apply his mind, for publication, to these high autobiographical themes. He was being interviewed by Terry Coleman of the *Guardian* who put to him the suggestion that twice, in 1968 and in 1974, he had gone over the precipice. Back at once came the retort that there was a great contrast between the two occasions: 'In 1968 I didn't know there was a precipice. It was an elephant pit—but in 1974 I drove over the precipice knowing that the road I was on was bound to take me over a precipice, and telling everyone, and myself, "Look, there is the end of my public life." '

'Telling everyone' must be dismissed as an exaggeration; that is never the Enoch Powell way. Telling and arguing with himself, in the true 'loner' style, would be more accurate. But the conclusion still stands. He did believe that in deserting his own party and inviting the electorate to vote 'Labour' he was committing political suicide, and, according to most of the precedents, he was correct in that judgement. Joseph Chamberlain was never forgiven by his old associates for a far less abrupt and barefaced breach of allegiance.

In this sense the whole Ulster period was a kind of life after death, an uncovenanted bonus, a man playing with all his consummate talents a quite unexpected role. All else was made subordinate to the service of the people who sent him to represent them in the British Parliament, and for this task his grand rejection of Heathite Conservatism was no handicap at all. He had ceased to be a loner, and was quite entitled to parry the charge, as he did, that he, like Joseph Chamberlain, had become a political failure.

PART SEVEN
On Travel and Places

ELEVEN WRITERS on mobility, large and small, and the sights and novelties it brings: one, Hazlitt, straddles the eighteenth and nineteenth centuries; four others utterly Victorian, Butler, Dickens, Henry James and Ruskin; two, Belloc and Conrad, come from the early part of the twentieth century; some have international perspectives, such as Mann, Camus and Bowles. All contribute to the Essay in what may count as its most delightful incarnation.

Today, the travel 'piece', Essay or article forms part of an industry. Arguably it always did. Horace and Pausanius and Ptolemy may have been accurately classified as poets or historians or geographers; nevertheless their mobility informed their classical disciplines. Essays about travel and places have several qualities in common, one of which, a certain wistfulness, seems particularly useful. It provides nostalgia (best when suitably restrained), atmosphere, reflection—characteristics which the writers feel able to let off the leash, whereas in their other disciplines, as novelists or critics, they can never have such luxury.

This explains how Hazlitt can permit himself an observation like 'I cannot see the wit of walking and talking at the same time'; how the more habitually reserved Thomas Mann, after a journey on a liner calling to several antiquarian ports, can feel frivolously, 'I shall henceforth be able to hold my own in company, that is certain'; why the customarily rigorous Paul Bowles feels at liberty to include 'a little essay composed by a candidate for a post in one of the public services, entitled simply: *The Cow*'.

Finally, by way of *envoi*, I have included Virginia Woolf's *The Modern Essay*, itself the introduction to a collection of Essays. I have included it for a number of reasons, all of them within the ethic of the form, some already stated in the Introduction. Many of the points she makes will be found inherently in the contents of the previous seventy contributions. And her inclusion keeps a little tongue-in-cheek faith with Bacon's beginning in doubt, ending in certainty, as well as with all the worthy teachers who insisted that a perfect essay should end where it began.

On Going a Journey

WILLIAM HAZLITT

One of the pleasantest things in the world is going a journey; but I like to go by myself. I can enjoy society in a room; but out of doors, nature is company enough for me. I am then never less alone than when alone.

The fields his study, nature was his book.

I cannot see the wit of walking and talking at the same time. When I am in the country, I wish to vegetate like the country. I am not for criticising hedgerows and black cattle. I go out of town in order to forget the town and all that is in it. There are those who for this purpose go to watering-places and carry the metropolis with them. I like more elbow-room and fewer incumbrances. I like solitude, when I give myself up to it, for the sake of solitude; nor do I ask for

> *a friend in my retreat,*
> *Whom I may whisper, solitude is sweet.*

The soul of a journey is liberty, perfect liberty, to think, feel, do, just as one pleases. We go a journey chiefly to be free of all impediments and of all inconveniences; to leave ourselves behind, much more to get rid of others. It is because I want a little breathing-space to muse on indifferent matters, where Contemplation

> *May plume her feathers and let grow her wings,*
> *That in the various bustle of resort*
> *Were all too ruffled, and sometimes impair'd,*

that I absent myself from the town for a while, without feeling at a loss the moment I am left by myself. Instead of a friend in a post-chaise or in a Tilbury, to exchange good things with and vary the same stale topics over again, for once let me have a truce with impertinence. Give me the clear blue sky over my head, and the green turf beneath my feet, a winding road before me, and a three hours' march to dinner—and then to thinking! It is hard if I cannot start some game on these lone heaths. I laugh, I run, I leap, I sing for joy. From the point of yonder rolling cloud, I plunge into my past being and revel there, as the sunburnt Indian plunges headlong into the wave that wafts him to his native shore. Then long-forgotten things, like 'sunken wrack and sumless treasuries', burst upon my eager sight, and I begin to feel, think, and be myself again. Instead of an awkward silence, broken by attempts at wit or dull commonplaces, mine is that undisturbed silence of the heart which alone is perfect eloquence. No one likes puns, alliterations, antitheses, argument, and analysis better than I do; but I sometimes had rather be without them. 'Leave, oh, leave me to my repose!' I have just now other business in hand, which would seem idle to you, but is with me 'very stuff of the conscience'. Is not this wild rose sweet without a comment? Does not this daisy leap to my heart set in its coat of emerald? Yet if I were to explain to you the circumstance that has so endeared it to me, you would only smile. Had I not better then keep it to myself, and let it serve me to brood over, from here to yonder craggy point, and from thence onward to the far-distant horizon? I should be but bad company all that way, and therefore prefer being alone. I have heard it said that you may, when the moody fit comes on, walk or ride on by yourself and indulge your reveries. But this looks like a breach of manners, a neglect of others, and you are thinking all the time that you ought to rejoin your party. 'Out upon such half-faced fellowship,' say I. I like to be either entirely to myself, or entirely at the disposal of others; to talk or be silent, to walk or sit still, to be sociable or solitary. I was pleased with the observation of Mr Cobbett's, that 'he thought it a bad French custom to drink our wine with our meals, and that an Englishman ought to do only one thing at a time'. So I cannot talk and think, or indulge in melancholy musing and lively conversation by fits and starts. 'Let me have a companion of my way,' says Sterne, 'were it but to remark how the shadows lengthen as the sun declines.' It is beautifully said; but in my opinion, this continual comparing of notes interferes with the involuntary impression of things upon the mind and hurts the sentiment. If you only hint what you feel in a kind of dumb show, it is insipid; if you have to explain it, it is making a toil of a pleasure. You cannot read the book of nature without being perpetually put to the trouble of translating it for the benefit of others. I am for the synthetical method on a journey, in preference to the analytical. I am content to lay in a stock of ideas then, and to examine and anatomise them afterwards. I want to see my vague notions float like the down of the thistle before the breeze, and not to have them entangled in the briars and thorns of controversy. For once, I like to have it all my own way; and this is impossible unless you are alone, or in such company as I do not covet. I have no objection to argue a point with anyone for twenty miles of measured road, but not for pleasure.

If you remark the scent of a beanfield crossing the road, perhaps your fellow-traveller has no smell. If you point to a distant object, perhaps he is short-sighted, and has to take out his glass to look at it. There is a feeling in the air, a tone in the colour of a cloud which hits your fancy, but the effect of which you are unable to account for. There is then no sympathy, but an uneasy craving after it, and a dissatisfaction which pursues you on the way, and in the end probably produces ill humour. Now I never quarrel with myself, and take all my own conclusions for granted till I find it necessary to defend them against objections. It is not merely that you may not be of accord on the objects and circumstances that present themselves before you—these may recall a number of objects and lead to associations too delicate and refined to be possibly communicated to others. Yet these I love to cherish, and sometimes still fondly clutch them, when I can escape from the throng to do so. To give way to our feelings before company, seems extravagance or affectation; and, on the other hand, to have to unravel this mystery of our being at every turn, and to make others take an equal interest in it (otherwise the end is not answered) is a task to which few are competent. We must 'give it an understanding, but no tongue'. My old friend C——, however, could do both. He could go on in the most delightful explanatory way over hill and dale, a summer's day, and convert a landscape into a didactic poem or a Pindaric ode. 'He talked far above singing.' If I could so clothe my ideas in sounding and flowing words, I might perhaps wish to have someone with me to admire the swelling theme; or I could be more content, were it possible for me still to hear his echoing voice in the woods of All-Foxden. They had 'that fine madness in them which our first poets had'; and if they could have been caught by some rare instrument, would have breathed such strains as the following.

> Here be woods as green
> As any, air likewise as fresh and sweet
> As when smooth Zephyrus plays on the fleet
> Face of the curled streams, with flow'rs as many
> As the young spring gives, and as choice as any;
> Here be all new delights, cool streams and wells,
> Arbours o'ergrown with woodbines, caves and dells;
> Choose where thou wilt, whilst I sit by and sing.
> Or gather rushes, to make many a ring
> For thy long fingers; tell thee tales of love;
> How the pale Phoebe, hunting in a grove,
> First saw the boy Endymion, from whose eyes

She took eternal fire that never dies;
How she convey'd him softly in a sleep,
His temples bound with poppy, to the steep
Head of old Latmos, where she stoops each night,
Gilding the mountain with her brother's light,
To kiss her sweetest.

'*The Faithful Shepherdess*'

Had I words and images at command like these, I would attempt to wake the thoughts that lie slumbering on golden ridges in the evening clouds; but at the sight of nature my fancy, poor as it is, droops and closes up its leaves, like flowers at sunset. I can make nothing out on the spot: I must have time to collect myself.

In general, a good thing spoils out-of-door prospects; it should be reserved for table-talk. L—— is for this reason, I take it, the worst company in the world out of doors; because he is the best within. I grant, there is one subject on which it is pleasant to talk on a journey; and that is, what one shall have for supper when we get to our inn at night. The open air improves this sort of conversation or friendly altercation by setting a keener edge on appetite. Every mile of the road heightens the flavour of the viands we expect at the end of it. How fine is it to enter some old town, walled and turreted, just at approach of nightfall, or to come to some straggling village, with the lights streaming through the surrounding gloom; and then after inquiring for the best entertainment that the place affords, to 'take one's ease at one's inn'! These eventful moments in our lives' history are too precious, too full of solid, heart-felt happiness to be frittered and dribbled away in imperfect sympathy. I would have them all to myself, and drain them to the last drop; they will do to talk of or to write about afterwards. What a delicate speculation it is, after drinking whole goblets of tea,

The cups that cheer, but not inebriate,

and letting the fumes ascend into the brain, to sit considering what we shall have for supper—eggs and a rasher, a rabbit smothered in onions, or an excellent veal-cutlet! Sancho in such a situation once fixed on cow-heel; and his choice, though he could not help it, is not to be disparaged. Then, in the intervals of pictured scenery and Shandean contemplation, to catch the preparation and the stir in the kitchen—*Procul, O procul este profani!* These hours are sacred to silence and to musing, to be treasured up in the memory, and to feed the source of smiling thoughts hereafter. I would not waste them in idle talk; or if I must have the integrity of fancy broken in upon, I would rather it were by a stranger than a friend. A stranger takes his hue and character from the time and place; he is a part of the furniture and costume of an inn. If he is a Quaker, or from the West Riding of Yorkshire, so much the better. I do not even try to sympathise with him, and he breaks no squares. I associate nothing with my travelling companion but present objects and passing events. In his ignorance of me and my affairs, I in a manner forget myself. But a friend reminds one of other things, rips up old grievances, and destroys the abstraction of the scene. He comes in ungraciously between us and our imaginary character. Something is dropped in the course of conversation that gives a hint of your profession and pursuits; or from having someone with you that knows the less sublime portions of your history, it seems that other people do. You are no longer a citizen of the world: but your 'unhoused free condition is put into circumspection and confine'. The *incognito* of an inn is one of its striking privileges—'Lord of one's self, uncumber'd with a name.' Oh! it is great to shake off the trammels of the world and of public opinion—to lose our importunate, tormenting, everlasting personal identity in the elements of nature, and become the creature of the moment, clear of all ties—to hold to the universe only by a dish of sweet-breads, and to owe nothing but the score of the evening—and no longer seeking for applause and meeting with contempt, to be known by no other title than *the Gentleman in the parlour*! One may take one's choice of all characters in this romantic state of uncertainty as to one's real pretensions, and become indefinitely respectable and negatively right-worshipful. We baffle prejudice and disappoint conjecture; and from being so to others, begin to be objects of curiosity and wonder even to ourselves. We are no more those hackneyed commonplaces that we appear in the world; an inn restores us to the level of nature and quits scores with society! I have certainly spent some enviable hours at inns—sometimes when I have been left entirely to myself and have tried to solve some metaphysical problem, as once at Witham Common, where I found out the proof that likeness is not a case of the association of ideas—at other times, when there have been pictures in the room, as at St Neot's (I think it was), where I first met with Gribelin's engravings of the Cartoons, into which I entered at once, and at a little inn on the borders of Wales, where there happened to be hanging some of Westall's drawings, which I compared triumphantly (for a theory that I had, not for the admired artist) with the figure of a girl who had ferried me over the Severn, standing up in a boat between me and the twilight—at other times I might mention luxuriating in books, with a peculiar interest in this way, as I remember sitting up half the night to read *Paul and*

Virginia, which I picked up at an inn at Bridgewater, after being drenched in the rain all day; and at the same place I got through two volumes of Madame D'Arblay's *Camilla*. It was on the 10th of April 1798, that I sat down to a volume of the *New Eloise*, at the inn at Llangollen, over a bottle of sherry and cold chicken. The letter I chose was that in which St Preux describes his feelings as he first caught a glimpse from the heights of the Jura of the Pays de Vaud, which I had brought with me as a *bon bouche* to crown the evening with. It was my birthday, and I had for the first time come from a place in the neighbourhood to visit this delightful spot. The road to Llangollen turns off between Chirk and Wrexham; and on passing a certain point, you come all at once upon the valley, which opens like an amphitheatre, broad, barren hills rising in majestic state on either side, with 'green upland swells that echo to the bleat of flocks' below, and the River Dee babbling over its stony bed in the midst of them. The valley at this time 'glittered green with sunny showers', and a budding ash-tree dipped its tender branches in the chiding stream. How proud, how glad I was to walk along the high road that overlooks the delicious prospect, repeating the lines which I have just quoted from Mr Coleridge's poems! But besides the prospect which opened beneath my feet, another also opened to my inward sight, a heavenly vision, in which were written, in letters large as Hope could make them, these four words, LIBERTY, GENIUS, LOVE, VIRTUE; which have since faded into the light of common day, or mock my idle gaze.

The beautiful is vanished, and returns not.

Still I would return some time or other to this enchanted spot; but I would return to it alone. What other self could I find to share that influx of thoughts of regret and delight, the fragments of which I could hardly conjure up to myself, so much have they been broken and defaced! I could stand on some tall rock and overlook the precipice of years that separates me from what I then was. I was at that time going shortly to visit the poet whom I have above named. Where is he now? Not only I myself have changed; the world, which was then new to me, has become old and incorrigible. Yet will I turn to thee in thought, O sylvan Dee, in joy, in youth and gladness as thou then wert; and thou shalt always be to me the river of Paradise, where I will drink the waters of life freely!

There is hardly anything that shows the short-sightedness or capriciousness of the imagination more than travelling does. With change of place we change our ideas; nay, our opinions and feelings. We can by an effort indeed transport ourselves to old and long-forgotten scenes, and then the picture of the mind revives again; but we forget those that we have just left. It seems that we can think but of one place at a time. The canvas of the fancy is but of a certain extent, and if we paint one set of objects upon it, they immediately efface every other. We cannot enlarge our conceptions, we only shift our point of view. The landscape bares its bosom to the enraptured eye, we take our fill of it and seem as if we could form no other image of beauty or grandeur. We pass on and think no more of it; the horizon that shuts it from our sight, also blots it from our memory like a dream. In travelling through a wild, barren country, I can form no idea of a woody and cultivated one. It appears to me that all the world must be barren, like what I see of it. In the country we forget the town, and in town we despise the country. 'Beyond Hyde Park', says Sir Fopling Flutter, 'all is a desert.' All that part of the map that we do not see before us is a blank. The world in our conceit of it is not much bigger than a nutshell. It is not one prospect expanded into another, county joined to county, kingdom to kingdom, land to seas, making an image voluminous and vast—the mind can form no larger idea of space than the eye can take in at a single glance. The rest is a name written in a map, a calculation of arithmetic. For instance, what is the true signification of that immense mass of territory and population, known by the name of China to us? An inch of paste-board on a wooden globe, of no more account than a China orange! Things near us are seen of the size of life: things at a distance are diminished to the size of the understanding. We measure the universe by ourselves, and even comprehend the texture of our own being only piecemeal. In this way, however, we remember an infinity of things and places. The mind is like a mechanical instrument that plays a great variety of tunes, but it must play them in succession. One idea recalls another, but it at the same time excludes all others. In trying to renew old recollections, we cannot as it were unfold the whole web of our existence; we must pick out the single threads. So in coming to a place where we have formerly lived and with which we have intimate associations, everyone must have found that the feeling grows more vivid the nearer we approach the spot, from the mere anticipation of the actual impression: we remember circumstances, feelings, persons, faces, names that we had not thought of for years; but for the time all the rest of the world is forgotten—To return to the question I have quitted above.

I have no objection to go to see ruins, aqueducts, pictures, in company with a friend or a party, but rather the contrary, for the former reason reversed. They are intelligible matters and will bear talking about. The sentiment here is not tacit, but communicable and overt. Salisbury Plain is barren of criticism, but Stonehenge will bear a discussion antiquarian, picturesque, and philosophical. In setting out on a party of pleasure, the first consideration always is where we shall go to; in taking a solitary ramble, the question is what we shall meet with by the way. 'The mind is its own place'; nor are we anxious to arrive at the end of our journey. I can myself do the honours indifferently well to works of art and curiosity. I once took a party to Oxford with no mean *éclat*—showed them that seat of the Muses at a distance,

The glistering spires and pinnacles adorn'd

descanted on the learned air that breathes from the grassy quadrangles and stone walls of halls and colleges—was at home in the Bodleian; and at Blenheim quite superseded the powdered ciceroni that attended us, and that pointed in vain with his wand to common-place beauties in matchless pictures.—As another exception to the above reasoning, I should not feel confident in venturing on a journey in a foreign country without a companion. I should want at intervals to hear the sound of my own language. There is an involuntary antipathy in the mind of an Englishman to foreign manners and notions that requires the assistance of social sympathy to carry it off. As the distance from home increases, this relief, which was at first a luxury, becomes a passion and an appetite. A person would almost feel stifled to find himself in the deserts of Arabia without friends and countrymen; there must be allowed to be something in the view of Athens or old Rome that claims the utterance of speech; and I own that the Pyramids are too mighty for any single contemplation. In such situations, so opposite to all one's ordinary train of ideas, one seems a species by one's-self, a limb torn off from society, unless one can meet with instant fellowship and support.—Yet I did not feel this want or craving very pressing once, when I first set my foot on the laughing shores of France. Calais was peopled with novelty and delight. The confused, busy murmur of the place was like oil and wine poured into my ears; nor did the mariners' hymn, which was sung from the top of an old crazy vessel in the harbour, as the sun went down, send an alien sound into my soul. I only breathed the air of general humanity. I walked over 'the vine-covered hills and gay regions of France', erect and satisfied; for the image of man was not cast down and chained to the foot of arbitrary thrones; I was at no loss for language, for that of all the great schools of painting was open to me. The whole is vanished like a shade. Pictures, heroes, glory, freedom, all are fled: nothing remains but the Bourbons and the French people!—There is undoubtedly a sensation in travelling into foreign parts that is to be had nowhere else; but it is more pleasing at the time than lasting. It is too remote from our habitual associations to be a common topic of discourse or reference, and, like a dream or another state of existence, does not piece into our daily modes of life. It is an animated but a momentary hallucination. It demands an effort to exchange our actual for our ideal identity; and to feel the pulse of our old transports revive very keenly, we must 'jump' all our present comforts and connections. Our romantic and itinerant character is not to be domesticated. Dr Johnson remarked how little foreign travel added to the facilities of conversation in those who had been abroad. In fact, the time we have spent there is both delightful and in one sense instructive; but it appears to be cut out of our substantial, downright existence, and never to join kindly on to it. We are not the same, but another, and perhaps more enviable individual, all the time we are out of our own country. We are lost to ourselves, as well as our friends. So the poet somewhat quaintly sings,

Out of my country and myself I go.

Those who wish to forget painful thoughts, do well to absent them-selves for a while from the ties and objects that recall them; but we can be said only to fulfil our destiny in the place that gave us birth. I should on this account like well enough to spend the whole of my life in travelling abroad, if I could anywhere borrow another life to spend afterwards at home!

En Route

THOMAS MANN

translated by Dr William Rose

I have been *en route* for weeks, which seem to me like years. I am
tossed about on the seas, I am the Flying Dutchman. There echo in
my ears the two *motifs* with the help of which Wagner has depicted so
impressively the figure of the unhappy man: the quiet, dreary one
which pictures the monotonous waste of the motionless sea, and the
ballad-like refrain, *Hoi ho* and *Hoi he*, with which the overture opens.
I have known the eternal ocean in both its moods, drowsy and
turbulent, I have seen the sun playing on its blue surface and the moon
on its slumbering gloom, and for hours at a time, with the wind
howling and the canvas cracking, I have gazed into its turmoil, while
the bow of the pounding, heaving ship hurled its weight against the
waves that the tempest rolled toward it, and the whole fore part of the
ship was sprayed with white froth. In the morning I have the ocean
poured hot into my bath, and afterwards I eat porridge, eggs, and
excellent marmalade for breakfast. Occasionally I go ashore, to
submit myself to the influence of famous architecture, to observe the
manners of foreign peoples, and so to extend the narrow limits of my
education. Soon, however, as for Senta's pale lover, the cry again
resounds, 'To sea! To sea!'

It is a pleasure voyage of the Hamburg steamer *General San Martin*
in the Mediterranean, the second it has undertaken this year. There is
to be a third, and all the berths are already taken. I am not surprised:
the *General* is an excellent boat, well cared for and exceedingly
comfortable, not so large as the more frequently mentioned *Peer
Gynt,* 6,500 tons, if I am not mistaken, but commodious enough,
with its dining hall and Winter Garden, its cosy saloons, its broad
promenade deck, with room for about a hundred and sixty passengers without crowding. They live very well and are served by an
army of white jackets; the food, which is luxurious, is eaten not
without ceremony, we dress for seven o'clock dinner, there is an
orchestra, and sometimes a dance on the deck which is decorated with
flags and strewn with talcum powder. I will not describe everything,
since it might act as a social incitement, as the approving description of an orgy of post-war capitalism, with *nouveaux riches* in the

gleaming *cabines de luxe*. It *is* like that. It *is* something of the sort. But it is also a German vessel, which shows our flag on the high seas and in foreign ports, with a captain whose earnestness and qualities are written on his brow, with courteous officers, good-natured crew, and an atmosphere of Hamburg matter-of-factness and neatness that is very soothing after the exotic oddities to which it carries us.

I do not occupy a *cabine de luxe*, and I am glad. I was given a respectable cabin on the boat-deck, which formerly belonged to the ship's doctor, a narrow but practically fitted little room with a writing table and numerous spacious drawers under the bed and in the chest. I am comfortable, but not too comfortable, and that is as it should be. My deck-chair for reading stands in front of the door.

I went aboard in Venice. Heavens, how moved I was to see the beloved town once more, after having only borne it in my heart for thirteen years! The slow journey in a gondola from the station to the steamer, with strange companions, through night and wind, will always be among my dearest and most fantastic memories. I listened again to its stillness, the mysterious beating of water against its silent palaces. I was again impressed by its air of distinction in death. The façades of churches, squares and steps, bridges and alleys, with isolated pedestrians, appeared unexpectedly and glided away. The gondoliers exchanged cries. I was at home. The steamer, which lay before the Piazzetta, was not sailing till the following evening. In the morning I went into the town, to the Piazza, to San Marco, through the streets. In the afternoon I stood on deck and surveyed the *ensemble* I love; the columns with the lion and the saint, the Arabic witchery and Gothic style of the palace, the showy projecting side of the fairy temple. I was certain that nothing I might see on the coming journey would be able to surpass this picture; my departure was really painful.

Now I am *en route*, for I know not how long. It is the strangest tour of inspection that I have ever undertaken. We are gaining such knowledge of the world as is achieved by sailors. We anchor here and there, we examine the ports, and again put out to sea. We oscillate between two continents, change our climate as we change our clothes—our clothes according to the climate—and our education is being extended to a degree we had not divined. How easy I shall find it in future to speak about Cattaro, when the conversation at dinner-parties turns that way. Perhaps I could use a little art and skilfully turn the conversation in that direction, in order to enjoy my globe-trotting experiences. The entrance to that narrow and picturesque little southern town is unusual and fjord-like, skirted by mountains at the foot of which nestle charming villages. It rained while we were there, but it was much warmer than, for example, in Turkey, and nothing prevented us from going ashore and setting our exploratory feet on the soil of Jugoslavia. I could not make anything of the Cathedral façade. There is a Gothic rose-window over the portal, but there are also Romance *motifs*. In any case the total effect is magnificent. A very tasteful *dix-huitième* appears among the public buildings and the better class *bourgeois* houses of Cattaro. A large number of the sons of the Black Mountains, Montenegrins, had come down to the market-place and lent colour and animation to the picture by their national costume. We departed enriched.

What do you think! I have been in Egypt! Lesseps in a dress-coat stands on the great mole at Port Said. Some disliked the statue, but my view was that he could not very well have been set there dressed as a Greek god or as Amon-Ra. Finally they agreed that the correct thing would have been a morning-coat. We drove past his work, the Suez Canal, in a special train. The best thing I got out of it was *Aïda,* and I tried to whistle some bars of this melodious opera while we rolled along the traffic artery which forms a blue path in the desert sand. We went to Cairo, a town pulsing turbulently with oriental life. We lunched in an English hotel and roared out toward the pyramids of Gizeh in a charabanc, eagerly blinking at the land and the people, our eyes protected by coloured spectacles against the dust and sun of Africa.

I did not see much. I was surrounded by Arabs, men and youths, a gang compared with whom the tip-hunters of Southern Italy are veritable British aristocrats.

They have only one thought in their minds—baksheesh, and with all the means in their power, including a dreadful shrieking, they make this interest prevail over any other which might have brought us to Egypt. We really have to ward them off with the fly-fan which is bought immediately on landing for protection against the real flies; but they are worse than the real ones. Neither in the streets of Cairo, where they assail your ears as peddlers of mummy fragments, scarabs, postcards, and all manner of dubious souvenirs; nor in the desert, as donkey drivers, shoe-cleaners, and beggars, do they leave you in peace for a single moment. Yet one cannot get seriously angry with them. They are picturesque and jolly. Often good-looking, in an African way. They have teeth such as I have never seen in my life. One can see their incredible dentures from a distance as white strips gleaming in their dark faces.

The women appear to have no part in public life. Enveloped in black, nun-like, one sees them walking along, a water jar on their heads, lying when it is empty, upright when it is full. The men and boys maintain the field, and they are a noisy nuisance. Even the children, often indescribably droll creatures, with amulets on their foreheads and sucking a piece of sugar cane or a cracknel, are generally seen in the arms of men. My donkey had three names—Bismarck, Maurice, and Dooley, according to circumstances, as the owner explained to me candidly while he trotted along at my side and examined my purse to see how much English silver it contained. In Capri I once rode on a donkey named Michelangelo, and it was very odd to hear the driver continually trying to spur him on to greater effort with the cry, 'Courage, Michelangelo!' At any rate it was the name of a national hero, a proud name, only one and there was an end of it. But this one—varying according to circumstances—was entirely lacking in character and bore all the marks of obsequiousness in the interests of the tourist industry, amusing but contemptible. For the rest, Bismarck was a delightful beast, whitey-grey, small, with a large head and humorous eyes, clever, tough, intelligent, like most donkeys in this country. But I ought not to have said so. I ought not to have praised him. It cost me a lot of money.

We were in Luxor, in Carnac, in the royal graves of Thebes. A sleeping-car took us there and back by night. It is difficult to understand how this strip of land between two deserts, watered by the Nile, where rye, poppy, cotton, and sugar grow, could have nourished the culture whose ruins I saw jutting up in the burning heat of a sky from which not a drop of rain had fallen in three years. I walked in the dust amid these lotus and papyrus columns, those pylons, whose surfaces are so magically full of pictures and eternal inscriptions. I also descended with the others into the close atmosphere of the suites of chambers which comprised the tombs of the sons of the sun in the mountains at the edge of the Libyan desert, although it made me feel uncomfortable. I feel sure that every right-minded person will feel as I did, in the dusty heat of these chambers driven far and deep in the mountain, whose dry air has kept the colours of the wall-paintings so incredibly fresh throughout the years. A shameful feeling of intrusion oppresses one all the time. These people planned all their lives, and omitted no precaution, to prevent what is now happening. Amenophis IV, by whose glass-covered mummy in its coffin of porphyry I stood deeply moved for some time—the fine features of the young king are fully recognisable as they were in life, the dried-up arms crossed on the breast—had two false tomb-chambers with false royal mummies placed before his real one, to make protection certain. He was successful for a time; science was for long content with the first chamber, and then with the second. Finally, however, his ruse was detected after all, and he was himself discovered. It is a shame that cries to eternity.

The tomb of Tutankhamen has been completely emptied. Only the gilded casing of the mummy remains. He was completely equipped for eternity down there and thought that he was secure with his domestic furniture.

I saw some of the treasures in the museum at Cairo, above all the chair with the golden lions' feet and the back painted with figures, a work of exceeding grace. Is it right and proper that such beauty of human feeling should again be made fruitful, or ought it, in accordance with a will whose majesty could not be destroyed by any passing of the centuries, never to have been revealed to our eyes?

A dilemma.

The East—yes, yes, I *have* absorbed it. I carry away timeless pictures, which have not changed since the days of Isis and the falcon-headed gods. I saw the brown men of Kemi draw up their buckets on the clayey shores of the Nile, the ploughman till with primitive instruments the ground that has been fertilised with sacred memories, the ox turning the water-wheel. I saw the camel, white, shabby, useful, old—with thousands of years in the gaze of its grotesque, wise, serpent-like head—I still see it, loaded, with turbaned rider, one behind the other, winding along the horizon in a long line, I shall always see it when I want to. The East *has* become mine.

On board, on board! You will perhaps think that Constantinople is somewhat inaccessible? Not at all. You only need to bathe in warm sea water in the morning for a couple of days, to put on a dinner-jacket in the evening, you pass unawares through the Dardanelles and the Sea of Marmora, and you have arrived. To be sure there may be a gale *en route* and the sea may be rough, so that the dining-room is always half empty, and gets even emptier during the course of the meal, and you learn to appreciate the heartening qualities of vermouth. Then the boat is late, but only a couple of hours. And to make up for it I had on my arrival a stimulating surprise—an official reception by the Turkish port-authorities! I was invited into the smoking-room and introduced to the almond-eyed police officers. One of them made a speech about various things, which the other interpreted, and I gathered that they were extremely pleased to greet me in their town and very much hoped that my sojourn would be agreeable. I replied in fluent German that this was my first visit to Turkey and that I was looking forward with the greatest eagerness to visiting their celebrated capital; that I heartily appreciated the courtesy of their welcome. The exchange of compliments continued for a time. Finally I received a special recommendation on my passport in writing that went from right to left. There did not ensue any practical consequences or advantages for me, but I should like to know how the Turks discovered that I was coming.

The view of Constantinople from the sea is magnificent. The minarets look like Faber pencils with little round tops. The Hagia Sophia possesses six of them. They ought not to be spoken of jestingly. The sanctuary, which has had such a chequered fate, is one of the most majestic buildings in the world; Allah is great there, and the floor is covered with carpets that arouse the envy of the amateur. San Marco on a gigantic scale. Nevertheless I remain faithful to the golden mysteriousness of my temple.

I saw other mosques, heard the Koran chanted, and the muezzin calling to prayer to all the four points of the compass from his crow's nest, saw the Moslems touching the ground with their foreheads with a gentle and beautiful movement. I saw also the Jeré-Batan cistern, the pillared subterranean vault in the water, a fantastic sight. I drove through the country, fertile, though inadequately cultivated, out to where, high above the blue Bosphorus, above the park of the summer residence of the German Embassy, lies the cemetery dedicated to the Germans who fell in the Dardanelles. On the cross of one hangs the burst life-belt in which he was washed ashore. Field-Marshal von der Goltz is also buried there.

The town itself is a disappointment. The economic decay is perceptible; there are no elegant shops; the Great Bazaar is a rag market; Pera Street is tedious; it is a mistake to have seen first the stream of oriental life in Cairo. The males, from the boy of five to the old man, all wear the fez (the low one, mostly dark red, and not the tall one of the Egyptians which is usually of a brighter colour). But the difference in outlook among the population, the division into old and young Turks, is obvious in the women, who are to be seen walking partly muffled up, in strict accordance with the faith, partly unveiled, in accordance with enlightened opinion. They get on well with each other. The emancipated woman is seen walking tolerantly with the traditionalist, the pious one with the liberal, whose lips are possibly of the coral of Paris.

Athens? I was there. I glided after another stormy night into the Piraeus, was rowed ashore, and drove in a Buick up to the Acropolis. I did not go so far as to have myself photographed in front of the caryatids of the Erechtheum, like many of my companions. But otherwise the way I wandered about among the noble ruins was no less vulgar and contemptible.

All the same, it is impossible to describe the sense of kinship, of intellectual elegance, of the youthfulness of Europe, with which these divine remains inspired us after the forms of Nile culture. All cultivated sentimentality apart—it is no trifling matter to look down from the citadel and out upon Salamis and the sacred way. It is, ultimately, the beginning of all of us, it is veritably the heroic land of our youth. We put off the sultry East, our soul became clear and serene, there arose a vision of mankind which often fell but climbed again and again toward the sun. Where I stood one feels that he alone is truly the son of Europe whose soul can in its best hours find its way back to Hellas. One breathes there the fervent wish that the Persians, in whatever shape they come, may always be hurled back.

All honour to Stinnes! I have seen magnificent things, and I returned on his capitalistic pleasure barque with admiration, love, and a human pride of youth in my heart. I saw the original Eleusine relief (with the Eros), I saw the reflecting Athene, the bronze Ephebes of Anticythera and that incomparable marble—half eaten away by the sea to which it had been thrown by barbarians—the youth bending to throw the discus; to stroke that wonderfully modelled back with one's hand is an intellectual and sensual delight. The way in which Phidias, also called Pheidias, was able to make the thinnest of garments cling in the most delicate folds to the soft figure of a woman, is really amazing. It is a pity that so much talent was combined with human weaknesses about which it would, perhaps, be better to remain silent. In confidence—he purloined materials and died in prison.

We are steering for Messina and, after visiting the celebrated Taormina, are to proceed to Naples to examine the progress which has been made in the excavations at Pompeii. If anyone thinks we are leaving Algiers, he is mistaken. We shall cast a short but keen glance at the essentials. We shall anchor before Malaga and betake ourselves to Granada, inspecting the Alhambra as well as attending, with mixed feelings, a bull fight. We shall run into Barcelona and take the serpentine route by coach to Monsarrat. Our pleasure trip ends in Genoa, but that is a long way ahead, though at times I am inclined to wish it were less. The good living and all the variegated superficiality are beginning to bore me. And it is cold, for except in Egypt we have arrived everywhere too early in the season for this year's weather. We are now in the Ionian Sea, and I am sitting in my winter clothing and have turned on the steam heating of my respectable cabin. I was spared the more serious stages of sea-sickness, but my stomach is often inclined to hyper-acidity and uneasiness.

I shall henceforth be able to hold my own in company, that is certain. I shall be able to speak like a book based on observation, hasty though it was. I am impatient to enjoy this social advantage. I wish the time had come.

Christmas Day at Sea

JOSEPH CONRAD

Theologically Christmas Day is the greatest occasion for rejoicing offered to sinful mankind; but this aspect of it is so august and so great that the human mind refuses to contemplate it steadily, perhaps because of its own littleness, for which, of course, it is in no way to blame. It prefers to concentrate its attention on ceremonial observances, expressive generally of goodwill and festivity, such, for instance, as giving presents and eating plum-puddings. It may be said at once here that from the conventional point of view the spirit of Christmas Day at sea appears distinctly weak. The opportunities, the materials too, are lacking. Of course, the ship's company get a plum-pudding of some sort, and when the captain appears on deck for the first time the officer of the morning greets him with a 'Merry Christmas, sir', in a tone only moderately effusive. Anything more would be, owing to the difference in station, not correct. Normally he may expect a return for this in the shape of a 'The same to you' of a nicely graduated heartiness. He does not get it always, however.

One Christmas morning, many years ago (I was young then and anxious to do the correct thing), my conventional greeting was met by a grimly scathing 'Looks like it, doesn't it?' from my captain. Nothing more. A three days' more or less thick weather had turned frankly into a dense fog, and I had him called according to orders. We were in the chops of the Channel, with the Scilly Isles on a vague bearing within thirty miles of us, and not a breath of wind anywhere. There the ship remained wrapped up in a damp blanket and as motionless as a post stuck right in the way of the wretched steamboats groping blindly in and out of the Channel. I felt I had behaved tactlessly; yet how rude it would have been to have withheld the season's greeting from my captain!

It is very difficult to know what is the right thing to do when one is young. I suffered exceedingly from my gaucherie; but imagine my disgust when in less than half an hour we had the narrowest possible escape from a collision with a steamer which, without the slightest warning sound, appeared like a vague dark blot in the fog on our bow. She only took on the shape of a ship as she passed within twenty yards of the end of our jib-boom, terrifying us with the furious screeching of her whistle. Her form melted into nothing, long before the end of the beastly noise, but I hope that her people heard the simultaneous yell of execration from thirty-six throats which we sent after her by way of a Christmas greeting. Nothing more at variance with the spirit of peace and goodwill could be imagined; and I must add that I never saw a whole ship's company get so much affected by one of those 'close calls' of the sea. We remained jumpy all the morning and consumed our Christmas puddings at noon with restless eyes and straining ears as if under the shadow of some impending marine calamity or other.

On shore, of course, a calamity at Christmas time would hardly take any other shape than that of an avalanche—avalanche of unpaid bills. I think that it is the absence of that kind of danger which makes Christmas at sea rather agreeable on the whole. An additional charm consists in there being no worry about presents. Presents ought to be unexpected things. The giving and receiving of presents at appointed times seems to me a hypocritical ceremony, like exchanging gifts of Dead Sea fruit in proof of sham good-fellowship. But the sea of which I write here is a live sea; the fruits one chances to gather on it may be salt as tears or bitter as death, but they never taste like ashes in the mouth.

In all my twenty years of wandering over the restless waters of the globe I can only remember one Christmas Day celebrated by a present given and received. It was, in my view, a proper live sea transaction, no offering of Dead Sea fruit; and in its unexpectedness perhaps worth recording. Let me tell you first that it happened in the year 1879, long before there was any thought of wireless messages, and when an inspired person trying to prophesy broadcasting would have been regarded as a particularly offensive nuisance and probably sent to a rest-cure home. We used to call them mad-houses then, in our rude, cave-man way.

The daybreak of Christmas Day in the year 1879 was fine. The sun began to shine some time about four o'clock over the sombre expanse of the Southern Ocean in latitude 51; and shortly afterwards a sail was sighted ahead. The wind was light, but a heavy swell was running. Presently I wished a 'Merry Christmas' to my captain. He looked still sleepy, but amiable. I reported the distant sail to him and ventured the opinion that there was something wrong with her. He said, 'Wrong?' in an incredulous tone. I pointed out that she had all her upper sails furled and that she was brought to the wind, which, in that region of the world, could not be accounted for on any other theory. He took the glasses from me, directed them towards her stripped masts resembling three Swedish safety matches, flying up and down and waggling to and fro ridiculously in that heaving and austere wilderness of countless water-hills, and returned them to me without a word. He only yawned. This marked display of callousness gave me a shock. In those days I was generally inexperienced and still a comparative stranger in that particular region of the world of waters.

The captain, as is a captain's way, disappeared from the deck; and after a time our carpenter came up the poop-ladder carrying an empty small wooden keg, of the sort in which certain ship's provisions are packed. I said, surprised, 'What do you mean by lugging this thing up here, Chips?'—'Captain's orders, sir,' he explained, shortly.

I did not like to question him further, and so we only exchanged Christmas greetings and he went away. The next person to speak to me was the steward. He came running up the companion-stairs: 'Have you any old newspapers in your room, sir?'

We had left Sydney, N.S.W., eighteen days before. There were several old Sydney *Heralds, Telegraphs,* and *Bulletins* in my cabin, besides a few home papers received by the last mail. 'Why do you ask, steward?' I enquired naturally. 'The captain would like to have them,' he said.

And even then I did not understand the inwardness of these eccentricities. I was only lost in astonishment at them. It was eight o'clock before we had closed with that ship, which, under her short canvas and heading nowhere in particular, seemed to be loafing aimlessly on the very threshold of the gloomy home of storms. But long before that hour I had learned from the number of the boats she carried that this nonchalant ship was a whaler. She was the first whaler I had ever seen. She had hoisted the Stars and Stripes at her peak, and her signal flags had told us already that her name was: '*Alaska*—two years out from New York—east from Honolulu—two hundred and fifteen days on the cruising ground.'

We passed, sailing slowly, within a hundred yards of her; and just as our steward started ringing the breakfast-bell, the captain and I held aloft, in good view of the figures watching us over her stern, the keg, properly headed up and containing, besides an enormous bundle of old newspapers, two boxes of figs in honour of the day. We flung it far out over the rail. Instantly our ship, sliding down the slope of a high swell, left it far behind in our wake. On board the *Alaska* a man in a fur cap flourished an arm; another, a much be-whiskered person, ran forward suddenly. I never saw anything so ready and so smart as the way that whaler, rolling desperately all the time, lowered one of her boats. The Southern Ocean went on tossing the two ships like a juggler his gilt balls, and the microscopic white speck of the boat seemed to come into the game instantly, as if shot out from a catapult on the enormous and lonely stage. That Yankee whaler lost not a moment in picking up her Christmas present from the English wool-clipper.

Before we had increased the distance very much she dipped her ensign in thanks, and asked to be reported 'All well, with a catch of three fish.' I suppose it paid them for two hundred and fifteen days of risk and toil, away from the sounds and sights of the inhabited world, like outcasts devoted, beyond the confines of mankind's life, to some enchanted and lonely penance.

Christmas Days at sea are of varied character, fair to middling and down to plainly atrocious. In this statement I do not include Christmas Days on board passenger ships. A passenger is, of course, a brother (or sister) and quite a nice person in a way, but his Christmas Days are, I suppose, what he wants them to be: the conventional festivities of an expensive hotel included in the price of his ticket.

On Getting Respected in Inns and Hotels

HILAIRE BELLOC

To begin at the beginning is, next to ending at the end, the whole art of writing; as for the middle you may fill it in with any rubble that you choose. But the beginning and the end, like the strong stone outer walls of medieval buildings, contain and define the whole.

And there is more than this: since writing is a human and a living art, the beginning being the motive and the end the object of the work, each inspires it; each runs through organically, and the two between them give life to what you do.

So I will begin at the beginning and I will lay down this first principle, that religion and the full meaning of things has nowhere more disappeared from the modern world than in the department of Guide Books.

For a Guide Book will tell you always what are the principal and most vulgar sights of a town; what mountains are most difficult to climb, and, invariably, the exact distances between one place and another. But these things do not serve the End of Man. The end of man is Happiness, and how much happier are you with such a knowledge? Now there are some Guide Books which do make little excursions now and then into the important things, which tell you (for instance) what kind of cooking you will find in what places, what kind of wine in countries where this beverage is publicly known, and even a few, more daring than the rest, will give a hint or two upon hiring mules, and upon the way that a bargain should be conducted, or how to fight.

But with all this even the best of them do not go to the moral heart of the matter. They do not give you a hint or an idea of that which is surely the basis of all happiness in travel. I mean, the art of gaining respect in the places where you stay. Unless that respect is paid you you are more miserable by far than if you had stayed at home, and I would ask anyone who reads this whether he can remember one single journey of his which was not marred by the evident contempt which the servants and the owners of taverns showed for him wherever he went?

It is therefore of the first importance, much more important than any question of price or distance, to know something of this art; it is not difficult to learn, moreover it is so little exploited that if you will but learn it you will have a sense of privilege and of upstanding among your fellows worth all the holidays which were ever taken in the world.

Of this Respect which we seek, out of so many human pleasures, a facile, and a very false, interpretation is that it is the privilege of the rich, and I even knew one poor fellow who forged a cheque and went to gaol in his desire to impress the host of the 'Spotted Dog', near Barnard Castle. It was an error in him, as it is in all who so imagine. The rich in their degree fall under this contempt as heavily as any, and there is no wealth that can purchase the true awe which it should be your aim to receive from waiters, serving-wenches, boot-blacks, and publicans.

I knew a man once who set out walking from Oxford to Stow-in-the-Wold, from Stow-in-the-Wold to Cheltenham, from Cheltenham to Ledbury, from Ledbury to Hereford, from Hereford to New Rhayader (where the Cobbler lives), and from New Rhayader to the end of the world which lies a little west and north of that place, and all the way he slept rough under hedges and in stacks, or by day in open fields, so terrified was he at the thought of the contempt that awaited him should he pay for a bed. And I knew another man who walked from York to Thirsk, and from Thirsk to Darlington, and from Darlington to Durham, and so on up to the border and over it, and all the way he pretended to be extremely poor so that he might be certain the contempt he received was due to nothing of his own, but to his clothes only: but this was an indifferent way of escaping, for it got him into many fights with miners, and he was arrested by the police in Lanchester; and at Jedburgh, where his money did really fail him, he had to walk all through the night, finding that no one would take in such a tatterdemalion. The thing could be done much more cheaply than that, and much more respectably, and you can acquire with but little practice one of many ways of achieving the full respect of the whole house, even of that proud woman who sits behind glass in front of an enormous ledger; and the first way is this:

As you come into the place go straight for the smoking-room, and begin talking of the local sport: and do not talk humbly and tentatively as so many do, but in a loud authoritative tone. You shall insist and lay down the law and fly into a passion if you are contradicted. There is here an objection which will arise in the mind of every niggler and boggler who has in the past very properly been covered with ridicule and become the butt of the waiters and stableyard, which is, that if one is ignorant of the local sport, there is an end to the business. The objection is ridiculous. Do you suppose that the people whom you hear talking around you are more learned than yourself in the matter? And if they are do you suppose that they are acquainted with your ignorance? Remember that most of them have read far less than you, and that you can draw upon an experience of travel of which they can know nothing; do but make the plunge, practising first in the villages of the Midlands, I will warrant you that in a very little while bold assertion of this kind will carry you through any tap-room or bar-parlour in Britain.

I remember once in the holy and secluded village of Washington under the Downs, there came in upon us as we sat in the inn there a man whom I recognised though he did not know me—for a journalist—incapable of understanding the driving of a cow, let alone horses: a prophet, a socialist, a man who knew the trend of things and so forth: a man who had never been outside a town except upon a motor bicycle, upon which snorting beast indeed had he come to this inn. But if he was less than us in so many things he was greater than us in this art of gaining respect in inns and hotels. For he sat down, and when they had barely had time to say good day to him he gave us in minutest detail a great run after a fox, a run that never took place. We were fifteen men in the room; none of us were anything like rich enough to hunt, and the lie went through them like an express. This fellow 'found' (whatever that may mean) at Gumber Corner, ran right through the combe (which, by the way, is one of those bits of land which have been stolen bodily from the English people), cut down the Sutton Road, across the railway at Coates (and there he showed the cloven hoof, for your liar always takes his hounds across the railway), then all over Egdean, and killed in a field near Wisborough. All this he told, and there was not even a man there to ask him whether all those little dogs and horses swam the Rother or jumped it. He was treated like a god; they tried to make him stop but he would not. He was off to Worthing, where I have no doubt he told some further lies upon the growing of tomatoes under glass, which is the main sport of that district. Similarly, I have no doubt, such a man would talk about boats at King's Lynn, murder with violence at Croydon, duck shooting at Ely, and racing anywhere.

Then also if you are in any doubt as to what they want of you, you can always change the scene. Thus fishing is dangerous for even the poor can fish, and the chances are you do not know the names of the animals, and you may be putting salt-water fish into the stream of

Lambourne, or talking of salmon upon the Upper Thames. But what is to prevent you putting on a look of distance and marvel, and conjuring up the North Atlantic for them? Hold them with the cold and the fog of the Newfoundland seas, and terrify their simple minds with whales.

A second way to attain respect, if you are by nature a silent man, and one which I think is always successful, is to write before you go to bed and leave upon the table a great number of envelopes which you should address to members of the Cabinet, and Jewish money-lenders, dukes, and in general any of the great. It is but slight labour, and for the contents you cannot do better than put into each envelope one of those advertisements which you will find lying about. Then next morning you should gather them up and ask where the post is: but you need not post them, and you need not fear for your bill. Your bill will stand much the same, and your reputation will swell like a sponge.

And a third way is to go to the telephone, since there are telephones nowadays, and ring up whoever in the neighbourhood is of the greatest importance. There is no law against it, and when you have the number you have but to ask the servant at the other end whether it is not somebody else's house. But in the meanwhile your night in the place is secure.

And a fourth way is to tell them to call you extremely early, and then to get up extremely late. Now why this should have the effect it has I confess I cannot tell. I lay down the rule empirically and from long observation, but I may suggest that perhaps it is the combination of the energy you show in early rising, and of the luxury you show in late rising: for energy and luxury are the two qualities which menials most admire in that governing class to which you flatter yourself you belong. Moreover the strength of will with which you sweep aside their inconvenience, ordering one thing and doing another, is not without its effect, and the stir you have created is of use to you.

And the fifth way is to be Strong, to Dominate and to Lead. To be one of the Makers of this world, one of the Builders. To have the more Powerful Will. To arouse in all around you by mere Force of Personality a feeling that they must Obey. But I do not know how this is done.

First Impressions of London

HENRY JAMES

There is a certain evening that I count as virtually a first impression—the end of a wet, black Sunday, twenty years ago, about the first of March. There had been an earlier vision, but it had turned grey, like faded ink, and the occasion I speak of was a fresh beginning. No doubt I had a mystic prescience of how fond of the murky modern Babylon I was one day to become; certain it is that as I look back I find every small circumstance of those hours of approach and arrival still as vivid as if the solemnity of an opening era had breathed upon it. The sense of approach was already almost intolerably strong at Liverpool, where, as I remember, the perception of the English character of everything was as acute as a surprise, though it could only be a surprise without a shock. It was expectation exquisitely gratified, superabundantly confirmed. There was a kind of wonder indeed that England should be as English as, for my entertainment, she took the trouble to be; but the wonder would have been greater, and all the pleasure absent, if the sensation had not been violent. It seems to sit there again like a visiting presence, as it sat opposite to me at breakfast at a small table in a window of the old coffee-room of the Adelphi Hotel—the unextended (as it then was), the unimproved, the unblushingly local Adelphi. Liverpool is not a romantic city, but that smoky Saturday returns to me as a supreme success, measured by its association with the kind of emotion in the hope of which, for the most part, we betake ourselves to far countries.

It assumed this character at an early hour—or rather indeed twenty-four hours before—with the sight, as one looked across the wintry ocean, of the strange, dark, lonely freshness of the coast of Ireland. Better still, before we could come up to the city, were the black steamers knocking about in the yellow Mersey, under a sky so low that they seemed to touch it with their funnels, and in the thickest, windiest light. Spring was already in the air, in the town; there was no rain, but there was still less sun—one wondered what had become, on this side of the world, of the big white splotch in the heavens; and the grey mildness, shading away into black at every pretext, appeared in itself a promise. This was how it hung about me,

between the window and the fire, in the coffee-room of the hotel—
late in the morning for breakfast, as we had been long disembarking.
The other passengers had dispersed, knowingly catching trains for
London (we had only been a handful); I had the place to myself, and I
felt as if I had an exclusive property in the impression. I prolonged it, I
sacrificed to it, and it is perfectly recoverable now, with the very taste
of the national muffin, the creak of the waiter's shoes as he came and
went (could anything be so English as his intensely professional back?
it revealed a country of tradition), and the rustle of the newspaper I
was too excited to read.

I continued to sacrifice for the rest of the day; it didn't seem to me a
sentient thing, as yet, to inquire into the means of getting away. My
curiosity must indeed have languished, for I found myself on the
morrow in the slowest of Sunday trains, pottering up to London with
an interruptedness which might have been tedious without the conversation of an old gentleman who shared the carriage with me and to
whom my alien as well as comparatively youthful character had
betrayed itself. He instructed me as to the sights of London, and
impressed upon me that nothing was more worthy of my attention
than the great cathedral of St Paul. 'Have you seen St Peter's in Rome?
St Peter's is more highly embellished, you know; but you may
depend upon it that St Paul's is the better building of the two.' The
impression I began with speaking of was, strictly, that of the drive
from Euston, after dark, to Morley's Hotel in Trafalgar Square. It
was not lovely—it was in fact rather horrible; but as I move again
through dusky, tortuous miles, in the greasy four-wheeler to which
my luggage had compelled me to commit myself, I recognise the first
step in an initiation of which the subsequent stages were to abound in
pleasant things. It is a kind of humiliation in a great city not to know
where you are going, and Morley's Hotel was then, to my imagination, only a vague ruddy spot in the general immensity. The immensity was the great fact, and that was a charm; the miles of housetops
and viaducts, the complication of junctions and signals through
which the train made its way to the station had already given me the
scale. The weather had turned to wet, and we went deeper and deeper
into the Sunday night. The sheep in the fields, on the way from
Liverpool, had shown in their demeanour a certain consciousness of
the day; but this momentous cab-drive was an introduction to rigidi-
ties of custom. The low black houses were as inanimate as so many
rows of coal-scuttles, save where at frequent corners, from a gin-
shop, there was a flare of light more brutal still than the darkness. The
custom of gin—that was equally rigid, and in this first impression the
public-houses counted for much.

Morley's Hotel proved indeed to be a ruddy spot; brilliant, in my recollection, is the coffee-room fire, the hospitable mahogany, the sense that in the stupendous city this, at any rate for the hour, was a shelter and a point of view. My remembrance of the rest of the evening—I was probably very tired—is mainly a remembrance of a vast four-poster. My little bedroom-candle, set in its deep basin, caused this monument to project a huge shadow and to make me think, I scarce knew why, of *The Ingoldsby Legends*. If at a tolerably early hour the next day I found myself approaching St Paul's, it was not wholly in obedience to the old gentleman in the railway-carriage: I had an errand in the City, and the City was doubtless prodigious. But what I mainly recall is the romantic consciousness of passing under Temple Bar and the way two lines of *Henry Esmond* repeated themselves in my mind as I drew near the masterpiece of Sir Christopher Wren. 'The stout, red-faced woman' whom Esmond had seen tearing after the staghounds over the slopes at Windsor was not a bit like the effigy 'which turns its stony back upon St Paul's and faces the coaches struggling up Ludgate Hill'. As I looked at Queen Anne over the apron of my hansom—she struck me as very small and dirty, and the vehicle ascended the mild incline without an effort—it was a thrilling thought that the statue had been familiar to the hero of the incomparable novel. All history appeared to live again and the continuity of things to vibrate through my mind.

To this hour, as I pass along the Strand, I take again the walk I took there that afternoon. I love the place today, and that was the commencement of my passion. It appeared to me to present phenomena and to contain objects, of every kind, of an inexhaustible interest: in particular it struck me as desirable and even indispensable that I should purchase most of the articles in most of the shops. My eyes rest with a certain tenderness on the places where I resisted and on those where I succumbed. The fragrance of Mr Rimmel's establishment is again in my nostrils; I see the slim young lady (I hear her pronunciation), who waited upon me there. Sacred to me today is the particular aroma of the hairwash that I bought of her. I paused before the granite portico of Exeter Hall (it was unexpectedly narrow and wedge-like), and it evokes a cloud of associations which are none the less impressive because they are vague; coming from I don't know where—from *Punch*, from Thackeray, from old volumes of *The Illustrated London News* turned over in childhood; seeming connected with Mrs Beecher Stowe and *Uncle Tom's Cabin*. Memorable is a rush I made into a glover's at Charing Cross—the one you pass going eastward, just before you turn into the station; that, however, now that I think of it, must have been in the morning, as soon as I issued from the hotel. Keen within me was a sense of the importance of deflowering, of despoiling the shop.

A day or two later, in the afternoon, I found myself staring at my fire, in a lodging of which I had taken possession on foreseeing that I should spend some weeks in London. I had just come in, and, having attended to the distribution of my luggage, sat down to consider my habitation. It was on the ground-floor, and the fading daylight reached it in a sadly damaged condition. It struck me as stuffy and unsocial, with its mouldy smell and its decoration of lithographs and wax-flowers—an impersonal black hole in the huge general blackness. The uproar of Piccadilly hummed away at the end of the street, and the rattle of a heartless hansom passed close to my ears. A sudden horror of the whole place came over me, like a tiger-pounce of homesickness which had been watching its moment. London was hideous, vicious, cruel, and above all overwhelming; whether or no she was 'careful of the type' she was as indifferent as nature herself to the single life. In the course of an hour I should have to go out to my dinner, which was not supplied on the premises, and that effort assumed the form of a desperate and dangerous quest. It appeared to me that I would rather remain dinnerless, would rather even starve than sally forth into the infernal town, where the natural fate of an obscure stranger would be to be trampled to death in Piccadilly and his carcass thrown into the Thames. I did not starve, however, and I eventually attached myself by a hundred human links to the dreadful, delightful city. That momentary vision of its smeared face and stony heart has remained memorable to me, but I am happy to say that I can easily summon up others.

Ramblings in Cheapside

SAMUEL BUTLER

Walking the other day in Cheapside I saw some turtles in Mr Sweeting's window, and was tempted to stay and look at them. As I did so, I was struck not more by the defences with which they were hedged about, than by the fatuousness of trying to hedge that in at all which, if hedged thoroughly, must die of its own defencefulness. The holes for the head and feet through which the turtle leaks out, as it were, on to the exterior world, and through which it again absorbs the exterior world into itself—'catching on' through them to things that are thus both turtle and not turtle at one and the same time—these holes stultify the armour and show it to have been designed by a creature with more of faithfulness to a fixed idea, and hence onesidedness, than of that quick sense of relative importances and their changes, which is the main factor of good living.

The turtle obviously had no sense of proportion; it differed so widely from myself that I could not comprehend it; and as this word occurred to me, it occurred also that until my body comprehended its body in a physical material sense, neither would my mind be able to comprehend its mind with any thoroughness. For unity of mind can only be consummated by unity of body; everything, therefore, must be in some respects both knave and fool to all that which has not eaten it, or by which it has not been eaten. As long as the turtle was in the window and I was in the street outside, there was no chance of our comprehending one another.

Nevertheless, I knew that I could get it to agree with me if I could so effectually buttonhole and fasten on to it as to eat it. Most men have an easy method with turtle soup, and I had no misgiving but that if I could bring my first premise to bear I should prove the better reasoner. My difficulty lay in this initial process, for I had not with me the argument that would alone compel Mr Sweeting to think that I ought to be allowed to convert the turtles—I mean I had no money in my pocket. No missionary enterprise can be carried on without any money at all, but even so small a sum as half a crown would, I suppose, have enabled me to bring the turtle partly round, and with many half-crowns I could in time no doubt convert the lot, for the turtle needs must go where the money drives. If, as is alleged, the world stands on a turtle, the turtle stands on money. No money, no turtle. As for money, that stands on opinion, credit, trust, faith— things that, though highly material in connection with money, are still of immaterial essence.

The steps are perfectly plain. The men who caught the turtles brought a fairly strong and definite opinion to bear upon them, that passed into action, and later on into money. They thought the turtles would come that way, and verified their opinion; on this, will and action were generated, with the result that the men turned the turtles on their backs and carried them off. Mr Sweeting touched these men with money, which is the outward and visible sign of verified opinion. The customer touches Mr Sweeting with money, Mr Sweeting touches the waiter and the cook with money. They touch the turtle with skill and verified opinion. Finally, the customer applies the clinching argument that brushes all sophisms aside, and bids the turtle stand protoplasm to protoplasm with himself, to know even as it is known.

But it must be all touch, touch, touch; skill, opinion, power, and money, passing in and out with one another in any order we like, but still link to link and touch to touch. If there is failure anywhere in respect of opinion, skill, power, or money either as regards quantity or quality, the chain can be no stronger than its weakest link, and the turtle and the clinching argument will fly asunder. Of course, if there is an initial failure in connection, through defect in any member of the chain, or of connection between the links, it will no more be attempted to bring the turtle and the clinching argument together, than it will to chain up a dog with two pieces of broken chain that are disconnected. The contact throughout must be conceived as absolute; and yet perfect contact is inconceivable by us, for on becoming perfect it ceases to be contact, and becomes essential, once for all inseverable, identity. The most absolute contact short of this is still contact by courtesy only. So here, as everywhere else, Eurydice glides off as we are about to grasp her. We can see nothing face to face; our utmost seeing is but a fumbling of blind finger-ends in an over-crowded pocket.

Presently my own blind finger-ends fished up the conclusion, that as I had neither time nor money to spend on perfecting the chain that would put me in full spiritual contact with Mr Sweeting's turtles, I had better leave them to complete their education at someone else's expense rather than mine, so I walked on towards the Bank. As I did so it struck me how continually we are met by this melting of one existence into another. The limits of the body seem well defined enough as definitions go, but definitions seldom go far. What, for example, can seem more distinct from a man than his banker or his solicitor? Yet these are commonly so much parts of him that he can no more cut them off and grow new ones, than he can grow new legs or arms; neither must he wound his solicitor; a wound in the solicitor is a very serious thing. As for his bank—failure of his bank's action may be as fatal to a man as failure of his heart. I have said nothing about the medical or spiritual adviser, but most men grow into the society that surrounds them by the help of these four main tap-roots, and not only into the world of humanity, but into the universe at large. We can, indeed, grow butchers, bakers, and greengrocers, almost *ad libitum*, but these are low developments, and correspond to skin, hair, or finger-nails. Those of us again who are not highly enough organised to have grown a solicitor or banker can generally repair the loss of whatever social organisation they may possess as freely as lizards are said to grow new tails; but this with the higher social, as well as organic, developments is only possible to a very limited extent.

The doctrine of metempsychosis, or transmigration of souls—a doctrine to which the foregoing considerations are for the most part easy corollaries—crops up no matter in what direction we allow our thoughts to wander. And we meet instances of transmigration of body as well as of soul. I do not mean that both body and soul have transmigrated together, far from it; but that, as we can often recognise a transmigrated mind in an alien body, so we not less often see a body that is clearly only a transmigration, linked on to someone else's new and alien soul. We meet people every day whose bodies are evidently those of men and women long dead, but whose appearance we know through their portraits. We see them going about in omnibuses, railway carriages, and in all public places. The cards have been shuffled, and they have drawn fresh lots in life and nationalities, but anyone fairly well up in medieval and last-century portraiture knows them at a glance.

Going down once towards Italy I saw a young man in the train whom I recognised, only he seemed to have got younger. He was with a friend, and his face was in continual play, but for some little time I puzzled in vain to recollect where it was that I had seen him before. All of a sudden I remembered he was King Francis I of France. I had hitherto thought the face of this king impossible, but when I saw it in play I understood it. His great contemporary Henry VIII keeps a restaurant in Oxford Street. Falstaff drove one of the St Gothard diligences for many years, and only retired when the railway was opened. Titian once made me a pair of boots at Vicenza, and not very good ones. At Modena I had my hair cut by a young man whom I perceived to be Raffaello. The model who sat to him for his celebrated Madonnas is first lady in a confectionery establishment at Montreal. She has a little motherly pimple on the left side of her nose that is misleading at first, but on examination she is readily recognised; probably Raffaello's model had the pimple too, but Raffaello left it out—as he would.

Handel, of course, is Madame Patey. Give Madame Patey Handel's wig and clothes, and there would be no telling her from Handel. It is not only that the features and the shape of the head are the same, but there is a certain imperiousness of expression and attitude about Handel which he hardly attempts to conceal in Madame Patey. It is a curious coincidence that he should continue to be such an incomparable renderer of his own music. Pope Julius II was the late Mr Darwin. Rameses II is a blind woman now, and stands in Holborn, holding a tin mug. I never could understand why I always found myself humming 'They oppressed them with burthens' when I passed her, till one day I was looking in Mr Spooner's window in the Strand, and saw a photograph of Rameses II. Mary Queen of Scots wears surgical boots and is subject to fits, near the Horse Shoe in Tottenham Court Road.

Michelangelo is a commissionaire; I saw him on board the *Glen Rosa,* which used to run every day from London to Clacton-on-Sea and back. It gave me quite a turn when I saw him coming down the stairs from the upper deck, with his bronzed face, flattened nose, and with the familiar bar upon his forehead. I never liked Michelangelo, and never shall, but I am afraid of him, and was near trying to hide when I saw him coming towards me. He had not got his commissionaire's uniform on, and I did not know he was one till I met him a month or so later in the Strand. When we got to Blackwall the music struck up and people began to dance. I never saw a man dance so much in my life. He did not miss a dance all the way to Clacton, nor all the way back again, and when not dancing he was flirting and cracking jokes. I could hardly believe my eyes when I reflected that this man had painted the famous 'Last Judgement' and had made all those statues.

Dante is, or was a year or two ago, a waiter at Brissago on the Lago Maggiore, only he is better-tempered-looking, and has a more intellectual expression. He gave me his ideas upon beauty: *'Tutto ch' è vero è bello,'* he exclaimed, with all his old self-confidence. I am not afraid of Dante. I know people by their friends, and he went about with Virgil, so I said with some severity, *'No, Dante, il naso della Signora Robinson è vero, ma non è bello'*; and he admitted I was right. Beatrice's name is Towler; she is waitress at a small inn in German Switzerland.

I used to sit at my window and hear people call 'Towler, Towler, Towler', fifty times in a forenoon. She was the exact antithesis to Abra; Abra, if I remember, used to come before they called her name, but no matter how often they called Towler, everyone came before she did. I suppose they spelt her name Taula, but to me it sounded Towler; I never, however, met anyone else with this name. She was a sweet, artless little hussy, who made me play the piano to her, and she said it was lovely. Of course I only played my own compositions; so I believed her, and it all went off very nicely. I thought it might save trouble if I did not tell her who she really was, so I said nothing about it.

I met Socrates once. He was my muleteer on an excursion which I will not name, for fear it should identify the man. The moment I saw my guide I knew he was somebody, but for the life of me I could not remember who. All of a sudden it flashed across me that he was Socrates. He talked enough for six, but it was all in *dialetto*, so I could not understand him, nor, when I had discovered who he was, did I much try to do so. He was a good creature, a trifle given to stealing fruit and vegetables, but an amiable man enough. He had had a long day with his mule and me, and he only asked me five francs. I gave him ten, for I pitied his poor old patched boots, and there was a meekness about him that touched me. 'And now, Socrates,' said I at parting, 'we go on our several ways, you to steal tomatoes, I to filch ideas from other people; for the rest—which of those two roads will be the better going, Our Father which is in Heaven knows, but we know not.'

I have never seen Mendelssohn, but there is a fresco of him on the terrace, or open-air dining-room, of an inn at Chiavenna. He is not called Mendelssohn, but I knew him by his legs. He is in the costume of a dandy of some five-and-forty years ago, is smoking a cigar, and appears to be making an offer of marriage to his cook. Beethoven both my friend Mr H. Festing Jones and I have had the good fortune to meet; he is an engineer now, and does not know one note from another; he has quite lost his deafness, is married, and is, of course, a little squat man with the same refractory hair that he always had. It was very interesting to watch him, and Jones remarked that before the end of dinner he had become positively posthumous. One morning I was told the Beethovens were going away, and before long I met their two heavy boxes being carried down the stairs. The boxes were so squat and like their owners that I half thought for a moment that they were inside, and should hardly have been surprised to see them spring up like a couple of Jacks-in-the-box. *'Sono indentro?'* said I, with a frown of wonder, pointing to the boxes. The porters knew what I meant, and laughed. But there is no end to the list of people whom I have been able to recognise, and before I had got through it myself, I found I had walked some distance, and had involuntarily paused in front of a second-hand bookstall.

I do not like books. I believe I have the smallest library of any literary man in London, and I have no wish to increase it. I keep my books at the British Museum and at Mudie's, and it makes me very angry if anyone gives me one for my private library. I once heard two ladies disputing in a railway carriage as to whether one of them had or had not been wasting money. 'I spent it in books,' said the accused, 'and it's not wasting money to buy books.' 'Indeed, my dear, I think it is,' was the rejoinder, and in practice I agree with it. Webster's Dictionary, Whitaker's Almanack, and Bradshaw's Railway guide should be sufficient for any ordinary library; it will be time enough to go beyond these when the mass of useful and entertaining matter which they provide has been mastered. Nevertheless, I admit that sometimes, if not particularly busy, I stop at a second-hand bookstall and turn over a book or two from mere force of habit.

I know not what made me pick up a copy of Aeschylus—of course in an English version—or rather I know not what made Aeschylus take up with me, for he took me rather than I him; but no sooner had he got me than he began puzzling me, as he has done any time this forty years, to know wherein his transcendent merit can be supposed to lie. To me he is, like the greater number of classics in all ages and countries, a literary Struldbrug, rather than a true ambrosia-fed immortal. There are true immortals, but they are few and far between; most classics are as great impostors dead as they were when living, and while posing as gods are, five-sevenths of them, only Struldbrugs. It comforts me to remember that Aristophanes liked Aeschylus no better than I do. True, he praises him by comparison with Sophocles and Euripides, but he only does so that he may run down these last more effectively. Aristophanes is a safe man to follow, nor do I see why it should not be as correct to laugh with him as to pull a long face with the Greek professors; but this is neither here nor there, for no one really cares about Aeschylus; the more interesting question is how he contrived to make so many people for so many years pretend to care about him.

Perhaps he married somebody's daughter. If a man would get hold of the public ear, he must pay, marry, or fight. I have never understood that Aeschylus was a man of means, and the fighters do not write poetry, so I suppose he must have married a theatrical manager's daughter, and got his plays brought out that way. The ear of any age or country is like its land, air, and water; it seems limitless, but is really limited, and is already in the keeping of those who naturally enough will have no squatting on such valuable property. It is written and talked up to as closely as the means of subsistence are bred up to by a teeming population. There is not a square inch of it but is in private hands, and he who would freehold any part of it must do so by purchase, marriage, or fighting, in the usual way—and fighting gives the longest, safest tenure. The public itself has hardly more voice in the question who shall have its ear, than the land has in choosing its owners. It is farmed as those who own it think most profitable to themselves, and small blame to them; nevertheless, it has a residuum of mulishness which the land has not, and does sometimes dispossess its tenants. It is in this residuum that those who fight place their hope and trust.

Or perhaps Aeschylus squared the leading critics of his time. When one comes to think of it, he must have done so, for how is it conceivable that such plays should have had such runs if he had not? I met a lady one year in Switzerland who had some parrots that always travelled with her and were the idols of her life. These parrots would not let anyone read aloud in their presence, unless they heard their own names introduced from time to time. If these were freely interpolated into the text they would remain as still as stones, for they thought the reading was about themselves. If it was not about them it could not be allowed. The leaders of literature are like these parrots; they do not look at what a man writes, nor if they did would they understand it much better than the parrots do; but they like the sound of their own names, and if these are freely interpolated in a tone they take as friendly, they may even give ear to an outsider. Otherwise they will scream him off if they can.

I should not advise anyone with ordinary independence of mind to attempt the public ear unless he is confident that he can out-lung and out-last his own generation; for if he has any force, people will and ought to be on their guard against him, inasmuch as there is no knowing where he may not take them. Besides, they have staked their money on the wrong men so often without suspecting it, that when there comes one whom they do suspect it would be madness not to bet against him. True, he may die before he has out-screamed his opponents, but that has nothing to do with it. If his scream was well pitched, it will sound clearer when he is dead. We do not know what death is. If we know so little about life which we have experienced, how shall we know about death which we have not—and in the nature of things never can? Everyone, as I said years ago in *Alps and Sanctuaries,* is an immortal to himself, for he cannot know that he is dead until he is dead, and when dead how can he know anything about anything? All we know is, that even the humblest dead may live long after all trace of the body has disappeared; we see them doing it in the bodies and memories of those that come after them; and not a few live so much longer and more effectually than is desirable, that it has been necessary to get rid of them by Act of Parliament. It is love that alone gives life, and the truest life is that which we live not in ourselves but vicariously in others, and with which we have no concern. Our concern is so to order ourselves that we may be of the number of them that enter into life—although we know it not.

Aeschylus did so order himself; but his life is not of that inspiriting kind that can be won through fighting the good fight only—or being believed to have fought it. His voice is the echo of a drone, drone-begotten and drone-sustained. It is not a tone that a man must utter or die—nay, even though he die; and likely enough half the allusions and hard passages in Aeschylus of which we can make neither head nor tail are in reality only puffs of some of the literary leaders of his time.

The lady above referred to told me more about her parrots. She was like a Nasmyth hammer going slow—very gentle, but irresistible. She always read the newspaper to them. What was the use of having a newspaper if one did not read it to one's parrots?

'And have you divined', I asked, 'to which side they incline in politics?'

'They do not like Mr Gladstone,' was the somewhat freezing answer; 'this is the only point on which we disagree, for I adore him. Don't ask more about this, it is a great grief to me. I tell them everything,' she continued, 'and hide no secret from them.'

'But can any parrot be trusted to keep a secret?'

'Mine can.'

'And on Sundays do you give them the same course of reading as on a weekday, or do you make a difference?'

'On Sundays I always read them a genealogical chapter from the Old or New Testament, for I can thus introduce their names without profanity. I always keep tea by me in case they should ask for it in the night, and I have an Etna to warm it for them; they take milk and sugar. The old white-headed clergyman came to see them last night; it was very painful, for Jocko reminded him so strongly of his late . . .'

I thought she was going to say 'wife', but it proved to have been only of a parrot that he had once known and loved.

One evening she was in difficulties about the quarantine, which was enforced that year on the Italian frontier. The local doctor had gone down that morning to see the Italian doctor and arrange some details. 'Then perhaps, my dear,' she said to her husband, 'he is the quarantine.' 'No, my love,' replied her husband. 'The quarantine is not a person, it is a place where they put people'; but she would not be comforted, and suspected the quarantine as an enemy that might at any moment pounce out upon her and her parrots. So a lady told me once that she had been in like trouble about the anthem. She read in her Prayer Book that in choirs and places where they sing 'here followeth the anthem', yet the person with this most mysteriously sounding name never did follow. They had a choir, and no one could say the church was not a place where they sang, for they did sing—both chants and hymns. Why, then, this persistent slackness on the part of the anthem, who at this juncture should follow his papa, the rector, into the reading-desk? No doubt he would come some day, and then what he would be like? Fair or dark? Tall or short? Would he be bald and wear spectacles like papa, would he be young and good-looking? Anyhow, there was something wrong, for it was announced that he would follow, and he never did follow; therefore there was no knowing what he might not do next.

I heard of the parrots a year or two later as giving lessons in Italian to an English maid. I do not know what their terms were. Alas! since then both they and their mistress have joined the majority. When the poor lady felt her end was near she desired (and the responsibility for this must rest with her, not me) that the birds might be destroyed, as fearing they might come to be neglected, and knowing that they could never be loved again as she had loved them. On being told that all was over, she said 'Thank you', and immediately expired.

Reflecting in such random fashion, and strolling with no greater method, I worked my way back through Cheapside and found myself once more in front of Sweeting's window. Again the turtles attracted me. They were alive, and so far at any rate they agreed with me. Nay, they had eyes, mouths, legs, if not arms, and feet, so there was much in which we were both of a mind, but surely they must be mistaken in arming themselves so very heavily. Any creature on getting what the turtle aimed at would overreach itself and be landed not in safety but annihilation. It should have no communion with the outside world at all, for death could creep in wherever the creature could creep out; and it must creep out somewhere if it was to hook on to outside things. What death can be more absolute than such absolute isolation? Perfect death, indeed, if it were attainable (which it is not), is as near perfect security as we can reach, but it is not the kind of security aimed at by any animal that is at the pains of defending itself. For such want to have things both ways, desiring the livingness of life without its perils, and the safety of death without its deadness, and some of us do actually get this for a considerable time, but we do not get it by plating ourselves with armour as the turtle does. We tried this in the Middle Ages, and no longer mock ourselves with the weight of armour that our forefathers carried in battle. Indeed the more deadly the weapons of attack become the more we go into the fight slug-wise.

Slugs have ridden their contempt for defensive armour as much to death as the turtles their pursuit of it. They have hardly more than skin enough to hold themselves together; they court death every time they cross the road. Yet death comes not to them more than to the turtle, whose defences are so great that there is little left inside to be defended. Moreover, the slugs fare best in the long run, for turtles are dying out, while slugs are not, and there must be millions of slugs all the world over for every single turtle. Of the two vanities, therefore, that of the slug seems most substantial.

In either case the creature thinks itself safe, but is sure to be found out sooner or later; nor is it easy to explain this mockery save by reflecting that everything must have its meat in due season, and that meat can only be found for such a multitude of mouths by giving everything as meat in due season to something else. This is like the Kilkenny cats, or robbing Peter to pay Paul; but it is the way of the world, and as every animal must contribute in kind to the picnic of the universe, one does not see what better arrangement could be made than the providing each race with a hereditary fallacy, which shall in the end get it into a scrape, but which shall generally stand the wear and tear of life for some time. *'Do ut des'* is the writing on all flesh to him that eats it; and no creature is dearer to itself than it is to some other that would devour it.

Nor is there any statement or proposition more invulnerable than living forms are. Propositions prey upon and are grounded upon one another just like living forms. They support one another as plants and animals do; they are based ultimately on credit, or faith, rather than the cash of irrefragable conviction. The whole universe is carried on on the credit system, and if the mutual confidence on which it is based were to collapse, it must itself collapse immediately. Just or unjust, it lives by faith; it is based on vague and impalpable opinion that by some inscrutable process passes into will and action, and is made manifest in matter and in flesh: it is meteoric—suspended in mid-air; it is the baseless fabric of a vision so vast, so vivid, and so gorgeous that no base can seem more broad than such stupendous baselessness, and yet any man can bring it about his ears by being over-curious; when faith fails, a system based on faith fails also.

Whether the universe is really a paying concern, or whether it is an inflated bubble that must burst sooner or later, this is another matter.

If people were to demand cash payment in irrefragable certainty for everything that they have taken hitherto as paper money on the credit of the bank of public opinion, is there money enough behind it all to stand so great a drain even on so great a reserve? Probably there is not, but happily there can be no such panic, for even though the cultured classes may do so, the uncultured are too dull to have brains enough to commit such stupendous folly. It takes a long course of academic training to educate a man up to the standard which he must reach before he can entertain such questions seriously, and by a merciful dispensation of Providence university training is almost as costly as it is unprofitable. The majority will thus be always unable to afford it, and will base their opinions on mother wit and current opinion rather than on demonstration.

So I turned my steps homewards; I saw a good many more things on my way home, but I was told that I was not to see more this time than I could get into twelve pages of the *Universal Review*; I must therefore reserve any remark which I think might perhaps entertain the reader for another occasion.

Brokers' and Marine-Store Shops

CHARLES DICKENS

When we affirm that brokers' shops are strange places, and that if an authentic history of their contents could be procured, it would furnish many a page of amusement, and many a melancholy tale, it is necessary to explain the class of shops to which we allude. Perhaps when we make use of the term 'Brokers' Shop', the minds of our readers will at once picture large, handsome warehouses, exhibiting a long perspective of French-polished dining-tables, rosewood chiffoniers, and mahogany wash-hand-stands, with an occasional vista of a four-post bedstead and hangings, and an appropriate foreground of dining-room chairs. Perhaps they will imagine that we mean a humble class of second-hand furniture repositories. Their imagination will then naturally lead them to that street at the back of Long Acre, which is composed almost entirely of brokers' shops; where you walk through groves of deceitful, showy-looking furniture, and where the prospect is occasionally enlivened by a bright red, blue, and yellow hearthrug, embellished with the pleasing device of a mail-coach at full speed, or a strange animal, supposed to have been originally intended for a dog, with a mass of worsted-work in his mouth, which conjecture has likened to a basket of flowers.

This, by the by, is a tempting article to young wives in the humbler ranks of life, who have a first-floor front to furnish—they are lost in admiration, and hardly know which to admire most. The dog is very beautiful, but they have a dog already on the best tea-tray, and two more on the mantelpiece. Then, there is something so genteel about that mail-coach; and the passengers outside (who are all hat) give it such an air of reality!

The goods here are adapted to the taste, or rather to the means, of cheap purchasers. There are some of the most beautiful *looking* Pembroke tables that were ever beheld: the wood as green as the trees in the Park, and the leaves almost as certain to fall off in the course of a year. There is also a most extensive assortment of tent and turn-up bedsteads, made of stained wood, and innumerable specimens of that base imposition on society—a sofa bedstead.

A turn-up bedstead is a blunt, honest piece of furniture; it may be slightly disguised with a sham drawer; and sometimes a mad attempt is even made to pass it off for a bookcase; ornament it as you will, however, the turn-up bedstead seems to defy disguise, and to insist on having it distinctly understood that he is a turn-up bedstead, and nothing else—that he is indispensably necessary, and that being so useful, he disdains to be ornamental.

How different is the demeanour of a sofa bedstead! Ashamed of its real use, it strives to appear an article of luxury and gentility—an attempt in which it miserably fails. It has neither the respectability of a sofa, nor the virtues of a bed; every man who keeps a sofa bedstead in his house, becomes a party to a wilful and designing fraud—we question whether you could insult him more, than by insinuating that you entertain the least suspicion of its real use.

To return from this digression, we beg to say, that neither of these classes of brokers' shops forms the subject of this sketch. The shops to which we advert, are immeasurably inferior to those on whose outward appearance we have slightly touched. Our readers must often have observed in some by-street, in a poor neighbourhood, a small dirty shop, exposing for sale the most extraordinary and confused jumble of old, worn-out, wretched articles, that can well be imagined. Our wonder at their ever having been bought, is only to be equalled by our astonishment at the idea of their ever being sold again. On a board, at the side of the door, are placed about twenty books—all odd volumes; and as many wine-glasses—all different patterns; several locks, an old earthenware pan, full of rusty keys; two or three gaudy chimney-ornaments—cracked, of course; the remains of a lustre, without any drops; a round frame like a capital O, which has once held a mirror; a flute, complete with the exception of the middle joint; a pair of curling-irons; and a tinder-box. In front of the shop window are ranged some half-dozen high-backed chairs, with spinal complaints and wasted legs; a corner cupboard; two or three very dark mahogany tables with flaps like mathematical problems; some pickle-jars, some surgeons' ditto, with gilt labels and without stoppers; an unframed portrait of some lady who flourished about the beginning of the thirteenth century, by an artist who never flourished at all; an incalculable host of miscellanies of every description, including bottles and cabinets, rags and bones, fenders and street-door knockers, fire-irons, wearing apparel and bedding, a hall-lamp, and a room-door. Imagine, in addition to this incongruous mass, a black doll in a white frock, with two faces—one looking up the street, and the other looking down, swinging over the door; a board with the squeezed-up inscription 'Dealer in marine stores', in lanky white letters, whose height is strangely out of proportion to their width;

and you have before you precisely the kind of shop to which we wish to direct your attention.

Although the same heterogeneous mixture of things will be found at all these places, it is curious to observe how truly and accurately some of the minor articles which are exposed for sale—articles of wearing apparel, for instance—mark the character of the neighbour-hood. Take Drury Lane and Covent Garden for example.

This is essentially a theatrical neighbourhood. There is not a potboy in the vicinity who is not, to a greater or less extent, a dramatic character. The errand-boys and chandler's-shop-keepers' sons are all stage-struck: they 'gets up' plays in back kitchens hired for the purpose, and will stand before a shop-window for hours, con-templating a great staring portrait of Mr Somebody or other, of the Royal Coburg Theatre, 'as he appeared in the character of Tongo the Denounced'. The consequence is, that there is not a marine-store shop in the neighbourhood, which does not exhibit for sale some faded articles of dramatic finery, such as three or four pairs of soiled buff boots with turn-over red tops, heretofore worn by a 'fourth robber', or 'fifth mob'; a pair of rusty broadswords, a few gauntlets, and certain resplendent ornaments, which, if they were yellow instead of white, might be taken for insurance plates of the Sun Fire Office. There are several of these shops in the narrow streets and dirty courts, of which there are so many near the national theatres, and they all have tempting goods of this description, with the addition, perhaps, of a lady's pink dress covered with spangles; white wreaths, stage shoes, and a tiara like a tin lamp reflector. They have been purchased of some wretched supernumeraries, or sixth-rate actors, and are now offered for the benefit of the rising generation, who, on condition of making certain weekly payments, amounting in the whole to about ten times their value, may avail themselves of such desirable bargains.

Let us take a very different quarter, and apply it to the same test. Look at a marine-store dealer's, in that reservoir of dirt, drunkenness, and drabs: thieves, oysters, baked potatoes, and pickled salmon— Ratcliff Highway. Here, the wearing apparel is all nautical. Rough blue jackets, with mother-of-pearl buttons, oil-skin hats, coarse checked shirts, and large canvas trousers that look as if they were made for a pair of bodies instead of a pair of legs, are the staple commodities. Then, there are large bunches of cotton pocket-handkerchiefs, in colour and pattern unlike any one ever saw before, with the exception of those on the backs of the three young ladies without bonnets who passed just now. The furniture is much the same as elsewhere, with the addition of one or two models of ships, and some old prints of naval engagements in still older frames. In the window are a few compasses, a small tray containing silver watches in clumsy thick cases; and tobacco-boxes, the lid of each ornamented with a ship, or an anchor, or some such trophy. A sailor generally pawns or sells all he has before he has been long ashore, and if he does not, some favoured companion kindly saves him the trouble. In either case, it is an even chance that he afterwards unconsciously repurchases the same things at a higher price than he gave for them at first.

Again: pay a visit with a similar object, to a part of London, as unlike both of these as they are to each other. Cross over to the Surrey side, and look at such shops of this description as are to be found near the King's Bench prison, and in 'the Rules'. How different, and how strikingly illustrative of the decay of some of the unfortunate residents in this part of the metropolis! Imprisonment and neglect have done their work. There is contamination in the profligate denizens of a debtor's prison; old friends have fallen off; the recollection of former prosperity has passed away; and with it all thoughts for the past, all care for the future. First, watches and rings, then cloaks, coats, and all the more expensive articles of dress, have found their way to the pawnbroker's. That miserable resource has failed at last, and the sale of some trifling article at one of these shops has been the only mode left of raising a shilling or two, to meet the urgent demands of the moment. Dressing-cases and writing-desks, too old to pawn but too good to keep; guns, fishing-rods, musical instruments, all in the same condition; have first been sold, and the sacrifice has been but slightly felt. But hunger must be allayed, and what has already become a habit is easily resorted to, when an emergency arises. Light articles of clothing, first of the ruined man, then of his wife, at last of their children, even of the youngest, have been parted with, piecemeal. There they are, thrown carelessly together until a purchaser presents himself, old, and patched and repaired, it is true; but the make and materials tell of better days; and the older they are, the greater the misery and destitution of those whom they once adorned.

The Extension of Railways in
the Lake District

JOHN RUSKIN

The evidence collected in the following pages, in support of their pleading, is so complete, and the summary of his cause given with so temperate mastery by Mr Somervell, that I find nothing to add in circumstance, and little to reinforce in argument. And I have less heart to the writing even of what brief preface so good work might by its author's courtesy be permitted to receive from me, occupied as I so long have been in efforts tending in the same direction, because, on that very account, I am far less interested than my friend in this local and limited resistance to the elsewhere fatally victorious current of modern folly, cruelty, and ruin. When the frenzy of avarice is daily drowning our sailors, suffocating our miners, poisoning our children, and blasting the cultivable surface of England into a treeless waste of ashes, what does it really matter whether a flock of sheep, more or less, be driven from the slopes of Helvellyn, or the little pool of Thirlmere filled with shale, or a few wild blossoms of St John's Vale lost to the coronal of English spring? Little to anyone; and—let me say this, at least, in the outset of all saying—*nothing to me*. No one need charge me with selfishness in any word or action for defence of these mossy hills. I do not move, with such small activity as I have yet shown in the business, because I live at Coniston (where no sound of the iron wheels by Dunmail Raise can reach me), nor because I can find no other place to remember Wordsworth by, than the daffodil margin of his little Rydal marsh. What thoughts and work are yet before me, such as he taught, must be independent of any narrow associations. All my own dear mountain grounds and treasure-cities, Chamouni, Interlachen, Lucerne, Geneva, Venice, are long ago destroyed by the European populace; and now, for my own part, I don't care what more they do; they may drain Loch Katrine, drink Loch Lomond, and blow all Wales and Cumberland into a heap of slate shingle; the world is wide enough yet to find me some refuge during the days appointed for me to stay in it. But it is no less my duty, in the cause of those to whom the sweet landscapes of England are yet precious, and to whom they may yet teach what they taught me, in early boyhood, and would still if I had it now to learn—it is my duty to plead with what earnestness I may, that these sacred sibylline books may be redeemed from perishing.

But again, I am checked, because I don't know how to speak to the persons who *need* to be spoken to in this matter.

Suppose I were sitting, where still, in much-changed Oxford, I am happy to find myself, in one of the little latticed cells of the Bodleian Library, and my kind and much-loved friend, Mr Coxe, were to come to me with news that it was proposed to send nine hundred excursionists through the library every day, in three parties of three hundred each; that it was intended they should elevate their minds by reading all the books they could lay hold of while they stayed—and that practically scientific persons accompanying them were to look out for and burn all the manuscripts that had any gold in their illuminations, that the said gold might be made of practical service; but that he, Mr Coxe, could not, for his part, sympathise with the movement, and hoped I would write something in deprecation of it! As I should then feel, I feel now, at Mr Somervell's request that I would write him a preface in defence of Helvellyn. What could I say for Mr Coxe? Of course, that nine hundred people should see the library daily, instead of one, is only fair to the nine hundred, and if there is gold in the books, is it not public property? If there is copper or slate in Helvellyn, shall not the public burn or hammer it out—and they say they will, of course—in spite of us? What does it signify to *them* how we poor old quiet readers in this mountain library feel? True, we know well enough—what the nine hundred excursionist scholars don't—that the library can't be read quite through in a quarter of an hour; also, that there is a pleasure in real reading, quite different from that of turning pages; and that gold in a missal, or slate in a crag, may be more precious than in a bank or a chimney-pot. But how are these practical people to credit us—these, who cannot read, nor ever will; and who have been taught that nothing is virtuous but care for their bellies, and nothing useful but what goes into them?

Whether to be credited or not, the real facts of the matter, made clear as they are in the following pages, can be briefly stated for the consideration of any candid person.

The arguments in favour of the new railway are in the main four, and may be thus answered.

1. 'There are mineral treasures in the district capable of development.'

Answer. It is a wicked fiction, got up by whosoever has got it up, simply to cheat shareholders. Every lead and copper vein in Cumberland has been known for centuries; the copper of Coniston does not pay; and there is none so rich in Helvellyn. And the main central volcanic rocks, through which the track lies, produce neither slate nor haematite, while there is enough of them at Llanberis and Dalton to roof and iron-grate all England into one vast Bedlam, if it honestly perceives itself in need of that accommodation.

2. 'The scenery must be made accessible to the public.'

Answer. It is more than accessible already; the public are pitched into it head-foremost, and necessarily miss two-thirds of it. The Lake scenery really begins, on the south, at Lancaster, where the Cumberland hills are seen over Morecambe Bay; on the north, at Carlisle, where the moors of Skiddaw are seen over the rich plains between them and the Solway. No one who loves mountains would lose a step of the approach, from these distances, on either side. But the stupid herds of modern tourists let themselves be emptied, like coals from a sack, at Windermere and Keswick. Having got there, what the new railway has to do is to shovel those who have come to Keswick to Windermere, and to shovel those who have come to Windermere to Keswick. And what then?

3. 'But cheap and swift transit is necessary for the working population, who otherwise could not see the scenery at all.'

Answer. After all your shrieking about what the operatives spend in drink, can't you teach them to save enough out of their year's wages to pay for a chaise and pony for a day, to drive Missis and the Baby that pleasant twenty miles, stopping when they like, to unpack the basket on a mossy bank? If they can't enjoy the scenery that way, they can't any way; and all that your railroad company can do for them is only to open taverns and skittle grounds round Grasmere, which will soon, then, be nothing but a pool of drainage, with a beach of broken gingerbeer bottles; and their minds will be no more improved by contemplating the scenery of such a lake than of Blackpool.

4. What else is to be said? I protest I can find nothing, unless that engineers and contractors must live. Let them live, but in a more useful and honourable way than by keeping Old Bartholomew Fair under Helvellyn, and making a steam merry-go-round of the lake country.

There are roads to be mended, where the parish will not mend them, harbours of refuge needed, where our deck-loaded ships are in helpless danger; get your commissions and dividends where you know that work is needed, not where the best you can do is to persuade pleasure-seekers into giddier idleness.

The arguments brought forward by the promoters of the railway may thus be summarily answered. Of those urged in the following pamphlet in defence of the country as it is, I care only myself to direct the reader's attention to one (see pp. 27, 28), the certainty, namely, of the deterioration of moral character in the inhabitants of every district penetrated by a railway. Where there is little moral character to be lost, this argument has small weight. But the Border peasantry of Scotland and England, painted with absolute fidelity by Scott and Wordsworth (for leading types out of this exhaustless portraiture, I may name Dandie Dinmont and Michael), are hitherto a scarcely injured race, whose strength and virtue yet survive to represent the body and soul of England before her days of mechanical decrepitude and commercial dishonour. There are men working in my own fields who might have fought with Henry V at Agincourt without being discerned from among his knights; I can take my tradesmen's word for a thousand pounds; my garden gate opens on the latch to the public road, by day and night, without fear of any foot entering but my own, and my girl-guests may wander by road, or moorland, or through every bosky dell of this wild wood, free as the heather bees or squirrels.

What effect, on the character of such a population, will be produced by the influx of that of the suburbs of our manufacturing towns, there is evidence enough, if the reader cares to ascertain the facts, in every newspaper on his morning table.

And now one final word concerning the proposed beneficial effect on the minds of those whom you send to corrupt us.

I have said I take no selfish interest in this resistance to the railroad. But I do take an unselfish one. It is precisely because I passionately wish to improve the minds of the populace, and because I am spending my own mind, strength, and fortune, wholly on that object, that I don't want to let them see Helvellyn while they are drunk. I suppose few men now living have so earnestly felt—none certainly have so earnestly declared—that the beauty of nature is the blessedest and most necessary of lessons for men; and that all other efforts in education are futile till you have taught your people to love fields, birds, and flowers. Come then, my benevolent friends, join with me in that teaching. I have been at it all my life, and without pride, do solemnly assure you that I know how it is to be managed. I cannot indeed tell you, in this short preface, how, completely, to fulfil so glorious a task. But I can tell you clearly, instantly, and emphatically, in what temper you must set about it. *Here* are you, a Christian, a gentleman, and a trained scholar; *there* is your subject of education—a Godless clown, in helpless ignorance. You can present no more blessed offering to God than that human creature, raised into faith, gentleness, and the knowledge of the works of his Lord. But observe this—you must not hope to make so noble an offering to God of that which doth cost you nothing! You must be resolved to labour, and to lose, yourself, before you can rescue this overlaboured lost sheep, and offer it alive to its Master. If then, my benevolent friend, you are prepared to take O UT your two pence, and to give them to your hosts here in Cumberland, saying—'Take care of him, and whatsoever thou spendest more, I will repay thee when I come to Cumberland myself,' on *these* terms—oh my benevolent friends, I am with you, hand and glove, in every effort you wish to make for the enlightenment of poor men's eyes. But if your motive is, on the contrary, to put two pence into your own purse, stolen between the Jerusalem and Jericho of Keswick and Ambleside, out of the poor drunken traveller's pocket—if your real object, in your charitable offering, is, not even to lend unto the Lord by *giving* to the poor, but to lend unto the Lord by making a dividend out of the poor—then, my pious friends, enthusiastic Ananias, pitiful Judas, and sanctified Korah, I will do my best, in God's name, to stay your hands, and stop your tongues.

The Wind at Djemila

ALBERT CAMUS

translated by Ellen Conroy Kennedy

There are places where the mind dies so that a truth which is its very denial may be born. When I went to Djemila, there was wind and sun, but that is another story. What must be said first of all is that a heavy, unbroken silence reigned there—something like a perfectly balanced pair of scales. The cry of birds, the soft sound of a three-hole flute, goats trampling, murmurs from the sky were just so many sounds added to the silence and desolation. Now and then a sharp clap, a piercing cry marked the upward flight of a bird huddled among the rocks. Any trail one followed—the pathways through the ruined houses, along wide, paved roads under shining colonnades, across the vast forum between the triumphal arch and the temple set upon a hill—would end at the ravines that surround Djemila on every side, like a pack of cards opening beneath a limitless sky. And one would stand there, absorbed, confronted with stones and silence, as the day moved on and the mountains grew purple surging upward. But the wind blows across the plateau of Djemila. In the great confusion of wind and sun that mixes light into the ruins, in the silence and solitude of this dead city, something is forged that gives man the measure of his identity.

It takes a long time to get to Djemila. It is not a town where you stop and then move further on. It leads nowhere and is a gateway to no other country. It is a place from which travellers return. The dead city lies at the end of a long, winding road whose every turning looks like the last, making it seem all the longer. When its skeleton, yellowish as a forest of bones, at last looms up against the faded colours of the plateau, Djemila seems the symbol of that lesson of love and patience which alone can lead us to the world's beating heart. There it lies, among a few trees and some dried grass, protected by all its mountains and stones from vulgar admiration, from being pictur-esque, and from the delusions of hope.

We had wandered the whole day in this arid splendour. The wind, which we had scarcely felt at the beginning of the afternoon, seemed to increase as the hours went by, little by little filling the whole countryside. It blew from a gap in the mountains, far to the East, rushing from beyond the horizon, leaping and tumbling among the stones and in the sunlight. It whistled loudly across the ruins, whirled through an amphitheatre of stones and earth, bathing the heaps of pock-marked stone, circling each column with its breath and spreading out in endless cries on the forum, open to the heavens. I felt myself whipping in the wind like a mast, hollowed at the waist. Eyes burning, lips cracking, my skin became so dry it no longer seemed mine. Until now, I had been deciphering the world's handwriting on my skin. There, on my body, the world had inscribed the signs of its tenderness or anger, warming with its summer breath or biting with its frosty teeth. But rubbed against for so long by the wind, shaken for more than an hour, staggering from resistance to it, I lost consciousness of the pattern my body traced. Like a pebble polished by the tides, I was polished by the wind, worn through to the very soul. I was a portion of the great force on which I had drifted, then much of it, then entirely it, confusing the throbbing of my own heart with the great sonorous beating of this omnipresent natural heart. The wind was fashioning me in the image of the burning nakedness around me. And its fugitive embrace gave me, a stone among stones, the solitude of a column or an olive tree in the summer sky.

The violent bath of sun and wind drained me of all strength. I scarcely felt the quivering of wings inside me, life's complaint, the weak rebellion of the mind. Soon, scattered to the four corners of the earth, self-forgetful and self-forgotten, I am the wind and within it, the columns and the archway, the flagstones warm to the touch, the pale mountains around the deserted city. And never have I felt so deeply and at one and the same time so detached from myself and so present in the world.

Yes, I am present. And what strikes me at this moment is that I can go no further—like a man sentenced to life imprisonment, to whom everything is present. But also like a man who knows that tomorrow will be the same, and every other day. For when a man becomes conscious of what he is now, it means he expects nothing further. If there are landscapes like moods, they are the most vulgar. All through this country I followed something that belonged not to me but to it, something like a taste for death we both had in common. Between the columns with their now lengthening shadows anxieties dissolved into the air like wounded birds. And in their place came an arid lucidity. Anxiety springs from living hearts. But calm will hide this living heart: this is all I can see clearly. As the day moved forward, as the noises and lights were muffled by the ashes falling from the sky, deserted by myself, I felt defenceless against the slow forces within me that were saying no.

Few people realise that there is a refusal that has nothing to do with renunciation. What meaning do words like future, improvement, good job have here? What is meant by the heart's progress? If I obstinately refuse all the 'later on's' of this world, it is because I have no desire to give up my present wealth. I do not want to believe that death is the gateway to another life. For me, it is a closed door. I do not say it is a step we must all take, but that it is a horrible and dirty adventure. Everything I am offered seeks to deliver man from the weight of his own life. But as I watch the great birds flying heavily through the sky at Djemila, it is precisely a certain weight of life that I ask for and obtain. If I am at one with this passive passion, the rest ceases to concern me. I have too much youth in me to be able to speak of death. But it seems to me that if I had to speak of it, I would find the right word here between horror and silence to express the conscious certainty of a death without hope.

We live with a few familiar ideas. Two or three. We polish and transform them according to the societies and the men we happen to meet. It takes ten years to have an idea that is really one's own—that one can talk about. This is a bit discouraging, of course. But we gain from this a certain familiarity with the splendour of the world. Until then, we have seen it face to face. Now we need to step aside to see its profile. A young man looks the world in the face. He has not had time to polish the idea of death or of nothingness, even though he has gazed on their full horror. That is what youth must be like, this harsh confrontation with death, this physical terror of the animal who loves the sun. Whatever people may say, on this score at least, youth has no illusions. It has had neither the time nor the piety to build itself any. And I don't know why, but faced with this ravined landscape, this solemn and lugubrious cry of stone, Djemila, inhuman at nightfall, faced with this death of colours and hope, I was certain that when they reach the end of their lives, men worthy of the name must rediscover this confrontation, deny the few ideas they had, and recover the innocence and truth that gleamed in the eyes of the Ancients face to face with destiny. They regain their youth, but by embracing death. There is nothing more despicable in this respect than illness. It is a remedy against death. It prepares us for it. It creates an apprenticeship whose first stage is self-pity. It supports man in his great effort to avoid the certainty that he will die completely. But Djemila . . . and then I feel certain that the true, the only, progress of civilisation, the one to which a man devotes himself from time to time, lies in creating conscious deaths.

What always amazes me, when we are so swift to elaborate on other subjects, is the poverty of our ideas on death. It is a good thing or a bad thing, I fear it or I summon it (they say). Which also proves that everything simple is beyond us. What is blue, and how do we think 'blue'? The same difficulty occurs with death. Death and colours are things we cannot discuss. Nonetheless, the important thing is this man before me, heavy as earth, who prefigures my future. But can I really think about it? I tell myself: I am going to die, but this means nothing, since I cannot manage to believe it and can only experience other people's death. I have seen people die. Above all, I have seen dogs die. It was touching them that overwhelmed me. Then I think of flowers, smiles, the desire for women, and realise that my whole horror of death lies in my anxiety to live. I am jealous of those who will live and for whom flowers and the desire for women will have their full flesh and blood meaning. I am envious because I love life too much not to be selfish. What does eternity matter to me. You can be lying in bed one day and hear someone say: 'You are strong and I owe it to you to be honest: I can tell you that you are going to die'; you're there, with your whole life in your hands, fear in your bowels, looking the fool. What else matters: waves of blood come throbbing to my temples and I feel I could smash everything around me.

But men die in spite of themselves, in spite of their surroundings. They are told: 'When you get well . . . ,' and they die. I want none of that. For if there are days when nature lies, there are others when she tells the truth. Djemila is telling the truth tonight, and with what sad, insistent beauty! As for me, here in the presence of this world, I have no wish to lie or be lied to. I want to keep my lucidity to the last, and gaze upon my death with all the fullness of my jealousy and horror. It is to the extent I cut myself off from the world that I fear death most, to the degree I attach myself to the fate of living men instead of contemplating the unchanging sky. Creating conscious deaths is to diminish the distance that separates us from the world and to accept a consummation without joy, alert to rapturous images of a world forever lost. And the melancholy song of the Djemila hills plunges this bitter lesson deeper in my soul.

Toward evening, we were climbing the slopes leading to the village and, retracing our steps, listened to explanations: 'Here is the pagan town; this area outside the field is where the Christians lived. Later on . . .' Yes, it is true. Men and societies have succeeded one another in this place; conquerors have marked this country with their non-commissioned officer's civilisation. They had a vulgar and ridiculous idea of greatness, measuring the grandeur of their empire by the surface it covered. The miracle is that the ruin of their civilisation is the very negation of their ideal. For this skeleton town, seen from high above as evening closes in and white flights of pigeons circle round the triumphal arch, engraved no signs of conquest or ambition on the sky. The world always conquers history in the end. The great shout of stone that Djemila hurls between the mountains, the sky, and the silence—well do I know its poetry: lucidity, indifference, the true signs of beauty or despair. The heart tightens at the grandeur we've already left behind. Djemila remains with its sad watery sky, the song of a bird from the other side of the plateau, the sudden, quick scurrying of goats along the mountainside, and, in the calm, resonant dusk, the living face of a horned god on the pediment of an altar.

A Visit to Ancient Egypt

AUBREY MENEN

I like going to Egypt. I like wandering among the temples and tombs of the ancient Egyptians. It reminds me that Madison Avenue must be taken seriously. It is a stern fact, and we should never forget it. The ancient Egyptians built up a civilisation just as preposterous as the one that Madison Avenue has built for us. It did not collapse: it did not evolve into a better thing. It lasted, exactly as it was, for six thousand years. And it was firmly founded on the power of advertising. That is a solemn enough thought. But there is one more solemn still. The advertisements outlasted the civilisation. They are still there.

In one of the main squares of Cairo, outside the central railway station, is a colossal statue thirty-two feet high. It has been brought from a ruin and set up there by the present rulers of Egypt, and it is perfectly preserved. It shows the Pharaoh Rameses II. His mummy, which has been found, shows much the same cast of features, so we know that the statue is a good portrait of him.

Rameses II had this enormous statue carved from a single block of stone. His object was to impress his own and future generations with his wealth, his power, and his beauty. He had the statue made to ensure that he would never be forgotten. If the world were a just place such egotism would be punished, and Rameses II would have sunk into oblivion like a hundred other Pharaohs of whom we know barely their names. On the contrary, he has succeeded. Everybody going through the square three thousand one hundred and eighty-five years after his death, thinks of him. It has paid to advertise.

But this is high-class advertising. The statue is a work of art. Rameses II made it, in the terms of Madison Avenue, a prestige job. There is another advertisement, not far away, which is as vulgar and banal as any electric sign in Times Square. Some twenty minutes' drive from the railway station brings you to the Great Pyramid of Cheops. The Great Pyramid is a vast pile of stone without the least pretensions to beauty or to anything except size. Pharaohs before Cheops had built pyramids, but modest ones. Cheops decided to build the biggest pyramid that had ever been seen. His aim was exactly the same as that of Rameses II, but where Rameses had taste,

Cheops had none. All the same, he succeeded. He succeeded better than Rameses II, for there cannot be a literate person in the world who has not heard about the Great Pyramid or seen a picture of it. Advertising once more paid, as it always does, and the brasher it is the better. That, I remember, was the first lesson taught me when I worked in an advertising agency myself.

I worked for six happy moon-struck months in that agency before I defected to the real world. I am not a family man. I have no children. But I have always felt that my six months among advertisers made me understand a child's mind. I know what makes one child say to another, 'My father's car is a million billion trillion times better than your father's car.' I know why a child deliberately makes up a story and then is capable of believing it so intensely that he is afraid to go to bed. I know why children can sit together and wonder just how high was Jack's beanstalk, for I have spent days earnestly discussing a problem just as unreal. It all comes back to me when I visit Egypt, for the ancient Egyptians, like my colleagues in the agency, were children who spent their lives amid the most preposterous fairy tales ever to have come from the human mind. They built a way of life out of pure nonsense, and had the money to persuade the world to take them seriously. Egypt is littered with their gigantic toys.

The biggest of these is the Sphinx. A great deal of nonsense has been talked about the Sphinx for a very long time. It is said to be mysterious, when in fact it is no more mysterious than a billboard. It is said to be a goddess who asked a riddle of all passers-by and ate them when they could not give the right answer—a gruesome story invented by the Greeks about a thousand years after the statue was made. It was said to have a hidden meaning which would only be discovered when it was fully dug out of the sand. It has now been dug out. Nothing has been discovered except its vast lion's body, sprawling seventy yards across the desert, and its colossal paws like two vast city walls. The meaning of this immense piece of carved stone has never been in doubt to anybody who can bring himself to believe the plain facts. It is a piece of propaganda. Its face is not that of a goddess or a woman. It is the portrait of the Pharaoh who had it carved. His name was Khafre. The statue looks toward the east to remind the world that Khafre's name meant The-One-Who-Shines-Like-The-Sun. The face has a gigantic lion's body to show that Khafre was a strong king with the money and the power to have the monstrosity carved at his bidding.

He was not quite as successful in his advertising as Cheops. The sand drifted round his Sphinx until it was almost covered. Khafre's name might have been forgotten had not another Pharaoh, Amenhopis IV, dreamed that the monument came to him and asked to be dug out. The Egyptians, again like children, had a profound faith in the reality of dreams. Amenhopis immediately granted the Sphinx's request, dug away the sand, and set up a stone between its paws to say what he had done. On that stone he mentioned the name of the Pharaoh, whose portrait loomed in the sky above it. Since no other reference to the Sphinx has ever been found, without that monument the Sphinx might truly have a secret, and, in the circumstances, an ironic one. But luck was on Khafre's side. We remember him. You are thinking about him now, as I am, in spite of ourselves. We know nothing else about him whatever, except that he made the Sphinx. But it is enough for his purpose.

From the time Khafre raised the Sphinx to the time Amenhopis cleaned it up, the stupendous interval of one thousand four hundred years had passed. Yet there were still Pharaohs. Instead of such monuments as the Great Pyramid and the Sphinx bringing the state down in financial ruin or maddening the people into changing their system of government, Egypt was richer than ever. The Pharaohs were still masters of their people and they governed as absolutely as their predecessors. Nothing had changed, except the site of the capital. Khafre ruled from Memphis, a place in the north of Egypt which has disappeared. Amenhopis ruled from Thebes, a town in the south, which, in part, still remains. The Pharaohs built a series of indestructible monuments there, even more overwhelming in their size than the Sphinx. It is in Thebes that you come closest to knowing this extraordinary people.

Thebes is now called Luxor. It is a village set among palm trees on the banks of the Nile. It is kept very clean. At sunset it looks as pretty as a picture postcard and it is obvious that some authority or other has gone to a deal of trouble to see that it does. The climate of Luxor is agreeable in the winter and for a long time it has been fashionable to go there. Some of the fashionable tourists have written their impressions of the monuments.

There was the travel-writer Strabo, for instance, who described it as it was at the time of his visit. When Strabo was writing about Thebes, Jesus of Nazareth was approximately twenty years old. Another traveller instructed, or encouraged, a female poet in his entourage to scribble a few verses on one of the statues, mentioning his name. He was the Roman Emperor Hadrian and the lady's indifferent verses can still be read. The tourist who goes to Luxor can look forward, therefore, to seeing a place which an emperor travelled a thousand miles to see, and which was a famous travel sight when Mary and Joseph fled into Egypt.

Two thousand years of tourists have been perfectly right. The ruins at Luxor are, in my opinion, the most overwhelming sight that antiquity has left us. They are as vast as buildings seem in dreams. They are the most arrogant and impressive piece of propaganda ever made.

The first thing to do in Luxor, however, is not to see the ruins but to stand on the bank of the Nile and look to the other side. There is a narrow strip of vegetation that is stopped by a line of abrupt cliffs. Beyond this lies the desert. Behind you lies another strip of vege-tation, not a mile wide, with some gigantic ruins, and then, again, the desert. Thebes lies before you and behind you. There are two cities, each in its way as splendid as the other. The one behind you was built for the living. The other, across the Nile, was built for the dead. For the Egyptians, the one across the Nile was by far the more important.

People have always believed that there is some sort of life after death. It has been the constant hope and the occasional fear of the greater part of the human race. All the same, it has been generally agreed that since no one has ever come back from the grave to tell us, we do not really know what life after death is like. Attempts to guess at it, among adults, have always petered out in harps, houris, or hell fire. But the Egyptians were never adults. They had the directness of children. They settled the problem that has concerned the profoun-dest thinkers in the simplest possible manner. Life after death, they decided, was exactly like life before it. A child today will ask if he can take his puppy dog to heaven. The Egyptians answered that he most certainly could. He could take his spinning top and his toy horse as well. He could take anything he fancied, even, in certain circum-stances, his nurse. For children, this is a disarming belief. For full-grown Pharaohs, it was preposterous.

It is important to understand that the Egyptians meant exactly what they said. The afterlife was not, as with the Christians, a vague but real reward for a good life or a bad one. It was not, as with the Mohammedans, a place of cool repose for the warriors of Islam. To the Egyptians there was nothing spiritual about it. In later times, there was some notion of a judgement in which the soul of the dead would be weighed against his good deeds. But this was never taken too seriously. In any case, the dead person could always escape judgement by making the right remarks at the right time. Lest he should forget them, they were written in plain hieroglyphics, on the inside of his coffin. Apart from this, the Egyptian heaven was purely materialistic. You live the life you lived on earth, on your own bed, in your own clothes, wearing your own jewellery, waited upon by your own servants, eating the food you always liked and listening to your favourite tunes. If you had a turn for business or farming, you could go about that, too, in the old familiar way.

The Egyptian made sure that all this would happen with the relentlessly wrong logic of twelve-year-olds. When you died, you took your best pieces of furniture with you. That is to say, they were put in your tomb beside you by your family. You took your best clothes and your best jewellery. You had models made of your favourite servants, which would leap to life in the next world on your saying the right magic text, supplied on a papyrus scroll called the Book of the Dead, or written on the walls of your tomb to read while you were walking about and easing your limbs prior to entering heaven. Harps and zithers were supplied for music making, pots full of food for banquets, ointment to make you smell nice at feasts, checkerboards for gambling—in short, all the apparatus for a spacious and easy standard of living. As for business, you had models made of your clerks, your farmhands, your granaries, your ships, all with the appropriate workmen doing their appointed tasks. At your command, these would grow from foot-high wooden figures to living men and women who would go on making money for you for ever and ever.

Besides all these things, you needed, of course, your body. This necessity was most elaborately taken care of. You were mummified by expert embalmers. Since your lungs, heart, liver and other organs would not keep as well as your outer self—and you would, naturally, need these to enjoy your food and your banquets—these were removed and preserved in jars. The jars were handily disposed round your sarcophagus, so that your organs were ready to bounce back inside you as soon as you pushed up the lid.

All this vast variety of objects, including your own corpse, were stored away in a tomb of two, three or even four chambers, cut into the solid rock of the cliff faces across the Nile. In a materialist heaven you had to make a good impression and make it quickly. You therefore arranged—for the wise man spent years preparing his own tomb—for a good deal of gold and jewels to be buried with you. To prevent these being stolen, your tomb was sealed with a stone and the site covered in a great pile of rock debris. This was supposed to deceive robbers. It did not. Of all the tombs that have been explored, only one of any value had not been looted. The robberies went on during the very same ages that other burials were taking place. Tomb-making and tomb-robbing were conducted simultaneously. It brings to mind, in its naïvety, the picture of a group of children elaborately burying a sparrow and watching, blankly, as the dog digs it up again.

But although Thebes of the dead is a city of empty tombs, it is a deeply interesting place to visit. The high brown cliffs are approached by a causeway, built for dragging the sarcophagi on sleds to their resting places. The causeway turns a corner into the Valley of the Kings, a bleak and stony place, sun-drenched and silent. Here and there on the slopes are trenches. Down into these run steep ramps made for the sarcophagi to slide down. Below is the entrance to the tomb, no bigger than a normal door to a house. Indeed, the tomb itself is a house cut into the rock, with corridors, rooms, closets and a bedroom where the master slept until his inevitable and joyous awakening to a life of pleasure. These rooms and corridors were once crammed to the ceiling with treasure and household goods. They are empty now, but the wall paintings, astonishingly preserved in the dry Egyptian air, are still there to delight the spectator's eye with a hundred vivid and highly realistic scenes of life after death.

In one tomb, and in one alone, the dead man still lies, awaiting his promised resurrection. He was an unimportant Pharaoh called Tutankhamen. He lived in troubled times; he died young; he was buried in haste. It seems that the site of his tomb was forgotten by everybody, including the robbers. When it was discovered in 1926, it was intact. The king lay on a nest of coffins, two of which were of gold and lapis lazuli. The coffins were in a series of shrines. Outside the shrines was piled a houseful of furniture and ornaments, including a throne of gold. The treasure has been carried off to the museum in Cairo, but the king remains. We have evidence that at least one of the people who prepared his tomb did not seriously believe that his master would rise and inspect his work. There is a tarnished patch on one of the shrines, where the gold leaf had been adulterated. The gilder had cheated, secure in the belief that nobody would know he had done so until long after the tomb was sacked. It is surprising that nobody else seems to have followed his example.

The city of the dead has a profound effect upon the city on the other bank of the Nile, the living Thebes. If being dead was nothing but an eternity of material joys, the ancient Egyptian saw no reason why he should not wallow in them when he was alive. Whatever it was you wanted—a gold and lapis-lazuli collar, rare spices, an ivory bed—you could enjoy it now, and you *could* take it with you. Materialism, as a way of life, could go no further. An American might well think he owed himself a Cadillac, but no American has yet, so far as I know, been buried in one. Religiously inclined or not, he would consider it improper.

The city of Thebes was the greatest centre of luxury trades in the ancient world. Homer, who had a taste for high living himself, remarks that the precious objects in Thebes were more numerous than grains of sand. Now we know from our own experience that an economy based on a high rate of consumption can be kept going only by keeping the buyer in a mood to consume. A whole profession of men expert in whetting our appetites has grown up around us. They assure us, almost every minute of our waking day, that it is right and proper to consume as much as we can. If they find we are not doing it, they gently, humorously berate us.

In Thebes, the persuaders—and the profession existed there in full force—went further still. They assured the public that materialism was not only the way of the world; it was also the way of heaven. They set up a perpetual Christmas. Religion, they said, was purely a matter of giving sumptuous gifts to the gods. The gods themselves were innumerable, and unimportant. What mattered was that they should be given an unending supply of costly presents. Now since the gods were only stone statues, the gifts had to be received by someone on the statue's behalf. The persuaders said that they themselves should receive the gifts. Thus arose the most astonishing, the most rapacious and most powerful priesthood in the history of the world.

I call them priests, but they were much more. They were an *élite*, such as the Communist party members are in Russia, who controlled the thoughts and the daily lives of every inhabitant of the country. They invented the Egyptian religion, unashamedly adding to it whatever suited their purpose. They invented the laws. They invented gods by the hundred. They invented rituals of worship, and they invented the heaviest system of ecclesiastical taxation in history. They even invented the Pharaoh, by declaring that the supreme ruler of Egypt was, in fact, a god himself: that is, if he gave them enough gifts. If he did not—and a few rebelled—they dethroned him and put somebody more respectful in his place. Lastly, they invented the most stupendous temples ever built. Let us visit one.

Karnak is a tiny Arab village on either side of a sandy road that leads out of Luxor. We drive along the road for five minutes and come suddenly to a vast open space. On either side of us is a great avenue of sphinxes. Each sphinx crouches on a pedestal, and is bigger than a man. This was the boulevard that led from the city of Thebes to its major temple, the Great Temple of Amon at Karnak. On our right is its majestic entrance.

It is a vast wall, tapering toward the top and divided into two parts by a gateway. Its shape, its gigantic size, the boldness of the conception show that nobody was meant to go through such an entrance without being struck with awe. Nobody, I think, ever has.

Immediately after the gateway comes a courtyard. It is so huge that the spectator seems to shrink, while the great gate itself, looking back at it, is diminished to an ordinary doorway. Massive columns, bulging at the top, stand on all sides like an army. We cross the courtyard and come to another doorway, as vast as the first. We go through it and, like generations of visitors before us, we are dumbfounded.

We are in the great Hypostyle Hall. The Pharaohs who built it—it took nine of them—intended that nothing of its sort could be seen anywhere else in the world. Their world was small compared with ours. But there is still nothing to compare with it. The Hypostyle Hall is three hundred and thirty feet long by a hundred and eighty feet wide. It is filled with thirty-four colossal columns, holding up a stone roof seventy-five feet from the floor. The columns are fifty feet in circumference. Such figures are hard to grasp, but there is a better way of judging the scale of this immense work: fifty grown persons could stand, with space to be at their ease, on the flat tops of each of the central columns.

The columns are placed close together, leaving only narrow paths between them, except in the middle of the hall, where they fall back to leave a processional road. Once off this road and among the columns, you can get lost, as in a forest of gigantic trees. Not content with raising a tremendous piece of architecture in stone, the Pharaohs painted each of the pillars from top to bottom with symbols, texts and religious scenes. Some of the paintings still remain. They are sufficient to let us see that when the hall was new it could have been read like a coloured storybook.

Four more gateways, diminishing in size, lead into the temple proper, where few but the Pharaoh and the temple priests ever came. The scale of the architecture here is much smaller. Grandeur stopped where the people stopped. The sanctuary is no more than a set of rooms, an apartment for the statue of the god Amon, who was bathed, dressed and offered gifts and food every day to the sound of music.

But there is no feeling of solemnity. There is no sense of the mysteries of religion. Nor could there very well be. The walls of the inner sanctuary are as pragmatical as the advertising pages of a magazine. They show innumerable processions, each led by a Pharaoh, and each Pharaoh is followed by a long line of retainers, every one of whom is bringing a gift for the god. The decoration is a sacerdotal hint to the reigning Pharaoh and it is a hint as broad as a barge.

The Pharaohs obliged handsomely. At one time the priesthood was so rich that they owned one-third of the wealth of Egypt. But the arrangement worked two ways. The reigning Pharaoh donated immense treasure to the priests. They, in return, allowed the Pharaoh to use the temple as a propaganda machine.

We can best see how this was done by leaving the Great Temple of Karnak and going to the temple of Amon at Luxor. It is smaller, though still massive. It has much the same entrance. But in front of it stand six colossal statues, two of them seated, the others standing. These are statues of Rameses II and they had exactly the same purpose as his statue in Cairo. They told the worshipper, six times over before he even set foot in the temple, that Rameses II was a mighty man. On the gateway itself is a bas-relief, much in the style of a formalised poster, which narrates one of Rameses II's famous victories. Inside the temple, the propaganda grows even more insistent. In one of the courtyards there are no less than thirteen gigantic statues, this time of the Pharaoh Amenhophis III. They are seated. They stare straight ahead. Their expression is one of utter calm. Their physique is that of giant athletes. Nobody in real life ever sat so impressively, nobody ever had such calves and biceps, nobody ever had such an expression of godlike tranquillity. But massive lumps of stone insist thirteen times that Amenhophis had all these things: and the whole affair is so big that you believe it, at least while you are standing by the huge feet of these monstrous advertisements.

The Pharaohs were much given to describing their own personalities, but we are quite unable to gather from the inscriptions they have left behind what a Pharaoh was really like. The inscriptions are about as self-critical as the pronouncements of a heavy-weight boxer on the day before a fight.

We would, in fact, know nothing about the Pharaohs at all except their triumphs, if it were not for the fact that there is one rent in the curtain of favourable propaganda. One of these great men was a woman.

Her name was Hatshepsut and we are not at all sure how she managed to clamber onto the throne of Egypt. It happened, after all, three thousand five hundred years ago and all we have to go by is a handful of inscriptions on temple walls. But it appears that she was the wife of a temple priest, Thutmose, who had some slender claim to the throne since he was the son of the reigning Pharaoh through an obscure concubine. According to the inscription he had carved on the temple at Karnak, one day he was suddenly wafted up to heaven and there was crowned by the sun god himself. We need not believe this. But this accession, it seems, did not lack drama. In one of the courtyards of the temple was a spot on which only the Pharaoh could stand. On a great feast day, the priests, who were weary of the reigning king, stood Thutmose on this significant spot, under the nose of the Pharaoh, who abdicated. Thutmose thus became the absolute master of everybody in Egypt, except his wife.

She, too, had a claim to the throne. She was of royal blood. She was beautiful, and she was an aggressive woman. She rallied a party of nobles round her, made up of men who disliked Thutmose as the tool of priests, and got herself made co-regent with her husband.

But this did not satisfy her. She decided that it was time she wore the breeches, which were, in this instance, the elaborately folded loincloth of the divine kings of Egypt. She insisted that although she was a woman, she was also Pharaoh. Since the Pharaohs played a large part in all religious ceremonies, this created havoc not only in the court but in the temples. Egypt, which for centuries had been accustomed to the rule of a man, now was forced to bow to the caprices of a woman who, moreover, gloried in her femininity.

After five years of chaos, the old Pharaoh who had abdicated in the temple allied himself with another of his sons and threw Thutmose and Hatshepsut off the throne. The old man's son was also called Thutmose, and I shall refer to him as Thutmose II.

The old king and Thutmose II now embarked on a campaign against Hatshepsut, so childish as to be incredible if the evidence were not still clearly before our eyes. Hatshepsut, as deep a believer in publicity as any male Pharaoh, had filled Thebes with monuments and reliefs glorifying herself. The old Pharaoh and Thutmose II now ordered that everywhere Hatshepsut had put her name, it should be chiselled out and their own put in its place. Where the figure of the face of the queen had been carved, that had to be chiselled out too.

As a result, they made Hatshepsut immortal. You cannot erase from stone without leaving clear evidence of what you have done. The outline of Hatshepsut with all her features hacked away is pointed out to every visitor today. The blank space where her name had been is the most interesting feature of the bas-reliefs in the temples she built. The best that can be said for the infantile rage of Thutmose II and his father is that Hatshepsut must have been a terrible woman to put up with.

And they were not finished with her. The old man died and the brawling broke out once more. Thutmose II fell ill, and perhaps in a final attempt to keep the woman off the throne, he made overtures of peace to her husband, the other Thutmose. It was a mistake. The two Thutmoses reigned together for three years and then Hatshepsut was back, this time for good.

Officially, she had equal power with her husband. In fact, she was supreme. An inscription says: 'The Divine Consort, Hatshepsut, adjusted the affairs of (Egypt) according to her own decisions. Egypt was made to labour with bowed head for her, the excellent child of god, who came forth from him.'

It will be seen that she had solved the problem of being a woman and the son of a god at the same time. She solved it in the feminine manner: that is, she ignored it completely. Her bosom friend was an architect. She set him to build her a magnificent temple on the other bank of the Nile, where it can still be seen. On the walls, she had carved the whole story, illustrated with bas-reliefs of her divine birth. She had herself shown as a *boy*. She also showed herself being acknowledged as a *queen* by the old Pharaoh who was the father of her husband. She reigned for twenty-one years, filling the court with her favourites, and indulging in such womanly pastimes as sending vast expeditions in search of rare perfumes. Then she died. Thutmose ruled alone at last.

He has left a permanent record of his impressions of married life. Following the example set him, he hacked out Hatshepsut's name wherever he found it and built walls round the obelisk which she had put up in the temple of Karnak so that nobody could see it. But Hatshepsut had the last word. The wall has fallen down. Her obelisk still stands.

Such, then, were the Pharaohs in real life. Yet when they moved in procession through the vast courtyards of their temples, or were glimpsed between the gigantic statues, everybody, except the priests, thought them gods. Perhaps when they stood underneath one of their towering statues, they thought so too. The temptation to do so must have been strong. The Pharaohs were by far the most successful rulers of the ancient world and two immense statues, known to us as the Colossi of Memnon, stand on the plain in the dead city of Thebes to witness that the Pharaohs were by far the richest. Not even the Romans could afford to erect statues to themselves as big as these. They bear witness, for me, to another fact: there is no idea so silly that you cannot persuade a great number of people to believe it is true. As they told me in my advertising agency, all it needs is time, money and a sense of dedication. The Egyptians were the first people in the world to have all three.

Notes Mailed at Nagercoil

PAUL BOWLES

I have been here in this hotel now for a week. At no time during the night or day has the temperature been low enough for comfort; it fluctuates between 95 and 105 degrees, and most of the time there is absolutely no breeze, which is astonishing for the seaside. Each bedroom and public room has the regulation large electric fan in its ceiling, but there is no electricity; we are obliged to use oil lamps for lighting. Today at lunchtime a large Cadillac of the latest model drove up to the front door. In the back were three little men wearing nothing but the flimsy dhotis they had draped around their loins. One of them handed a bunch of keys to the chauffeur, who then got out and came into the hotel. Near the front door is the switch box. He opened it, turned on the current with one of the keys, and throughout the hotel the fans began to whir. Then the three little men got out and went into the dining room where they had their lunch. I ate quickly, so as to get upstairs and lie naked on my bed under the fan. It was an unforgettable fifteen minutes. Then the fan stopped, and I heard the visitors driving away. The hotel manager told me later that they were government employees of the State of Travancore, and that only they had a key to the switch box.★

Last night I awoke and opened my eyes. There was no moon; it was still dark, but the light of a star was shining into my face through the open window, from a point high above the Arabian Sea. I sat up, and gazed at it. The light it cast seemed as bright as that of the moon in northern countries; coming through the window, it made its rect-angle on the opposite wall, broken by the shadow of my silhouetted head. I held up my hand and moved the fingers, and their shadow too was definite. There were no other stars visible in that part of the sky; this one blinded them all. It was about an hour before daybreak, which comes shortly after six, and there was not a breath of air. On such still nights the waves breaking on the nearby shore sound like

★Subsequently Travancore and Cochin have merged to make the province of Kerala.

great, deep explosions going on at some distant place. There is the boom, which can be felt as well as heard, and which ends with a sharp rattle and hiss, then a long period of complete silence, and finally, when it seems that there will be no more sound, another sudden boom. The crows begin to scream and chatter while the darkness is still complete.

The town, like the others here in the extreme south, gives the impression of being made of dust. Dust and cow-dung lie in the streets, and the huge crows hop ahead of you as you walk along. When a gust of hot wind wanders in from the sandy wastes beyond the town, the brown fans of the palmyra trees swish and bang against each other; they sound like giant sheets of heavy wrapping paper. The small black men walk quickly, the diamonds in their earlobes flashing. Because of their jewels and the gold thread woven into their dhotis, they all look not merely prosperous, but fantastically wealthy. When the women have diamonds, they are likely to wear them in a hole pierced through the wall of one nostril.

The first time I ever saw India I entered it through Dhanushkodi. An analogous procedure in America would be for a foreigner to get his first glimpse of the United States by crossing the Mexican border illegally and coming out into a remote Arizona village. It was God-forsaken, uncomfortable, and a little frightening. Since then I have landed as a bonafide visitor should, in the impressively large and unbeautiful metropolis of Bombay. But I am glad that my first trip did not bring me in contact with any cities. It is better to go to the villages of a strange land before trying to understand its towns, above all in a complex place like India. Now, after travelling some eight thousand miles around the country, I know approximately as little as I did on my first arrival. However, I've seen a lot of people and places, and at least I have a somewhat more detailed and precise idea of my ignorance than I did in the beginning.

If you have not taken the precaution of reserving a room in advance, you risk having considerable difficulty in finding one when you land in Bombay. There are very few hotels, and the two or three comfortable ones are always full. I hate being committed to a reserva-tion because the element of adventure is thereby destroyed. The only place I was able to get into when I first arrived, therefore, was something less than a first-class establishment. It was all right during the day and the early hours of the evening. At night, however, every square foot of floor space in the dark corridors was occupied by sleepers who had arrived late and brought their own mats with them; the hotel was able in this way to shelter several hundred extra guests each night. Having their hands and feet kicked and trodden on was apparently a familiar enough experience to them for them never to make any audible objection when the inevitable happened.

Here in Cape Comorin, on the other hand, there are many rooms and they are vast, and at the moment I am the only one staying in the hotel.

It was raining. I was on a bus going from Alleppey to Trivandrum, on my way down here. There were two little Indian nuns on the seat in front of mine. I wondered how they stood the heat in their heavy robes. Sitting near the driver was a man with a thick, fierce moustache who distinguished himself from the other passengers by the fact that in addition to his dhoti he also wore a European shirt; its scalloped tail hung down nearly to his knees. With him he had a voluminous collection of magazines and newpapers in both Tamil and English, and even from where I sat I could not help noticing that all this reading matter had been printed in the Soviet Union.

At a certain moment, near one of the myriad villages that lie smothered in the depths of the palm forests there, the motor suddenly ceased to function, and the bus came to a stop. The driver, not exchanging a single glance with his passengers, let his head fall forward and remain resting on the steering wheel in a posture of despair. Expectantly the people waited a little while, and then they began to get down. One of the first out of the bus was the man with the moustache. He said a hearty goodbye to the occupants in general, although he had not been conversing with any of them, and started up the road carrying his umbrella, but not his armful of printed matter. Then I realised that at some point during the past hour, not foreseeing the failure of the motor and the mass departure which it entailed, he had left a paper or magazine on each empty seat—exactly as our American comrades used to do on subway trains three decades ago.

Almost at the moment I made this discovery, the two nuns had risen and were hurriedly collecting the 'literature'. They climbed down and ran along the road after the man, calling out in English: 'Sir, your papers!' He turned, and they handed them to him. Without saying a word, but with an expression of fury on his face, he took the bundle and continued. But it was impossible to tell from the faces of the two nuns when they returned to gather up their belongings whether or not they were conscious of what they had done.

A few minutes later everyone had left the bus and walked to the village—everyone, that is, but the driver and me. I had too much luggage. Then I spoke to him.

'What's the matter with the bus?'

He shrugged his shoulders.

'How am I going to get to Trivandrum?'

He did not know that, either.

'Couldn't you look into the motor?' I pursued. 'It sounded like the fan belt. Maybe you could repair it.'

This roused him sufficiently from his apathy to make him turn and look at me.

'We have People's Government here in Travancore', he said. 'Not allowed touching motor.'

'But who *is* going to repair it, then?'

'Tonight making telephone call to Trivandrum. Making report. Tomorrow or other day they sending inspector to examine.'

'And then what?'

'Then inspector making report. Then sending repair crew.'

'I see.'

'People's Government,' he said again, by way of helping me to understand. 'Not like other government.'

'No,' I said.

As if to make his meaning clearer, he indicated the seat where the man with the large moustache had sat. 'That gentleman Communist.'

'Oh, really?' (At least, it was all in the open, and the driver was under no misapprehension as to what the term 'People's Government' meant.)

'Very powerful man. Member of Parliament from Travancore.'

'Is he a good man, though? Do the people like him?'

'Oh, yes, sir. Powerful man.'

'But is he *good*?' I insisted.

He laughed, doubtless at my ingenuousness. 'Powerful man all rascals,' he said.

Just before nightfall a local bus came along, and with the help of several villagers I transferred my luggage to it and continued on my way.

Most of the impressively heavy Communist vote is cast by the Hindus. The Moslems are generally in less dire economic straits, it is true, but in any case, by virtue of their strict religious views, they do not take kindly to any sort of ideological change. (A convert from Islam is unthinkable; apostasy is virtually non-existent.) If even Christianity has retained too much of its pagan décor to be acceptable to the puritanical Moslem mind, one can imagine the loathing inspired in them by the endless proliferations of Hindu religious art with its gods, demons, metamorphoses and avatars. The two religious systems are antipodal. Fortunately the constant association with the mild and tolerant Hindus has made the Moslems of India far more understanding and tractable than their brothers in Islamic countries further west; there is much less actual friction than one might be led to expect.

During breakfast one morning at the Connemara Hotel in Madras the Moslem head waiter told me a story. He was travelling in the Province of Orissa, where in a certain town there was a Hindu temple which was noted for having five hundred cobras on its premises. He decided he would like to see these famous reptiles. When he had got to the town he hired a carriage and went to the temple. At the door he was met by a priest who offered to show him around. And since the Moslem looked prosperous, the priest suggested a donation of five rupees, to be paid in advance.

'Why so much?' asked the visitor.

'To buy eggs for the cobras. You know, we have five hundred of them.'

The Moslem gave him the money on condition that the priest let him see the snakes. For an hour his guide dallied in the many courtyards and galleries, pointing out bas-reliefs, idols, pillars and bells. Finally the Moslem reminded him of their understanding.

'Cobras? Ah, yes. But they are dangerous. Perhaps you would rather see them another day?'

This behaviour on the priest's part had delighted him, he recalled, for it had reinforced his suspicions.

'Not at all,' he said. 'I want to see them now.'

Reluctantly the priest led him into a small alcove behind a large stone Krishna, and pointed into a very dark corner.

'Is this the place?' the visitor asked.

'This is the place.'

'But where are the snakes?'

In a tiny enclosure were two sad old cobras, 'almost dead from hunger,' he assured me. But when his eyes had grown used to the dimness he saw that there were hundreds of eggshells scattered around the floor outside the pen.

'You eat a lot of eggs,' he told the priest.

The priest merely said: 'Here. Take back your five rupees. But if you are asked about our cobras, please be so kind as to say that you saw five hundred of them here in our temple. Is that all right?'

The episode was meant to illustrate the head waiter's thesis, which was that the Hindus are abject in the practice of their religion; this is the opinion held by the Moslems. On the other hand, it must be remembered that the Hindu considers Islam an incomplete doctrine, far from satisfying. He finds its austerity singularly comfortless, and deplores its lack of mystico-philosophical content, an element in which his own creed is so rich.

I was invited to lunch at one of the cinema studios in the suburbs north of Bombay. We ate our curry outdoors; our hostess was the star of the film then in production. She spoke only Marathi; her husband, who was directing the picture, spoke excellent English. During the course of the meal he told how, as a Hindu, he had been forced to leave his job, his home, his car and his bank account in Karachi at the time of partition, when Pakistan came into existence, and emigrate empty-handed to India, where he managed to remake his life. Another visitor to the studio, an Egyptian, was intensely interested in his story. Presently he interrupted to say: 'It is unjust, of course.'

'Yes,' smiled our host.

'What retaliatory measures does your govenment plan to take against the Moslems left here in India?'

'None whatever, as far as I know.'

The Egyptian was genuinely indignant. 'But why not?' he demanded. 'It is only right that you apply the same principle. You have plenty of Moslems here still to take action against. And I say that, even though I am a Moslem.'

The film director looked at him closely. 'You say that *because* you are a Moslem,' he told him. 'But we cannot put ourselves on that level.'

The conversation ended on this not entirely friendly note. A moment later packets of betel were passed around. I promptly broke a tooth, withdrew from the company and went some distance away into the garden. While I, in the interests of science, was examining the mouthful of partially chewed betel leaves and areca nut, trying to find the pieces of bicuspid, the Egyptian came up to me, his face a study in scorn.

'They are afraid of the Moslems. That's the real reason,' he whispered. Whether he was right or wrong I was neither qualified nor momentarily disposed to say, but it was a classical exposition of the two opposing moral viewpoints—two concepts of behaviour which cannot quickly be reconciled.

Obviously it is a gigantic task to make a nation out of a place like India, what with Hindus, Parsees, Jainists, Jews, Catholics and Protestants, some of whom may speak the arbitrarily imposed national idiom of Hindi, but most of whom are more likely to know Gujarati, Marathi, Bengali, Urdu, Telugu, Tamil, Malayalam or some other tongue instead. One wonders whether any sort of unifying project can ever be undertaken, or, indeed, whether it is even desirable.

When you come to the border between two provinces you often find bars across the road, and you are obliged to undergo a thorough inspection of your luggage. As in the United States, there is a strict control of the passage of liquor between wet and dry districts, but that is not the extent of the examination.

Sample of conversation at the border on the Mercara–Cannanore highway:

'What is in there?' (Customs officer.)

'Clothing.' (Bowles.)

'And in that?'

'Clothing.'

'And in all those?'

'Clothing.'

'Open all, please.'

After eighteen suitcases have been gone through carefully: 'My God, man! Close them all. I could charge duty for all of these goods, but you will never be able to do business with these things here anyway. The Moslem men are too clever.'

'But I'm not intending to sell my clothes.'

'Shut the luggage. It is duty-free, I tell you.'

A professor from Raniket in North India arrived at the hotel here the other day, and we spent a good part of the night sitting on the window seat in my room that overlooks the sea, talking about what one always talks about here: India. Among the many questions I put to him was one concerning the reason why so many of the Hindu temples in South India prohibit entry to non-Hindus, and why they have military guards at the entrances. I imagined I knew the answer in advance: fear of Moslem disturbances. Not at all, he said. The principal purpose was to keep out certain Christian missionaries. I expressed disbelief.

'Of course,' he insisted. 'They come and jeer during our rituals, ridicule our sacred images.'

'But even if they were stupid enough to want to do such things,' I objected, 'their sense of decorum would keep them from behaving like that.'

He merely laughed. 'Obviously you don't know them.'

The post office here is a small stifling room over a shop, and it is full of boys seated on straw mats. The postmaster, a tiny old man who wears large diamond earrings and gold-rimmed spectacles, and is always naked to the waist, is also a professor; he interrupts his academic work to sell an occasional stamp. At first contact his English sounds fluent enough, but soon one discovers that it is not adapted to conversation, and that one can scarcely talk to him. Since the boys are listening, he must pretend to be omniscient, therefore he answers promptly with more or less whatever phrase comes into his head.

Yesterday I went to post a letter by airmail to Tangier. 'Tanjore,' he said, adjusting his spectacles. 'That will be four annas.' (Tanjore is in South India, near Trichinopoly.) I explained that I hoped my letter would be going to Tangier, Morocco.

'Yes, yes,' he said impatiently. 'There are many Tanjores.' He opened the book of postal regulations and read aloud from it, quite at random, for (although it may be difficult to believe) exactly six minutes. I stood still, fascinated, and let him go on. Finally he looked up and said: 'There is no mention of Tangier. No airplanes go to that place.'

'Well, how much would it be to send it by sea mail?' (I thought we could then calculate the surcharge for air mail, but I had misjudged my man.)

'Yes,' he replied evenly. 'That is a good method, too.'

I decided to keep the letter and post it in the nearby town of Nagercoil another day. In a little while I shall have several to add to it, and I count on being able to send them all together when I go. Before I left the post office I hazarded the remark that the weather was extremely hot. In that airless attic at noon it was a wild understatement. But it did not please the postmaster at all. Deliberately he removed his glasses and pointed the stems at me.

'Here we have the perfect climate,' he told me. 'Neither too cold nor too cool.'

'That is true,' I said. 'Thank you.'

In the past few years there have been visible quantitative changes in the life, all in the one direction of Europeanisation. This is in the smaller towns; the cities of course have long since been Westernised. The temples which before were lighted by bare electric bulbs and coconut oil lamps now have fluorescent tubes glimmering in their ceilings. Crimson, green, and amber floodlights are used to illumine bathing tanks, deities, the gateways of temples. The public-address system is the bane of the ear these days, even in the temples. And it is impossible to attend a concert or a dance recital without discovering several loudspeakers in operation, whose noise completely destroys the quality of the music. A mile before you arrive at the cinema of a small town you can hear the raucous blaring of the amplifier they have set up at its entrance.

This year in South India there are fewer men with bare torsos, dhotis and sandals: more shirts, trousers and shoes. There is at the same time a slow shutting-down of services which to the Western tourist make all the difference between pleasure and discomfort in travelling, such as the restaurants in the stations (there being no dining-cars on the trains) and the showers in the first-class compartments. A few years ago they worked; now they have been sealed off. You can choke on the dust and soot of your compartment, or drown in your own sweat now, for all the railway cares.

At one point I was held for forty-eight hours in a concentration camp run by the Ceylon government on Indian soil. (The euphemism for this one was 'screening camp'.) I was told that I was under suspicion of being an 'international spy'. My astonishment and indignation were regarded as almost convincing in their sincerity, thus proof of my guilt.

'But who am I supposed to be spying *for*?' I asked piteously.

The director shrugged. 'Spying for international,' he said.

More than the insects or the howling of pariah dogs outside the rolls of barbed wire, what bothered me was the fact that in the centre of the camp, which at that time housed some twenty thousand people, there was a loudspeaker in a high tower which during every moment of the day roared forth Indian film music. Fortunately it was silenced at ten o'clock each evening. I got out of the hell-hole by making such violent trouble that I was dragged before the camp doctor, who decided that I was dangerously unbalanced. The idea in letting me go was that I would be detained further along, and the responsibility would fall on other shoulders. 'They will hold him at Talaimannar,' I heard the doctor say. 'The poor fellow is quite mad.'

Here and there, in places like the bar of the Hotel Metropole at Mysore, or at the North Coorg Club of Mercara, one may still come across vestiges of the old colonial life; ghosts in the form of incredibly sunburned Englishmen in jodhpurs and boots discussing their hunting luck and prowess. But these visions are exceedingly rare in a land that wants to forget their existence.

The younger generation in India is intent on forgetting a good many things, including some that it might do better to remember. There would seem to be no good reason for getting rid of their country's most ancient heritage, the religion of Hinduism, or of its most recent acquisition, the tradition of independence. This latter, at least insofar as the illiterate masses are concerned, is inseparable not only from the religious state of mind which made political victory possible, but also from the legend which, growing up around the figure of Gandhi, has elevated him in their minds to the status of a god.

The young, politically-minded intellectuals find this not at all to their liking; in their articles and addresses they have returned again and again to the attack against Gandhi as a 'betrayer' of the Indian people. That they are motivated by hatred is obvious. But what do they hate?

For one thing, subconsciously they cannot accept their own inability to go on having religious beliefs. Then, belonging to the group without faith, they are thereby forced to hate the past, particularly the atavisms which are made apparent by the workings of the human mind with its irrationality, its subjective involvement in exterior phenomena. The floods of poisonous words they pour forth are directed primarily at the adolescents: it is an age group which is often likely to find demagoguery more attractive than common sense.

There are at least a few of these enlightened adolescents in every town; the ones here in Cape Comorin were horrified when, by a stratagem, I led them to the home of a man of their own village named Subramaniam, who claims that his brother is under a spell. (They had not imagined, they told me later, that an American would believe such nonsense.) According to Subramaniam, his brother was a painter who had been made art-director of a major film studio in Madras. To substantiate his story he brought out a sheaf of very professional sketches for film sets.

'Then my brother had angry words with a jealous man in the studio,' said Subramaniam, 'and the man put a charm on him. His mind is gone. But at the end of the year it will return.' The brother presently appeared in the courtyard; he was a vacant-eyed man with a beard, and he had a voluminous turkish towel draped over his head and shoulders. He walked past us and disappeared through a doorway.

'A spirit doctor is treating him . . .' The modern young men shifted their feet miserably; it was unbearable that an American should be witnessing such shameful revelations, and that they should be coming from one in their midst.

But these youths who found it so necessary to ridicule poor Subramaniam failed to understand why I laughed when, the conversation changing to the subject of cows, I watched their collective expression swiftly change to one of respect bordering on beatitude. For cow-worship is one facet of popular Hinduism which has not yet been totally superseded by twentieth-century faithlessness. True, it has taken on new forms of ritual. Mass cow worship is often practised now in vast modern concrete stadiums, with prizes being distributed to the owners of the finest bovine specimens, but the religious aspect of the celebration is still evident. The cows are decorated with garlands and jewellery, fed bananas and sugar-cane by people who have waited in line for hours to be granted that rare privilege, and when the satiated animals can eat no more they simply lie down or wander about, while hundreds of young girls perform sacred dances in their honour.

In India, where the cow wishes to go, she goes. She may be lying in the temple, where she may decide to get up, to go and lie instead in the middle of the street. If she is annoyed by the proximity of the traffic streaming past her, she may lumber to her feet again and continue down the street to the railway station, where, should she feel like reclining in front of the ticket window, no one will disturb her. On the highways she seems to know that the drivers of trucks and buses will spot her a mile away and slow down almost to a stop before they get to her, and that therefore she need not move out from under the shade of the particular banyan tree she has chosen for her rest. Her superior position in the world is agreed upon by common consent.

The most satisfying exposition I have seen of the average Hindu's feeling about this exalted beast is a little essay composed by a candidate for a post in one of the public services, entitled simply: *The Cow*. The fact that it was submitted in order to show the aspirant's mastery of the English language, while touching, is of secondary importance.

The Cow

The cow is one wonderful animal, also he is quadruped and because he is female he gives milk—but he will do so only when he has got child. He is same like God, sacred to Hindu and useful to man. But he has got four legs together. Two are foreward and two are afterwards.

His whole body can be utilised for use. More so the milk. What it cannot do? Various ghee, butter, cream, curds, whey, kova and the condensed milk and so forth. Also, he is useful to cobbler, watermans and mankind generally.

His motion is slow only. That is because he is of amplitudinous species, and also his other motion is much useful to trees, plants as well as making fires. This is done by making flat cakes in hand and drying in the sun.

He is the only animal that extricates his feedings after eating. Then afterwards he eats by his teeth whom are situated in the inside of his mouth. He is incessantly grazing in the meadows.

His only attacking and defending weapons are his horns, especially when he has got child. This is done by bowing his head whereby he causes the weapons to be parallel to ground of earth and instantly proceeds with great velocity forwards.

He has got tail also, but not like other similar animals. It has hairs on the end of the other side. This is done to frighten away the flies which alight on his whole body and chastises him unceasingly, whereupon he gives hit with it.

The palms of his feet are so soft unto the touch, so that the grasses he eats would not get crushed. At night he reposes by going down on the ground and then he shuts his eyes like his relative the horse which does not do so. This is the cow.

The moths and night insects flutter about my single oil lamp. Occasionally, at the top of its chimney, one of them goes up in a swift, bright flame. On the concrete floor in a fairly well-defined ring around the bottom of my chair are the drops of sweat that have rolled off my body during the past two hours. The doors into both the bedroom and the bathroom are shut; I work each night in the dressing-room between them, because fewer insects are attracted here. But the air is nearly unbreathable with the stale smoke of cigarettes and bathi sticks burned to discourage the entry of winged creatures. Today's paper announced an outbreak of bubonic plague in Bellary. I keep thinking about it, and I wonder if the almost certain eventual victory over such diseases will prove to have been worth its price: the extinction of the beliefs and rituals which gave a satisfactory meaning to the period of consciousness that goes between birth and death. I doubt it. Security is a false god; begin making sacrifices to it and you are lost.

L'Envoi

The Modern Essay

VIRGINIA WOOLF

As Mr Rhys truly says, it is unnecessary to go profoundly into the history and origin of the essay—whether it derives from Socrates or Siranney the Persian—since, like all living things, its present is more important than its past. Moreover, the family is widely spread; and while some of its representatives have risen in the world and wear their coronets with the best, others pick up a precarious living in the gutter near Fleet Street. The form, too, admits variety. The essay can be short or long, serious or trifling, about God and Spinoza, or about turtles and Cheapside. But as we turn over the pages of these five little volumes, containing essays written between 1870 and 1920, certain principles appear to control the chaos, and we detect in the short period under review something like the progress of history.

Of all forms of literature, however, the essay is the one which least calls for the use of long words. The principle which controls it is simply that it should give pleasure; the desire which impels us when we take it from the shelf is simply to receive pleasure. Everything in an essay must be subdued to that end. It should lay us under a spell with its first word, and we should only wake, refreshed, with its last. In the interval we may pass through the most various experiences of amusement, surprise, interest, indignation; we may soar to the heights of fantasy with Lamb or plunge to the depths of wisdom with Bacon, but we must never be roused. The essay must lap us about and draw its curtain across the world.

So great a feat is seldom accomplished, though the fault may well be as much on the reader's side as on the writer's. Habit and lethargy have dulled his palate. A novel has a story, a poem rhyme; but what art can the essayist use in these short lengths of prose to sting us wide awake and fix us in a trance which is not sleep but rather an intensification of life—a basking, with every faculty alert, in the sun of pleasure? He must know—that is the first essential—how to write. His learning may be as profound as Mark Pattison's, but in an essay it must be so fused by the magic of writing that not a fact juts out, not a dogma tears the surface of the texture. Macaulay in one way, Froude in another, did this superbly over and over again. They have blown more knowledge into us in the course of one essay than the innumerable chapters of a hundred text-books. But when Mark Pattison has to tell us, in the space of thirty-five little pages, about Montaigne, we feel that he had not previously assimilated M. Grün. M. Grün was a gentleman who once wrote a bad book. M. Grün and his book should have been embalmed for our perpetual delight in amber. But the process is fatiguing; it requires more time and perhaps more temper than Pattison had at his command. He served M. Grün up raw, and he remains a crude berry among the cooked meats, upon which our teeth must grate for ever. Something of the sort applies to Matthew Arnold and a certain translator of Spinoza. Literal truth-telling and finding fault with a culprit for his good are out of place in an essay, where everything should be for our good and rather for eternity than for the March number of the *Fortnightly Review*. But if the voice of the scold should never be heard in this narrow plot, there is another voice which is as a plague of locusts—the voice of a man stumbling drowsily among loose words, clutching aimlessly at vague ideas, the voice, for example of Mr Hutton in the following passage:

Add to this that his married life was brief, only seven years and a half, being unexpectedly cut short, and that his passionate reverence for his wife's memory and genius—in his own words, 'a religion'—was one which, as he must have been perfectly sensible, he could not make to appear otherwise than extravagant, not to say an hallucination, in the eyes of the rest of mankind, and yet that he was possessed by an irresistible yearning to attempt to embody it in all the tender and enthusiastic hyperbole of which it is so pathetic to find a man who gained his fame by his 'dry-light' a master, and it is impossible not to feel that the human incidents in Mr Mill's career are very sad.

A book could take that blow, but it sinks an essay. A biography in two volumes is indeed the proper depository; for there, where the licence is so much wider, and hints and glimpses of outside things make part of the feast (we refer to the old type of Victorian volume), these yawns and stretches hardly matter, and have indeed some positive value of their own. But that value, which is contributed by the reader, perhaps illicitly, in his desire to get as much into the book from all possible sources as he can, must be ruled out here.

There is no room for the impurities of literature in an essay. Somehow or other, by dint of labour or bounty of nature, or both combined, the essay must be pure—pure like water or pure like wine, but pure from dullness, deadness, and deposits of extraneous matter. Of all writers in the first volume, Walter Pater best achieves this arduous task, because before setting out to write his essay ('Leonardo da Vinci') he has somehow contrived to get his material fused. He is a learned man, but it is not knowledge of Leonardo that remains with us, but a vision, such as we get in a good novel where everything contributes to bring the writer's conception as a whole before us. Only here, in the essay, where the bounds are so strict and facts have to be used in their nakedness, the true writer like Walter Pater makes these limitations yield their own quality. Truth will give it authority; from its narrow limits he will get shape and intensity; and then there is no more fitting place for some of those ornaments which the old writers loved and we, by calling them ornaments, presumably despise. Nowadays nobody would have the courage to embark on the once famous description of Leonardo's lady who has

learned the secrets of the grave; and has been a diver in deep seas and keeps their fallen day about her; and trafficked for strange webs with Eastern merchants; and, as Leda, was the mother of Helen of Troy, and, as Saint Anne, the mother of Mary . . .

The passage is too thumb-marked to slip naturally into the context. But when we come unexpectedly upon 'the smiling of women and the motion of great waters', or upon 'full of the refinement of the dead, in sad, earth-coloured raiment, set with pale stones', we sud- denly remember that we have ears and we have eyes, and that the English language fills a long array of stout volumes with innumerable words, many of which are of more than one syllable. The only living Englishman who ever looks into these volumes is, of course, a gentleman of Polish extraction. But doubtless our abstention saves us much gush, much rhetoric, much high-stepping and cloud-prancing, and for the sake of the prevailing sobriety and hard-headedness we should be willing to barter the splendour of Sir Thomas Browne and the vigour of Swift.

Yet, if the essay admits more properly than biography or fiction of sudden boldness and metaphor, and can be polished till every atom of its surface shines, there are dangers in that too. We are soon in sight of ornament. Soon the current, which is the life-blood of literature, runs slow; and instead of sparkling and flashing or moving with a quieter impulse which has a deeper excitement, words coagulate together in frozen sprays which, like the grapes on a Christmas tree, glitter for a single night, but are dusty and garish the day after. The temptation to decorate is great where the theme may be of the slightest. What is there to interest another in the fact that one has enjoyed a walking tour, or has amused oneself by rambling down Cheapside and looking at the turtles in Mr Sweeting's shop win- dow? Stevenson and Samuel Butler chose very different methods of exciting our interest in these domestic themes. Stevenson, of course, trimmed and polished and set out his matter in the traditional eighteenth-century form. It is admirably done, but we cannot help feeling anxious, as the essay proceeds, lest the material may give out under the craftsman's fingers. The ingot is so small, the manipulation so incessant. And perhaps that is why the peroration—

To sit and contemplate—to remember the faces of women without desire, to be pleased by the great deeds of men without envy, to be everything and everywhere in sympathy and yet content to remain where and what you are—

has the sort of insubstantiality which suggests that by the time he got to the end he had left himself nothing solid to work with. Butler adopted the very opposite method. Think your own thoughts, he seems to say, and speak them as plainly as you can. These turtles in the shop window which appear to leak out of their shells through heads and feet suggest a fatal faithfulness to a fixed idea. And so, striding unconcernedly from one idea to the next, we traverse a large stretch of ground; observe that a wound in the solicitor is a very serious thing; that Mary Queen of Scots wears surgical boots and is subject to fits near the Horse Shoe in Tottenham Court Road; take it for granted that no one really cares about Aeschylus; and so, with many amusing anecdotes and some profound reflections, reach the peroration, which is that, as he had been told not to see more in Cheapside than he could get into twelve pages of the *Universal Review*, he had better stop. And yet obviously Butler is at least as careful of our pleasure as Stevenson; and to write like oneself and call it not writing is a much harder exercise in style than to write like Addison and call it writing well.

But, however much they differ individually, the Victorian essayists yet had something in common. They wrote at greater length than is now usual, and they wrote for a public which had not only time to sit down to its magazine seriously, but a high, if peculiarly Victorian, standard of culture by which to judge it. It was worth while to speak out upon serious matters in an essay; and there was nothing absurd in writing as well as one possibly could when, in a month or two, the same public which had welcomed the essay in a magazine would carefully read it once more in a book. But a change came from a small audience of cultivated people to a larger audience of people who were not quite so cultivated. The change was not altogether for the worse. In volume three we find Mr Birrell and Mr Beerbohm. It might even be said that there was a reversion to the classic type, and that the essay by losing its size and something of its sonority was approaching more nearly the essay of Addison and Lamb. At any rate, there is a great gulf between Mr Birrell on Carlyle and the essay which one may suppose that Carlyle would have written upon Mr Birrell. There is little similarity between *A Cloud of Pinafores*, by Max Beerbohm, and *A Cynic's Apology,* by Leslie Stephen. But the essay is alive; there is no reason to despair. As the conditions change so the essayist, most sensitive of all plants to public opinion, adapts himself, and if he is good makes the best of the change, and if he is bad the worst. Mr Birrell is certainly good; and so we find that, though he has dropped a considerable amount of weight, his attack is much more direct and his movement more supple. But what did Mr Beerbohm give to the essay and what did he take from it? That is a much more complicated question, for here we have an essayist who has concentrated on the work and is without doubt the prince of his profession.

What Mr Beerbohm gave was, of course, himself. This presence, which has haunted the essay fitfully from the time of Montaigne, had been in exile since the death of Charles Lamb. Matthew Arnold was never to his readers Matt, nor Walter Pater affectionately abbreviated in a thousand homes to Wat. They gave us much, but that they did not give. Thus, some time in the nineties, it must have surprised readers accustomed to exhortation, information, and denunciation to find themselves familiarly addressed by a voice which seemed to belong to a man no larger than themselves. He was affected by private joys and sorrows, and had no gospel to preach and no learning to impart. He was himself, simply and directly, and himself he has remained. Once again we have an essayist capable of using the essayist's most proper but most dangerous and delicate tool. He has brought personality into literature, not unconsciously and impurely, but so consciously and purely that we do not know whether there is any relation between Max the essayist and Mr Beerbohm the man. We only know that the spirit of personality permeates every word that he writes. The triumph is the triumph of style. For it is only by knowing how to write that you can make use in literature of your self; that self which, while it is essential to literature, is also its most dangerous antagonist. Never to be yourself and yet always—that is the problem. Some of the essayists in Mr Rhys' collection, to be frank, have not altogether succeeded in solving it. We are nauseated by the sight of trivial personalities decomposing in the eternity of print. As talk, no doubt, it was charming, and certainly the writer is a good fellow to meet over a bottle of beer. But literature is stern; it is no use being charming, virtuous, or even learned and brilliant into the bargain, unless, she seems to reiterate, you fulfil her first condition—to know how to write.

This art is possessed to perfection by Mr Beerbohm. But he has not searched the dictionary for polysyllables. He has not moulded firm periods or seduced our ears with intricate cadences and strange melodies. Some of his companions—Henley and Stevenson, for example—are momentarily more impressive. But *A Cloud of Pinafores* has in it that indescribable inequality, stir, and final expressiveness which belong to life and to life alone. You have not finished with it because you have read it, any more than friendship is ended because it is time to part. Life wells up and alters and adds. Even things in a book-case change if they are alive; we find ourselves wanting to meet them again; we find them altered. So we look back upon essay after essay by Mr Beerbohm, knowing that, come September or May, we shall sit down with them and talk. Yet it is true that the essayist is the most sensitive of all writers to public opinion. The drawing-room is the place where a great deal of reading is done nowadays, and the essays of Mr Beerbohm lie, with an exquisite appreciation of all that the position exacts, upon the drawing-room table. There is no gin about; no strong tobacco, no puns, drunkenness, or insanity. Ladies and gentlemen talk together, and some things, of course, are not said.

But if it would be foolish to attempt to confine Mr Beerbohm to one room, it would be still more foolish, unhappily, to make him, the artist, the man who gives us only his best, the representative of our age. There are no essays by Mr Beerbohm in the fourth or fifth volumes of the present collection. His age seems already a little distant, and the drawing-room table, as it recedes, begins to look rather like an altar where, once upon a time, people deposited offerings—fruit from their own orchards, gifts carved with their own hands. Now once more the conditions have changed. The public needs essays as much as ever, and perhaps even more. The demand for the light middle not exceeding fifteen hundred words, or in special cases seventeen hundred and fifty, much exceeds the supply. Where Lamb wrote one essay and Max perhaps writes two, Mr Belloc at a rough computation produces three hundred and sixty-five. They are very short, it is true. Yet with what dexterity the practised essayist will utilise his space—beginning as close to the top of the sheet as possible, judging precisely how far to go, when to turn, and how, without sacrificing a hair's-breadth of paper, to wheel about and alight accurately upon the last word his editor allows! As a feat of skill it is well worth watching. But the personality upon which Mr Belloc, like Mr Beerbohm, depends suffers in the process. It comes to us not with the natural richness of the speaking voice, but strained and thin and full of mannerisms and affectations, like the voice of a man shouting through a megaphone to a crowd on a windy day. 'Little friends, my readers,' he says in the essay called 'An Unknown Country', and he goes on to tell us how—

There was a shepherd the other day at Findon Fair who had come from the east by Lewes with sheep, and who had in his eyes that reminiscence of horizons which makes the eyes of shepherds and of mountaineers different from the eyes of other men... I went with him to hear what he had to say, for shepherds talk quite differently from other men.

Happily this shepherd had little to say, even under the stimulus of the inevitable mug of beer, about the Unknown Country, for the only remark that he did make proves him either a minor poet, unfit for the care of sheep, or Mr Belloc himself masquerading with a fountain pen. That is the penalty which the habitual essayist must now be prepared to face. He must masquerade. He cannot afford the time either to be himself or to be other people. He must skim the surface of thought and dilute the strength of personality. He must give us a worn weekly halfpenny instead of a solid sovereign once a year.

But it is not Mr Belloc only who has suffered from the prevailing conditions. The essays which bring the collection to the year 1920 may not be the best of their authors' work, but, if we except writers like Mr Conrad and Mr Hudson, who have strayed into essay writing accidentally, and concentrate upon those who write essays habitually, we shall find them a good deal affected by the change in their circumstances. To write weekly, to write daily, to write shortly, to write for busy people catching trains in the morning or for tired people coming home in the evening, is a heart-breaking task for men who know good writing from bad. They do it, but instinctively draw out of harm's way anything precious that might be damaged by contact with the public, or anything sharp that might irritate its skin. And so, if one reads Mr Lucas, Mr Lynd, or Mr Squire in the bulk, one feels that a common greyness silvers everything. They are as far removed from the extravagant beauty of Walter Pater as they are from the intemperate candour of Leslie Stephen. Beauty and courage are dangerous spirits to bottle in a column and a half; and thought, like a brown paper parcel in a waistcoat pocket, has a way of spoiling the symmetry of an article. It is a kind, tired, apathetic world for which they write, and the marvel is that they never cease to attempt, at least, to write well.

But there is no need to pity Mr Clutton Brock for this change in the essayists's conditions. He has clearly made the best of his circumstances and not the worst. One hesitates even to say that he has had to make any conscious effort in the matter, so naturally has he effected the transition from the private essayist to the public, from the drawing-room to the Albert Hall. Paradoxically enough, the shrinkage in size has brought about a corresponding expansion of individuality. We have no longer the 'I' of Max and of Lamb, but the 'we' of public bodies and other sublime personages. It is 'we' who go to hear the *Magic Flute*; 'we' who ought to profit by it; 'we', in some mysterious way, who, in our corporate capacity, once upon a time actually wrote it. For music and literature and art must submit to the same generalisation or they will not carry to the farthest recesses of the Albert Hall. That the voice of Mr Clutton Brock, so sincere and so disinterested, carries such a distance and reaches so many without pandering to the weakness of the mass or its passions must be a matter of legitimate satisfaction to us all. But while 'we' are gratified, 'I', that unruly partner in the human fellowship, is reduced to despair. 'I' must always think things for himself, and feel things for himself. To share them in a diluted form with the majority of well-educated and well-intentioned men and women is for him sheer agony; and while the rest of us listen intently and profit profoundly, 'I' slips off to the woods and the fields and rejoices in a single blade of grass or a solitary potato.

In the fifth volume of modern essays, it seems, we have got some way from pleasure and the art of writing. But in justice to the essayists of 1920 we must be sure that we are not praising the famous because they have been praised already and the dead because we shall never meet them wearing spats in Piccadilly. We must know what we mean when we say that they can write and give us pleasure. We must compare them; we must bring out the quality. We must point to this and say it is good because it is exact, truthful, and imaginative:

Nay, retire men cannot when they would; neither will they, when it were Reason; but are impatient of Privateness, even in age and sickness, which require the shadow: like old Townsmen: that will still be sitting at their street door, though thereby they offer Age to Scorn...

and to this, and say it is bad because it is loose, plausible, and commonplace:

With courteous and precise cynicism on his lips, he thought of quiet virginal chambers, of waters singing under the moon, of terraces where taintless music sobbed into the open night, of pure maternal mistresses with protecting arms and vigilant eyes, of fields slumbering in the sunlight, of leagues of ocean heaving under warm tremulous heavens, of hot ports, gorgeous and perfumed...

It goes on, but already we are bemused with sound and neither feel nor hear. The comparison makes us suspect that the art of writing has for backbone some fierce attachment to an idea. It is on the back of an idea, something believed in with conviction or seen with precision and thus compelling words to its shape, that the diverse company which includes Lamb and Bacon, and Mr Beerbohm and Hudson, and Vernon Lee and Mr Conrad, and Leslie Stephen and Butler and Walter Pater reaches the farther shore. Very various talents have helped or hindered the passage of the idea into words. Some scrape through painfully; others fly with every wind favouring. But Mr Belloc and Mr Lucas and Mr Squire are not fiercely attached to anything in itself. They share the contemporary dilemma—that lack of an obstinate conviction which lifts ephemeral sounds through the misty sphere of anybody's language to the land where there is a perpetual marriage, a perpetual union. Vague as all definitions are, a good essay must have this permanent quality about it; it must draw its curtain round us, but it must be a curtain that shuts us in, not out.

Acknowledgements

Every effort has been made to contact copyright holders; in the event of an inadvertent omission or error, the editorial department should be notified at The Folio Society, 202 Great Suffolk Street, London SE1 1PR.

The editor wishes to thank the following writers, publishers and literary representatives for their permission to use copyright material:

'Living on Capital' from *For Love and Money* by Jonathan Raban, 1987, reprinted by permission of Collins Harvill and Aitken and Stone Ltd.

'An Irish Schooling' by Seán O'Faoláin reprinted by permission of A. P. Watt Ltd and Curtis Brown Ltd, New York.

'Hot-Water-Bottle Love: Cheltenham Ladies College' by Theodora Benson. Copyright Theodora Benson 1934. Reproduced by permission of Curtis Brown Ltd, London.

'Not Cricket' by Michael Holroyd first appeared in *Summer Days: Writers on Cricket*, edited by Michael Meyer (Eyre Methuen, 1981). Reprinted by permission of the author.

'Single-handed and Untrained' from *Required Writing* by Philip Larkin. Copyright © 1982, 1983 by Philip Larkin. Reprinted by permission of Faber and Faber Ltd and Farrar, Strauss and Giroux, Inc.

'As Old as the Century' by V. S. Pritchett. Reprinted by permission of the Peters, Fraser & Dunlop Group Ltd.

'The Privileges of 10 April 1840' by Stendhal. Translated by Cyril Connolly and first published in *Horizon*, 1947. Reprinted by permission of Rogers, Coleridge & White Ltd.

'On the Power of the Imagination' from *Essays* by Montaigne, translated by J. M. Cohen (Penguin Classics, 1958), copyright © J. M. Cohen, 1958. Reprinted by permission of Penguin Books Ltd.

'Concerning Busybodies' by Plutarch. From *Selected Essays of Plutarch* translated by T. G. Tucker (1913). Reprinted by permission of Oxford University Press.

'Mr Smyllie, Sir' by Patrick Campbell first appeared in the *Spectator*. Reprinted by permission of Lady Glenavy.

'The Gardener's August' from *The Gardener's Year* by Karel Čapek, 1931. Reprinted by permission of Unwin Hyman Ltd.

'Going out for a Walk' from *And Even Now* by Max Beerbohm, 1920. Reprinted by permission of Mrs Eva Reichmann.

'Food of the Gods' by A. A. Milne. Copyright A. A. Milne 1929, reproduced by permission of Curtis Brown Ltd, London.

ACKNOWLEDGEMENTS

'The Church Supper' from *Plnck and Lnck*, 1925 by Robert Benchley. Reproduced by permission of Henry Holt and Company.

'The Reach of Imagination' by Jacob Bronowski. First published in the *Proceedings of the American Academy of Arts and Letters and National Institute*, Second Series, Number Seventeen, 1967. Reprinted by permission of the American Academy and Institute of Arts and Letters.

'Machines and the Emotions' from *Sceptical Essays* by Bertrand Russell, 1928. Reprinted by permission of Unwin Hyman Ltd.

'Selected Snobberies' from *Music at Night* by Aldous Huxley. Copyright 1931 by Aldous Huxley. Reprinted by permission of Mrs Laura Huxley, The Hogarth Press and Harper & Row, Publishers, Inc.

'How to Name a Dog' from *The Beast in Me and Other Animals* by James Thurber. Copyright © 1948 James Thurber. Copyright © 1975 Helen Thurber and Rosemary A. Thurber. Reprinted by permission of Rosemary A. Thurber and Hamish Hamilton Ltd.

'A Note on the Way' from *Abinger Harvest* by E. M. Forster, 1936. Reprinted by permission of Edward Arnold.

'Exclusion' from *Afterthought* by Elizabeth Bowen. Copyright © Elizabeth Bowen 1962. Reproduced by permission of Curtis Brown Ltd, London.

'Decline of the English Murder' from *Shooting an Elephant and Other Essays* by George Orwell, copyright 1950 by Sonia Brownell Orwell, renewed 1978 by Sonia Pitt-Rivers, reprinted by permission of the estate of the late Sonia Brownell Orwell, Martin Secker & Warburg and Harcourt Brace Jovanovich, Inc.

'Bohemia' from *The Best of Alan Coren* by Alan Coren, 1980. Reprinted by permission of the author.

'Beatrix Potter' from *The Lost Childhood, and Other Essays* by Graham Greene. Copyright 1951, renewed © 1979 by Graham Greene. Reprinted by permission of Viking Penguin, a division of Penguin Books USA, Inc. and Laurence Pollinger Ltd.

'Cyril Connolly at Fifty' from *Tynan Right and Left* by Kenneth Tynan, 1967. Reprinted by permission of Methuen London.

'Frying the Flag' from *Esprit de Corps* by Lawrence Durrell, 1957. Reprinted by permission of Faber and Faber Ltd.

'On Shakespeare' from *Enthusiasms* by Bernard Levin, 1983. Reprinted by permission of Jonathan Cape Ltd and Curtis Brown Ltd, London.

'The Swirling Cape and the Low Bow' from *The Road to Miltown* by S. J. Perelman, 1957. Reprinted by permission of the Liz Darhansoff Literary Agency.

'Rodin' from *Pen Portraits and Reviews* by George Bernard Shaw, 1932. Reprinted by permission of the Society of Authors on behalf of the Bernard Shaw Estate.

'My View of History' from *Civilization on Trial* by Arnold Toynbee, 1948. Reprinted by permission of Oxford University Press.

ACKNOWLEDGEMENTS

'The Genealogy of Hitler' from *The Poisoned Crown* by Hugh Kingsmill, 1944. Reprinted by permission of Lady Hopkinson.

'Pink Triangle and Yellow Star' from *Pink Triangle and Yellow Star* by Gore Vidal. © 1976, 1977, 1978, 1979, 1980, 1981, 1982 by Gore Vidal. Reprinted by permission of William Heinemann Ltd and William Morris Agency, Inc. on behalf of the author.

'Faith, Knowledge and Peace' from *What I think* by Adlai Stevenson. Copyright © 1954, 1955, 1956 by R. Keith Kane. Reprinted by permission of Adlai E. Stevenson and Harper & Row, Publishers, Inc.

'Enoch Powell' from *Loyalists and Loners* by Michael Foot, 1986. Reprinted by permission of the author.

'En Route' (*'Unterwegs'*) from *Gesammelte Werke in dreizehn Bänden, Reden und Aufsätze 3* © 1960, 1974 S. Fischer Verlag GmbH, Frankfurt am Main by Thomas Mann, translated by Dr William Rose, 1925. Reprinted by permission of S. Fischer Verlag.

'On Getting Respected in Inns and Hotels' from *On Nothing and Kindred Subjects* by Hilaire Belloc, 1908. Reprinted by permission of the Peters, Fraser & Dunlop Group Ltd.

'The Wind at Djemila' from *Lyrical and Critical Essays* by Albert Camus, translated by Ellen Conroy Kennedy. © Copyright 1968 by Alfred A. Knopf, Inc. © Copyright 1967 by Hamish Hamilton Ltd. Reprinted by permission of Hamish Hamilton Ltd and Alfred A. Knopf, Inc.

'Notes Mailed at Nagercoil' from *Their Heads are Green* by Paul Bowles. Copyright © 1982, by Paul Bowles. Reprinted by permission of Peter Owen Ltd and William Morris Agency, Inc.

'The Modern Essay' from *The Common Reader* by Virginia Woolf, 1925, The Hogarth Press. Reprinted by permission of the Executors of the Virginia Woolf Estate, and Harcourt Brace Jovanovich, Inc.

The editor also wishes to thank the following for their editorial and/or research assistance: Sue Bradbury, Richard Cohen, Sheila Jordan, Rachel Scott, Carolyn Smith, Anthony Whittome—and Phillida and Jonathan Gili, and the Executors of the late Reynolds Stone for permission to reproduce the wood engravings by Reynolds Stone.

Biographical Notes

ADDISON, JOSEPH 1672–1719: Essayist, poet, chronicler of English poetry, civil servant, politician, dramatist in theatre and opera, friend of Swift and Steele: author of popular observations in *Tatler* and the *Spectator* (both founded during his lifetime). 'Statesman, yet friend to truth!' wrote Pope, 'of soul sincere,/In action faithful, and in honour clear.'

BACON, FRANCIS 1561–1626: Viscount St Albans; philosopher, diplomat, logician, historian, politicised civil servant, law officer accused of taking bribes. 'I have taken all knowledge to be my province', he wrote; Izaak Walton called him 'the great Secretary of Nature and all learning'; though others observed that he had 'the eye of a viper'.

BARBELLION, W. N. P: The pseudonym of Bruce Frederick Cummings, 1889–1919, English journalist-turned-natural historian. Stricken with a sclerotic ailment, he kept detailed accounts of his mood changes and depressions. His consuming glooms may be traced in his nom-de-plume— the initials 'W. N. P.' derive from Kaiser Wilhelm, Nero and Pontius Pilate, in his opinion three of the world's greatest failed egotists.

BEERBOHM, MAX 1872–1956: Henry Maximilian; author of one novel, *Zuleika Dobson*, many caricatures; literary socialite, parodist, rhymer and observer of the avant-garde, drama critic and broadcaster with a gift for mimicking famous literary styles. Lytton Strachey said of him, 'He has the most remarkable and seductive genius—and I should say about the smallest in the world.'

BELLOC, HILAIRE 1870–1953: Joseph Hilary Pierre; French birth, English education; conforms to a popular apprehension of the word 'essayist', but practised politics (as a Liberal MP), verses, historical biography, travel books and sedulous Roman Catholicism. Frequently considered in the same breath as Chesterton (q.v.). 'Conscious of being decrepit and forgetful, but not of being a bore,' wrote Evelyn Waugh.

BENCHLEY, ROBERT 1889–1945: American humourist; theatre critic of *Life* and the *New Yorker*; member of the celebrated Algonquin Round Table, talker and, occasionally, actor; self-deprecator in the interests of humour— 'Drawing on my fine command of language I said nothing.'

BENSON, THEODORA 1906–68: The Hon. Eleanor Theodora Roby; novelist: *Salad Days*, *Glass Houses*, *Lobster Quadrille*; humorist, short story writer; non-fiction chronicler of women's fortunes in war; essayist and observer of the social foibles of British society; 'Who she is I can't make out,' James Lees-Milne wrote in his diary. 'Speaks slowly, as though drugged, with eyes shut.'

BOWEN, ELIZABETH 1899–1973: credited as one of the writers who, along with James Joyce, raised the short story to art form. Often dividing her time between her native Cork and London she wrote powerful and intense fictional accounts of the middle classes, often laced with a peasant awareness of the supernatural, and fine, thoughtful prose discussion of the writer's art.

BOWLES, PAUL b. 1910, New York, resides in Tangier; music critic, composer, novelist; author of several highly-regarded nihilistic works of fiction—*The Sheltering Sky, Let it Come Down*—as well as several translations, travel essays, memoirs, verses, short stories, songs, ballet, opera. A cult has formed around him among young film-makers, musicians and journalists.

BRONOWSKI, JACOB 1908–74: Polish-born poet, humanist, scientist, philosopher; early interest in mathematical aspects of biology; investigated famously *The Effects of Atomic Bombs at Hiroshima and Nagasaki* and thereby influenced the movement towards disarmament; a regular contributor to the Brains Trust broadcasts, his reputation as a populariser and clarifier of complex matters came to wide recognition in the 1973 BBC television series *The Ascent of Man*.

DE BURY, RICHARD 1281–1345: Benedictine monk, Dean of Wells, Bishop of Durham, tutor to the Prince of Wales, later Edward III; bibliophile extraordinary, diplomat—to the Pope and to Scotland—and establisher of libraries at Oxford and Durham (modelled on the Sorbonne library); set himself to rescue valuable manuscripts from destruction; believed that books purveyed a certain spiritual distinction: 'No one can serve books and Mammon.'

BUTLER, SAMUEL 1835–1902: writer, and dilettante in music and painting; fame arrived at thirty-seven when he published *Erewhon*, consolidated by *The Way of All Flesh*. Other works challenged Darwin; suggested that the *Iliad* and *Odyssey* were composed by a Sicilian woman; put forward an early theory of general unconscious memory. 'The phrase "unconscious humour" is the one contribution I have made to the current literature of the day.'

CAMPBELL, PATRICK 1913–80: Patrick Gordon, the 3rd Baron Glenavy; journalist, broadcasting personality, wit, humorous columnist; career began on *Irish Times*; in London became a television broadcaster, egregious owing to a stammer; and a nationally renowned Autolycus-like columnist: 'He could toss up a trifle of experience', wrote the *Times* obituarist, 'and keep it in the air with great dexterity for minutes before letting it spin away into fantasy.'

CAMUS, ALBERT 1913–60: Algerian-born novelist, essayist, playwright; Nobel Prize for Literature, 1957; his novel *L'Etranger* was translated as *The Outsider*, the study 'of an absurd man in an absurd world'; co-edited with Sartre a publication of left-wing philosophies; wrote with increasing nihilism and pessimistic irony; died in a car accident. 'A single sentence will suffice for modern man—he fornicated and read the newspapers.'

ČAPEK, KAREL 1890–1938: born Bohemia, educated Prague, Berlin, Paris, son of a doctor; novelist with romantic though realistic leanings, playwright with science-fiction and futuristic inclinations, his work reflected the same concerns as that of H. G. Wells and George Orwell, with, sometimes, greater vision than the one, edgier satire than the other. He variously discussed a society taken over by machines, the puniness of political man, the perils of totalitarian rule.

CARLYLE, THOMAS 1795–1881: essayist and historian; brought massive energy to bear upon nineteenth-century letters; wrote a biography of Schiller, translated Goethe, wrote a history of the French Revolution; lectured widely and famously, proved a leader of fashion in thought, a challenger of received history, a humorous memoirist. A man of huge spirit and irascibility, he founded, with others, the London Library because the British Museum statutorily could not let him take books home. Tennyson called him, 'A poet to whom Nature has denied the faculty of verse.'

CHESTERTON, G. K. 1874–1936: Gilbert Keith; London-born journalist, novelist, essayist, critic, versifier; creator of the shrewd, misleadingly bemused priest-sleuth, Father Brown; wrote, lectured, argued with great energy, wit and success, all of which receded after his conversion to Roman Catholicism in 1922; most likely to be remembered for his lighter work than for his robust polemics: at his funeral Belloc (q.v.) said, 'He will not occur again.'

COBBETT, WILLIAM 1763–1835: soldier, countryman, amateur grammarian, Tory MP for Oldham, creator of what became Hansard. His *Rural Rides* and *Advice to Young Men* delighted as many people as were antagonised by his *History of the Reformation* or his political activities: according to John Stuart Mill, 'There were two sorts of people he could not endure, those who differed from him and those who agreed with him.'

CONRAD, JOSEPH 1857–1924: Teodor Josef Konrad Korzeniowski; novelist and short story writer, whose early work was dominated by the sea; Ukrainian-born of Polish parents. After twenty years at sea he settled to full-time writing and waited long for critical or public acclaim. Through books such as *Almayer's Folly* and *Lord Jim* appreciation burgeoned. 'I read you', wrote Henry James (q.v.) in a letter, 'as I listen to rare music—with deepest depths of surrender, and out of those depths I emerge slowly and reluctantly again to acknowledge that I return to life.'

COREN, ALAN 1938– : humorist, columnist, broadcaster; editor, *Punch*, *The Listener*; widely-published commentator on television and topical matters; irreverent, hugely amusing in conversation as in print. Influenced by twentieth-century Americans such as S. J. Perelman, (q.v.) much of Coren's humour derives from iconoclasm perpetuated upon popular culture; when the American Senate contemplated not retiring septuagenerian CIA agents, Coren wrote, '[James] Bond tensed in the darkness and reached for his teeth.'

COWPER, WILLIAM 1731–1800: poet and barrister; depressive, prone to nervous breakdown, he temporarily saved himself by enjoying the literary attentions of some ladies under whose encouragement he almost ceased writing doom-filled hymns, and turned to satires, translations from Homer and somewhat detached pre-Wordsworthian poems. Dismissed by Hazlitt: 'He shakes hands with Nature with a pair of fashionable gloves on.'

DICKENS, CHARLES 1812–70: Charles John Huffham; son of a navy clerk;

throughout his successful career as a novelist he continued to practise the journalism, though by essay rather than reportage, by which he came to writing; indeed, a series of 'essays', *Sketches by Boz*, brought him to his earliest prominence and thereafter the form, whenever he used it, proved redolent of his novels especially in atmosphere and details of place.

DURRELL, LAWRENCE b. 1912, India: Lawrence George; novelist, journalist, diplomat, playwright, poet; prolific, with considerable vitality; best-known for the *Alexandria Quartet* of novels written 1957 to 1960, which he called 'an investigation of modern love'. A wide strain of experiment runs through his work, much of which is located in the Mediterranean where he has spent many years. A writer of luxuriant prose (too ornate for some critics) into which he heaps ideas, Durrell's first novel was published when he was twenty-three.

FELLTHAM, OWEN 1602?–68: Suffolk-born minor essayist on 'moral' themes; *Resolves, Divine, Morall, Politicall* was compared unfavourably with Bacon (q.v.); poet, contemporary of Ben Jonson to whose elegies he contributed; he wrote amusingly of 'The Vices and Virtues of the Inhabitants' of the Low Countries; Latinist, Royalist and Anglican: 'My books have been my delight and my recreation but not my trade, though perhaps I could wish they had.'

FIELDING, HENRY 1707–54: began as a comic playwright and farceur, then theatrical author-manager; publisher of periodicals to which he also contributed; satirist and political journalist and attacker of literary or intellectual pretensions; novelist, with *Tom Jones* (1749), for which his beloved wife inspired Sophie Western, as she also did the eponymous *Amelia* (1751). Dr Johnson (q.v.) called him 'a blockhead, a barren rascal', and Byron called him 'the prose Homer of human nature'.

FOOT, MICHAEL 1913– : Rt Hon. Michael Mackintosh, MP; leader British Labour Party 1980–83; writer, critic, journalist, orator, Swiftian, compassionate political activist; Secretary of State for Employment, 1974–76; Leader, House of Commons, 1976–79; Hon. Fellow, Wadham College, Oxford; biographer of Aneurin Bevan; commentator upon, campaigner against, denials of human rights or threats to quality of modern life. Regarded as the most compelling parliamentary speaker of his age.

FORSTER, E. M. 1879–1970: Edward Morgan; novelist, essayist and critic; author of finely modulated novels such as *A Room with a View* (1908), *Howard's End* (1910), *A Passage to India* (1924); librettist of the Britten opera, *Billy Budd* (1951). Though now secure in literary repute his work provoked contemporarily violent criticism: Lytton Strachey (q.v.) called him a mediocre man 'who will come to no good; in the meantime he's treated rudely by waiters and is not really admired, even by middle-class dowagers'.

GOLDSMITH, OLIVER 1730–74: educated through charity at Trinity College, Dublin, and after a little medical study settled in London to practise—with no success whatsoever—as a doctor. Turned to writing plays, novels and essays, became a humorous, good-natured 'citizen of the world'. His play, *She Stoops to Conquer*, and his novel, *The Vicar of Wakefield*, guarantee his literary immortality. 'No man was more foolish when he had not a pen in his hand, nor more wise when he had,' said Dr Johnson (q.v.).

GREENE, GRAHAM 1904– : Henry Graham; consistently successful from the 1920s to the 1980s with novels and narratives he calls 'entertainments'; *Brighton Rock* (1938), *The Power and the Glory* (1940), *The Heart of the Matter* (1948), *The End of the Affair* (1951), and others which brought him a level of critical and popular success unequalled by any British contemporary. The essay chosen in this anthology exhibits an infrequently acknowledged sense of humour.

HAZLITT, WILLIAM 1778–1830: essayist with painterly talents; almost as famous for his friendships with Wordsworth and Coleridge (who described Hazlitt's manners as 'ninety-nine in a hundred singularly repulsive') as for his literary and theatrical criticisms and miscellaneous, elegantly-written observations, *pace* 'On Going a Journey'. He made the reputation of the actor Edmund Kean and, though frequently poverty-stricken and repulsive to many, including a wife who bade him farewell on their return from honeymoon, he died saying, 'Well, I've had a happy life.'

HOLROYD, MICHAEL 1935– : Michael de Courcy Fraser; biographer of Hugh Kingsmill (q.v.), Lytton Strachey (q.v.), Augustus John and George Bernard Shaw (q.v.); took the art of biography up to a new plateau, critically and commercially. Influential contributor to contemporary literary debate, lecturer, belle-lettrist. Valued contributor to the book world in activities on behalf of the Book Trust, Society of Authors, British Council, etc.

HUME, DAVID 1711–76: Scottish philosopher; historian, politician; his works were generally more successful after his death—while alive his views provoked hostility, though positively influenced French thinkers such as Voltaire and Rousseau, whom Hume befriended. His chief works included *Enquiry Concerning Human Understanding*, *Essays Political and Moral* and a gigantic six-volume *History of England*. Described himself as 'a sober, discreet, virtuous, regular, quiet, good-natured man of bad character'.

HUNT, LEIGH 1784–1859: Leigh James Henry; essayist and poet, Liberal newspaper editor and friend of Keats and Shelley whom he first published. The model for Mr Skimpole in *Bleak House*, he cut a London dash as the quintessential man of letters whose home entertained every writer of note. One of the pioneers of light essay writing, he libelled the Prince Regent, serving nearly three years in jail, and caused Byron to call him 'a good man, with some poetical elements in his chaos'.

HUXLEY, ALDOUS 1894–1963: Aldous Leonard; novelist, essayist, would-be mystic; described by Elizabeth Bowen (q.v.) as 'at once the truly clever person and the stupid person's idea of the clever person', his novels and lectures led to edgily divided opinion on his merits. Novels such as *Crome Yellow* (1921) and *Point Counter-Point* (1928) made him intellectually fashionable and precociously notorious.

JAMES, HENRY 1843–1916: New York-born, of Irish ancestry and educated in Europe; novelist, travel writer, critic; author of elegant though mannered novels such as *Portrait of a Lady*, *The Ambassadors*, *The Golden Bowl*; his subtle—if stylised—prose creates lasting impressions, atmospheres and characters. Arnold Bennett said, 'he writes like an angel': T. S. Eliot called him an 'extraordinarily clever but negligible curiosity'.

JEFFERIES, RICHARD 1848–87: a farmer's son who ran away from home, he became a journalist and amateur naturalist whose best work lay in the observation of his native fields and hedgerows. One novel, *Bevis, The Story of a Boy* received wide attention, though his fiction never proved as popular as his country notebooks. Called 'Looney Dick' by his Wiltshire neighbours, alarmed at his face-down communing with the earth on the Downs in summer.

JOHNSON, DR SAMUEL 1709–84: 'a writer of dictionaries, a harmless drudge', essayist, editor, clubman; born Lichfield, hugely intelligent, frequently depressed; shrewd, energetic and committed (if often irascibly) to his friends; the most intimately observed figure—by James Boswell—in English letters. Eccentric and memorable in conversation, with a wide coterie of friends and acquaintances, his achievements are now seen as his *Dictionary* (1755), his *Lives of the Poets* (1779–81) and his personality as evidenced by Boswell.

KINGSMILL, HUGH 1889–1949: critic, anthologist, essayist; man of letters; insufficiently-recognised literary commentator on Matthew Arnold, on *After Puritanism—The Return of William Shakespeare*, 1929, on Frank Harris, D. H. Lawrence; collaborator with William Gerhardie (on *Casanova*, 1933) and Malcolm Muggeridge (*Talking of Dick Whittington*, 1947); stylish and perceptive, the subject of an excellent study (1964) by Michael Holroyd (q.v.).

LAMB, CHARLES 1775–1834: poet, essayist, critic; Londoner and occasional lunatic from a family afflicted with insanity; renowned chiefly for *Tales from Shakespear* (1807) and *Essays of Elia* in two volumes, 1823 and 1833. Dramatist, too, balladeer and letter-writer, much-loved friend of Coleridge, Hazlitt (q.v.), de Quincey, and Wordsworth who called him 'the frolic and the gentle'.

LARKIN, PHILIP 1922–88: Philip Arthur; poet and librarian; first poems appeared in 1944/45, novels *Jill* and *A Girl in Winter*, 1946 and 1947; thereafter concentrated on verse with some criticism and essays. Influenced by Yeats, Graves and Auden; librarian at Hull University. Self-satirising, self-effacing, self-disciplined, his brief insights opened wide views, his images, entirely of their time, illuminated wider horizons. A pithy critic, he described many modern novels as having 'a beginning, a muddle and an end'.

LEVIN, BERNARD 1928–   : Henry Bernard; journalist and author; columnist for *The Times*; literary, drama and music critic, broadcaster and (apparently) philologist; enthusiastic Wagnerian and Shakespearean, may achieve immortality for his pendent clauses, long (very, very) sentences and immensely enjoyable essay style; aphoristic and provocative, he once described a play as having 'the depth of a cracker-motto and the drama of a dial-a-recipe service'.

LUCAS, E. V. 1868–1938: Edward Verrall; essayist, assistant editor of *Punch*, biographer (of Charles Lamb, q.v.) and editor of the letters of Lamb and his mad matricidal sister Mary; originally a bookseller's assistant in Brighton, his essays, (light) novels and memoirs frequently, though untediously, re-visit bookshops. Anthologist and travel writer, he typified a sort of man-of-letters frequently found in a progression from the Edwardians to the 1930s—unmoving though energetic, engaging though passionless.

MACAULAY, LORD 1800–59: Thomas Babington, 1st Baron; parliamentarian, essayist, historian; impressive Victorian; most frequently published in *The Edinburgh Review*; contributed learned pieces on writers and politicians to *Encyclopaedia Britannica*; an acerbic critic, he wrote the renowned *Lays of Ancient Rome* and the massive five-volume *History of England* while occupying such eminent positions as war secretary and paymaster; unpopular owing to his self-confidence, Matthew Arnold called him 'the great apostle of the Philistines'.

MANN, THOMAS 1875–1955: novelist, born in Germany, Nobel Prize 1929 (for *The Magic Mountain*), emigrated to the United States, 1933, fleeing Nazism; died Switzerland; success came at twenty-six with *Buddenbrooks*, a four-generation novel in which men of action are superseded by men of imagination and ideas—but the family dies out. Most famous work now *Death in Venice*, owing to the successful film; influenced by the philosophers Nietzsche and Schopenhauer, and (perhaps most of all) by Goethe.

MENEN, AUBREY 1912–89: drama critic, essayist and novelist; advertising film-maker; travel writer with studies of India, Venice, London, Naples; drama critic and experimental theatre impresario and director; educationalist—in pre-independence India; combined an amateur interest in archaeology with creative output.

MILNE, A. A. 1882–1956: Alan Alexander; while at Cambridge edited the undergraduate magazine *Granta*; joined the staff of *Punch* and wrote numerous articles, essays, plays and novels, all of which disappeared in the shadows of his children's books addressed to his own son, Christopher Robin. *When We Were Very Young*, and the Pooh books, involving a bear with some other characters including a pig and a donkey, made him continuingly successful in the world of children's literature.

MONTAIGNE, MICHEL DE 1533–92: Michel Eyquem de; (see Introduction); born at Perigord, after legal studies and pleasurable digressions in chateau society and at court in Paris became a city councillor of Bordeaux and then inherited the family estates, from which time, at the age of thirty-eight, he developed a hitherto dilettante interest in literature. On his personal medallion he had inscribed the words, *'Que sais-je?'* ('What do I know?').

NASHE, THOMAS 1567–1601: satirist; early contributor to the adventure-novel genre with *The Unfortunate Traveller*, generally known as *Jacke Wilton*; vituperative anti-Puritan—an attitude which landed him in jail, then forced him out of London. Satirised in his turn as Ingenioso, an out-of-favour writer, a contemporary said of him, 'his jests [are] but the dregs of common scurrility, the shreds of the theatre, or the off-scourings of new pamphlets'.

O'FAOLÁIN, SEÁN 1900– : John Whelan, born Cork; novelist, critic, biographer (of Irish political figures) and, principally, short story writer, on which he has also theorised (*The Short Story*, 1948). His stories interrogate the lives of individuals, mainly rural, during and after the 1916–22 period of conflict and civil war in southern Ireland: is seen at his best when discussing the pressures of a dogmatically conforming society upon the sexual and religious choices of the individual limited by his small community. Has also written wry and charming memoirs, *Vive-moi!* (1964).

OKAKURA-KAKUZO 1862–1913: Japanese-born curator, fine arts administrator and observer of aesthetics; civil servant with responsibilities for musical education in late nineteenth-century Tokyo; curator Chinese and Japanese depts, Boston Museum of Fine Arts, 1910; on his return to Tokyo presided over commissions on archaeology and art exchange between East and West; Professor of Aesthetics, Imperial University; author of *The Awakening of Japan*, 1904; *The Ideals of the East*, 1904; *The Book of Tea*, 1906.

ORWELL, GEORGE 1903–50: *nom-de-plume* of Eric Arthur Blair; journalist, essayist, polemicist; author of the political satires *Animal Farm* (1945) and *Nineteen Eighty-Four* (1949); after early experience as a policeman in Burma, resolved to campaign against all forms of 'man's dominion over man'. Called variously 'Don Quixote on a bicycle' and 'a kind of saint', an 'emotional public schoolboy' and 'a silly billy', he endowed the language with phrases such as 'Doublethink' and 'Big Brother is watching you'.

PATER, WALTER 1839–94: Walter Horatio; essayist, aesthete, pre-Raphaelite and don; his *Studies in the History of the Renaissance* (1873) established his reputation, after which he influenced a generation of writers, most notably Oscar Wilde. He enjoyed the friendship of an artistic circle which included Swinburne, the Rossettis, Aubrey Beardsley, who like others admired his prose style and his lucid, discursive tutoring—although Max Beerbohm (q.v.) said 'he laid out every sentence as in a shroud', and Samuel Butler (q.v.) said his style was like an old woman who has 'had herself enamelled. The bloom is nothing but powder and paint and the odour is cherry-blossom'.

PERELMAN, S. J. 1904–79: Sidney Joseph; humorist; born New York, and for forty-five years contributed to the *New Yorker*; associated with the Marx brothers for whom he wrote scripts, his surreal style, his play on words and his popular-culture targets early made him a loved and respected figurehead among humorists; books such as *Crazy Like a Fox* and *Westward Ha!* brought him a wider audience.

PLUTARCH AD c.46–c.125: Greek biographer, Delphic priest (see Introduction), whose *Moral Tales* still provoked discussion among the Renaissance scholars, and whose biographical work, *Parallel Lives*, provided Shakespeare's sources, most notably in *Julius Caesar*, *Antony & Cleopatra* and *Coriolanus*. A prototypical Essayist whose discourses engaged with diverse subjects—religion, social habits, thought, criticism—Plutarch was Montaigne's (q.v.) model and central stimulus.

PRITCHETT, V. S. 1900– : Sir Victor Sawdon; short story writer, novelist, biographer of Balzac (1973), Turgenev (1977), Chekhov (1988). Knighted for his services to literature, his wide and energetic output displays close observation of English suburbia's fractional passions, especially in his short stories—a craft which he has defined thus: 'the novel tends to tell us everything whereas the short story tells us only one thing and that, intensely.'

RABAN, JONATHAN 1942– : essayist, novelist, critic and travel writer, acclaimed for *Arabia: a Journey through the Labyrinth*, and *Old Glory*, his journey on the Mississippi, said by the *New York Times* to be 'more successful than ninety-nine per cent of books about America'. *Coasting*, in which he described a voyage round the coast of Britain, selflessly underplayed—for the sake of writing about it—the hazards of sailing alone in waters that included the perils of the Atlantic and the unpredictabilities of the Irish sea and the English Channel. His novel-writing abilities have been described as 'nothing short of awesome'.

RUSKIN, JOHN 1819–1900: critic of Architecture and Art, protean and herculean letter-writer, utopian protagonist of civil and social causes; first Slade professor of Art at Oxford, author of many travel pieces including the prodigious three-volume *The Stones of Venice*. With eulogies of Turner and defences of the pre-Raphaelites he became (and perhaps remains) the single most influential critic in the history of art in Britain. Popularly famous too, not least on account of the remark for which the painter Whistler sued: 'I never expected to hear a coxcomb ask two hundred guineas for flinging a pot of paint in the public's face.'

RUSSELL, BERTRAND 1872–1970: Bertrand Arthur William, 3rd Earl Russell; philosopher; though his earliest fame came with his two *Principles/ Principia* works on mathematics, his polymathic capacities—education, politics, literature (for which he won the Nobel Prize in 1950)—put his name before a wider public than philosophers typically enjoy. Provocative, controversial, pessimistic, D. H. Lawrence, who also called him 'the enemy of all mankind', said, 'It isn't that life has been too much for him, but too little.'

SHAW, GEORGE BERNARD 1856–1950: critic, playwright, lecturer, reformist, correspondent, wit, novelist, essayist, failed sufferer of fools; alleged misogynist; largely self-taught in all his fields of intellectual activity; indefatigable and (largely) endearing self-publicist, a puncturer of humbug who often ran the risk of becoming that which he attacked, and an unsubduable opponent of the shallow and opportune. 'Mr Shaw has no enemies,' said Oscar Wilde, 'but is intensely disliked by all his friends.'

STEELE, RICHARD 1672–1729: Sir Richard; soldier, politician, essayist, playwright, thinking man; Dublin-born, originator of the *Tatler*. A moralising sentimentalist, he safely romanticised comic aspects of society to sermonise on the values of Christian family life and the sweetness of womanhood. 'He maintained a perpetual struggle between reason and appetite,' said Cibber.

STENDHAL 1783–1842: one of the many pseudonyms—he used nearly two hundred—of Marie Henri Beyle; soldier, journalist, novelist, biographer (of Rossini and Haydn); also proficient in drama, essay, criticism, travel writing, but above all the novel; profoundly influential upon French nineteenth-century literature; a confident narrator and satirist: did not suffer the fate suggested in his own aphorism, 'The more one pleases generally, the less one pleases profoundly.'

STEVENSON, ADLAI 1900–65; Adlai Ewing; American lawyer and Democratic statesman; founder-contributor to the United Nations, governor of Illinois; loser in two successive presidential elections against Eisenhower; undramatic in personality, philosophical in politics, his obituarists called him 'as unexceptional as a glass of decent Beaujolais' and a reminder to the world of the Cold War 'that there was another America—sensitive, self-critical, thoughtful and visionary'.

STEVENSON, R. L. 1850–94: Robert Louis (originally—and pronounced—'Lewis'); 'the Dying Wanderer'; Scottish novelist, poet, essayist, traveller; romantic in output, hard-nosed in achievement; a dearly attractive figure, whose adventure novels, *Treasure Island* and *Kidnapped*, retain their original alertness; fought appalling ill-health to gain the stature he had always wanted as writer and man of letters, defeating his own view, 'Whatever else we are intended to do we are not intended to succeed: failure is the fate allotted.'

STRACHEY, LYTTON 1880–1932: Giles Lytton; essayist and biographer of Queen Victoria (1921) *inter alia* (see Introduction); member of the informal Bloomsbury Group (founded 1905), free-thinking intellectuals whose pleasures, they insisted, resided in rational discussion and the easy association of human beings. Strachey's greatest success, *Eminent Victorians* (1918), influenced the direction of biography. More admired than loved, he incensed many with pronouncements such as, 'I write very slowly, and in faultless sentences.'

SWIFT, JONATHAN 1667–1745: Dean of St Patrick's Cathedral, Dublin; pamphleteer, satirist, author of *Gulliver's Travels*, cousin of John Dryden, scourge of political opportunists and despots; melancholy and uncertain lover; versifier and polemicist; associate of Addison (q.v.) and Steele (q.v.). Beloved pastor of his city flock, though they irritated him: once when they forgathered outside his Deanery 'to witness an eclipse of the sun', he sent them away saying it had been 'postponed'.

THACKERAY, W. M. 1811–63: William Makepeace; journalist, editor of periodicals (*The Cornhill Magazine*), novelist—*The Luck of Barry Lyndon* (1844), *Vanity Fair* (1847), *Pendennis*, (1848); with a sad personal life—death among his children, madness in his wife—he nevertheless sculpted a brave face for himself, illustrated his own books, while lecturing and writing humorously. Auden wrote, 'William Makepeace Thackeray/Wept into his daiquiri/When he heard St Johns Wood/Thought he was no good.'

THURBER, JAMES 1894–1961: James Grover, Ohio-born humorist, cartoonist, fabulist, playwright, long associated with *The New Yorker*, of whose editor, Harold Ross, he wrote an amusing account, *The Years with Ross* (1959). Best known works include *Is Sex Necessary* (1929), *My World and Welcome to It* (1942), in which appeared his most famous single piece, *The Secret Life of Walter Mitty* (filmed with Danny Kaye), and *The Thurber Carnival* (1945). 'You can fool too many of the people', he said, 'too much of the time.'

TOYNBEE, ARNOLD 1889–1975: civil service diplomat, Byzantine scholar, historian; between 1934 and 1955 he published *A Study of History* in ten volumes, investigating cyclical imperatives of destruction and renewal in the civilising of mankind; advocated union of man through spiritual and religious initiatives, through political rationalisation rather than confrontation; feared for the demise of Western civilisation; rated humanity's prospects of survival as 'considerably better when we were defenceless against tigers than they are today when we have become defenceless against ourselves'.

TYNAN, KENNETH 1927–80: drama critic, principally of the *Observer* newspaper—in the eyes of some he was the most significant critical voice of twentieth-century theatre; a stylist of intelligence and perceptive wittiness, he contributed to the formation of contemporary British theatre not just by his writings but in his capacity as founding prime mover and later Literary Manager of the National Theatre; constructively undermined the principle of censorship: 'A critic', he wrote, 'is a man who knows the way but cannot drive the car.'

VIDAL, GORE 1925– : American essayist, novelist, dramatist and commentator on literature and politics; in one series of novels, including *Washington D.C.* (1967), *Burr* (1974) and *Lincoln* (1984), he has been 'writing my country's biography'. Hailed by critics as 'one of the most important stylists of contemporary American prose', his observations of American mores are contained in his more acerbic works such as *Myra Breckinridge* (1968) and *Duluth* (1983); deliverer of aphorisms: 'Whenever a friend succeeds—a little something in me dies.'

WOOLF, VIRGINIA 1882–1941: (see Introduction); diarist, belletrist, novelist; publisher; wife of Leonard, core members of the Bloomsbury Group; (see Strachey); literary Modernist, experimentalist, whose artistic reputation, suggested initially by perceptive criticism, reached fruition in three novels, *Mrs Dalloway* (1925), *To the Lighthouse* (1927) and *The Waves* (1931). A prolific and daring critic and correspondent, she by no means gained comprehensive approval of her talent. Edith Sitwell 'thought nothing of her writing: I considered her a beautiful little knitter', and Wyndham Lewis wrote of one of her novels, 'The time has come to take the cow by the horns.'

STONE, REYNOLDS: (ENGRAVINGS) 1909–79; Alan Reynolds; engraver, letter-cutter, painter; son of an Eton College housemaster, first became interested in typography when at Cambridge *via* the Cambridge University Press; took part in a revival of classical lettering; commissions included the Churchill, T. S. Eliot and Benjamin Britten memorials, masthead for *The Times*, coat-of-arms for HMSO, the British passport symbol, £5 and £10 notes for the Bank of England—and The Folio Society logo. A painter of great delicacy, he developed in woodcuts those themes and motifs he first investigated in watercolours.